C000001206

1 MONTH OF
FREE
READING

at

www.ForgottenBooks.com

By purchasing this book you are eligible for one month membership to ForgottenBooks.com, giving you unlimited access to our entire collection of over 1,000,000 titles via our web site and mobile apps.

To claim your free month visit:

www.forgottenbooks.com/free175310

ISBN 978-0-483-27004-6
PIBN 10175310

This book is a reproduction of an important historical work. Forgotten Books uses
state-of-the-art technology to digitally reconstruct the work, preserving the original format
whilst repairing imperfections present in the aged copy. In rare cases, an imperfection in
the original, such as a blemish or missing page, may be replicated in our edition. We do,
however, repair the vast majority of imperfections successfully; any imperfections that
remain are intentionally left to preserve the state of such historical works.

THE FORUM

VOL. XLV

January, 1911—June, 1911

MITCHELL KENNERLEY
LONDON AND .NEW YORK
MCMXI

AP
2
.F8
v.45

THE FORUM
FOR JANUARY 1911

THE HUMAN DRIFT

JACK LONDON

" The Revelations of Devout and Learn'd
Who rose before us, and as Prophets Burn'd,
Are all but stories, which, awoke from Sleep,
They told their comrades, and to Sleep return'd."

HE history of civilization is a history of wandering, sword in hand, in search of food. In the misty younger world we catch glimpses of phantom races, rising, slaying, finding food, building rude civilizations, decaying, falling under the swords of stronger hands, and passing utterly away. Man, like any other animal, has roved over the earth seeking what he might devour; and not romance and adventure, but the hunger-need, has urged him on his vast adventures. Whether a bankrupt gentleman sailing to colonize Virginia or a lean Cantonese contracting to labor on the sugar plantations of Hawaii, in each case, gentleman and coolie, it is a desperate attempt to get something to eat, to get more to eat than he can get at home.

It has always been so, from the time of the first pre-human anthropoid crossing a mountain-divide in quest of better berry-bushes beyond, down to the latest Slovack, arriving on our shores to-day, to go to work in the coal mines of Pennsylvania. These migratory movements of peoples have been called drifts, and the word is apposite. Unplanned, blind, automatic, spurred on by the pain of hunger, man has literally drifted his way around the planet.

There have been drifts in the past, innumerable and forgotten, and so remote that no records have been left, or composed of such low-typed humans or pre-humans that they made no scratchings on stone or bone and left no monuments to show that they had been. These early drifts we conjecture and know must have occurred, just as we know that the first upright-walking brutes were descended from some kin of the quadrumana through having developed " a pair of great toes out of two opposable thumbs." Dominated by fear, and by their very fear accelerating their development, these early ancestors of ours, suffering hunger-pangs very like the ones we experience to-day, drifted on, hunting and being hunted, eating and being eaten, wandering through thousand-year-long odysseys of screaming primordial savagery, until they left their skeletons in glacial gravels, some of them, and their bone-scratchings in cavemen's lairs.

There have been drifts from east to west and west to east, from north to south and back again, drifts that have criss-crossed one another, and drifts colliding and recoiling and caroming off in new directions. From Central Europe the Aryans have drifted into Asia, and from Central Asia the Turanians have drifted across Europe. Asia has thrown forth great waves of hungry humans from the prehistoric " round-barrow " " broad-heads " who overran Europe and penetrated to Scandinavia and England, down through the hordes of Attila and Tamerlane, to the present immigration of Chinese and Japanese that threatens America. The Phoenicians and the Greeks, with unremembered drifts behind them, colonized the Mediterranean. Rome was engulfed in the torrent of Germanic tribes drifting down from the north before a flood of drifting Asiatics. The Angles, Saxons, and Jutes, after having drifted whence no man knows, poured into Britain, and the English have carried this drift on around the world. Retreating before stronger breeds, hungry and voracious, the Eskimo has drifted to the inhospitable polar regions, the Pygmy to the fever-rotten jungles of Africa. And in this day the drift of the races continues, whether it be of Chinese into the Philippines and the Malay Peninsula, of Europeans to the United States, or of Americans to the wheat-lands of Manitoba and the North-west.

Perhaps most amazing has been the South Sea Drift. Blind,

fortuitous, precarious as no other drift has been, nevertheless the islands in that waste of ocean have received drift after drift of the races. Down from the mainland of Asia poured an Aryan drift that built civilizations in Ceylon, Java, and Sumatra. Only the monuments of these Aryans remain. They themselves have perished utterly, though not until after leaving evidences of their drift clear across the great South Pacific to far Easter Island. And on that drift they encountered races who had accomplished the drift before them, and they, the Aryans, passed, in turn, before the drift of other and subsequent races whom we to-day call the Polynesian and the Melanesian.

Man early discovered death. As soon as his evolution permitted, he made himself better devices for killing than the old natural ones of fang and claw. He devoted himself to the invention of killing devices before he discovered fire or manufactured for himself religion. And to this day, his finest creative energy and technical skill are devoted to the same old task of making better and ever better killing weapons. All his days, down all the past, have been spent in killing. And from the fear-stricken, jungle-lurking, cave-haunting creature of long ago, he won to empery over the whole animal world, because he developed into the most terrible and awful killer of all the animals. He found himself crowded. He killed to make room, and as he made room ever he increased and found himself crowded, and ever he went on killing to make more room. Like a settler clearing land of its weeds and forest bushes in order to plant corn, so man was compelled to clear all manner of life away in order to plant himself. And, sword in hand, he has literally hewn his way through the vast masses of life that occupied the earth space he coveted for himself. And ever he has carried the battle wider and wider, until to-day not only is he a far more capable killer of men and animals than ever before, but he has pressed the battle home to the infinite and invisible hosts of menacing lives in the world of micro-organisms.

It is true, that they that rose by the sword perished by the sword. And yet, not only did they not all perish, but more rose by the sword than perished by it, else man would not to-day be overrunning the world in such huge swarms. Also, it must not be forgotten that they who did not rise by the sword did not rise at all.

They were not. In view of this, there is something wrong with
Doctor Jordan's war-theory, which is to the effect that the best being
sent out to war, only the second best, the men who are left, remain
to breed a second best race, and that, therefore, the human race
deteriorates under war. If this be so, if we have sent forth the best
we bred and gone on breeding from the men who were left, and if
we have done this for ten thousand millenniums and are what we
splendidly are to-day, then what unthinkably splendid and god-like
beings must have been our forebears those ten thousand millenniums
ago. Unfortunately for Doctor Jordan's theory, those ancient
forebears cannot live up to this fine reputation. We know them for
what they were, and before the monkey cage of any menagerie we
catch truer glimpses and hints and resemblances of what our ancestors really were long and long ago. And by killing, incessant
killing, by making a shambles of the planet, those apelike creatures
have developed even into you and me. As Henley has said in *The
Song of the Sword:*

> " *The Sword*
> *Singing—*
> Driving the darkness,
> Even as the banners
> And spears of the Morning;
> Sifting the nations,
> The Slag from the metal,
> The waste and the weak
> From the fit and the strong;
> Fighting the brute,
> The abysmal Fecundity;
> Checking the gross
> Multitudinous blunders,
> The groping, the purblind
> Excesses in service
> Of the Womb universal,
> ˙The absolute drudge."

As time passed and man increased, he drifted ever farther afield
in search of room. He encountered other drifts of men, and the
killing of men became prodigious. The weak and the decadent fell

under the sword. Nations that faltered, that waxed prosperous in fat valleys and rich river deltas, were swept away by the drifts of stronger men who were nourished on the hardships of deserts and mountains and who were more capable with the sword. Unknown and unnumbered billions of men have been so destroyed in prehistoric times. Draper says that in the twenty years of the Gothic war, Italy lost 15,000,000 of her population; " and that the wars, famines, and pestilences of the reign of Justinian diminished the human species by the almost incredible number of 100,000,000." Germany, in the Thirty Years' War, lost 6,000,000 inhabitants. The record of our own American Civil War need scarcely be recalled.

And man has been destroyed in other ways than by the sword. Flood, famine, pestilence, and murder are potent factors in reducing population—in making room. As Mr. Charles Woodruff, in his *Expansion of Races*, has instanced: In 1886, when the dikes of the Yellow River burst, 7,000,000 people were drowned. The failure of crops in Ireland, in 1848, caused 1,000,000 deaths. The famines in India of 1896-7 and 1899-1900 lessened the population by 21,-000,000. The T'ai'ping rebellion and the Mohammedan rebellion, combined with the famine of 1877-8, destroyed scores of millions of Chinese. Europe has been swept repeatedly by great plagues. In India, for the period of 1903 to 1907, the plague deaths averaged between one and two millions a year. Mr. Woodruff is responsible for the assertion that 10,000,000 persons now living in the United States are doomed to die of tuberculosis. And in this same country ten thousand persons a year are directly murdered. In China, between three and six millions of infants are annually destroyed, while the total infanticide record of the whole world is appalling. In Africa, now, human beings are dying by millions of the sleeping sickness.

More destructive of life than war, is industry. In all civilized countries great masses of people are crowded into slums and labor-ghettos, where disease festers, vice corrodes, and famine is chronic, and where they die more swiftly and in greater numbers than do the soldiers in our modern wars. The very infant mortality of a slum parish in the East End of London is three times that of a middle class parish in the West End. In the United States, in the last

fourteen years, a total of coal-miners, greater than our entire standing army, has been killed and injured. The United States Bureau
of Labor states that during the year 1908, there were between 30,000
and 35,000 deaths of workers by accidents, while 200,000 more were
injured. In fact, the safest place for a workingman is in the army.
And even if that army be at the front, fighting in Cuba or South
Africa, the soldier in the ranks has a better chance for life than the
workingman at home.

And yet, despite this terrible roll of death, despite the enormous
killing of the past, and the enormous killing of the present, there
are to-day alive on the planet a billion and three-quarters of human
beings. Our immediate conclusion is that man is exceedingly fecund
and very tough. Never before have there been so many people in
the world. In the past centuries the world's population has been
smaller; in the future centuries it is destined to be larger. And this
brings us to that old bugbear that has been so frequently laughed
away, and that still persists in raising its grisly head—namely, the
doctrine of Malthus. While man's increasing efficiency of food-pro-
duction, combined with colonization of whole virgin continents, has
for generations given the apparent lie to Malthus' mathematical
statement of the Law of Population, nevertheless the essential significance of his doctrine remains and cannot be challenged. Population *does* press against subsistence. And no matter how rapidly
subsistence increases, population is certain to catch up with it.

When man was in the hunting stage of development, wide areas
were necessary for the maintenance of scant populations. With the
shepherd stage, the means of subsistence being increased, a larger
population was supported on the same territory. The agricultural
stage gave support to a still larger population; and, to-day, with
the increased food-getting efficiency of a machine civilization, an
even larger population is made possible. Nor is this theoretical.
The population is here, a billion and three-quarters of men, women,
and children, and this vast population is increasing on itself by leaps
and bounds.

A heavy European drift to the New World has gone on and is
going on; yet Europe, whose population a century ago was 170,000,-
000, has to-day 500,000,000. At this rate of increase, provided that

subsistence is not overtaken, a century from now the population of Europe will be 1,500,000,000. And be it noted of the present rate of increase in the United States that only one-third is due to immigration, while two-thirds is due to excess of births over deaths. And at this present rate of increase, the population of the United States will be 500,000,000 in less than a century from now.

Man, the hungry one, the killer, has always suffered for lack of room. The world has been chronically overcrowded. •Belgium with her 572 persons to the square mile is no more crowded than was Denmark when it supported only 500 palæolithic people. According to Mr. Woodruff, cultivated land will produce 1,600 times as much food as hunting land. From the time of the Norman Conquest, for centuries Europe could support no more than twenty-five to the square mile. To-day Europe supports eighty-one to the square mile. The explanation for this is that for the several centuries after the Norman Conquest her population was saturated. Then, with the development of trading and capitalism, of exploration and exploitation of new lands, and with the invention of labor-saving machinery, and the discovery and application of scientific principles, was brought about a tremendous increase in Europe's food-getting efficiency. And immediately her population sprang up.

According to the census of Ireland, of 1659, that country had a population of 500,000. One hundred and fifty years later, her population was 8,000,000. For many centuries the population of Japan was stationary. There seemed no way of increasing her food-getting efficiency. Then, sixty years ago, came Commodore Perry, knocking down her doors and letting in the knowledge and machinery of the superior food-getting efficiency of the Western world. Immediately upon this rise in subsistence began the rise of population; and it is only the other day that Japan, finding her population once again pressing against subsistence, embarked, sword in hand, on a westward drift in search of more room. And, sword in hand, killing and being killed, she has carved out for herself Formosa and Korea, and driven the vanguard of her drift far into the rich interior of Manchuria.

For an immense period of time China's population has remained at 400,000,000—the saturation point. The only reason that the Yellow River periodically drowns millions of Chinese is that there is no other land for those millions to farm. And after every such catastrophe the wave of human life rolls up and new millions flood out upon that precarious territory. They are driven to it, because they are pressed remorselessly against subsistence. It is inevitable that China, sooner or later, like Japan, will learn and put into application our own superior food-getting efficiency. And when that time comes, it is likewise inevitable that her population will increase by unguessed millions until it again reaches the saturation point. And then, inoculated with Western ideas, may she not, like Japan, take sword in hand and start forth colossally on a drift of her own for more room? This is another reputed bogie—the Yellow Peril; yet the men of China are only men, like any other race of men, and all men, down all history, have drifted hungrily, here, there and everywhere over the planet, seeking for something to eat. What other men do, may not the Chinese do?

But a change in the affairs of man has long been coming. The more recent drifts of the stronger races, carving their way through the lesser breeds to more earth-space, have led to peace, ever to wider and more lasting peace. The lesser breeds, under penalty of being killed, have been compelled to lay down their weapons and cease killing among themselves. The scalp-taking Indian and the head-hunting Melanesian have been either destroyed or converted to a belief in the superior efficiency of civil suits and criminal prosecutions. The planet is being subdued. The wild and the hurtful are either tamed or eliminated. From the beasts of prey and the cannibal humans down to the death-dealing microbes, no quarter is given; and daily, wider and wider areas of hostile territory, whether of a warring desert-tribe in Africa or a pestilential fever-hole like Panama, are made peaceable and habitable for mankind. As for the great mass of stay-at-home folk, what percentage of the present generation in the United States, England, or Germany, has seen war or knows anything of war at first hand? There was never so much peace in the world as there is to-day.

War itself, the old red anarch, is passing. It is safer to be a soldier than a workingman. The chance for life is greater in an active campaign than in a factory or a coal mine. In the matter of killing, war is growing impotent, and this in face of the fact that the machinery of war was never so expensive in the past nor so dreadful. War-equipment to-day, in time of peace, is more expensive than of old in time of war. A standing army costs more to maintain than it used to cost to conquer an empire. It is more expensive to be ready to kill, than it used to be to do the killing. The price of a Dreadnought would furnish the whole army of Xerxes with killing weapons. And, in spite of its magnificent equipment, war no longer kills as it used to when its methods were simpler. A bombardment by a modern fleet has been known to result in the killing of one mule. The casualties of a twentieth century war between two world-powers are such as to make a worker in an iron-foundry turn green with envy. War has become a joke. Men have made for themselves monsters of battle which they cannot face in battle. Subsistence is generous these days, life is not cheap, and it is not in the nature of flesh and blood to indulge in the carnage made possible by present-day machinery. This is not theoretical, as will be shown by a comparison of deaths in battle and men involved, in the South African War and the Spanish American War on the one hand, and the Civil War or the Napoleonic Wars on the other.

Not only has war, by its own evolution, rendered itself futile, but man himself, with greater wisdom and higher ethics, is opposed to war. He has learned too much. War is repugnant to his common sense. He conceives it to be wrong, to be absurd, and to be very expensive. For the damage wrought and the results accomplished, it is not worth the price. Just as in the disputes of individuals the arbitration of a civil court instead of a blood feud is more practical, so, man decides, is arbitration more practical in the disputes of nations.

War is passing, disease is being conquered, and man's food-getting efficiency is increasing. It is because of these factors that there are a billion and three-quarters of people alive to-day instead of a billion, or three-quarters of a billion. And it is because of these factors that the world's population will very soon be two billions and climbing rapidly toward three billions. The lifetime of the generation is increasing steadily. Men live longer these days. Life is not so precarious. The newborn infant has a greater chance for survival than at any time in the past. Surgery and sanitation reduce the fatalities that accompany the mischances of life and the ravages of disease. Men and women, with deficiencies and weaknesses that in the past would have effected their rapid extinction, live to-day and father and mother a numerous progeny. And high as the food-getting efficiency may soar, population is bound to soar after it. The " abysmal fecundity " of life has not altered. Given the food, and life will increase. A small percentage of the billion and three-quarters that live to-day may hush the clamor of life to be born, but it is only a small percentage. In this particular, the life in the man-animal is very like the life in the other animals.

And still another change is coming in human affairs. Though politicians gnash their teeth and cry anathema, and men, whose superficial book-learning is vitiated by crystallized prejudice, assure us that civilization will go to smash, the trend of society, to-day, the world over, is toward socialism. The old individualism is passing. The state interferes more and more in affairs that hitherto have been considered sacredly private. And socialism, when the last word is said, is merely a new economic and political system whereby more men can get food to eat. In short, socialism is an improved food-getting efficiency.

Furthermore, not only will socialism get food more easily and in greater quantity, but it will achieve a more equitable distribution of that food. Socialism promises, for a time, to give all men, women, and children all they want to eat, and to enable them to eat all they want as often as they want. Subsistence will be pushed back, temporarily, an exceedingly long way. In consequence, the flood of life will rise like a tidal wave. There will be more marriages and more children born. The enforced sterility that obtains to-day for many millions, will no longer obtain. Nor will the fecund millions in the slums and labor-ghettos, who to-day die of all the ills. due to chronic underfeeding and overcrowding, and who die with their fecundity largely unrealized, die in that future day when the increased food-getting efficiency of socialism will give them all they want to eat.

It is undeniable that population will increase prodigiously—just as it has increased prodigiously during the last few centuries, following upon the increase in food-getting efficiency. The magnitude of population in that future day is well-nigh unthinkable. But there is only so much land and water on the surface of the earth. Man, despite his marvelous accomplishments, will never be able to increase the diameter of the planet. The old days of virgin continents will be gone. The habitable planet, from ice-cap to ice-cap, will be inhabited. And in the matter of food-getting, as in everything else, man is only finite. Undreamed efficiencies in food-getting may be achieved, but, soon or late, man will find himself face to face with Malthus' grim law. Not only will population catch up with subsistence, but it will press against subsistence, and the pressure will be pitiless and savage. Somewhere in the future is a date when man will face, consciously, the bitter fact that there is not food enough for all of him to eat.

When this day comes, what then? Will there be a recrudescence of old obsolete war? In a saturated population life is always cheap, as it is cheap in China, in India, to-day. Will new human drifts take place, questing for room, carving earth-space out of crowded life? Will the Sword again sing:

> " Follow, O follow, then,
> Heroes, my harvesters!
> Where the tall grain is ripe
> Thrust in your sickles!
> Stripped and adust
> In a stubble of empire,
> Scything and binding
> The full sheaves of sovranty."

Even if, as of old, man should wander hungrily, sword in hand, slaying and being slain, the relief would be only temporary. Even if one race alone should hew down the last survivor of all the other races, that one race, drifting the world around, would saturate the planet with its own life and again press against subsistence. And in that day, the death rate and the birth rate will have to balance. Men will have to die, or be prevented from being born. Undoubtedly a higher quality of life will obtain, and also a slowly decreasing fecundity. But this decrease will be so slow that the pressure against subsistence will remain. The control of progeny will be one of the most important problems of man and one of the most important functions of the state.

Disease, from time to time, will ease the pressure. Diseases are parasites, and it must not be forgotten that just as there are drifts in the world of man, so are there drifts in the world of micro-organisms —hunger-quests for food. Little is known of the micro-organic world, but that little is appalling; and no census of it will ever be taken, for there is the true, literal " abysmal fecundity." Multitudinous as man is, all his totality of individuals is as nothing in comparison with the inconceivable vastness of numbers of the micro-organisms. In your body, or in mine, right now, are swarming more individual entities than there are human beings in the world to-day. It is to us an invisible world. We only guess its nearest confines. With our powerful microscopes and ultramicroscopes, enlarging diameters twenty thousand times, we catch but the slightest glimpses of that profundity of infinitesimal life.

Little is known of that world, save in a general way. We know that out of it arise diseases, new to us, that afflict and destroy man. We do not know whether these diseases are merely the drifts, in a fresh direction, of already-existing breeds of micro-organisms, or whether they are new, absolutely new, breeds themselves just spontaneously generated. The latter hypothesis is tenable, for if spontaneous generation still occurs on the earth, it is far more likely to occur in the form of simple organisms than of complicated organisms.

Another thing we know, and that is that it is in crowded populations that new diseases arise. They have done so in the past. They do so to-day. And no matter how wise are our physicians and bacteriologists, no matter how successfully they cope with these invaders, new invaders continue to arise—new drifts of hungry life seeking to devour us. And so we are justified in believing that in the saturated populations of the future, when life is suffocating in the pressure against subsistence, new, and ever new, hosts of destroying micro-organisms will continue to arise and fling themselves upon earth-crowded man to give him room. There may even be plagues of unprecedented ferocity that will depopulate great areas before the wit of man can overcome them. And this we know: that no matter how often these invisible hosts may be overcome by man's becoming immune to them through a cruel and terrible selection, new hosts will ever arise of these micro-organisms that were in the world before he came and that will be here after he is gone.

After he is gone? Will he then some day be gone, and this planet know him no more? Is it thence that the human drift in all its totality is trending? God Himself is silent on this point, though some of His prophets have given us vivid representations of that last day when the earth shall pass into nothingness. Nor does science, despite its radium speculations and its attempted analysis of the ultimate nature of matter, give us any other word than that man will pass. So far as man's knowledge goes, law is universal. Elements react under certain unchangeable conditions. One of these conditions is temperature. Whether it be in the test tube of the laboratory or the workshop of nature, all organic chemical reactions take place only within a restricted range of heat. Man, the latest of the ephemera, is pitifully a creature of temperature, strutting his brief day on the thermometer. Behind him is a past wherein it was too warm for him to exist. Ahead of him is a future wherein it will be too cold for him to exist. He cannot adjust himself to that future, because he cannot alter universal law, because he cannot alter his own construction or the molecules that compose him.

It would be well to ponder these lines of Herbert Spencer's which follow, and which embody, possibly, the widest vision the scientific mind has ever achieved :

" Motion as well as Matter being fixed in quantity, it would seem that the change in the distribution of Matter which Motion effects, coming to a limit in whichever direction it is carried, the indestructible Motion thereupon necessitates a reverse distribution. Apparently, the universally-co-existent forces of attraction and repulsion, which, as we have seen, necessitate rhythm in all minor changes throughout the Universe, also necessitate rhythm in the totality of its changes—produce now an immeasurable period during which the attractive forces predominating, cause universal concentration, and then an immeasurable period during which the repulsive forces predominating, cause universal diffusion—alternate eras of Evolution and Dissolution. *And thus there is suggested the conception of a past during which there have been successive Evolutions analogous to that which is now going on; and a future during which successive other Evolutions may go on—ever the same in principle but never the same in concrete result.*"

That is it—the most we may know—alternate eras of evolution and dissolution. In the past there have been other evolutions similar to that one in which we live, and in the future there may be other similar evolutions—that is all. The principle of all these evolutions remains, but the concrete results are never twice alike. Man was not; he was; and again he will not be. In the eternity which is beyond our comprehension, the particular evolution of that solar satellite we call the "Earth" occupies but a slight fraction of time. And of that fraction of time man occupies but a small portion. All the whole human drift, from the first ape-man to the last savant, is but a phantom, a flash of light and a flutter of movement across the infinite face of the starry night.

When the thermometer drops, man ceases—with all his lusts and wrestlings and achievements; with all his race-adventures and race-tragedies; and with all his red killings, billions upon billions of human lives multiplied by as many billions more. This is the last word of Science, unless there be some further, unguessed word which Science will some day find and utter. In the meantime it sees no farther than the starry void, where the "fleeting systems lapse like foam." Of what ledger-account is the tiny life of man in a vastness where stars snuff out like candles and great suns blaze for a time-tick of eternity and are gone?

And for us who live, no worse can happen than has happened to the earlier drifts of man, marked to-day by ruined cities of foreign civilizations—ruined cities, which, on excavation, are found to rest on ruins of earlier cities, city upon city, and further cities, down to a stratum where, still earlier, wandering herdsmen drove their flocks, and where, even preceding them, wild hunters chased their prey long after the cave-man and the man of the squatting-place cracked the knuckle-bones of wild animals and vanished from the earth. There is nothing terrible about it. With Richard Hovey, when he faced death, we can say: "Behold! I have lived!" And with another and greater one, we can lay ourselves down with a will. The one drop of living, the one taste of being, has been good; and perhaps our greatest achievement will be that we dreamed immortality, even though we failed to realize it.

THE ITALIANS IN THE UNITED STATES

ALBERTO PECORINI

THERE are something like 2,000,000 Italians in the United States, and of these considerably more than 500,000 are living in the City of New York, so that the Italian problem—if, indeed, an Italian problem exists—may be said to be centred here. The Italian population of New York is increasing at the rate of at least 50,000 per year, while the approximate 4,000,000 of other nationalities, native and foreign, grows at the rate of only 200,000 per year. This increase among the Italians began with the year 1903, and continued until 1907. One effect of the bank panic of that year was to cause an exodus to Italy, as a result of which the Italian population of the city remained stationary until last year. In 1909, however, the increase was again approximately 50,000; and, similar conditions as at present continuing to exist, the same annual growth is likely to continue for at least ten years more. It is probable, therefore, that taking the natural growth of the present population with the increase from Italy into consideration, the Italian population in 1917 or 1918 will number 1,000,000 of the potential 6,000,000 residents of New York City, or one-sixth of the population, instead of one-eighth, as they are to-day. It is more difficult to predict the growth of the Italian population in the United States outside of New York City, but the ratio is likely to remain about the same as at present.

The Italians are here; they are coming, and it is worth while to consider what effect this great tide of immigration of one nationality is likely to have upon the well-being of New York City in particular and the country in general. I believe that the United States have derived benefit from the coming of the hundreds of thousands of my countrymen who are already here, and that that benefit will become increasingly manifest with the advent of additional hundreds of thousands. The average American to-day, however, feels somewhat uneasy when he thinks of the immense number of Italian immigrants crowding into New York and other large cities of the East, although there was a time when the Italian immigrant was received

with open arms in the metropolis. During the years which preceded
the Italian revolution, Italy was not a safe place for Italian patriots;
and, although the majority of them preferred to follow Mazzini to
England, many came to America. In 1849, as soon as the news of
the liberal policy adopted by Pius IX reached New York, a mass
meeting was held at which several of the greatest living Americans
were present to help the cause of the unification of Italy. Those
were what may be called the heroic times of Italian immigration—
when Garibaldi lived in a poor frame house on Staten Island and
worked as a candle maker in a shop in Bleecker Street. Before 1879
most of the Italians of New York were from Northern Italy, but
after that year immigrants from the South and from Sicily came
in very large numbers, and with the recent rapid growth of the
Italian population attention has been attracted by the condition of
the Italian quarters, by the personal appearance of the Italian laborer, and by the headlines in the newspapers about Italian criminals.
Thus the former sympathy with the Italian disappeared to a large
extent, and many Americans have gone to the other extreme and actually oppose Italian immigration.

Before coming to a definite conclusion as to the value of the
Italian in the community, is it not well that the American people
should know all the facts concerning him in order that final judgment
may be impartial? It is only by facts that a clear interpretation of
the life of the whole mass of the members of the race, as distinguished
from that of only a small part of it, may be had.

Conditions existing in New York may be said to approximate
those of the other American cities in which the Italians have made
their homes. In New York, although they are scattered throughout
the five boroughs, there are several quarters that may be considered
as distinctively Italian, of which three are in Manhattan, two in
the Bronx, and five in Brooklyn. In Manhattan there are two
Italian settlements in the lower part of the city, one on the east side
with its centre in Mulberry Street, and the other on the west side
with its centre in Bleecker Street; uptown the Italian quarter is
known as " Little Italy," and its centre is Jefferson Park in Harlem.
The population both of " Little Italy " and the Mulberry Street
settlements are almost entirely from Southern Italy and Sicily,

while in that centring on Bleecker Street there are a large number of Italians from the North. In the Bronx are two Italian quarters: one with its centre in Morris Avenue near 150th Street, and the other near Bedford Park and 200th Street. In Brooklyn the oldest Italian quarter is to be found between Atlantic Avenue and Hamilton Avenue, and the others are in Navy Street; in Williamsburg; in Flatbush, and at the west end of Coney Island.

Life in these Italian settlements is to a large extent explained by the composition of the population. Four-fifths of the Italians of New York come from centres of less than 10,000 population, and are therefore entirely new to the active and exciting life of a great city. American students of social conditions have referred to the Italian settlements of New York as cities within a city. As a matter of fact, they are a collection of small villages, with all the characteristics of village life. In one street will be found peasants from one Italian village; in the next street the place of origin is different and distinct, and diffcrent and distinct are manners, customs and sympathies. Entire villages have been transplanted from Italy to one New York street, and with the others have come the doctor, the grocer, the priest, and the annual celebration of the local patron saint. The acute rivalry between village people, who have not developed and can scarcely be expected to develop in a short period what may be called " city consciousness," is perhaps the most important cause of the lack of coherence in the Italian mass, which makes impossible united and persistent effort on its part in any direction, economic, social or political.

In the Italian quarters the life is that of the tenement. The families are usually large, and in most of them boarders are taken with a view to eking out the payment of the rent. There are tenements occupied by Italians in New York in which eight and ten men sleep in one room, with not more than 1,500 cubic feet of air to breathe, for eight or nine hours. Very often a whole family occupies a single sleeping room, children over fourteen years of age sleeping with their parents or with smaller brothers and sisters. The first consequence of this overcrowding is an astonishing decline in physical strength. Thousands of Italians who come to New York robust and healthy go back every year to their native country to die.

The records of the Board of Health show that the death rate among the Italians in New York is higher than that of any other nationality, being no less than 36.43 in the thousand, as against an average of 18.71, the next highest being that of the Irish, 23.55, and the lowest that of the Germans, 12.13, while that of native Americans is 13.98. Consumption and bronco-penumonia are the most fatal diseases among adult Italians, and diphtheria and measles (both easily cured if treated in time) the principal causes of the high death rate among the children, because of the ignorance of the Italian mothers.

Ignorance is, indeed, the cause of most of the evils of Italian immigration in this country. Almost 50 per cent. of all Italian adults in New York are illiterate; and, as a whole, they form a mass of faithful and honest workers—the most useful, and in a certain sense the most needed, if not the most desirable. These are the men who excavate the subways, clean the streets, work at the cement foundations of the skyscrapers, and build the great railway stations. Their ignorance, however, creates a number of problems that otherwise would not exist. Not being able to make their own contracts, they must depend on some boss or " padrone "; they work when and where he sends them, and take what he gives them. Not being able to read or write, they must hire somebody to indite letters to Italy and send money to the family there. This somebody is the " banker "—a curious product of the Italian quarter. The banker receives the mail of his clients, who are usually from the same village as himself; he writes their letters, sends their money, sells them steamship and railway tickets, acts as notary public; he goes with them to the Italian consulate to arrange matters for them there; he is, in fact, adviser of the ignorant Italian in all his business affairs. Quite a number of these bankers have absconded with the money of their patrons, and the marvel is, when the ignorance of the Italian mass is taken into consideration, that so many of the bankers are honest. Perhaps the circumstance that a victimized Italian, more particularly if he is from the South, is likely to take the law into his own hands when he finds his despoiler rather than hale him into court, may have some bearing on this phase of the matter. Very often the banker and the padrone, as well as the grocer and the real estate man, are themselves half-illiterate, though they have a decided advantage over the laborer in that they have lived longer in the country and have some knowledge of their environment and of American methods. With the increase of their business, however, they are compelled to employ educated assistants—and Italian professional talent is cheap in New York. There are Italian lawyers and professional men, with diplomas from renowned universities, acting as clerks to half-illiterate bankers and contractors at salaries of from $6 to $10 per week.

Aside from the professional men, the half-illiterate man of business, and the laborer, there is still another intermediate Italian-American type, somewhat above the others in education, but not sufficiently cultivated to associate with the university graduates. He is the son of the little merchant in Italy, who has been through the elementary schools, but could not meet the requirements of the high school; the man who served three years in the army, and went to prison for making fun of his peasant corporal, and who finally landed in America without any trade, and, what is worse, with no inclination or intention to work. A new land, a new environment, often works wonders, and some of these derelicts find fields of honest activity in trade and industry, but a large number of them unite with the few criminals escaped from Italy, and form a class of half-educated malefactors—the "Black Handers," if you care thus to term them. To these outlaws the poor, illiterate laborer and his prosperous half-illiterate boss fall an equally easy prey, and on them they manage to subsist. The laborer they exploit and swindle at every turn, and occasionally succeed in robbing him of all his savings as he is about to take the steamer home. The boss is duped and despoiled in many ingenious ways. These predal opportunists flatter him in magnificent articles published in weekly newspapers and magazines that are born and die in the Italian quarters with wonderful rapidity; they get money for subscriptions to and advertisements in newspapers that are never published at all; they take his part in foolish quarrels with equally vain competitors for the presidency of a society, perhaps, or over a decoration expected from the Italian Government; and, after all other expedients have been employed, they demand money with threatening letters, kidnap his children, or put a stick of dynamite in his cellar.

In another way does ignorance among the Italians in this country breed criminals. The children born in this country of the Italian illiterate laborer never see a book or a newspaper in their homes, until they bring them there from the public schools. These children cannot help making comparisons between the palatial surroundings of the school and the squalid tenements in which they live; between the intelligence, knowledge and grace of the teachers and the ignorance and bad manners of their own parents. The illiterate Calabrian or Sicilian has a much larger grounding of sound common sense than his American child who has studied history, geography, arithmetic, and a number of other beautiful things, but the youngster who has reached the eighth grade becomes vain of his knowledge and too often looks with disdain upon his unlettered parents. If the illiterate father succeeds in swearing falsely as to the age of his child, and sends him to work at the age of twelve, the chances are that he will make of him an honest and industrious worker and a second-rate citizen. If, however, the boy goes on to the ninth grade, he too often breaks from the influence of his parents, when he begins a career of idleness in the pool-room, continues it in the saloon, and ends in the reformatory or the jail. The breaking up of family ties results even more disastrously in the case of girls, but fortunately natural instinct keeps them more securely under the influence of the mother. The young American-educated Italian criminals already constitute a much graver problem than the uneducated criminal from Italy, or the older Italian criminals created by environment in this country.

What proportion of the 50,000 Italian pupils of the public schools in New York, and of the 5,000 in the parochial schools, are subject to the process of demoralization described above, it is difficult to estimate. Even in well-to-do Italian families, however, there are not a few parents who complain bitterly of the system of American education, and of the degree of liberty manifested by children in their relations with fathers and mothers. There are, of course, many Italian children who take advantage of the opportunities offered them in this country that would never have been theirs in Italy. A number of young Italians have been graduated from Columbia University, and there is even a society of Italian students, most of them attending Columbia and the City College, that numbers a hundred members. On the whole, nevertheless, the Italians of the second generation in America pay more heavily than the second generation of settlers from north-western Europe that preceded them, the price of the sudden change from the environment of their parents. The relatively few successful youths of Italian parentage and American birth and education are lost to the Italian population of New York; they are not interpreters of American life and American ideals, as they should be.

At this point I feel that I ought to make an apology to the Italians of America. They may justly say that I have drawn a dark picture; that I have presented the very worst features of Italian life here. This I have done purposely, for, thus far, one of the most discouraging features of the situation has been the lack of serious and zealous study, by the Italians, of conditions among themselves in the new land. On the whole, however, the Italian outlook in the United States is encouraging. First of all, Italian immigration is improving. The day of the organ-grinder, once the only representative of his race, has passed forever, and that of the ignorant peasant is rapidly passing. Illiteracy is diminishing, and with it the evils of which it has been the principal cause. The Italians who have come to New York in recent years—and, as has been noted, conditions among the Italians here are approximately those in other American cities—have not all been mere manual laborers, but in a large measure representatives of the different trades. There are to-day in the city fifteen thousand Italian tailors, many of them employed in the best establishments of Fifth Avenue and Broadway, earning from $40 to $100 per week. Almost one half of the barbers in New York are Italians, and satisfaction with their cleanliness and skill is general. There are thousands of printers, mechanics, bricklayers, electricians and carpenters at work here, and their employers will testify that they are among the most sober, honest and industrious of workmen.

The rising movement among the Italians has been noticed especially·in trade and industry. The retail fruit business is to a large extent, and the artificial flower industry almost entirely, in their hands. Italian hotels and restaurants are popular with Americans, and the Italian 50-cent *table d'hôte* is conceded to be the best to be had for that amount. Italians are prominent in the contracting business, although contractors generally can not be considered the most desirable class of Italians, many of them being utterly uneducated and taking advantage of the ignorance of the laborers of their race. Italian importers and merchants are no longer small storekeepers, importing a few barrels of wine or boxes of macaroni from their native villages, to be distributed among purchasers from the same villages; they are members of well-organized and powerful firms, with offices on Broadway and elsewhere side by side with those of important American merchants and importers. Four-fifths of all the trade between Italy and the United States, which amounts to $100,000,000 per year, passes through New York, and the greater part of it is controlled by Italians, from the importation of raw silk to that of lemons, olive oil and macaroni.

The number of Italian bankers doing a legitimate business among their countrymen in New York, especially since the enactment of the law compelling them to give a bond to the state, is increasing every day. There are at present more than a hundred of these bankers in New York; and, while most of their business is that of steamship agents and notaries public, there are several important financial institutions among them. One of these, founded in 1865, occupies fine quarters in Wall Street. The number of the bankers of the old irresponsible type is rapidly decreasing, partly on account of the decrease of ignorance among the Italian masses, but more particularly because of the establishment here of the Italian Savings Bank and of an agency of the Bank of Naples. On the first of the year the Savings Bank held total deposits of $2,395,750.71, divided among 11,170 depositors. The agency of the Bank of Naples, which was established by the Italian Government to facilitate the transfer of money from Italian immigrants here to their families at home, under normal conditions sends to Italy $5,000,000 annually—and about $2,000,000 is sent each year through the Post Office. Italian business men have in the banking field, as their particular financial organ, the Savoy Trust Company, founded five years ago as the Italian-American Trust Company. This institution has a capital of $500,000; and, although during the panic of 1907 its deposits dwindled to an insignificant amount, it weathered the storm, and is prospering to-day in its handsome offices on Broadway, with deposits of $2,000,000. An institution that is inspiring and directing Italian trade in New York is the Italian Chamber of Commerce, which, in existence for many years, has recently been reorganized and is now controlled by younger and more capable men.

Italian professional men are involved in the general uplift. The lawyers of to-day, although many of them are bad enough, are a great improvement upon their fellows of only ten years ago. Formerly, when actions were brought for damages in case of accident, the lawyer who appeared for the complainant was in the pay of the individual or corporation responsible for the casualty; he would accept ridiculously small compensation on behalf of his client, and then divide that with the unfortunate laborer who had been injured, or with his family in the event of his death. This practice, once the rule, still exists as an exception. There are almost 400 Italian physicians in New York, and by far the majority of them are respectable and able men. Competition among them has been somewhat severe in the past, and it is yet to some extent. However the Italian Medical Association of New York was recently formed, with headquarters in the Metropolitan Building, and at its first annual banquet, held at the Hotel Astor, the Italian doctors demonstrated that vast possibilities exist among them for serious, organized effort for the good of the Italian masses.

The professional men suggest the artists. There are, of course, the Italian operatic " stars," who are attracted by the high prices offered by the American impresarios, but who do not come to stay. Those artists who remain are the musicians, the teachers of music and the decorators. The musicians have already made their presence felt, having practically abolished the monopoly held for years by German bands and orchestras; the decorators are already asserting themselves as against artists of other nationalities, and their work may be seen in the handsomest theatres and the finest hotels. And among the artists, may I be pardoned if I mention the cooks? They claim that theirs comes first among the *beaux arts*, and a great many of us agree with them. Well, Italian cooks are already employed in large numbers in the most fashionable restaurants and hotels, and the day is not far off when they will destroy the monopoly of the French *chefs des cuisines* as they ended that of the German musicians.

That the Italian Government has done a great deal for the Italian immigrants in America cannot be denied. The Society for Italian Immigrants, which protects ignorant arrivals from thieves and swindlers and gives them food and shelter for 50 cents a day until they may find work, is largely subsidized by the Italian Government, as is the Home for Italian Immigrants, established by the St. Raphael Society under the presidency of Archbishop Farley. The Italian Government also maintains an Italian labor bureau in New York for the distribution of immigration, and an Italian inspectorate of immigration informs the Government at Rome of the conditions of labor in this country. The Italian Government further has subscribed $60,000 toward the fund for the erection of an Italian hospital in New York.

The Roman Catholic Church is, of course, the most important religious agency among the Italians in America. There are about fifty Italian churches of this denomination and more than eighty priests in New York. Various Protestant denominations have also established churches and missions throughout the Italian quarters, twenty of which are now in operation. Grace Episcopal Church, the Methodist Episcopal Church of Jefferson Park, and the Presbyterian Church in University Place, have been particularly successful in social work among the Italians. Settlement work exclusively among Italians, both in Manhattan and Brooklyn, has had a far-reaching influence, the Richmond Hill House in the former borough being a centre of activity.

The most important educational centre for Italians in New York at present is the great English and trade school, recently established by the Children's Aid Society in the two large buildings formerly used by the Five Points House of Industry, in Worth Street. Here nearly 500 Italians of both sexes may be found every evening. There are classes in English, stenography, typewriting, sewing, cooking, sign painting and printing, as well as a gymnasium, club rooms, a library and a large auditorium. The Young Men's Christian Association has also done a great deal in the way of evening classes for Italians, half the membership of the Bowery branch, for instance, being of that race. The Italians are further receiving efficient help from the Board of Education in the matter of evening schools and lectures in Italian, and it is a cause for regret that these schools and lectures are not patronized as are those in the Jewish quarters. For the last eight years there has been an Italian member of the Board of Education.

It is to be regretted that the Italian press, by reason of a mistaken idea of patriotism, is not serving as an interpreter of American life and ideals to its constituency. Nevertheless the Italian press has followed the general movement forward, though it has not led it. There are six Italian daily newspapers in New York with a circulation varying from 10,000 to 30,000 copies per day. About half of these newspapers have a larger circulation out of than in the city, and all have special agents hunting for subscribers in the smaller towns, the mining districts and the labor camps. The first Italian newspapers consisted merely of translations from American journals, and even now the Italian press has no local news service of its own, while almost every daily imposes upon itself a great sacrifice for its cable service from Italy. While a great part of the advertising of the Italian newspapers comes from steamship companies, professional men, importers and merchants, there is still too large a proportion from fake doctors, real estate swindlers, and alleged brokers who sell to the immigrant the stock of companies that do not exist. However, there are two Italian dailies that enjoy the distinction of having refused money offered for political support at the last municipal election, and of having helped the Fusion cause without recompense—a startling reform in Italian journalism. It is to be hoped that in the future the Italian press may not confine its benevolent activities to the providing of the city with monuments to Italian worthies, but that it will attempt to instruct the Italian masses with regard to their duties in their new environment.

That Italians to-day are coming to America in families in much larger numbers than ever before is a most encouraging sign. Accustomed and attached to family life, the Italian is lost without it. The proportion of Italian women coming to the country is much greater than it was, and Italian life in American cities is little by little losing the appearance of impermanence it presented when a small number of families, each with a large number of men boarders, was the rule. Another encouraging feature of the situation is that Italian books are coming into the United States in much larger quantities than in the past, one dealer in Broadway having imported as many as a million volumes last year, three-fourths of which were fairy tales and popular novels, the literary pabulum of artisan families in Italy. The Italian uplift in New York may further be said to have found expression in the formation of an up-to-date men's club, with a handsome house near Fifth Avenue. The Italian Club has more than 350 members, with an initiation fee of $100, and it boasts of having sold $600 worth of champagne to its members last New Year's Eve—thus measuring a long step forward in the arts of civilization.

So much for the urban Italian. One of the arguments urged against the race, that they are a failure in the United States, because, having been engaged in agricultural pursuits at home they turn to other labor here, is rather proof of their value to their adopted country. On this point may be cited an interesting paradox in the history of immigration, to be found in the fact that during a decade of agricultural expansion in the United States, from 1870 to 1880, her greatest immigration was from the industrial countries of north-western Europe, Great Britain and Ireland, Norway, Sweden and Germany, while, during a like period of industrial expansion, from 1895 to 1905, her principal immigration was from south-eastern Europe, Greece, Italy, Austria, Hungary, Poland and Russia. The riddle is easily read: forty years ago the crying need of the country was for agricultural workers; hence the immigrants from north-western Europe went to the West and settled there. Immigration from south-eastern Europe, and particularly from Italy, was at its height at the time of the demand here for mill workers and unskilled laborers of all kinds in the building industries fifteen years ago, and hence the Italians crowded into the large cities of the north-east, and were employed chiefly in manufactures. The Italian working population of the United States today is approximately 1,200,000, of whom 67 per cent. were engaged in agriculture at home, while only 6.60 per cent. of them are actually engaged in agriculture here. If, then, the Italian immigrants have been an agricultural failure in the United States, they have been an industrial success, and moreover have proved their capacity to "make good" in either pursuit, the fact being that their occupatiou here depends upon economic conditions, and not upon any particular preference of their own.

The small percentage of Italians engaged in agriculture in this country have developed in three distinct fields—truck farming, extensive agriculture, and fruit raising. During the last ten years a considerable number of farms, abandoned by Americans who have gone west or entered business in the cities, have been occupied by Italians in Western New York and the New England States. Truck farming has been carried on to a greater extent, however, in New Jersey, Pennsylvania and the Carolinas. In Ohio there are Italian truck farmers in the vicinity of Cincinnati and Cleveland, and fruits are raised by Italians in large quantities near the former city. The vicinity of Chicago, in Illinois, has also a large number of Italian farmers, many of whom make sausages after the Italian fashion, which, being sold in the east, seriously menace the trade in the imported Italian kind. Recently the Long Island railroad has established an experimental agricultural station, where Italians have been successfully raising vegetables. Long Island, like New Jersey, Western New York and the lower part of the Connecticut Valley, will in the next few years see an even greater number of Italian farmers raising vegetables on land neglected or abandoned by native Americans.

The second field in which the Italian has been tried out as an agricultural laborer in the United States is in what I have termed extensive agriculture. Italians are not numerous in the wheat and corn fields of the Dakotas and Kansas, but they have gone in considerable numbers to the cotton, sugar cane, and tobacco fields of the south and south-west. Of the 30,000 Italians in Louisiana, about one-half are working on sugar and cotton plantations. Reports from the famous farm colony of Sunny Side, in Arkansas, founded by the late Austin Corbin, in which many Italians are employed, show that in spite of adverse conditions they are much more than holding their own in competition with the negro. Very few

Italians have penetrated into Alabama, although they are raising vegetables and tobacco in two agricultural colonies in that state. Texas, on the contrary, is a wide open and inviting field for the Italian, and already 15,000 of them are engaged in agriculture there.

It is, however, in fruit culture that the Italian agriculturist has been the most successful in the New World. Almost every Italian owning a farm raises fruit to some extent, but the great fruit-bearing country for them is California, in which state are 60,000 Italians, of whom fully one-half are engaged in agriculture. Vines of all kinds have been imported from the most celebrated wine-producing districts of Europe, and for the last few years the American tourist has been drinking London claret produced by the Italian in California.

As to the future of the Italian engaged in agriculture, the country need have no misgivings; for he loves the soil and his most ardent desire is to own his little piece of land as soon as possible. The need of the urban Italian is a civic need. There are only a little more than 15,000 voters among the half million Italians in New York, approximately 3 per cent., while the proportion among other foreign nationalities varies from 15 per cent. to 25 per cent. The naturalized Italians are mostly of the class of laborers, small storekeepers and petty contractors. The better elements have not as yet identified themselves with the community in which they live, in which their children were born, in which they own millions of dollars' worth of real estate, and pay millions annually in taxes. There is not an Italian holding an important municipal office. These conditions are abnormal, unhealthful, and they may become disastrous; they must be changed. Desirable Italian residents must become American citizens, and must take away the direction of their politics and the protection of their interests from the dealers in votes. Thus far relations between the Italian voter and the political parties have existed only at election time, and the better class of Italians have lost confidence in them.

To get votes is political propaganda; to make citizens an educational process. Citizens are needed far more than voters. To organize all educational agencies at present working among the Italians, and make them transform this inert, dead mass into a living progressive force, is an immediate necessity. A million unassimilated Italians in New York, with three millions in the United States, only a few years hence, will not tend to lessen the burden of government in the city or the nation. The problem of making a citizen of the Italian is not an insoluble one. It is only a question of going to work with a sincere desire to help, not to exploit; recognizing the bad side of Italian-American life, but giving full credit for the good. The Italian is certainly capable of contributing his full quota to the best life of the Republic, and it should be the task of earnest Americans to bring that consummation about. Only thus may what seems now a peril be made a blessing.

A SPRING-SONG IN A CAFÉ

WITTER BYNNER

As gray, on the table, lay his hand
As the root of a tree in a barren land,
   Or a rope that lowers the dead.

As gray as a gravestone was his head,
And as gray his beard as dusty grain;
   But his eyes were as gray as the rain,—

As gray as the rain that warms the snow,
The bridegroom who brings, to the grass below,
   A breath of the wedding-day.

O his eyes were the gray of a rain in May
That shall waken and mate a dead May-queen,
Shall marry and quicken a queen of the May
   When all the graves are green!

"LITTLE DARLING"

ROSE STRUNSKY

ONE morning when I was living in Ebba's house in Helsingfors, she herself brought in the coffee to my room and sat down on my bed. When Ebba did that it meant she had news which she could not possibly keep a minute longer.

"What is it?" I asked.

"Maljutka is in Finland and I am permitted to telephone to him."

"Well?" I said.

"Well, I am so happy. I feel as if my son had suddenly come back to me."

"Maljutka?" I asked. "That is a child's nickname in Russian, is it not? Doesn't it mean 'little darling'?"

"Yes, though he is not a child at all, but a handsome young corporal, turned revolutionist. I never knew his name and so of course I had to call him 'Maljutka.' Now everyone calls him that."

"Tell me about him."

"I can't. But he is wonderful. He has nerves of iron. You will see he will do great things yet—for that matter he has already done them."

"What?" I asked.

"You have heard of Valentine, have you not? Do you remember when he was sentenced to death in Sebastopol last August? It was Maljutka who got him out. A lot of Party people were there planning all kinds of desperate ways of getting out Valentine; even blowing a hole in the prison wall with a bomb and dashing up on a charger to rescue him was seriously thought of. You see, apart from all sentimental considerations they needed him. He was not a private; he was a leader, a general. The government knew full well who he was, but they did not know just what he had done, so they indicted him for organizing the Sebastopol mutiny. 'You can hang me for plotting against your ministers,' he said, 'but not for the mutiny. That did not happen to be in my department.' It did not bother the authorities much and they sentenced him to death, by hanging, preferably."

"Preferably!" and I gulped the coffee. "If they preferred it, why didn't they do it?"

The story that Valentine had been sentenced to death last year made no impression on me now. I had heard it before and I knew he was free, so I could afford to joke.

"Silly goose," said Ebba. "Don't you know that there is no capital punishment in Russia, except by special grace and under martial law? Well, they didn't have the special grace last year nor the martial law, and ergo they hadn't any hangmen on hand."

"They have managed to pick up a big enough force by now," I sniffed.

"Yes, but can you imagine the bother they had getting them! Can you imagine the authorities hunting high and low over the realm for a hangman and offering fifty, seventy-five, one hundred rubles for the job, and no one showing up! That's a picture for you."

"And in comes your Maljutka," I interrupted; "promises to do it, but doesn't, and runs off with Valentine and the hundred rubles and the rope."

Ebba looked horrified. "Maljutka offering to do it!" She seemed ready to strike me.

"By the way," I said, to change the trend this story had taken; "what did the authorities prefer next to the hanging?"

"Shooting."

"Oh! and after that exhibition in the War, they couldn't trust their sharpshooters to shoot straight. Was that it?"

"Not a bit of it," said Ebba. "Valentine was in the fortress, and the captain couldn't bring himself to stain the army by shooting a civilian. He heard there was a Circassian who would do the hanging, and he sent out messengers high and low for him. The brute would come in daily to Valentine's cell and tell his troubles to him. 'It is awfully hard getting him,' he would say. 'I don't know but you are to be shot after all,' and Valentine would coax to be shot. 'My father was Governor of Warsaw. You might give me military honors.'

" It was true that the army was in his blood, for he dreaded the hanging and prayed each night for the shooting. However, the captain still had his hopes in the Circassian and would come daily to tell of his disappointments or his progress."

" Pleasant for Valentine," I muttered.

" The captain did not want to torture Valentine. It was Valentine's natural sympathetic nature, which made the captain go to him with his troubles. There is that spell about Valentine—well, but that does not matter here.

" One day the captain came in, joyous. They had found the Circassian and he was coming in a few days, and he wanted to be congratulated. ' Nothing like perseverance,' etc. Valentine blanched. The captain looked at him well and went out. ·· Things were getting on and there were to be no more breaks. The situation began to look official. Everyone loved Valentine and had talked with him, and the captain had winked at it, because he was guilty himself; but now strict silence was enforced.

" Here is where Maljutka comes in, bless him. He was corporal over the corridor where Valentine sat, and he adored him. He racked his brains how to save him, and was in constant communication with Valentine's friends. The captain, whether he was suspicious of Maljutka's friendliness to Valentine, or whether he thought it was more official to change the personnel around him, put Maljutka in charge of another corridor. Maljutka was desperate. He had one plan—to dress Valentine up like a soldier and just to march out with him from the fortress. If it went, good; if not, well—it were better to die with him. But to carry this out Maljutka had to be near Valentine. He went to the captain with tears in his eyes. His heart was broken, he said. They had sullied his honor; his loyalty had been questioned. He must be returned to his corridor, confidence must be restored to him, or he would blow his brains out right there in front of the captain. The captain was pleased with such gallant sentiments and put him back at his old post.

" The next night the prisoners were given their weekly bath. Maljutka brought Valentine a soldier's costume and a razor. The room was crowded, yet Valentine had to shave himself and put on his costume unnoticed. ' It was the quickest shave in my life,' he said afterwards. He managed it all by turning to a corner, and shaved and dressed himself somehow. That is Valentine for you. And behold him walking out arm-in-arm with that trusted soldier, Maljutka, Corporal-whatever-his-name-is. Some day I will ask it. It will be famous yet. Well, they walked down five flights of stairs, with sentinels at each turning, and past the captain's office, and down to the court, through one gate and to the next, and so on and so on, not too leisurely nor too hastily, but determinately, as soldiers bent for the canteen. And sentinels, sentinels everywhere—thirty in all. And to each one there was a salute and a password to say, and Maljutka kept his back as stiff and straight as the best of corporals do, and his voice never trembled. And so they left the fortress and took the train for Roumania and crossed over to Paris, and from there back to Copenhagen for the boat to Helsingfors, and here they both came one fine morning ready for work again. Oh, the little darling! Do you wonder I love him?"

I put my cup down. "Can't I meet him?" I asked.

"If he comes here, of course. Meanwhile I can only telephone to him."

I came in rather abruptly one evening into Ebba's pink and white drawing-room and found Volodya and a tall youth sitting on the divan in front of the table, intent upon a sheet of pink paper they were trying to decipher. Ebba was also sitting near the table and looking quietly on, with her head resting on her hand. The young man was startled when I entered and covered the paper. He glanced quickly at Ebba.

"It is all right," she said. "That is the American girl I told you about. This is Maljutka," she said to me.

We shook hands. There was something striking in his stiffness. He carried his head very high and straight, and there was a prominent "Adam's apple" in his neck—"A neck that would break in the noose, not bend," I said to myself, and shuddered. I would have given anything not to have had that thought, but try as I would all evening, I could not drive the picture of a straight back and a broken neck out of my mind. There was no apparent reason for thoughts so gruesome. All were seemingly in good spirits, and even Volodya's wistful little smile gave place to hearty laughter often during the evening. We talked gaily. The paper was a peasant's passport which they were trying to copy.

"I will become a peasant as soon as I write this police captain's name," said Maljutka. "Such calligraphy! And why he wrote the genitive instead of the instrumental I don't know. It may be ignorance and it may be a catch. Of all the stupid things, the passport's the worst. As if it could possibly keep anyone from going anywhere or being anything he wants to. See," he said to me, "if a wild American can copy this name. I personally have been too well trained to make even a semblance of it."

I tried it.

"Oh, that is too wild," he said. "Where did they teach you that?"

"Chocatah," I answered.

Maljutka shook his head. "There is no such place on the map."

"It makes a larger dot on the map," I answered, "than a lot of towns in Russia which I could name." I had just come from a trip on the Volga, and I could say the whole time-table by heart. We had a match to see who knew more of each other's country. I quizzed, and they both fell on Angel's Camp and Hell's Kitchen.

Maljutka rose stiffly and I stopped laughing, for my lurid thought came back to me. He accused me of unfair American methods. "After this revolution," he said, "I am going to America myself to study geography."

"Good," I said; "and I will meet you under the Statue of Liberty." But in my heart I felt it would never be.

"What do you say, Volodya?" he cried. "The Statue of Liberty! Will you come, too?"

Volodya's little fine smile came back to him. "I suppose you will get there some day," he said. "You always were lucky."

Ebba looked at me. "Volodya's conception of luck," she muttered, "is at least not commonplace."

I wondered why she said it, and whether she felt about Maljutka as I did.

"I know good luck from bad by bitter experience," Volodya answered; "but here, Maljutka, you sing a pretty farewell song for the ladies, and I will write you your passport. There isn't much time before that train goes."

Maljutka was from the South and he made his g's and h's very soft. He had a good strong tenor, and he sang a love song from one of Tchaykowsky's operas. His dark eyes shone with a tender light as he sang, but his straight military bearing brought back the picture of the noose and the broken neck to me, and I wished he would stop singing. His good face and happy nature stood unmistakably for life, and the fact that he would kill and might be killed was unbearable to me. I wanted to cry out and I clasped my hands nervously.

"You love Tchaykowsky?" Maljutka asked me. "He is truly a great melody maker."

"Yes, I love harmony," I answered.

It was time for them to go and Maljutka turned to Ebba and took from his pocket a little jumping-jack which looked laughably like the Czar, and a Mauser revolver. "Keep these things for me till I come back," he said to Ebba, "and don't give that Mauser to anybody until I call for it myself in person. And the jumping-jack is kind of precious," and he gave it a little twist. "He looks so much like Kolie* I couldn't resist buying him."

Ebba locked the Mauser and the jumping-jack in her white enameled desk, and the men went away.

I saw Maljutka again and practically for the last time a few days later. I woke very early one morning, dressed and went into the drawing-room. In the dim morning light of winter I saw someone sitting huddled on the pink and white satin divan. The figure rose when I came in and I recognized Maljutka. He was dressed, half peasant, half workman, in high leather boots and a sheepskin coat. He looked like a young, strong peasant from the interior who had come to work in the city.

"I have just come on the night train from St. Petersburg. I think I was followed there."

My heart sank. "You are not going back?" I asked.

"Oh, yes, I must, and to-day. I am going to get another passport and some new clothes. I shall go back as a gentleman. I will come in this afternoon to let you see how nice I can look."

* Kolie is a nickname for Nicholas.

He came in as he promised, in the afternoon. He wore a frock-coat and a top hat and yellow kid gloves.

"Are you going to be married?" Ebba asked.

"In yellow gloves?" and he looked at her scornfully. "No, madam. In my country they marry in white. I am only a noble-man going to church," and he bowed.

"He is so ridiculous and such a little darling!" Ebba said, and we all laughed. "While you so assiduously go to church, I shall go to the country with the whole family."

"And the American girl, too," I added. "I want to see a Finnish Christmas."

And so after some more light talk he was gone again. The visit seemed ordinary except that he shook hands with me rather warmly, and Ebba kissed him.

The next day we were off to Ebba's villa, which lay in the heart of Finland. The house was thirty-five miles from the nearest railway station at the head of a little lake. We went the thirty-five miles by sleigh, through beautiful pine woods covered with thick white snow. The stillness and whiteness of the northern winter lay over all and we glided silently over the whiteness. Toward evening a large silver moon arose, changing the landscape to nile green, and throwing emeralds and diamonds on the snow-covered roads and trees. We drove on in silence, except once when I said to Ebba, looking straight at her, "Where is Maljutka now, I wonder?" But she only com-pressed her lips and said nothing.

Late at night we reached the house. It was large, brilliantly lighted, and seemed to send out long rays of welcome through the white pine trees. Such peace and beauty were here. I forgot the city and the Russian government and the fight. I drew the sharp air in through my teeth. I reveled in the stillness and the uublem-ished scene.

"I am reborn," I said to Ebba the next morning. "I have thrown the city from me like a bad dream."

"And I have brought it with me," she said. "All night I could not sleep for worry. Maljutka's going off in those yellow gloves meant something serious. I can hardly wait for the mail."

In the evening we went to the village, or to the church as they

called it, for our mail. The post-office, the smith and the soda-water
maker all settled around the district church, and so one went "to
the church" for all country needs. It lay about three miles from
the villa, and the road to it was over low hills covered with pine
woods. Ebba gave me a pair of long Lappish skis and we glided
quickly over the heavy snow.

"Do you know," she said, "ever since I was a child I have
dreaded the woods in winter? The trees look to me like the dead
dressed in their shrouds. The tall trees are the men and they bend
down and whisper to the short scrubby little women-folk. See that
tall big pine with outstretched arms imploring the little juniper
bush. They are buried alive and they move and talk in their shrouds.
It is ghastly!" she cried out, and glided swiftly down the hill, hardly
touching the ground with her little poles. At the post-office she
put the skis deftly up against the wall and entered.

"Here is a newspaper and a postcard in an envelope addressed
in Volodya's hand," she said when she came out. "I think I had
better open them at home. I do not like to here," and she looked
nervous.

She went very quickly and I followed. I could see her bent back
and her rigid arms as she grasped her poles. There was fear and
strength in her attitude. I was full of conjectures, and for the first
time that day I remembered that there was a strange outside world
where a fight to the death was going on.

When we reached the house she tore the envelope open and took
out the card. A low groan came from her and she handed it to me.

"I knew him," she said. "They called him Vladimir. He was
beautiful."

It was a picture postcard of a severed head. There was a hole in
the left temple, the mouth was distorted and the head looked as if
it had been beaten. But the eyes were closed, which gave it a peaceful look. At the foot of the card was printed, "The head of the
unknown slayer of the President of the Court-martial, Morosoff,
kept for identification." I did not understand what it meant. I
held the card in my hand and looked at Ebba. She was standing,
still in her furs, reading the newspaper. Her face was livid and fur-
rowed with great pain.

" What is it, Ebba? " I cried.

" It happened last Sunday," she said, " in that church where Maljutka went in his yellow gloves; but there is not a word about him. Evidently he got away. Vladimir shot at the President and then they say he shot himself. It looks more as if they had beaten him to death. At any rate, he is dead, and they have found absolutely nothing on him. They haven't the least idea who he is or where he comes from, and so they are keeping his head, and have ordered all the janitors to come and look at it. So far no one has recognized it. The killing has made a great sensation in Petersburg. They are talking of restricting the court-martial. If only they do not identify him, it would be a great gain, for they would be unable to locate his comrades."

We talked of nothing else but of Vladimir's act all night. She was unhappy over him and over Maljutka.

" Poor beautiful boy," she kept repeating. " And Maljutka, he was in it somehow," she said. " Yet they would not send two men to do one shooting. It must have been that someone else, who did not come, was expected. No doubt that is how Maljutka got away. Though he might have got away anyhow, he is that kind," she said with pride. " Volodya is right. Maljutka was born lucky. But oh, how I hated his going away in those yellow gloves." And she smiled, though her eyes were full of tears. " How wonderful it would be if they really failed in tracing Vladimir. What a victory over that government with its army of secret police."

From that day on we went daily to the church in our anxiety for more news.

" A letter from Volodya," Ebba announced about ten days later. " I do not like letters from Volodya. He only writes when there is news, and the only news a revolutionist has is the last—arrested or dead. The letter is thick." She weighed it and felt it in her hand. " And from St. Petersburg." She put it in her pocket and started home nervously, in the same way as when she first received the news of the killing of Morosoff. At home she hesitated a long time before opening the letter. Then it occurred to her that perhaps Maljutka was arrested. She opened the letter quickly.

" It is in cipher," she said. " Yes, he was arrested. Arrested together with Boris Ivanowich yesterday when walking on the street in St. Petersburg. They were followed by a spy who pointed them out to a gendarme. They were brought to the Fortress. Nothing was found on them, and Maljutka refused to give his name or disclose his identity. However, they seem to know all about Boris Ivanowich. There is no hope for him. But Volodya seems to' think that Maljutka is perfectly safe. 'They will never find out who he is and the government would not hang an unknown man. They can keep him but not hang him, and that is Maljutka and luck,' she read from the letter.

"'Of course between you and me it is only justice,' Ebba read on. 'The government holds him for the Morosoff affair, but it was much higher bait he was after. It would not be right that he should fall over something he did not mean to do. But of course one cannot explain that to the authorities.'

"'The strange thing about the case is the spy. He seems to have been a waiter in that hotel where we were all staying a month ago in Finland. He was a Finn, too. How he came to rush down to Petersburg and identify Vladimir, I don't know. There is some mystery there. Anyway, he did, and moreover, he gave a minute description of the other four. Now they have two of us. As for me, I never noticed the waiter and I haven't the least idea how he looks. But he ought to be done away with. That is up to you people in Finland since he is a Finn.'"

Ebba put the letter down. "That's all," she said, "except some more assurances about Maljutka. 'He is as safe as if he were at home with his own mother,'" and Ebba smiled bitterly. But on the whole she seemed happy at these assurances. She was hungry and eager for hope. She kept arguing the case. "If they do not know who he is they cannot have anything against him. Suppose that waiter does say he lived with Vladimir, that does not prove he was in the same plot. Besides, they cannot hang a man because one man testifies against him. They have got to have some real proof. Anybody might go and point out anybody, but that is not proof."

Days passed, and though we could get no more news, the thought of Maljutka was not once out of Ebba's mind. Every evening we went to the church for the mail. These trips grew fearful to me.

Ebba's dread of the snow-covered trees passed over to me. It was as if we went each night over an army of dead to get news of one about to join them. It could not be that Maljutka would live. There were omens of death. We were living in a strange world of death. Had we been in the city, perhaps I too would have hoped. We did not speak of release, for that we knew could not be when once arrested in Russia. But there must be a semblance of justice in taking a life; there must be evidence and witnesses and proofs. That thought seemed useless. It did not comfort. Ebba on the other hand grew more hopeful as the days passed. "There is a fitness about things," she said. "Volodya is right; Maljutka will not die. He cannot. The life force is too strong in him."

It was almost three weeks after the news of his arrest. Ebba had succeeded in buoying herself up to the extent that she was not only sure that no harm would come to Maljutka, but that he would even be released. We were taking our daily trips to the church.

"See the beautiful white world around us!" she cried. "I love my Finnish winters. They teach us the meaning of life, they are so earnest and serious. They are like deep-thinking philosophers, and we who are born in them take on all their earnestness and seriousness. We never chatter empty-headed like those of the South. We have been taught to think and feel, and that is why it is so hard for us to talk. Now, this minute, if I could only express what I feel with you here, a stranger come from over the seas, living my life with me, going with me over these hills which you have never heard or dreamed of before, and anxious in common with me over the fate of one so far away from your own world! It ought to be strange and hard to understand, yet it seems very natural. I can't understand why it should be so natural for you to be here, and for me to have you here."

"Understand?" I said. "Why try to understand? Life is everywhere. Everywhere there are men and women and children and birth and death. There is one life all over the world, even in the whole universe, I suppose."

"No, no!" Ebba cried. "It is different here. Perhaps it was meant to be the same, but man has made it different. You haven't the Russian youth, who, for four generations, lived and died for one idea —Liberty. You haven't Maljutkas and Volodyas in America."

"No," I answered, "but we shall have them as soon as we need them. It must be so, for just as natural as it is for you to have me here, so is it for me to be here. This life here is not stranger than my own deserts and ranches. I live and suffer and enjoy here as there."

"Have you such sunsets?" she cried.

The sun was a red mouth which sent out tongues of flame even to the east. The white trees seemed dripping with blood. I shuddered, "No," I said, "not like that. We never have them blood-red on such terrible whiteness."

"Why blood-red? Rose-red, rather," she corrected me. "However, if I were not happy this minute I think I would say my trees look like murdered dead in bloody shrouds. But now they are just trees—beautiful trees, covered with the white snow and the sunset.— The church at last," she called out, and made the turn sharply.

I entered the post-office with her.

"Again a letter from Volodya," she said, and tore the envelope open quickly and nervously, bending under the little lamp to read the letter. I saw that her face became pale and her hands trembled violently. She said nothing, finished the reading, nodded her head to me, and went out. I followed. Outside it was already dark.

"They were both hanged yesterday at sunrise," she whispered to me between her set teeth. "Maljutka and Boris Ivanowich—together —two scaffolds—they were very brave. The officer held them up as examples to the soldiers. He said if the soldiers had fought half as bravely in Manchuria as these two died, they would not have lost the War." Ebba gave a little low sarcastic laugh. "Brave! Maljutka and Boris Ivanowich, brave! What else did they expect?"

I thought I had prepared myself for the blow with all manners of omens, yet in reality I was unprepared. My heart seemed to stop. All was black before me. I clutched Ebba's hand and held it.

"Tell me," I asked. "How did it happen? Did they find out who he was—what he had done?"

"No."

"Then how did they hang him?"

"Just so—Russia."

"No evidence?"

"That waiter, Volodya says, though his wife said she could not remember him. Also there was an isvostchik who said he thought he took someone to the church that Sunday who looked like Maljutka. So there you are. It wasn't the witnesses; it was his intelligence and courage which condemned him—they dare not leave such men alive. I should have known that they would kill him as soon as he was arrested. It was Volodya who filled me with hope; and, well—that was natural, I suppose. Come quickly."

She started off, almost without warning, and was far ahead of me in a twinkling. "How they have learned to bear things!" I said to myself, as I watched her small dark figure ahead of me.

Again she was in the midst of the army of the dead. And I, too, I was alone with the dead. I shuddered and grew afraid. Suddenly I saw her stop and look around nervously. She was saying something to me which from the distance I could not hear. When I came up, I saw that her eyes stared strangely.

"I can't stand it!" she said. "Why should I resign myself and bear things? I want to shout aloud! I want to cry out against the universe! Look at them all here in the wood, all with broken necks, all hanged, all of them! Do you not see them?"

Did I not see them! The tall ones standing in the woods were all Maljutkas, with straight backs and broken necks.

"They are ghosts!" Ebba muttered. "I can hear them cry out. They have come up here to remind us of our work. You see this road running through them? They made it for us and we must walk on it."

The wood swayed as the wind blew through the trees. A light snow fell from the branches and overhead the cold winter stars twinkled impassively.

"You have no dead making paths for you in America," Ebba continued. "But our dead are with us and fight with us. We are better off than you. Ah, Maljutka, my little darling!"

Again she started off, gliding on the white snow, swiftly, and again she held the poles, not fearfully as before, but with strength and purpose. She sped on boldly and I followed, my eyes fixed on her, daring to look neither to the right nor left, for I feared this strange road with the shrouded trees.

THE PURPOSE OF WOMANHOOD

C. W. SALEEBY, M.D.

LITTLE is yet known, though much is asserted, for this or that end, regarding the differences between men and women. By this we mean, of course, the natural as distinguished from the nurtural differences—to use the antithetic terms so usefully adapted by Sir Francis Galton from Shakespeare. But it is rarely easy to disentangle the effects of nature from those of nurture, all the phenomena, physical and psychical, of all living creatures being not the sum but the product of these two factors. The sharp allotment of this or that feature to nature or to nurture alone is therefore always wholly wrong: and the nice estimation of the relative importance of the natural as compared with the nurtural factors must necessarily be difficult, especially for the case of mankind, where critical observation, on a large scale, and with due control, of the effects of environment upon natural potentialities, is still lacking.

But, at least, we may unhesitatingly declare and insist upon *the* one indisputable and all-important distinction between man and woman. We must not commit the error of regarding this distinction as qualitative so much as quantitative: by which I mean that it really is neither more nor less than a difference in the proportions of two kinds of vital expenditure. Nor must we commit the still graver error of asserting, without qualification, that such and such, and that only, is the ideal of womanhood, and that all women who do not conform to this type are morbid, or, at least, abnormal. It takes all sorts to make a world, we must remember. Further, the more we learn, especially thanks to the modern experimental study of heredity, regarding the constitution of the individual of either sex, the more we perceive how immensely complex and how infinitely variable that constitution is. Nay more, the evidence regarding both the higher animals and the higher plants inclines us to the view, not unsupported by the belief of ages, that woman is even more complex in constitution than man, and therefore no less liable to vary within wide limits. On what one may term organic analysis, comparable to the chemist's analysis of a compound, woman is found to be more complex, composed of even more and more various elementary atoms, so to say, than man.

And if these new observations upon the nature of femaleness were not enough to warn the writer who should rashly propose, after the fashion of the unwise, who on every hand lay down the law on this matter, to state once and for all exactly what, and what only, every woman should be, we find that another long-held belief as to the relative variety of men and women has lately been found baseless. It was long held, and is still generally believed—in consequence of that universal confusion between the effects of nature and of nurture to which we have already referred—that women are less variable than men, that they vary within much narrower limits, and that the bias toward the typical, or mean, or average, is markedly greater in the case of women than of men. A vast amount of idle evidence is quoted in favor of a proposition which seems to have some *a priori* plausibility. It is said—of course, without any allusion to nurture, education, environment, opportunity—that such extreme variations as we call genius are much commoner amongst men than women: and then that the male sex also furnishes an undue proportion of the insane—as if there were no unequal incidence of alcohol and other great factors of insanity, upon the two sexes. Nevertheless, observant members of each sex will either contradict one another on this point according to their particular opportunities, or will, on further inquiry, agree that women vary surely no less generally than men, at any rate within considerable limits, whatever may be the facts of colossal genius. Indeed, we begin to perceive that differences in external appearance, which no one supposes to be less general among women than among men, merely reflect internal differences; and that, as our faces differ, so do ourselves, every individual of either sex being, in fact, not merely a peculiar variety, but the solitary example of that variety—in short, unique. The analysis of the individual now being made by experimental biology lends abundant support to this view of the higher forms of life—the more abundant, the higher the form. So vast, as yet quite incalculably vast, is the number of factors of the individual, and such are the laws of their transmission in the germ-cells, that the mere mathematical chances of a second identical throw, so to speak, resulting in a second individual like any other, are practically infinitely small. The greater physiological complexity of woman, as compared with man, lends especial force to the argument in her case. The remarkable phenomena of "identical twins," who alone of human beings are substantially identical, lend great support to this proposition of the uniqueness of every individual: for we find that this unexampled identity depends upon the fact that the single cell from which every individual is developed, having divided into two, was at that stage actually separated into two independent cells, each producing a complete individual of absolutely identical germinal constitution. In no other case can this be asserted; and thus this unique identity confirms the doctrine that otherwise all individuals are indeed unique.

Nevertheless, there remains the fact that, in the variety which is normally included within the female sex, there is yet a certain character, or combination of characters, upon which, indeed, distinctive femaleness depends. It will in due course be our business to discuss the subordinate and relatively trivial differences between the sexes, whether native or acquired; but we shall encounter nothing of any moment compared with the distinction now to be insisted upon.

One may well suggest that insistence is necessary, for never, it may be supposed, in the history of civilization was there so widespread or so effective a tendency to declare that, in point of fact, there are no differences between men and women except that, as Plato declared, woman is in all respects simply a weaker and inferior kind of man. Great writer though Plato was, what he did not know of biology was eminently worth knowing, and his teaching regarding womanhood and the conditions of motherhood in the ideal city is more fantastically and ludicrously absurd than anything that can be quoted, I verily believe, from any writer of equal eminence. If, indeed, the teaching of Plato were correct, there would be no purpose in this article. If a girl is practically a boy, we are right in bringing up our girls to be boys. If a woman is only a weaker and inferior kind of man, those women—themselves, as a rule, the nearest approach to any evidence for this view—who deny the weakness and inferiority and insist upon the identity, are justified. Their error and that of their supporters is twofold.

In the first place, they err because, being themselves, as we have convincing reasons to see, of an aberrant type, they judge women and womanhood by themselves, and especially by their abnormal psychological tendencies—notably the tendency to look upon motherhood much as the lower type of man looks upon fatherhood. It requires closer and more intimate study of this type than we can spare space for—more, even, than the state of our knowledge yet permits —in order to demonstrate how absurd is the claim of women thus peculiarly constituted to speak for their sex as a whole.

But, secondly, those women and men who assert the doctrine of the identity of the sexes are led to err, not because it can really be hidden from the most casual observer that there is a profound distinction between the sexes, apart from the case of the defeminized woman—but because, by a surprising fallacy, they confuse the doctrine of sex-equality with that of sex-identity; or, rather, they believe that only by demonstrating the doctrine that the sexes are substantially identical, can they make good their plea that the sexes should be regarded as equal. The fallacy is evident, and would not need to detain us but for the fact that, as has been said, the whole tendency of the time is toward accepting it—the recent biological proof of the fundamental and absolute difference between the sexes being unknown as yet to the laity. Yet surely, even were the facts less salient, or even were they other than they are, it is a pitiable failure of logic to suppose, as is daily supposed, that in order to prove woman man's equal one must prove her to be really identical in all essentials, given, of course, equal conditions. Controversialists on both sides, and even some of the first rank, are content to accept this absurd position.

The one party seeks to prove that woman is man's equal because Rosa Bonheur and Lady Butler have painted, Sappho and George Eliot have written, and so forth; in other words, that woman is man's equal because she can do what he can do: any capacities of hers which he does not share being tacitly regarded as beside the point or insubstantial.

The other party has little difficulty in showing that, in point of fact, men do things admittedly worth doing of which women are on the whole incapable; and then triumphantly, but with logic of the order which this party would probably call " feminine," it is assumed that woman is not man's equal because she cannot do the things he does. That she does things vastly better and infinitely more important which he cannot do at all, is not a point to be considered; the baseless basis of the whole silly controversy being the exquisite assumption, to which the woman's party have the folly to assent, that only the things which are common in some degree to both sexes shall be taken into account, and those peculiar to one shall be ignored.

It is my most solemn conviction that the cause of woman, which is the cause of man, and the cause of the unborn, is by nothing more gravely and unnecessarily prejudiced and delayed than by this doctrine of sex-identity. It might serve some turn for a time, as many another error has done, were it not so palpably and egregiously false. Advocated as it is mainly by either masculine women or unmanly men, its advocates, though in their own persons offering some sort of evidence for it, are of a kind which is highly repugnant to less abnormal individuals of both sexes. Hosts of women of the highest type, who are doing the silent work of the world, which is nothing less than the creation of the life of the world to come, are not merely dissuaded from any support of the woman cause by the spectacle of these palpably aberrant and unfeminine women, but are further dissuaded by the profound conviction arising out of their woman's nature, that the doctrine of sex-identity is absurd. Many of them would rather accept their existing status of social inferiority with its thousand disabilities and injustices than have anything to do with women who preach " Rouse yourselves, women, and be men!" and who themselves illustrate only too fearsomely the consequences of this doctrine.

Certainly not less disastrous, as a consequence of this most unfortunate error of fact and of logic, is the alienation from the woman's cause of not a few men whose support is exceptionally worth having. There are men who desire nothing in the world so much as the exaltation of womanhood, and who would devote their lives to this cause, but would vastly rather have things as they are than aid the movement of " Woman in Transition "—if it be transition from womanhood to something which is certainly not womanhood and at best a very poor parody of manhood except in cases almost infinitely rare. I have in my mind a case of a well-known writer, a man of the highest type in every respect, well worth enlisting in the army that fights for womanhood to-day, whose organic repugnance to the defeminized woman is so intense, and whose perception of the distinctive characters of real womanhood and of their supreme excellence is so acute that, so far from aiding the cause of, for instance, woman's suffrage, he is one of its most bitter and unremitting enemies. There must be many such—to whom the doctrine of sex-identity, involving the repudiation of the excellences, distinctive and exquisite, of women, is an offence which they can never forgive.

I desire briefly to refer to the work of a very remarkable woman, scarcely known at all to the reading public, either in Great Britain or in America, and never alluded to by the feminist leaders in those countries, though her works are very widely known on the Continent of Europe, and, with the whole weight of biological fact behind them, are bound to become more widely known and more effective as the years go on. I refer to the Swedish writer, Ellen Key, one of whose works, though by no means her best, has at last been translated into English. All her books are translated into German from the Swedish, and are very widely read and deeply influential in determining the course of the woman's movement in Germany. To supplement this brief article, I earnestly commend the reader of any age or sex to study Ellen Key's *Century of the Child.** It is necessary and right to draw particular attention to the teaching of this woman since it is urgently needed in Anglo-Saxon countries at this very time, and almost wholly unknown, but for this minor work of hers and an occasional allusion—as in an article contributed by Dr. Havelock Ellis to the *Fortnightly Review* some few years ago. Especial importance attaches to such teaching as hers when it proceeds from a woman whose fidelity to the highest interests, even to the unchallenged autonomy, of her sex cannot be questioned, attested as it is by a lifetime of splendid work. The present controversy in Great Britain would be profoundly modified in its course and in its character if either party were aware of Ellen Key's work. The most questionable doctrines of the English feminists would be already abandoned by themselves if either the wisest among them, or their opponents, were able to cite the evidence of this great Swedish feminist, who is certainly at this moment the most powerful and the wisest living pro- .

* G. P. Putnam's Sons: London and New York, 1909,

tagonist of her sex.   From a single chapter of the book, to which it
may be hoped that the reader will refer, there may be quoted a few
sentences which will suffice to indicate the reasons why Ellen Key
dissociated herself some ten years ago from the general feminist
movement, and will also serve as an introduction from the practical
and instinctive point of view to the scientific argument regarding the
nature and purpose of womanhood.   Hear Ellen Key :—

" Doing away with an unjust paragraph in a law which concerns
woman, turning a hundred women into a field of work where only ten
were occupied before, giving one woman work where formerly not one
was employed—these are the mile-stones in the line of progress of the
woman's rights movement.   It is a line pursued without consideration
of feminine capacities, nature and environment.

" The exclamation of a woman's rights champion when another
woman had become a butcher, ' Go thou and do likewise,' and an
American young lady working as an executioner, are, in this connection, characteristic phenomena.

" In our programme of civilization, we must start out with the
conviction that motherhood is something essential to the nature of
woman, and the way in which she carries out this profession is of value
for society.   On this basis we must alter the conditions which more
and more are robbing woman of the happiness of motherhood and are
robbing children of the care of a mother.

" I am in favor of real freedom for woman; that is, I wish her to
follow her own nature, whether she be an exceptional or an ordinary
woman . . . I recognize fully the right of the feminine individual to
go her own way, to choose her own fortune or misfortune.   I have
always spoken of women collectively and of society collectively.

" From this general, not from the individual, standpoint, I am
trying to convince women that vengeance is being exacted on the
individual, on the race, when woman gradually destroys the deepest
vital source of her physical and psychical being, the power of motherhood.

" But present-day woman is not adapted to motherhood; she will
only be fitted for it when she has trained herself for motherhood and
man is trained for fatherhood. Then man and woman can begin together to bring up the new generation out of which some day society
will be formed.   In it the completed man—the superman—will be
bathed in that sunshine whose distant rays but color the horizon of
to-day."

SOCIALISTIC TENDENCIES IN ENGLAND

GEORGE BOURNE

WEEK by week the rumor increases that Socialism is making wonderful advances in England. Everyone is ready to affirm it; you can hardly look at a newspaper without coming upon some allusion to it; from America and the Continent the news of it begins to travel back: the tale is so persistent, nay, is gaining so much the complexion of a commonplace, as to leave no room for doubt that something strange must be going on in England to account for it; and yet, when one looks around for the circumstances which would justify such a general persuasion, at first sight it is puzzling to make out precisely what they are.

A great deal of the talk—and that, too, the most convinced in its tone—will not stand a moment's examination. To take a recent example: no sooner had the news arrived that a republic had been set up in Portugal, than it began to be said in England that that change was the work of Socialists and that England's turn would come next, by reason of the spread of Socialism in England. The people who expressed this belief probably had no real opinion on the matter; with the examples of France and America before them, they still had failed to perceive that republics might have nothing to do with Socialism; they had simply hit upon a remark to make which sounded apposite to the occasion. Yet this is a fair specimen of half the talk that goes on; and it is clear that, in so far as the rumor about the advance of Socialism is spread by empty phrasing like this, there is next to nothing in it. The same may be said of pronouncements like that of Lord Rosebery, some twelve months ago. If one may believe the reports of his speech, his lordship permitted himself to say that Socialism in England was threatening to destroy capital, ruin " the home "; corrupt the morality of the nation, overturn its religion. I have not the report of the speech by me to give its exact words; but though I miss their eloquence, that was what I understood them to mean. At about the same time much the same opinion was expressed by a learned professor at Cambridge University—the bearer, he, of a world-famous name; so that the talk does

not lack august support. One must suppose, however, that these
high personages are too uplifted above ordinary life and opinion
to know anything about it, or they would never say that the English
are in danger of committing themselves to such uncomfortable
courses. The prophecy of impending anarchy is too ridiculous to
be received. Ignorance and panic are the parents of it, or ignorance and political infatuation. It reminds one of what an au-
thropologist—Mr. Andrew Lang, I think—once wrote about the
primitive savage. With a sharpened flint and a block of wood, it
was affirmed, any savage might carve out an idol which would
frighten him into fits when it was finished. So with this alarmist
tale about a Socialism which is to destroy religion and break up the
home: those who spread it are the victims of a terror which their
own darkened fancies have conjured up.

But, apart from such disordered and irresponsible prophesying,
the evidence is still extremely questionable. It appears that the
name " Socialism " is habitually given to projects which, albeit of
a reforming character, are not regarded by their promoters as anything but Radicalism. And the difference is fundamental. For
whereas your true Socialist condemns our existing system of competitive industry as unsound from top to bottom, and proposes to
replace it with a collective system, your Radical on the contrary
seeks to establish the existing system more securely, by remedying
the defects which weaken it. He regards it as a building which has
gone askew and needs wedging up; and although the wedges he
would insert for that end are furiously denounced as the " thin end
of the wedge " of Socialism, it remains to be proved that they are
that. At least the Radical is not of that opinion. His wedges
have no very thick end. He hopes to go on in the present way, only
more happily. Of all the Radicals in England who welcome with
enthusiasm the new taxes on unused land, it may be doubted if one
in five hundred would countenance the socialistic plan of dispossess-
ing all land-owners of their property and giving it over to the state.

And when one turns to the ranks of avowed Socialists, to discover who they are and where they are to be found, one comes upon
a fact which, if it were appreciated, must decidedly weaken the force
of the public rumor. It is quite true that several Members of Parlia-

ment acknowledge themselves Socialists; true too—and for the moment this looks more like the real thing—that the greater Labor organizations have professed a sort of academic adhesion to the Socialist doctrine. This should be conclusive, so far as Labor goes. Yet, very oddly, it is not conclusive. For the present Labor platform, when closely scrutinized, proves to be based upon a very unsocialistic acceptance of private ownership in capital and land, and of the existing industrial organization. Hardly even on the " thin end of the wedge " theory, for instance, can the agitation for an eight hours' day be understood as an attempt to deprive capitalists of their property; hardly can the use of " conciliation boards " be regarded as a step toward taking the organization of industry out of private hands altogether and committing it to state control. These are no devices of Socialism: they are Radical measures for making the present arrangements run more smoothly. On this very point unbending Socialists—to judge by the offensive terms in which their organs refer to the Labor Leaders—are very sore. They feel that their name has been stolen; for if the great trades have nominally gone over to Socialism, in practice they have rather captured the Socialist sign-board and put it up over a Radical shop-window. No doubt many individual members of the Trades Unions are Socialists in theory; but that is a different thing. Many middle-class people too are Socialists. If all who truly accept the theory of Socialism could be counted up, the number would run into thousands. Yet what are thousands, in a population of forty millions? If numbers are to be considered, England looks as much like going over to the Salvation Army as to Socialism.

II

But if the rumor is not justified by facts, so far as genuine Socialism is concerned, it is not therefore to be dismissed as unworthy of attention. The truth is that the prevailing talk, ill-informed or alarmist though it may be, is a distorted and grotesque reflection of a movement in the under-currents of popular feeling, which is probably as momentous as any that has occurred in England's history. Something, certainly, is spreading very vigorously; some-

thing well deserving to be investigated, whether it be called Socialism or by any other name.

To come to the point: that which is giving rise to all the talk
is a growth of ideas—ideas whose outcome it is as impossible to
foresee as it is impossible to doubt that it will be far-reaching.
These ideas differ from the theory of Socialism in much the same
way as a holiday-maker's first dreams of travel differ from one of
Messrs. Cook's Tourist Programmes. The tourist programme is a
definite and ready-made idea of something that might be carried
out; a published idea; an idea which has done growing and now
waits to be accepted. Anybody may be acquainted with its main outlines; an earl or a professor of science might add it to their other
stock of information and take no harm at all. And so with the idea
of Socialism. It is a programme of certain economic arrangements,
the details of which no doubt may be varied slightly or elaborated
more fully, but the essential features of which can no longer " grow "
and can only be approved or disapproved. Like a boat on the sea-
beach, separated from the ideas which gave it birth and shaped it,
there it lies—a finished product of invention for anybody to examine; for anybody to use too, if he will; but wanting in force or
initiative of its own.

In strongest possible contrast, the truly growing ideas, full of
force, and in fact providing the impulse of the new movements of
England's life, are no more definite and not much more theoretical
than a would-be holiday-maker's dreams of travel. Instead of being
powerless, they may rather be said to be power itself—power to
recognize new aspects in old things. Such ideas are they as those
by which a doctor appreciates the obscure symptoms of disease, or a
musician the harmonies unnoticed by other people, or a sailor the
significance of the clouds. For better illustration, say that they are
like those conceptions which nowadays sway the English in their attitude toward the old " half-timbered " buildings of the Elizabethan period. Where the Mid-Victorians saw in those places little
save unprofitable inconvenience deserving to be pulled down, something even worse than inconvenience is discovered by the modern idea
of the hygienic importance of light and air; but on the other hand,
ideas of picturesqueness in shape and color, and of the lovable sen-

timent belonging to things associated with so many generations of English life, discover precious values in overhanging wall and crooked gable and steep roof, and induce the owners to preserve what their forefathers would have destroyed without a qualm. An example perhaps even better still may be found in the modern attitude with regard to the treatment of animals. It is not on theory that people are apt to sicken now at sight of an ill-used horse or a tormented bullock; but because of an idea which recognizes, in the sensitive bodies of animals, an attribute transcending their utility; a something which at all costs should be inviolate; a sort of sacredness, of which men of an earlier period had, literally, " no idea."

And the growth of so-called Socialism in England proceeds out of ideas of just this quality—powers of recognition very new and unfamiliar and ill-defined, but yet strong, as we see, even in this rudimentary state. They are rooted in taste and feeling; conscience is concerned to cherish them, because they discern for it what is beautiful, or sacred, or happy, or just, or stately. New members, they are, of an old and illustrious family. For the ideas of honor, and of " playing the game "; and those of patriotism; and the Scottish and Irish and Welsh ideas which recognize the splendor of nationality; belong to the same stock, as indeed does the American idea of " The Union," or the German one of " The Fatherland." But in these new ones the English have struck out lines of recognition which, it is true, their poets—Wordsworth, Blake, Byron—were following a century ago, but which it has taken almost the succeeding century to popularize. Amongst the things previously but little noticed, which begin to be understood now, the paramount importance of obscure and lowly people may be mentioned, and the greatness of the qualities they exhibit, and the rich possibilities of development in them, if they had a proper chance to develop. The value of physical health as a national asset is another subject of recognition, while yet others have to do with the orderliness, cleanliness, comeliness even, of streets and of homes. The old idea of national prosperity is as it were filling out in details: where earlier generations were keen enough to value the place of England amongst the Powers, the present generation has ideas touching the place of the English in England. And then, entwining in closest growth with all this, are ideas—more theoretical perhaps, or perhaps more imaginative—as to what people ought to live for, and what benefits ought in common fairness to reward the endless labor of the wage-earning classes. Should there not be found somehow, should there not be conceived and realized, a happiness to make industry worth while? Ought not men and women to have leisure to live? And ought not the riches of art, and the refreshment of games, and the delight of gardens and pleasant places, to be available so that leisure may be enjoyed? One sees the seeds of some such ideas germinating everywhere; and even of ideas picturing conditions in which labor itself would be as pleasant as leisure. Truly, new ideas are not lacking in England. It would be easy to instance others; but I have said enough to show that the stir of approaching change is caused by no programme or ready-made doctrine, but by idea-powers which multitudes of English men and women are exercising almost spontaneously, as they go about their daily affairs.

III

But now note the inevitable result of this activity. All up and down England the life of the people is coming under review; the relations between the classes are being re-examined, and the effects of old laws and customs. And most of all the nation is focusing its attention upon Poverty, looking into the varied manifestations of it, searching out its causes, and generally testing it by the new ideas of what is fit for the sacred life in human bodies and fit for the English as a people. No observant person who has lived in England during the last ten years can have failed to notice the great awakening of the national conscience in this direction. It is as though poverty had just been discovered; as though it were a new thing in the country. But what is really new is the play of luminous ideas over it. A generation ago—scarcely more than that—the majority of the English regarded it very much as they regarded the ill-treatment of animals, recognizing its existence but not its shame. That apathy, however, is past. Seeing it in the increasing light of their new ideas, people are daily more shocked at the aspects of poverty, where slums reek with it and where work-houses try in vain to cover

it up. With growing displeasure they view the scandals that attend
it—the unemployment, the sweating; and the abominable diseases
which it fosters, and the crimes and vices into which it drives men
and women who have no other solace, or no other means of livelihood.
In fine, poverty, we may say, is being dragged out from its old haunts
to come up for trial, and to receive judgment too; for on every charge
preferred against it, it is found guilty.

IV

Of course this is not all. It is only the beginning of a further
growth of ideas, which are the outward and visible sign of the inward
spiritual grace of the others. Here the new movement pushes up
into the daylight and becomes public. But just as the blade and
ears of the growing wheat differ from its roots, so these upper idea-
growths differ from those we have considered hitherto. Those were
vague ideas connected with taste and feelings; dreamy, "Utopian."
These, on the contrary, are "practical" ideas of definite action to
be taken, definite things to be done. Without stopping to investigate poverty thoroughly, ardent spirits everywhere are formulating plans or programme-ideas for dealing with it piece-meal. The
fact that Socialists look upon their efforts with contempt, as of experts watching amateurs, disturbs them not at all. They care nothing about Socialism; they are impatient to be at work; and the
vast diversity of the projects which are taken up is proof of the
spontaneity of the movement. It is endemic, not epidemic. It is
springing up everywhere. There is no concerted plan of attack
upon poverty as a whole; the attacking parties have hardly realized
that poverty as a whole is the true enemy; but each directs its attention upon some detailed scandal without regard to what others
may be doing elsewhere. In one detail, indeed—that which had to
do with impoverished age—a programme has not only been devised
but carried into practice; and the Old Age Pensions Act, costing
some eight million pounds a year, proves what compulsive force is in
these new ideas; for the English are not exactly burning to spend
their money. As a rule, however, the projects have not got beyond
the stage of discussion, or have not yet got far. Schemes for feed-

ing necessitous school-children, and for providing better dwelling-
houses for the poorer workers, and for state-insurance against unemployment, are amongst the most conspicuous of them; but the new
leaven may be seen working in hundreds of other directions.   It inspires alike the lowliest and the loftiest programmes; the most parochial, and the most far-reaching.   The advocates of extreme measures, such as that for the national endowment of motherhood, have
no monopoly of the modern spirit; you may trace the stir of its
energies just as well, amongst the supporters of Dr. Barnardo's
Homes, or of Prison Missions, or of societies for promoting a return to the system of apprenticeship; and even in the self-sacrifice
of those quiet people in many an English village, who give their
evenings to the management of "Institutes" or "Boys' Clubs,"
because they cannot bear to stand by and do nothing while poverty
ruins the youth of the village.   Such activities, though not all
equally well-considered and effective, are all symptomatic of the new
English attitude toward poverty.   The movement is a siege conducted on no plan, by assailants whose zeal is their only qualification
for taking part in it.

V

Were it not for one reason, it would seem that none but scare-
mongers could pretend to see "Socialism" in such a medley of un-
directed activity as this.   It is true that, inasmuch as poverty is inherent in the present economic system, some modification of that
system must be expected to follow any movement against poverty.
But Socialism does not propose to modify: it proposes to recast.
Instead of demanding that those who control wealth should control
it more patriotically so that there shall be less poverty, it would give
the control of wealth into the hands of the state, so that there
should be no poverty at all.   That is how Socialism differs from
the partial schemes now agitating the country.   And when one considers how those schemes are supported by people who, for the most
part, dislike the name of Socialism and have no intention of inquiring into its nature, it seems at first unjust that the name they dislike
should be so freely bestowed upon their plans.

But it must be remembered that popular movements are very apt to gain a sort of independent momentum of their own. The ideas at the back of them, continuing to grow, continue to push them forward; at the same time the resistance of the circumstances with which they come into contact forces them into special channels; and eventually the movements exhibit " tendencies " which are not to be withstood, even though they may be disapproved, by the people who originated them. Now, it is far from impossible that this will happen in the present case. Diverse as are the " programmes " in hand, they almost all converge upon economic reform; and the farther they go, the likelier they are to merge into some more comprehensive programme. Resistance from without—I mean, the refusal of poverty to yield to unorganized attacks—can hardly fail to have this result. Meanwhile, amidst the " inward spiritual " ideas which give force to the whole movement, a formidable one is coming to the front in the shape of a new recognition—the recognition of responsibility. After answering, for centuries, " No," to the question " Am I my brother's keeper? " the English in great numbers are beginning to have an idea that the answer is " Yes." It is a change fraught with far consequences. From the uneasy feeling that one's-self may be partly responsible for poverty, there is but a step or so to the recognition of national responsibility for it; and once a man is there he cannot easily escape hearing of the Socialist programme, awaiting his attention. And it is the suspicion of this tendency that is so disturbing to those whose ideas are backward in growth. Instinctively they dread the recognition of national or any collective responsibility. You may hear them repudiating it, roundly asserting that poverty is the fault of the poor and the poor alone. Or you may note the formulæ invented as weapons to fight off the new conception. " Parental responsibility," for instance, is a phrase very useful for this purpose. Children in need of medical attendance must not be given it at the public cost, because that would weaken the sense of responsibility in their parents. So it is argued; and yet the same people who use the argument—namely, school managers and so on—are actually organizing private charity to supply funds for giving the very assistance which their own argument says should not be given. The inference is clear. Parental responsibility has been thought of, because people fear the recognition of collective responsibility. They are shy of the collective principle. They do not see where it is to end; but at a guess they say " Socialism." And little though they know of Socialism, and far though England seems from accepting that programme, it would be foolish to deny that the guess looked plausible. At any rate the tendency to recognize national responsibility for poverty, and consequently for the economic conditions which breed it, grows unceasingly.

At this point it should be noted that, upon the edges of this central movement, numerous groups of ideas are forming in regard to other and happier subjects than poverty, and are pointing toward a collective responsibility of municipalities rather than of the whole state. Nay, they point beyond responsibility, to the propriety of a collective seizing of opportunity. For in fact a considerable degree of municipal responsibility has long been acknowledged and approved. It is quite a familiar idea. Everybody understands that the disposal of sewage, the cleansing of streets, the battle with infectious disease, the policing of the criminal classes, and so on, are tasks for collective action; but the new ideas are going further. Would it not be proper, they suggest, for local authorities, with their great collective powers, to lay out public gardens, support municipal bands, keep up picture galleries, provide swimming baths? Throughout England ideas of this kind are gathering force; ideas constructive rather than remedial; ideas not of mitigating evil but of providing good; and these programmes, too, do not fail to rouse suspicion in those minds in which the Utopian or tasteful ideas are undeveloped. Wherever they are mooted, there are sure to be timorous people who cannot see the point, cannot recognize it, have " no idea " of the good that is sought, but smell in it the danger which they call " Socialism."

VI

When the matter is viewed in this light, one illusion disappears; that, namely, which ascribes the growth to the present Liberal government. That it has become much more apparent since the return of the Liberals to office is quite true; but to imagine that they could create in men's minds all this growth of idea-power is to attribute to them an influence which no government possesses. If the Liberal government has given a more practical turn to ideas which had long been waiting for the opportunity of becoming practical, that is as much as it must be blamed or praised for. The growth began earlier. The preceding period of Conservative inattention to social matters was in fact a period favorable to the germinating of ideas in much greater diversity than would have been possible, had each idea from the start been tempted to become practical. When there was so little prospect of doing anything at all, men could indulge themselves in rich dreams of what might be done, some day. They had time to cultivate tastes—tastes for art and the sunshine of life; tastes for color and comeliness in human affairs. Under the Conservative rule there were more dreamy philosophers and fewer practical politicians than now; but the dreams they were dreaming were bound in the long run to make them dislike the actualities they saw; and now under the Liberal rule the dreamers are waking up to begin work. The opening for work, however, has been made only in "Radical" directions; and the genuine Socialist programme appears to be not greatly in demand.

At the same time, it would be idle to pretend that it is so unpopular as it was, say, five years ago. Most curiously, the principal effect of the ignorant agitation against a fancied Socialism has been to break down one of the barriers which kept people from inquiring into the real thing. The name of Socialism has not lost all its terrors yet; but it has lost many of them, since it has been bandied about so recklessly, and applied so readily to all sorts of projects which large numbers of the English have at heart; and as a consequence the programme begins to receive attention in quarters where it could hardly have been mentioned with safety a little while ago. Not in a quarter of a century have avowed Socialists been able to do so much for their cause as the fatuity of their opponents has effected in five years.

That fatuity indeed should be watched. It is a source of danger. The enemies of Socialism can do nothing either to check the growing ideas of which I have been speaking, or to alter the Socialist programme; nor is it easy to see what they could do, to prevent the

new growth from entering into the programme and vitalizing it, if
that should prove to be the tendency of the times. But they might,
by an access of fatuity, stimulate into sudden growth a wholly different crop of ideas—revolutionary, vindictive—which would fore-
stall the other growth, and use Socialism for violent ends. In the
industrial centres, where capital appears to be planning to crush
organized labor and reduce the working population to political im-
potence, such revolutionary ideas as these are particularly likely
to spring up. And there stands the programme of Socialism, waiting to be used. Note that. It is common property. It is at anybody's disposal; should the overburdened workers once be persuaded
that all other avenues of well-being are closed to them, there is nothing to prevent them from trying this one as a last resource. If
capital is foolish, such a situation may easily be produced; and if
one considers how much foolishness on the side of capital is betrayed in the ignorant talk of the day, one must admit it to be not
quite impossible that some day England may wake up to find real
Socialism on the move, driven by ideas not hopeful and kindly, but
desperate and angry. It is of course questionable if such ideas
could carry out the constructive part of Socialism; but its destructive proposals they could unquestionably carry out to the bitter end.

VII

At present, however, in most parts of England revolutionary
ideas are quiescent, and if there is any real movement toward Socialism, it is a movement of merely Radical ideas. Will they ever get
any great distance on the way? It is impossible to say; but provided that their humane intention is understood, there is no great
objection to regarding their advance as something more than a tendency. Call it, rather, the arrival of the Pilgrim Fathers of Socialism, destined to make a "New England"—at home. Foreshad-
owed dimly in the "programme-idea," the real Socialist State stands
unexplored, waiting for colonists—waiting for ameliorative ideas to
come; the small achievements of Radicalism being but primitive settlements on its fringes.

That, at least, is a point of view; and not one that should excite alarm. For one notes that the little changes which have been accomplished, whether they are Socialism or not, are on the whole acceptable. Everybody for example is glad at heart, though some few still shake their heads, at the thought that the aged poor are getting state pensions. It is the programme of any change that disturbs people in England, and not the accomplished thing. Invariably, while a project of collective action is under discussion, there are people ready to see in it the thin end of a wedge. The establishment of the police force had its detractors at the time; state education, because its programme is constantly developing, still has them. But as one after another the ameliorative projects become established facts the propriety of them is admitted by all save the very few. In general those who make the opposition are wanting in imaginative idea-power rather than in good-will; they fail to recognize the advantages of a scheme until it has been carried out. Then they approve it, and transfer their opposition to the next scheme. It is becoming a common thing in English towns for the District Council or municipality to buy land and make it into public gardens. And the same thing always happens; so long as the plan is under discussion there is opposition to it: it is " Socialism." But as soon as the gardens are laid out, there come public-spirited offers from the ranks of the opposition to put up drinking fountains and garden-seats. I have lately heard of another curious example of the same sort of thing. Notwithstanding the reluctance of the members of a certain school-authority, it has been decided to provide dinners at the school for the poorer scholars, below cost price, and to make up the difference out of the local rates. That proved to be the only decent thing to do. In other words, an idea of decency as to the nourishment of children has grown up in prudent brains and, Socialism or no Socialism, insists on having its way. For many other projects as yet disapproved a similar success may be anticipated. The Individualist theory still holds its own in England; inspires still the outcry against " Socialism "; but the Collectivist spirit grows, with the results that we see. The aged poor have pensions paid to them; starving children begin to be fed; little patches of garden beauty make their appearance in the dingy quarters of England's old towns.

WHISTLER AND VERITY

HALDANE MACFALL

OF a surety Art is for Art's Sake; as an Ass is for an Ass's Sake.

But when a man shall tell you a door-scraper is for a door-scraper's sake, be you sure, and he sure, what you mean by door-scraping.

When a school arose, but a while ago, that had for its battle-cry Art for Art's sake, it really meant that Art was for Craft's sake—that the goal of Art lay solely in the beauty of its Craftsmanship. These sneered at the " subject " of a work of Art as being of little or no importance! The handling of the craftsmanship was to be the sole aim in a work of art—indeed, alone created it into a work of art. This blasphemy to art were as though one said that the Creator made the body of man as the supreme achievement—that man's character and soul, his emotions, his passions and his yearnings, were of little or no account. They would have " the play of Hamlet without the Prince of Denmark." In the shallows of their confusion, in the deeps of their ignorance, what they said was this: that if a master-hand paint a wall white, by his mastery of trick-of-thumb he creates Art! That if a man speak beautiful words signifying nothing, he creates the poetic! That if an exquisite harmony of blues and grays and greens and such-like be set upon a piece of canvas with such skill as to please the eye, and produce a sense of beauty, these thereby create a work of art! That nothing else signifies but the exquisite handling of a medium!

The curse of the mere pursuit of Craftsmanship, in mistake for Art, lies like a blight upon artistic endeavor to-day, and has ever created the decay of Art.

The concept has, perhaps, reached to its fullest danger in that Whistler, a superb artist, uttered it in the exquisite falsehood of his famous oration, the *Ten O'clock*. But the Whistler who employed the Art of painting of which he was a master, was a far different Whistler from the Whistler who employed the art of prose, of which he was only a craftsman, not an artist. Whistler, by the words of his mouth, would have us believe that it is the province of Art to say Nothing very Beautifully. His instincts and his practice, his genius, made no such mistake. No man's hand and brain ever gave his mouth the lie in more frank and splendid insolence than did his. When Whistler stepped out of his province, as a superb artist in color, into the realm of literature, he came into a kingdom in which his sense of artistry in color led him by instinct to astounding craftsmanship of words—he employed words as he would have employed color; and in the doing proved how absolutely the methods of the two arts are one. But he failed in that his instincts could not produce Art in letters, as surely as they were unable to produce anything but Art in painting. He gave to the world, clothed in exquisite raiment of words, modeled with consummate craftsmanship, a book of Criticism of Art which is as sorry a Falsity as was ever written by a great artist on his art—a book that, were it not a falsity, would condemn his superb art out of his own mouth—a book that has destroyed the potential power to create art in more young painters of his following than any one of the many fatuous works written aforetime has wronged a great man's disciples and turned them from the splendor of his ways.

Whistler was a master of emotional statement in color. He gave himself wholly to the right instinct which impels an artist to utter the revelation of life in such terms as his skill of hand can best essay. In the presence of nature he took from her the mood of the thing seen, the emotion it aroused in his senses; and he set it down with so fine and subtle a craftsmanship in color that the harmonies of his paint arouse in us these same emotions. The mere dross of the paint and canvas falls from it; and there is revealed to us that which is above paint and canvas—the mood of the thing seen, the hour of the day, the whole subtle significance of it all, wrought into perfect utterance by the skill of a master. And this wondrous miracle of the hand's craft being so, we are tempted in our blindness of understanding to seek for it in the mere beauty of the clay of the body that held it—and we are dullard enough to raise the exquisite craftsmanship of the paint on the canvas to the exalted state of the emotion that it creates. And, if we be but brazen enough to bray, we cry out that the sensation is the Little—the clotted pigment, the flowing oil, the warp and woof of the canvas the Great!

It were no mitigation of our humiliation to plead that Whistler himself, when he was talking, should have avowed falsities for his creed which his conduct and practice were incapable of committing. Nay, was it not Whistler who gave us the most foolish definition of Art uttered by man's mouth? He said that Art was the Science of the Beautiful—which were no mean definition of Craft; and had been no bad definition of Art but that Art is not a Science and is not Beauty. It is of the wisdom of the wiseacre who defined a Crab as a scarlet reptile that walks backwards—which were not so bad, were it a reptile, were it scarlet, and did it walk backwards!

Nor is it the least significant of Whistler's career that, whilst in following his instinct for artistic utterance in painting, he was incapable of a falsity; so, in attempting to utter himself in literature, he mastered and achieved complete and consummate skill in the craftsmanship of words but to betray the fact that he had no instinct to create Art in literature! He debauched the province of Art by essaying to misuse its craftsmanship to express ideas which he had not the skill to turn into terms of living Art. And so deep in falsity were the foundations of his literary utterance that he could but build a structure of Falsities upon them. And it is not the least fantastic part of his defeat that the most precious passage in his literary craftsmanship should have contained flagrant falsities, petty conceit, and mean understanding. Scan it for a moment:—

" And when the evening mist clothes the riverside with poetry, as with a veil, and the poor buildings lose themselves in the dim sky, and the tall chimneys become campanili, and the warehouses are palaces in the night, and the whole city hangs in the heavens, and fairy-land is before us—then the wayfarer hastens home; the working man and the cultured one, the wise man and the one of pleasure, cease to understand, as they have ceased to see; and Nature, who, for once, has sung in tune, sings her exquisite song to the artist alone, her son and her master—her son in that he loves her, her master in that he knows her."

Here is a man priding himself on his " poetry," wholly unsuspecting that poetry, like all other forms of Art, should not conceal but reveal—glorying in things not looking like what they are but like what they are not—as though a warehouse or a chimney should not have as noble a significance as a palace or campanile!—unable to realize the real romance, but seeking exultantly the rather the false idea—

and, not content with a bridge not looking like a bridge or what not, not content with a false impression, pouring his scorn upon others in that they do not see falsely with him! Of a mind so petty and a conceit so vast that he insolently accuses all but the artist of being unable to see the exquisite beauty of the vision of nature; incapable of realizing that multitudes see it with as deep and reverent, with as subtle and exquisite eyes and senses as he, though they may not have been granted the great gifts to utter the thing seen! So set on exalting the artist that he denies him to be a wayfarer, a worker, cultured, wise, or capable of pleasure! Indeed, it would be difficult to count the swarming falsities, hiving like bees, in that short passage; difficult to discover a single phrase of unadulterated truth in it! The exquisite tricks of craftsmanship of it cover a raw sentimentality, mawkish as a seducer's love-letters, vulgar as lard, contemptible and ill-seen. But of true Art, not a tittle. For true Art cannot lie.

And as Whistler wrote of Art but to belittle it, so he belittled his manhood and betrayed smallness of soul in the pages of that paltry confession of his pettinesses in the affected volume of his *Gentle Art of Making Enemies,* wherein, essaying to bring his fellows into contempt, he betrays into what shallows he could stoop his great and astounding genius, even whilst he punished his contemptible revilers and sapped the pretention of the pompous. Think of a man publishing a whole volume to prove the cleverness of the paltriness of his soul!

It was exactly in his confusing Art with Beauty, that Whistler fell short of the vastnesses. There are far greater, far more profound emotions than such as are aroused by mere beauty; and it was just in these very majestic qualities, in the sense of the sublime and of the immensities, before which his exquisite and subtle genius stood mute. But at least one of the greater senses was given to him in abundance —the sense of mystery. His splendid instinct told him that suggestion was the soul of craftsmanship, and kept him from the blunder of mimicry. He never overstated the details of life. Out of the mystic twilight he caught the haunting sense of its half-revelations and its elusiveness; and was granted an exquisite emotional use of color to utter these subtleties; and in the seeing he caught a glimpse of the hem of the garment of the Great Designer.

THE PROBLEM OF DIVORCE

RHETA CHILDE DORR

The United States used to be described in Europe as " The Land of the Dollar." The term was applied half enviously and half contemptuously. Just now the United States is known in Europe as " The Land of Easy Divorce," and the title carries with it small envy and very genuine contempt. They believe, over there, that American husbands and wives change their marital partners as easily and as lightly as they change partners at a dance. A prospect of improved social or financial standing, a fit of temper, a sentimental aberration, any kind of a whim—and off to the divorce courts. That is what they think about American marriages, in Europe.

In the United States there exists a large public which heartily agrees with this opinion. A considerable class of people indorse the statement made some time ago, that " *Marriage, as an institution, hardly exists among us, any more than in the fifth century at Rome, when twenty wives in succession was not thought an extravagance.*" Another group of Americans share with Cardinal Gibbons the opinion that " *The reckless facility with which divorce may be procured in every state in the Union, except South Carolina, is a blot on the name of the law in our land.*"

Not all of this large public believes with Cardinal Gibbons that divorce, in any circumstances, is a positive evil, and should never be tolerated at all. Few people outside the Catholic communion hold this extreme view. But most thoughtful Americans have an uneasy suspicion that far too many divorces are granted in the United States. They may not be as worried about it as Mrs. Humphry Ward, who wrote a novel to demonstrate that American divorce laws indicate a state of social anarchy which is rapidly disintegrating the very foundations of the Republic. But they do suspect that the well-worn phrase, the " divorce evil," describes a condition of affairs gravely menacing to the home, and to society at large.

Nobody has known exactly what to do about it. A few panaceas have been offered. A Christian bishop, a year or two ago, sent out the gentle suggestion that divorced persons should be socially ostracized, denied all fellowship with the happily married. National conventions of churchmen have denounced divorce in the sternest possible terms. Nearly all the Christian bodies have agreed to prevent, as far as possible, the remarriage of divorced persons. National congresses of lawyers have been called to discuss uniform divorce laws as a check on divorce. Many states have made their marriage laws more rigid in the hope of preventing marriages likely to end in separation.

None of these suggestions or experiments has made the slightest impression on the situation. The " divorce evil " has continued to flourish and to expand until at the present time the fondest pair of lovers in the land face the fact that there is at least one chance in twelve that they will never celebrate their silver wedding. In some states the chance is one *in six*.

We are a nation disgraced in the eyes of the world as a people holding the marriage bond in contempt. Rational considerations, it would seem, should impel the Government to make frequent investigations into the facts of marriage and divorce. But in all the history of the United States only two such investigations have been made. The first one, carried on in 1887 by the Department of Labor, under Commissioner Carroll D. Wright, was sadly barren of results. Certain facts were disclosed in regard to divorce. The one fact that, in the twenty years between 1867 and 1887, a total of 328,716 marriages had been dissolved, seemed appalling enough. Still, nobody could tell precisely how appalled he ought to be, because of the paucity of certain other related facts. In the period which produced those 328,716 divorces, how many marriages had taken place? The investigators reported that in most states this important fact could never be determined. Many states had no records of marriages, and in most of the others the records were so carelessly and incompletely kept as to be practically without worth.

Some states required marriage licenses; others required none. Many states lacked compulsory requirements for returning and recording marriages. Others had the requirements, but attached no penalty to non-observance of the law. Thus in one county of a state the investigators found more licenses than marriages; in the next county they found more marriages than licenses. No state had very much information about marriage. People just married and some of them, an unknown proportion of them, afterwards sought divorces. If there was any reason why this country should produce a divorce crop twice as large as any European country, that reason remained undiscovered. If there were any new social forces operating on those 328,716 married and divorced pairs, those forces remained undisclosed.

Yet there must be some explanation. We have no divorce statistics back of 1867, but we know that previous to the Civil War divorce was rare. What began to happen in 1867? What has been happening ever since? We must find out before we can take a single step toward coping with our divorce problem. And let us agree to call it a problem, instead of an evil. Prejudgments are always unfair and very frequently incorrect.

The second federal examination into the facts concerning marriage and divorce, begun in 1906 under the direction of the Bureau of the Census, was completed this year. The report, recently issued in a large volume entitled *Statistics of Marriage and Divorce*, makes it possible, for the first time in our history, for us to sit down quietly, with at least some of the facts before us, to diagnose our marital unrest.

In this report fairly complete marriage returns are made. The states have progressed wonderfully in this regard since 1887. To-day every state in the Union, except South Carolina and New Jersey, requires marriage licenses. New Jersey requires a license in case one or both parties to the marriage are non-residents of the state. Every state, except South Carolina, now keeps records of marriages. South Carolina is the one state in the Union where no divorce is allowed.

A taste for reading and analyzing statistics is rarely natural, nor is it very frequently even acquired. It is hardly possible that this latest volume of the census will have a large popular circulation. But the facts contained in its closely printed pages of tabulated figures are so interesting, so suggestive, so valuable, that they deserve to be given the very widest publicity. Every man and woman in the United States ought to know them, ought to think about them, talk about them, reform their social ideals if need be, readjust their lives in accordance with them. Not otherwise are we ever going to solve our problem.

The first fact to be noted is that, while our marriage rate has increased in the twenty years between 1887 and 1906, our divorce rate has increased even more briskly. According to the Census of 1890, there was a married population in the United States of 22,447,-769, with an annual average of 33,197 divorces. That is, there was one divorce to every 676 of married population. According to the Census of 1900, there was a married population of 27,770,101, with an annual divorce record of 55,502, or one divorce to every 500 of married population. Between 1887 and 1906 the record of divorces reaches the amazing total of 945,625. Nearly a million American marriages went to pieces in twenty years. That is, disruption overtook 47,281 marriages a year, 3,940 a month—more than 130 a day.

No one section of the country produces a much larger divorce crop than another. Louisiana, with its large Catholic population, Mormon Utah and Unitarian Massachusetts furnish similar figures. Broadly speaking, the divorce rate rises as we cross the map westward, but, on the whole, the rate is fairly even throughout the country. The rate is slightly larger in cities than in the country, but divorce is by no means a city problem.

It is astonishing to find that divorce laws, stringent or liberal, affect the rate very slightly. New Hampshire, Utah and South Dakota show almost exactly the same proportion of divorces per population and per marriages. New York with its one cause for divorce and New Jersey with its half dozen causes show a rate nearly identical.

This would appear to prove the charge, so often made, that most of our divorces are sought in states offering bargain counter decrees. But such is not the case. A small proportion of divorces, less than twenty per cent., are migratory. The great majority of unhappily mated apparently cannot afford to take long vacations in fashionable divorce colonies. In fact they are not all rich people nor do a considerable number of them ornament the stage. For the most part, they are plain, middle-class people. They seek relief from their marital bonds among their neighbors, in their own towns.

Another popular fiction—that Americans rush into marriage and out again, impetuously and without reflection—is disproved by actual figures. We all know the class to whom marriage is a joke, those who get married in balloons, in store windows, or on the stage after the performance. The convivial pairs who wake up a "marrying parson" at two o'clock in the morning are also familiar, as is likewise the anarchistic millionaire class, to whom the whim of the moment is the only law in the universe. This population, however conspicuous, is very small. The ordinary American marries in good faith and actually makes an effort to stay married. The statistics show that the average marriage ending in divorce endures from seven to ten years. The largest number of divorces are granted at the end of the fourth year of marriage, and the number does not decrease very much until the sixteenth year. Along about the twentieth to the twenty-fifth year the divorce rate takes a little spurt. After that it declines. Still, from 1887 to 1906, two hundred and eighty-seven marriages were found that collapsed after enduring for fifty years.

Women, not men, are the more frequent movers in divorce proceedings. Two-thirds of all the divorces granted in this country since 1887 were given to aggrieved wives.

The largest contributing cause was desertion. More than one-third of all divorces granted to women, and nearly one-half of all divorces granted to men, were for desertion. At this point you get your first gleam of light on the problem of divorce.

About two-thirds of all American divorces were granted for desertion. The marriage had actually been dissolved from one to three years before action was brought at all. In other words, most of our divorces were mere legal ratifications of something which had previously taken place. No statistics can determine how many of these desertions were cold blooded and cowardly abandonments, and how many of them were separations for cause, or by arrangement.

But—very few divorces were contested. This would seem to indicate that both parties were weary of the bond, or at least, retained a very feeble interest in it. That the majority of those who do contest suits are willing to be free is evident from the slight nature of the average contest made.

Seldom does it appear that a change of marital partners is the object of the divorce. Divorced persons in the United States remarry not much more frequently than widowed persons. And this is rather remarkable since divorced persons are likely to be younger than widowed persons, presumably more attractive—in a word, more marriageable. One marriage, however, really seems to be enough for most of those whose romances end in a divorce court.

Divorce is not a very profitable arrangement to the average American woman. Alimony is granted in only about thirteen per cent. of all cases; in more than eighty per cent. of suits brought by women, alimony is not even asked for. According to the census bulletin, *Statistics of Women at Work*, more than half the divorced women in the United States are self-supporting. In a large number of cases they are supporting children.

After this, you can hardly escape the suspicion that the great majority of American divorces are separations by mutual consent. The events which led to that mutual consent are beyond the power of any census enumerator to determine.

This knowledge does not make any simpler the solution of the divorce problem. If we found the chief contributing cause to be adultery, cruelty or intemperance, we might find something to do about it. But adultery, while furnishing a frequent cause for divorce of husbands against wives, is far down in the scale in suits of wives against husbands. After desertion, cruelty appears in women's suits as the most frequent cause. Intemperance hardly appears at all. It is shown in five per cent. of women's suits and only one per cent. in men's.

What is to be done with a nation of people that will not continue to wear marriage bonds after mutual love and respect between husband and wife is dead? What is the use of unifying divorce laws? What is the good of congresses of lawyers and clergymen? Why go to the trouble of forbidding religious marriage to divorced persons? Apparently, the Americans are a people that will not accept any marriage but a happy one. What can be done with such an extraordinary race?

In the discussion of the divorce problem, we very seldom go beyond the question of whether divorce itself is right or wrong. Churchmen usually confine their arguments to a passage from the Gospel according to St. Matthew, wherein Christ is quoted as forbidding husbands to divorce their wives. Whether or no wives were to be allowed to divorce their husbands is not stated. Some churchmen go back to the Garden of Eden and show that Adam possessed only one wife, and never got a divorce from her. Whether these arguments really bear on the subject, it is absolutely certain that they do not at all affect the problem as it exists to-day.

The strongest argument brought against divorce is that it breaks up homes, and is therefore unsocial, and dangerous to the community. This argument seems weakened by the evidence that two-thirds of all divorces are granted for desertion. The home, in two-thirds of all instances, was already broken up.

The truth is that behind every divorce there lies concealed a big, human story. Stranger than fiction, many of them are; some, sadder than death. Not one person who reads these lines but has personal knowledge of one or more of these stories.

Nearly a third of all divorces granted to women have cruelty as the chief contributing cause. Now cruelty, it is known, is often the merest excuse, given to conceal the real cause for divorce. Physical brutality on the part of husbands is common enough, however, and many genuine cases are carried to the divorce courts. Read some actual evidence. A neighbor is testifying.

" When I got to the door she had stopped screaming. But after I got into the room he was still beating her over the head and body with a stick. She was insensible and covered with blood. He had torn most of the clothes off her, and I truly believe was trying to kill her."

" Who, besides yourself, was in the room? "

" Annie, the oldest girl, and two of the boys. They were crying and screaming."

" What happened next? "

" I grasped him by the arms from behind—I'm pretty strong— and threw him away from her. Then more people came, and some one fetched the policeman."

This story is offered to those people who advocate separation but not divorce. The man in the case had recently returned after a sepa- ration of two years, brought about on account of his dissolute habits. The wife thought herself free, but one day the husband turned up and begged to be taken back, assuring her that he had fully reformed. A week later he was drinking and one night, after she had refused to give him money to buy more drink, he turned on her and beat her almost to death. Was divorce in this case—a typical one—an evil, or was it a good? Was this home broken up because divorce thrust out of it a brutal husband and father?

A prominent lawyer in New York, after eighteen years of marriage, more or less uncongenial, discovered that the mother of his three children had become addicted to drugs. When under their influence her conduct was frequently disgraceful. The woman refused to go to a sanitarium for treatment and several times made scenes in public, accusing her husband of conspiracy against her freedom. After a year or two of this kind of martyrdom the husband obtained a divorce. During the trial, which was as sensational as the woman could make it, the eldest daughter, a sensitive girl of sixteen, broke down nervously and for months lingered on the brink of insanity. Was divorce in this case an evil, or was it a social duty?

These are extreme cases, in which divorce seems to have been positively necessary. We do not know how necessary or how unnecessary the average divorce is because the real facts are usually concealed. Sometimes the real facts are so extraordinary that no divorce laws cover them, and hence they are not brought forth, as in the case of a woman now well known in the literary world. This woman married, very soon after leaving college, a civil engineer whom she met while traveling in the West. He seemed a fine, manly chap, and the young woman married him with every prospect for a happy union. After her marriage she made a very disquieting discovery. The man's moral nature had in it a strange twist. He had not the slightest notion of truth or veracity. He was a congenital liar. He lied about everything, great and trivial. The camp cook sneered at him behind his back and his colleagues openly despised him. The young wife, who had accompanied her husband on a long surveying trip into the mountains, found herself in an intolerable positiou. She must defend her husband, shield him, corroborate his fictions, become a liar herself for his sake, or she must quarrel with him. She struggled blindly with the situation until the expedition was at an end. Then she left her husband and began to earn her

living with her pen. He divorced her—for desertion. What should
that woman have done? Borne children to a man without honor?

After all the most serious aspect of this problem is not the individual happiness of the men and women involved. The real concern
of the state is for the children of mismated couples. If divorce is bad
for such children, if we could prove that it is bad, then we ought to
forbid divorce altogether.

A strong effort was made by the investigators for the recent
census report, to determine the number of children who were affected
by the 945,625 divorces obtained between 1887 and 1906, and also
to determine just how they were affected. This was difficult because
not all the records were complete in regard to children. In nearly
twenty per cent. of recorded divorces no mention of children appears.
About forty per cent. mention that there were no children, and something over thirty-nine per cent. state that children were involved.
The disposition of the children, being, as a rule, entirely outside the
actual divorce proceedings, is frequently not made a matter of record.
As a matter of usage, however, we know that the children are nearly
always awarded the mother. Women, it will be remembered, obtain
the divorces and are counted innocent parties in two-thirds of all divorce cases. If there is any significance in this, it must mean that
American courts are convinced that association with drunken, delinquent, or irresponsible fathers is not good for children.

In Europe, be a father ever so dissolute, his paternal rights, so-
called, are always recognized. He is commonly awarded all his sons
after they have passed their seventh year. In this country, the rights
of the children rather than of either parent, are protected. We are
coming more and more to recognize that an essential right of all children is a healthy, clean and harmonious environment in which to grow
to manhood and womanhood.

We used to be keenly interested in the question of heredity, especially in its bearings on crime, disease, and vagrancy. Some years
ago eminent evolutionists made a remarkabble study* of the descendants of two men. One of these men was the great New England
theologian, Jonathan Edwards; the other was a notorious drunkard
and criminal, a man named Max Jukes. These studies, extending

* *Science of Penology*, Bois. Putnam's, 1901.

over one hundred and fifty years, show an astonishing persistence of family traits. The Edwards descendants, almost without exception, were of a high and noble type. Hundreds of them received high honors as clergymen, educators, jurists, and statesmen, all were upright and useful citizens.

The record of the Jukes family is one of almost unbroken immorality and crime. Through six generations, its members were uniformly criminals, drunkards, vagrants, degenerates and prostitutes. They intermarried, and came at length to form a sort of community by themselves, a thieves' nest of poverty, vice, and crime.

The records of these families have stood for years as evidence of hereditary transmission of family traits; but lately our faith in the transmission of physical, mental, and moral characteristics has been rudely shaken. Science has demonstrated that viciousness is not propagated through heredity, but is a product of environment and example. If a Jukes baby had been taken at birth and placed in an Edwards cradle, its chances for reaching high eminence in law, science, or statesmanship would have been limited only by the amount of brain matter it was born with. If an Edwards infant had been dropped into a Jukes cradle, the career of an unusually clever criminal would have been instantly inaugurated. There are exceptions to this law, but they are rare.

We are beginning to realize that the only way to deal with vicious families is to break them up. The state often takes children away from immoral and brutal parents. The divorce court often takes immoral and brutal parents away from children, thus giving the children a chance to grow up in a favorable environment.

No one can possibly doubt that every child is entitled to a home with two parents in it—two parents who love instead of hate each other. There is no case recorded of a home like that being broken up by divorce.

What is the matter with Americans that they do not have more happy marriages? Why are marriages in Europe more successful than they are in this country? That is the real problem we have to solve. Divorce is no more an evil than headache is a disease. Both are symptoms.

We assume that European marriages are more successful than

American marriages, because divorce is comparatively rare in Europe. England, Scotland, and Wales had in 1900 a population about half as large as that of the United States. In that year, 743 divorces were granted in the United Kingdom, not including Ireland, where there occurred only one divorce. In 1900 our *annual average* of divorces was 55,502.

Perhaps, if we examine into the reasons why only 743 divorces were granted in Great Britain in 1900, we may get some light on why we demanded and obtained 55,502.

In Great Britain a man may divorce his wife for a single act of infidelity. A woman may divorce her husband for persistent infidelity, provided that in addition he has brutally assaulted her—and she can bring witnesses to prove it; or if he has been guilty of unnatural crime—and she can prove it; or if he has wilfully deserted her for at least two years.

Divorce on these conditions may be obtained in Great Britain, if the parties have money enough to go to London, where the only divorce court in the kingdom is held; if they can pay costs amounting usually from $300 to $500; and, in case the suit is defended, if they can give security for the opposition's costs. Pending the trial of a divorce suit, even when brought by a wife, the children of the marriage are placed in charge of the husband. Even after it is proved that a man has been unfaithful, brutal, or unspeakably evil enough to warrant giving his wife a divorce, the children may be awarded to him part of the time.

This is a fair sample of the divorce laws of Europe. Everywhere, with the possible exception of Switzerland, the laws are notoriously in favor of the man and against the woman. There is hardly a country in Europe which does not legalize the double standard of morals, hardly one where it is possible for a woman to remove her own property, her earnings, her children, or her person from the possession of a man, however unfit he may be to live with. In fact, it is impossible for the woman to protect herself unless she is possessed of great wealth and great influence, and the man's offences are of a really scandalous nature.

In the United States, except in Texas and North Carolina, the laws make no distinction whatever between the offences of a husband

and the offences of a wife. In the two states mentioned, adultery has to be aggravated by desertion before a woman can divorce her husband. This is a curious left-over from the European tradition. Everywhere else in America the laws are perfectly fair to women.

Divorce is allowed in most states for the following reasons: Adultery, cruelty, desertion, conviction of felony, neglect to provide, or impotency. Any one of these means a gross breach of the marriage contract. Men and women are protected in all their other contracts. It appears to accord with American sense of justice that they ought also to be protected in the contract which most intimately concerns life and destiny.

Nowhere in the United States is divorce so costly that only the rich can buy justice. Nowhere does divorce mean to a good mother the loss of her children. A comparison of the laws of Europe and the laws of the United States invites the question, on which side of the world is a loftier ideal of marriage shown? Where are the rights of women and children the better protected?

The solution of our divorce problem lies in securing a better relation between men and women in every department of life. It is an anomaly in this republic that there should be any distinctions on account of sex. It is absurd that women should receive lower wages than men for equal work performed or equal service given. It is unfair to deny women their share in public housekeeping. It is unjust to tax them and at the same time refuse them citizenship.

American women are as well educated, as intelligent, as moral, as conscientious, and within their opportunities, as efficient as American men. Once this is fully recognized; once the last vestige of sex prejudice and sex contempt vanishes from custom and from the statute books; once the same standard of morals is recognized in society as it is in the law; once it is made at least as easy for women as for men to earn an honorable living; once marriage on absolutely equal terms is made possible—no moral or physical advantage on the side of the husband, no parasitism allowed on the part of the wife:

Then it will be perfectly safe to attach a divorce coupon to every marriage certificate, with permission for both parties to tear it off at will.

THREE AMERICAN POETS *

RICHARD LE GALLIENNE

Three volumes of new-born American poetry, published within a week or two of each other, just come into my hands, force upon me the reiteration of a protest and an affirmation, which I—and not I only— have made so often of late that it already seems a form of indignant platitude. Reviewing in this same magazine, a short time ago, *The Younger Choir*—a selection from the writings of one small group of younger American poets—and reviewing elsewhere Mr. Charles Hanson Towne's notable *Manhattan,* I could not but exclaim upon the strange and unutterably stupid superstitition that poetry in America is dead, and that, generally speaking, " there are no poets nowadays."

The three poets whom I propose to appreciate once more victoriously remind one of the opacity of a public that asks, or pretends to ask, for poetry, yet cannot see it when it is there shining and singing, so to say, under its very nose, or, if it sees it, churlishly refuses to buy. " If there were dreams to sell . . . who then would buy! "

There are dreams to sell to-day as of old, more dreams, perhaps, than ever; but Beddoes was right—where are the buyers?

Yes! the fault is with the public—not with the poets. There are, perhaps, more good poets—I say good, not, of course, great—in the world at this moment than there have ever been before in its history, and America is entitled to a proud percentage of them. It would, indeed, be almost safe to say that there are more poets in the world to-day than there are readers, or at all events, buyers, of poetry; and that, under the conditions, poets manage to get published at all is a circumstance which shows the modern publisher in an unaccustomed light, as a quixotic lover of literature: for not one volume of poetry in a hundred can possibly pay its expenses, and even poets with well-established names, to whom important reviews devote columns of appreciation, know to their cost, or rather the cost of their publishers, that fame is more cry than wool, and that, unless a poet can contrive to

---

* *Flower o' the Grass,* by Ada Foster Murray (Mrs. H. M. Alden), Harper & Brothers; *Poems,* by Dorothy Landers Beall, Mitchell Kennerley; *The Town Down the River,* Edwin Arlington Robinson, Charles Scribner's Sons.

feed, clothe and house himself on his laurels, it is likely to go hard with him in a world, which, as Villon sang, will

> "... grind him to the dust with poverty,
> And build him statues when he comes to die."

The public only cares for poetry that has some national or moral or mawkishly sentimental theme—or, may be, makes some momentarily sensational appeal. The best in its great " popular " poets it knows nothing of. It knows Tennyson by *The Charge of the Light Brigade*, and *The May Queen*, but probably never heard of *The Lotus Eaters*, or *Lucretius*. Similarly it knows Longfellow by his grotesque *Excelsior*, and knows nothing of his

> " Spanish sailors with bearded lips
> And the magic of the sea,"—

all that finer gift of his which has been obscured for even true lovers of poetry by what one can only describe as his horrible popularity.

The three poets who are the occasion of all this righteous indignation have, I fear, little factitious popularity to hope for from the nature of their themes. They are just—poets. They have no special " message," nor are they " prophets " of anything in particular. One of them, indeed, Mr. Robinson, has been brought as nearly in touch with " the great heart of the public " as the appreciation of Mr. Roosevelt could bring him. How near that is I have no means of knowing. Mr. Roosevelt would seem to occupy the same position of general *arbiter librorum* which Mr. Gladstone—sharing the honors with Queen Victoria—held in England. A word from Mr. Gladstone made the fame of Mrs. Humphry Ward, and, perhaps to his greater credit, it made the—Anglo-Saxon—fame of Marie Bashkirtseff. I hope, for Mr. Robinson's sake, that Mr. Roosevelt's fiat on literary matters has a like potency in America. But, unaided by some such reverberating advocate, I fear that Mr. Robinson's muse, alike with the muses of Miss Beall and Miss Murray, will not " put money in " his " purse," or in that of his publishers—for the very good (and discouraging) reason that all three volumes are too good poetry to appeal to the bad taste and general ignorance of the so-called " reading public "—God-a-mercy!

If this prognostication should prove unduly pessimistic, I shall thank their publishers for letting me know; for, indeed, it would be cheering news, faith for cloudy days, to hear that such good, even fine, and, in some instances, remarkable, poetry, had actually—sold.

The theme of Miss Beall's singing is stated with the characteristic dogmatism and naïveté of that surging youth which flowers and flashes on every page of a book which I venture to surmise is her first book of "Poems"—a wonderful first book.   Some day, when, as again so divinely young, she says in her dedication to a friend, " all my world shall read me," she will probably call this book as Dante—or rather Rossetti for him—called his *Vita Nuova*—

> " the song
> Which first of all he made, when young."

But, to return to the theme of Miss Beall's singing:

> " Chopin was wise
> To write of loving.   'Tis the only theme
> For life and inspiration!"

(I don't think, by the way, that there is a single love-song in Mr. Robinson's volume!)

Love! love! love! like the voice of some reiterative bird in a wood, that one word rings from end to end of Miss Beall's volume. Too often, for some tastes perhaps grown a little middle-aged,—" and therefore, blest and wise,"—she substitutes the words " desire " and " passion " and comes at last to their natural literary destination—" surrender." These three words,—or rather the lush use of them—Miss Beall will, doubtless, outgrow, and leave to certain corybantic lady-novelists, who, for the time being at least, have destroyed their poetic value. Love! love! love!   This is Miss Beall's theme ; love all the more voluble, naturally, because it is love, for the most part, famished and expectant, or fed and disillusioned.   Three long " confessional " poems—*Revelation, To Him that Knocketh, This Woman—and This Man,*—two of them professedly dramatic,—develop and illustrate Miss Beall's thesis. In *Revelation*, Miss Beall, after the mysterious manner of many young woman poets, writes as a man—writes the love-diary, so to say, of a

man who loves a woman in vain, and realizes that he has lost her by
excess of . . . no! let me rather say by lack of idealistic reserve.

> " We who have found a certain rare, great love
> Must keep it sacred in a sacred place
> Of ideality! No passion's wind
> Must rage among those silences! "

So speaks Miss Beall in somewhat transparent masculine disguise.
In *This Woman—and This Man*, we have the inverse situation—
and the far truer and finer poem—of the woman whose love begins—
as all fine love must—in the idealism of " desire," renouncing the
flesh, like some youthful anchorite, next " surrendering " to it in the
form of some highly transfigured unworthy masculine object of devotion, next face-down before the crucifix of outraged idealism, and ultimately reconciled to a sort of autumnal compromise between the
dream and the fact of love.

> " With the white dawn came peace. I saw my woe
> Futile and foolish. All my wickedness
> Of judgment where Eternity must judge.
> I turned to him and all the tenderness
> Of all my loving leaped into my eyes.
> ' My spirit is too hungry. Love, forgive! '
> My heart flamed up to greet me and above
> The pure dawn touched us very sacredly! "

In *To Him that Knocketh*—artistically the most promising thing
in Miss Beall's book—we have, if one may use the expression, a sturdier variant of Miss Beall's chosen theme—the forbidden, or un-
answered, cry of the cloistered or neglected maiden for love.

Now, if Miss Beall's subject-matter were all, I should hardly have
taken up so much space with her name; for, to speak plainly, the bitter
naked cry of the un-mated or ill-mated, or recently adolescent literary
woman, is becoming an offence against literary decency. The world is
weary of the sexual dreams and disillusionments of disappointed
literary ladies. One sighs for the blush upon these emotional disclosures with which, after a long and painful discussion between
herself and the traditional reticence, eternally sacred, of her woman-

hood, Mrs. Browning took from a sequestered drawer certain "Love-Sonnets from the Portuguese," and placed them in the hands of Robert Browning. They had been written for him—for him only. Yet she blushed as she gave them to him—gave them at last after a struggle with herself, at which our modern ladies of the literary confessional must surely smile. For these ladies not only do not hide away their love-sonnets in sequestered drawers, but, on the contrary, they run out into the market-place with them and read them aloud without even a painted blush, to the wide and weary world.

Mrs. Browning would surely never have unlocked that drawer if she could have realized what flood-gates of feminine emotionalism—to put it mildly—she thus let loose upon the long-suffering future.

But I must not seem to confuse Miss Beall with her subject-matter, or those literary ladies aforesaid. Immediately to set such possible misapprehension right, let me quote :

> " Her heart is great as all the universe
> For suffering and childhood! You should see
> How lovingly she touches the round heads
> Of the small parish children. Here, I thought,
> Is a sweet mother-nature, long frustrate
> Of its true loving. O my Lady, you
> Who would so gladly fold a rose-small form
> Into your eager arms, God fore-ordained
> That you should clasp the whole, weak, weary world
> Into a great embrace of sympathy!
> You are a little mother of us all,
> My gentle-fingered Lady, my dear love!
>
> I walked along beside her, marveling
> That such great love as mine were unexpressed."

This is from *Revelation*. Miss Beall, you will understand, is writing as a man. Listen, with what magic she can speak as a woman—in *This Woman—and This Man:*

> " To-night he comes. O little kindly star
> Hung quaintly at the window of my soul,
> Shine silverly! And tho' my pain doth mar
> This chamber of my spirit, make me whole,

Cleanse me and fashion me! O infinite
White light of beauty, glorify my night!

To-night he comes and in that little word
I do unroll the carpet of my dreams
Before this arrogant and gracious lord
Who has so stormed my spirit. O meseems,
This is a world of tenderness! Afar,
Ten thousand lovers worship thee, my star.

I do so love him that my heart would pray
Great pain for him, soul-tearing agony,
That I might kiss his suffering away
And blot his woe out with vast sympathy.
Yet if he suffer, all my tenderness
Doth bleed great drops of life-red bitterness!"

And, allow me, turning over her pages, to gather single lines and
passages such as these:

" My letters followed her like silver gulls"—
" Whose touch is music, and whose coming, light "—
" Furtive as fear in a wide wilderness "—
                              " the cry
Vain, weak, insistent, wherewith finite minds
Do storm the fortress of infinity "—
" Happiness compassed in a single sound "—
                              " I lie
Among the gentle grasses. I can hear
Them tug against the fetters of their roots"—
" . . . the slow penitent rain . . ."
" Peace, and a little foothold for my soul."

Such lines and passages are no exceptions in Miss Beall's book, but so
to speak, the very grass we tread on. She has, indeed, a remarkable
fecundity of imagery, not mere fanciful imagery, but that powerful
metaphorical imagery which comes of the large grasp and deep insight of the profounder poetic imagination. The obvious influence of
George Meredith shows that her muse has been nourished on the great

masters, and been gifted to catch something of their large accent. It is impossible to read *This Woman—and This Man*, without realizing how much *Modern Love* has meant to Miss Beall's poetic development. Indeed, the poem numbered " xxii " is almost a replica of the opening poem of *Modern Love*, as also that numbered "xxiii" no less clearly re-echoes another of the most characteristic dramatic moments of Meredith's great poem. From a metrical point of view, it is interesting to note that Miss Beall's favorite form is what one might call a sonnet in blank verse—a " moment " presented in fourteen unrhymed lines, and it says no little for her art that one is hardly conscious of the omission of the rhymes.

Miss Ada Foster Murray, with whose haunting and distinguished verses we have been familiar, for some time, in those magazines that still recognize distinction, is no *sturm und drang* singer such as Miss Beall, though she often strikes chords of deep emotion and even passion—but with her, to use her own fine phrase, it is the " rich Indian summer of the heart." For the most part, her mood is elegiac, or at least retrospective, but, at the same time, as her brilliant lighter verses particularly illustrate, she has learnt from life to wear her rue with a philosophic gaiety which gives her verse that peculiar piquancy which comes, for some natures, of the humanizing effects of experience. Indeed, she seems to have achieved that wisdom which consists in almost entirely forgetting one's self; and her best poems are either impersonal pictures of nature—particularly nature in autumn—done with a rare combination of delicate precision and profound poignancy, or tender remembrances of young creatures to whom early has been given that sleep promised to those beloved of the gods. Take this perfect little elegy, quite classic in its simplicity: *Her Dwelling Place—*

> " Amid the fairest things that grow
> My lady hath her dwelling-place;
> Where runnels flow, and frail buds blow
> As shy and pallid as her face.
>
> The wild, bright creatures of the wood
> About her fearless flit and spring;
> To light her dusky solitude
> Comes April's earliest offering.

The calm Night from her urn of rest
Pours downward an unbroken stream;
All day upon her mother's breast
My lady lieth in a dream.

Love could not chill her low, soft bed
With any sad memorial stone;
He put a red rose at her head—
A flame as fragrant as his own."

And, again, what a delicately observed picture is this of *Autumn*, with its frail exquisitely placed detail, and its subtle appropriateness of mood:

"The dandelions that made glad the spring
Return to brighten autumn's dimmer way;
Queen Anne's shrunk laces to their thin stems cling,
Pale yellow butterflies about them stray.

Above the spent flame of the goldenrod
The smouldering embers of the sumac burn,
And flakes of fire upon the ashen sod
Mark where the leaves to native dust return.

A tremulous light the smoky ether fills,
As from a censer silver wreaths arise;
Above the altar of the turquoise hills
Ascend strange shapes in mists of sacrifice.

Pile high the pyre, the flaming faggots bring,
To one vast urn the shining dust consign!
The gentle wraiths of summer-time and spring
Shall hover near, involving powers benign.

While ancient spirits hidden in the tree,
Waiting the touch that breaks the silent spell,
Guard even now the tender mystery
Of leaf and bloom, spring's folded miracle."

I haven't space to quote from Miss Murray's lighter verse, though such delightful things as *A Manhattan Love-Song*, and *After the*

Wedding, cannot fail to find a place eventually in some anthology of American *vers de société*.

Mr. Robinson, also, as I have hinted, has passed the period of his *sturm und drang*. He, too, has gone through the mill—in a man's way; and his book is not a book of love-songs. It is occupied almost exclusively with men who have gone through the mill also: Lincoln, Napoleon, Theodore Roosevelt (the particular god of his idolatry), and certain sad, cynical, good-hearted men, comrades in the misfortunes of existence, with whom he has been accustomed to foregather at " Calverly's "—

> " We go no more to Calverly's,
>   For there the lights are few and low;
>   And who are there to see by them,
>   Or what they see, we do not know."

Leffingwell, Clavering, and Lingard are the names of these friends —of whose individualities and fates Mr. Robinson gives us somewhat too cryptic glimpses—in a literary medium compounded of Browning and Mr. A. E. Housman—of *The Shropshire Lad*. I don't mean that Mr. Robinson is a mere imitator of either of these two poets—for he has a very marked individuality of his own—he is a poet of steel and grit, refreshingly bracing after the too much honeycomb provided us by some of our younger poets; but he has none the less been markedly influenced by Browning and Housman, and their influence has resulted in somewhat too stringent and tight-packed a style, in too many dark sayings and drastic abbreviations of his meaning. So far, he is a poet of vividly etched lines rather than of complete poems, flashes of insight, and lightning glimpses of character. His characterizations of Lincoln in *The Master* are particularly searching:

> " Shrewd, hallowed, harassed, and among
>   The mysteries that are untold,
>   The face we see was never young
>   Nor could it ever have been old.
>
> For he to whom we had applied
>   Our shopman's test of age and worth,
>   Was elemental when he died,
>   As he was ancient at his birth:

> The saddest among kings of earth,
> Bowed with a galling crown, this man
> Met rancor with a cryptic mirth,
> Laconic—and Olympian."

"Cryptic mirth" would be no bad description of a certain persimmon humor which pervades Mr. Robinson's volume, in such delightful characterizations as this of *Miniver Cheevy:*

> "Miniver cursed the commonplace
> And eyed a khaki suit with loathing;
> He missed the mediæval grace
> Of iron clothing.
>
> Miniver scorned the gold he sought,
> But sore annoyed was he without it;
> Miniver thought, and thought, and thought,
> And thought about it.
>
> Miniver Cheevy, born too late,
> Scratched his head and kept on thinking;
> Miniver coughed, and called it fate,
> And kept on drinking."

Or this tender *vale* for Clavering:

> "He clung to phantoms and to friends,
> And never came to anything.
> He left a wreath on Cubit's grave.
> I say no more for Clavering."

Perhaps what I have been trying to say of Mr. Robinson's point of view is best expressed in this whimsical sketch of Shadrach O'Leary:

> "O'Leary was a poet—for a while:
> He sang of many ladies frail and fair,
> The rolling glory of their golden hair,
> And emperors extinguished with a smile.
> They foiled his years with many an ancient wile,
> And if they limped, O'Leary didn't care:
> He turned them loose and had them everywhere,
> Undoing saints and senates with their guile.

> But this was not the end. A year ago
> I met him—and to meet was to admire:
> Forgotten were the ladies and the lyre,
> And the small, ink-fed Eros of his dream.
> By questioning I found a man to know—
> A failure spared, a Shadrach of the Gleam."

Whatever the value of **Mr. Robinson's** muse, it is assuredly not that of a " small, ink-fed Eros." As I said before, there is not one love-poem in his volume, though he has a very beautiful dirge *For a Dead Lady*—

> " The forehead and the little ears
>   Have gone where Saturn keeps the years;
>   The heart where roses could not live
>   Has done with rising and with falling "—

and he has a charming poem to a baby.

A PLATFORM FOR WOMEN

REBECCA J. LOSE

[As the woman's suffrage movement is continuously conspicuous, a clear and concise statement of the principles involved, as they appear to the advocates of the cause, seems desirable.   The following " Platform " is not issued with the authority of any political organization, but it should provide a reasonable basis for discussion.— Editor.]

WHEREAS; It is evident that the question of the right of women to full citizenship with men is regarded with:
  1. Indifference,
  2. Misapprehension,
  3. Hostility: *and*
WHEREAS; We believe the said indifference, misapprehension and hostility to be due largely:
  1. To a lack of intelligent interest in the subject,
  2. To the inborn distrust of the race for things untried,
  3. To a disregard of the fact that the centre of gravity is changing in matters industrial and economic,
  4. To an antiquated and unscientific view of the origin and growth of the human race: *and*
WHEREAS; We have become deeply impressed with the desirability of a more complete and dispassioned understanding of the question:
THEREFORE; Confiding in the ultimate intelligence, patriotism and discriminating justice of the race, we submit the following statement of our beliefs to the candid judgment of all men.
First: That we hold the axiom of the American people, that governments derive their just powers only from the consent of the governed, to be as true to-day as yesterday.
Second: That, also to-day as yesterday, taxation without representation is tyranny.
Third: That taxation must be regarded, not alone as the levying of stated sums upon stated values, but must be understood as including every act of legislation that affects life, every act that regulates values or opportunities; and that it also includes penalties,

the penalties of ignorance and neglect and of wilfully wrong decisions.

Fourth: That we hold the right of woman to full citizenship with man to lie in the fact that her share in the stake of government is the same as that of man, her risk the same, her life, liberty and happiness as valuable, not only to herself, but to the state.

Fifth: That, whilst we realize that, as of old, prudence dictates that governments should not be changed for light or transient reasons, we submit that from this day forth, woman's share in the stake of government must be considered; that no legislation can hereafter hold that fails to take her into account; that no question can ever again be decided permanently and rightfully that excludes her from its consideration.

Sixth: That we hold the law to have lagged already by reason of its failure to perceive and to estimate at its true value the economic and industrial changes of recent years, changes that have enormously affected the life, the condition and the capacity of women.

Seventh: That, the old law of force having been outlived, we hold that no longer is the individual man in any sense the necessary protector of the individual woman; that the law, the delegated fist of primeval days, must hereafter protect alike the man and the woman.

Eighth: That we regard as extraneous the argument that women are rightfully excluded from a participation in the functions of government because of their inability to enforce their decisions, should the sexes, by any chance, be arrayed against each other; holding that any line, arbitrarily dividing mankind, no matter upon what basis drawn, would find upon one side the stronger and upon the other side the weaker.

Ninth: That we also regard as idle the demand that women pledge themselves to better conditions; that none can predicate the future; that men and women, being made of like clay, will probably for all time be actuated by like motives, and be subject to like inducements, one with another.

Tenth: That no sentimental reason holds against the admission of women to the rights and privileges of citizenship; that the various arguments of this sort,—the doubled vote, the possible confusion, the ignorance of women of the machinery of government, the added burden, etc., etc.,—are, all alike, to be disregarded as not touching the real question at any point.

Eleventh: That, in conclusion, we re-affirm our belief in the absolute, inherent right of women to full and equal citizenship with men; said citizenship to carry with it the same privileges, and to be subject to the same conditions as are laid upon men under like circumstances, and to none other.

EDGAR CHAMBLESS AND HIS RUNAWAY TOWN *

GERALD STANLEY LEE

THE thing that came to me first when someone told me about Roadtown, was not any particular interest in the town itself, but a very great and immediate curiosity about the man who could have thought of it. I wondered how he came to. I thought how happy he must have been when, that first day, it all came over him. Owing, perhaps, to certain æsthetic pre-judgments and partialities, his idea did not quite seem important to me at once, but it did seem important to me that there should be, tucked away on this planet somewhere, a man who was really living to-day in my own generation and whom I had not seen, who could think of such a thing. The idea itself, this particular one, might or might not be important, but I could not but feel that any mind that could face a whole broadside of modern civilization so naïvely, so freshly and as if it had never been faced before, and that could conceive an idea offhand, with such boldness, with such a noble sweep of implications and inferences and with such a range of vision in it, and yet could conceive it at the same time with such quietness and thoroughness—must be an important mind. I decided that if that mind was still in New York the next time I went down, I would hunt it up in its little pigeonhole in the big city and get a look at it.

Mr. Chambless called on me not long afterward and in an alcove in one of the New York clubs, with his long roll of Roadtown in his hand and with a fine self-forgetfulness and forgetfulness of me, and with his long legs and his long arms and his eager eyes all sweeping graciously about him, he sat and talked.

Then a thing happened, which, as it turned out, proved to be the determining and conclusive factor in my attitude toward Mr. Chambless's important mind.

He bored me.

But he bored me beautifully.

There was not a single second while he was doing it when even in

* A book about " Roadtown," by Edgar Chambless, is published by the author, 150 Nassau Street, New York. $1.25 net, postpaid.

the utmost depths of my helplessness, as I watched his eyes and watched my mind struggling with his mind, my heart did not cry out within me, " Go on, go on, old boy, I glory in you! I envy you. I am proud of you and proud of being in the same world with you. May God's name be praised! " In short, I am bound to record that the one thing I have to say with regard to Edgar Chambless's boring me is that he emerged from it in my eyes a great man.

If there is anybody else who will bore me in the same way that Edgar Chambless did that day, who will leave me at the end of it in the same attitude toward the world and toward my own work, so that I come home singing to do it, they will be welcome. If there is some other man who will bore me so that when I wake up in the night and think of this old world of ours lying out there in its vast blanket of darkness, I shall find myself thinking of *him* a minute, as I think of Chambless—thinking what a great world it is that such people are born in it, men who build the lives of the next generation—if there is anybody else who will bore me so that with this strange happiness I shall find myself thinking of them suddenly when I hear church bells ringing or see young children playing, I wish they would do it.

One does not like, to-day, to call anyone a great man in so many words. It seems almost like hitting a man in the dark from behind to say to people that he is a great man. It makes him lonesome suddenly, and separates him helplessly from other people. And no really great man would like it. I would rather say that Edgar Chambless is a man who is working day and night in a great spirit on the fate of the world.

All the rest follows. When once you have caught a man's spirit and when once after a long groping or thirsting you have found him, and when once you have drunk deep at his single-heartedness and have seen that here is a man who has packed his world into one big, summing-up idea, an idea to which he is devoting his life and sacrificing himself and sacrificing everybody about him, there is not anything one can say or anything that all the world can do to keep that idea, in one form or another, from coming to pass.

And now that Mr. Chambless has written and published his book about Roadtown, perhaps I need not say that Mr. Chambless's book does not bore me, and that it could not bore anybody. The most lovable absent-mindedness in the world can be managed on paper. One can come to, any time, in a book, and go back and be sorry if one wants to, and cut it out. This is what Mr. Chambless has done. For that matter, what Mr. Chambless has to say about Roadtown, whether in conversation or in writing, is really and always has been, taken as a whole, absorbingly interesting. I have merely meant to intimate in making my main point about Mr. Chambless that my own interest in machinery, like some other people's, is selective. Probably I like to take for granted now and then in thinking of machinery, or in being talked to about it, too many cogs and things. It does not need to be said that the bleak places or streaks of mechanics which might keep Mr. Chambless's conversation, at least with me at times, like any other inventor's, from being too monotonously interesting, are all left out in his book.

I have wanted to say something about Mr. Chambless and his book, when it would be timely. But the subject is large and dazzling, and keeps coming back, and there will be no end to it, if I go further. There is one striking fact, however, I would like to mention with regard to Mr. Chambless's appearance as an author. It is a fact which is going to make many people read his book, who might think they were merely going to glance at it.

We have quite a few men who are writing books to-day, who seem, judging from their books, to have interesting minds. But what Mr. Chambless does in his book is to make his readers' minds interesting. He is not merely being original. He makes other people original. He sets them to talking back. Before they know it, they set to work on his book themselves—they begin building Roadtowns of their own. And the more they get to work on their own Roadtowns, I am inclined to think, the more seriously they will take Mr. Chambless's. He has not finished his idea. But he has made room in it for all the world to help. He has had a thought that it will take cities to think out, and great men and geniuses, architects, artists, inventors, and statesmen, and women and children—all grappling with civilization and with their own lives—will help on Edgar Chambless's book.

In the meantime he has made a tremendous start.

THE NEW MACHIAVELLI

H. G. WELLS

CHAPTER THE FOURTH

THE HOUSE IN WESTMINSTER

V

POLLING day came after a last hoarse and dingy crescendo. The excitement was not of the sort that makes one forget one is tired out. The waiting for the end of the count has left a long blank mark on my memory, and then everyone was shaking my hand and repeating: "Nine hundred and seventy-six."

My success had been a foregone conclusion since the afternoon, but we all behaved as though we had not been anticipating this result for hours, as though any other figures but nine hundred and seventy-six would have meant something entirely different. "Nine hundred and seventy-six!" said Margaret. "They didn't expect three hundred."

"Nine hundred and seventy-six," said a little short man with a paper. "It means a big turn over. Two dozen short of a thousand, you know."

A tremendous hullabaloo began outside, and a lot of fresh people came into the room.

Isabel, flushed but not out of breath, Heaven knows where she had sprung from at that time of night! was running her hand down my sleeve almost caressingly, with the innocent bold affection of a girl. "Got you in!" she said. "It's been no end of a lark."

"And now," said I, "I must go and be constructive."

"Now you must go and be constructive," she said.

"You've got to live here," she added.

"By Jove, yes," I said.

"I shall read all your speeches."

She hesitated.

"I wish I was you," she said, and said it as though it was not exactly the thing she was meaning to say.

"They want you to speak," said Margaret, with something unsaid in her face.

"You must come out with me," I answered, putting my arm through hers, and felt someone urging me to the French windows that gave on the balcony.

"If you think—" she said, yielding gladly.

The Mayor of Kinghamstead, a managing little man with no great belief in my oratorical powers, was sticking his face up to mine.

"It's all over," he said, "and you've won. Say all the nice things you can and say them plainly."

I turned and handed Margaret out through the window and stood looking over the Market place, which was more than half filled with swaying people. The crowd set up a roar of approval at the sight of us, tempered by a little booing. Down in one corner of the square a fight was going on for a flag, a fight that even the prospect of a speech could not instantly check. "Speech!" cried voices, "speech!" and then a brief "boo-oo-oo" that was drowned in a cascade of shouts and cheers. The conflict round the flag culminated in the smashing of a pane of glass in the chemist's window and instantly sank to peace.

"Gentlemen voters of the Kinghamstead Division," I began.

"Votes for women!" yelled a voice, amidst laughter,—the first time I remember hearing that memorable war cry.

"Three cheers for Mrs. Remington!"

"Mrs. Remington asks me to thank you," I said, amidst further uproar and reiterated cries of "speech!"

Then silence came with a startling swiftness.

Isabel was still in my mind, I suppose. "I shall go to Westminster," I began. I sought for some compelling phrase and could not find one. "To do my share," I went on, "in building up a great and splendid civilization."

I paused, and there was a weak gust of cheering, and then a renewal of booing.

"This election," I said, "has been the end and the beginning of much. New ideas are abroad—"

"Chinese labor!" yelled a voice, and across the square swept a wildfire of hooting and bawling.

It is one of the few occasions when I quite lost my hold on a speech. I glanced sideways and saw the mayor of Kinghamstead speaking behind his hand to Parvill. By a happy chance Parvill caught my eye.

"What do they want?" I asked.

"Eh?"

"What do they want?"

"Say something about general fairness—the other side," prompted Parvill, flattered but a little surprised by my appeal. I pulled myself hastily into a more popular strain with a gross eulogy of my opponent's good taste.

"Chinese labor!" cried the voice again.

" You've given that notice to quit," I answered.

The Market Place roared delight, but whether that delight expressed hostility to Chinamen or hostility to their practical enslavement no student of the General Election of 1906 has ever been able to determine. Certainly one of the most effective posters on our side displayed a hideous yellow face, just that and nothing more. There was not even a legend to it. How it impressed the electorate we did not know, but that it impressed the electorate profoundly there can be no disputing.

VI

Kinghamstead was one of the earliest constituencies fought, and we came back—it must have been Saturday—triumphant but very tired, to our house in Radnor Square. In the train we read the first intimations that the victory of our party was likely to be a sweeping one.

Then came a period when one was going about receiving and giving congratulations and watching the other men arrive, very like a boy who has returned to school with the first batch after the holidays. The London world reeked with the general election; it had invaded the nurseries. All the children of one's friends had got big maps of England cut up into squares to represent constituencies and were busy sticking gummed blue labels over the conquered red of Unionism that had hitherto submerged the country. And there were also orange labels, if I remember rightly, to represent the new Labor party, and green for the Irish. I engaged myself to speak at one or two London meetings, and lunched at the Reform, which was fairly tepid, and dined and spent one or two tumultuous evenings at the National Liberal Club, which was in active eruption. The National Liberal became feverishly congested towards midnight as the results of the counting came dropping in. A big green-baize screen had been fixed up at one end of the large smoking-room with the names of the constituencies that were voting that day, and directly the figures came to hand, up they went, amidst cheers that at last lost their energy through sheer repetition, whenever there was record of a Liberal gain. I don't remember what happened when there was a Liberal loss; I don't think that any were announced while I was there.

How packed and noisy the place was, and what a reek of tobacco and whiskey fumes we made! Everybody was excited and talking, making waves of harsh confused sound that beat upon one's ears, and every now and then hoarse voices would shout for someone to speak. Our little set was much in evidence. Both the Cramptons were in, Lewis, Bunting Harblow. We gave brief addresses attuned to this excitement and the late hour, amidst much enthusiasm.

"Now we can *do* things!" I said amidst a rapture of applause. Men I did not know from Adam held up glasses and nodded to me in solemn fuddled approval as I came down past them into the crowd again.

Men were betting whether the Unionists would lose more or less than two hundred seats.

"I wonder just what we shall do with it all," I heard one sceptic speculating. . . .

After these orgies I would get home very tired and excited, and find it difficult to get to sleep. I would lie and speculate about what it was we *were* going to do. One hadn't anticipated quite such a tremendous accession to power for one's party. Liberalism was swirling in like a flood. . . .

I found the next few weeks very unsatisfactory and distressing. I don't clearly remember what it was I had expected; I suppose the fuss and strain of the general election had built up a feeling that my return would in some way put power into my hands, and instead I found myself a mere undistinguished unit in a vast but rather vague majority. There were moments when I felt very distinctly that a majority could be too big a crowd altogether. I had all my work still before me, I had achieved nothing as yet but opportunity, and a very crowded opportunity it was at that. Everyone about me was chatting parliament and appointments; one breathed distracting and irritating speculations as to what would be done and who would be asked to do it. I was chiefly impressed by what was unlikely to be done and by the absence of any general plan of legislation to hold us all together. I found the talk about parliamentary procedure and etiquette particularly trying. We dined with the elder Cramptons one evening, and old Sir Edward was lengthily sage about what the House liked, what it didn't like, what made a good impression and what a bad one. "A man shouldn't speak more than twice in his first session, and not at first on too contentious a topic," said Sir Edward. "No.

"Very much depends upon manner. The House hates a lecturer. There's a sort of airy earnestness——"

He waved his cigar to eke out his words.

"Little peculiarities of costume count for a great deal. I could name one man who spent three years living down a pair of spatterdashers. On the other hand—a thing like that—if it catches the eye of the *Punch* man, for example, may be your making."

He went off into a lengthy speculation of why the House had come to like an originally unpopular Irishman named Biggar. . . .

The opening of Parliament gave me some peculiar moods. I began to feel more and more like a branded sheep. We were sworn in in batches, dozens and scores of fresh men, trying not to look too fresh under the inspection of policemen and messengers, all of us carrying new silk hats and wearing magisterial coats. It is one of my vivid memories from this period, the sudden outbreak of silk hats in the smoking-room of the National Liberal Club. At first I thought there must have been a funeral. Familiar faces, that one had grown to know under soft felt hats, under bowlers, under liberal-minded wide brims, and above artistic ties and tweed jackets, suddenly met one, staring with the stern gaze of self-consciousness, from under silk hats of incredible glossiness. There was a disposition to wear the hat much too forward I thought, for a good parliamentary style.

There was much play with the hats all through; a tremendous competition to get in first and put hats on coveted seats. A memory hangs about me of the House in the early afternoon, an inhuman desolation inhabited almost entirely by silk hats. There were yards and yards of empty green benches with hats and hats and hats distributed along them, resolute-looking top hats, lax top hats with a kind of shadowy grin under them, sensible top hats brim upward and one scandalous incontinent that had rolled from the front Opposition bench right to the middle of the floor. A headless hat is surely the most soulless thing in the world, far worse even than a skull. . . .

At last, in a leisurely muddled manner we got to the Address; and I found myself packed in a dense elbowing crowd to the right of the Speaker's chair; while the attenuated Opposition, nearly leaderless after the massacre, tilted its brim to its nose and sprawled at its ease amidst its empty benches.

There was a tremendous hullabaloo about something, and I craned to see over the shoulder of the man in front. " Order, order, order ! "

" What's it about ? " I asked.

The man in front of me was clearly no better informed, and then I gathered from a slightly contemptuous Scotchman beside me that it was Chris Robinson had walked between the honorable member in possession of the House and the Speaker. I caught a glimpse of him blushingly whispering about his misadventure to a colleague. He was just that same little figure I had once assisted to entertain at Cambridge, but gray-haired now, and still it seemed with the same knitted muffler he had discarded for a reckless half-hour while he talked to us in Hatherleigh's rooms.

It dawned upon me that I wasn't particularly wanted in the House, and that I should get all I needed of the opening speeches next day from the *Times*.

I made my way out and was presently walking rather aimlessly through the outer lobby.

I caught myself regarding the shadow that spread itself out before me, multiplied itself in blue tints of various intensity, shuffled itself like a pack of cards under the many lights, the square shoulders, the silk hat, already worn with a parliamentary tilt backward; I found I was surveying this statesmanlike outline with a weak approval. "A *member!*" I felt the little cluster of people that were scattered about the lobby must be saying.

"Good God!" I said in hot reaction, "what am I doing here?"

It was one of those moments, infinitely trivial in themselves, that yet are cardinal in a man's life. It came to me with extreme vividness that it wasn't so much that I had got hold of something as that something had got hold of me. I distinctly recall the rebound of my mind. Whatever happened in this Parliament, I at least would attempt something. "By God!" I said, "I won't be overwhelmed. I am here to do something, and do something I will!"

But I felt that for the moment I could not remain in the House.

I went out by myself with my thoughts into the night. It was a chilling night, and rare spots of rain were falling. I glanced over my shoulder at the lit windows of the Lords. I walked, I remember, westward, and presently came to the Grosvenor Embankment and followed it, watching the glittering black rush of the river and the dark, dimly lit barges round which the water swirled. Across the river was the hunched sky-line of Doulton's potteries, and a kiln flared redly. Dimly luminous trams were gliding amidst a dotted line of lamps, and two little trains crawled into Waterloo station. Mysterious black figures came by me and were suddenly changed to the commonplace at the touch of the nearer lamps. It was a big confused world, I felt, for a man to lay his hands upon.

I remember I crossed Vauxhall Bridge and stood for a time watching the huge black shapes in the darkness under the gasworks. A shoal of coal barges lay indistinctly on the darkly shining mud and water below, and a colossal crane was perpetually hauling up coal into mysterious blacknesses above, and dropping the empty clutch back to the barges. Just one or two minute black featureless figures of men toiled amidst these monster shapes. They did not seem to be controlling them, but only moving about among them. These gas works have a big chimney that belches a lurid flame into the night, a livid shivering bluish flame, shot with strange crimson streaks. . . .

On the other side of Lambeth Bridge broad stairs go down to the lapping water of the river; the lower steps are luminous under the lamps, and one treads unwarned into thick soft Thames mud. They seem to be purely architectural steps, they lead nowhere, they have an air of absolute indifference to mortal ends.

Those shapes and large inhuman places—for all of mankind that one sees at night about Lambeth is minute and pitiful beside the industrial monsters that snort and toil there—mix up inextricably with my memories of my first days as a legislator. Black figures drift by me, heavy vans clatter, a newspaper rough tears by on a motor bicycle, and presently, on the Albert Embankment, every seat has its one or two outcasts huddled together and slumbering.

"These things come, these things go," a whispering voice urged upon me, "as once those vast unmeaning Saurians whose bones encumber museums came and went, rejoicing noisily in fruitless lives." . . .

Fruitless lives!—was that the truth of it all? . . .

Later I stood within sight of the Houses of Parliament in front of the colonnades of St. Thomas's hospital. I leant on the parapet close by a lamp-stand of twisted dolphins,—and I prayed!

I remember the swirl of the tide upon the water, and how a string of barges presently came swinging and bumping round as high-water turned to ebb. That sudden change of position and my brief perplexity at it, sticks like a paper pin through the substance of my thoughts. It was then I was moved to prayer. I prayed that night that life might not be in vain, that in particular I might not live in vain. I prayed for strength and faith, that the monstrous blundering forces in life might not overwhelm me, might not beat me back to futility and a meaningless acquiescence in existent things. I knew myself for the weakling I was, I knew that nevertheless it was set for me to make such order as I could out of these disorders, and my task cowed me, gave me at the thought of it a sense of yielding feebleness. . . .

"Break me, O God," I prayed at last, "disgrace me, torment me, destroy me as you will, but save me from self-complacency and little interests and little successes and the life that passes like the shadow of a dream."

Book the Third

THE HEART OF POLITICS

CHAPTER THE FIRST

The Riddle for the Statesman

I

I HAVE been planning and replanning, writing and rewriting, this next portion of my book for many days. I perceive I must leave it raw edged and ill joined. In doing it I have learnt something of the impossibility of History. For all I have had to tell is the story of one man's convictions and aims and how they reacted upon his life; and I find it too subtle and involved and intricate for the doing. I find it tax all my powers to convey even the main forms and forces in that development. It is like looking through moving media of changing hue and variable refraction at something vitally unstable. Broad theories and generalizations are mingled with personal influences, with prevalent prejudices, and not only colored but altered by phases of hopefulness and moods of depression. The web is made up of the most diverse elements, beyond treatment multitudinous. . . . For a week or so I desisted altogether, and walked over the mountains and returned to sit through the warm soft mornings among the shaded rocks above this little perched-up house of ours, discussing my difficulties with Isabel, and I think on the whole complicating them further in the effort to simplify them to manageable and stateable elements.

Let me, nevertheless, attempt a rough preliminary analysis of this confused process. A main strand is quite easily traceable. This main strand is the story of my obvious life, my life as it must have looked to most of my acquaintances. It presents you with a young couple, bright, hopeful, and energetic, starting out under Altiora's auspices to make a career. You figure us well dressed and active, running about in motor-cars, visiting in great people's houses, dining amidst brilliant companies, going to the theatre, meeting in the lobby. Margaret wore hundreds of beautiful dresses. We must have had an air of succeeding meritoriously during that time.

We did very continually and faithfully serve our joint career. I thought about it a great deal, and did and refrained from doing ten thousand things for the sake of it. I kept up a solicitude for it, as it were by inertia, long after things had happened and changes occurred in me that rendered its completion impossible. Under certain very artless pretences, we wanted steadfastly to make a handsome position in the world, achieve respect, *succeed*. Enormous unseen changes had been in progress for years in my mind and the realities of my life, before our general circle could have had any inkling of their existence, or suspected the appearances of our life. Then suddenly our proceedings began to be deflected, our outward unanimity visibly strained and marred by the insurgence of these so long-hidden developments.

That career had its own hidden side, of course; but when I write of these unseen factors I do not mean that but something altogether broader. I do not mean the everyday pettinesses which gave the cynical observer scope and told of a narrower, baser aspect of the fair but limited ambitions of my ostensible self. This " sub-careerist " element noted little things that affected the career, made me suspicions of the rivalry of so-and-so, propitiatory to so-and-so, whom, as a matter of fact, I didn't respect or feel in the least sympathetic toward, guarded with that man, who for all his charm and interest wasn't helpful, and a little touchy at the appearance of neglect from that. No; I mean something greater, and not something smaller, when I write of a hidden life.

In the ostensible self who glowed under the approbation of Altiora Bailey, and was envied and discussed, praised and depreciated, in the House and in smoking-room gossip, you really have as much of a man as usually figures in a novel or an obituary notice. But I am tremendously impressed now in the retrospect by the realization of how little that frontage represented me, and just how little such frontages do represent the complexities of the intelligent contemporary. Behind it, yet struggling to disorganize and alter it altogether, was a far more essential reality, a self less personal, less individualized, and broader in its references. Its aims were never simply to get on; it had an altogether different system of demands and satisfactions. It was critical, curious, more than a little unfeeling—and relentlessly illuminating.

It is just the existence and development of this more generalized self-behind-the-frontage that is making modern life so much more subtle and intricate to render and so much more hopeful in its relations to the perplexities of the universe. I see this mental and spiritual hinterland vary enormously in the people about me, between a type which seems to keep, as people say, all its goods in the window, to others who, like myself, come to regard the ostensible existence more and more as a mere experimental feeder and agent for that greater personality behind. And this back-self has its history and phases, its crises and happy accidents and irrevocable conclusions, more or less distinct from the adventures and achievements of the ostensible self. It meets persons and phrases, it assimilates the spirit of a book, it is startled into new realizations by some accident that seems altogether irrelevant to the general tenor of one's life. Its increasing independence of the ostensible career makes it the organ of corrective criticism; it accumulates disturbing energy. Then it breaks our overt promises and repudiates our pledges, coming down at last like an overbearing mentor upon the small engagements of the pupil.

In the life of the individual it takes the rôle that the growth of philosophy, science, and creative literature may play in the development of mankind.

II

It is curious to recall how Britten helped to shatter that obvious, lucidly explicable presentation of myself upon which I had embarked with Margaret. He returned to revive a memory of adolescent dreams and a habit of adolescent frankness; he reached through my shallow frontage as no one else seemed capable of doing, and dragged that back-self into relation with it.

I remember very distinctly a dinner and a subsequent walk with him which presents itself now as altogether typical of the quality of his influence.

I had come upon him one day while lunching with Somers and Sutton at the Playwrights' Club, and had asked him to dinner on the spur of the moment. He was oddly the same curly-headed, red-faced ventriloquist, and oddly different, rather seedy as well as untidy, and at first a little inclined to make comparisons with my sleek successfulness. But that disposition presently evaporated, and his talk was good and fresh and provocative. And something that had long been straining at its checks in my mind flapped over, and he and I found ourselves of one accord.

Altiora wasn't at this dinner. When she came matters were apt to become confusedly strenuous. There was always a slight and ineffectual struggle at the end on the part of Margaret to anticipate Altiora's overpowering tendency to a rally and the establishment of some entirely unjustifiable conclusion by a *coup-de-main*. When, however, Altiora was absent, the quieter influence of the Cramptons prevailed; temperance and information for its own sake prevailed excessively over dinner and the play of thought. . . . Good Lord! what bores the Cramptons were! I wonder I endured them as I did. They had all of them the trick of lying in wait conversationally; they had no sense of self-exposures, the gallant experiments in statement that are necessary for good conversation. They would watch one talking with an expression exactly like peeping through bushes. Then they would, as it were, dash out, dissent succinctly, contradict some secondary fact, and back to cover. They gave one twilight nerves. Their wives were easier but still difficult at a stretch; they talked a good deal about children and servants, but with an air caught from Altiora of making observations upon sociological types. Lewis gossiped about the House in an entirely finite manner. He never raised a discussion; nobody ever raised a discussion. He would ask what we thought of Evesham's question that afternoon, and Edward would say it was good, and Mrs. Willie, who had been behind the grille, would think it was very good, and then Willie, parting the branches, would say rather conclusively that he didn't think it was very much good, and I would deny hearing the question in order to evade a profitless statement of views in that vacuum, and then we would cast about in our minds for some other topic of equal interest. . . .

On this occasion Altiora was absent, and to qualify our Young Liberal bleakness we had Mrs. Millingham, with her white hair and her fresh mind and complexion, and Esmeer. Willie Crampton was with us, but not his wife, who was having her third baby on principle; his brother Edward was present, and the Lewises, and of course the Bunting Harblows. There was also some other lady. I remember her as pale blue, but for the life of me I cannot remember her name.

Quite early there was a little breeze between Edward Crampton and Esmeer, who had ventured an opinion about the partition of Poland. Edward was at work then upon the seventh volume of his monumental Life of Kosciusko, and a little impatient with views perhaps not altogether false but betraying a lamentable ignorance of accessible literature. At any rate, his correction of Esmeer was magisterial. After that there was a distinct and not altogether delightful pause, and then some one, it may have been the pale-blue lady, asked Mrs. Lewis whether her aunt Lady Carmixter had returned from her rest-and-sun-cure in Italy. That led to a rather anxiously sustained talk about regimen, and Willie told us how he had profited by the no-breakfast system. It had increased his power of work enormously. He could get through ten hours a day now without inconvenience.

"What do you do?" said Esmeer abruptly.

"Oh! no end of work. There's all the estate and looking after things."

"But publicly?"

"I asked three questions yesterday. And for one of them I had to consult nine books!"

We were drifting, I could see, toward Doctor Haig's system of dietary, and whether the exclusion or inclusion of fish and chicken were most conducive to high efficiency, when Britten, who had refused lemonade and claret and demanded Burgundy, broke out, and was discovered to be demanding in his throat just what we Young Liberals thought we were up to?

"I want," said Britten, repeating his challenge a little louder, "to hear just exactly what you think you are doing in Parliament?"

Lewis laughed nervously, and thought we were "Seeking the Good of the Community."

"*How?*"

"Beneficent Legislation," said Lewis.

"Beneficent in what direction?" insisted Britten. "I want to know where you think you are going."

"Amelioration of Social Conditions," said Lewis.

"That's only a phrase!"

"You wouldn't have me sketch bills at dinner?"

"I'd like you to indicate directions," said Britten, and waited.

"Upward and On," said Lewis with conscious neatness, and turned to ask Mrs. Bunting Harblow about her little boy's French.

For a time talk frothed over Britten's head, but the natural mischief in Mrs. Millingham had been stirred, and she was presently echoing his demand in lisping, quasi-confidential undertones. "What *are* we Liberals doing?" Then Esmeer fell in with the revolutionaries.

To begin with, I was a little shocked by this clamor for fundamentals—and a little disconcerted. I had the experience that I suppose comes to every one at times of discovering oneself together with two different sets of people with whom one has maintained two different sets of attitudes. It had always been, I perceived, an instinctive suppression in our circle that we shouldn't be more than vague about our political ideals. It had almost become part of my morality to respect this convention. It was understood we were all working hard, and keeping ourselves fit, tremendously fit, under Altiora's inspiration, Pro Bono Publico. Bunting Harblow had his under-secretaryship, and Lewis was on the verge of the Cabinet, and these things we considered to be in the nature of confirmations. . . . It added to the discomfort of the situation that these plunging inquiries were being made in the presence of our wives.

The rebel section of our party forced the talk.

Edward Crampton was presently declaring—I forget in what relation: "The country is with us."

My long-controlled hatred of the Cramptons' stereotyped phrases about the Country and the House got the better of me. I showed my cloven hoof to my friends for the first time.

" We don't respect the Country as we used to do," I said. " We haven't the same belief we used to have in the will of the people. It's no good, Crampton, trying to keep that up. We Liberals know as a matter of fact—nowadays every one knows—that the monster that brought us into power has, among other deficiencies, no head. We've got to give it one—if possible with brains and a will. That lies in the future. For the present if the country is with us, it means merely that we happen to have hold of its tether."

Lewis was shocked. A " mandate " from the Country was sacred to his system of pretences.

Britten wasn't subdued by his first rebuff; presently he was at us again. There were several attempts to check his outbreak of interrogation; I remember the Cramptons asked questions about the welfare of various cousins of Lewis who were unknown to the rest of us, and Margaret tried to engage Britten in a sympathetic discussion of the Arts and Crafts exhibition. But Britten and Esmeer were persistent, Mrs. Millingham was mischievous, and in the end our rising hopes of Young Liberalism took to their thickets for good, while we talked all over them of the prevalent vacuity of political intentions. Margaret was perplexed by me. It is only now I perceive just how perplexing I must have been. " Of course," she said with that faint stress of apprehension in her eyes, " one must have aims." And, " it isn't always easy to put everything into phrases." " Don't be long," said Mrs. Edward Crampton to her husband as the wives trooped out. And afterwards when we went upstairs I had an indefinable persuasion that the ladies had been criticising Britten's share in our talk in an altogether unfavorable spirit. Mrs. Edward evidently thought him aggressive and impertinent, and Margaret with a quiet firmness that brooked no resistance took him at once into a corner and showed him Italian photographs by Coburn. We dispersed early.

I walked with Britten along the Chelsea back streets towards Battersea Bridge—he lodged on the south side.

" Mrs. Millingham's a dear," he began.

" She's a dear."

" I liked her demand for a hansom because a four-wheeler was too safe."

" She was worked up," I said. " She's a woman of faultless character, but her instincts, as Altiora would say, are anarchistic—when she gives them a chance."

" So she takes it out in hansom cabs."

" Hansom cabs."

" She's wise," said Britten. . . .

" I hope, Remington," he went on after a pause, " I didn't rag

your other guests too much. I've a sort of feeling at moments——
Remington, those chaps are so infernally not—not bloody. It's
part of a man's duty sometimes at least to eat red beef and get drunk.
How is he to understand government if he doesn't? It scares me to
think of your lot—by a sort of misapprehension—being in power.
A kind of neuralgia in the head, by way of government. I don't understand where *you* come in. Those others—they've no lusts.
Their ideal is anæmia. You and I, we had at least a lust to take hold
of life and make something of it. They—they want to take hold
of life and make nothing of it. They want to cut out all the stimu-
lants. Just as though life was anything else but a reaction to stimulation!" . . .

He began to talk of his own life. He had had ill-fortune through
most of it. He was poor and unsuccessful, and a girl he had
been very fond of had been attacked and killed by a horse in a
field in a very horrible manner. These things had wounded and
tortured him, but they hadn't broken him. They had, it seemed
to me, made a kind of crippled and ugly demi-god of him. He
was, I began to perceive, so much better than I had any right
to expect. At first I had been rather struck by his unkempt look,
and it made my reaction all the stronger. There was about
him something, a kind of raw and bleeding faith· in the deep
things of life, that stirred me profoundly, as he showed it. My set
of people had irritated him and 'disappointed him. I discovered at
his touch how they irritated me. He reproached me boldly. He
made me feel ashamed of my easy acquiescences as I walked in my
sleek tall neatness beside his rather old coat, his rather battered hat,
his sturdier shorter shape, and listened to his denunciations of our
self-satisfied New Liberalism and Progressivism.

" It has the same relation to progress—the reality of progress
—that the things they paint on door panels in the suburbs have to
art and beauty. There's a sort of filiation. . . . Your Altiora's
just the political equivalent of the ladies who sell traced cloth for embroidery ; she's a dealer in Refined Social Reform for the Parlor.
The real progress, Remington, is a graver thing and a painfuller
thing and a slower thing altogether. Look! *that* "—and he pointed
to where under a hoarding in the light of a gas lamp a dingy woman
stood lurking—" was in Babylon and Nineveh. Your little lot make
believe there won't be anything of the sort after this Parliament!
They're going to vanish at a few top notes from Altiora Bailey!
Remington!—It's foolery. It's prigs at play. It's make-believe,
make-believe! Your people there haven't got hold of things, aren't
beginning to get hold of things, don't know anything of life at all,
shirk life, avoid life, get in little bright clean rocms and talk big over

your bumpers of lemonade while the Night goes by outside—untouched. Those Crampton fools slink by all this,"—he waved at the woman again—" pretend it doesn't exist, or is going to be banished root and branch by an Act to keep children in the wet outside public-houses. Do you think they really care, Remington? *I* don't. It's make-believe. What they want to do, what Lewis wants to do, what Mrs. Bunting Harblow wants her husband to do, is to sit and feel very grave and necessary and respected on the Government benches. They think of putting their feet out like statesmen, and tilting shiny hats with becoming brims down over their successful noses. Presentation portrait to a club at fifty. That's their Reality. That's their scope. They don't, it's manifest, *want* to think beyond that. The things there *are*, Remington, they'll never face! the wonder and the depth of life,—lust, and the night-sky,—pain."

"But the good intention," I pleaded, " the Good Will!"

"Sentimentality," said Britten. "No Good Will is anything but dishonesty unless it frets and burns and hurts and destroys a man. That lot of yours have nothing but a good will to think they have good will. Do you think they lie awake of nights searching their hearts as we do? Lewis? Crampton? Or those neat, admiring, satisfied little wives? See how they shrank from the probe!"

"We all," I said, " shrink from the probe."

"God help us!" said Britten. . . .

"We are but vermin at the best, Remington," he broke out, " and the greatest saint only a worm that has lifted its head for a moment from the dust. We are damned, we are meant to be damned, coral animalculæ building upward, upward in a sea of damnation. But of all the damned things that ever were damned, your damned shirking, temperate, sham-efficient, self-satisfied, respectable, make-believe, Fabian-spirited Young Liberal is the utterly damnedest." He paused for a moment, and resumed in an entirely different note: " Which is why I was so surprised, Remington, to find *you* in this set!"

"You're just the old plunger you used to be, Britten," I said. " You're going too far with all your might for the sake of the damns. Like a donkey that drags its cart up a bank to get thistles. There are depths in Liberalism——"

"We were talking about Liberals."

"Liberty!"

"Liberty! What do *your* little lot know of liberty?"

"What does any little lot know of liberty?"

"It waits outside, too big for our understanding. Like the night and the stars. And lust, Remington! lust and bitterness! Don't I know them? with all the sweetness and hope of life bitten and

trampled, the dear eyes and the brain that loved and understood—
and my poor mumble of a life going on! I'm within sight of being
a drunkard, Remington! I'm a failure by most standards! Life
has cut me to the bone. But I'm not afraid of it any more. I've
paid something of the price, I've seen something of the meaning."

He flew off at a tangent. " I'd rather die in Delirium Tremens,"
he cried, " than be a Crampton or a Lewis. . . ."

" Make-believe. Make-believe." The phrase and Britten's squat
gestures haunted me as I walked homeward alone. I went to
my room and stood before my desk and surveyed papers and files and
Margaret's admirable equipment of me.

I perceived in the lurid light of Britten's suggestions that so it
was Mr. George Alexander would have staged a statesman's private
room. . . .

III

I was never at any stage a loyal party man. I doubt if party
will ever again be the force it was during the eighteenth and nineteenth centuries. Men are becoming increasingly constructive and
selective, less patient under tradition and the bondage of initial circumstances. As education becomes more universal and liberating,
men will sort themselves more and more by their intellectual temperaments and less and less by their accidental associations. The past
will rule them less; the future more. It is not simply party but
school and college and county and country that lose their glamour.
One does not hear nearly as much as our forefathers did of the " old
Harrovian," " old Arvonian," " old Etonian " claim to this or that
unfair advantage or unearnt sympathy. Even the Scotch and the
Devonians weaken a little in their clannishness. A widening sense of
fair play destroys such things. They follow freemasonry down—
freemasonry of which one is chiefly reminded nowadays in England
by propitiatory symbols outside shady public-houses. . . .

There is, of course, a type of man which clings very obstinately
to party ties. These are the men with strong reproductive imaginations and no imaginative initiative, such men as Cladingbowl, for example, or Dayton. They are the scholars-at-large in life. For them
the fact that the party system has been essential in the history of
England for two hundred years gives it an overwhelming glamour.
They have read histories and memoirs, they see the great gray pile
of Westminster not so much for what it is as for what it was, rich
with dramatic memories, populous with glorious ghosts, phrasing itself inevitably in anecdotes and quotations. It seems almost scandalous that new things should continue to happen, swamping with
strange qualities the savor of these old associations.

That Mr. Ramsay Macdonald should walk through Westminster Hall, thrust himself, it may be, through the very piece of space that once held Charles the Martyr pleading for his life, seems horrible profanation to Dayton, a last posthumous outrage, and he would, I think, like to have the front benches left empty now for ever, or at most adorned with laureated ivory tablets, "Here Dizzy sat," and "On this Spot William Ewart Gladstone made his First Budget Speech." Failing this, he demands, if only as signs of modesty and respect on the part of the survivors, meticulous imitation. "Mr. G.," he murmurs, "would not have done that," and laments a vanished subtlety even while Mr. Evesham is speaking. He is always gloomily disposed to lapse into wonderings about what things are coming to, wonderings that have no grain of curiosity. His conception of perfect conduct is industrious persistence along the worndown, well-marked grooves of the great recorded days. So infinitely more important to him is the documented, respected thing than the elusive present.

Cladingbowl and Dayton do not shine in the House, though Cladingbowl is a sound man on a committee, and Dayton keeps the *Old Country Gazette*, the most gentlemanly paper in London. They prevail, however, in their clubs at lunch time. There, with the pleasant consciousness of a morning's work free from either zeal or shirking, they mingle with permanent officials, prominent lawyers, even a few of the soberer type of business men, and relax their minds in the discussion of the morning paper, of the architecture of the West End, of the latest public appointments, of golf, of holiday resorts, of the last judicial witticisms and forensic "crushers." The New Year and Birthday honors lists are always very sagely and exhaustively considered, and anecdotes are popularly and keenly judged. They do not talk of the things that are really active in their minds, but in the formal and habitual manner they suppose to be proper to intelligent but still honorable men. Socialism, individual money matters, and religion are forbidden topics, and sex and women only in so far as they appear in the law courts. It is to me the strangest of conventions, this assumption of unreal loyalties and traditional respects, this repudiation and concealment of passionate interests. It is like wearing gloves in summer fields, or bathing in a gown, or falling in love with the heroine of a novel, or writing under a pseudonym, or becoming a masked Tuareg. . . .

It is not, I think, that men of my species are insensitive to the great past that is embodied in Westminster and its traditions; we are not so much wanting in the historical sense as alive to the greatness of our present opportunities and the still vaster future that is possible to us. London is the most interesting, beautiful, and wonderful city in the world to me, delicate in her incidental and multitudinous littleness, and stupendous in her pregnant totality: I cannot bring myself to use her as a museum or an old bookshop. When I think of Whitehall that little affair on the scaffold outside the Banqueting Hall seems trivial and remote in comparison with the possibilities that offer themselves to my imagination within the great gray Government buildings close at hand.

It gives me a qualm of nostalgia even to name those places now. I think of St. Stephen's tower streaming upward into the misty London night and the great wet quadrangle of New Palace Yard, from which the hansom cabs of my first experiences were ousted more and more by taxicabs as the second Parliament of King Edward the Seventh aged; I think of the Admiralty and War Office with their tall Marconi masts sending out invisible threads of direction to the armies in the camps, to great fleets about the world. The crowded, darkly shining river goes flooding through my memory once again, on to those narrow seas that part us from our rival nations; I see quadrangles and corridors of spacious gray-toned offices in which undistinguished little men and little files of papers link us to islands in the tropics, to frozen wildernesses gashed for gold, to vast temple-studded plains, to forest worlds and mountain worlds, to ports and fortresses and lighthouses and watchtowers and grazing lands and corn lands all about the globe. Once more I traverse Victoria Street, grimy and dark, where the Agents of the Empire jostle one another, pass the big embassies in the West End with their flags and scutcheons, follow the broad avenue that leads to Buckingham Palace, witness the coming and going of troops and officials and guests along it from every land on earth. . . . Interwoven in the texture of it all, mocking, perplexing, stimulating beyond measure, is the gleaming consciousness, the challenging knowledge: " You and your kind might still, if you could but grasp it here, mould all the destiny of Man! "

IV

My first three years in Parliament were years of active discontent. The little group of younger Liberals to which I belonged was very ignorant of the traditions and qualities of our older leaders, and quite out of touch with the mass of the party. For a time Parliament was enormously taken up with moribund issues and old quarrels. The early Educational legislation was sectarian and unenterprising, and the Licensing Bill went little further than the attempted rectification of a Conservative mistake. I was altogether for the nationalization of the public-house, and of this end the Bill gave no intimations. It was just beer-baiting. I was recalcitrant almost from the beginning, and spoke against the Government so early as the second reading of the first Education Bill, the one the Lords rejected in 1906. I went a little beyond my intention in the heat of speaking,—it is a way with inexperienced men. I called the Bill timid, narrow, a mere sop to the jealousies of sects and little-minded people. I contrasted its aim and methods with the manifest needs of the time.

I am not a particularly good speaker; after the manner of a writer I worry to fine my meaning too much; but this was one of my successes. I spoke after dinner and to a fairly full House, for people were already a little curious about me because of my writings. Several of the Conservative leaders were present and stayed, and Mr. Evesham, I remember, came ostentatiously to hear me, with that engaging friendliness of his, and gave me at the first chance an approving " Hear, Hear! " I can still recall quite distinctly my two futile attempts to catch the Speaker's eye before I was able to begin, the nervous quiver of my rather too prepared opening, the effect of hearing my own voice and my subconscious wonder as to what I could possibly be talking about, the realization that I was getting on fairly well, the immense satisfaction afterward of having on the whole brought it off, and the absurd gratitude I felt for that encouraging cheer.

Addressing the House of Commons is like no other public speaking in the world. Its semi-colloquial methods give it an air of being easy, but its shifting audience, the comings and goings and hesitations of members behind the chair—not mere audience units, but men who matter—the desolating emptiness that spreads itself round the man who fails to interest, the little compact, disciplined crowd in the strangers' gallery, the light, elusive, flickering movements high up behind the grille, the wigged, attentive, weary Speaker, the table and the mace and the chapel-like Gothic background with its sombre shadows, conspire together, produce a confused, uncertain feeling in me, as though I was walking upon a pavement full of trap-doors and patches of uncovered morass. A misplaced, well-meant " Hear, Hear! " is apt to be extraordinarily disconcerting, and under no other circumstances have I had to speak with quite the same sideways twist that the arrangement of the House imposes. One does not recognize one's own voice threading out into the stirring brown. Unless I was excited or speaking to the mind of some particular person in the House, I was apt to lose my feeling of an auditor. I had no sense of whither my sentences were going, such as one has with a public meeting well under one's eye. And to lose one's sense of an auditor is for a man of my temperament to lose one's sense of the immediate, and to become prolix and vague with qualifications.

V

My discontent with the Liberal party and my mental exploration of the quality of party generally is curiously mixed up with certain impressions of things and people in the National Liberal Club. The National Liberal Club is Liberalism made visible in the flesh—and Doulton-ware. It is an extraordinary big club done in a bold, wholesale, shiny, marbled style, richly furnished with numerous paintings, steel engravings, busts, and full-length statues of the late Mr. Gladstone; and its spacious dining-rooms, its long, hazy, crowded smoking-room with innumerable little tables and groups of men in armchairs, its magazine room and library upstairs, have just that undistinguished and unconcentrated diversity which is for me the Liberal note. The pensive member sits and hears perplexing dialects and even fragments of foreign speech, and among the clustering masses of less insistent whites his roving eye catches profiles and complexions that send his mind afield to Calcutta or Rangoon or the West Indies or Sierra Leone or the Cape. . . .

I was not infrequently that pensive member. I used to go to the Club to doubt about Liberalism.

About two o'clock in the day the great smoking-room is crowded with countless little groups. They sit about small round tables, or in circles of chairs, and the haze of tobacco seems to prolong the great narrow place, with its pillars and bays, to infinity. Some of the groups are big, as many as a dozen men talk in loud tones; some are duologues, and there is always a sprinkling of lonely, dissociated men. At first one gets an impression of men going from group to group and as it were linking them, but as one watches closely one finds that these men just visit three or four groups at the outside, and know nothing of the others. One begins to perceive more and more distinctly that one is dealing with a sort of human mosaic; that each patch in that great place is of a different quality and color from the next and never to be mixed with it. Most clubs have a common link, a lowest common denominator in the Club Bore, who spares no one, but even the National Liberal bores are specialized and sectional. As one looks round one sees here a clump of men from the North Country or the Potteries, here an island of South London politicians, here a couple of young Jews ascendant from Whitechapel, here a circle of journalists and writers, here a group of Irish politicians, here two East Indians, here a priest or so, here a clump of old-fashioned Protestants, here a little knot of eminent Rationalists indulging in a blasphemous story *sotto voce*. Next them are a group of anglicized Germans and highly specialized chess-players, and then two of the oddest-looking persons—bulging with documents and intent upon extraordinary business transactions over long cigars. . . .

I would listen to a stormy sea of babblement, and try to extract some constructive intimations. Every now and then I got a whiff of politics. It was clear they were against the Lords—against plutocrats—against Cossington's newspapers—against the brewers. . . . It was tremendously clear what they were against. The trouble was to find out what on earth they were *for!* . . .

As I sat and thought, the streaked and mottled pillars and walls, the various views, aspects, and portraits of Mr. and Mrs. Gladstone, the partitions of polished mahogany, the yellow-vested waiters, would dissolve and vanish, and I would have a vision of this sample of miscellaneous men of limited, diverse interests and a universal littleness of imagination enlarged, unlimited, no longer a sample but a community, spreading, stretching out to infinity—all in little groups and duologues and circles, all with their special and narrow concerns, all with their backs to most of the others.

What but a common antagonism would ever keep these multitudes together? I understood why modern electioneering is more than half of it denunciation. Let us condemn, if possible, let us obstruct and deprive, but not let us do. There is no real appeal to the commonplace mind in " Let us do." That calls for the creative imagination, and few have been accustomed to respond to that call. The other merely needs jealousy and hate, of which there are great and easily accessible reservoirs in every human heart. . . .

I remember that vision of endless, narrow, jealous individuality very vividly. A seething limitlessness it became at last, like a waste place covered by crawling locusts that men sweep up by the sackload and drown by the million in ditches. . . .

Grotesquely against it came the lean features, the sidelong shy movements of Edward Crampton, seated in a circle of talkers close at hand. I had a whiff of his strained, unmusical voice, and behold! he was saying something about the " Will of the People. . . . "

The immense and wonderful disconnectednesses of human life! I forgot the smoke and jabber of the club altogether; I became a lonely spirit flung high by some queer accident, a stone upon a ledge in some high and rocky wilderness, and below as far as the eye could reach stretched the swarming infinitesimals of humanity, like grass upon the field, like pebbles upon unbounded beaches. Was there ever to be in human life more than that endless struggling individualism? Was there indeed some giantry, some immense valiant synthesis, still to come—or present it might be and still unseen by me, or was this the beginning and withal the last phase of mankind? . . .

I glimpsed for a while the stupendous impudence of our ambitions, the tremendous enterprise to which the modern statesman is implicitly addressed. I was as it were one of a little swarm of would-be reef

builders looking back at the teeming slime upon the ocean floor. All
the history of mankind, all the history of life, has been and will be the
story of something struggling out of the indiscriminated abyss,
struggling to exist and prevail over and comprehend individual lives
—an effort of insidious attraction, an idea of invincible appeal. That
something greater than ourselves, which does not so much exist as
seek existence, palpitating between being and not-being, how marvelous it is! It has worn the form and visage of ten thousand different
Gods, sought a shape for itself in stone and ivory and music and wonderful words, spoken more and more clearly of a mystery of love, a
mystery of unity, dabbling meanwhile in blood and cruelty beyond
the common impulses of men. It is something that comes and goes,
like a light that shines and is withdrawn; is withdrawn so completely
that one doubts if it has ever been. . . .

VI

I would mark with a curious interest the stray country member of
the club up in town for a night or so. My mind would be busy with
speculations about him, about his home, his family, his reading, his
horizons, his innumerable fellows who didn't belong and never came
up. I would fill in the outline of him with memories of my uncle and
his Staffordshire neighbors. He was perhaps Alderman This or
Councillor That down there, a great man in his ward, J.P. within
seven miles of the boundary of the borough, and a God in his home.
Here he was nobody, and very shy, and either a little too arrogant or
a little too meek toward our very democratic mannered but still liveried
waiters. Was he perhaps the backbone of England? He over-ate
himself lest he should appear mean, went through our Special Dinner
conscientiously, drank, unless he was teetotal, of unfamiliar wines, and
did his best, in spite of the rules, to tip. Afterwards, in a state of
flushed repletion, he would have old brandy, black coffee, and a
banded cigar, or in the name of temperance omit the brandy and have
rather more coffee, in the smoking-room. I would sit and watch that
stiff dignity of self-indulgence, and wonder, wonder. . . .

An infernal clairvoyance would come to me. I would have visions
of him in relation to his wife, checking always, sometimes bullying,
sometimes being ostentatiously " kind "; I would see him glance furtively at his domestic servants upon his staircase, or stiffen his upper
lip against the reluctant, protesting business employee. We imaginative people are base enough, heaven knows, but it is only in rare moods
of bitter penetration that we pierce down to the baser lusts, the viler
shames, the everlasting lying and muddle-headed self-justification of
the dull.

I would turn my eyes down the crowded room and see others of him and others. What did he think he was up to? Did he for a moment realize that his presence under that ceramic glory of a ceiling with me meant, if it had any rational meaning at all, that we were jointly doing something with the nation and the empire and mankind? . . . How on earth could any one get hold of him, make any noble use of him? He didn't read beyond his newspaper. He never thought, but only followed imaginings in his heart. He never discussed. At the first hint of discussion his temper gave way. He was, I knew, a deep, thinly-covered tank of resentments and quite irrational moral rages. Yet withal I would have to resist an impulse to go over to him and nudge him and say to him, " Look here! What indeed do you think we are doing with the nation and the empire and mankind? You know—*Mankind!* "

I wonder what reply I should have got.

So far as any average could be struck and so far as any backbone could be located, it seemed to me that this silent, shy, replete, sub-angry, middle-class sentimentalist was in his endless sub-species and varieties and dialects the backbone of our party. So far as I could be considered as representing anything in the House, I pretended to sit for the elements of *him*. . . .

VII

For a time I turned toward the Socialists. They at least had an air of coherent intentions. At that time Socialism had come into politics again after a period of depression and obscurity, with a tremendous *éclat*. There was visibly a following of Socialist members to Chris Robinson; mysteriously uncommunicative gentlemen in soft felt hats and short coats and square-toed boots who replied to casual advances a little surprisingly in rich North Country dialects. Members became aware of a " seagreen incorruptible," as Colonel Marlow put it to me, speaking on the Address, a slender twisted figure supporting itself on a stick and speaking with a fire that was altogether revolutionary. This was Philip Snowden, the member for Blackburn. They had come in nearly forty strong altogether, and with an air of presently meaning to come in much stronger. They were only one aspect of what seemed at that time a big national movement. Socialist societies, we gathered, were springing up all over the country, and every one was inquiring about Socialism and discussing Socialism. It had taken the Universities with particular force, and any youngster with the slightest intellectual pretension was either actively for or brilliantly against. For a time our Young Liberal group was ostentatiously sympathetic. . . .

When I think of the Socialists there comes a vivid memory of certain evening gatherings at our house. . . .

These gatherings had been organized by Margaret as the outcome of a discussion at the Baileys'. Altiora had been very emphatic and uncharitable upon the futility of the Socialist movement. It seemed that even the leaders fought shy of dinner parties.

" They never meet each other," said Altiora, " much less people on the other side. How can they begin to understand politics until they do that? "

" Most of them have totally unpresentable wives," said Altiora, " totally!" and quoted instances, " and they *will* bring them. Or they won't come! Some of the poor creatures have scarcely learnt their table manners. They just make holes in the talk. . . . "

I thought there was a great deal of truth beneath Altiora's outburst. The presentation of the Socialist case seemed very greatly crippled by the want of a common intimacy in its leaders; the want of intimacy didn't at first appear to be more than an accident, and our talk led to Margaret's attempt to get acquaintance and easy intercourse afoot among them and between them and the Young Liberals of our group. She gave a series of weekly dinners, planned, I think, a little too accurately upon Altiora's model, and after each we had as catholic a reception as we could contrive.

Our receptions were indeed, I should think, about as catholic as receptions could be. Margaret found herself with a weekly houseful of insoluble problems in intercourse. One did one's best, but one got a nightmare feeling as the evening wore on.

It was one of the few unanimities of these parties that everyone should be a little odd in appearance, funny about the hair or the tie or the shoes or more generally, and that bursts of violent aggression should alternate with an attitude entirely defensive. A number of our guests had an air of waiting for a clue that never came, and stood and sat about silently, mildly amused but not a bit surprised that we did not discover their distinctive Open-Sesames. There was a sprinkling of manifest seers and phophetesses in shapeless garments, far too many, I thought, for really easy social intercourse, and any conversation at any moment was liable to become oracular. One was in a state of tension from first to last; the most innocent remark seemed capable of exploding resentment, and replies came out at the most unexpected angles. We Young Liberals went about puzzled but polite to the gathering we had evoked. The Young Liberals' tradition is on the whole wonderfully discreet, superfluous steam is let out far away from home in the Balkans or Africa, and the neat, stiff figures of the Cramptons, Bunting Harblow, and Lewis, either in extremely well-cut morning coats indicative of the House, or in what is sometimes written of as "faultless evening dress," stood about on those evenings, they and their very quietly and simply and expensively dressed little wives, like a datum line amidst lakes and mountains.

I didn't at first see the connection between systematic social reorganization and arbitrary novelties in dietary and costume, just as I didn't realize why the most comprehensive constructive projects should appear to be supported solely by odd and exceptional personalities. On one of these evenings a little group of rather jolly-looking pretty young people seated themselves for no particular reason in a large circle on the floor of my study, and engaged, so far as I could judge, in the game of Hunt the Meaning, the intellectual equivalent of Hunt the Slipper. It was not unusual to be given hand-bills and printed matter by our guests, but there I had the advantage over Lewis, who was too tactful to refuse the stuff, too neatly dressed to pocket it, and had no writing-desk available upon which he could relieve himself in a manner flattering to the giver. So that his hands got fuller and fuller. A relentless, compact little woman in what Margaret declared to be an extremely expensive black dress has also printed herself on my memory; she had set her heart upon my contributing to a weekly periodical in the lentil interest with which she was associated, and I spent much time and care in evading her.

Mingling with the more hygienic types were a number of Anti-Puritan Socialists, bulging with bias against temperance, and breaking out against austere methods of living all over their faces. Their manner was packed with heartiness. They were apt to choke the approaches to the little buffet Margaret had set up downstairs, and there engage in discussions of Determinism—it always seemed to be Determinism—which became heartier and noisier, but never acrimonious even in the small hours. It seemed impossible to settle about this Determinism of theirs—ever. And there were worldly Socialists also. I particularly recall a large, active, buoyant, lady-killing individual with an eyeglass borne upon a broad black ribbon, who swam about us one evening. He might have been a slightly frayed actor, in his large frock-coat, his white waistcoat, and the sort of black and white check trousers that twinkle. He had a high-pitched voice with aristocratic intonations, and he seemed to be in a perpetual state of interrogation. "What are we all he-a for?" he would ask only too audibly. "What are we doing he-a? What's the connection?"

What *was* the connection?

We made a special effort with our last assembly in June, 1907. We tried to get something like a representative collection of the parliamentary leaders of Socialism, the various exponents of Socialist thought and a number of Young Liberal thinkers into one room.   Dorvil came, and Horatio Buleh; Featherstonehaugh appeared for ten minutes and talked charmingly to Margaret and then vanished again; there was Wilkins the novelist and Toomer and Dr. Tumpany.   Chris Robinson stood about for a time in a new comforter, and Magdeberg and Will Pipes and five or six Labor members.   And on our side we had our particular little group, Bunting Harblow, Crampton, Lewis, all looking as broadminded and open to conviction as they possibly could, and even occasionally talking out from their bushes almost boldly.   But the gathering as a whole refused either to mingle or dispute, and as an experiment in intercourse the evening was a failure.   Unexpected dissociations appeared between Socialists one had supposed friendly.   I could not have imagined it was possible for half so many people to turn their backs on everybody else in such small rooms as ours.   But the unsaid things those backs expressed broke out, I remarked, with refreshed virulence in the various organs of the various sections of the party next week.

I talked, I remember, with Dr. Tumpany, a large young man in a still larger professional frock-coat, and with a great shock of very fair hair, who was candidate for some North Country constituency. We discussed the political outlook, and, like so many Socialists at that time, he was full of vague threatenings against the Liberal party.   I was struck by a thing in him that I had already observed less vividly in many others of these Socialist leaders, and which gave me at last a clue to the whole business.   He behaved exactly like a man in possession of valuable patent rights, who wants to be dealt with.   He had an air of having a corner in ideas.   Then it flashed into my head that the whole Socialist movement was an attempted corner in ideas. . . .

VIII

Late that night I found myself alone with Margaret amid the débris of the gathering.

I sat before the fire, hands in pockets, and Margaret, looking white and weary, came and leant upon the mantel.

" Oh Lord! " said Margaret.

I agreed.   Then I resumed my meditation.

" Ideas," I said, " count for more than I thought in the world."

Margaret regarded me with that neutral expression behind which she was accustomed to wait for clues.

" When you think of the height and depth and importance and

wisdom of the Socialist ideas, and see the men who are running them," I explained. . . . "A big system of ideas like Socialism grows up out of the obvious common sense of our present conditions. It's as impersonal as science. All these men——They've given nothing to it. They're just people who have pegged out claims upon a big intellectual No-Man's-Land—and don't feel quite sure of the law. There's a sort of quarrelsome uneasiness. . . . If we professed Socialism do you think they'd welcome us? Not a man of them! They'd feel it was burglary. . . ."

"Yes," said Margaret, looking into the fire. "That is just what *I* felt about them all the evening. . . . Particularly Dr. Tumpany."

"We mustn't confuse Socialism with the Socialist," I said; "that's the moral of it. I suppose if God were to find He had made a mistake in dates or something, and went back and annihilated everybody from Owen onward who was in any way known as a Socialist leader or teacher, Socialism would be exactly where it is and what it is to-day—a growing realization of constructive needs in every man's mind, and a little corner in party politics. So, I suppose, it will always be. . . . But they *were* a damned lot, Margaret!"

I looked up at the little noise she made. "*Twice!*" she said, smiling indulgently, "to-day!" (Even the smile was Altiora's.)

I returned to my thoughts. They *were* a damned human lot. It was an excellent word in that connection. . . .

But the ideas marched on, the ideas marched on, just as though men's brains were no more than stepping-stones, just as though some great brain in which we are all little cells and corpuscles was thinking them! . . .

"I don't think there is a man among them who makes me feel he is trustworthy," said Margaret; "unless it is Featherstonehaugh."

I sat taking in this proposition.

"They'll never help us, I feel," said Margaret.

"Us?"

"The Liberals."

"Oh, damn the Liberals!" I said. "They'll never even help themselves."

"I don't think I could possibly get on with any of these people," said Margaret, after a pause.

She remained for a time looking down at me and, I could feel, perplexed by me, but I wanted to go on with my thinking, and so I did not look up, and presently she stooped to my forehead and kissed me and went rustling softly to her room.

I remained in my study for a long time with my thoughts crystallizing out. . . .

It was then, I think, that I first apprehended clearly how that opposition to which I have already alluded of the immediate life, and the mental hinterland of a man can be applied to public and social affairs. The ideas go on—and no person or party succeeds in embodying them. The reality of human progress never comes to the surface, it is a power in the deeps, an undertow. It goes on in silence while men think, in studies where they write self-forgetfully, in laboratories under the urgency of an impersonal curiosity, in the rare illumination of honest talk, in moments of emotional insight, in thoughtful reading, but not in everyday affairs. Everyday affairs and whatever is made an everyday affair, are transactions of the ostensible self, the being of habits, interests, usage. Temper, vanity, hasty reaction to imitation, personal feeling, are their substance. No man can abolish his immediate self and specialize in the depths; if he attempt that, he simply turns himself into something a little less than the common man. He may have an immense hinterland, but that does not absolve him from a frontage. That is the essential error of the specialist philosopher, the specialist teacher, the specialist publicist. They repudiate frontage; claim to be pure hinterland. That is what bothered me about Codger, about those various schoolmasters who had prepared me for life, about the Baileys and their dream of an official ruling class. A human being who is a philosopher in the first place, a teacher in the first place, or a statesman in the first place, is thereby and inevitably, though he bring God-like gifts to the pretence—a quack. These are attempts to live deep-side shallow, inside out. They produce merely a new pettiness. To understand Socialism, again, is to gain a new breadth of outlook; to join a Socialist organization is to join a narrow cult which is not even tolerably serviceable in presenting or spreading the ideas for which it stands. . . .

I perceived I had got something quite fundamental here. It had taken me some years to realize the true relation of the great constructive ideas that swayed me not only to political parties, but to myself. I had been disposed to identify the formulæ of some one party with social construction, and to regard the other as necessarily anti-constructive, just as I had been inclined to follow the Baileys in the self-righteousness of supposing myself to be wholly constructive. But I saw now that every man of intellectual freedom and vigor is necessarily constructive-minded nowadays, and that no man is disinterestedly so. Each one of us repeats in himself the conflict of the race between the splendor of its possibilities and its immediate associations. We may be shaping immortal things, but we must sleep and answer the dinner gong, and have our salt of flattery and self-approval. In politics a man counts not for what he is in moments of imaginative expansion, but for his common, workaday, selfish self, and political parties are held together not by a community of ultimate aims, but by the stabler bond of an accustomed life. Everybody almost is for progress in general, and nearly everybody is opposed to any change, except in so far as gross increments are change, in his particular method of living and behavior. Every party stands essentially for the interests and mental usages of some definite class or group of classes in the existing community, and every party has its scientific-minded and constructive leading section, with well-defined hinterlands formulating its social functions in a public-spirited form, and its superficial-minded following confessing its meannesses and vanities and prejudices. No class will abolish itself, materially alter its way of life, or drastically reconstruct itself, albeit no class is indisposed to coöperate in the unlimited socialization of any other class. In that capacity for aggression upon other classes lies the essential driving force of modern affairs. The instincts, the persons, the parties, and vanities sway and struggle. The ideas and understandings march on and achieve themselves for all—in spite of every one. . . .

The methods and traditions of British politics maintain the form of two great parties, with rider groups seeking to gain specific ends in the event of a small Government majority. These two main parties are more or less heterogeneous in composition. Each, however, has certain necessary characteristics. The Conservative Party has always stood quite definitely for the established propertied interests. The land-owner, the big lawyer, the Established Church, and latterly the huge private monopoly of the liquor trade which has been created by temperance legislation, are the essential Conservatives. Interwoven now with the native wealthy are the families of the great international usurers, and a vast miscellaneous mass of financial enterprise. Outside the range of resistance implied by these interests, the Conservative Party has always shown itself just as constructive and collectivist as any other party. The great landowners have been as well-disposed toward the endowment of higher education, and as willing to coöperate with the Church in protective and mildly educational legislation for children and the working class, as any political section. The financiers, too, are adventurous-spirited and eager for mechanical progress and technical efficiency. They are prepared to spend public money upon research, upon ports and harbors and public communications, upon sanitation and hygienic organization. A certain rude benevolence of public intention is equally characteristic of the liquor trade. Provided his comfort leads to no excesses of temperance, the liquor trade is quite eager to see the common man prosperous, happy, and with money to spend in a bar. All sections of the party are aggressively patriotic and favorably inclined to the idea of an upstanding, well-fed, and well-exercised population in uniform. Of course there are reactionary landowners and old-fashioned country clergy, full of localized self-importance, jealous even of the cottager who can read, but they have neither the power nor the ability to retard the constructive forces in the party as a whole. On the other hand, when matters point to any definitely confiscatory proposal, to the public ownership and collective control of land, for example, or state mining and manufactures, or the nationalization of the so-called public-house or extended municipal enterprise, or even to an increase of the taxation of property, then the Conservative Party presents a nearly adamantine bar. It does not stand for, it *is*, the existing arrangement in these affairs.

Even more definitely a class party is the Labor Party, whose immediate interest is to raise wages, shorten hours of labor, increase employment, and make better terms for the working-man tenant and working-man purchaser. Its leaders are no doubt constructive minded, but the mass of the following is naturally suspicious of education and discipline, hostile to the higher education, and—except for an obvious antagonism to employers and property owners—almost destitute of ideas. What else can it be? It stands for the expropriated multitude, whose whole situation and difficulty arise from its individual lack of initiative and organizing power. It favors the nationalization of land and capital with no sense of the difficulties involved in the process; but, on the other hand, the equally reasonable socialization of individuals which is implied by military service is steadily and quite naturally and quite illogically opposed by it. It is only in recent years that Labor has emerged as a separate party from the huge hospitable caravanserai of Liberalism, and there is still a very marked tendency to step back again into that multitudinous assemblage.

For multitudinousness has always been the Liberal characteristic. Liberalism never has been nor ever can be anything but a diversified crowd. Liberalism has to voice everything that is left out by these other parties. It is the party against the predominating interests. It is at once the party of the failing and of the untried; it is the party of decadence and hope. From its nature it must be a vague and planless association in comparison with its antagonist, neither so constructive on the one hand, nor on the other so competent to hinder the inevitable constructions of the civilized state. Essentially it is the party of criticism, the " Anti " party. It is a system of hostilities and objections that somehow achieves at times an elusive common soul. It is a gathering together of all the smaller interests which find themselves at a disadvantage against the big established classes, the leasehold tenant as against the landower, the retail tradesman as against the merchant and moneylender, the Nonconformist as against the Churchman, the small employer as against the demoralizing hospitable publican, the man without introductions and broad connections against the man who has these things. It is the party of the many small men against the fewer prevailing men. It has no more essential reason for loving the Collectivist state than the Conservatives; the small dealer is doomed to absorption in that just as much as the large owner; but it resorts to the state against its antagonists as in the Middle Ages common men pitted themselves against the barons by siding with the king. The Liberal Party is the party against " class privilege " because it represents no class advantages, but it is also the party that is on the whole most set against Collective control because it represents no established responsibility. It is constructive only so far as its antagonism to the great owner is more powerful than its jealousy of the state. It organizes only because organization is forced upon it by the organization of its adversaries. It lapses in and out of alliance with Labor as it sways between hostility to wealth and hostility to public expenditure. . . .

Every modern European state will have in some form or other these three parties: the resistant, militant, authoritative, dull, and unsympathetic party of establishment and success, the rich party; the confused, sentimental, spasmodic, numerous party of the small, struggling, various, undisciplined men, the poor man's party; and a third party sometimes detaching itself from the second and sometimes reuniting with it, the party of the altogether expropriated masses, the proletarians, Labor. Change Conservative and Liberal to Republican and Democrat, for example, and you have the conditions in the United States. The Crown or a dethroned dynasty, the Established Church or a dispossessed church, nationalist secessions, the personalities of party leaders, may break up, complicate, and confuse the self-expression of these three necessary divisions in the modern social drama, the analyst will make them out none the less for that. . . .

And then I came back as if I came back to a refrain;—the ideas go on—as though we are all no more than little cells and corpuscles in some great brain beyond our understanding. . . .

So it was I sat and thought my problem out. . . . I still remember my satisfaction at seeing things plainly at last. It was like clouds dispersing to show the sky. Constructive ideas, of course, couldn't hold a party together alone, " interests and habits, not ideas," I had that now, and so the great constructive scheme of Socialism, invading and inspiring all parties, was necessarily claimed only by this collection of odds and ends, this residuum of disconnected and exceptional people. This was true not only of the Socialist idea, but of the scientific idea, the idea of veracity—of human confidence in humanity —of all that mattered in human life outside the life of individuals. . . . The only real party that would ever profess Socialism was the Labor Party, and that in the entirely one-sided form of an irresponsible and non-constructive attack on property. Socialism in that mutilated form, the teeth and claws without the eyes and brain, I wanted as little as I wanted anything in the world.

Perfectly clear it was, perfectly clear, and why hadn't I seen it before? . . . I looked at my watch, and it was half-past two.

I yawned, stretched, got up and went to bed.

(To be continued)

THE FORTIFICATION OF THE PANAMA CANAL

H. A. AUSTIN

THIS is a question which Congress will have to settle at the present session, and although the Administration is exerting every effort to induce that body to make the necessary appropriations to begin the erection of fortifications at the entrances to the canal, the adoption of the policy of fortification is meeting with considerable opposition by many prominent members of both the House and Senate.

Ever since the United States undertook the construction of the Panama Canal there has been a great deal of discussion on the subject of whether or not the canal should be fortified. Notwithstanding this diversity of opinion, our Government seems to have proceeded on the assumption that it had the right to erect such fortifications and Congress is now called upon to decide whether that assumption is correct. The "Taft Fortification Board," which several years ago was created by authority of Congress to report upon the state of our sea-coast defences and submit suggestions for new projects, recommended that certain fortifications be installed at the entrances to the canal, and the Joint Army and Navy Board, appointed last year to visit the Canal Zone for the purpose of reporting on the subject, recommended that an appropriation of several million dollars be asked of Congress for the purpose of erecting sea-coast defences there.

The report of this latter board was submitted to Congress at its last session, but owing to the diversity of opinion as to the advisability of fortifying the canal, no action was taken upon the report.

Now that the matter is reaching a climax, it is arousing the public interest of other nations, and before the question is finally settled, we may expect to hear rumors of contemplated protests by European and Asiatic nations, in case the Government adheres to the policy of fortification. In fact, Philippe Buneau-Varilla, who is now in France, and who was the representative of the Republic of Panama in the negotiations of 1903 for the transfer to the United States of the canal property and rights, controverts the right of the United States in time of peace to erect fortifications in the vicinity of the canal. This view is also taken by many members of Congress.

It is the purpose of this article to present the arguments of both sides to the controversy, and to draw therefrom what are thought to be logical and reasonable conclusions.

The subject is divisible into two phases; the first involving the question of our legal and moral right; the second, the question of policy.

In order to comprehend fully the legal and moral side of the question, it is necessary to consider not only the international treaties in which this country has engaged, but to study briefly the political conditions existing prior to and at the time such treaties were made.

The first treaty of importance affecting the construction of a canal in Central America connecting the Atlantic and Pacific oceans was entered into between the United States and New Granada (now the Republic of Colombia) in 1846. While this treaty has little bearing upon the question of our right to fortify the canal, its principal provisions will be noted. In substance, it was stipulated that the United States guaranteed the neutrality of any " means of transit " across the Isthmus of Panama, in return for which the Government of New Granada granted to the citizens and vessels of the United States the free use, on terms of equality with the citizens and vessels of New Granada, of any such " means of transit " between the two oceans as might be constructed. As stated before, no reference was made in the treaty to the right of the United States to fortify the canal, and therefore it is not necessary to discuss this treaty at length.

The Clayton-Bulwer treaty of 1850, between the United States and Great Britain, has a direct bearing on the question at issue, and in order that its terms may be fully understood, it is well not only to cite its principal provisions, but to refer briefly to the events which led up to the negotiation of the treaty.

To those who have not given the subject any special study, the question naturally arises: Why should the United States enter into an agreement with Great Britain, in regard to the construction of a canal on the American Continent, to the exclusion of other European powers? To answer this question it is necessary to consider the relations between the United States and Great Britain at the time the Clayton-Bulwer treaty was negotiated. The feeling existing between the two nations was far from amicable. In 1823 the Monroe Doctrine was asserted by this country, by which it was made known to the world that the United States would not countenance the acquiring of additional territory on the Western Hemisphere by any European nation or coalition of nations. In its final analysis, this doctrine is simply one of self-preservation. The same doctrine (without a name) was asserted by Japan in regard to Manchuria and Korea immediately prior to the Russo-Japanese war. It was at that time a bulwark of the perpetuity of our freedom and national existence. On the other hand, Great Britain had interests in the Mosquito Coast region of Central America and her influence in that section had been more than once manifested. Both nations realized the need of a canal across the Isthmus, but each was jealous of the other getting control of such a canal in case it should be constructed.

Such a state of affairs existed in 1850, and the relations between the two countries became so strained that rumors of war were afloat in both the United States and Great Britain. The Clayton-Bulwer treaty was in the nature of a compromise, and, it has been said, was a potent factor in averting war at that time. But it was simply an attempt to settle certain controverted matters which had become acute, and was not entirely satisfactory to the United States at the time of its ratification or at any time during the fifty years it was in force.

By the terms of the treaty, the United States and Great Britain agreed that neither would obtain or maintain for itself any exclusive control over a ship canal across the Isthmus; that neither would ever erect or maintain any fortifications commanding the canal or in the vicinity thereof; that neither party would ever occupy, fortify, colonize, assume or exercise any dominion over Nicaragua, Costa Rica, the Mosquito Coast, or any other part of Central America; that vessels of both nations traversing the canal in case of war between the contracting parties, should be exempt from blockade, detention or capture by either of the belligerents. The two nations guaranteed the neutrality of the canal so that it might be forever open and free. They engaged to invite other nations to enter into similar stipulations, and in order to establish a general principle, they agreed to extend their protection, not alone to a canal at Nicaragua (at that time it was assumed that any canal contemplated would be constructed through Nicaragua), but to any other " practicable communications " which might be contemplated by way of Tehuantepec or Panama.

There can be no doubt that under the terms of this treaty the United States was prohibited from erecting fortifications on the canal, and this prohibition received the acquiescence of our citizens generally for more than a decade after the promulgation of the treaty.

At the time of the negotiation of the Clayton-Bulwer treaty, the value of the canal as a commercial enterprise seems to have been paramount. Little or no consideration was given to the military value of such a waterway. In fact, it was not until after the Civil War, when the people of this country began to realize to some extent the importance of the United States among the great nations of the world, that this phase of the question received any serious consideration. As the nation recovered from the shock of that war, a decided change in public sentiment, as regards the construction of an Isthmian canal, seems to have manifested itself. In the light of the attitude which Great Britain and other European nations had assumed during the Civil War, and the revival of interest in the

Monroe Doctrine, the terms of the Clayton-Bulwer treaty became very distasteful to many of our citizens. But the treaty remained in force for over fifty years before being abrogated, although repeated attempts were made to bring about this result.

The Spanish-American war, resulting in our acquiring island possessions and coaling stations in both oceans, emphasized more fully than ever before the military value to this country of a canal connecting the Atlantic and Pacific oceans, and the crystallizing of public sentiment in favor of the United States owning and exclusively controlling such a canal finally brought about negotiations between Great Britain and the United States looking toward the abrogation or modification of the Clayton-Bulwer treaty.

In 1900, Secretary of State Hay and Lord Pauncefote, the British Ambassador to this country, drafted a new treaty which modified the Clayton-Bulwer treaty in several important respects. In this draft it was agreed that the United States should construct, own and have exclusive control of the canal, should be the sole guarantor of its neutrality, but that the waterway should be open and free to all nations; the United States was prohibited from erecting any fortifications at the canal, and other nations were invited to adhere to the provisions of the treaty. When the treaty came before the Senate, that body struck out the clause inviting other nations to adhere to its provisions, and inserted one " for securing by its own forces the defence of the United States and the maintenance of public order." The provision prohibiting fortifications was not stricken out, but the treaty was not ratified by both nations and was, therefore, never in force.

In 1902, another treaty was drafted by Secretary Hay and Lord Pauncefote which was ratified by both countries and is now in force. This treaty is similar to the first Hay-Pauncefote treaty, except that it is silent in regard to the right of the United States to fortify the canal. The fact that this prohibition was stipulated in the first draft and omitted in the final ratified treaty has a significant bearing on the question of our right to fortify the canal. As far as Great Britain is concerned, under the terms of the treaty it is not conceivable that that nation could offer any objections to our erecting fortifications if we saw fit to do so, except under the neutrality clause, which will be considered later. The treaty is silent in regard to either party occupying, colonizing, assuming or exercising any dominion over any of the Central American republics. This omission was no doubt due to the fact that Great Britain had long since ceased to exercise any influence in the internal affairs of those countries, and the Monroe Doctrine having never been openly assailed by other nations, it was considered unnecessary to continue such a provision in the treaty. No mention is made in the final draft of the Hay-Pauncefote treaty as to vessels of Great Britain traversing the canal, in case of war between the contracting parties, being exempt from blockade, detention or capture by the United States. Under the treaty the United States is the sole guarantor of the neutrality of the canal.

There remains to be considered the treaty between the United States and the Republic of Panama, made subsequently to the Hay-Pauncefote treaty.

The only provision in this treaty which needs mention here is that which stipulates that if at any time it should become necessary to employ armed forces for the safety or protection of the canal, the United States shall have the right to establish fortifications. While this treaty was made with a small republic, and is, of course, binding only upon the two contracting parties, it may be said that it is a notification to all nations that the United States assumes the right to fortify the canal should it see fit to do so.

The Hay-Pauncefote treaty of 1902 and the treaty between this country and Panama (the Hay-Buneau-Varilla treaty) are the only ones now in force, and our treaty rights may be gathered from these two documents. With no other nation have we a treaty regarding the construction, maintenance or control of the Panama Canal.

Now that our treaty rights have been set forth, it may be well to consider briefly the opinions of our public officials and others in regard thereto. In the consideration of the question of our right under these treaties to erect fortifications on the canal, considerable discussion centres around the meaning of the term " neutrality." As stated above, the United States is the sole guarantor of the neutrality of the canal. Those opposed to the policy of fortification contend that under this guarantee the United States is bound to keep the canal open to the passage of vessels of all nations at all times, in peace and war, not only in case of war between two or more foreign nations, but also in case any one or more of them should be at war with this country. That for this reason, if for no other, we are prohibited from erecting fortifications on the canal or from using more military force than is necessary to protect it against lawlessness and disorder. On the other hand, the proponents of the policy of fortification contend that the term "neutrality," as applied in this instance, simply means that in so far as other belligerents are concerned, the canal will be open to the vessels of both nations at all times on equal terms; but that in case of war between the United States and Great Britain, or any other nation, it would not be expected that this country would allow its opponent's vessels free passage through the canal if such transit would be detrimental to our defence or of advantage to our enemy from a military standpoint.

Another controverted point in regard to our treaty rights is the clause in the Panama treaty granting us the right to erect fortifications, if at any time it should become necessary to employ armed forces for the safety or protection of the canal. Buneau-Varilla, who represented the Republic of Panama in the negotiation of the treaty with that republic, now claims—and in this he is upheld by some of our own citizens—that under this clause the United States cannot establish permanent fortifications in time of peace; that such authorization is merely an accessory of the right to use military force to protect the canal when the necessity arises for such protection. Many of our prominent public officials, however, take the view that the United States has the right to decide upon the measures necessary to secure the safety and protection of the canal, and also the means to be employed for guaranteeing its neutrality, and that should it consider it necessary, in the accomplishment of both of these ends, to place permanent fortifications at the entrances to the canal in time of peace, it has the legal and moral right to do so.

Turning now from the legal right to the question of policy, there are two phases to consider in this connection. The first is, the strategical value of the canal to us in case of war; the second, the canal as an objective of an enemy having in view its capture for its own use during war, as a prize of war when peace is secured, or as the basis of a claim for indemnity at the conclusion of hostilities.

Under this phase, the arguments against fortification may be summed up as follows: That the canal is a point on a line of sea communications, and its defence should be purely a naval one, to be made as far from it as possible; that control of the sea is the principal factor in its defence, capture or destruction; that if an enemy secured control of the sea, either on the Atlantic or Pacific, the canal would be of no use to our navy, for it would be blockaded, in which case fortifications at its entrances would not interfere with such a blockade. In other words, that if the navy could not protect the canal without fortifications, it could not do so with them. It is also argued that guns at the entrances to the canal, no matter how powerful, would not prevent small raiding parties from landing elsewhere in the vicinity out of range of the coast guns and destroying the canal by the use of dynamite or attacking the forts in rear; that the danger of a hostile fleet passing through the canal is visionary, unless the enemy first got possession, for the ships when once in the canal would be at the mercy of the lock-tenders; that if a portion of our army was located on the Isthmus, it would need open communications with the United States, and if the enemy had control of the sea this would be impossible, and fortifications would be of no use in this respect; that no damage could be done to the locks and dams by a hostile fleet outside, for these are out of range of gun fire from the respective harbors; that the danger of bombardment to an unfortified canal is imaginary, as the laws of war forbid it.

On the other hand, it is claimed by those who favor fortification that strategically the canal in the hands of an enemy at the outbreak of war might cripple the United States from the outset; that is, if our fleet were all in one ocean, on the side opposite the theatre of war, it would be compelled to go around the Horn, thus giving a formidable enemy the opportunity to inflict great damage along our seacoast before its arrival in the theatre of war; or, if the fleet was divided, one-half would be paralyzed in the distant ocean while the enemy, with a superior naval force, might deal with the other half in the near ocean. Another cogent reason advanced against the proposition that the defence of the canal rests with the navy is that this would deprive it of its principal asset—mobility—and compel it to remain in passive defence in one locality, when its principal function is, owing to its mobility, that of acting on the offensive; that in order to protect the canal, it would be necessary to tie it to one locality or one area of waters, thus depriving it of its rôle as an offensive weapon. It is pointed out that economically and strategically, it would be inadvisable to use so expensive a weapon as the navy to perform duties which could as well be performed by a much less expensive weapon, such as would be afforded by adequate land defences; also that in case the canal was the objective of an enemy, his navy would probably make a feint with a portion of his naval force at attacking some part of our continental coast and that if our fleet followed his lead, the canal, in case it was unfortified, would be open to raid by another portion of the enemy's fleet. If, however, our battle fleet remained on guard at the canal, the enemy could attack the rest of our coast without danger of naval interference.

Having presented some of the main arguments in favor of and against the policy of fortifying the canal, it is now proposed to " sum up the evidence " and draw a few conclusions therefrom.

It is believed that, despite assertions to the contrary, there is no limitation upon the power and right of this Government to erect fortifications on the waterway should it see fit to do so. The public press of Great Britain admits that that Government has tacitly consented to such action by the United States, although censuring the Administration for its weakness in abrogating the Clayton-Bulwer treaty. While the Republic of Panama may now take the view that no right to fortify the canal in time of peace was granted to the United States under the Hay-Buneau-Varilla treaty, it is not conceivable that this country must wait until the actual necessity— war—exists before taking steps to secure its defence and protection. With no other country than these two has the United States any treaty affecting the Panama Canal; there is no unwritten law against erecting fortifications there, and at no time has this country ever given any pledge or even intimation, since the abrogation of the Clayton-Bulwer treaty, that it would abstain from treating the canal as a part of our territory or as a factor in our military equipment. The United States has, in its assertion of the Monroe Doctrine, as well as in the exertion of its good offices in the domestic affairs of the Central and South American republics, demonstrated to the world its policy of extending a protecting hand over its sister republics on this Hemisphere, and as a factor in the carrying out of this policy, the Panama Canal is of great importance. Considering all these things, it is believed that we have a just and equitable right to protect the canal by the erection of permanent fortifications, or by any other legitimate means we may see fit to adopt.

As regards the guarantee of neutrality, rather than prohibiting fortifications on the canal, such a guarantee carries with it, by inference if not by letter, the right to adopt such measures as may be necessary to insure that guarantee being fulfilled. In only two ways can that object be obtained; that is, in order to enforce the dictates of the guarantor, the power must either be present at the canal in the form of permanent fortfications, or by the presence of our navy in waters contiguous to the canal, at least until we secured absolute control of the sea on both sides, and, as stated above, to compel the navy alone to defend the canal would be to deprive it of its principal function of acting in the offensive. Concerning the argument that it is needless to fortify the canal because the navy can defend it, such an argument has never been urged in regard to erecting fortifications in the vicinity of our large commercial centres along our continental sea-coast, and yet the two cases seem to be analogous.

Assuming, then, that we have a legal and moral right to erect permanent fortifications on the canal, let us now consider the question of policy.

It is impossible to consider the Panama Canal in the light of a purely commercial enterprise. Any consideration of the value of the waterway naturally involves the question of the strategic advantage afforded the United States by its use in time of war.

The completion of the canal will undoubtedly lessen the necessity of such large additions to our navy as would be required if we were compelled to maintain a battle fleet in both oceans. And without the means of rapidly transferring our fleet from one ocean to the other, this country, in case of sudden outbreak of war, would be confronted with a serious problem. It is a matter of simple mathematical calculation to demonstrate that with our battle fleet on the opposite ocean to the theatre of war, and the canal closed to the transit of our vessels, a formidable enemy could make a quick dash across the ocean and inflict considerable damage along our coasts, to say nothing of our insular possessions, before the fleet could reach the theatre of operations. But with possession of the canal during hostilities assured to us, our battle fleet would be available, within a short time, for service in either ocean.

In this connection, another important factor in our national defence presents itself. It is a well-known fact that the United States is lamentably lacking in its ability to secure, in a short time, sufficient merchant marine for use as transports, colliers and cruisers in time of war. It is probable that should a sudden war occur, necessitating our sending strong reinforcements to our outlying possessions, we should be unable to transport an army of 100,000 men without calling upon all of our merchant marine on both coasts, and should the canal fall into the hands of an enemy and compel us, in concentrating our battle fleet and transports, to sail around the Horn instead of passing through the Isthmus, it would place us at a very great disadvantage.

Therefore, in view of the great strategic importance of the canal to this country, to neglect to take every precautionary measure to prevent it from falling into the possession of an enemy in time of war, would certainly be most unwise.

It has been argued that even though the United States should erect fortifications at the entrances to the canal, it would not absolutely insure its security, for it would be exposed in time of war to attack from the inside by small raiding parties. While this is no doubt true, yet it would be no less exposed to such attack without fortifications at the terminal points; and it is assumed that with war impending, the United States would take every precaution to guard against attacks of this character, either with or without fortifications at the entrances.

Another important fact must be here considered; that is, the necessity, in case the canal was blockaded at one exit, of our battle fleet being able, in passing through the waterway, to debouch in

battle formation, and this could not be done except under the protection of the land armament. With adequate defences at the two
entrances to the canal, a hostile fleet could be kept at such a distance
as to allow our fleet to form in line of battle after passing out of
the canal; whereas, without such fortifications, the enemy's fleet
could approach so near the mouth of the canal as to be able to crush
our fleet in detail as it emerged.

It is contended by those opposed to the policy of fortification,
that even should fortifications be erected on the canal, the United
States would have to maintain, in time of war, a large mobile force
in the Canal Zone, and to do this, open communications with this
country would have to be maintained; that this could not be done
if the enemy had control of the sea, for the canal would be blockaded. It is hardly conceivable that any possible enemy would secure
command of the sea on both oceans, and with the enemy holding control in but one ocean, we should always have a safe line of communications open to us. With adequate fortifications, no hostile fleet
could pass through the canal, nor is it probable that an attempt
would be made to bombard the forts with this purpose in view, for
history teaches us that since the application of steam to navigation,
out of thirty-eight cases in which sea-coast fortifications have been
bombarded by hostile vessels, in only six cases have the attacks met
with success. Therefore, should the canal be fortified and the enemy
have control of the sea on one side, the canal would be self-sustaining
for an indefinite period of time.

Regarding the assumption that our enemy would fail, for sentimental reasons, or because of treaty agreements, to attack the canal
with a view to securing it for its own use, or depriving us of its use,
the assumption is not borne out by past history. It is reasonably
probable that in case we became involved in war with another nation
with which we have a treaty regarding the canal, the provisions of
such a treaty, upon the opening of hostilities, would be declared
null and void.

Finally, it may be said that if the canal is fortified, even though
we may not be able to use it ourselves, it is an assured fact that no
enemy can use it against us, and the same thing can not be said of it
if we fail to erect adequate fortifications at its entrances.

There are other points in favor of fortifying the canal which might be presented, but it is believed that the above fully substantiate the contention that the United States has the legal and moral right to erect such fortifications, and that as a matter of policy it would be unwise to neglect to avail ourselves of this right.

In concluding this article, reference must be made to the matter of the expense of the proposed defences. It is estimated that the cost of the sea-coast fortifications recommended by the Panama Canal Board would reach a total of $12,000,000. This is little more than the cost of a modern battleship of the Dreadnought type, and considering the initial cost of the construction of the canal, such a sum is small as the expense of insuring its safety in time of war. Should the canal fall into the hands of an enemy and remain in its possession at the close of war, the amount of indemnity which we should be required to pay. to regain possession would be many times this amount. Or, should an enemy, if victorious, retain the waterway as a prize of war, our loss in the original outlay of nearly half a billion of dollars and in the loss of profits accruing from tolls, would make the expense of erecting adequate fortifications appear an insignificant sum.

THE MESSAGE OF TOLSTOY

ARCHIBALD HENDERSON

I DO not believe anyone can do Tolstoy a greater disservice than to write about him as a man of letters. There is, and there will be, no dearth of devotees who will immortalize the artist who had not yet learned what is art; and bemoan, in accents of refined regret, the perversion of his talents to the service of the religion of the future and the humanity of a purer era. Is it for nothing that, in our day, a man—weak, faulty, illogical, inconsistent—has arisen who, struggling bitterly and blithely to a self-mastery and a self-discipline that had in them something of the saintly, pierced the veil of art and saw there human service—or nothing?

There is no stranger inconsistency in all of Tolstoy's life than this. The art of the great masters—Turgenev, Maupassant, Hugo —fired his fancy, sent the blood into his cheeks, drove him to a frenzy of creative activity. And yet he denied that ideal of pure creative productivity, put it away from him as an evil thing, and with the intense concentration of the anchorite chained his soaring soul to the dread problems of virtue and self-purification, humanity and life, religion and immortality. Temperament again and again re-asserted itself, burst the cruel bonds of self-annihilation, and poured itself forth in rapturous contemplation of that ancient art whose highest content is internal harmony, unvexed with problems of individual destiny or cosmic ruin.

The real struggle was never in abatement. Tolstoy expressed in his own person as no man in modern times has expressed it, the clear conviction that men must live with ever widening aims and ever increasing purpose. We are marching to-day, as Brunetière put it, toward the socialization, the moralization of literature. Tolstoy realized and expressed in enduring form—in his writings, in his life—the supreme conviction that man's greatest need, man's highest duty, is to devote the talents that germinate within him to purposes that transcend and surpass all purely personal purposes and aims. That same conviction has animated Bernard Shaw in his vehement declaration that he who devotes himself solely to art for art's sake is a fool in the scriptural sense, an utterly hopeless fool, a man in a state of damnation. Personal talent, in Tolstoy's view, is not an individual possession, but a public trust. It is that great God-given instrumentality by which man may be enabled not to raise himself above his fellows to a position of aristocratic eminence in art, but to raise his fellow-man to a consciousness of human brotherhood that will bring all men together in common sympathy and common unity for the universal welfare.

I am no Tolstoyan. I would celebrate, not Tolstoyism, but Tolstoy. And even thus, the reservations are almost as overwhelming as the affirmations. For Tolstoy, in many ways, was a survival of strangely monastic asceticism foreign to the spirit of our day and time. His most splendid trait was at once his besetting sin: self-reliance. Enthusiastic, vehement, passionate in conviction, he passed violently from one stage of development to another—sometimes deepening, widening his volume and content of spiritual consciousness, yet oftentimes narrowing and fossilizing his energies with rabid dogmatism and intolerance that re-creates the spirit of the Hebrew prophets of old. With all his self-mortification, his dreary yet enlightening struggle toward an almost superhuman self-mastery, he never put away from him the mania of certitude. Torn from their moorings—surroundings of wealth, leisure, self-indulgence—by Tolstoy's fierce assumption ·of infallibility, men and women tried to follow his strange counsels of perfection. Almost without exception, they came to grief in the end—Tolstoyism broke in their hands even though their faith in Tolstoy remained undimmed. The Tolstoy colonies—established in many parts of the world—went to ruin, in many cases pitiable ruin. For those who sought to put Tolstoyan principles into effect in a world of competition, of industrial organization, found that sweetness and light will not suffice for the earning of bread or the satisfaction of the needs of life.

When I recall Tolstoy's own struggle, so often a victorious struggle, for a humility of spirit that was almost sublime, I shrink from a criticism that may sound both trivial and over-confident. But facts are more eloquent than any words. And the facts themselves speak here with unerring certainty. Tolstoyism has failed—

and will, I believe, always fail—because it does not take into account the industrial organization of modern society. How sad—and indeed, how futile—were Tolstoy's own efforts to exemplify his doctrines in his own life and conduct! I honor him far more in the breach of his avowed principles than in their observance. Almsgiving he vehemently condemned as tacit support of prevailing conditions of civilization and government; yet he created a systematic scheme of petty almsgiving without a parallel in modern times. He preached that property was theft, with a ferocity almost inhuman in one who could be so gentle, so humble and so mild; and yet his life was one long subterfuge—a specious shifting to the shoulders of his wife and family of the burdens which his conscience forbade him to endure. With staggering inconsequence, he reproved men and women for conducting and directing hospitals and asylums for the poor, the homeless, the parentless; and yet when famine devastated his land and struck down his people by tens of thousands, he threw himself ardently into the struggle, rallied around him his family and all right-minded men and women who would coöperate in the work, and for days, weeks, months and years, without cessation, gave his life unstintedly to the hazardous, dreary, enervating task of relieving the horrible sufferings and tortures of his people. Preaching Christian Anarchism of an exalted type, he theoretically defied government, authority, taxation and all the functions incident to the administration of the modern state. And yet he did not hesitate to memorialize the Czar to give Russia a better government; publicly advocated the candidacy of Mr. Bryan for President of the United States; maintained his estates and allowed taxes to be paid in his name; heartily approved the plan of putting into effect by governmental power the Single Tax theories of Henry George; and in a thousand other ways belied the doctrines he preached with such high seriousness, such passionate vehemence, such unwithered confidence.

Shall we thus upbraid Tolstoy for his inconsistency—and scornfully print the ancient truth that faith without works is dead? Not for one moment. We must remember that it was a case of Tolstoy *contra mundum*. In his most imperfect, yet most perfectly, most divinely human way, he failed to put into practice his inhuman theories. The logic of his position demanded separation from his family, demanded absolute renunciation of property, demanded the production with his own hands of more than he actually consumed. He went as far as he was able—as far, indeed, as the very breaking point of human endurance; but the law-giver of a new dispensation failed utterly to give any sort of adequate exemplification of the operation of those laws. If all the force of spiritual conviction, of resolute will, of stubborn certainty lodged in Tolstoy's being could not carry him over the barriers he had himself erected, the conclusion is reasonable—is inevitable—that it was humanly impossible. Tolstoy furnishes the most lamentably conclusive proof of the fallacy of Tolstoyism.

The most signal evidence of Tolstoy's greatness consists in the tremendous fact that, though failing to achieve his own principles in his own person, Tolstoy came to be regarded as the most remarkable figure of modern times. If we acknowledge the bankruptcy of Tolstoyism, its total failure to bring Tolstoy's interpretation of Christian principles into accord with the life of his time, shall we then fall back upon the declaration that Tolstoy has set an example to the modern world which all men would do well to follow? Just that way the greatest danger lies. For it is not easy to disengage from the vast complexity of Tolstoy's futile attempt at over-simplification of life, those doctrines and dogmas in respect to conduct which accord both with the reality of civilization and the highest ideals of our day. Tolstoy enjoyed the untold advantage—an advantage which seems actually incalculable—of the most strategic position for the enunciation of his doctrines that Western civilization can offer. It is inconceivable that Tolstoy could have lived and flourished, could have exercised one tithe of the influence he unquestionably exerted, had he lived in England or in America. In either country, the sturdy common sense, the ingrained practicability of the common people would have offered an absolutely impervious obstacle to the acceptance of his theories. The Anglo-Saxon race demands of its reformers fertile suggestions of direct practical value in the business of carrying on the affairs of life—whether of commerce, or politics, or sociology, or religion. It is the man who has something demonstrably useful to offer, something which not only can be, but actually is, put to practical use for public service, who commends himself to the great mass of the people. In England or in America, Tolstoy would have been regarded as a visionary, a freak, perhaps even a madman; his doctrines would have been done to death with ridicule by the press, the comic papers, the practical men of affairs. The very welfare of the mass of the workers in America would have offered an insuperable barrier to the acceptance of his monkish, early Christian and primitive conceptions of a life of agrarian simplicity, without definite purpose or rational organization.

It was because Tolstoy lived in Russia, still a century behind other Western nations in freedom, in civilization, in humanity of outlook, that his doctrines found fertile soil in which to germinate and flourish. At the door lay the opportunity for putting into practice Tolstoy's ascetic, primitive ideas. I do not doubt the statement that ninety-nine hundredths of the working classes in Russia do not actually produce enough to support themselves and their families comfortably. Tolstoy was *vox clamantis in deserto*—passionately calling upon the rich to desert their banquet halls, their wealth, their luxury and their vices, and go forth to prepare the way of the Lord. If his own life was fatally inconsistent, if his colonies were blown away like chaff by the wind of their own futility, if his doctrines fell of their own weight and shattered before the irreducible facts of actuality, it is as nothing to the fact that Tolstoy stood forth as a great humanizing force in a land of despotism, tyranny, and oppression. Like a prophet of old, the true backer of a people, he spoke forth with unexampled boldness in behalf of justice, of humanity, of liberty. With great-hearted simplicity, with true Christian humility, he again and again openly addressed the Czar, not as ruler, but as fellow-man, urging him to act humanely and wisely, to outride the selfish counsels of sycophantic advisers, to devote his great power, not to buttressing his despotic throne, but to protecting and caring for his people. "Little Father" was the traditional title, bestowed with tragic irony upon the sovereign who had his subjects brutally shot down in the streets when they came to petition him for redress of wrongs. It was Tolstoy who was the great father of his people, indicting with trenchant, splendid words of scriptural authority the atrocities of a government which created the very insurrectionism it throttled with merciless mailed hand.

There are two great qualities which pronounce Tolstoy a great man and a great writer in the larger sense of our time. First of these qualities was a boldness, an undaunted courage which had behind it the complete readiness of supreme self-sacrifice. I do not believe that Tolstoy would or could have been one whit braver had he been one of Christ's own disciples who, living, followed His footsteps. He bore the excommunication of the Russian Church with a spiritual equanimity that can only be called supreme. He defied the evil temporal powers of his country, his race, and his age with such magnificent audacity that even the Czar dared not touch him. For well he knew that Tolstoy courted martyrdom, imprisonment, even death—for that would turn the force of humanitarian sentiment, not only throughout Russia, but throughout the civilized world, against the horrors of Russian autocracy. No man, of whatever race or clime, who has read Tolstoy's works and pondered those great appeals against tyranny, injustice and oppression, can withhold a feeling of profound admiration for the exalted spiritual heroism of the man.

The other great quality which has given Tolstoy so great a hold upon the consciousness of the modern world is his spirit of infinite earnestness and sincerity. His life is a succession of spiritual conflicts, in which, now rising, now falling to rise again, he perpetually ascends to greater and ever greater heights of spiritual self-surrender and Christian self-mastery. There is something horrifying, at times revolting, in Tolstoy's complete absorption in the concerns of his own spiritual development. The man who could desert his wife when she was in the throes of child-birth, in order to find solitude for working out a problem of spiritual stress through which he happened to be passing, strikes an Anglo-Saxon as heathenish, inhuman in utter selfishness. This indeed was his besetting sin—his setting the development of the individual soul above all other interests, however imperative, however humanely obligatory. Tolstoy spent a lifetime in the herculean struggle to understand himself. Had he sought with equal fervor and earnestness to understand others, he would have been a greater man and a greater Christian. There is something almost inexplicable in the workings of conscience which prompted Tolstoy to condemn almsgiving; and yet when charged with inconsistency, he confessed that, though the beggars might spend the pennies he gave them for vodka, he himself was spiritually refreshed by the mere act of benevolence.

For England and the United States, Tolstoy offers a lesson at once immediate and unmistakable. In England, scandals are surreptitiously covered up; reformation is tardy and proceeds through the slow operation of political opinion; subserviency to rank and position devitalizes the healthy stamina of the people in all classes of society below the highest; marriage is wellnigh indissoluble, resulting in a widespread double standard of life which is winked at by public sentiment; the working man, by the tens, almost hundreds of thousands, wanders the streets vainly seeking employment for his talent and his labor; women clamor for the vote against the veto of a premier, in face of impressive parliamentary support; evils lurk at every hand to stifle the freedom of the people, to debauch their views, to deprive them of the means of livelihood, to rob them of the fruits of their labor. In the United States, the lords of protection still sit entrenched in the citadels of their wealth, laughing the lowly to scorn as he reads the message of a President defending a tariff bill which a united nation has risen to destroy. Northern proclaimers of the equality madness socially speak the negro race with fairness; but deprive them of the right to live by refusing them membership in the labor unions. Southern negro haters go about the country prophesying the great race conflict of the future; and prevent strife between the races by the prediction that the inevitable solution of the negro problem is for the white race to exterminate the black race with Winchesters and Gatling guns. The Northern man preaches equality but refuses to practise it. The Southern man allows the negro laborer to work side by side with the white laborer; but does not give him a square deal in the courts of law. Race animosity slumbers everywhere in the breast of the white race, needing only some dastardly outrage to break forth in hideous carnivals of crime, a blot on our civilization and a shame on our race. North and South, East and West—there is no distinction; once the embers are fanned into flame, the vengeance of the mob knows no check, and innocent men and women are done to death in a frenzy of racial rage. Everywhere labor wages its immitigable conflict with capital, protected by law, defended by publicists, protected by government. New York to-day would be the financial centre of the world were it not for a financial system of hazard and monumental uncertainty which from time to time plunges a sound business nation at large in disastrous and wide-spread panic. Insidious foes to freedom and justice are lurking near at hand, ready to show themselves when circumstances shall throw those weaker than themselves into their power.

Tolstoy stood forth in Russia in advocacy of that great weapon which the common people have discovered and must use in their own defence in the days that are to come. Tolstoy was the apostle of publicity. Without abating one jot or tittle of the facts, without sparing friend or foe, without respecting persons, even to the Czar himself, Tolstoy flung forth the naked truth, and bade defiance to consequences and to the future. English conservatism is withering up from fear of publicity. Instead of covering up their numerous scandals, instead of winking at their degenerating double standards of public and private morality, they should throw such questions open to public gaze, invite the wholesome judgment of corporate common sense, and trust, not simply to the slow-moving operation of their great legal and judicial system, but to the immediate and voluntary expression of public standards of rectitude. In the era of publicity now dawning in England—the era of such critical and practical reformers as Lloyd George, Sidney Webb and Bernard Shaw, socialistic, radical, demagogic though they may be—these will, I believe, awaken a sense of the importance of publicly facing national dangers and insidious social evils, and of submitting their arbitrament and solution to the Referendum of an intelligent electorate.

To the United States, Tolstoy as publicist speaks with equally certain and clarion tones. America to-day enjoys in the eyes of the civilized world an unsavory, an almost unholy reputation, not so much on account of the evils of her civilization, but on account of what Americans have publicly said of their own country. The fundamental falsity and insidious deception of the English and foreign press in regard to American affairs are colossal and appalling. The great majority of the correspondents of English and foreign papers located in America are, however speciously disguised, yellow journalists, giving jaundiced views of conditions and of circumstances by reporting only those things which will flatter foreign vanity and tend to confirm the foreign view that America is a modern survival of the later decadence of the Roman Empire.   The fighting magazines in America have raked the country fore and aft with the muck rake, uncovering scandals with fearlessness of consequences; but only too often artistically darkening the picture and omitting mention of the unremitting efforts of right-minded men to cure the social ills.   What America needs is not more publicity, but better publicity; not exposure of more scandals, but more truthful exposure of social conditions, emphasizing the great efforts at social reform and pointing the way to cure the evils exposed.   More than all, America needs the sort of publicity that Tolstoy gave to conditions in Russia.   Let the great men of our day—the Charles W. Eliots, the Arthur T. Hadleys, the Woodrow Wilsons—let the greatest men of our day study the sociologic features of our civilization—not only study them, but tell us—tell America—tell the whole world what should be done, what must be done, to realize on American soil that great dream of independence, of social solidarity, of democratic freedom, which animated the founders of the American Republic.

DANAE'S SONG

FREDERIC MANNING

Thou, whom the gray seas bare more fierce than they,
O bitter Love! Have pity on his weeping,
Smite me with pain; lo, I am all thy prey.
Sleep thou, my son, as all the world is sleeping;
Sleep thou, my babe; and sleep, thou cruel sea;
And sleep, O grief, within the heart of me.

Bitter thy fruit, O Love, thy crown is pain!
Sweet were thy words to me, thy soft caresses.
Child of my heart, O gain beyond all gain,
Sleep, while I shelter thee with arms and tresses!
Sleep thou, my babe; and sleep, thou cruel sea;
And sleep, O grief, within the heart of me.

Yea, I am thine, O Love. I am thy spoil!
Sleep thou, my son, sleep softly till the morrow!
Love, who hast snared me in thy golden toil,
Still the loud seas though thou still not my sorrow!
Sleep thou, my babe; and sleep, thou cruel sea;
And sleep, O grief, within the heart of me.

THE FLASH

MRS. HAVELOCK ELLIS

Dollie Hosking was considerably upset. All the yellow cream on thirty pans of milk had "bucked." It was why she hated June. Thirty gallons of milk and all the trouble thrown in, only fit to give to the pigs! Her new gray dress seemed a far-off possibility. Her mother let her keep a quarter of the money from the dairy for herself, and she had been saving for weeks for an Irish poplin upon which she had set her heart. She opened the windows, meshed with fine wire instead of glass, wider.

"Cats can't do more than the sun has done," she murmured. A bee buzzed in at once and settled on the first long pat of butter on a huge slate containing about fifty pounds. The white-washed dairy, the blue-gowned girl and the yellow cream and butter made heat seem a blessing and not a disaster to a casual onlooker.

"You here, this time of day?" said Dollie suddenly, as she caught sight of a bronzed face in the doorway. "I've no time to talk now. Everything almost be turned sour and I wish I'd stayed in London and never come home to silly work like this."

Amos Trewin pushed the door wider open as he came in and sat sideways on the corner of a large slate slab. He was one of the local sailors and Gavose Head could not boast of a braver one. His large tanned face was very serious as he took in the situation. His gray eyes softened suddenly as he looked at Dollie.

"What's bucked milk?" he queried. His strong white teeth made his smile a sort of challenge. He put his hands in his flapping trouser pockets and crossed one leg over the other. "If you be all right, what's the odds?"

"Don't be silly," retorted Dollie. "It's more to me than you know. I'd counted on something as meant something else."

This cryptic sentence made Amos knit his brows.

"It's real disaster to me," Dollie added.

Amos kicked the leg of the table with his heel.

"I want to save you from disasters," he said.

Dollie tossed her pretty head and readjusted a band of velvet nestling in the coils of her hair. She bent toward Amos to do this and he said softly:

"You've a neck like an alderney, somehow, Dollie. Them low collars be real perky."

"Those collars," said Dollie kindly. She patted her low muslin collar as she spoke.

"You've the advantage," said Amos, "being in London a year."

"I only wish I'd stayed," sighed Dollie. "No, I don't, though," she added as she hummed the tune of a waltz.

"Thanks be it was not meant," said Amos. "I felt all the time you was away like a boat neither steady at anchor nor yet well out to sea. When you came home it was like fair sailing and big catches."

Dollie put a milking stool and bucket under the table on which Amos sat and slowly hung up some milk-cans on hooks in the stone wall. She wheeled suddenly round and tapped the young sailor on the shoulder.

"Stop saying those things, Amos," she said slowly. "I shall never marry you—never, never," she added emphatically. "You won't believe it, but I know it's true."

"Kiss me!" he cried passionately. An impulse seized her as she saw his outstretched arms. She came toward him and took his head between her long cool hands and looked in his eyes.

"I want to," she said, "and yet it's not fair."

"Leave that to me," he said, and his face grew very tender. "I'll take all the risks, whatever they are."

He unlocked her hands and drew her toward him. She felt his limbs trembling, and yet, such was his love of her, she knew that because she had put him on his word about this matter of kissing he would keep himself from what he craved till she gave it willingly. Dollie half despised and half respected him for this self-control. Amos was a novice with regard to women. Love was a simple thing to him; so simple that it boded failure from the outset. It meant doing the will of the woman he worshiped—no more and no less. He knew nothing of passion's waywardness, its subtle cruelties or its strange inconsistencies. He had loved Dollie ever since he could remember anything. He had always felt her as part of himself.

She was like the sea was to him, something intimate and familiar yet with new ways every time you looked and thought about things. Like his prayers or the thought of his mother she was mixed up in all he did. Out in the boat at night she had become one with the sky, the storms, the sunrises and sunsets. When his mates chaffed him because he was so quiet he could not tell them he was happiest when he was picturing the times ahead to be lived with Dollie. That she had become a sort of lady by living in London for a year as a lady's maid only enhanced his feeling for her. She was now not only a holy thing to him, but a sort of queen. These last months he had never had her face out of his mind. She had come from London prettier than ever, glad to be away from the noise and the dirt, she declared, and hungering for cream and pasties and honeysuckle and all the things Amos and she liked the best. He had taken her one glorious February night by moonlight in his boat, and she had told him she loved him more than anyone else. It was all so at one with the big moon and the stars and the lapping water against the boat that neither of them spoke much.

Amos told her some of the things in his heart and she listened with a quiet smile on her face that made him lean over his oars and just say " home " to her. He never knew why he said it, but expected he got the same feeling a youngster has in the nest after its mother has fed it. As they were putting in he said lamely: " I wanted to say more but it won't come. We belong—that's near enough."

They had walked to her mother's farm and scarcely said even good-night and he had never thought of kissing her. But Amos was at peace. When he was fishing or cleaning his boat and hauling in big or little catches his face had a glow about it and his mates chaffed him and called him " Moses " because the Bible said that after being up on the Mount, Moses had to wear a veil like a woman to hide the things he knew which would show on his countenance. That was only four months ago, but these last two months a change seemed to have come over Dollie. Amos had grown restless and perplexed and he did not know why. A certain wistfulness had crept into her eyes and her large tender mouth seemed to be drooping a little at the corners. There had been an unusually early catch of pilchards for

the time of year, and as Amos had flung the silver fish in shoals from
his boat into the gullies that morning he had suddenly made up his
mind to go straight to the girl he loved and have a "forthright"
talk with her. Now, as he found himself with her head on his breast
he seemed utterly incapable of speech or action. Dollie drew herself
away from him, and laughed bitterly. He had not even kissed her
in spite of his passionate cry to her.

"Oh, you know nothing!" she cried, "nothing! And yet—oh
dear, oh dear! Why should you?"

"Dollie!" gasped Amos. "I don't want to scare you nor yet
break my word, but the heart in me be bursting for—for——" He
never finished. The look in Dollie's eyes stopped him. They seemed
misty and strange. With a savage stamp of her foot she faced
Amos.

"This is calf love," she said. "I know the difference and the
sooner you know it too the better. This isn't strong enough even
to brighten Sunday with, much less year in and year out. It's not
sufferable. It's only—only driving me mad for what," she hesitated, "for what—Oh! Amos! Don't stare like that. Can't you
see that it's not you I love a bit, though you talked me into saying
so once! I'm not a bit in love with you any more than I am with
brother Jack. And yet," shrinking from the look in his eyes, "I'm
certain sure I'm fonder of you than anyone else in the world in a
manner of speaking, but I'm too used to you somehow. You never
maze me."

"Maze you!" echoed Amos in a low voice. "Maze you! It's
what I've tried never to do."

She laughed almost merrily.

"Well! you've succeeded," she said. "I'm as quiet as a lamb
in the fields with its mother when I'm with you."

Amos was very puzzled.

"What call is there to be any other?" he said. She noticed how
gray his face was and how tired his eyes had grown.

"Don't let me bother you, Amos," she said kindly. "Just leave
me be."

"That's out of the reckoning now," he said. "We be one."

"No! no!" she cried. "That's not true. You are my companion, but not that. It will allus be so now." She shivered. "It will never be that way between you and me."

"What way?" he asked in a dull voice.

"Oh! can't you see something 'ave happened to me? I'm—I'm —too alive for you. Amos, Amos, can't you guess and then just leave it all alone? Talk won't help either of us."

"I'm no nearer understanding," said Amos.

"I can't speak plainer," said Dollie. "I'm always reckoning with things that have nothing to do with you at all. Now do you understand?"

"I can't sum it up," said Amos. "You've been part and parcel of all my thoughts and strivings ever since I can remember. What 'ave befallen us at all? From babies you and me belong together."

His face had changed so much that Dollie got a little nervous, and the more she realized how he was suffering the more irritated she grew.

"You're a fool, Amos," she said. "Anyone but you would have seen all along."

"I've allus been backward at scenting danger, even in the boat," said Amos thoughtfully. "Seemly, I can't haul this unbeknowns thing on deck."

Dollie stamped her foot.

"You've got to sweetheart somewhere else," she said brutally, "and the sooner the better. Maybe we'll be real friends again when you're married."

"Married!" cried Amos. "And not to you?"

Dollie was really angry now and his white face made her want to slap it.

"Don't make me loathe you, Amos." She spoke slowly as she stooped to pick up a hairpin which had fallen on the floor.

He got down quickly from the bench. He shook himself like a big dog and faced her.

"That's an uplong word, I reckon," he said quietly. "I've never made no use of it myself, but it 'ave somehow made me see things. It's a word that be mostly used against what be very low and evil, ain't it, like snakes and toads and such? I've never reck-oued myself on them lines, partly because my thoughts 'ave been mostly of you. That's allus kept me clean and fair in my dealin's and not wayward and flighty."

Dollie looked at the man before her. Some realization of his nature was slowly dawning on her.

"Amos," she said gently, "I wish it had been you, but it won't never be different now."

"Who's the man?" he asked suddenly.

"That's to me," she said. "No one like the chaps hereabouts."

"A swell?" he demanded. "A Londoner?"

"A man who knows how to behave," she said meaningly.

"Damn him!" said Amos in such a deliberate way that Dollie started. She had never heard Amos swear before and she had never seen anyone with so white a face. She was frightened.

"That's foolish," she said, "and not a bit like you belong."

"It comes natural," said Amos. "All in me be turning black."

Dollie put her hands on the man's shoulders and looked in his eyes.

"It's one of them things," she said, "we've no call to quarrel with. If I could get loose from the thought of him by day and night and then come to you I'd do it. But I can't."

Amos caught her passionately in his arms as he cried, "I'll rob him of this anyway," and he kissed her full on her mouth. With the agony of death in his heart and without another word he let her go and passed out of the dairy.

"He'm more alive than I thought, after all," she muttered when she could recover herself. "What wonderful dreamy ways he've got, and even his slowness has the feeling of lightning somehow."

Dollie knew little of life and less of love, though if you had told her so she would have laughed.

The young squire of the neighboring village, home from a tour abroad, in April, had found her one day in his woods, picking primroses. The sun was unusually hot for April and sport being scarce he had let a sudden impulse conquer him and made violent love to this woodland girl. That she was his for the asking he never doubted and he thanked his lucky stars afterwards that he had not been fool enough to take more than her kisses. But such kisses! He felt in his first youth when he thought about them.

Cecil Fairthorne had not lived his twenty-seven years without realizing that women, at heart, were really without any moral sense. He never implied to himself or his friends that they were deliberately immoral, for he honestly believed they had a very rigid code they held to in theory and struggled to carry out in practice; but he had come to the conclusion that any man who was determined to overcome their puritanism could easily do it, because it was not radical in women but something imposed on them from without by so-called civilization. Without undue arrogance he smilingly remembered his own particular conquests. When he thought about Dollie at all, which he often did, as she had really charmed him, he knew he had only to appear again and like an over-ripe peach she would literally fall into his mouth. He imagined he was being magnanimous when really he was forcing himself to avoid complications when he vowed he would not see her again.

Dollie, on her part, simply had longed and waited for the day when he would return, for she never doubted that he would come back. Analysis was as foreign to Dollie as to Amos. She had been passionately kissed and the whole of her budding womanhood had suddenly blossomed. Dollie was just twenty-two and the one thing she was quite sure of was that she was as much in love as it was possible to be. She thought about the young squire every moment she dared let her mind roam from her immediate work. When scalding milk or making butter she had to give some of her thought to the temperature of the milk and the watching for the slowly widening line round the yellow milk in the nearly boiling pan which showed when the Cornish cream had " come." In the mechanical making of butter, however, after it was weighed into big yellow pound mounds she could let her fancies free while she lustily beat it into shape and squeezed all the water out of it. To every pat went a delicious dream. Every squeeze of the butter between the wooden " hands " was a little sob of longing. Sometimes she laughed softly to herself as she glanced in the mirror in the dairy and saw how radiant her face was and how white her neat collar and apron against her blue dress. Often she hummed a waltz and took her dress in each hand as if for a minuet and moved slowly and softly to the thoughts in her heart. As she danced slowly round the large tables on which were the big pans of milk and cream she smiled happily. Had ever anyone had such kisses on their lips before, she wondered? Her nostrils dilated. She was thinking of the verbena scent about her lover's clothes and the faint odor about his hair. Why had she been so blessed? Life was too glorious for words, she thought, and love the one thing in it that mattered. No wonder she had forgotten Amos. What had he to do with this heavenly swirl of her thoughts wherein were kisses like a madness and glances like fire! She stopped dancing and leaned a moment against the white-washed wall. If only he would come in then and there and sit for a moment where Amos had sat! Only for a moment though. He would soon take her up in his strong arms and stop her mouth with his kisses till she could scarcely breathe. Her breath came quickly as she thought of it. He would ask no permission. He was not so foolish. He would just take what he wanted and what she longed to give and not stare in the silly way Amos did as if he was half afraid of her. How she would work and make all the butter possible so that she could buy that soft gray dress at Lander's shop. The mere thought of it made her slap the butter fiercely and quickly. So much butter, so many more yards for her dress. She meant to have it by next week in spite of the fact that her aunt had died at an awkward time. He might come any day, who could tell? The gray would do for half mourning, and she could put a black velvet bow under her new muslin and lace collar and that would make the dress look even nicer and not vex her mother. She only stopped for a glass of milk and a bit of saffron cake for her lunch, and by three o'clock forty pounds of butter had been made and placed in stiff white papers with the sides turned up like clean collars round the amber-colored lengths of butter.

"It would have been double but for the 'bucking,'" she said sadly. She was washing her hands before leaving her dairy when her mother spoke to her from the door.

"Come out, Dorothy Rosewarne, do."

Her mother always gave her the full baptismal name whenever anything was wrong or she was cross, so Dollie hurried out of the dairy. She went into the kitchen and saw Andrew Martin standing by the fire with a strange look on his face. Her mother was opening and shutting drawers rapidly. As she turned she faced her daughter.

"Dorothy Rosewarne," she said, "Amos be gone dead."

Dollie never moved. She had not in the least grasped the meaning of the words.

"Drownded two hours since," went on her mother. "I'm looking for winding sheets. Sakes, girl! ain't you a bit sorry? You was such companions. It's a whish job, sure enough."

Dollie stood where she was and never even opened her mouth. Her feet and legs felt like lead. She tried to speak, but only coughed.

"Give me a goody," she gasped at last. "My throat be dry."

Her mother hunted in a box on the chimney piece and gave her a bit of broken peppermint. Dolly bit it up and said how strong it was, and she wondered if they heard her for her voice seemed so far away. She noticed a big inkspot on the table and asked who had done it. No one answered.

"What took him?" she demanded as Andrew Martin stared first at the table and then at her.

"Nobody knows," said Martin. "He went out all alone and Jim Stevens was looking out to sea soon after and he saw through his long glasses that a boat had gone keel up and a man was seemly clinging to it. They got to him faster than speech can tell, but he was dead and blood was all about his mouth."

"Blood!" cried Dollie, and a dreadful pain came in the back of her neck and at the top of her head.

"Iss!" said Andrew Martin. "We found out the meanin' of that by and by. When Amos come to the quay for his boat we asked him what was wrong. He'd a handkerchief to his mouth.

"'Tooth out,' he said."

"His teeth were so—so—white," stammered Dollie.

"Iss! grand, sure enough!" said Andrew. "He were only boasting the other day that he'd never had one out and never had no pain in them. Dr. Mayne went to see the chemist after he'd viewed the body. He gave a queer account of Amos. He thought he'd gone mad, he said."

"Mad!" cried Mrs. Hosking. "Amos mad! A sounder lad never put foot into his mother's knitted stockings."

"I quite thinks with you, Mrs. Hosking," said Andrew. "I'm only telling you what he said when he showed the doctor the tooth."

"What was wrong with the tooth?" asked Dollie as a horrid pain nipped her in her left side.

"There was nothing wrong, that was just the queer part," said Andrew. "He said as how Amos had come to him and said 'pull out my tooth, please,' and the dentist asked him which one was paining, and he said Amos laughed in a funny way and said 'that's what I want it to do.' Mr. Kenyon told Amos to open his mouth, and when the poor lad pointed to a big double fanger the dentist said he never tugged so hard in his life and that Amos never so much as groaned! 'No, young man,' he said to him afterwards when Amos wanted to know how much it was, 'I'll take no money. Your pluck is payment enough. Be careful you don't catch cold. What you wanted a grand tooth like that out for baffles me.' He said Amos had a very stern look on him at the time, but he thought it was because of the jerk he'd given him, for he said he had nearly pulled his head off."

Dollie had listened with her mouth a little open and her head on one side. The whole meaning of things had suddenly changed for her as she realized that at the moment her impulse was to run to Amos himself and ask what it meant. She had always turned to him about everything. A feeling of terror crept over her. Where was Amos? Why was he not there to explain and to help? Her habit of grumbling at him returned. Why was he not here to comfort her? Why had he died? What was she to do? What had she done? At this thought shivers ran down her back and she shook like a willow in the wind. Her teeth chattered and she nearly fell.

"Steady, girl!" said Mrs. Hosking, "you're feeling it after all. You was playmates, sure enough. Fortitude be a solace in the face of sudden death, for it's got to be met."

"Amos, Amos!" whispered Dollie.

"It ain't no manner of use calling, Dorothy Rosewarne," said Mrs. Hosking. "Amos be passed round land and out of earshot."

"They do say, down-a-long," said Andrew, "as he did it on purpose."

Dollie moved to a chair close by and sat down. She had never noticed before that Andrew had stubbly hair growing out of his ears. Her eyes were riveted on them as she asked mechanically: "What for?"

"Nobody will reckon that up," said Andrew. "A more God-fearin', civil-spoken neighbor never breathed than Amos Trewin. He might 'ave been took faintey when he was puttin' up the sail of his boat seein' as he lost so much blood, but no one will ever make me believe he did it purposely. His face be peaceful enough, but we closed down the eyes for they'd a rare and pitiful look in them. Give me the winding sheets, Mrs. Hosking, and let me go."

Dollie walked over to the big kitchen grate and poked the fire. Then she mechanically put out her hands. Her mother noticed the action.

"It be rare and cold for just on July and the dog days," she said, "and Death adds to it. My blessed Life! Who'd have thought Amos, of all people, would have been took, for I'll never believe he did this of his own free will! He were a man of men, was Amos. I thought once, Dollie, as you and him was sparking."

Dollie pushed the door of the grate with her foot. She wished she could stop the incessant twittering of birds outside and the silly hum of the bees on the jasmine by the window. A faint smell of honeysuckle made her feel quite sick, and the glare of the sun made her wish it was night. There seemed nothing to do and nothing left anywhere. Never once had the thought of the young squire crossed her mind.

When her mother suggested, two days later, that it was only neighborly to go and see Amos in his coffin, Dollie began to realize something of what had befallen her. The dreariness of a desert seemed about her. She was as incapable of going to see her lover dead as she had been of giving herself to him when he was alive. She knew now in a dull aching way that Amos was really a part of herself. She could not go and see herself dead. The thing was unimaginable. Dollie knew nothing about the law of affinity. All she did was to wonder if, when Amos declared they belonged to one another, this was what he meant and that they really were one person in two bodies. If not, why did she feel so strange and forlorn? Perhaps that was the very reason Amos had never "mazed" her. No one could maze themselves. She felt her own limbs were half dead already and her energy gone. Whatever she did, she did mechanically. The gray dress, the delicious kisses, her dancing and singing seemed far away things that did not matter now. She nearly quarreled with her mother the day he was buried, for she refused to go to the funeral. She fled to the woods instead. The faces of the neighbors and the semi-festivities of a village funeral grated on every nerve in her body. She had put on a white linen dress and a black bow and wandered from the atmosphere of death and mourning. She felt she would like to wear weeds, for a great tenderness was mingling with her dull ache for Amos. She felt she wished he knew how like a widow she felt. As she sat on the trunk of a tree with her hand shading her face from the sun she whispered her dead lover's name. A voice rang on the air.

"I've come at last, you see!"

Dollie jumped up from her seat by a fallen tree and before she could realize anything she was in a man's arms and her mouth was captured. She could not move. Kiss after kiss held her motionless and limp. Cecil Fairthorne was enraptured at her sudden yielding. She had almost fainted, he was afraid, from sudden joy. He wished she would look up and resist a little, as she did before, because it fed his passion and he knew delay was merely whetting his desires. He wanted this girl. He had come home the night before and by accident had found her in the very wood of their first love-making. He expected she often went there alone. He smiled at her infatuation and he owned his own was nearly as great. Dollie stirred his pulses as only one woman had ever done, and she was dead years ago. Dollie's purity and absurd unconsciousness of either good or evil fascinated him. He remembered her clinging kisses before—kisses that had almost sucked his prudence away. He had been wise all these weeks, but the memory of her had often made him restless. He meant to have her now and let consequences take care of themselves. He meant to have a June feast of her kisses. How ready she was! She was quiescent now, but he knew these moods in women. This lovely apathy was the languor of mid-summer, but implied the scorching heat and abandonment which was a part of nature's summer festival.

"Strange!" he whispered as he let her go and stood facing her. "How could I have stayed away all this time? I've read my newspaper every morning and yet I've missed this day after day."

Dollie did not speak. Her soul was speaking instead. What had befallen her? Her mouth was hurting from Cecil's kisses, and yet if ice had been pressed to them instead of his lips she could not have felt less responsive. Cecil smiled to himself. What magnificent actresses women were, he pondered. Nothing she could have done would have roused him more. She was fencing and he had made up his mind. The longer the delay, the more delicious the surrender.

"Come and sit down," he said happily. She seated herself at once where he pointed. He stood a moment looking down upon her.

"God!" he cried, "you women are the most intoxicating things in the whole world." He stretched out his arms and then flung them upwards and lengthways, showing the whiteness of shirt between his waistcoat and sleeve. "What a day, and what a beauty you are, my girl!"

He suddenly dropped his arms and put his hands in his pockets as he smiled at her and went on.

"If one did not love or hunt in this weather, one would soon go mad."

Dollie was looking steadily at him in a strangely wistful way.

"You're only mazing yourself," she said.

Cecil sat down by Dollie's side. How bewitching she was with her clean length of limb and her face rounded for kisses. He had almost forgotten the quality of her voice with the interrogative lilt of the Cornish at the end of her sentences. How full of natural charm she was! She had the ways of a lady, too, a lady born and bred. A sudden impulse mastered him.

"Would you marry me?"

"No!" she said.

Her answer was so cold and deliberate that he started even in the midst of wondering why he had already forgotten his prudence by such a question. He caught her hands.

"I'll give you three No's," he said merrily, "and then—"

She was carrying coquettishness to absurdity, for she did not look even flattered. He stopped and looked at her questioningly. She wrenched her hands from his and stood up.

"Leave me be, please," she said quietly.

The man laughed.

"Love never waits," he said.

"Love!" she cried. "Oh! don't!" There was a wail in her voice.

Cecil was growing a little bit impatient. Dalliance was one thing, rebellion quite another. Cecil Fairthorne was growing to regard himself as an adept in the gentle art of making love. The man who took a woman at her word instead of taking her was of course a fool. Every woman hated a tyrant in theory and adored him in practice. All was fair in these things—even force. His lips tightened.

"Look here, darling!" he cried. "I've not kept away for two months to be treated like this now." He swung forward and caught her to him. Dollie simply bit his arm, not fiercely, but deliberately.

"Leave go," she said sternly as she lifted her face and saw him wince.

"Not likely!" said Cecil hotly. "By Gad! your white young teeth can bite, my lady."

The pressure of her warm, lithe body, the pain of the bite, the sun, the belief in her need for surrender and his need to conquer, urged him to caresses which blended impudence with assurance. Dollie looked in his face, imprisoned as she was. What she saw there brought a cry of pain and terror. It was desire, but it was something else too which Dollie could not measure. It was something so fateful, so awesome, so devilish,—so it seemed to her,— that death and it got mixed in her fear of this man and she thought he was going to kill her.

As if in answer to her thought, for she was too hysterical to speak, he bent over her face and almost whispered in her ear:

"It is inevitable. There is no escape for either of us. You

might as well try to bite iron into shape as change me now." He forced her backwards, his arms still holding her. Every breath in her seemed drawn from some unknown depth. She felt herself sinking—sinking into some horrible nightmare of imprisonment where even her voice forsook her. She sank toward the ground and he let her lie on the moss-covered earth with his arms still round her. A smile of triumph broke the tension of his face.

"Say you're happy, girl," he whispered.

She was so torn with terror that she seemed to cease breathing, but she made frantic movements with her hands and body in order to try to escape. This only goaded him to frenzy.

"You tigress!" he cried. "Delicious, maddening tigress, but you're caged at last. Nothing can save you now, and you know you love it—love it." He unlocked his arms for a moment and knelt on the ground for a second to recover himself. Dollie leaped to her feet and tried to run, but her limbs were heavy and the terror in her heart kept her standing like a wild animal at bay. Cecil flung himself upon her and in less time than can be imagined a primitive fight of the man for the woman he had stolen had begun. Dollie could never quite recall the few moments it lasted. She only knew she had to give some lame excuse of narrow lanes in unknown by-paths in the woods she knew by heart, to account for her torn dress and bruised hands. A wild bull, she had explained, had followed her and frightened her into places she had never known before. It was destruction to her clothes, bruises on her flesh or a horrible mutilation and death, she had added, and her word had never been questioned.

Cecil Fairthorne had reverted to the methods by which we imagine our savage ancestors showed their love of a woman by knocking her down and slaking their own thirst regardless of any protest from the captured. Dollie, in one tremendous realization, grasped at last the whole situation. Intuitive woman as she was, she knew force now was of no avail from her side of the conflict. She tried subterfuge and pleaded for time and mercy. The answer was virile enough.

"The time is now!" said Cecil. "Mercy is what a woman in love, loathes."

The word " loathes " roused her. Where had she heard it lately? Why did it hurt like these kisses hurt? Oh! how frightened she was! Would he never let her go? Her hair was all down her face like fire. Both their breaths were coming in long, suffocating gasps, hers from terror, his from desire. A sudden jerk of his hands away from her made them both reel. She fell and he stood over her laughing as only those laugh who conquer for self and without glory. He stood a second and she lay prone, suffocating with terror as she watched his next movement. " Amos, Amos, save me! " she wailed.

What had happened? She never knew. She heard Cecil mutter something and stand still with his hand over his eyes. She took her moment and like one of the swallows of a late summer she fled and never stopped till she reached her home. No one was back from the funeral nor were they likely to be yet. She locked herself in her room and took out the key. She knelt down, but said no prayer. Nothing would come into her head. She felt very dumb and faint. She poured out some water from the bottle on her little washstand and drank it. Then she opened the window and shivered. A sudden thought came to her. She drew a galvanized bath from under her bed and half filled it with cold water. She undressed slowly, thinking of nothing but just getting her sponge and soap and whether she had brought in her towels which were drying on the currant bushes. She bathed and put on clean clothes and the blue dress Amos loved so, and then she knelt again and found she could pray. A skylark outside was filling the air with his song. A great peace stole over her.

" My own Love," she said softly, at last, just as if Amos was there. Somehow she felt he was. She tidied her room, put her torn clothes in the washing basket and sat at the open window. The long, black uneven line of mourners returning to Mrs. Trewin's cottage could not see her, but she saw them. Her blue dress and white pinafore would have shocked them. Amos always loved her in her " grown up pinney," as he called it, but neither it nor the dress belonged to funeral feasts. The whole intricate meaning of love and desire was unfolded to Dollie now. So much she had heard and seen in her short life stood clearly out to her at last. The frantic struggle of the afternoon, the tension of flight and ultimate safety, the

cleansing by the cold water and the deliverance following her prayer
had turned Life, Love and Death into definite things which had been
faced and understood. Love and Death were mostly to do with
Amos, thought Dollie. Life seemed quite a separate thing, a thing
of struggle and fear needing great patience and prayerfulness.
She felt very wise and very grown up and caught herself pitying
all the girls she knew.

"They'm all giddy with foolish hopes," she said. "Perhaps,
like me, they'll never know their right hand from their left till both
are tied fast."

Dollie went to a little drawer and drew out a photograph of
Amos when he was a small boy. Her mouth softened as she looked
at it. The big wide eyes and square mouth made the tears come.
At last she sobbed quietly. His large hat with strings and two
enormous bows of silk over his ears made her put her hand to her
heart. Were many people as foolish as she had been, she wondered?
Did lots of folk run after "fancical" things and let real things go
by? ‧ She put the photograph back in her drawer and took out a
clean handkerchief instead from a little case half filled with dry lav-
ender. Perhaps she was letting something real slip now by sitting
there in a blue dress when her mother expected her to go to the funeral tea and help things through for Mrs. Trewin? She was just
thinking of herself again. That would never do. She hurriedly
changed into an old black dress she had not worn since she had been
back from London, and went downstairs and across to the cottage
where Amos had lived. The guests were preparing to go, but lingered a little when Dollie appeared.

"Two things do never happen but a third do follow," Andrew
Martin was saying. "The young squire be the second disaster this
week, and they two will be followed by some third trouble, sure
enough."

"The young squire? What of him?" asked Dollie sharply.

Andrew placed his hands on his knees and looked at Dollie. "He
can't seemly give no account of the thing himself, but Doctor says
as it looks a bit like sunstroke and a bit like blindness, but he hopes
it is neither and that it will pass."

"What happened?" asked Dollie indifferently. Cecil Fairthorne had become a stranger to her in a few hours, so completely can passion die when love deals the blow.

"He were found faintey in Seller's Copse," said Andrew. "One of his keepers happened on him. The young squire said all he knew of it, when he got a bit himself, was that a flash of lightning fiercer than he'd ever seen nearly blinded him as he was standing looking at something in the air. The funny part in the concern is that there was not a cloud in the sky in the afternoon. The young squire swears there was no thunder with the flash, but may be he got faint and does not remember much."

"It might have been a sign," said Mrs. Trewin.

"A sign Amos lives perhaps," said Dollie quietly, "as it happened at his buryin'!"

"He'd prove that to we, not to the squire, Dorothy Rosewarne," said Mrs. Hosking. "There'd be no meanin' in that, for signs be tokens. Now if it had come to you it would have been more reasonable." There was a suspicion of banter even in her funereal tone. "To take the sight away from a young man as Amos did not even know would have no meaning at all."

"What blinds one may give sight to another," said Dollie softly.

"Now that's the sort of saying poor Amos might have made use of," said Andrew Martin.

THE MYSTERY OF "FIONA MACLEOD" *

RICHARD LE GALLIENNE

In the fascinating memoir of her husband, which Mrs. William Sharp has written with so much dignity and tact, and general biographic skill, she dwells with particular fondness of recollection on the two years of their life at Phenice Croft, a charming cottage they had taken in the summer of 1892 at Rudgwick in Sussex, seven miles from Horsham, the birthplace of Shelley. Still fresh in my memory is a delightful visit I paid them there, and I was soon afterwards to recall with special significance a conversation I had with Mrs. Sharp, as four of us walked out one evening after dinner in a somewhat melancholy twilight, the glow-worms here and there trimming their ghostly lamps by the wayside, and the nightjar churring its hoarse lovesong somewhere in the thickening dusk.

" Will," Mrs. Sharp confided to me, was soon to have a surprise for his friends in a fuller and truer expression of himself than his work had so far attained, but the nature of that expression Mrs. Sharp did not confide—more than to hint that there were powers and qualities in her husband's make-up that had hitherto lain dormant, or had, at all events, been but little drawn upon.

Mrs. Sharp was thus vaguely hinting at the future " Fiona Macleod," for it was at Rudgwick, we learn, that that so long mysterious literary entity sprang into imaginative being with *Pharais*. *Pharais* was published in 1894, and I remember that early copies of it came simultaneously to myself and Grant Allen, with whom I was then staying, and how we were both somewhat *intrigué* by a certain air of mystery which seemed to attach to the little volume. We were both intimate friends of William Sharp, but I was better acquainted with Sharp's earlier poetry than Grant Allen, and it was my detection in *Pharais* of one or two subtly observed natural images, the use of which had previously struck me in one of his

---

* *William Sharp* (*Fiona Macleod*). A Memoir, compiled by his wife, Elizabeth A. Sharp. (Duffield & Co.)
The Writings of Fiona Macleod. Uniform edition. Arranged by Mrs. William Sharp. (Duffield & Co.)

Romantic Ballads and Poems of *Phantasy*, that brought to my mind in a flash of interpretation that Rudgwick conversation with Mrs. Sharp, and thus made me doubly certain that "Fiona Macleod" and William Sharp were one, if not the same. Conceiving no reason for secrecy, and only too happy to find that my friend had fulfilled his wife's prophecy by such fuller and finer expression of himself, I stated my belief as to its authorship in a review I wrote for the London *Star*. My review brought me an urgent telegram from Sharp, begging me, for God's sake, to shut my mouth—or words to that effect. Needless to say, I did my best to atone for having thus put my foot in it, by a subsequent severe silence till now unbroken; though I was often hard driven by curious inquirers to preserve the secret which my friend afterwards confided to me.

When I say "confided to me," I must add that in the many confidences William Sharp made to me on the matter, I was always aware of a reserve of fanciful mystification, and I am by no means sure, even now, that I, or any of us—with the possible exception of Mrs. Sharp—know the whole truth about "Fiona Macleod." Indeed it is clear from Mrs. Sharp's interesting revelations of her husband's temperament that "the whole truth" could hardly be known even to William Sharp himself; for, very evidently, in "Fiona Macleod" we have to deal not merely with a literary mystification, but with a psychological mystery. Here it is pertinent to quote the message written to be delivered to certain of his friends after his death: "This will reach you," he says, "after my death. You will think I have wholly deceived you about Fiona Macleod. But, in an intimate sense this is not so, though (and inevitably) in certain details I have misled you. Only, it is a mystery. I cannot explain. Perhaps you will intuitively understand or may come to understand. 'The rest is silence.' Farewell. WILLIAM SHARP."

"It is only right, however, to add that I, and I only, was the author—in the literal and literary sense—of all written under the name of 'Fiona Macleod.'"

"Only it is a mystery. I cannot explain." Does "I cannot explain" mean "I must not explain," or merely just what it says? I am inclined to think it means both; but, if so, the "must not" would refer to the purely personal mystification on which, of course, none would desire to intrude, and the " cannot " would refer to that psychological mystery which we are at liberty to investigate.

William Sharp's explanation to myself—as I believe to others of his friends—was to the same tenor as this posthumous statement. He and he only had actually *written* the " Fiona Macleod " fantasies and poems, but—yes! there was a real Fiona Macleod as well. She was a beautiful cousin of his, living much in solitude and dreams, and seldom visiting cities. Between her and him there was a singular spiritual kinship, which by some inexplicable process, so to say, of psychic collaboration, had resulted in the writings to which he had given her name. They were hers as well as his, his as well as hers. Several times he even went so far as to say that Miss Macleod was contemplating a visit to London, but that her visit was to be kept a profound secret, and that he intended introducing her to three of his friends and no more—George Meredith, W. B. Yeats, and myself. Probably he made the same mock-confidence to other friends, as a part of his general scheme of mystification. On one occasion, when I was sitting with him in his study, he pointed to the framed portrait of a beautiful woman which stood on top of a revolving book-case, and said " That is Fiona! " I affected belief, but, rightly or wrongly, it was my strong impression that the portrait thus labeled was that of a well-known Irish lady prominently identified with Home Rule politics, and I smiled to myself at the audacious white lie. Mrs. Sharp, whose remembrance of her husband goes back to " a merry, mischievous little boy in his eighth year, with light-brown curly hair, blue-gray eyes, and a laughing face, and dressed in a tweed kilt," tells us that this " love not only of mystery for its own sake, but of mystification also " was a marked characteristic of his nature—a characteristic developed even in childhood by the necessity he always felt of hiding away from his companions that visionary side of his life which was almost painfully vivid with him, and the sacredness of which in late years he felt compelled to screen under his pseudonym.

That William Sharp's affirmation of an actual living and breathing " Fiona Macleod " was however virtually true is confided by this significant and illuminating passage in Mrs. Sharp's biography. Mrs. Sharp is speaking of a sojourn together in Rome during the spring of 1891, in which her husband had experienced an unusual exaltation and exuberance of vital and creative energy.

"There, at last," she says, "he had found the desired incentive towards a true expression of himself, in the stimulus and sympathetic understanding of the friend to whom he dedicated the first of the books published under his pseudonym. This friendship began in Rome and lasted throughout the remainder of his life. And though this new phase of his work was at no time the result of collaboration, as certain of his critics have suggested, he was deeply conscious of his indebtedness to this friend, for—as he stated to me in a letter of instructions, written before he went to America in 1896, concerning his wishes in the event of his death—he realized that it was 'to her I owe my development as "Fiona Macleod," though in a sense of course that began long before I knew her, and indeed while I was still a child,' and that, as he believed, 'without her there would have been no "Fiona Macleod."' Because of her beauty, her strong sense of life and of the joy of life; because of her keen intuitions and mental alertness, her personality stood for him as a symbol of the heroic women of Greek and Celtic days, a symbol that, as he expressed it, unlocked new doors in his mind and put him 'in touch with ancestral memories' of his race. So, for a time, he stilled the critical, intellectual mood of William Sharp to give play to the development of this new-found expression of subtle emotions, towards which he had been moving with all the ardor of his nature."

From this statement of Mrs. Sharp one naturally turns to the dedication of *Pharais* to which she refers, finding a dedicatory letter to "E. W. R." dealing for the most part with "Celtic" matters, but containing these more personal passages:—

"Dear friend," the letter begins, "while you gratify me by your pleasure in this inscription, you modestly deprecate the dedication to you of this study of alien life—of that unfamiliar island-life so alien in all ways from the life of cities, and, let me add, from that of the great mass of the nation to which, in the communal sense, we both belong. But in the Domhan-Tòir of friendship there are resting-places where all barriers of race, training, and circumstances fall away in dust. At one of these places we met, a long while ago, and found that we loved the same things, and in the same way."

The letter ends with this: "There is another Pàras (Paradise) than that seen of Alastair of Innisròn—the Tir-Nan-Oigh of friendship. Therein we both have seen beautiful visions and dreamed dreams. Take, then, out of my heart, this book of vision and dream."

"Fiona Macleod," then, would appear to be the collective name given to a sort of collaborative Three-in-One mysteriously working together: an inspiring Muse with the initials E. W. R.; that psychical "other self" of whose existence and struggle for expression William Sharp had been conscious all his life; and William Sharp, general *littérateur*, as known to his friends and reading public. "Fiona Macleod" would seem to have always existed as a sort of spiritual prisoner within that comely and magnetic earthly tenement of clay known as William Sharp, but whom William Sharp had been powerless to free in words, till, at the wand-like touch of E. W. R.—the creative stimulus of a profound imaginative friendship—a new power of expression had been given to him—a power of expression strangely missing from William Sharp's previous acknowledged writings.

To speak faithfully, it was the comparative mediocrity, and occasional even positive badness, of the work done over his own name that formed one of the stumbling-blocks to the acceptance of the theory that William Sharp *could* be "Fiona Macleod." Of course, his work had been that of an accomplished widely-read man of letters, his life of Heine being perhaps his most notable achievement in prose; and his verse had not been without intermittent flashes and felicities, suggestive of smouldering poetic fires, particularly in his *Sospiri di Roma;* but, for the most part, it had lacked any personal force or savor, and was entirely devoid of that magnetism with which William Sharp was so generously endowed. In fact, its disappointing inadequacy was a secret source of distress to the innumerable friends who loved him with a deep attachment to which the many letters making one of the delightful features of Mrs. Sharp's biography bear witness. In himself William Sharp was so prodigiously a personality, so conquering in the romantic flamboyance of his sun-like vitality, so overflowing with the charm of a finely sensitive, richly nurtured temperament, so essentially a poet in all he felt and did and said, that it was impossible patiently to accept his writings as any fair expression of himself. He was, as we say, so much more than his books—so immeasurably and delightfully more—that, compared with himself, his books practically amounted to nothing; and one was inclined to say of him in one's heart, as one does sometimes say of such imperfectly articulate artistic natures: "What a pity he troubles to write at all! Why not be satisfied with being William Sharp? Why spoil 'William Sharp' by this inadequate and misleading translation?"

The curious thing, too, was that the work he did over his own name, after "Fiona Macleod" had escaped into the freedom of her own beautiful individual utterance, showed no improvement in quality, no marks of having sprung from the same mental womb where it had lain side by side with so fair a sister. But, of course, one can readily understand that such work would naturally lack spontaneity of impulse, having to be done, more or less, against the grain, from reasons of expediency: so long as "Fiona Macleod" must remain a secret, William Sharp must produce something to show for himself, in order to go on protecting that secret, which would, also, be all the better kept by William Sharp continuing in his original mediocrity. Of this dual activity, Mrs. Sharp thus writes with much insight:—

"From then till the end of his life," she says, "there was a continual play of the two forces in him, or of the two sides of his nature: of the intellectually observant, reasoning mind—the actor, and of the intuitively observant, spiritual mind—the dreamer, which differentiated more and more one from the other, and required different conditions, different environment, different stimuli, until he seemed to be two personalities in one. It was a development which, as it proceeded, produced a tremendous strain on his physical and mental resources, and at one time between 1897-8 threatened him with a complete nervous collapse. And there was for a time distinct opposition between those two natures which made it extremely difficult for him to adjust his life, for the two conditions were equally imperative in their demands upon him. His preference, naturally, was for the intimate creative work which he knew grew out of his inner self; though the exigencies of life, his dependence on his pen for his livelihood, and moreover, the keen active interest 'William Sharp' took in all the movements of the day, literary and political, at home and abroad, required of him a great amount of applied study and work,"

The strain must indeed have been enormous, and one cannot but feel that much of it was a needless, even trivial " expense of spirit," and regret that, when " Fiona Macleod " had so manifestly come into her own, William Sharp should have continued to keep up the mystification, entailing as it did such an elaborate machinery of concealment, not the least taxing of which must have been the necessity of keeping up " Fiona Macleod's " correspondence as well as his own. Better, so to say, to have thrown William Sharp overboard, and to have reserved the energies of a temperament almost abnormally active, but physically delusive and precarious, for the finer productiveness of " Fiona Macleod." But William Sharp deemed otherwise. He was wont to say " Should the secret be found out, Fiona dies," and in a letter to Mrs. Thomas A. Janvier,—she and her husband being among the earliest confidants of his secret—he makes this interesting statement: " I can write out of my heart in a way I could not do as William Sharp, and indeed I could not do so if I were the woman Fiona Macleod is supposed to be, unless veiled in scrupulous anonymity. . . . This rapt sense of oneness with nature, this *cosmic ecstasy* and elation, this wayfaring along the extreme verges of the common world, all this is so wrought up with the romance of life that I could not bring myself to expression by my outer self, insistent and tyrannical as that need is . . . My truest self, the self who is below all other selves, and my most intimate life and joys and sufferings, thoughts, emotions and dreams, *must* find expression, yet I cannot save in this hidden way . . . "

Later he wrote: " Sometimes I am tempted to believe I am half a woman, and so far saved as I am by the hazard of chance from what a woman can be made to suffer if one let the light of the common day illuminate the avenues and vistas of her heart . . . "

At one time, I thought that William Sharp's assumption of a feminine pseudonym was a quite legitimate device to steal a march on his critics, and to win from them, thus disguised, that recognition which he must have been aware he had failed to win in his own person. Indeed, it is doubtful whether if he had published the " Fiona Macleod " writings under his own name, they would have received fair critical treatment. I am very sure that they would not; for there is quite a considerable amount of so-called " criticism " which is really foregone conclusion based on personal prejudice, or biassed preconception, and the refusal to admit (employing a homely image) that an old dog does occasionally learn new tricks. Many well-known writers have resorted to this device, sometimes with considerable success. Since reading Mrs. Sharp's biography, however, I conclude that this motive had but little, if any, influence on William Sharp, and that his statement to Mrs. Janvier must be taken as virtually sincere.

A certain histrionism, which was one of his charms, and is inseparable from imaginative temperaments, doubtless had its share in his consciousness of that " dual nature " of which we hear so much, and it is difficult sometimes to take his presentation of it with " Celtic " seriousness. Take, for example, this letter to his wife, when, having left London, precipitately, in response to the call of the Isles, he wrote: " The following morning we (for a kinswoman was with me) stood on the Greenock pier waiting for the Hebridean steamer, and before long were landed on an island, almost the nearest we could reach that I loved so well." Mrs. Sharp dutifully comments: " the ' we ' who stood on the pier at Greenock is himself in his dual capacity; his ' kinswoman ' is his other self." Later he writes, on his arrival in the Isle of Arran: " There is something of a strange excitement in the knowledge that two people are here: so intimate and yet so far off. For it is with me as though Fiona were asleep in another room. I catch myself listening for her step sometimes, for the sudden opening of a door. It is unawaredly that she whispers to me. I am eager to see what she will do—particularly in *The Mountain Lovers*. It seems passing strange to be here with her alone at last . . . "

I confess that this strikes me disagreeably. It is one thing to be conscious of a " dual personality "—after all, consciousness of dual personality is by no means uncommon, and it is a commonplace that, spiritually, men of genius are largely feminine—but it is another to dramatize one's consciousness in this rather childish fashion. There seems more than a suspicion of pose in such writing: though one cannot but feel that William Sharp was right in thinking that the real " Fiona Macleod " was asleep at the moment. At the same time, William Sharp seems unmistakably to have been endowed with

what I suppose one has to call " psychic " powers—though the word
has been " soiled with all ignoble use "—and to be the possessor in a
considerable degree of that mysterious " sight " or sixth sense attributed to men and women of Gaelic blood.   Mrs. Sharp tells a cu-
rions story of his mood immediately preceding that flight to the
Isles of which I have been writing.   He had been haunted the night
before by the sound of the sea.   It seemed to him that he heard it
splashing in the night against the walls of his London dwelling.
So real it had seemed that he had risen from his bed and looked out
of the window, and even in the following afternoon, in his study, he
could still hear the waves dashing against the house.   " A telegram
had come for him that morning," writes Mrs. Sharp, " and I took it
to his study.   I could get no answer.   I knocked, louder, then
louder,—at last he opened the door with a curiously dazed look in
his face.   I explained.   He answered: ' Ah, I could not hear you for
the sound of the waves!' "

His last spoken words have an eerie suggestiveness in this connection.   Writing of his death on the 12th of December, 1905,
Mrs. Sharp says: " About three o'clock, with his devoted friend Alec
Hood by his side, he suddenly leant forward with shining eyes and
exclaimed in a tone of joyous recognition, ' Oh, the beautiful
" Green Life " again!', and the next moment sank back in my arms
with the contented sigh, ' Ah, all is well!' "

" The green life " was a phrase often on Sharp's lips, and stood
for him for that mysterious life of elemental things to which he was
almost uncannily sensitive, and into which he seemed able strangely
to merge himself, of which too his writings as " Fiona Macleod "
prove him to have " invisible keys."   It is this, so to say, conscious
pantheism, this kinship with the secret forces and subtle moods of
nature, this responsiveness to her mystic spiritual " intimations,"
that give to those writings their peculiar significance and value.   In
the external lore of nature William Sharp was exceptionally learned.
Probably no writer in English, with the exceptions of George Meredith
and Grant Allen, was his equal here, and his knowledge had been
gained as such knowledge can only be gained, in that receptive period
of an adventurous boyhood of which he has thus written: " From fifteen to eighteen I sailed up every loch, fjord, and inlet in the Western

Highlands and islands, from Arran and Colonsay to Skye and the Northern Hebrides, from the Rhinns of Galloway to the Ord of Sutherland. Wherever I went I eagerly associated myself with fishermen, sailors, shepherds, gamekeepers, poachers, gypsies, wandering pipers, and other musicians." For two months he had "taken the heather" with, and had been "star-brother" and "sun-brother" to, a tribe of gypsies, and in later years he had wandered variously in many lands, absorbing the wonder and the beauty of the world. Well might he write to Mrs. Janvier: "I have had a very varied, and, to use a much abused word, a very romantic life in its internal as well as in its external aspects." Few men have drunk so deep of the cup of life, and from such pure sky-reflecting springs, and if it be true, in the words of his friend Walter Pater, that "to burn ever with this hard gem-like flame, to maintain this ecstasy, is success in life," then indeed the life of William Sharp was a nobly joyous success.

And to those who loved him it is a great happiness to know that he was able to crown this ecstasy of living with that victory of expression for which his soul had so long travailed, and to leave behind him not only a lovely monument of star-lit words, but a spiritual legacy of perennial refreshment, a fragrant treasure-house of recaptured dreams, and hallowed secrets of the winds of time: for such are *The Writings of 'Fiona Macleod.'*

THE NEW ART IN PARIS

MARIUS DE ZAYAS

I THOUGHT I had formed a complete idea of the movement in French Art, principally in so far as painting was concerned, through the exhibitions that the Photo-Secession of New York held of the works of some of the artists who belong to this movement. There, I studied their works as well as the impressions they produced on the American public, and the judgments that the art critics published in the New York press. But I was mistaken. In spite of the efforts of Mr. Steichen, who selects in Paris the works of this kind that are shown in New York, and in spite of the heroism of Mr. Stieglitz, who gives them frank hospitality, both having undertaken this enterprise for art's sake, and to break the chains that tie the spirit of the artists to the rock of the Academy, the exhibitions of the Photo-Secession give but a faint idea of the intensity of this movement.

That is why, as soon as I arrived in Paris, I hastened to ratify my opinion, profiting by the excellent opportunity offered me by the " Salon d'Automne," which had just opened, and in which I could see in ensemble, what I had only seen in small fragments in the New York exhibitions. At the same time I had the opportunity to see if the critics here were as intransient, and if the French public was as excited as the American over the insurrectionary movement of the artists.

I must begin by telling my readers that the Society of the Salon d'Automne is legally constituted, and its object is to further, from the general point of view, the development of fine arts, in all the manifestations of painting, sculpture, engraving, architecture, and applied arts, holding to that end an annual exhibition which takes place in the autumn, from which it derives its name.

This exposition takes place in the so-called Grand Palais of the Champs Elysées, from the first of October to the eighth of November, and in it may participate both French and foreign artists, with one restriction: that the works sent have not been exhibited before in any of the Paris Salons.

So frank and noble is the hospitality offered to the artists foreign to the association, that its regulations limit the works of its associates to two contributions per section and place no restriction upon those of the non-associates, the object being to allow to all the young unknown talents, and to all the artistic efforts, an opportunity to manifest themselves freely.

I wanted first to get an idea of the ensemble, and afterwards to study the details, which is a system just as good as any other. But I could not understand anything. I looked, but did not see: it seemed to me as if I were in the Tower of Babel of painting, in which all the languages of technique, color, and subjects, were spoken in an incoherent and absurd manner, and I began to surmise that this Salon was nothing but a *charge d'atelier*, peculiar to the humorous artists. There were artists here from almost every part of the world, like Matisse, French; Matthes, German; Steichen, American; Bondy, Austrian; Borgeaud, Swiss; Borjeson, Swedish; Bottlik, Hungarian; Cardona, Spanish; Gill, English; Gottlieb, Polish; Halpert, Russian; Hohlenberg, Danish; Alcorta, Brazilian; and of many other nationalities.

Wearily I sat down on a bench, and closed my eyes. It seemed to me I was the victim of an atrocious nightmare. Everywhere I saw flocks of butterflies mixed with rare birds, with colossal vampires, and with other supernatural beings. And afterwards appeared a multitude of geometrical figures, curves, triangles, ellipses, squares, cones, rhombs, and I heard voices, which told me: " This is the head of a satyr; this is a torso of a nymph; this other is an arm; this succession of geometrical figures forms the faithful portrait of a woman of rare beauty; those octagonal spots constitute a landscape." That was an obsession.

But, was there not something more, besides that which I perceived in my rapid passage through the galleries?

The public increased, and increased. The galleries were full; every one was contemplating the pictures, some with abstraction, others with curiosity, and others with a mocking air. But no one was scandalized, no one protested in a loud voice; which made me meditate, and persuade myself that in these works there was something more than that which my first impression gave me.

I went through the galleries again, and I stopped before a group

in which a person of respectable appearance gave some explanations
to several people who listened to him with apparent pleasure.

" One must not make fun of what one cannot understand, only
because one cannot understand it. We must not laugh at the rules of
' cubism,' at the pyramids upon the parallelopipeds, nor at the theories that a triangle has an equal value in painting with a beautiful
blue, or an hexagonal with a burnt sienna. Worse things the philosophers of the Positivism make you swallow every day and you don't
protest. Let us put aside the exaggerations peculiar to all systems,
to every school which revolutionizes, seeking the truth either in the
future or in the past. This Salon is not a school properly speaking,
it is a neutral field for all the strugglers in art, and here is admitted
everything that is brought, without regard to the trademark. A man
may believe in the theory of ' cubism,' he must demonstrate here its
exactitude, or at least its conveniences. Another may believe in metaphysical painting, without form or contour, when he brings his work
here we will see what there is in it to impress us. This painting
could be taken for a plate of spinach, or for a sunset, that other one
could be called the *Rape of the Sabines,* as well as *A Family of Croco-
diles Sleeping their Siesta on the Banks of a River.* That does not
matter. This is only a question of optics, of conventionalism. What
matters is that the artist should tell us what he wanted to make, and
that we should find out if he accomplished it."

That was to me the thread of Ariadne. A very thin and fragile
thread, it is true, but, if I pulled not too strongly, it could help me out
of the labyrinth.

What are these people aiming at? To find the truth, not the
absolute truth, but the artistic truth, reproducing the outer nature as
they see it, if not through their temperament, at least through their
theories.

They want to go back to the past, to the primitive art, for they
consider it less conventional, more spontaneous, more like the truth, if
not more truthful.

But they are groping as if they were studying the ground before
entering fully into it. They are making rehearsals that shock us, because they are against all we have seen and learned. They find
massed against them the academic dogmas and their believers, who

are unable to think, to have their own ideas, and who repeat what they have heard, refusing to investigate anything that would disturb the opinions they have inherited.

I have gone several times to study this movement, which is to me more revolutionary than evolutionary, in which I have not yet found any manifestation that can convince me of having its source direct in nature. I do not know whether anything will come out of it; I do not dare to predict that it will pass, as a fashion does, in time. I do not become enthusiastic with the noisy applause and dithyrambs of the admirers of this revolution, nor do the affronts and insults of its deprecators impress me.

In art, as in politics, both manifestations on the part of the public are of no account, and the final result is the only one that counts. In every innovator there is something of a redeemer, and every redeemer is crucified by those he wants to redeem. This is a fatal law. Apotheosis may come later, for after the Calvary comes the Tabor; but, for the present, they have to undergo the *Via Crucis*, stopping at all its stations.

The main point of the fundamental idea of the founders of the Salon d'Automne is the development of the personality of each artist, emancipating them from the Academies, offering them all the necessary resources for its accomplishment.

But it seems to me that the artists have not known how to take advantage of this opportunity offered to them, and that in an unconscious way they are grouping themselves into a school. I notice that they are officiating at the altars of Greco, Cézanne and Gauguin, if not all, at least the majority of them. Perhaps this is due to the difficulty inherent in complete and sudden emancipation; the present is the fatal consequence of the past. Speaking from my personal point of view, the movement is a sequel, a new form of the primitive; it does not limit itself to painting and the other plastic arts, but extends itself to literature and music, as I have found in the same Salon d'Automne, where they have been giving Literary and Musical Matinées.

A long and narrow hall, somewhat dark, and very cold; a special audience, not very numerous, composed for the most part of the poets affiliated with the new school of *libre-versistes;* all with an air of mystic abstraction. Up front a kind of platform, on which the yellow light of two enormous lamps fights against the gray light that enters through the wide windows, making more undefined the dark shadows which move in this atmosphere. These shadows are the artists who are going to give conferences, or to read selected pieces of the most conspicuous apostles of the new literary creed.

I felt as if I were present at one of those mysterious sessions of the Eleusinian Priests, or in a " venta " of Carbonari, or at a religious ceremony of the primitive Christians in the Catacombs of Rome. It looked somewhat ghostly, somewhat mystic, like a masonic initiation: it looked like anything you wish, but like nothing that would bring to the imagination the idea of Parnassus, of Helicon, of Hippocrene, and Castalia.

No one speaks; they murmur: no one walks; they glide. The shadows which move up stage, whose names are favorably known, and applauded in the world of reality, are M. Joubé, of the Théâtre de l'Odéon; Mmes. René Rocher and Jouvey; Mlle. Blanche Albane, of the Théâtre Sarah Bernhardt; Mme. Marguerite Jules-Martin, and Mlle. Marcelle Schmidt.

How great is the influence of the atmosphere of a place! None of those professional actors, so full of action on the stage, remembered their profession; or perhaps they are so consummate that they remembered it only too well, and transformed body and soul, adapting them to their surroundings. They observed great parsimony of action; the body almost rigid, all the mimic concentrated in the face, all the gamut of passion left to the vocal organs alone.

Here are some of the suggestive titles of the poems, and the names of their authors, which figured on the programme: *Hymn to the Lie,* by Arennes; *The Dead,* by Batilliot; *Faetoente,* by Jean-Marc Bernard; *Pride,* by Billet; *In the Clear Nights,* by Clary; *The Dance of the Sparks,* by Dévigne; *The Transfigurators,* by Louis Martin; *The Glory,* by Martin; *Dawn upon Paris,* by Poinsot; *The Song of the Wind,* by Jean Robert; *The Verb,* and *The Love,* by D'Ivermont.

I don't know if it was the effect of the atmosphere I was in, or of the people I was surrounded by, or of the way in which the artists rendered the compositions, or of the true merit of them. The fact is that I felt deeply impressed with this necromantic literary session, with poetry, mostly melancholic, which reminded me of the Hebrew harps which hang from the Babylonic salices, through whose strings murmur the mournful breezes of the Euphrates.

It is a poetry in which there is more twilight than light; sensations rather than thoughts. It is not the work of energetic thinkers, but of neurasthenic dreamers, unprecise, vague, lovers of sorrow who seek in suffering the voluptuosities they cannot find in passion. These poets believe themselves incomprehensible, and they do not try to make themselves understood: they are ultra-sensitive, and they make us feel. They make music with words, and we shall see later that the musicians endeavor to play words with harmony. They neither rebel nor submit; they deliver themselves to contemplation, like a St. Lawrence who composes himself on his grate.

I have been unable to find out what kind of metrical art they have adopted. I perceive that their verses are dissimilar, some very long, like the hexameters, perhaps longer; others very short, of only four or five syllables; but all are of a perfect rhythm, and the recitation of them seems like a μελοποιία in which the accompaniment of the lyre can be guessed without being heard.

The men and women recited in the same diapason, the only difference was the tone.

I don't know what this poetry of tears and lamentations, mixture of all the feminine exquisiteness and all the desires of a virile soul, aims at. I don't know if this art is decaying, or rising. I have not had either time or wish to inquire if it violates the rules set by Boileau, or if it observes them rigorously. That does not matter; I know that it is an art whose object is emotion, and that it awakens, moves, and multiplies it. It makes me feel, and that is all I ask of it. It is something new and beautiful at the same time.

As I said before, the poets who are in this movement make music with words, and the musicians want to render words with harmony. The concerts given in the Grand Palais prove it. The composers I refer to, have also the tendency toward what they take for primitive art: they have no use for the established culture, combination, deformations, and returns to the musical themes. In a word, they declare themselves to be against the music they call scientific, and against the scholastic canons; entering without reserve into the

" autodidaxy," with an overflow of sensations, and without taking into consideration any of the other means of expression. P. Dupin is one of the apostles of this system, and in his *Sabina, Quatuor á cordes,* develops it extensively. He neglects the counterpoint, substituting for it the introduction of a musical entanglement of secondary melodies, which gives the illusion of a complex polyphony. Dupin believes that as far as the *quatuor á cordes* is concerned, he has created a new manner: the descriptive one. This is the main objective of the neologists.

I find the tendency still more accentuated in *Royauté,* a poem by Stuart Merrill, which initiates itself with the chime of the " grave bells " of the submerged town. The " King of the Olden Times " dreams of his submerged treasures, and of the vanity of his glory. . . But suddenly the trumpets of the Old Pride awaken. Afterwards everything becomes calm. It is the awaiting, outside of life, for the day in which " he will draw his sign in the sky." At last the heroic spirit appears: hope of conquests, thirst of victory. Then a melody difficult to define, is heard, and it cannot be known whether it is " the trumpets of the tempest," or " the iron bells " of the submerged city, tolling mournfully. I declare ingenuously that I did not understand a *single word* of this musical poem.

I comprehend better *The Lamentation of Ariadne,* a work by Madame de Noailles. These lamentations are exhaled musically, through screams of passion and despair, while the piano answers with the murmur of the wind through the trees.

According to my way of considering the fine arts, all tendency to make music either philosophical or descriptive is an offence against its inner nature. Music is not and cannot be more than sound, that is to say, melodies and harmonies, through which we can express affections, sensations, and passions. But there can never be demonstrated through it, either a mathematical theorism, or a philosophical principle, nor can a historical point be elucidated, nor can a landscape be described, if words are not added to it. The field of the domain of music is large enough without entering the fields of its sister arts.

I don't mean to imply that in this musical movement there is not a great deal of indisputable merit, which belongs essentially to music, without metaphysical distinctions of any kind.

After having seen and heard so much of these three arts, I consider what Paris is: a unique city; with a unique public, and with a unique soul.

In no other artistic centre of the world is there a greater liberality in making concessions to the thinking genius, nor are so many projects admitted to discussion, nor so many attempts and systems shown, without scandalizing the public, who do not listen to the outcry of the scholastic conventionalisms. Here any one who has an idea on art or science, can express it to the public without fear of persecution, being sure that someone will shelter, consider, examine, and weigh it, finishing by sanctioning, and even adopting it, if it shows true merit: if not, they prove it to be impracticable, unjust, or noxious, and exclude it.

But no one is denied a Tribune in which to speak, a Salon in which to exhibit, or a Hall in which to produce his musical creations. The public, supreme judge, not on account of its knowledge, but on account of the weight of its decision, is the one which pronounces the final sentence, reserving the right to revise it later.

This tolerance is based on a great artistic and scientific capacity, on an unrivaled knowledge, which constitutes the greatest glory of thinking France.

All these thoughts were in my mind when, leaving the Salon d'Automne, I was crossing the magnificent bridge of Alexander III, upon which a large multitude was standing, peering over the parapet of the Seine.

Those men and women, who like myself came from the galleries of the Grand Palais, with their souls shaken by the strong impressions caused by the paintings, by the recitations, or by the music, with their spirit full of new ideas and ideals, stopped, joining the idlers, to contemplate the waters of the river.

"How many fools there are in this, the most spiritual city in the world!" I said to myself. And without thinking, I also stopped, increasing the number of fools.

A gray river, a gray sky, a gray atmosphere. The last dashes of an autumnal light, of leaden color, showing in the distance the towers of Notre Dame. Carriages, automobiles, and all kinds of vehicles passing in all directions, on both sides of the river. Some small boats, used for carrying passengers, going up and down its waters, giving more life to them. . . .

No, those people were not fools: they were a part of the intellectual, contemplative Parisian people, who find in everything its true value. The river which swiftly and quietly flows on its course, is an idyl; the river that flows threatening destruction, is an epic strophe.

There, there was a picture, a poem, and a symphony; and the Parisian public knew how to see and appreciate that picture, that poem, and that symphony. Yes, only among these people can exist the Salon d'Automne, and the Museum of the Louvre, the Grand Opera and the Music Hall of the Grand Palais, the Academy and the School of *libre-versistes*. This is not a town, but a soul. This is not a people, but an intelligence.

ON WITH THE DANCE

SHAEMAS O SHEEL

Dancing has been the most deeply buried temple of all the arts amid the sands of desert days. There is a peculiar significance in this, for dancing is at once the most elementary of the arts and the one which belongs most truly to all men; that it of all has been most nearly lost epitomizes the tragedy of the general turning-away from art. And equally significant of the conditions upon which the arts may return is the fact that this most democratic of them all is returning to us by way of the example of a few highly-trained, specializing individuals. Progress, which is the virtue of change, has its immitigable laws just as tradition, which is the virtue of unchanging things, has its indecadent qualities. We can re-create an ancient art in modern times not in ancient ways, but in modern. That which under natural conditions was developed by all the people must be revived and restored under artificial conditions by a few specialists who shall be teachers.

The revival of dancing is also significant of the abiding, though often forgotten, need of the world for its arts, and of the strange immortality of the arts themselves. Within a very few years several great dancers have come to summon the world, who must have trained through long periods separately and without a common plan; yet with the effectiveness of a planned simultaneity they have appeared, as it were in a company. And the response of the public has been the welcome we give to an advent long desired.

My own introduction to this momentous movement was by way of the incomparably greatest of its exponents, Isadora Duncan. Perhaps but two or three other hours of my life have been as important to me as that in which I first saw her; one of those hours in which an invisible beneficent hand is known upon the helm of destiny. In that hour I sensed the manifold meanings and implications of the dance, and its beauties; since then I have studied it carefully and lovingly, and I venture to write about it because I am sure of its almost first importance to modern life.

Of Isadora Duncan I have written elsewhere at length. She is the greatest of the dancers, not because she does what they all do supremely well, but because she does a different thing, and one which is related to the works of the others as the teaching of a John Baptist or a Francis of Assisi is related to the preaching of a Chrysostom or a Fénelon; better, as the poetry of a Shakespeare is related to the verse of a Hood or a Praed. The dancing of Isadora Duncan is a great symbol, one of the few superlative artistic expressions of eternal spiritual glories. Her endowment is no mere talent for the consummation of exterior beauties; she has genius of the finest kind. One of the selected sibyls, to her is given wisdom and understanding. The deep disease of the soul of the world, its wasting, anæmic illness since it ate of the weeds of prudery and was torn by the tusks of brute supremacy and went astray on the hard roads of materialism, is known to her, and she has a great pity; and with devoted effort, through the consecrating trials of toil and rejection, she has fitted herself to be a physician of the spirit. She brings us pure delicate wine from the vineyard of beauty, and she will not mix and mingle with it any sharp strange bitters to sting our jaded taste. She comes garlanded with meadow-flowers, but they are from Arcady, and she will not wear the orchids that have beguiled us, as she thinks, too long. In her manner is nothing either of decadence or of the gigantic, splendid but futile mechanism of Wagner; she is of the company of Chopin, Mallarmé, Maeterlinck, Symons, Yeats, Debussy, all who have held to the slender infrangible cord of the eternal essential tradition. She recalls things that the most ancient memory of the mind had forgotten, and startles our forgotten spiritual memories from a sleep of centuries. What glorious things she makes the soul remember! Once we were young, and the leaping blades of our desire striking the granite facts of life lit lively fires of wonder; we were simple, so that when the moving beauty of nature and the joy of each other's company stirred us to ecstasies, we gave a free and natural expression to them: we danced: and we danced as the movements of waves and branches and the postures of hill and plain suggested, and as the exquisite beauties of our own bodies (actually known to us!) suggested. These memories take form in the dancing of Duncan; her curious, exquisite, subtle movements are as the drifting of a leaf over the ground, as the drifting of a mist over the still surface of a pool in the morning; but it is not only forms she recalls: the very state of the soul in that time is recovered, as we watch her, and once more we have a sense that hears the gods.

But it is not only the memory of innocence and wonder that this woman reveals; no less than the priestess of the purest rite is she a prophetess of the sublimest aspirations. In the forms of her work she does not restrict herself to Grecian dances, but interprets also Beethoven and Chopin; and the spiritual significance of her varied expressions, being consistently pure and great, is of eternal value. It were like losing the way to Olympus in loitering before a bas-relief of the gods to consider her work only as a memory and take from it no inspiration. Because—as I believe, having tested her work and failed to find a flaw—because Isadora Duncan is one of the great artists of all times, she has been able to become in her dances a symbol of the soul of man in its earthly maze; a visible form of the spirit's qualities and adventures, its wonders, fears, angers, joys, its loves, trials and triumphs. From her, for all that we seem so ill-attuned, even the most cultured of us dulled to such fine touches, we must receive much strength to aspiration and effort for beauty's sake: for, as she has proved,—what the poets always know—the soul of the race is not dead but sleeping, and wakes ever responsive to the true touch.

One who is often compared with Isadora Duncan is Maud Allan, and the comparison is natural as to external aspects, but with regard to spirit and significance there is no comparison, as there is no comparison between the poet of deep content as well as perfected form, and the-versifier who displays as great ingenuity of metre and rhyme for the mere illustration of a passing topic. Maud Allan is a beautiful woman, and perhaps the most graceful in motion of all living humanity. Besides these qualifications she has a great dramatic talent; and her accomplishment is the accomplishment of an actress using gestures and steps in place of speech. Her art I have elsewhere called dramatic dancing. She has no purpose of suggesting wonderful things, but only of making a flowing or rushing beauty before the eyes, or telling a definite story in an unmistakable pantomime. *A Vision of Salome,* which is a little silent play,

is most characteristic of her work, and proves her an intelligent
actress, but also proves the imperfection of her art-sense, else she
could never do both this and her Grecian dances.   More consistent
with the latter are her dances to the Peer Gynt music, but they are
also dramatic, not symbolic.   Her greatest achievement is the dance
to the music of the Death of Ase, wherein while wisely refraining
from an attempt to suggest the mother of Peer Gynt, yet building
up her individual interpretation in a purely dramatic way, she
sweeps the emotions, like the fingers of a master on the lower chords
of a lyre, to a tremendous climax.   But in vain shall we await a
whisper at the soul from Maud Allan's dancing; we should nevertheless be grateful for the boon of visible beauties of graceful motion
and posture.

    The art of Ruth St. Denis is also dramatic dancing, more
frankly avowed, taking the form of brief acts amid illustrative
stage-settings and a supporting company.   It is a little special art-
form, and since it is very beautiful and has its own suggestive qualities, we may be thankful for it, though it is not greatly pertinent to
a consideration of the revival of the dance.   It is a delightful memory, though not an inspiration or a hope.   The rites at the temple
of this subtle interpreter of Hindoo manners are varied, and not
for the senses only, but for the spirit.   An order of thought and
an order of imagination having for us the value of great difference
from our own are finely suggested, and we may from this little series
of stage-pictures and rhythmic dumb-shows gain some understanding of the strange sensuous sacrificial East—the East where sacrifice is garlanded and veiled in sensuousness, while the revels of sense
are understrained by the warning drums of sacrifice.   In the very
austerity of the Yogi's Attainment there is known the secret presence of sensuous beauty, as though it would not be denied part in
any service of truth; and the gross atmosphere of the Nautch revels
betrays a feverish futile effort to escape, in the obvious and carnal,
the inevitable presence of sacrifice in the very inner soul of each
reveler.   Other dances more subtly blend the two motives, especially
that splendid Dance of the Five Senses.   Here the goddess herself
is lured from her altar by the jewels and wine, the flowers and incense
of her service, and she dances, as these stir in turn each of her senses,

with the restrained intensity of bodily delight which only a woman of the Orient feels, and the end is utter weariness and complete renunciation. But this praise, which I cannot help paying, is a digression, for, in spite of her great bodily beauty and her delicate, courageous use of it, in spite of her skill as a dancer—I remember with delight the simple kicking step of the Dance of Sound—in spite of her fascinating suppleness—those flowing arms!—and her soothing plasticity under the rhythms of the music; in spite of her suggestion of a few secrets of the strange sensuous sacrificial East, Ruth St. Denis helps little in the preparation for a new advent of universal dancing.

It seems to me too that very little of general impulse toward this advent can be caught from the dancers of the ballet mode, though so charming and capable exponents of this have recently helped in the first service of awakening interest in the dance as a form of art. But the technique of the ballet is a specialized and artificial one admitting no adaptation to popular purposes, and indeed in part a technique of deformity and unhealthiness. The ballet-dancer is an entertainer only, a performer in the places where we take our pleasures indolently, post-prandially, merely as spectators. Adeline Genée, the petite and delicate Danish woman with so piquant a face and such delightful hair, though she triumphed over her environment—one of the most horrible managerial crimes of this commercial day having cast her like a pearl, or at least a flower, among swine—till she suggested fairy-tales and elvish things, yet could have inspired no one with a desire to help to right the wrong of our general neglect of the dance. As to Anna Pavlowa and Mikail Mordkin—

I think that Pavlowa is greater than Genée precisely in the degree in which she is a more beautiful, a more perfectly proportioned woman. I think that Genée is greater than Pavlowa precisely in the degree in which her more winsome personality induces in her spectators a greater fascination—an exquisite fascination that is a real affection. In point of technique the two are equal; the greater prestige of the Russian woman is the adventitious effect of her connection with so impressive an institution as the Imperial Russian Ballet. It is true that Genée has not discovered to us an ability to perform other than ballet-dances; but there is no reason to believe that she could not, and on the other hand Pavlowa and Mordkin, though capable of a very high art, continue to dance very wretched ballets, and to produce programmes of a hybrid and pernicious character. While it is impossible for me to understand how an audience of cultured people can receive an illusion of artistic pleasure from an incongruous performance in which a few beautiful moments are lost in hours of error, I see that such things happen, and I greatly fear that Pavlowa and Mordkin are becoming dangerous obstacles to the progress of the revival of dancing, and to the induction of a wider understanding of the art's greater meanings. It is unfortunate, for Mordkin's illustration of the grace of motion possible to men, though lacking both subtlety and breadth, is yet salutary; and Pavlowa has such beauty and charm, and such splendid technique, that it is distressing to register anything against her. But these two have chosen to mingle ballet-dancing and dramatic dancing in such a way that the resultant is a pretentious fallacy unduly impressive to those who fail to note the greater possibilities being neglected. I have nothing to say against *Coppelia*, which is of the delicate quality of a fairy tale or a whimsical exquisite willow-pattern. But *Giselle*—that product of a period when art-concepts had gone to seed, an incoherent, lugubrious, artificial pantomime that rasped the nerves till it succeeded in producing a horrible similitude of pathos—against such products and such productions, as a lover of the dance I cry out! Also I would at least question the desirability of *Aziade*, that elaborately-staged playlet, which was pretentious but not pathetic, sensational but never really sensuous, and which concealed a little genuine dancing amid a lot of rather ridiculous acting. It is for Pavlowa and Mordkin to delight and inspire us by dramatic dances without the adventitious and fatal assistance of elaborate acts, gorgeous scenery and large companies, and in ballets of simplicity and delicacy; and they should also develop the qualities they display in the *Bacchanal*. That is a dance of dances—Pavlowa and Mordkin to Glazvunow's *Bacchanal!* The glory of the madness of wine in the veins of youth, the dangerous delirious freedom and the perilous passion of it, the sudden flood of wildness that is one of the disguises of beauty—the liberation of vigorous limbs, the inspired command of impetuous and languorous steps, graceful swayings and gestures, head-tossings and arm-wavings and thrillings ecstatic of all the body—done so spiritedly, so perfectly, with such wild sweet suggestions of the very joy of life!. I can as fervently wish for more performances of this *Bacchanal*, and for the development, through gay and grave, of the style to which it belongs, as I can pray for deliverance, my own and every man's, from *Giselle* and all such bathetic outrages.

The latest of the dancers who have come with words of the one message is the Countess Thamara de Swirsky, a young Russian noblewoman, who, after entertaining and subsequently excoriating the wealthy folk of Newport, has for the sake of reaching a larger public, subjected herself to the trying conditions of the vaudeville stage. Shortened, deprived of proportion, squeezed into twenty minutes, her three dances are not in such circumstances to be justly appraised. She has a stately beauty, and she knows how to drape it perhaps better than any of the other dancers. In her *Tanagra* tableaux she is a veritable living Hellenic woman, a Dorian, one of the strong and golden-haired ones who conquered Greece and gave it glory, and were akin to the ancestors of the Russians, for it is not by accident that the Russians have always looked toward Greece, but because they found the glorious bright records of their own gods there.

Yet, though she looks the woman of Hellas, and postures with fine suggestiveness of Hellenic things, the Countess de Swirsky is a Slav; her interpretation of the Glazvunow *Bacchanal* is purely Slavic, with a certain temper in it which even a Dorian could never have felt. It is not as satisfactory as Pavlowa's *Bacchanal*, but whether Swirsky actually failed to bind the hap-hazard of the music into a sure though wild rhythm, or whether the mere physical condition of a small stage made it seem so, I am not able to say. In the *Bat* dance the Countess created beautiful rhythms both with her sweeping wings and with her competent feet. I await a performance of greater extent which shall tell us more of Thamara de Swirsky's qualities; for the present I know that she has beauty, talent, intelligence, youth, ambition and the love of her art. She will probably tend to develop modern and original dances rather than to revive ancient forms; she promises, as she studies, learns and perfects, to be one of the leaders of the new movement.

One more individual dancer whom it is most important to consider is a man, and for that reason I have reserved him for the last, and because he is not widely known as a dancer, but as a courageous, and in the public view eccentric, protestant against modern dress; and as a producer of Greek drama in accordance with living Greek tradition. Of course I refer to Raymond Duncan. Of his work as a whole, and its possible meanings, I have written enthusiastically elsewhere; here I would only recall that in the course of his productions of *Alcestis* and *Electra* he dances as the chorus danced in the ancient theatre, and does it worthily. I have not seen him attempt other sorts of dancing, elaborate efforts of stepping and swaying, and perhaps a man would have to be more beautiful than he is to do these things. But not even his own sister can either present the visible beauty of Hellenic posturing or suggest the spirit of Greek tragedy as he can. I do not think he will ever accomplish the miracle, which is his sister's, of showing us, in the seeming of a dance of the body, the very essential flow of moods through the spirit, in all its subtle variations, from ecstatic joy to vague terror in the face of baffling destinies; because Raymond Duncan is not subtly attuned to the moods, and is fascinated by external beauties. He senses the sublimity of destiny rather as a towering dark immuring cliff, than as an imponderable bewildering veil behind which there are moving mysteries and magic things. It is his to induce a majestic dramatic awe, by means of a recovery of the strange and wonderful gestures of the Greek dancers; gestures which were pure symbols, not of spiritual things, but, with definite and conventional applications, of the emotions and passions of man. This is so important a recovery that I hope a wide public will soon have the opportunity of seeing this lone evangel of many outcast creeds in the rôle of dancer.

For it is the dance as a force in that new propagandum of Art which is eagerly seeking the generous conquest of all men, in which we must be interested. It were nothing to us more than a puppet-show, if it were only a passing amusement, if it remained only on the stage, if it were a sort of easel-picture, made ineffective when taken from its special frame, and from under its special light, useless for the gracing of our halls and courts. I think we should welcome each new manifestation which is a true dance, distinct from the romp of the music-hall and the slouch of the ball-room, because each can move us in different ways, or awaken different companies of us. That Pavlowa has captivated her thousands and Genée her tens of thousands is well, for to watch them is to be summoned to consider beauty of motion, and at least delicacy of suggestion, and to appreciate them is to add more than a mite to one's æsthetic stores. And many doubtless are made, by the experience of seeing these artists of the ballet, more receptive of those whose art seems at first more difficult of appreciation by the majority, yet has in fact a surer appeal, since it awakens the desire of emulation. The eager flow of appreciation that went out to Isadora Duncan, Maud Allan, the Countess de Swirsky, and the Anna Pavlowa of the *Bacchanal* has its source in the impulse natural to every human being to express emotional states and fluctuations by movements of the whole body; an impulse banned and chained by social custom, but still rebelliously alive—poor captive, it leaped in wistful recognition of its own glorious possibilities if only we would in self-mercy liberate it! Everyone who saw these beautifully simple natural dance-expressions of the moods and the emotions knew in the heart that he or she often wanted and needed to do just so. And the wild hope came that perhaps some day again we might do so without incurring society's verdict of insanity.

But the enlistment of many of us in the ranks of dancers is not the ultimate result to be sought. As the dance must not stop at the proscenium arch, so also it must not stop with its own performance, but must be a contribution to the evolution of an art of life. The first spark which the public has caught from the light of the individual dancers has kindled a wide and active interest in folk-dancing, and this may have far-reaching effects. Beyond their obvious beneficent physical results,—erect carriage, light step, vigorous flow of blood,—folk-dances are conventionalized, but naturally conventionalized, expressions of the emotions, and the exercise of them must tend to reëstablish the emotions in life. The impetuous and barbaric Polish and Hungarian dances mean pride and passion and desire, and the less spectacular Irish dances mean joyousness and a

subtle pursuit of rhythm.   And there is the magic word in which all
the secrets of the dance are summed up—rhythm!

It has been a matter of entire unconcern to us that we have gone
about the daily work and the daily pleasure with no thought of
rhythmic motion or rhythmic speech, and we have done things unnecessarily and worn unnecessary things which have made rhythmic
speech and motion impossible; and the very idea of rhythm has been
absent from our minds unless in some special moments when with an
effort we have recaptured it for the basis of a sort of appreciation
of poetry or music.   That rhythm should be the very fact of our
speech, our actions and our every thought; that unless it is so, we
are forever incapable of finding the true path to that goal of beauty
which is our deepest secret desire, has been a lost and wandering
truth.   Yet till this wandering truth is set in its place in the heavens
that sway our destiny, we shall be in darkness, our conquests hollow,
our arts futile, and our destiny itself awry.   And the muse of the
dance hastens to us not to gain our plaudits for her grace, but to
bear this star in her hands and set it before our eyes, and bid us un-
cover and restore the temple and the universal rites of rhythm.   In
that temple all miracles may be accomplished.   A couple of years
ago there was in Paris a young woman of rather ordinary character
and endowments, in her usual moments, who, being put in a hyp-
notic trance, danced spontaneously to various suggestions—music
of Gluck, Schubert, Chopin and Tschaikowsky, humorous dialogues,
tragic recitals and heroic speeches—with absolute, significant and
beautiful plasticity to every instantaneous suggestion.   Similarly,
may not the secret of the miracles of the saints and of the Christ be
only a more perfect correspondence with the eternal rhythms?   Is
not rhythm, indeed, the essence of religion?   And social justice and
fraternity must be based on a rhythmic reconciliation of individuals
and groups now out of tune.   A race which could dance communally
could not be divided into masters and slaves.

Here is the art, which, once accepted, is both the most imperious and the most encouraging, the opener of most doors, come to
our door on eager feet.   We can indeed mock it by insincere imitations of its technique while closing our lives to its influence; but
once we really understand and love it and accept and practise it as

an art, we must turn to the ways of beauty and seek to be always of the company of the flowers on that way, moving to the breath and the music of the old winds of time. These things we must do as we come to understand the essence of the dance, and I, being of the children of faith, can believe that by the running feet and the swaying arms of the little band who have providentially appeared, we are being awakened to a lasting spell in which we shall do all the acts of thought and of motion between the cradle and the grave in an ecstasy of rhythm; and strife and hatred, cruelty and stupidity, with the wrongs that rest on them, and they are all wrongs, can no longer be. For to live rhythmically is to live beyond the possibility of error. And while the day of every man's perfection in the rite is sadly distant, may we not indeed believe that the revelation has come, and that it rests with us who have the vision to spread it and to fill the ears of the world with the joyous cry, On With The Dance!

WOMAN IN PROFILE

MARIAN COX

" A pageant of profiles! " said Prince Dolmar, as he stood beside his friend, within the embrasure of a window in a club overlooking Fifth Avenue, and watched the motors and carriages passing by in the vivid autumn air.

" The profile of the American woman already interests me," he went on, in his whimsical, ebullient mood, " and, so far, that is all I have had the chance to see of her. I have been in New York but a few days and yet have seen more profiles of women here than I have ever observed in London, Paris or Berlin. Has the American woman mastered the art of the profile? In her fugitive activities and vivacities she seems to promise so. She is always coming or just going and is never really there, or anywhere. Can even marriage make of her a permanent factor? I doubt it. Therein consists her charm. Really I am beginning to fancy that I may find my ideal here. My ideal would be found in the woman who has mastered the art of the profile."

" Is it an Art? " queried Sydney Waite, the one friend and cicerone of the Prince in the city.

" An Art indeed. And if you will listen to me patiently I will explain why and how. The woman gifted with the art of the profile would not only be my ideal, but would be the supreme feminine personality of to-day. She would make her position—of superior class and fortune—a thing of romance, instead of the mere feeding trough it now signifies. The great woman of modern times must be she who presents only the profile view of herself and life. She would be a stamp of grace upon democracy; and would make thrones issue from the thoughts of moribund minds. She would be but a profile; a half-revelation; far more stimulating to the taste of to-day than could be a Venus, arising in entire revelation from her ocean concealment. Venus would be a bore. Art has improved her by omitting her arms; thus we still flock to see her statue; but a living complete Venus could not long hold the modern attention. Men now desire their loves overdraped. To their wives they give wings, saying: ' Now hide yourself beneath these and let me alone '; to their mistresses they give the concealment of silks, satins and silence. And if possession of the latter were as legitimate as in ancient times, men would lose all desire for them. A harem is the dullest and most moral place in the world. Where religion has made polygamy a duty, it has taken away all its charm, and made faithfulness to one a lawless sensuality attractive to everyone imbued with imagination. Nowadays if a thing is to remain desirable and precious to man, it must be separated and secreted, like gems wrapped in jeweler's cotton, instead of, as in antiquity, heaped together and carried openly in salvers and urns. That is why I say the woman of the profile must become the great romantic figure of to-day. She will suit the spirit of her times, the XX Century, as Aspasia suited the Golden Age, Agnes Sorel the XV Century, Du Barry the XVIII Century, and Flora, Republican Rome. For she alone can bring a thrill of poetry into its leveling prose. She will redirect man's imagination from mechanics and the conquest of the air, to Ovid's art and a renaissance of gallantry. Only the woman in profile can achieve this. And why? Because the full face is bourgeois and hopelessly matter-of-fact, whereas the side face piques the inert fancy as it seems to say: ' I am in the attitude of passing visions—hold me if you can. I am placed like the faces of deities when stamped upon the metal for the greedy handling of men. I am in the pose of a queen when mingling with her people, giving but half to one side, half to the other, and thus saluted, venerated, idolized, by those subjects who could never endure the full revelation of aught they worshiped ' . . . Ah, the woman who is endowed with a beautiful profile has no shadow upon the other side but that of a crown. More than any other influence, I believe that of a woman's profile has created the havoc of love in man. Invariably it stirs him to seek—the other side; and the entire impetus of love in a man consists in the seeking. Where there is nothing to seek, when all is given, there is nothing to love. The tragedy of marriage is that a man always sees in full face the woman he has wooed in profile. A bench for two lovers, a ride, a walk together, gets its charm because of the profile. Whereas the breakfast table, the conjugal bed and *tête-à-têtes* get their boredom because of the full face. No woman can look reproach at a man with her profile. Nor can it give him candor, simplicity, honesty—three things he really detests in woman. But it does give him illusions, dreams, inspirations: the aliment of love. I believe that more men have married because of their ideal of a woman's profile at their hearth-side than from any other motive. Disappointment comes when they discover that in marriage the profile turns away and becomes a full face that—talks!"

"I agree with you there," ejaculated Sydney, who was married.

"For silence belongs only to the profile, and no man has ever yet had enough of silence in his marriage, or enough of speech in his courtship. The art of the profile is really the great art for woman to-day. The woman is an artist who succeeds in leaving in a man the memory of a profile. Man never wants to retain anything of a woman but a picture, anyway, a picture upon which can wax his sentimentality. He does not want to be loved. Witness the unreciprocated loves of the great women whom genius endowed with a rare capacity for love; from Sappho to Mary Wollstonecraft they are recorded, proving that man does not desire to be loved, only to love. His chief need in life is to adore. One cannot adore the full face; and women maintain the full-face view when they love. Only profiles can be wooed. The full face belongs to the gynæceum. Between the two there is the difference between a fresco and a map. The first is suggestive art, the second, experienced routes. A man looks for flaws in the full-face, but never does aught but admire the profile. They appeal to obverse sides of his nature. If it had not been for some few beautiful women who have had the cleverness to remain as profiles to men, men would never have accorded to women the homage of their respect. We respect only the half-revealed. And love must have respect as one of its components, otherwise it degenerates into the vulgar or the flabby. The great empress Catherine understood this; and was clever enough to kill her lovers after they had lost the profile view of her in the full one; for she realized that love, in them, could never again be so ardent. Sooner or later in every man's heart there is enshrined the profile of some woman who is never dethroned until he has seen all sides of her, and so thereafter is presented by memory in full view. I doubt whether Adam would have accepted the fatal fruit from Eve if he had not been surveying her in profile as she plucked it."

"Must you go to Genesis to prove the importance of your theory?"

"Observation of the modern woman is sufficient to establish it. She bids fair to forget the power of the profile, and to reveal and give too much of herself. I fancy the American women are, at present, respected by their men more than are the women of other nations, simply because the American men, as yet, have had no time to study anything of her but her profile. In Europe, too, she is only a profile; and that is why all discuss her more than they do their own womankind. Is there more than the profile to her? Or is she really a metallic goddess blank upon the other side? This surmise is what interests us foreigners in the American woman. Little is known of her. She does not figure in your history, save as a nebulous background. There is something about her so callous and yet so artificial, so piquantly naïve and yet *poseuse*. Really your American woman is but a profile, as yet. Thence she is interesting and adorable, so long as she makes us dream of the other side. But what if there is no other side to her? What if she is hiding indigence instead of affluence? What if she can never love, and so can never present to man the full view? Will her profile then lose any of its charm? . . . I have come to discover these things for myself. I shall marry one of your Americans, the one who is most master of the profile, for I could love her; but I shall cure my love by discovering the truth of her full view."

"So, love, too, you must have?" asked his auditor, now surveying the Prince with his shrewd, appraising, American eye, which ever sought the defect before its valuations, in order to be absolved from the emotional burden of admiration. Sydney admired the extraordinary gifts of mind and person of the Prince to such an extent that it appeased him to realize that his debt-ridden indigence placed him in a position of marketability which depreciated his value to that of a pound of flesh.

The obvious marketability of Prince Dolmar had aroused prejudice and disparagement among the men of the clubs, into which Sydney Waite had introduced him, and it was whispered among them that Sydney, a New York plutocrat of one generation ambitious for social extensions abroad, was financing the destitute nobleman upon a quest for the golden girl whose plethoric coffers would resurrect the ancient glories of his defunct house. This was covertly resented by the men and rendered them impervious to the brilliant personality of the Prince and to his blithe espousal of his own cause and aim.

"Wait until you have secured your heiress, and you will see them change," Sydney would say to him, "for Americans can resist anything but success."

For reasons of his own, reasons Jesuitical, pertaining to that lust of power rife in the circles in which he moved, Sydney had undertaken to instigate the success of the Prince in another one of the great marriages of international significance, consolidating royalty with dollars. Thus when he regarded him at the end of his expatiation upon woman's profile and queried, "So love, too, you must have?" it was with an anxious foreboding before complications. Strange to say, though the Prince claimed to be flagrantly mercenary, there was an incorrigible romanticism in his nature which, at times, bewildered and annoyed those who, like Sydney, were interested in seeing him accept life as an algebraic formula whose ever-besought x must be—wealth. For it alone could solve his difficulties and reinstate him in his own.

"Love, too, why not?" replied the Prince. "The profiles of your women are so promising I am beginning to dream, in spite of myself, that I can find one uniting lovability with suitability."

"Do not expect too much; it is the tragedy of youth to want everything. Besides I have already selected the heiress for you. You are to meet her at dinner to-night. She is the richest young woman in her own right, in the Metropolis, and is so strenuously American that America is not big enough for her ambition; hence she is looking for a Prince Charming who will transport her across the seas from where she can safely snowball the statue of Bartholdi. It is amusing to see how our women, when emancipated by wealth from pretence, reveal themselves as curious little anarchs against liberty. Once established in Europe they are the greatest sticklers for form, ceremony, and aristocracy. The name of the one you are to meet to-night is Cynthia Marlowe. She is a relative of my wife."

"So it is all arranged!" said the Prince with a sigh. It was his goal; his duty, personal, political, ancestral. One can do nothing without money. The politeness of kings is leisure, not punctuality, and their morality consists in immunity from the sordid motives and needs of others. How could these royal prerogatives be secured save through the agencies of wealth? In the past, thrones were built of gold, but to-day they are built upon gold. Dispossessed, the Prince felt that he had a right to come ino his own through the ministrations of another. All that he appropriated would be his due. Then why did he sigh? What did he surrender for the triumph of this marriage? Merely the secret ritual, the hidden pomps, of the imponderable Ideal. And to what did ideals lead save to exile from all sympathy, comprehension, and participation in the world? The Prince loved the world in the way we love the thing that has made us suffer sufficiently to inspire us with the desire to master it. So now he shrugged his shoulders and said:

" Very well. It is understood. I will marry her if the settlements can be arranged. I leave it all to you."

Sydney was equal to the charge. That night the Prince and Cynthia met; both prepared to accept a personage far inferior to that which they discovered, hence their courtship was initiated in the auspiciousness of surprise.

Cynthia Marlowe, in personality, was staunch, sallow and strident; and affected the extreme of smartness in attire and manner. She had watchful eyes, an indiscreet mouth, unable to close over its stores, and a shapely nose whose nostrils had each a little nick in them, as though worn there by her constant scenting for victims for snubs. In character she was the typical American woman, as the possession of great wealth evolves her. She was enpanoplied in suspicions regarding everything of her own nationality, and was so much like all her social compatriots that her chief aim in life was to distinguish herself from them. Thus she expended her energies and time in a calculating vigil of life. She was vigilant against any abrogation from her wealth and social position, a thing so precarious in the headless chaos of New York society that its quest wholly consumes the feminine natures in futile strife with each other, and refused to know any one whose limitations of purse or visiting list opened them to the suspicion of wanting something from her. Americans want so much themselves that they cannot tolerate any want in another. But vig-

ilance absorbed only a portion of her energies; the rest was expended
in calculations as to ways and means of procuring more self-aggran-
dizement. She was a patronizer of the arts, like all the ambitious
plutocrats of her country, but not a patron: that is, she would give
a surplus of admiration or money to any form of art or artist already
in their ultimate of rank, beyond any need of her or others, but had
no more perception or regard for the uncirculating mintage of art's
gold than has a cowslip for a comet. Philanthropy, also, she adopted;
for it was fashionable, and kept her name and picture in the papers;
but she made her secretary select all the philanthropies to which
she so liberally contributed, and protect her vigorously from learning, reading or hearing anything of them. She had now been out
five seasons in New York society and had concluded that no fields to
conquer were there: everything was too readily and exclusively accorded to the open sesame of wealth. This was not flattering or inspiring to the personal powers she fancied she possessed, and her
virile blood, inherited from pioneer ancestors, tingled in somnolence
and boredom until she resolved upon a marriage that would trans-
plant her into vast, alien, foreign spheres, whose reluctance to absorb
her would stimulate all her faculties and energies. This is the secret
of the American woman's love of deracination. She must have something to overcome; antagonism arms her. The Father of her Country
is suitably emblemized by an axe, and this little implement dancing in
her corpuscles is the root of her wanderlust and activities.

In a week the Prince and Cynthia were formally engaged. The
journals waxed flamboyant over their *fiançailles*. The wife of Sydney
Waite negotiated for the rent of one of the great houses in the
Faubourg St. Germain, for the coming season; and everyone sought
to wine and dine the *fiancés*. They were seen, admired, and envied,
everywhere. Snapshots were taken of them as they stood in the ro-
tunda of the Metropolitan and at the Horse Show; and they were described at all the great functions and festivities. Cynthia lost her
former strained or *blasé* expression and became urbane and merry,
with a novel little air of proprietorship over her blond Prince. And
he, too, manifested all the signs of one whose hopes are consummated.

Ever affable, smiling, loquacious, magnetic from the springs of
inner felicity, he charmed everyone by the promiscuity of his bril-

liancy, which they called his democracy, until his popularity became unprecedented. The débutantes called him " Prince Charming " to his face, and the dowagers sent him flowers, and dreamed of a return in strawberry leaves at his table in Paris next season.

Cynthia had ordered her trousseau and preparations for the nuptials were in full sway when suddenly a peculiar change became noticeable in the Prince. His former demeanor made the change still more striking than otherwise it might have been. At first it was observed that he was absent-minded, listless, unnaturally silent and preoccupied, as though brooding over some deep problem or haunting thought. Often when addressed he did not reply or seem to hear, and on the streets he frequently passed his friends without sign of recognition. Then it became unmistakably evident that he was avoiding all his former associates. He was seen no more in public and his absence was remarked in the houses and clubs previously frequented by him. He declined all invitations and those already accepted were broken by brief notes from him. Even these in a few instances he neglected to send, and his absence from several dinners where he was expected, made his strange behavior still more generally commented upon. Within two weeks he became a mystery. A mystery over which curiosity agitated itself in vain, for the only ones who could have elucidated it at the time, Cynthia or Sydney, were inaccessible. Sydney was away on a fortnight's hunting trip in Canada, and Cynthia, after she had appeared a few times in the world, unattended by the Prince, and been questioned about him, had also suddenly secluded herself and refused to be communicated with by anyone. But though non-committal or evasive to inquiries, she had appeared so smiling and gay that the report was circulated of her having broken the engagement because of some belated revelations concerning the private affairs of the Prince. And this was the news that greeted Sydney upon his arrival.

He hastened at once to Cynthia for an explanation. He, too, immediately attributed the cause to her; for he knew the financial plight of the Prince too well to attribute to him any change of mind regarding the hymeneal masterpiece, so artfully contrived.

He was received by Cynthia in her Louis Seize boudoir of rose *fané* and gold. She looked worn and peevish; her complexion was

mottled; and the little nicks in her nostrils were enlarged from the inflation of their restive breathing. They suggested the idea to Sydney
of little taut reins arched over the steed of her evident distemper.
But in a moment she gave vent to her agitation:

"You ask what is the matter with the Prince and me, when I was
just about to send for you and ask you to find out the same for me!
We have had no quarrel, no misunderstanding, no difficulties of any
kind, and yet all of a sudden he has ceased to come to see me, or to
go out with me, or even to answer my notes or give me any explanation
whatsoever of his strange, his unpardonable behavior. What am I
to think? Does he want to break our engagement? If so, he has
taken an outrageous method of doing so. Or has something happened to him which he is fearful of revealing to me and which troubles
him to the point of mental irresponsibility for his present conduct?
Perhaps some affair, some threat, or debt, greater than those he has
confessed to? You see, Sydney, how I am giving him every benefit of
the doubt. I have waited patiently during these terrible past weeks
for an explanation. But now I can bear it no longer. His treatment
of me is too humiliating. You must go to him at once and take this
message: if by to-morrow afternoon he does not come to me and
fully and satisfactorily explain, I shall not marry him! No; nor
shall I ever see him or communicate with him again!"

The last sentences weakened from a tremolo in her voice, and her
glaucous eyes became suffused with tears.

"There are still many eligible princes left," she added, plain-
tively. "But only one Prince Dolmar. I know that. That is
why I have stood so much from him. Ah, there is no one else in the
world like him. He makes even his money difficulties seem picturesque instead of sordid as they would seem in an American. Even
in rags he would be crowned by romance. He is so handsome, brilliant, charming, and while he has treated me so shamefully it has
made me realize that I—I *really* love him!"

Then she swore Sydney to secrecy while she admitted that she
would overlook and forgive anything from the Prince if he would
but return to her; and charged Sydney with the achievement of this
end, urging him to go immediately to him with her message.

The Prince had a small suite in one of the fashionable bachelor apartments just off the Avenue, and Sydney found him there, sunken in the depths of a commodious chair, smoking and reading Hazlitt's *Liber Amoris.*

He greeted Sydney with a curious self-conscious manner, as though merely annoyed at the interruption his entrance caused in some phantom panorama of thought, from which he could not sufficiently disentangle himself even to realize the presence of his friend. Sydney observed with speechless amazement the change wrought in the entire personality of the Prince.

The open, mercurial, exuberant light of his former self seemed to have been completely extinguished upon the surface, and to have fallen down, deep into some profound recess of his spirit, where it smouldered in an intensity of dejection, in an avidity of despair, which licked its hurts and its solitude in a sombre solace.

His face had the set morose look of one whose life is deflected inwards; its lineaments appeared wasted and parched as though from the preying upon them of insomnia's incubi, and his eyes were congested from the strain of prolonged brooding. Over his whole person was that atmosphere of an unreachable and cherished solitude of soul which frustrates the step of approaching worldliness and disarms all its knowledge like some vision of a Jacob battling with an angel in the midst of modern men.

Sydney was bewildered and shocked.

"Why, what is the matter, old fellow?" he involuntarily exclaimed. "Are you ill or in trouble?"

"Ill!" replied the Prince, with an intonation of irony, "yes, that is it; I daresay, I am ill."

"In what way?"

"Mentally, spiritually, and so,—physically."

"I am awfully sorry to hear this. But why did you not let me know before, or Cynthia?" Sydney said perfunctorily; then went on, gravely, "Really, Dolmar, illness does not excuse your actions toward Cynthia. There must be some deeper reason than that. You must explain yourself definitely. She is indignant, outraged, and has sent me here to-day with the message that if you do not fully explain by to-morrow at five—all is off between you!"

The Prince shrugged his shoulders and said, softly, "Kismet!"

"Do you mean to imply that you do not care? Dolmar, what in the name of Heaven is the matter with you?"

"Sydney, I will be frank with you. During the past weeks I have been going through a terrible conflict trying to decide whether or not I can go through with the mockery of this marriage. All of a sudden it has become distasteful, nay worse, repulsive, tragic, to me!"

"What has happened to make it so? Only a few weeks ago and it represented the goal of your ambitions, the acme of all success. What has happened to change you so?"

"Something has happened, I admit," he replied, slowly, as though verging on detachment into reverie.

"Come, confide everything to me. Have I not already proven myself your friend?"

"Indeed, yes, Sydney," said the Prince in a low, melancholy tone, "and believe me when I tell you that it has been only on your account that I have hesitated, in this strife of irresolution. I felt that I *must* marry Cynthia in order to pay my debt to you, while for my own part, I would prefer never to see her again."

Then in a changed voice he added abruptly:

"Sydney, I am in love."

"In *love!*" Sydney drew a whistling breath and surveyed him with mocking distrustful eyes. "With whom?"

"Alas, that I myself do not know!"

"You are jesting!"

"Do I look like one who jests?"

"Then you must be mad. How can you be in love when you say you do not even know with whom?"

"It is true. I do not know her name or anything about her, but I have *seen* her; and that is enough. I have seen her every few days during the past three weeks and that has been sufficient for me to recognize in her—beyond the cavil of a doubt—my ideal."

"The woman in profile?" queried Sydney, endeavoring to subdue his sarcasm until he had elicited the full particulars.

"Ah, you remember that! I am glad. Now you will understand. That realization of her, long before I ever saw her, should alone prove that it is Fate. He who thwarts fate disorganizes his life and self. I have seen this woman only in profile. But I know her as well as I know myself, for I have dreamed of her all my life."

"Where have you seen her?"

"There," he designated one end of the oblong chamber, "from that window. It directly faces some windows in a rear wing of the Hotel—and in one of them I found her."

Sydney could scarcely restrain his derision, but dared not betray it, as he saw that the Prince was in deadly earnest and grew more and more excited as he bestowed his confidence.

"In the one opposite my own. I never know when she will be there. Once or twice she has appeared on consecutive days and again several have elapsed before she is visible. She remains there for varying lengths of time, but never very long. And Sydney, there is a strangeness about the way she comes and goes from that window which mystifies me. It is most puzzling, mysterious, disquieting. And she herself is so strange, so thrillingly, inexplicably strange, that I cannot satisfy myself that I am not the victim of an hallucination. This doubt of myself, coupled with my infatuation, is either crazing or killing me! Oh, Sydney, it is really a godsend that you have come to me to-day. For perhaps you can prove whether or not I am beset by some unheard-of form of insanity, some perversion of vision, or maniacal delusion, or what!"

Impetuously, he arose.

"She may be there now. Come, let us see."

The two men went to the window and through the frail tracery of the sash curtain, looked beyond into the casement opposite, so near that it seemed within a deceptive arm's reach. Sydney started to draw aside the intervening net when the Prince arrested his hand.

"No, we must not be seen. Someone else is in that room who watches her constantly: a veritable Cerberus!—whether servant, guardian, father, or just what, I cannot for the life of me determine. But once, at the start, when I was unwary, he caught sight of me and immediately drew her away. For five days afterwards, she did not reappear. Since then I have been most cautious."

But as he was speaking Sydney was wholly absorbed in contemplation of what was visible opposite, beyond the high casement: a woman's face in profile, an exquisite face, impassive as though sculptured, and yet aglow with all the tints of life; and crowning it was a wealth of tawny hair whose tresses cradled each other in a slumbrous vivacity like that of covied serpents. She was looking down. Her lashes lay like a black butterfly at rest upon her cheeks. One could imagine her reading a Book of Hours, pictured by Clovio. She looked like a creature emerged from a missal, sealed away from the world by the golden clasp of a reliquary, but reigning over some effulgent refuge of life which could be reached by love's ladder of dreams.

"Do you see her?" whispered the Prince, as though he doubted the evidence of his own senses.

"Certainly," confirmed Sydney, himself doubting the reality of the apparition, so mysterious did it appear in its stillness, so fabulous in its rapt posture and supernalism.

"Then it is neither delusion, nor phantasy, nor am I mad!" The Prince drew a deep breath of relief. "But Sydney, she is always the same. She never turns to the window. She never looks out. She never moves except as she comes and goes. What do you make of it?"

"It is certainly odd," muttered Sydney, his brows drawn in perplexity, while a thrill of the inexplicable quivered through him. "There is certainly a woman there. Of that there can be no doubt."

"Look, here he comes. What is *he?*" cried the Prince, suddenly gripping Sydney's arm, as there appeared beside her a little old man, with a sinister face, brassy tinted and withered as a russet apple, a white goatee, and enormous black eyebrows, giving it a foreign appearance. He bent over the woman and seemed to be addressing her with words to which she vouchsafed no reply.

"What is he?" repeated the Prince, in an anxiety that summoned his friend to explain and dispel all the peculiarities of the sorcerous scene. "What is he—to her? Can you imagine?"

Sydney did not reply, so concentrated was his attention, and after an interval of silence, the Prince said to him, very low, "Sydney, the idea has just flashed upon me that he has hypnotized her. That at least could account for *her* demeanor. Observe closely all his movements—and let us see if this is not a solution."

The pantomime in the window had become still more wildly mys-

terious. The old man was now bending over her and touching her
hair with what seemed a strange befondlement or necromancy, until it
became evident that he was withdrawing hairpins from the coils of
her hair. Slowly, one by one, he proceeded to draw them forth
until at last all her hair tumbled down suddenly over her throat and
shoulders, like Danae's caressing shower of gold. Then he produced
a tortoise shell comb which he began to draw sinuously through the
thick rivulet.

"A *coiffeur!*" ejaculated Sydney, buoyantly recovering his
poise as he scented a humorous element in the affair.

"No; he *loves* her hair. You can see that in his every gesture.
To comb it is but some indulged folly of his dotage. . . . Sydney,
if it were not for her hair I would not believe her alive. But look at
it. How marvelous and living it is!"

And the two silently regarded the spectacle as though participating in some phenomenal event. The hair responded like a living
thing to the traffic of the comb; it sleekened from the strain of its
touch, it curled voluptuously upon its departure, it tossed hither and
thither in ethereal abandons beside the ravished track. The tresses
of the Villas, in which was confined all the essence of their lives, could
never have been more sumptuously vivific than this lady's hair; the be-
combed locks of the Rhine maid, high perched between St. Goar and
Oberwesel, could never have been so perilous to hazardous gaze as were
the sentient strands, the enshrouding scintillance of this lady's hair, to
the infatuate eyes of the romantic Prince.

"Good God!" burst from his trembling lips. "I can stand this
no longer!"

And he went and threw himself upon a lounge, burying his face
in a cushion. Sydney came and sat beside him, embarrassed because
he did not dare to laugh at the bewildering incongruity of a situation
which might bear such disastrous consequences to the whole future
of the obsessed Prince. He was frantically ransacking his mind for
some way to extricate the Prince from the amatory web of his own
devising, when he lifted his haggard, flushed face from the cushion
and said:

"Sydney, I know this is utterly absurd. But that makes no difference to me. I cannot throw it off. Love is a disease, and I fancied

I was immune from it because I have never loved before. Love is a disease of which only the morbid are victims. The morbid are those who have either a devastating excess or debilitant want of vitality in their constitution. Love, in both, is merely the craving for soundness, but only the unsound can love "——

"Ah, you are coming to your senses."

"Yes; love is a disease; it is disorganization of the individual will, which is replaced by an unconscious volition for self-destruction. Love began when identity was created from chaos, and its longings are ' to be undone,' to revert to primordial forms, to merge the aching self-consciousness into something vaster and stronger than itself. Its ecstasies are merely the electrifying vertigoes from the surrender of the will; ecstasies experienced as well by the martyrs in arenas or at the stake. A lover is the martyr of nature. Only those are capable of love who are wounded in the will to live; for love is but incipient degeneracy, emotive monomania, hyperæsthetic idealogy, psychic neurotism, paranoic obsession—yes, always a disease, betokening the abnormality of evolved, highly civilized man. Its agonized desires are only for cure, and it turns for cure to the one who can most hurt it, to the one who has depersonalized its will, to the one who has confused and broken its identity, to the one—beloved. We only love the thing that has the power to destroy us. I know this and yet—I love!"

"What are you going to do about it?"

"It depends upon her. First I must know her; then—I must have her!"

"Would you give up Cynthia for this?"

"Of course. What is the whole world to me now that I have recognized Fate?"

"But you have no money!"

"Ah, you Americans, you never let one forget money. Well, I can work. I have never had anything worth working for until I saw her."

"You are certainly mad!" cried Sydney in a sardonic gravity as he perceived the seriousness of an influence upon the Prince sufficiently strong to drive him even to work. For a troubled second he faced the havoc of his own plans and of the Prince's career, then a flash of illumination passed over his face.

" Dolmar, it is only the mystery and distance of this woman which attracts you. You will be disenchanted as soon as you meet her."

An incredulous smile lifted the moody corners of the Prince's lips.

" There is no chance of that. I know myself and her too well. But I must meet her; and it seems impossible even to find out who she is. Already I have inquired at the hotel and they profess a very suspicious ignorance of the inmates of the room whose locality I have precisely designated. And I have been taking all my meals in the café there, in the hope of encountering her, and have inquired of the waiters, but all in vain. I cannot glean the vestige of a fact concerning her. Sydney, perhaps you can do so for me? Find out who she is and then I can manage to convey a letter to her."

Sydney eagerly accepted the commission and took his departure. The next morning he returned.

" Well? " demanded the Prince, his whole soul tense and throbbing in the vocable. His fever-glazed eyes revealed a sleepless night and his whole attitude was one of petitioning impatience.

" I have found out everything. I will tell you all in a moment." He looked as though he were making some tremendous effort to restrain equivocal emotions. The muscles about his mouth were twitching and his gaze avoided the searching one of the Prince. Then he launched forth on a detailed recountal of how he had gone to the hotel and engaged a room for the night adjacent to the one which he discovered held the Prince's inamorata, of how he had questioned the servants and bribed—when suddenly the impatience of the Prince became ungovernable and he burst out:

" I don't want to hear how you managed it. Simply tell me *who* she is."

Sydney started to reply, when suddenly his face convulsed with laughter; his body shook in an uncontrollable spasm of laughter, and he laughed until he was as red as a gobbler's comb, the veins stood out on either side of his forehead, and from his fattened eyes streamed tears.

The Prince drew in his breath with a sibilant sound and towered in speechless indignation. About his violated spirit he drew the memory of his royalty like a garment of purple and ermine, from whose tattered dignity he enunciated in a deliberateness meant to be crushingly impressive:

"Sir, Prince Dolmar cannot be insulted by a mere plebeian."

"Oh, wait a moment, Dolmar," Sydney gasped, recovering from his laughter.

"I demand an apology."

"Listen. You will understand all in a moment. Have you ever heard of the Baron of Biarritz? Well, he is a rich and eccentric nobleman who had the singular experience of having married and lost, through death, seven successive wives. After the death of the last one he had a life-size likeness in wax made of each of them; and with these images of the beloved deceased, he has lived for many years in his château, on the Bay of Biscay, happy in the illusion of their life, amusing himself by sending to Paris for the latest fashions and jewels for his seraglio, a devoted polygamist, until all of a sudden it struck him that they were all too artificial save one. This one became his favorite. So much so that he has deserted the others, and eloped to America with her in order to try an experiment of monogamy, whose secrecy he has well-paid servants to maintain. Dolmar, the old man in the window is the Baron of Biarritz."

"And she?"

"Is the effigy of his favorite wife."

The Prince was silent a long while.

"Ichabod," he finally murmured, "the glory hath departed!"

Then with a crestfallen air he went over to the rack where hung his hat and coat and taking them down, said:

"I am going to Cynthia."

As they walked down the Avenue together, he broke a prolonged silence with the words:

"The Baron of Biarritz must be the only happy man in the world, for no one has disturbed his illusions."

To which his friend merely replied, as they stood at the stoop of Cynthia's house:

"Dolmar, I advise you never to look at any more profiles of women, except those upon the dollars your wife gives you. Only upon money is it safe to found romance, in these modern times."

THE ELDER GODS

A. E. JESSUP

FAR in the West, a Kingdom soars,
A world—lit by the dying sun—
Of ghostly seas and desert shores
    And deeds undone.

Where heavily and slow they fare,
—Those old dim shapes this world denied—
The Elder Gods whose creeds grew bare,
    And loveless, died.

Where Jove—a second Saturn now—
Upon a rocky eminence,
To heaven bemoans with cloudy brow
    His impotence.

And, wailing through deserted fanes,
As one who lives and yet would die,
Pan on his reedy flute complains
    To earth and sky.

And she whose smile mankind ensnared
There for her lost Adonis grieves,
While on her breasts, for kisses bared,
    Fall drifting leaves.

Through sombre groves of cypress sound
Sad murmuring rivulets, that rise
Where weeping Eos, sorrow-crowned,
    For Memnon cries.

Pale naiads throng the misty mere,
Locks loosed, wild eyes athirst for bliss;
Seeking a lover's face, they peer
    Where no love is.

Long, long it is since twilight cast
A withering shade along the sky;
The sun is quenched, and the cold blast
 Blows mockingly.

All silent now the old Gods sit,
Dull, witless, foolish-eyed they seem
As soulless tenements, where flit
 Shadow and dream.

Shadow of Godhead shattered, dream
Of old desires, and passions shed,
Like leaves upon an autumn stream
 Wrinkled and dead.

Eastward, in hope, each kneeleth now,
Muttering, " the dark will soon be gone,"
As giant trees to the tempest bow
 In unison.

She comes—the white Moon! Silently
Her form o'er frozen crests hath sailed;
Each God—a phantom Majesty—
 Standeth unveiled.

Naked, in fear, from crumbling thrones
Adown the gulf of Time they pour,
Where Lethe through her cavern moans
 For evermore.

And o'er the void where dead thoughts sink,
And all Remembrances find a grave,
Low-leaning sullenly they drink
 Its callous wave.

O, outcasts of Eternity,
O, glittering hosts of heaven, some day
Stripped of our prayers, ye too shall be
 Even as they!

EDITORIAL NOTES

THIS is an age of dreams—not of little dreams, personal, impracticable and evanescent; but of big dreams, translated into enduring facts by human skill and courage and devotion. As the old ideas of chivalry fade, new ideas are growing, strengthening, and becoming normal. The tumult and the shouting dies; the tinsel of tournaments is outmoded; to the sorry romance of war succeeds the real romance of commerce, of industry, of the world's work and the world's workers. Marvel follows marvel, by sea and land—and now, preëminently, in the air. The impossibilities of yesterday, are the commonplaces of to-day. A long generation ago, one man dreamed of separating two continents, and joining two civilizations. Thousands of laborers, toiling under a tropical sun, surrendered their lives because of that dream. The dreamer himself is dead, with the multitudes who served him and perished; but now, the dream has a name, known to the world. It is called the Suez Canal. And those who pass from West to East, or from East to West, have forgotten the desert that tried to engulf the dream; the shifting sands; the innumerable dangers and difficulties. They remember the tedious passage between the narrow banks under the sweltering sun. Yet how many thousands of miles of voyaging has that dream saved, for each of how many thousands of ships that sail the seas upon the world's business!

In our own time, within daily cognizance, another, bigger dream is steadily approaching fulfilment. Again two continents are being severed, that two oceans may be united. But few of us, who talk more or less glibly of the Panama Canal, and the question of its neutralization or effective defence, have any clear idea of the stupendous nature of this new wonder of the world; of the lives that have gone to its fashioning; of the heroism which kept men at the point of duty, not because of any hypothetical Field-Marshal's bâton, but because,—" By God, I am going to stand by!"

The following letter to the Editor of THE FORUM, from an official in the Department of Sanitation in the Canal Zone, has more than a personal and ephemeral interest.

" I have a letter to you in my office desk which I began some time in March—it is still unfinished. The first six months in this country you read state papers and write letters, the second six months you drop the papers, take daintily to magazines and write a few letters. The second year the *Saturday Evening Post* is your principal literary diet—and as for letters—well, to-morrow. The third year is not worth noting—I am in my fifth year—enough said——

" A recent writer has described us as ' The Exiles of Industry,' and he hit it about right. Shut out of the world in this God-forsaken country we come to have but one idea—' Dig the dirt out and put the concrete in,' and we of the Sanitary Department stand by to watch and nurse and protect the men like children that they may have the health and strength to do that one thing.

" We have lost all interest in the rest of the world; our job is the biggest ever undertaken by any nation, our country is doing it, and God help us, we are going to stand by until it is accomplished, or die in the attempt. That is the underlying influence that keeps every man here. Money is no compensation in this job; the canal will be dug because the 5,000 Americans who drop on their beds at night dead tired, crawl to the cold shower in the morning muttering, ' By God, I am going to stand by!' No one is ever rested, no one awakens with the feeling that they can lick the world, everyone kicks himself to work, and yet few shirk and they soon find that they are ostracized by their mates. I intended to resign in May and go home. When it came to the point horses could not have dragged me off the job. It has been hell since the first of April. Rain day and night and in spite of our efforts malaria has had a boom. So for this month we have had twenty-one deaths from malaria, a greater number than for any month for three years. This is largely due to the construction work and cannot be avoided. Two years ago Colonel Goethals adopted the army method and took the actual work out of our hands. Under Colonel Gergas I worked out the details of the reorganization. I thought then and I know now it was a great mistake. All our work now is done by request upon the Quartermaster and Division Engineer's Department. It is only a nuisance to them and they have no interest in it. Their own work comes first and ours when they can get to it. For three years we reduced the malarial rate 50 per cent. yearly; since the reorganization the rate has increased steadily until now it is higher than at any time during the American occupation. We are in a sense helpless and yet the army administration hold to the old theory that has pervaded the army since the days of the Romans. When will they ever learn the lesson demonstrated by the Japanese in the Russian war, viz., that sanitary work can only be done by sanitary men with an authority that can over-rule the staff officers? In the end we are going to win out and the Sanitary Department will come again to its own. It will be an object lesson that may reorganize all army methods. I have decided to hold on and see the canal completed unless I get knocked out for good in the meantime. I go into the hospital about every six months, but I soon get on my feet and am at it again. Four younger men who have work similar to mine have gone down and out, but the old man holds on and is good for more to come."

* * *

Clyde Fitch has been dead over a year. Had he lived much beyond forty-five, we should have seen a certain transformation in his technique, and a more pronounced purpose in his plots; for he was becoming deeply conscious of the fundamental truths of life, and he was eager to put strength into his dialogue in order to offset the delicacy and feminine flashes which the public always considered purely Fitchean. *The City* was his first, as it proved to be his last, effort in that direction.

Mr. Fitch often claimed that he was always measured in the public press by stereotyped phrases which clung to him because his manner was ever the same. He deplored the fact that the newspapers failed to give him credit for his close study of character, such as one finds in *The Girl with the Green Eyes* and in *The Truth*. Only after he was dead did the critics begin to realize the incommunicable flavor permeating his dramas. This flavor came partly from a close understanding of New York life, whether of the past or of the present; in *Captain Jinks of the Horse Marines* or in *Girls*. But it was in larger share the flavor of personality; no degree of profundity could ever have limited Clyde Fitch's enthusiasm while writing or rehearsing; he was quick in mind and in execution, and sometimes his very deftness and easy brilliancy were his undoing. He realized this; he tried his best to push back the numberless contracts and offers which claimed his time. When he died, he was in the whirl of popularity. In Europe he was disposing of play after play, some of which New York had rejected—as *The Woman in the Case*.

He took his success as naïvely as a boy, but he was planning to place more attention upon the message than he had heretofore done.

This may later have handicapped him, for passages of an ethical nature in *A Happy Marriage* retarded the action of the piece.

After all, the sum total of his work cannot be rejected from the body of dramatic literature; his very style is distinctive and is a measure of the man's outlook upon life. He told his story simply, directly, tenderly, and humorously. Only when he resorted to theatrical trickery did his work become uneven; and this unevenness accentuated the rich humanity and the kindly observation of his normal plays. One cannot call *The Stubbornness of Geraldine* a great drama, but it has a certain lively charm that no other playwright seems able to embody in a play. The temptation is to call such sentiment commonplace. *Granny* was full of it; so was *The Girl Who Has Everything.* Seeing these plays in succession, the theatre-goer would criticise their apparent resemblance. But an analysis would inevitably lead to the conclusion that the resemblance lay in the same personality behind them, and not in any monotony of detail.

Clyde Fitch was extravagant in his invention; he was careless in throwing a whole problem away within the limits of a line of dialogue. Such extravagance was indicative of his natural interest in all things bearing on human relationships; he brought the whole of life within the compass of home, and he gained his audiences by a seeming comradeship which made them feel that his windows overlooked the very housetops with which they themselves were familiar. He knew how to use the reporter's method; one could see this in *The Woman in the Case,* and in *The City.* But his usual method was literary, not journalistic; it was narrative in direct fashion, and not impressionistic. And because he knew his New York so well, he could afford to throw out those sparks of wit and humor which transcend a town, and are common to all provincial attitudes toward life. If he was cynical, it was friendly banter; he was never bitter. Yet looking deeper into the printed page of his published plays, it is apparent that he had had quite enough of society at the time of his death; that the city had made such demands upon his physical strength as to turn his desire toward the quietness of country life. There he would have started the larger work of a different kind from that characterizing his long list of popular plays. Whether he would have succeeded as well is a matter of futile speenlation.

He has been dead over a year, and he is missed; there is no one to take his place. A remark was once made by Thomas A. Edison to the effect that he hoped some day to have the time at his disposal for making a real contribution to science. But it is not easy to believe that anything he may do will ever surpass his actual genius in hitching his wagon to a star; in other words, in attaching a high imagination to practical conditions. So was it with Clyde Fitch. His personality is part of the work he did, and New York's duty is clearly defined, for he is in a sense the city's playwright. America has not yet understood what honor is due to such literary achievement. Its immediate reward was in the crowds that constituted a Fitch following for some fifty plays, mostly popular in their long " runs." Still, there is more to do, for now that he is dead, we know that something rare is taken from the theatre—something with a distinct literary value—light, no doubt, airy, and sometimes frothy, but none the less life with which we are all familiar.

The time is opportune for reviving some of those successes. Pinero's *Trelawny of ' The Wells '* is being revived. Why not *Captain Jinks of the Horse Marines?* And shall the excellence of *The Climbers* be overlooked? There is nothing old-fashioned in Clyde Fitch's attitude or in his workmanship; they will scarcely become out-of-date for many a decade. There are other artists much stronger, with theories of technique much more original. But Clyde Fitch's originality is to be found in his close connection with the material he used. His audiences were given much more of himself than they ever knew. And that is why they will never find any other plays quite like his.

*   *   *

There was a little gentle amusement, and a little genuine interest, on this side with regard to the traveling and sight-seeing achievements of Mr. W. R. Holt, the English journalist selected by the management of the London *Daily Mail* to represent them in connection with the recent record-breaking " round trip " of the Mauretania—an ocean-race against time which attracted exceptional attention in England. By the judicious use of special trains and automobiles, and with the incidental assistance of the Mauretania, Mr. Holt succeeded in traveling from London to Washington and back

in twelve days—the average rate of speed day and night being
twenty-three miles an hour. This is, of course, an astonishing
record in transit. Since his return, Mr. Holt has been publishing
some impressions under the title *Thirty-Eight Hours in America*.
Of President Taft, with whom he had an interview at Washington,
he writes:

" Imagine Athos taking up politics in his maturity, and you see
President Taft. A tall, straight, stalwart dragoon, dressed in a
beautifully cut morning coat. Popular caricatures show him as a fat
man; but he is not fat; he is big and bold and strong. He has a clear
eye, a transparent complexion, and a drooping yellow moustache.
His laugh is the jolliest thing I heard in America. . . . My own impression of the President was that of a strong, penetrating man, who
finds indulgence in his natural spirit of jollity as good a cloak as any
other for his inmost thoughts. He is an unmistakable diplomatist."

Mr. Holt adds little descriptive touches of the Vice-President and
Mr. Cannon:

" The Vice-President, Mr. Sherman, was genial but reserved. But
the Speaker of the House of Representatives, Mr. Joseph Cannon—
known throughout the United States as ' Uncle Joe '—is vigorous
enough to give a glow to the continent. He is over seventy, is forty
years old as a politician, and combines the vigor of youth with the
masterful ways of old age. He has a red face, a chin beard, and a
pair of bright, twinkling eyes, whose gleam is not dimmed by spectacles or glasses. He stuck a big cigar in the corner of his mouth,
pointing upwards; he paced his red throne-room like a fretful tiger;
and he addressed me as if I were a public meeting."

*   *   *

Nearly nine years after the death of Cecil Rhodes, comes his first
complete biography, by Sir Lewis Michell, at one time his confidential secretary, and later an executor of the famous will establishing
the Rhodes Scholarships. Under the title *The Life and Times of
the Right Honorable Cecil John Rhodes*, Sir Lewis Michell has tried
to paint a complete picture of a many-sided life. He has done his
work painstakingly, and, on the whole, adequately; nothing more
exhaustive or authoritative can very well be issued. But he has left
out a little color here and there—in the sky. For Rhodes was more
than a Cape politician and premier; an imperialist; a financier; a

man of millions. He was a man of destiny. Few romances of modern years can parallel this of the boy—not yet seventeen—who left home in June, 1870, and after what was then considered a record passage of seventy days, landed at Durban, Natal, on September 1st.

His eldest brother, Herbert, was already settled in Natal, experimenting in cotton-growing, and Cecil joined him. In two seasons, he learnt many of the secrets of cotton-growing; but the great diamond discoveries were now proving an irresistible lure to the adventurous, and in October, 1871, Cecil started for the nearest mine " in a Scotch cart drawn by a team of oxen, carrying with him a bucket and a spade, several volumes of the classics and a Greek lexicon—surely the strangest equipment for a youth in his teens, bound for a miners' camp! "

Here he found his opportunity, and made full use of it.

" A tall fair boy, blue-eyed, and with somewhat aquiline features, wearing flannels of the school playing field, somewhat shrunken with strenuous rather than effectual washings, that still left the color of the red veld dust—a harmony in a prevailing scheme. This was my first impression of Cecil John Rhodes.

" The burly man of later years was at this time a slender stripling, showing some traces of the delicacy that had sent him to the Cape. He had not long come to the Fields, and the impression made upon such a nature as his by the novel world in which he found himself must have been particularly penetrating. Fresh from home and school, he found himself amongst men of much experience in many walks of life; his self-reliance led him into competition with them; and good fortune, and his clear head, brought him out on top.

" Digging for diamonds sounds a fascinating Sindbad sort of occupation, but in reality it was far from velvety. The summer days were incredibly hot and the winter nights extremely cold, and we had nothing but a little canvas between us and these extremes. Added to which mining was just then very dangerous. The roads that had been left across the mine were tall causeways of crumbling tufa, sometimes sixty feet above the claims on either hand, and constantly falling, to the great danger of the workers below. Ox-carts and mule-carts, that lumbered along these perilous ways, not infrequently went over, and altogether the claims were not pleasant spots to work in.

" But they were pleasanter than the Sorting Places, where, in those primitive days, the digger sat amongst his Kafirs, in the blinding sun and dust, passing the sifted granules of tufa before his dazzled eyes. Great heaps and mounds of this débris grew round the vast basin of the mine, rising month by month as the excavated cavity of the crater grew deeper and deeper. Mound and mine were black with men moving and working with ant-like activity. And the cries and songs of the natives, the whirling of innumerable windlasses and the crash of buckets filled the air.

"From this high vantage one could see all the camp: gleaming patches of canvas, stretching away to the open veld, all shimmering in the noonday heat. I was working for some time near Rhodes's ground, and the picture of his tall delicate figure crumpled up on an inverted bucket, as he sat scraping his gravel surrounded by his dusky Zulus, lives in my memory.

"Many young men would have been content to float on this easy tide of good fortune, but it was not so with Cecil Rhodes. I remember his telling me that he had made up his mind to go to the University, it would help him in his career; also that it might be wise if he were to eat his dinners, the position of a barrister 'was always useful.' Then in his abrupt way he said, ' I dare say you think I am keen about money: I assure you I wouldn't greatly care if I lost all I have to-morrow, it's the game I like '; and so, shortly after, he went to Oxford, but before going he made several investments in claims and also in diamonds; he became very interested in old De Beers, and used to speak of it as a ' nice little mine.'

"Then he went to Oriel and lived the life of the usual under-graduate—with a difference. I stayed with him at Oxford some years later and saw this difference, but I doubted at the time that his college friends did; he played polo, a somewhat new game in those days, and worked and amused himself much as other men did, but I could not help thinking, as we sauntered up the High, of Kimberley far away, and all the schemes and deals that this strange undergraduate was engaged in while he lived amongst boys not yet entered upon the hard business of life.

"But this was, as I said before, some years after; for a cold, caught rowing on the Isis, suspended his University career for some time and sent him once more back to Africa.

"The voyage, however, set him up, and he arrived at Kimberley well, and keen for the contest. Here again Fortune had her eye on her friend, and brought him out at a favorable moment. Heavy rains had fallen that spring and had flooded the mines, and the digging community was rather helpless. The claims were by this time much sub-divided, being worked by men having little or no capital, and with small gangs of Kafirs; there was no machinery or any means of drain-ing the mines. Rhodes saw his chance; he managed to get hold of a practical engineer with whom he went down to the Colony and bought a couple of old engines of the threshing-machine order, and some centrifugal pumps, and sent in tenders to drain the two mines of Du Toit's Pan and old De Beers. There was no serious opposition, the tenders were accepted, and he was soon busily engaged pumping the two mines under a very satisfactory contract.

" It was not all quite smooth, however; the old agricultural machines were a bit asthmatic, and frequently broke down, and the practical engineer had his hands full to keep them in health and the mines dry. Then the fuel was a great difficulty, the radius of the wood supply was steadily retiring before the increasing demand, and at that date there was no coal; but Rhodes had a shaggy Basuto pony and an old yellow cart in which he scoured the country before sunrise to waylay the great Boer wood wagons as they lumbered to the Kimberley market. Yes, it was assuredly ' the game' that he loved.

" Until Rhodes finally took his degree he was continually going and coming between Oxford and Kimberley. His interests in the latter were, of course, always growing, and it is difficult to understand how he managed to keep his attention sufficiently fixed on his academic studies to enable him to pass.

" But Kimberley was his real university, and it was there that he graduated, it was there that he gained that insight into the intricacies of men's hearts that gave him in after years a power to govern their actions. If Africa was shaped by Rhodes in the days to come, it was because Africa shaped him in his youth.

" As I search my memory for the Rhodes of the early seventies, I seem to see a fair young man, frequently sunk in deep thought, his hands buried in his trousers pockets, his legs crossed and possibly twisted together, quite oblivious of the talk around him; then without a word he would get up and go out with some set purpose in his mind which he was at no pains to communicate. The same dual qualities that were to go with him through life were discernible now. He was a compound of moody silence and impulsive action. He was hot and even violent at times, but in working towards his ends he laid his plans with care and circumspection. He was fond of putting the case against himself. ' You will probably think so and so,' he would say, then he would balance his own contention against the view that he felt the devil's advocate would take; this habit of seeing the other side probably helped him much in his career. Few men are adequately aware what the other side thinks.

" The duality of his nature, the contemplative and the executive, had a curious counterpart in his voice, which broke, when he was excited, into a sort of falsetto, unusual in a man of his make; his laugh also had this falsetto note.

" In all his wide range he had no place for personal appearance; of this he was contemptuously indifferent.

" Almost a generation had passed away before I saw Cecil Rhodes again. In the meantime he had amplified the map of Africa, and had printed his name across a vast province. For good or evil, as men felt, his name had been bruited about the world as an empire-builder, a great financier, a man of vast schemes.

" I sat in the ante-room of a London hotel and waited for him. A murmur came to me through the folding doors, the deliberations of a joint-stock company reduced to one note. At length the door opened and the great man came across to where I was. We greeted and looked narrowly at each other, as men do who seek to strip away the disguise in which the years have clad them and see again the familiar face and figure. This burly frame, topped with the heavy-lined Napoleonic head—was this what time and the making of colonies had done with the stripling of yesterday?

" We talked, but we talked carefully, for many that we knew were dead, and others were ranged in opposing camps. Then I said to him, ' You, of all the men I have known, have made the biggest thing of life, you have written your name widest and highest. Now I want to know how you feel about it; have you enjoyed it? Has it been worth all the trouble? '

" He paused and looked at me, and then in the falsetto that I so well remembered, he said, ' Yes! I enjoyed it. Oh, yes! '—as though reassuring himself—' it has been worth the candle; ' then with a grim smile he added, ' When I thought Kruger was going to hang Frank, and I was not very sure they mightn't hang me too, I didn't like that.' Then again, with another change, he went on, as he walked up and down in his old impatient manner, ' No, the great fault of life is its shortness. Just as one is beginning to know the game, one has to stop.' In truth, it was *the game* he loved, and very soon he had to stop."

Of the boys who were reared in the quiet vicarage at Bishop's Stortford, the eldest, Herbert,—a strong, restless man,—is buried in far Nyasaland, where he perished by misadventure. Francis, who served in the Sudan campaign, at Suakim and Omdurman, in India and Uganda, was condemned to death by the Boer Government for his share in the Jameson Raid, but survived to be besieged in Ladysmith, and to die, six years later, in his brother's historic house at Groote Schuur. And Cecil, who stamped his sign-manual upon the greater part of a continent, lies in his tomb in the Matopo Hills —the tomb that he had chosen.

" After an early breakfast he rode with me to what he called ' The View of the World,' in order to point out the exact spot in which he desired to be buried, and he lay down there ' to see how it felt!' "

Just two other quotations. This, brief, but not without ethical significance:—

" On the Sunday afternoon we held an indaba of the indunas. We sat in a small group surrounded by at least fifty stalwart natives, and Rhodes, addressing them in their own language, said a few words to each chief. To some he spoke graciously, much to their delight. With others he was jocular, whereupon the whole assembly, after the immemorial custom of courtiers, laughed immoderately. To one man alone he was minatory and severe—a man who was reported to be still mischievously disposed. To him Rhodes addressed a few scathing remarks, till the fellow slowly changed from darkest bronze to ashen gray, and the beads of perspiration stood out upon his abashed forehead.

" Finally, he spoke to them collectively on a subject very near his heart—on the distinction drawn by white people between killing in fair fight and massacring unprotected non-combatants on lonely farms. On this theme he appeared to speak with real eloquence, and as the crowd, in excitement, closed in upon us, he put the crucial question, ' Will you promise never to kill our women and children again? ' An immediate, unanimous and unmistakable cry in the affirmative was given, but Rhodes looked disconcerted, and a smile flickered on the faces of those who knew the language, for the reply, as I afterwards ascertained, was ' We will kill no women, Inkoos, Baba, unless thou order it!' "

And this, long as it is, for it shows the wonderful insight and patience of the Master of Men—sometimes almost incredible to those of little knowledge.

" After some three hours the party returned and informed us that peace was in sight, as the chiefs had promised to call a big meeting of all the others not present for that day week, at a point some twenty-five miles further west in the hills. We at once set to work packing up, and trekked off next morning to fix our camp at the new place and be all ready by the day appointed. Colonel Plumer and his column followed us about a day later, Mr. Rhodes insisting that no troops should come nearer our camp than two miles, as he wished to show the rebels he had full confidence in their word that until they had discussed matters fully at the second indaba there would be no further fighting. It had been arranged that seven of us might attend this meeting, but that all of us should be unarmed, and this condition was agreed to on the understanding that the rebels should also carry no weapons.

" On the day appointed we set off, being accompanied by Mrs. Colenbrander and her sister, all of us being well mounted on horseback. The spot fixed was some two miles from our camp and about four from the fighting column. About fifteen to twenty natives were visible when we arrived, but suddenly some 400 to 500, armed to the teeth, came out of the bush and surrounded us. ' Keep on your horses,' shouted Mr. Colenbrander, and we all did save Mr. Rhodes, who dismounted and walked right up to the rebels, despite Colenbrander's entreaties, and began upbraiding them in no measured terms regarding their broken promise as to coming unarmed. ' How can I trust you? ' he questioned. ' You asked us to carry no guns and stated you would not, and what do I find? Until you lay them down, every one of you, I will not discuss a single point with you.'

" This led to much muttering among the ' amajacas ' (fighters), and they all looked very sulky. Calling up three or four of the older chiefs, Mr. Rhodes said, ' Why do you permit this? These young men are out of hand; you cannot control them, and yet you call yourselves their indunas.' ' Alas,' they replied, ' they *are* out of hand, but the young men of to-day are no longer to be controlled as they were when Lo Bengula was alive; they are too much for us.' ' Do not allow your authority to be set aside in such a fashion,' said Mr. Rhodes, ' I will stand by you. Order these amajacas to put down their guns at once, else we shall go back and the war will begin again.' Somewhat heartened, the chiefs went in among the impi while Rhodes walked up to a stone in the midst of them and sat down on it. The rest of us remained on our horses, thunderstruck at his actions and conversation, which was carried on in Matabele without the aid of an interpreter. In ten minutes or so, loud shouts of ' Inkosi ' (Master, Chief) went up, and all the arms were laid down.

" For the next three hours the chiefs poured out all their troubles, some of which Mr. Rhodes saw were genuine and promised to rectify. Others, he pointed out to them, were the result of their own folly. In the end a perfect understanding was arrived at, but before getting up Mr. Rhodes said to the chiefs, ' Are you all here, all the chiefs of the Matabele? ' They looked much upset at this question, then one of them came forward and said, ' No, Helae and Mapisa would not agree to come and meet you; they still want to fight.' ' Where do they live? ' said Mr. Rhodes, and on being told it was some eighteen miles further in the hills, he said, ' Well, tell them

I shall go to the door of their kraals and stay there till they come out.' Helae and Mapisa, it may be mentioned, controlled a very large number of Matabele, and had much influence.

"'And now,' he said, 'is it peace?'' 'Yebo, Inkosi, (Yes, Master) it is peace. We look at you now with white eyes. Hail, Lamula'mkunzi (separator of the Fighting Bulls), Lamula'mkunzi, Lamula'mkunzi,' shouted the impi, and the hills re-echoed the name given him by the natives, who were now overjoyed at the end of the war, but who a few minutes before were full of bitterness.

"Next morning we broke camp and trekked toward the strongholds of the two chiefs who had refused to come to the indaba—Helae and Mapisa. It took us three days' traveling to reach our objective, and Mr. Rhodes was full of hope that in a week the two recalcitrant chiefs would hand in their submission. Colonel Plumer's column followed, but was not allowed nearer than four miles, this being arranged so as to give confidence to the Matabele, many of whom were constantly coming to see their 'Father.' To a message sent them, the two chiefs vouchsafed no reply, so Mr. Rhodes said, 'Very well, we will sit here till they come out and seek us. It will not be long.' But it was not for six weeks (9th October, 1896), and those who know the impatient nature of Mr. Rhodes would have marveled at his persistency. Nothing seemed to trouble him save the one thing, the conquering of these two men. Many people urged him to give the matter up and leave one of his lieutenants to deal with it, but he would not. He had, he said, stated he would end the rebellion, and till these chiefs had submitted, the embers were still there."

Notice how the man who could bide his time so resolutely to achieve one fixed aim, was nevertheless always alert for new discoveries, new schemes. He finds that "View of the World" which made so great an impression on his imagination. In another instance, his practicality comes to the front. He sees an ideal place for a huge reservoir. At once, steps are taken to turn the possibility into a fact.

"One morning, in company with Earl Grey and Mr. George Wyndham, he went out riding, and when they came back about one o'clock, he was full of a discovery he had made. 'We found a hill in the Matopos,' he said, 'from which a perfectly wonderful view can be obtained. It may be considered one of the Views of the World. We must have a road made to it later on.' He talked of little else that night at dinner, and got both Lord Grey and Mr. Wyndham to describe it to us.

" Riding in another direction one morning, he found an ideal spot for conserving a large quantity of water, with some wonderfully rich soil underneath it. ' Providence,' he said, ' left this gap in the hills at this point for a purpose, and we must respond. Get a good engineer and arrange for him to prepare surveys for a dam and furnish us with an estimate of the cost.' Matters were put in hand, and before he died the dam was finished at a cost of thirty thousand pounds. When full it contains 987 million gallons of water, and is capable of irrigating a thousand acres of land which lies below its outlet.

" Having made up his mind to build the dam, Mr. Rhodes at once set to work and arranged all about clearing the land which it would dominate of stones and bush, and everything was planned out for the work to be commenced immediately after the chiefs gave in. Meanwhile, a man was sent to the Cape to buy machinery, implements, etc. Though apparently taking a long rest, Mr. Rhodes was really working quite hard, for his mind had to be occupied, and he threw himself into all such matters in his usual strenuous way.

" Day succeeded day, but still Helae and Mapisa were obdurate. No trace of impatience was, however, to be noted in Mr. Rhodes. The days were spent in all sorts of expeditions, and the evenings in discussing the development of Africa. One remark of his I remember, which might well be recorded: ' You cannot have real prosperity in South Africa,' he said, ' until you have first established complete confidence between the two races, and henceforth I shall make that part of my work, but all must help, all must help.'

" News of the outside world seldom reached us, and no one seemed to miss it. Some six weeks had elapsed since we came to the ' doors ' of the two rebel kraals, and all of us save Mr. Rhodes were much surprised when one evening just at dark a message came from the chiefs, carried by three of their councillors, to say they would come and talk to Mr. Rhodes shortly after sunrise the next day. ' Get everything ready to move to Bulawayo by noon to-morrow,' said Mr. Rhodes. ' Why,' said some one, ' how do you know they will submit?' ' How *did* I know, you mean?' was the reply; ' they have already submitted when their messengers are here.'

" Next morning the two chiefs with their head-men turned up about 7 o'clock, and in two hours everything had been settled. Helae put his points clearly, and Mr. Rhodes dealt fully with them, and they parted in the most friendly manner, and sure enough we were on the way to Bulawayo at 12 o'clock, and next day Mr. Rhodes was trekking to Salisbury."

THE NEW MACHIAVELLI

H. G. WELLS

CHAPTER THE FIRST

THE RIDDLE FOR THE STATESMAN

IX

My ideas about statecraft have passed through three main phases to the final convictions that remain. There was the first immediacy of my dream of ports and harbors and cities, railways, roads, and administered territories—the vision I had seen in the haze from that little church above Locarno. Slowly that had passed into a more elaborate legislative constructiveness, which had led to my uneasy association with the Baileys and the professedly constructive Young Liberals. To get that ordered life I had realized the need of organization, knowledge, expertness, a wide movement of coördinated methods. On the individual side I thought that a life of urgent industry, temperance, and close attention was indicated by my perception of these ends. I married Margaret and set to work. But something in my mind refused from the outset to accept these determinations as final. There was always a doubt lurking below, always a faint resentment, a protesting criticism, a feeling of vitally important omissions.

I arrived at last at the clear realization that my political associates, and I in my association with them, were oddly narrow, priggish, and unreal, that the Socialists with whom we were attempting coöperation were preposterously irrelevant to their own theories, that my political life didn't in some way comprehend more than itself, that rather perplexingly I was missing the thing I was seeking. Britten's footnotes to Altiora's self-assertions, her fits of energetic planning, her quarrels and rallies and vanities, his illuminating attacks on Cramptonism and the heavy-spirited triviality of such Liberalism as the Children's Charter, served to point my way to my present conclusions. I had been trying to deal all along with human progress as something immediate in life, something to be immediately attacked by political parties and groups pointing primarily to that end. I now began to see that just as in my own being there was the rather shallow, rather vulgar, self-seeking careerist, who wore an admirable silk hat and bustled self-consciously through the lobby, and a much greater and indefinitely growing unpublished personality behind him—my hinterland, I have called it—so in human affairs generally the permanent reality is also a hinterland, which is never really immediate, which draws continually upon human experience and influences human action more and more, but which is itself never the actual player upon the stage. It is the unseen dramatist who never takes a call. Now it was just through the fact that our group about the Baileys didn't understand this, that with a sort of frantic energy they were trying to develop that sham expert officialdom of theirs to plan, regulate, and direct the affairs of humanity, that the perplexing note of silliness and shallowness that I had always felt and felt now most acutely under Britten's gibes, came in. They were neglecting human life altogether in social organization.

In the development of intellectual modesty lies the growth of statesmanship. It has been the chronic mistake of statecraft and all organizing spirits to attempt immediately to scheme and arrange and achieve. Priests, schools of thought, political schemers, leaders of men, have always slipped into the error of assuming that they can think out the whole—or at any rate completely think out definite parts —of the purpose and future of man, clearly and finally; they have set themselves to legislate and construct on that assumption, and, experiencing the perplexing obduracy and evasions of reality, they have taken to dogma, persecution, training, pruning, secretive education, and all the stupidities of self-sufficient energy. In the passion of their good intentions they have not hesitated to conceal fact, suppress thought, crush disturbing initiatives and apparently detrimental desires. And so it is blunderingly and wastefully, destroying with the making, that any extension of social organization is at present achieved.

Directly, however, this idea of an emancipation from immediacy is grasped, directly the dominating importance of this critical, less personal, mental hinterland in the individual and of the collective mind in the race is understood, the whole problem of the statesman and his attitude toward politics gain a new significance, and become accessible to a new series of solutions. He wants no longer to " fix up," as people say, human affairs, but to devote his forces to the development of that needed intellectual life without which all his shallow attempts at fixing up are futile. He ceases to build on the sands, and sets himself to gather foundations.

You see, I began in my teens by wanting to plan and build cities and harbors for mankind; I ended in the middle thirties by desiring only to serve and increase a general process of thought, a process fearless, critical, real-spirited, that would in its own time give cities, harbors, air, happiness, everything at a scale and quality and in a light altogether beyond the match-striking imaginations of a contemporary mind. I wanted freedom of speech and suggestion, vigor of thought, and the cultivation of that impulse of veracity that lurks more or less discouraged in every man. With that I felt there must go an emotion. I hit upon a phrase that became at last something of a refrain in my speech and writings, to convey the spirit that I felt was at the very heart of real human progress—love and fine thinking.

(I suppose that nowadays no newspaper in England gets through a week without the repetition of that phrase.)

My convictions crystallized more and more definitely upon this. The more of love and fine thinking the better for men, I said; the less, the worse. And upon this fresh basis I set myself to examine what I as a politician might do. I perceived I was at last finding an adequate expression for all that was in me, for those forces that had rebelled at the crude presentations of Bromstead, at the secrecies and suppressions of my youth, at the dull unrealities of City Merchants', at the conventions and timidities of the Pinky Dinkys, at the philosophical recluse of Trinity and the phrases and tradition-worship of my political associates. None of these things was half alive, and I wanted life to be intensely alive and awake. I wanted thought like an edge of steel and desire like a flame. The real work before mankind now, I realized once and for all, is the enlargement of human expression, the release and intensification of human thought, the vivid utilization of experience and the invigoration of research—and whatever one does in human affairs has or lacks value as it helps or hinders that.

With that I had got my problem clear, and the solution, so far as I was concerned, lay in finding out the point in the ostensible life of politics at which I could most subserve these ends. I was still against the muddles of Bromstead, but I had hunted them down now to their essential form. The jerry-built slums, the roads that went nowhere, the tarred fences, litigious notice-boards and barbed wire fencing, the litter and the heaps of dumps, were only the outward appearances whose ultimate realities were jerry-built conclusions, hasty purposes, aimless habits of thought, and imbecile bars and prohibitions in the thoughts and souls of men. How are we through politics to get at that confusion?

We want to invigorate and reinvigorate education. We want to create a sustained counter effort to the perpetual tendency of all educational organizations toward classicalism, secondary issues and the evasion of life.

We want to stimulate the expression of life through art and literature, and its exploration through research.

We want to make the best and finest thought accessible to every one, and more particularly to create and sustain an enormous free criticism, without which art, literature, and research alike degenerate into tradition or imposture.

Then all the other problems which are now so insoluble, destitution, disease, the difficulty of maintaining international peace, the scarcely faced possibility of making life generally and continually beautiful, become—*easy*. . . .

It was clear to me that the most vital activities in which I could engage would be those which most directly affected the Church, public habits of thought, education, organized research, literature, and the channels of general discussion. I had to ask myself how my position as Liberal member for Kinghampstead squared with and conduced to this essential work.

CHAPTER THE SECOND

SEEKING ASSOCIATES

I

I HAVE told of my gradual abandonment of the pretensions and habits of party Liberalism. In a sense I was moving towards aristocracy. Regarding the development of the social and individual mental hinterland as the essential thing in human progress, I passed on very naturally to the practical assumption that we wanted what I may call "hinterlanders." Of course I do not mean by aristocracy the changing unorganized medley of rich people and privileged people who dominate the civilized world to-day, but as opposed to this, a possibility of coördinating the will of the finer individuals, by habit and literature, into a broad common aim. We must have an aristocracy—not of privilege, but of understanding and purpose —or mankind will fail. I find this dawning more and more clearly when I look through my various writings of the years between 1903 and 1910. I was already emerging to plain statements in 1908.

I reasoned after this fashion. The line of human improvement and the expansion of human life lies in the direction of education, and fine initiatives. If humanity cannot develop an education far beyond anything that is now provided, if it cannot collectively invent devices and solve problems on a much richer, broader scale than it does at the present time, it cannot hope to achieve any very much finer order or any more general happiness than it now enjoys. We must believe, therefore, that it *can* develop such a training and education, or we must abandon secular constructive hope. And here my peculiar difficulty as against crude democracy comes in. If humanity at large is capable of that high education and those creative freedoms our hope demands, much more must its better and more vigorous types be so capable. And if those who have power and leisure now, and freedom to respond to imaginative appeals, cannot be won to the idea of collective self-development, then the whole of humanity cannot be won to that. From that one passes to what has become my general conception in politics, the conception of the constructive imagination working upon the vast complex of powerful people, clever people, enterprising people, influential people, amidst whom power is diffused to-day, to produce that self-conscious, highly selective, open-minded, devoted aristocratic culture, which seems to me to be the necessary phase in the development of human affairs. I see human progress, not as the spontaneous product of crowds of raw minds swayed by elementary needs, but as a natural but elaborate result of intricate human interdependencies, of human energy and curiosity liberated and acting at leisure, of human passions and motives, modified and redirected by literature and art. . . .

But now the reader will understand how it came about that, disappointed by the essential littleness of Liberalism, and disillusioned about the representative quality of the professed Socialists, I turned my mind more and more to a scrutiny of the big people, the wealthy and influential people, against whom Liberalism pits its forces. I was asking myself definitely whether, after all, it was not my particular job to work through them and not against them. Was I not altogether out of my element as an Anti-? Weren't there big bold qualities about these people that common men lack, and the possibility of far more splendid dreams? Were they really the obstacles, might they not be rather the vehicles of the possible new braveries of life?

II

The faults of the Imperialist movement were obvious enough. The conception of the Boer War had been clumsy and puerile, the costly errors of that struggle appalling, and the subsequent campaign of Mr. Chamberlain for Tariff Reform seemed calculated to combine the financial adventurers of the Empire ·in one vast conspiracy against the consumer. The cant of Imperialism was easy to learn and use; it was speedily adopted by all sorts of base enterprises and turned to all sorts of base ends. But a big child is permitted big mischief, and my mind was now continually returning to the persua-

sion that after all in some development of the idea of Imperial patriotism might be found that wide, rough, politically acceptable expression of a constructive and philosophical movement such as no
formula of Liberalism supplied. The fact that it readily took vulgar
forms only witnessed to its strong popular appeal. Mixed in with
the noisiness and humbug of the movement there appeared a real regard for social efficiency, a real spirit of animation and enterprise.
There suddenly appeared in my world—I saw them first, I think, in
1908—a new sort of little boy, a most agreeable development of
the slouching, cunning, cigarette-smoking, town-bred youngster, a
small boy in a khaki hat, and with bare knees and athletic bearing,
earnestly engaged in wholesome and invigorating games up to and
occasionally a little beyond his strength—the Boy Scout. I liked the
Boy Scout, and I find it difficult to express how much it mattered to
me, with my growing bias in favor of deliberate national training,
that Liberalism hadn't been able to produce and had indeed never
even attempted to produce anything of this kind. . . ..

III

In those days there existed a dining club called—there was some
lost allusion to the exorcism of party feeling in its title—the Pentagram circle. It included Bailey and Dayton and myself, Sir Herbert Thorns, Lord Charles Kindling, Minns the poet, Gerbault the
big railway man, Lord Gane, fresh from the settlement of Framboya,
and Rumbold, who later became Home Secretary and left us. We
were men of all parties and very various experiences, and our object
was to discuss the welfare of the Empire in a disinterested spirit.
We dined monthly at the Mermaid in Westminster, and for a couple
of years we kept up an average attendance of ten out of fourteen.
The dinner-time was given up to desultory conversation, and it is odd
how warm and good the social atmosphere of that little gathering
became as time went on; then over the dessert, so soon as the waiters
had swept away the crumbs and ceased to fret us, one of us would
open with perhaps fifteen or twenty minutes' exposition of some
specially prepared question, and after him we would deliver ourselves
in turn, each for three or four minutes. When every one present
had spoken once talk became general again, and it was rarely we
emerged upon Hendon Street before midnight. Sometimes, as my
house was conveniently near, a knot of men would come home with
me and go on talking and smoking in my dining-room until two or
three. We had Fred Neal, that wild Irish journalist, among us
towards the end, and his stupendous flow of words materially pro-

longed our closing discussions and made our continuance impossible. I learned very much and very many things at those dinners, but more particularly did I become familiarized with the habits of mind of such men as Neal, Crupp, Gane, and the one or two other New Imperialists who belonged to us. They were nearly all, like Bailey, Oxford men, though mostly of a younger generation, and they were all mysteriously and inexplicably advocates of Tariff Reform, as if it were the principal instead of at best a secondary aspect of constructive policy. They seemed obsessed by the idea that streams of trade could be diverted violently so as to link the parts of the Empire by common interests, and they were persuaded, I still think mistakenly, that Tariff Reform would have an immense popular appeal. They were also very keen on military organization and with a curious little martinet twist in their minds that boded ill for that side of public liberty. So much against them. But they were disposed to spend money much more generously on education, and research of all sorts, than our formless host of Liberals seemed likely to do; and they were altogether more accessible than the Young Liberals to bold, constructive ideas affecting the universities and upper classes. The Liberals are abjectly afraid of the universities. I found myself constantly falling into line with these men in our discussions, and more and more hostile to Dayton's sentimentalizing evasions of definite schemes and Minns' trust in such things as the "Spirit of our People" and the "General Trend of Progress." It wasn't that I thought them very much righter than their opponents; I believe all definite party "sides" at any time are bound to be about equally right and equally lop-sided; but that I thought I could get more out of them and what was more important to me, more out of myself if I coöperated with them. By 1908 I had already arrived at a point where I could be definitely considering a transfer of my political allegiance.

These abstract questions are inseparably interwoven with my memory of a shining long white table, and our hock bottles and burgundy bottles, and bottles of Perrier and St. Galmier and the disturbed central trophy of dessert, and scattered glasses and nut-shells and cigarette-ends and menu-cards used for memoranda. I see old Dayton sitting back and cocking his eye to the ceiling in a way he had while he threw warmth into the ancient platitudes of Liberalism, and Minns leaning forward, and a little like a cockatoo with a taste for confidences, telling us in a hushed voice of his faith in the Destiny of Mankind. Thorns lounges, rolling his round face and round eyes from speaker to speaker and sounding the visible depths of misery whenever Neal begins. Gerbault and Gane were given to conversation in undertones, and Bailey pursued mysterious purposes in lisping whispers. It was Crupp attracted me most. He had, as people say, his eye on me from the beginning. He used to speak at me and drifted into a custom of coming home with me very regularly for an after-talk.

He opened his heart to me.

"Neither of us," he said, "are dukes, and neither of us are horny-handed sons of toil. We want to get hold of the handles, and to do that, one must go where the power is, and give it just as constructive a twist as we can. That's *my* Toryism."

"Is it Kindling's—or Gerbault's?"

"No. But theirs is soft, and mine's hard. Mine will wear theirs out. You and I and Bailey are all after the same thing, and why aren't we working together?"

"Are you a Confederate?" I asked suddenly.

"That's a secret nobody tells," he said.

"What are the Confederates after?"

"Making aristocracy work, I suppose. Just as, I gather, *you* want to do." . . .

The Confederates were being heard of at that time. They were at once attractive and repellent to me, an odd secret society whose membership nobody knew, pledged, it was said, to impose Tariff Reform and an ample constructive policy upon the Conservatives. In the press, at any rate, they had an air of deliberately organized power. I have no doubt the rumor of them greatly influenced my ideas. . . .

In the end I made some very rapid decisions, but for nearly two years I was hesitating. Hesitations were inevitable in such a matter. I was not dealing with any simple question of principle, but with elusive and fluctuating estimates of the trend of diverse forces and of the nature of my own powers. All through that period I was asking over and over again: how far are these Confederates mere dreamers? How far—and this was more vital—are they rendering lip-service to social organization? Is it true they desire war because it confirms the ascendancy of their class? How far can Conservatism be induced to plan and construct before it resists the thrust towards change? Is it really in bulk anything more than a mass of prejudice and conceit, cynical indulgence, and a hard suspicion of and hostility to the expropriated classes in the community?

That is a research which yields no statistics, an inquiry like asking what is the ruling color of a chameleon. The shadowy answer varied with my health, varied with my mood and the conduct of the people I was watching. How fine can people be? How generous? —not incidentally, but all round? How far can you educate sons beyond the outlook of their fathers, and how far lift a rich, proud, self-indulgent class above the protests of its business agents and so-licitors and its own habits and vanity? Is chivalry in a class possible?—was it ever, indeed, or will it ever indeed be possible? Is the progress that seems attainable in certain directions worth the retro-gression that may be its price?

IV

It was to the Pentagram Circle that I first broached the new conceptions that were developing in my mind. I count the evening of my paper the beginning of the movement that created the *Blue Weekly* and our wing of the present New Tory party. I do that without any excessive egotism, because my essay was no solitary man's production; it was my reaction to forces that had come to me very largely through my fellow-members; its quick reception by them showed that I was, so to speak, merely the first of the chestnuts to pop. The atmospheric quality of the evening stands out very vividly in my memory. The night, I remember, was warmly foggy when after midnight we went to finish our talk at my house.

We had recently changed the rules of the club to admit visitors, and so it happened that I had brought Britten, and Crupp introduced Arnold Shoesmith, my former schoolfellow at City Merchants', and now the wealthy successor of his father and elder brother. I remember his heavy, inexpressively handsome face lighting to his rare smile at the sight of me, and how little I dreamt of the tragic entanglement that was destined to involve us both. Gane was present, and Esmeer, a newly-added member, but I think Bailey was absent. Either he was absent, or he said something so entirely characteristic and undistinguished that it has left no impression on my mind.

I had broken a little from the traditions of the club even in my title, which was deliberately a challenge to the liberal idea: it was, " The World Exists for Exceptional People." It is not the title I should choose now—for since that time I have got my phrase of " mental hinterlander " into journalistic use. I should say now, " The World Exists for Mental Hinterland."

The notes I made of that opening have long since vanished with a thousand other papers, but some odd chance has preserved and brought with me to Italy the menu for the evening; its back black with the scrawled notes I made of the discussion for my reply. I found it the other day among some letters from Margaret and a copy of the 1909 Report of the Poor Law Commission, also rich with penciled marginalia.

My opening was a criticism of the democratic idea and method, upon lines such as I have already sufficiently indicated in the preceding sections. I remember how old Dayton fretted in his chair, and tushed and pished at that, even as I gave it, and afterwards we were treated to one of his platitudinous harangues, he sitting back in his chair with that small obstinate eye of his fixed on the ceiling, and a sort of cadaverous glow upon his face, repeating—quite regardless of all my reasoning and all that had been said by others in the debate —the sacred empty phrases that were his soul's refuge from reality. " You may think it very clever," he said, with a nod of his head to mark his sense of his point, " not to Trust in the People. *I* do." And so on. Nothing in his life or work had ever shown that he did trust in the people, but that was beside the mark. He was the party Liberal, and these were the party incantations.

After my preliminary attack on vague democracy I went on to show that all human life was virtually aristocratic; people must either recognize aristocracy in general or else follow leaders, which is aristocracy in particular, and so I came to my point that the reality of human progress lay necessarily through the establishment of freedoms for the human best and a collective receptivity and understanding. There was a disgusted grunt from Dayton, " Superman rubbish—Nietzsche. Shaw! Ugh! " I sailed on over him to my next propositions. The prime essential in a progressive civilization was the establishment of a more effective selective process for the privilege of higher education, and the very highest educational opportunity for the educable. We were too apt to patronize scholarship winners, as though a scholarship was toffee given as a reward for virtue. It wasn't any reward at all; it was an invitation to capacity. We had no more right to drag in virtue or any merit but quality than we had to involve it in a search for the tallest man. We didn't want a mere process for the selection of good as distinguished from gifted and able boys—" No, you *don't*," from Dayton —we wanted all the brilliant stuff in the world concentrated upon the development of the world. Just to exasperate Dayton further I put in a plea for gifts as against character in educational, artistic, and legislative work. " Good teaching," I said, " is better than good conduct. We are becoming idiotic about character."

Dayton was too moved to speak. He slewed round upon me an eye of agonized aversion.

I expatiated on the small proportion of the available ability that is really serving humanity to-day. " I suppose to-day all the thought, all the art, all the increments of knowledge that matter, are supplied so far as the English-speaking community is concerned by —how many?—by three or four thousand individuals. (" Less," said Thorns.) By, to be more precise, the mental hinterlands of three or four thousand individuals. We who know some of the band entertain no illusions as to their innate rarity. We know that they are just the few out of many, the few who got in our world of chance and confusion, the timely stimulus, the apt suggestion at the fortunate moment, the needed training, the leisure. The rest are lost in the crowd, fail through the defects of their qualities, become commonplace workmen and second-rate professional men, marry commonplace wives, are as much waste as the driftage of superfluous pollen in a pine forest is waste."

"Decent honest lives!" said Dayton to his bread-crumbs, with his chin in his necktie. "*Waste!*"

"And the people who do get what we call opportunity get it usually in extremely limited and cramping forms. No man lives a life of intellectual productivity alone; he needs not only material and opportunity, but helpers, resonators. Round and about what I might call the *real* men, you want the sympathetic coöperators, who help by understanding. It isn't that our—*salt* of three or four thousand is needlessly rare; it is sustained by far too small and undifferentiated a public. Most of the good men we know are not really doing the very best work of their gifts; nearly all are a little adapted, most are shockingly adapted to some second-best use. Now, I take it, this is the very centre and origin of the muddle, futility, and unhappiness that distresses us; it's the cardinal problem of the state—to discover, develop, and use the exceptional gifts of men. And I see that best done—I drift more and more away from the common stuff of legislative and administrative activity—by a quite revolutionary development of the educational machinery, but by a still more unprecedented attempt to keep science going, to keep literature going, and to keep what is the necessary spur of all science and literature, an intelligent and appreciative criticism going. You know none of these things have ever been kept going hitherto; they've come unexpectedly and inexplicably."

"Hear, hear!" from Dayton, cough, nodding of the head, and an expression of mystical profundity.

"They've lit up a civilization and vanished, to give place to darkness again. Now the modern state doesn't mean to go back to darkness again—and so it's got to keep its light burning." I went on to attack the present organization of our schools and universities, which seemed elaborately designed to turn the well-behaved, uncritical, and uncreative men of each generation into the authoritative leaders of the next, and I suggested remedies upon lines that I have already indicated in the earlier chapters of this story. . . .

So far I had the substance of the club with me, but I opened new ground and set Crupp agog by confessing my doubt from which party or combination of groups these developments of science and literature and educational organization could most reasonably be expected. I looked up to find Crupp's dark little eye intent upon me.

There I left it to them.

We had an astonishingly good discussion; Neal burst once, but we emerged from his flood after a time, and Dayton had his interlude. The rest was all close, keen examination of my problem.

I see Crupp now with his arm bent before him on the table in a way he had, as though it was jointed throughout its length like a lobster's antenna, his plump, short-fingered hand crushing up a walnut shell into smaller and smaller fragments. "Remington," he said, " has given us the data for a movement, a really possible movement. It's not only possible, but necessary—urgently necessary, I think, if the Empire is to go on."

" We're working altogether too much at the social basement in education and training," said Gane. " Remington is right about our neglect of the higher levels."

Britten made a good contribution with an analysis of what he called the spirit of a country and what made it. " The modern community needs its serious men to be artistic and its artists to be taken seriously." I remember his saying, " The day has gone by for either dull responsibility or merely witty art."

I remember very vividly how Shoesmith harped on an idea I had thrown out of using some sort of review or weekly to express and elaborate these conceptions of a new, severer, aristocratic culture.

" It would have to be done amazingly well," said Britten, and my mind went back to my school days and that ancient enterprise of ours, and how Cossington had rushed it. Well, Cossington had too many papers nowadays to interfere with us, and we perhaps had learnt some defensive devices.

" But this thing has to be linked to some political party," said Crupp, with his eye on me. " You can't get away from that. The Liberals," he added, " have never done anything for research or literature."

" They had a Royal Commission on the Dramatic Censorship," said Thorns, with a note of minute fairness. " It shows what they are made of," he added.

" It's what I've told Remington again and again," said Crupp, " we've got to pick up the tradition of aristocracy, reorganize it, and make it work. But he's certainly suggested a method."

" There won't be much aristocracy to pick up," said Dayton,

darkly to the ceiling, " if the House of Lords throws out the Budget."

" All the more reason for picking it up," said Neal. " For we can't do without it."

" Will they go to the bad, or will they rise from the ashes, aristocrats indeed—if the Liberals come in overwhelmingly? " said Britten.

" It's we who might decide that," said Crupp, insidiously.

" I agree," said Gane.

" No one can tell," said Thorns. " I doubt if they will get beaten."

It was an odd, fragmentary discussion that night. We were all with ideas in our minds at once fine and imperfect. We threw out suggestions that showed themselves at once for inadequate, and we tried to qualify them by minor self-contradictions. Britten, I think, got more said than any one. " You all seem to think you want to organize people, particular groups and classes of individuals," he insisted. " It isn't that. That's the standing error of politicians. You want to organize a culture. Civilization isn't a matter of concrete groupings; it's a matter of prevailing ideas. The problem is how to make bold clear ideas prevail. The question for Remington and us is just what group of people will most help this culture forward."

" Yes, but how are the Lords going to behave? " said Crupp. " You yourself were asking that a little while ago."

" If they win or if they lose," Gane maintained, " there will be a movement to reorganize aristocracy—Reform of the House of Lords, they'll call the political form of it."

" Bailey thinks that," said some one.

" The labor people want abolition," said some one.

" Let 'em," said Thorns.

He became audible, sketching a possible line of action.

" Suppose all of us were able to work together. It's just one of those indeterminate, confused, eventful times ahead when a steady jet of ideas might produce enormous results."

" Leave me out of it," said Dayton, " *if* you please."

" We should," said Thorns under his breath.

I took up Crupp's initiative, I remember, and expanded it.

" I believe we could do—extensive things," I insisted.

" Revivals and revisions of Toryism have been tried so often," said Thorns, " from the Young England movement onward."

" Not one but has produced its enduring effects," I said. " It's the peculiarity of English conservatism that it's persistently progressive and rejuvenescent."

I think it must have been about that point that Dayton fled our presence, after some clumsy sentence that I decided upon reflection was intended to remind me of my duty to my party.

Then I remember Thorns firing doubts at me obliquely across the table. " You can't run a country through its spoilt children," he said. " What you call aristocrats are really spoilt children. They've had too much of everything, except bracing experience."

" Children can always be educated," said Crupp.

" I said *spoilt* children," said Thorns.

" Look here, Thorns! " said I. " If this Budget row leads to a storm, and these big people get their power clipped, what's going to happen? Have you thought of that? When they go out lock, stock, and barrel, who comes in? "

" Nature abhors a vacuum," said Crupp, supporting me.

" Bailey's trained officials," suggested Gane.

" Quacks with a certificate of approval from Altiora," said Thorns. " I admit the horrors of the alternative. There'd be a massacre in three years."

" One may go on trying possibilities for ever," I said. " One thing emerges. Whatever accidents happen, our civilization needs, and almost consciously needs, a culture of fine creative minds, and all the necessary tolerances, opennesses, considerations, that march with that. For my own part, I think that is The Most Vital Thing. Build your ship of state as you will; get your men as you will; I concentrate on what is clearly my affair,—I want to ensure the quality of the quarter deck."

" Hear, hear! " said Shoesmith, suddenly—his first remark for a long time. " A first-rate figure," said Shoesmith, gripping it.

" Our danger is in missing that," I went on. " Muddle isn't ended by transferring power from the muddle-headed few to the muddle-headed many, and then cheating the many out of it again in the interests of a bureaucracy of sham experts. But that seems the limit of the liberal imagination. There is no real progress in a country except a rise in the level of its free intellectual activity. All other progress is secondary and dependent. If you take on Bailey's dreams of efficient machinery and a sort of fanatical discipline with no free-moving brains behind it, confused ugliness becomes rigid ugliness,—that's all. No doubt things are moving from looseness to discipline, and from irresponsible controls to organized controls— and also and rather contrariwise everything is becoming as people say, democratized; but all the more need in that, for an ark in which the living element may be saved."

" Hear, hear! " said Shoesmith, faint but pursuing.

It must have been in my house afterwards that Shoesmith became noticeable. He seemed trying to say something vague and difficult that he didn't get said at all on that occasion. "We could do immense things with a weekly," he repeated, echoing Neal, I think. And there he left off and became a mute expressiveness, and it was only afterwards, when I was in bed, that I saw we had our capitalist in our hands. . . .

We parted that night on my doorstep in a tremendous glow—but in that sort of glow one doesn't act upon without much reconsideration, and it was some months before I made my decision to follow up the indications of that opening talk.

V

I find my thoughts lingering about the Pentagram Circle. In my development it played a large part, not so much by starting new trains of thought as by confirming the practicability of things I had already hesitatingly entertained. Discussion with these other men so prominently involved in current affairs indorsed views that otherwise would have seemed only a little less remote from actuality than the guardians of Plato or the labor laws of More. Among other questions that were never very distant from our discussions, that came apt to every topic, was the true significance of democracy, Tariff Reform as a method of international hostility, and the imminence of war. On the first issue I can still recall little Bailey, glib and winking, explaining that democracy was really just a dodge for getting assent to the ordinances of the expert official by means of the polling booth. "If they don't like things," said he, "they can vote for the opposition candidate and see what happens then—and that, you see, is why we don't want proportional representation to let in the wild men." I opened my eyes—the lids had dropped for a moment under the caress of those smooth sounds—to see if Bailey's artful forefinger wasn't at the side of his predominant nose.

The international situation exercised us greatly. Our meetings were pervaded by the feeling that all things moved towards a day of reckoning with Germany, and I was largely instrumental in keeping up the suggestion that India was in a state of unstable equilibrium, that sooner or later something must happen there—something very serious to our Empire. Dayton frankly detested these topics. He was full of that old Middle Victorian persuasion that whatever is inconvenient or disagreeable to the English mind could be annihilated by not thinking about it. He used to sit low in his chair and look mulish. "Militarism," he would declare in a tone of the utmost moral fervor, "is a curse. It's an unmitigated curse." Then he would cough shortly and twitch his head back and frown, and seem astonished beyond measure that after this conclusive statement we could still go on talking of war.

All our Imperialists were obsessed by the thought of international conflict, and their influence revived for a time those uneasinesses that had been aroused in me for the first time by my continental journey with Willersley and by Meredith's *One of Our Conquerors.* That quite justifiable dread of a punishment for all the slackness, mental dishonesty, presumption, mercenary respectability and sentimentalized commercialism of the Victorian period, at the hands of the better organized, more vigorous, and now far more highly civilized peoples of Central Europe, seemed to me to have both a good and bad series of consequences. It seemed the only thing capable of bracing English minds to education, sustained constructive effort and research; but on the other hand it produced the quality of panic, hasty preparation, impatience of thought, a wasteful and sometimes quite futile immediacy. In 1909, for example, there was a vast clamor for eight additional Dreadnoughts—

" We want eight
And we won't wait,"

but no clamor at all about our national waste of inventive talent, our mean standard of intellectual attainment, our disingenuous criticism, and the consequent failure to distinguish men of the quality needed to carry on the modern type of war. Almost universally we have the wrong men in our places of responsibility and the right men in no place at all, almost universally we have poorly qualified, hesitating, and resentful subordinates, because our criticism is worthless and, so habitually as to be now almost unconsciously, dishonest. Germany is beating England in every matter upon which competition is possible, because she attended sedulously to her collective mind for sixty pregnant years, because in spite of tremendous defects she is still far more anxious for quality in achievement than we are. I remember saying that in my paper. From that, I remember, I went on to an image that had flashed into my mind. " The British Empire," I said, " is like some of those early vertebrated monsters, the Brontosaurus and the Atlantosaurus and such-like; it sacrifices intellect to character; its backbone, that is to say,—especially in the visceral region—is bigger than its cranium. It's no accident that things are so. We've worked for backbone. We brag about backbone, and if the joints are anchylosed so much the better. We're still but only half awake to our error. You can't change that suddenly."

" Turn it round and make it go backwards," interjected Thorns.

"It's trying to do that," I said, "in places."

And afterwards Crupp declared I had begotten a nightmare which haunted him of nights; he was trying desperately and belatedly to blow a brain as one blows soap-bubbles on such a mezozoic saurian as I had conjured up, while the clumsy monster's fate, all teeth and brains, crept nearer and nearer. . . .

I've grown, I think, since those days out of the urgency of that apprehension. I still think a European war, and conceivably a very humiliating war for England, may occur at no very distant date, but I do not think there is any such heroic quality in our governing class as will make that war catastrophic. The prevailing spirit in English life—it is one of the essential secrets of our imperial endurance—is one of underbred aggression in prosperity and diplomatic compromise in moments of danger; we bully haughtily where we can and assimilate where we must. It is not for nothing that our upper and middle-class youth is educated by teachers of the highest character, scholars and gentlemen, men who can pretend quite honestly that Darwinism hasn't upset the historical fall of man, that cricket is moral training, and that Socialism is an outrage upon the teachings of Christ. A sort of dignified dexterity of evasion is the national reward. Germany, with a larger population, a vigorous and irreconcilable proletariat, a bolder intellectual training, a harsher spirit, can scarcely fail to drive us at last to a realization of intolerable strain. So we may never fight at all. The war of preparations that has been going on for thirty years may end like a shamfight at last in an umpire's decision. We shall proudly but very firmly take the second place. For my own part, since I love England as much as I detest her present lethargy of soul, I pray for a chastening war—I wouldn't mind her flag in the dirt if only her spirit would come out of it. So I was able to shake off that earlier fear of some final and irrevocable destruction truncating all my schemes. At the most, a European war would be a dramatic episode in the reconstruction I had in view.

In India, too, I no longer foresee, as once I was inclined to see, disaster. The English rule in India is surely one of the most extraordinary accidents that has ever happened in history. We are there like a man who has fallen off a ladder on to the neck of an elephant, and doesn't know what to do or how to get down. Until something happens he remains. Our functions in India are absurd. We English do not own that country, do not even rule it. We make nothing happen; at the most we prevent things happening. We suppress our own literature there. Most English people cannot even go to this land they possess; the authorities would prevent it. If Messrs. Perowne or Cook organized a cheap tour of Manchester operatives, it would be stopped.   No one dare bring the average English voter face to face with the reality of India, or let the Indian native have a glimpse of the English voter.   In my time I have talked to English statesmen, Indian officials, and ex-officials, viceroys, soldiers, every one who might be supposed to know what India signifies, and I have prayed them to tell me what they thought we were up to there.   I am not writing without my book in these matters. And beyond a phrase or so about " even-handed justice "—and look at our sedition trials!—they told me nothing.   Time after time I have heard of that apocryphal native ruler in the north-west, who, when asked what would happen if we left India, replied that in a week his men would be in the saddle, and in six months not a rupee nor a virgin would be left in Lower Bengal.   That is always given as our conclusive justification.   But is it our business to preserve the rupees and virgins of Lower Bengal in a sort of magic inconclusiveness?   Better plunder than paralysis, better fire and sword than futility.   Our flag is spread over the peninsula, without plans, without intentions—a vast preventive.   The sum total of our policy is to arrest any discussion, any conferences that would enable the Indians to work out a tolerable scheme of the future for themselves. But that does not arrest the resentment of men held back from life. Consider what it must be for the educated Indian sitting at the feast of contemporary possibilities with his mouth gagged and his hands bound behind him!   The spirit of insurrection breaks out in spite of espionage and seizures.   Our conflict for inaction develops stupendous absurdities.   The other day the British Empire was taking off and examining printed cotton stomach wraps for seditious emblems and inscriptions. . . .

In some manner we shall have to come out of India.   We have had our chance, and we have demonstrated nothing but the appalling dullness of our national imagination.   We are not good enough to do anything with India.   Codger and Flack, and Gates and Dayton, Cladingbowl in the club, and the *Family Churchman* in the home, cant about " character," worship of strenuous force and contempt of truth; for the sake of such men and things as these, we must abandon in fact, if not in appearance, that empty domination.   Had we great schools and a powerful teaching, could we boast great men, had we the spirit of truth and creation in our lives, then indeed it might be different.   But a race that bears a sceptre must carry gifts to justify it.

It does not follow that we shall be driven catastrophically from India.   That was my earlier mistake.   We are not proud enough in our bones to be ruined by India as Spain was by her empire.   We may be able to abandon India with an air of still remaining there.

It is our new method. We train our future rulers in the public schools to have a very wholesome respect for strength, and as soon as a power arises in India in spite of us, be it a man or a culture, or a native state, we shall be willing to deal with it. We may or may not have a war, but our governing class will be quick to learn when we are beaten. Then they will repeat our South African diplomacy, and arrange for some settlement that will abandon the reality, such as it is, and preserve the semblance of power. The conqueror *de facto* will become the new " loyal Briton," and the democracy at home will be invited to celebrate our recession—triumphantly. I am no believer in the imminent dissolution of our Empire; I am less and less inclined to see in either India or Germany the probability of an abrupt truncation of those slow intellectual and moral constructions which are the essentials of statecraft.

VI

I sit writing in this little loggia to the sound of dripping water —this morning we had rain, and the roof of our little casa is still not dry, there are pools in the rocks under the sweet chestnuts, and the torrent that crosses the salita is full and boastful—and I try to recall the order of my impressions during that watching, dubious time, before I went over to the Conservative Party. I was trying— chaotic task!—to gauge the possibilities inherent in the quality of the British aristocracy. There comes a broad spectacular effect of wide parks, diversified by woods and bracken valleys, and dappled with deer; of great smooth lawns shaded by ancient trees; of big façades of sunlit buildings dominating the country side; of large fine rooms full of handsome, easy-mannered people. As a sort of representative picture to set off against those other pictures of Liberals and of Socialists I have given, I recall one of those huge assemblies the Duchess of Clynes inaugurated at Stamford House. The place itself is one of the vastest private houses in London, a huge clustering mass of white and gold salons with polished floors and wonderful pictures, and staircases and galleries on a Gargantuan scale. And there she sought to gather all that was most representative of English activities, and did, in fact, in those brilliant nocturnal crowds, get samples of nearly every section of our social and intellectual life, with a marked predominance upon the political and social side.

I remember sitting in one of the recesses at the end of the big salon with Mrs. Redmondson, one of those sharp-minded, beautiful rich women one meets so often in London, who seem to have done nothing and to be capable of everything, and we watched the crowd—uniforms and splendors were streaming in from a state ball—and exchanged information. I told her about the politicians and intellectuals, and she told me about the aristocrats, and we sharpened our wit on them and counted the percentage of beautiful people among the latter, and wondered if the general effect of tallness was or was not an illusion.

They were, we agreed, for the most part bigger than the average of people in London, and a handsome lot, even when they were not subtly individualized. "They look so well nurtured," I said, "well cared for. I like their quiet, well-trained movements, their pleasant consideration for each other."

"Kindly, good tempered, and at bottom utterly selfish," she said, "like big, rather carefully trained, rather pampered children. What else can you expect from them?"

"They are good tempered, anyhow," I witnessed, "and that's an achievement. I don't think I could ever be content under a bad-tempered, sentimentalizing, strenuous Government. That's why I couldn't stand the Roosevelt *régime* in America. One's chief surprise when one comes across these big people for the first time is their admirable easiness and a real personal modesty. I confess I admire them. Oh! I like them. I wouldn't at all mind, I believe, giving over the country to this aristocracy—given *something*——"

"Which they haven't got."

"Which they haven't got—or they'd be the finest sort of people in the world."

"That something?" she inquired.

"I don't know. I've been puzzling my wits to know. They've done all sorts of things—— "

"That's Lord Wrassleton," she interrupted, "whose leg was broken—you remember?—at Spion Kop."

"It's healed very well. I like the gold lace and the white glove resting, with quite a nice awkwardness, on the sword. When I was a little boy I wanted to wear clothes like that. And the stars! He's got the V.C. Most of these people here have at any rate shown pluck, you know—brought something off."

"Not quite enough," she suggested.

"I think that's it," I said. "Not quite enough—not quite hard enough," I added.

She laughed and looked at me. "You'd like to make us," she said.

"What?"

"Hard."

"I don't think you'll go on if you don't get hard."

" We shan't be so pleasant if we do."

" Well, there my puzzled wits come in again. I don't see why an aristocracy shouldn't be rather hard trained, and yet kindly. I'm not convinced that the resources of education are exhausted. I want to better this, because it already looks so good."

" How are we to do it? " asked Mrs. Redmondson.

" Oh, there you have me! I've been spending my time lately in trying to answer that! It makes me quarrel with "—I held up my fingers and ticked the items off—" the public schools, the private tutors, the army exams., the Universities, the Church, the general attitude of the country towards science and literature———"

" We all do," said Mrs. Redmondson. " We can't begin again at the beginning," she added.

" Couldn't one," I nodded at the assembly in general, " start a movement? "

" There's the Confederates," she said, with a faint smile that masked a gleam of curiosity. . . . " You want," she said, " to say to the aristocracy, ' Be aristocrats. *Noblesse oblige.*' Do you remember what happened to the monarch who was told to ' Be a King '? "

" Well," I said, " I want an aristocracy."

" This," she said, smiling, " is the pick of them. The backwoodsmen are off the stage. These are the brilliant ones—the smart and the blue. . . . They cost a lot of money, you know."

So far Mrs. Redmondson, but the picture remained full of things not stated in our speech. They were on the whole handsome people, charitable minded, happy, and easy. They led spacious lives, and there was something free and fearless about their bearing that I liked extremely. The women particularly were wide-reading, fine-thinking. Mrs. Redmondson talked as fully and widely and boldly as a man, and with those flashes of intuition, those startling, sudden delicacies of perception few men display. I liked, too, the relations that held between women and men, their general tolerance, their antagonism to the harsh jealousies that are the essence of the middle-class order. . . .

After all, if one's aim resolved itself into the development of a type and culture of men, why shouldn't one begin at this end?

VII

It is very easy indeed to generalize about a class of human beings, but much harder to produce a sample. Was old Lady Forthundred, for instance, fairly a sample? I remember her as a smiling, magnificent presence, a towering accumulation of figure and wonderful shimmering blue silk and black lace and black hair, and small fine features and chins and chins and chins, disposed in a big cane chair with wraps and cushions upon the great terrace of Champneys. Her eye was blue and hard, and her accent and intonation was exactly what you would expect from a rather commonplace dressmaker pretending to be aristocratic. I was, I am afraid, posing a little as the intelligent but respectful inquirer from below investigating the great world, and she was certainly posing as my informant. She affected a cynical coarseness. She developed a theory on the governance of England, beautifully frank and simple. " Give 'um all a peerage when they get twenty thousand a year," she maintained. " That's my remedy."

In my new rôle of theoretical aristocrat I felt a little abashed.

" Twenty thousand," she repeated with conviction.

It occurred to me that I was in the presence of the aristocratic theory currently working as distinguished from my as yet unformulated intentions.

" You'll get a lot of loafers and scamps among 'um," said Lady Forthundred. " You get loafers and scamps everywhere, but you'll get a lot of men who'll work hard to keep things together, and that's what we're all after, isn't ut? "

" It's not an ideal arrangement."

" Tell me anything better," said Lady Forthundred.

On the whole, and because she refused emphatically to believe in education, Lady Forthundred scored.

We had been discussing Cossington's recent peerage, for Cossington, my old schoolfellow at City Merchants', and my victor in the affair of the magazine, had clambered to an amazing wealth up a piled heap of energetically pushed penny and halfpenny magazines, and a group of daily newspapers. I had expected to find the great lady hostile to the new-comer, but she accepted him, she gloried in him.

" We're a peerage," she said, " but none of us have ever had any nonsense about nobility."

She turned and smiled down on me. " We English," she said, " are a practical people. We assimilate 'um."

" Then, I suppose, they don't give trouble? "

" Then they don't give trouble."

" They learn to shoot? "

" And all that," said Lady Forthundred. " Yes. And things go on. Sometimes better than others, but they go on—somehow. It depends very much on the sort of butler who pokes 'um about."

I suggested that it might be possible to get a secure twenty

thousand a year by at least detrimental methods—socially speaking.
" We must take the bad and the good of 'um," said Lady Forthundred, courageously. . . .

Now, was she a sample? It happened she talked. What was
there in the brains of the multitude of her first, second, third, fourth,
and fifth cousins, who didn't talk, who shone tall, and bearing themselves finely, against a background of deft, attentive maids and
valets, on every spacious social scene? How did things look to
them?

VIII

Side by side with Lady Forthundred, it is curious to put Evesham with his tall, bent body, his little-featured, almost elvish face,
his unequaled mild brown eyes, his gentle manner, his sweet, amazing
oratory. He led all these people wonderfully. He was always cu-
rions and interested about life, wary beneath a pleasing frankness
—and I tormented my brain to get to the bottom of him. For a
long time he was the most powerful man in England under the
throne; he had the Lords in his hand, and a great majority in the
Commons, and the discontents and intrigues that are the concomitants of an overwhelming party advantage broke against him as
waves break against a cliff. He foresaw so far in these matters
that it seemed he scarcely troubled to foresee. He brought political
art to the last triumph of naturalness. Always for me he has been
the typical aristocrat, so typical and above the mere forms of aristocracy, that he remained a commoner to the end of his days.

I had met him at the beginning of my career; he read some early
papers of mine, and asked to see me, and I conceived a flattered liking for him that strengthened to a very strong feeling indeed. He
seemed to me to stand alone without an equal, the greatest man in
British political life.

And what was he up to? What did *he* think we were doing with
Mankind? That I thought worth knowing.

I remember his talking on one occasion at the Hartsteins', at a
dinner so tremendously floriferous and equipped that we were almost
forced into duologues, about the possible common constructive purpose in politics.

" I feel so much," he said, " that the best people in every party
converge. We don't differ at Westminster as they do in the county
towns. There's a sort of extending common policy that goes on
under every government, because on the whole it's the right thing
to do, and people know it. Things that used to be matters of opinion become matters of science—and cease to be party questions."

He instanced education.

" Apart," said I, " from the religious question."

" Apart from the religious question."

He dropped that aspect with an easy grace, and went on with his general theme that political conflict was the outcome of uncertainty. "Directly you get a thing established, so that people can say, 'Now this is Right,' with the same conviction that people can say water is a combination of oxygen and hydrogen, there's no more to be said. The thing has to be done. . . ."

And to put against this effect of Evesham, broad and humanely tolerant, posing as the minister of a steadily developing constructive conviction, there are other memories.

Have I not seen him in the House, persistent, persuasive, indefatigable, and by all my standards wickedly perverse, leaning over the table with those insistent movements of his hand upon it, or swaying forward with a grip upon his coat lapel, fighting with a diabolical skill to preserve what are in effect religious tests, tests he must have known would outrage and humiliate and injure the consciences of a quarter—and that perhaps the best quarter—of the youngsters who come to the work of elementary education?

In playing for points in the game of party advantage Evesham displayed at times a quite wicked unscrupulousness in the use of his subtle mind. I would sit on the liberal benches and watch him, and listen to his urbane voice, fascinated by him. Did he really care? Did anything matter to him? And if it really mattered nothing, why did he trouble to serve the narrowness and passion of his side? Or did he see far beyond my scope, so that this petty iniquity was justified by greater, remoter ends of which I had no intimation?

They accused him of nepotism. His friends and family were certainly well cared for. In private life he was full of an affectionate intimacy; he pleased by being charmed and pleased. One might think at times there was no more of him than a clever man happily circumstanced, and finding an interest and occupation in politics. And then came a glimpse of thought, of imagination, like the sight of a soaring eagle through a staircase skylight. Oh, beyond question he was great! No other contemporary politician had his quality. In no man have I perceived so sympathetically the great contrast between warm, personal things and the white dream of statecraft. Except that he had it seemed no hot passions, but only interests and fine affections and indolences, he paralleled the conflict of my life. He saw and thought widely, and deeply; but at times it seemed to me his greatness stood over and behind the reality of his life, like some splendid servant, thinking his own thoughts, who waits behind a lesser master's chair. . . .

(To be continued.)

THE FORUM
FOR MARCH 1911

THE FORUM FOR TWENTY-FIVE YEARS

T is twenty-five years since the first number of THE FORUM was issued, in March, 1886. A generation has passed, with its promise, achievement, failure; the Nineteenth Century, which seemed through mere familiarity an era dominant and immutable, has been added to the counted centuries, and is already a memory; a new age has been born, a new world is in the making, and a new faith is growing in the hearts of men. Everywhere, to those who look with seeing eyes, are the signs and portents of the new order. Capital still clashes with labor; from continent to continent, the organization of industry becomes more complex and threatening; international jealousies still linger, fomented by the ignorant and careless; abuses and corruption are found notoriously in public and in private life. Yet the race progresses; the public conscience, less intolerant with regard to outward forms and observances, is more insistent in its demand for the broad view, the unselfish aim, the faithful and just discharge of duty. There are more men and women in the world to-day who would give their lives for an ideal, than there have ever been before; anarchist or patriot, missionary or physician, mediævalists or men of the Twentieth Century, they are numbered in the hosts of those who will sacrifice personal profit to principle; they are marching on—some, perhaps, with faltering steps and imperfect comprehension—to the achievement of the greater civilization. There have ever been visionaries: but to-day, ideals are becoming significantly normal; dreams are transmuted into deeds.

In 1886, Grover Cleveland was President of the United States; Queen Victoria had not yet seen the pageant of her first jubilee; William I was German Emperor, François Paul Jules Grévy the

Head of the French Republic, Humbert I King of Italy. They have gone. Four other Presidents have entered the White House, two Kings have sat on Queen Victoria's throne, two Kaisers have held the sceptre of the first War-lord. And of all the myriads of human beings who were then living, men, women, and children, more than two-fifths have passed away. In 1886, there were fifty-six millions of people in the United States; thirty-three millions of them are left, in the ninety-four millions of the present population. Twenty-three millions have died—the harvest of a quarter of a century. The Boer War has been fought and our war with Spain and in the Philippines. The air has been conquered. The Panama Canal has been brought into being. The genius of Edison and the great inventors has made the miraculous commonplace; automobiles, the phonograph, wireless telegraphy, aeroplanes, are among the products of these twenty-five years. Science has moved forward magnificently; the arts have followed—perhaps a little less conspicuously. New York has more than doubled her population: San Francisco has risen from ruins. There are eight more States in the Union, thirty-eight millions more people, fifty-six billions of dollars more wealth. The times change indeed, and the children of time and circumstance change with them. Perhaps it were unkind to suggest that while our imports and exports have doubled, while our wealth has doubled, and our population will soon have the same numerical distinction, the cost of living has increased in a corresponding ratio!

THE FORUM, which now celebrates its twenty-fifth anniversary, was founded by Mr. Isaac L. Rice, at one time lecturer in the School of Political Science at Columbia University, and later, instructor in the Law School. Mr. Rice, who had retired from Columbia in order to devote himself to railroad law, and to his business interests, had for some years been concerned with the idea of a magazine which should be preëminently a *public* magazine, a medium for the discussion, sanely and seriously, of all vital questions. When his partner, Mr. Nathan Bijur—now a Justice of the Supreme Court of New York State—communicated to him the fact that Mr. Lorettus S. Metcalf, long the managing editor of *The North American Review*, would be glad to undertake the literary direction of such a magazine, Mr. Rice at once entered into negotiations, and a definite arrangement was soon concluded. The title selected—THE FORUM—was sufficiently suggestive; the new review was to be open to the intelligent discussion of all legitimate topics, without bias, fear or favor. In a country where the experiment of democracy was being tried on a scale unprecedented in the history of the world, every undertaking which would further progress became more than a mere expression of personal effort or influence, and assumed a larger, and to some extent a national, importance. It is not easy for a young nation to become worthily articulate. In the stress and urgency of developing a country so vast and so unprecedentedly rich in natural resources, of assimilating the streams of immigrants, of building up a people and a political society that should have unity and stability, the tendency of the majority of men, both of fine and coarse fibre, was inevitably to action rather than to reflection. But the United States had now become more than an experimental republic in the west, which Europe regarded, tolerantly or critically, as embryonic and dubious; but to which the hordes of the submerged—pitiable products of those " old civilizations "—looked as to a haven beyond the seas; too often, a heaven beyond their attainment. She had become a World Force; had taken her place, for good or for evil, in the Congress of Powers; was beginning to realize, as she will learn to realize more and more, her special and high destiny—to lead the way where the nations shall follow; to vindicate democracy by making clear its trend and true completeness—liberty without license, equality without extravagance, fraternity without fanaticism; self-government and self-control; and a noble, just rejection of all indefensible principles and all unworthy actions. It is time that the rules which are observed by honorable men, as individuals, should regulate also the conduct of peoples and states. The brigandry of armed empires is as intolerable as the lawlessness of bandits and mobs. The day of insolent injustice—as between men or multitudes of men—is drawing to a close. The appeal is no longer from Festus to Cæsar, from the little lord to the greater lord, from the gunboat to the Dreadnought. It is from the conscience of man to the conscience of humanity. One appeal to force alone remains—the force of example. Let America compel the nations to follow her—by leading the way.

It was the desire of the founder of THE FORUM that the new review should serve the needs of the country by contributing, in degree, to the means by which she should become adequately articulate. In the conduct of the magazine, no policy of partisanship or special pleading was adopted; no precepts were offered dictatorially; no *ex cathedrâ* pronouncements were made. It was essentially *The Forum* —in which the People could discuss and debate. Any viewpoint of value could find expression. Orthodoxy was not a pre-requisite, if heterodoxy did not—as is occasionally its habit—disqualify itself by a too obtrusive disregard of the courtesies of custom and debate.

The first volume indicated the scope and possibilities of the new review, and prepared the way for its success and established position in American life. There were articles on Science, Religion, Government, Law, Education, Labor, Anarchism, Economics, and subjects of general or special importance. Among the contributors were Andrew Carnegie, Dr. Edward Everett Hale, Lieut. A. W. Greely, Professor Alexander Winchell, Thomas Wentworth Higginson, Bishop F. D. Huntington and Professor R. H. Thurston. Mr. Carnegie, in an article entitled *An Employer's View of the Labor Question*, offered definite suggestions for the amelioration of the relations between employer and employed, and concluded with a passage which may well be quoted here —:

" Whatever the future may have in store for labor, the evolutionist, who sees nothing but certain and steady progress for the race, will never attempt to set bounds to its triumphs, even to its final form of complete and universal industrial coöperation, which I hope is some day to be reached."

There is always a curious interest in reviewing the definite utterances of prominent men a generation ago, in the light of the actual achievements of the present, which they foresaw partly or in whole. Professor R. H. Thurston, in *The Limit of Speed in Ocean Travel*, made some remarkable speculations with regard to the development of ocean liners. The Etruria then represented " the best modern naval architecture; a ship of 520 feet length, 57 feet beam, 41 feet depth, and 8,000 tons measurement." The professor proceeded to estimate —not fantastically, but with careful consideration of the technical requirements—the possibilities of the future. In view of the records of the Mauretania and Lusitania, of the appearance of the new

Olympic and Titanic, and of the still more recent plans of the Cunard Line, the forecast has unusual interest at the present time. One cannot often compare so clearly the progress of a generation, with the previous expectations. Professor Thurston wrote:—

"It was asserted by a distinguished man of science, forty years ago, that no steamship could be made to cross the Atlantic because of the impossibility of carrying sufficient coal to supply the engines and boilers for the voyage. The prophecy was proved false almost as soon as it was uttered by the appearance in New York harbor of the Great Britain, the pioneer of the Cunard Line, after a passage of fourteen days and nine hours. . . . A more credible recent prediction was made in 1872 by a well-known naval architect, Mr. Robert Duncan, who stated that he anticipated that, before the end of the century, we should see crossing the Atlantic the ferry-boats of the ocean, 800 feet in length. The Great Eastern was 680 feet long, and the difference between that length and 800 feet is not now to be considered very great. Let us assume that such a ship may be constructed, the question arises, What would be her maximum possible speed?

"A steamer 800 feet in length, 80 feet beam, and of 25 feet draught of water, would weigh, complete and in sailing trim, about 38,000 tons, if given what may be considered as the best form to-day known for maximum speed. The fast ships of to-day exert about one and a half horse-power per ton to reach a speed of 20 sea miles an hour. With some little improvement, such as may be safely anticipated before the close of the century, this figure may be reduced somewhat, and a larger ship will have some advantage. Our later 'Leviathan' may be expected to demand about 35,000 horse-power at 20 knots. We will, however, aspire to 40 knots (about 47 miles). . . . At this enormous speed she would cross the Atlantic in about 80 hours, or less than three and a half days. . . . We may take the probable power demanded as not far from 250,000 horse-power."

The only comment necessary is in the form of the figures given below:—

	Gross Tonnage.	Horse-Power.	Length.	Beam.	Depth.
Mauretania } Lusitania	33,000	70,000	790	88	60
Olympic } Titanic	45,000	50,000	882	92	80

Lieut. A. W. Greely closes a paper on *The Future of Arctic Exploration* with the following passage, not without topical reference:—

" It is not improbable that the beginning of the twenty-first century will see a revival of interest and favor regarding this question of extended scientific polar research. If such renewal comes, let there be proper forethought, means and plan, so that never again shall our countrymen go forth on a hopeless quest, or under circumstances where ingenuity must supplement resources and personal qualities replace effective organization. Under such conditions American hearts would, as of old, be

' Strong in will
To strive, to seek, to find and not to yield.' "

So much—of brevity—for the first volume. In those which have followed, every phase of human activity and concern has been touched upon, from the relations of Church and State, to the relations of the sea-serpent and reality. James Bryce has written on the policy of annexation and on the teaching of civic duty; E. A. Freeman on the debt of the old world to the new; Theodore Roosevelt on the enforcement of law, on true American ideals, on the disappearance of big game in the West, on manly virtues and practical politics, on the law of civilization and decay, and on the meaning of " Americanism " —a characteristic list. Prince Peter Alexeievitch Kropotkin contributed two articles; W. D. Howells wrote on the nature of liberty, Charles W. Eliot on municipal misgovernment and on popular education, Woodrow Wilson on university training and citizenship, and other topics; and so through a long list of notable contributors. During the first four years, especially, many articles were published attacking political corruption; and in the selection of subjects for consideration, a certain higher purpose has always been apparent in the direction of THE FORUM. A brief list of some of the contributors who have attained international prominence is given here, for purposes of record.

SOME NOTABLE CONTRIBUTORS

Lyman Abbott	James Lane Allen
Jane Addams	William Archer
Felix Adler	Sir Edwin Arnold

Sir Walter Besant
Björnstjerne Björnson
Paul Bourget
James Bryce
Richard Burton
Bliss Carman
Andrew Carnegie
Georges Clémenceau
F. Marion Crawford
Charles W. Eliot
Anatole France
E. A. Freeman
E. L. Godkin
Edmund Gosse
Lieut. A. W. Greely
Arthur T. Hadley
Edward Everett Hale
Murat Halstead
Philip Gilbert Hamerton
J. Keir Hardie
Thomas Hardy
Benjamin Harrison
Frederic Harrison
Thomas Wentworth Higginson
George F. Hoar
Julia Ward Howe
William D. Howells
Sir Henry Irving
William James
Prince Kropotkin
Henry Labouchere
Andrew Lang
W. E. H. Lecky

Richard Le Gallienne
Henry Cabot Lodge
Pierre Loti
A. Maurice Low
Seth Low
Justin M'Carthy
A. T. Mahan
Edwin Markham
James Brander Matthews
George Meredith
Gen. Nelson A. Miles
Helena Modjeska
Charles Eliot Norton
Bishop Henry C. Potter
Jacob A. Riis
James Whitcomb Riley
Theodore Roosevelt
Lord Russell of Killowen
C. W. Saleeby
Gustav H. Schwab.
Anton Seidl.
John Sherman
Goldwin Smith
William T. Stead
Francis R. Stockton
William Graham Sumner
Algernon Charles Swinburne
Mark Twain
H. G. Wells
Horace White
Woodrow Wilson.
Louis Windmüller.
Carroll D. Wright

For sixteen years after its foundation, THE FORUM appeared monthly. In July, 1902, it was transformed into a quarterly, publishing in each issue a certain number of systematized reviews of the various phases of human activity, supplemented by several special articles. In July, 1908, it became a monthly again, but the system of reviews continued throughout 1909.

LORETTUS SUTTON METCALF, the first editor of THE FORUM, was born at Monmouth, Maine, in October, 1837. He was educated in the public schools at Monmouth and Boston. In 1899 he received the A.M. degree from Bates College, and a year later Iowa College conferred upon him the LL.D. In 1871 Mr. Metcalf became editor of *The Messenger* (Malden, Massachusetts), and during the next five years he controlled five weeklies near Boston. His connection with *The North American Review* commenced in 1876 and lasted till 1885, when the inception of THE FORUM was planned. He remained the editor until 1891, and has since founded and edited the *Florida Daily Citizen*.

WALTER HINES PAGE, editor from 1891 to 1895, was born at Cary, North Carolina, August 15th, 1855. He was educated at Bingham School and Randolph-Macon College, Virginia, and at Johns Hopkins University. From 1895 to 1899 he was literary adviser to Houghton, Mifflin and Company, and during the greater part of that time he was also editor of *The Atlantic Monthly*. In 1900 he assumed the editorship of *The World's Work*. He is a member of the well-known publishing firm of Doubleday, Page and Company, and the author of *The Rebuilding of Old Commonwealths*, published in 1902. For some time after Mr. Page's resignation the editorial direction remained in the hands of Mr. Isaac L. Rice, assisted by Mr. A. E. Keet, until the appointment of Dr. J. M. Rice.

JOSEPH M. RICE, editor for nearly ten years—from May, 1897, to April, 1907—was born at Philadelphia in 1857. He graduated at the College of the City of New York, and at the College of Physicians and Surgeons, and practised medicine in New York from 1881 to 1888. After studying psychology and pedagogics at the Universities of Jena and Leipzig he took over the control of THE FORUM, publishing many articles of his own on educational subjects. In 1903 he founded the Society for Educational Research.

FREDERIC T. COOPER, who succeeded Dr. Rice, was born in New York in 1864. He graduated from Harvard in 1886; Ph.D. Columbia, 1895. He was assistant instructor and assistant professor at Columbia and New York Universities, and became later the literary editor of *The Commercial Advertiser*. Dr. Cooper was followed by Dr. B. Russell Herts, who was born in New York in 1888 and graduated from Columbia in 1908. Dr. Herts was editor from the fall of 1909 until the summer of 1910, when THE FORUM passed under its present direction.

Isaac L. Rice, the founder of The Forum, and president, continuously, of The Forum Publishing Company, was born February 22nd, 1850. He was educated in Philadelphia and New York, and graduated from Columbia Law School in 1880. In 1902 he received the degree of LL.D. from Bates College. He founded the Academy of Political Science at Columbia, and was lecturer in the School of that name during 1882 and 1883, and instructor in the Law School from 1884 to 1886, when he resigned to devote himself to railroad law and to his widening business interests. For some time he was engaged as counsel and director of a number of railways. He subsequently projected and controlled many important undertakings, and is at present the head of a large group of companies, operating in various spheres of enterprise. He has contributed occasional essays to The Forum and other reviews, dealing with problems and principles of enduring importance.

It has been written—by a woman—that " he who casts on any set of duties the shadow of the *second best,* so far as he is successful, does more to influence the moral ideal than he who succeeds in passing a new law." This may appear, momentarily, a trifle cryptic; yet it represents precisely the underlying reason for the existence of The Forum. Men must move forward; they cannot be allowed to stagnate. The object of all reflection, all inquiry, all discussion and debate, is to discover, so far as possible, the principles of truth, and the means of progress toward the truth. To rest content with what seems moderately good, or relatively good, is intolerable, if there is a better which can be realized and interpreted in terms of life, activity, movement. For only the best is really good: as soon as we have perceived that any condition, or situation, or conduct of affairs, whether public or personal, local or of wide reference, is capable of improvement, we must discard the less and be content only with the greater. It is the defiance—not the ignorance—of this fundamental principle, which has permitted for so long the notorious scandals in municipal and national politics. Graft, greed, self-interest, ignorance, indifference, should be inconceivable, on a large scale, in a community which professes not merely to be civilized, but to be rational. In avoiding what may seem like self-righteousness, it is possible also to forfeit self-respect.

It will be the policy of The Forum, in the future, as in the past, to serve democracy by giving those who truly represent the people an opportunity to discuss questions of public and permanent interest; to ventilate legitimate grievances; to advocate, or seek for, the amelioration of all conditions which are not in accord with American ideas and ideals of justice and true fitness. And apart from political and general questions, The Forum will associate itself with that most important public service—the development of the national literature —by giving to all fine work, in poetry and in prose, an opportunity of recognition. But though the lessons of the past will not be ignored, and those outstanding movements which have enduring significance will be considered and reconsidered, the more definite aim will be to realize the needs and problems of the present and the possibilities of the future. There is ever a plethora of destructive or merely analytic criticism. This is the time, surely, for synthesis, for constructive statesmanship and constructive citizenship. In political or social life, in science and the arts, and in comprehensive philosophy, the outlook must be forward, rather than retrospective; the increasing purpose, creative or remedial. But reform based on facile enthusiasm, unregulated by reasoned inquiry and knowledge, is more hazardous than valuable. At this time, when there are so many pressing questions involving conflict between the individual and intrenched interests, it is necessary to realize clearly the distinction between liberty and license, and to avoid error, in judgment or policy.

In order to characterize especially the motives which prompted the founding of The Forum, we reprint an article written by Mr. Rice twenty-eight years ago, which summarizes his view of the philosophy of history and indicates the ends for which The Forum was founded and the lines which were to guide it. The progress of the world along these lines and within these years has not been less marvelons than that in the material arts. We need only point out in our own country the creation of the Interstate Commerce and Public Service Commissions, and the enactment of Employers' Liability laws; in France the separation of Church and State; in Turkey and Persia the establishment of democratic institutions, in Portugal of a Republic, in Russia of the Duma; in China the recognition of the will of the People; and in England the shaking to its foundations of the hereditary right to legislate.

A DEFINITION OF LIBERTY *

ISAAC L. RICE

THE conclusions arising from the history of the development of civil liberty in England, may, I contend, be summed up in two propositions: *First.* Civil liberty is the result of the restraint of the legally acknowledged and vested private rights of the more powerful individuals and classes of the community; provided, *Second.* That this restraint be exercised by the sovereign people.

First. Civil liberty as the result of the restraint of private rights.

That civil liberty is not generally supposed to be incompatible with the restraint of personal freedom, our penal statutes and prisons amply prove. It may, however, appear somewhat paradoxical to assert that it is also dependent on the restraint of rights of private property and private contracts. Nevertheless, the history of civil liberty in England conclusively shows that the right to convert all manner of relations into private property and the right to the unrestricted use of private property, are incompatible with the security of private property, and consequently incompatible with liberty itself; for such unrestricted rights are nothing less than instruments of oppression in the hands of the more powerful individuals and classes.

By the conquest of 1066 one individual became so powerful that, compared with him, all the other individuals and all classes of the community taken together, sink into insignificance. This was owing to the fact that at that period the idea of public relations was unknown, and that of unlimited private rights was recognized. And so William of Normandy, conquering England, acquired it as his private property in unrestricted ownership, with the incidental right of converting all relations springing out of the land into appurtenances of it. And thus, as owner, not only did he have a paramount title to the soil, so that all who occupied it held it by his good-will and pleasure, and subject to the conditions which, by contract, he chose to impose upon it; but likewise all the proceeds issuing out of land and constituting the movable property of the tenants became mere ap-

---

* Reprinted by the courtesy of *The North American Review* from its issue of January, 1883.

purtenances of the land, and were held by others only to the extent permitted by him. Consequently, whenever he required the possession of these movables, he was justified in seizing them by taxation or purveyance, as he merely took back his own. Since it was impossible fully to enjoy his property unless peace were kept in his domains, peace became an appurtenance of them, and there was an implied contract imposed upon all who were suffered by him to dwell upon them, not to commit an injury on the king's peace. Whoever broke the peace, therefore, committed a breach of the contract, under which alone he held anything whatever, and consequently forfeited all he held. If the king, in his mercy, allowed the offender to retain a portion when the offence was not too heinous, it was a matter of mercy, and called an amercement. And as it was difficult, or perhaps impossible, to maintain peace intact unless the tenants of his great manor dealt justly with each other, the dominion of the relations of justice as appendant to that of peace was one of the necessary appurtenances to the land. But, of course, this did not give a right to any one to compel the king to protect him against the injustice of his neighbor. This protection was always a favor which the king might grant, but for the granting of which he was justified in exacting a compensation. Just as necessary to the maintenance of peace was the control of the relations arising out of the commerce of his tenants among themselves, and with foreigners. Therefore, the dominion of markets, fairs, coinage, exchange, weights and measures, and many other things of this nature, became, likewise, a private right appurtenant to the land. It need hardly be said that the owner of this vast property might defend it against all enemies within and without, and that it was part of the contract of all his tenants to assist him in this defence, and that, in consequence, the dominion of war was also a necessary appurtenance of his ownership. These services he could exact either in the shape of men or money, or in necessaries, and could, of course, as owner, commute these one with another.

And this complete ownership had, by the time of King John, become, through the continued enjoyment of a century and a half, as thoroughly vested a right as it is possible to conceive. A complete proof of this is found in the fact that this king performed the extreme act of ownership—that of alienation. In 1213 he conveyed England with all its appurtenances to Pope Innocent, who reconveyed it to him in fee-farm subject to a rent of 1,000 marks; and that this conveyance and reconveyance were considered strictly within right is evidenced by the fact that the rent was paid throughout the reigns of Henry III, Edward I, and Edward II, and part of that of Edward III, for nearly a century and a quarter. And among the numberless other evidences of the king's vested rights of private property in the Kingdom of England, I shall only advance that as late as 1271, Edward I, while yet heir-apparent, devised the kingdom with all its appurtenances to his executors, to administer the same for the benefit of his heirs.

And this vast estate with its immense revenues, in the shape of reliefs, wardships, marriages, aids, and escheats, its direct issues of the land; and in the shape of taxation and purveyance, forfeiture and amercement, purchase money of judicial writs, tolls, customs, coinage, —its indirect issues; this vast estate, I repeat, was managed entirely on business principles—that is, on the basis of the self-interest of its owner.

His great officers and council, therefore, were nothing more nor less than his private servants, and any interference on the part of his tenants in regard to the appointment or removal of these was always resented as an unwarrantable impertinence. When Richard II was petitioned by Parliament to remove his chancellor, he replied indignantly that he would not remove the meanest scullion of his kitchen at their request. The answer shows that for the king the difference between a lord chancellor and a scullion was one in degree—not in kind—the one as the other being only his servant, and no one else's servant.

It was for the better collection of his revenues that he divided England into the bailiwicks of counties and hundreds, over which he set his sheriffs, escheators, and others, as his stewards or his farmers, responsible only to him, and holding their offices as tenements from the king, in fee, for life, or for a less estate by the various tenures in which land itself was held. And for the reason that the relation of the king to subjects was the private one of landlord and tenant, the Court of Exchequer, the guardian of his treasury, into which court all payments of whatever nature were collected, and all disbursements of whatever nature—whether for building of castles, manning of ships, or settling of butchers' and grocers' bills for the household—were indiscriminately rendered, was the highest court of the realm; where the capital justiciary presided, where the chancellor sold his writs, and whence the justices itinerant were sent all over England, to judge and to oversee the collection of taxes and rents, and secure faithful returns of the king's various revenues.

But such private rights and revenues, such ownership and management of an entire kingdom for the benefit of a single individual, were incompatible with civil liberty; for where one has absolute freedom, there all others can have none whatever. So, be the rights of their lord ever so vested, the interference with them ever so greatly to be reprehended, the tenants of the manor of England no sooner felt themselves strong enough, than they began the struggle to restrain these rights, in order that they might not be exercised to their ruin. By main force they extorted the Great Charter which restricted royal liberty, and diminished the royal revenue in every particular; and they clung to it, although it was quashed and cursed by the Pope as subversive of every principle of private property and vested rights. Yet the victory at Runnymede was only the first round in the struggle. It continued for nearly five hundred years thereafter, until, step by step, the king was not only restrained in the exercise of his private sovereign rights, but actually deprived of every vestige of them, and from an absolute owner of all England, was converted into a mere trustee, with the duty of executing for the public good, and in a regulated manner, the functions prescribed to him. I need hardly urge that each of these deprivations and conversions, though interfering with rights vested for centuries, is universally conceded to have been a step forward in the development of civil liberty.

The restraint of the king, however, was only one phase of this development; other elements of society required restriction no less than he. The most important of these was the Church—owner of the domain of conscience. For, absolute as the king might have been, his power only extended to temporalities—to matters of the body and this world: affairs of the soul, and concerning the Kingdom of Heaven, were sacred, and as the Middle Ages knew of no relations which might not be turned into property, were held by the Church in ownership. This ownership was moreover exceedingly profitable, and brought in large revenues in the form of tithes, payments for indulgences, dispensations, the control of probates of testaments, marriages, penalties for infringement of ceremonial laws and justice. And besides these general revenues of the national Church, the Pope, as Supreme Lord of the Church, had a vested right in many special revenues arising from provisions, translations, appeals, Peter's pence and other sources. And all these rights were again and again acknowledged and guaranteed by solemn charters, and designated collectively as the liberties of the Church.

But these liberties and rights proved tyrannical. A long struggle ensued, and after they had first been restrained, and then seized by the king, they were finally either abolished, or converted into the public rights and liberties of the nation.

And yet the restraint of both the sovereigns, spiritual and temporal, was not sufficient to secure civil liberty. It required restraint of subjects as well. In the first rank of these we may consider the king's officers, great and inferior, who had vested rights in their offices as tenements, held either in fee, or for life, or for a term of years, and generally for a valuable and legally valid consideration. Civil liberty was not reconcilable, however, with such vested private rights, and they were converted into public trusts, just as the king's had been. Akin to these were the rights of private persons to the various municipal offices in fee and for a less estate, and the rights of members of close corporations; also those of boroughs in Parliament. All of these were ruthlessly swept away in the progress of liberty.

But the rights of those whose station was altogether private, were just as unceremoniously interfered with. The great tenants held of their landlord not only the land with its incidents of relief, wardship, marriage, escheats, aids, and its villein population,—they also had let out to them the domains of peace, of justice, of commerce, with all the revenues (exceedingly important) attached to these tenements. As lords of their manors with respect to their own tenants and villeins, they, of course, held in their persons the right of defence of the same, and thus they became lords of the domain of war with respect to their neighbors; and their tenants were compelled to follow them in their expeditions, and assist them in their defence, or pay a commutation exactly as they themselves were bound to do toward their lord paramount, the king. So they could close up their possessions against strangers, and take toll for passage through them, on highways and on rivers. They were also possessed of the right of enlisting others besides their tenants under their banners by private contract, the right of liveries as it was called, which though occasioning considerable outlay was yet exceedingly beneficial to them, in enabling them to reimburse themselves with profit by disseizing their poorer neighbors or putting them under tribute.

All these valuable vested rights, no less than those of king, church, officers, corporations, and boroughs, were incompatible with civil liberty, and were abolished after long and bitter struggles.

In the midst of the struggles of crown, church, and nobles for the purpose of restraining one another, and of each to secure unrestrained mastery for itself, there arose another element—capital; which, in the measure that the others were mutually weakening each other, gained such power that the capitalistic class became the dominant one of the community. By means of its dominancy it secured to itself what may be termed freedom of commerce, a freedom which, like that of crown, church, and nobles, redounding to the advantage of a part of the community merely, proved incompatible with civil liberty. It brought in its train, not only the right of extreme exploitation of labor by capital, but also a general crowding downward and oppression of the less wealthy by the wealthiest. It became necessary, therefore, to limit its freedom and abolish some of the private rights that had been acquired, and had become vested through it; and the restraining process, begun about fifty years ago, has not as yet reached its final stage. Among the numerous acts of Parliament signalizing the progress in liberty by means of the limitation referred to, I shall only instance a few:

The right of contracting between masters and children and their guardians, and master and women generally, was restrained by a succession of factory and workshop laws, accompanied by a strict factory inspection, throwing private management open to public scrutiny under the sanction of public penalties; reducing the factory or workshop from being the castle of its lord to a quasi-public institution, and putting an end to his right of conducting his business according to strict "business principles" alone. The agricultural and mining interests and establishments of various other kinds were put under similar restraints. So the vested right of the employer to be free from responsibility for accidents to his workmen was abolished by the "Employers' Liabilities" act, and all acknowledgment of such supreme property in rotten hulks, as would permit the owner to send them to sea laden with human freight, was put an end to. The proprietors of animals were put under limitations of their property rights by various "Contagious Diseases" acts, and landlords were no less restricted by a complete sanitary code. In Ireland even the amount of rent which a landlord could charge was no longer left to his free arbitrament, and the remittal of all arrears beyond a certain term of years, decreed.* As it was thought oppressive that private individuals should operate telegraphs they were converted into public property; and railway corporations, though not yet so converted, have been much restrained. Moreover, as indirect means of restricting capital, trades-unions have been expressly sanctioned by statutes; and land-owners have been deprived of the vested right to improvements made by their tenants. All in all, we may say that the people of England have awakened to the fact that the acquired rights of capitalists are no more sacred than had been those of king, church, officers, and landlords, and as these were abolished so must those be, whenever the exercise of them becomes oppressive.

Second. Liberty requires a popular sovereignty.

By the conquest, as we have seen, the absolute sovereignty of England became vested in a single individual. One hundred and fifty years later, the tyrannies of this individual's successors had been heaped up to such a degree that the principal subjects revolted, extorted a charter by virtue of which the sovereign submitted to many restraints, and placed the means of enforcing these restraints in the hands of a committee. An individual sovereign, restrained by fear of the most powerful subjects, might seem to constitute a more liberal

---

* This portion of the land act has been assailed as depriving landlords of their property, and as being extreme Socialism; strangely enough, I think, when we remember that bankruptcy laws do a very similar thing, and yet no one dreams of calling them Socialistic.

form of government than an unrestrained one. In reality, however, it does not. The unsettling of the sovereignty only increases the number of tyrants, and proves to be a step backward rather than forward. And thus the committees charged with carrying out the Magna Carta under Henry III and Edward II, as well as all subsequent ones, were short-lived, and a restoration of the absolute sway of the king was always hailed as a diminution of tyranny. After the constitution had vibrated for over a hundred years between the unrestrained individual sovereign and the sovereign restrained by individuals, each party sought to draw over to itself the wealthier portions of the community, and thus was engendered the power of Parliament. When this body had become strong enough to exercise an important influence—that is, in the reign of Edward III—the third phase of our history is entered upon. It is characterized by the restraint of the sovereign through the influence of barons and knights in Parliament. This form of government was essayed for nearly one hundred and fifty years, and, like the preceding ones, was unable to bring about civil liberty. The oppression, indeed, which it exercised became unbearable, and again the absolute sovereignty was gladly permitted to reside with an individual; whom, it was hoped, the lessons of the past might have taught the necessity of restraining himself for the sake of his own safety. But Edward IV died without having secured the crown for his heir, and after a brief season, bordering on anarchy with its attendant horrors, the kingdom was conquered by Henry Tudor.

But the second conqueror was animated by motives different from those of the first. Instead of relying on the great and powerful nobles for his support—and to that end, still further enriching and exalting them—he schemed to overthrow and ruin them. This brought about a fifth phase in our history, in which the absolute sovereign, though still an individual, used his own unrestrained powers to restrain the great and wealthy oppressors of the people.

Many historians, too much engrossed with the idea that oppression can come only from the king, consider the period of the Tudors a retrograde movement in liberty, and are at a loss to understand how absolutism could be tamely submitted to by a people already experienced in parliamentary government. They forget that the sovereign is not necessarily the sole oppressor—and that he may even himself permit many oppressions, and yet relieve the people, if the oppressions are directed against those who are themselves oppressors. Fortunately, too, for the Tudors, the Reformation took place during their reign, and they fully availed themselves of it.

Until that event, the sovereignty of the kings, however absolute at times it might have been, was constantly hampered by the fact that it did not extend to spiritual matters, over which another lord, the Pope, had full control. This duality of the sovereignty, though it might have been beneficial for a time, was finally seen to be incompatible with progress in liberty, and so the assumption of church supremacy—of the headship in the domain of conscience, as well as in that of material things—proved of the most momentous advantage to the cause of liberty. The assumption, moreover, brought a new relation to the kingship itself—it involved a responsibility to an acknowledged Supreme Being, whose vicegerent on earth the king had become. It gave something peculiarly sacred to the character of sovereignty, which raised the sovereign from the condition of a private individual into the holder of a great public trust. It bore with it also another incident: the care of the poor, hitherto the wards of the monasteries. This care was a duty that could not be shirked, which was enforced by the irresistible pressure of circumstances, and which, therefore, required neither a committee nor a Parliament to compel the king to give it his attention. And thus the absolute sovereignty of the Tudors was of a nature entirely different from that of the Norman and the Plantagenet kings; and contained within itself something of a public character in which germs of liberty reside.

Yet the *jure divino* kingship, in spite of its high sense of duty, after a lengthy trial proved itself to be as incapable of actually securing civil liberty as the previous forms of sovereignty had been. Fortunately, by destroying the overweening power of the great Lords, it had proportionately raised the condition of the Commons; these, comprising a far greater portion of the people than the Lords, could, in a measure, be said to represent them, and were, therefore, better instruments for the advancement of liberty than the Lords had been. And so these very Commons, after having been the most subservient tool of absolutism; after having almost done away with themselves by giving the king's proclamations a force superior even to enacted statutes; after having empowered the king to devise his crown by will; after having changed even their creed again and again at the nod and beck of their master, gradually recover both their power and their sense of it, and, examining into the bases of the sovereignty of one by divine right and freely criticising them, totally deny their validity, and send the sovereign to the scaffold. The Restoration shows us the anomaly of a sovereign by divine right restrained by a Parliament—a condition too illogical to last. And when, finally, this sovereign goes so far as to attempt again to divest himself of his supremacy in the domain of conscience, in favor of a foreign lord, the whole people rise as one man, and, thoroughly satisfied that individual sovereignty in any form is incompatible with full liberty, abolish individual sovereignty, and replace it by that of the Parliament.

But was this transfer of the sovereignty from an individual to the wealthier classes of the community in their corporate capacity sufficient to ensure liberty? Certainly not. The reign of Parliament is signalized by the oppression of the unrepresented classes. The whole machinery of government was strained to enable capital to increase its profits by a proportionate increase of the miseries of labor. Parliamentary liberty became synonymous with unrestrained exploitation of the weaker by the stronger, of the employed by the employer, of wives by husbands, of children by parents.

All attempts on the part of the unrepresented to protect themselves against the encroachments of their rulers were checked by Draconic laws. Combinations of workmen for the purpose of bettering their conditions were forbidden by numerous and ever-recurring enactments. Not only were all contracts to combine for the purpose of lessening the hours of labor, or advancing wages, declared void, but they were put in the category of misdemeanors, and severe penalties were attached to them; indeed, the mere making of a request to assist such movements by money subscriptions was punished by imprisonment.

If a workman quitted his service before his time expired, he was guilty of a penal offence, and thus the employer was able to put on the screw at his pleasure, using for his guide nothing higher than his enlightened self-interest. And if the workmen, under these conditions, sought to flee from their inhuman surroundings by emigrating into more favorable countries, they were stopped by a most stringent law against enticing artificers out of the kingdom, and against exporting their tools. This kept a full supply of labor on hand, and made it cheap. On the other hand, manufacturers were expressly authorized to meet and elect inspectors of work; these inspectors were empowered to enter the dwellings of the workmen at all reasonable hours and examine their work, and if the work was not in compliance with the manifold statutes regulating the various kinds of work, enacted since the time of the Edwards, it was their duty to prosecute the workmen, and their unsupported oath was sufficient to convict. The laws of apprenticeship of Elizabeth were abolished, and the journeymen who had entered and completed their apprenticeship in obedience to, and in reliance upon these laws, were deprived of their valuable rights without one penny of compensation. The rights of the poorer classes to the soil were even less regarded than their rights to a fair return for their outlay of labor. Over four millions of acres of the common land of the kingdom were inclosed, that is, wrested from the poor and bestowed on the wealthy. While these freed themselves from all burdens on their land in regard to their lord, the king, they retained these burdens on copy-hold tenures on the land held of them, although their rights to those dues were less defensible than those of the king to dues from their tenures. For the loss of most of his rights they compensated the king, not by a tax on their lands, which gained everything, but by an excise, which they knew would fall chiefly on the poor, who gained nothing by their abolition.

All these tyrannical laws were supplemented by others, which made the want of visible means of subsistence a penal offence, and the workman who might refuse to work on inhuman terms was sent to the house of correction and publicly whipped.

The ruling classes, moreover, possessed a machinery for executing these laws to the utmost degree of exactness and rigidity. The justice of the peace, capitalist and landlord himself, and united by all family and social ties, and all the promptings of self-interest, with the legislature, was, to the poor man, a far more terrible tribunal than the Star Chamber had ever been to the rich. In the latter the accused was at least judged by men of his own rank and station, by his peers; but the poor man, like the king, had no peers, and his judges were instigated, not only by their duty to the sovereign, but also by an inborn antipathy and class hatred. Magna Carta and the Bill of Rights were empty names, and of no avail to the victim of the petty justice's summary jurisdiction. And besides his capacity as criminal judge, he was also empowered to interfere in all conflicts of a civil nature between employer and employees; and in all disputes between workman and master, he—himself frequently a master, and connected by all interests and ties with the master—was the arbiter. Even the finding of the rates of wages was intrusted to him; a precautionary measure, to shut out the oppressed from the last avenue of escape from their sad fate.

And now if we add to these sins of commission by parliamentary government, only the single one of omission, which permitted the barbarous clearing of estates—that is, the eviction of tenants from lands held and tilled by them in order to convert these into sheep walks and deer forests—and thus caused the destitution and starvation of thousands upon thousands of industrious citizens of the State for the purpose of increasing the already bloated wealth of the titular land-owner, and of making labor still cheaper in the cities, we have a picture of tyranny in the England of the House of Hanover to which that of the Tudor and the Plantagenet periods might seem preferable.

But the people did not seek to go back to the sovereignty of the barons or of the king, to feudalism or absolutism (by again narrowing the basis of the sovereignty) in order to find alleviation from oppression; on the contrary, profiting by the lessons of history, they widened the basis, and converted the sovereignty of individuals or classes into that of the people at large.

And this sovereignty carries within it all the potentialities required for the final consummation of a perfectly free condition of society; for, comprising in itself all the elements of society, it is logically not incapable of bringing about a complete harmony among them. That in the fifty years of its existence it has not entirely undone all the evils resulting from the oppressions of many hundred years of feudalism, of two hundred years of absolute monarchy, and of one hundred and fifty years of the sovereignty of capital, is natural. If it had done so it would have proceeded, indeed, too rapidly, and worked, itself, an oppression which might have led to a reaction. But that it has made an undoubted and substantial advance, the statute books testify; these indeed have completely altered their tone and have taken on the color of humanity as previously they had the color of barbarism. While formerly all combinations among workmen to better their conditions were treated as crimes, now they are expressly legalized and encouraged. While formerly the employers appointed their own creatures as inspectors, in order to oppress the workmen, now the government salaries a respectable class of agents in order to bring about an alleviation of their condition. While formerly the hours of labor were fixed so as to punish the laborer who worked less, they are now fixed so as to punish the capitalist who exacts more. While formerly land acts were for the purpose of evicting human beings in order to hasten the accumulation of capital in the hands of the favored classes, now the land acts are for the purpose of restraining eviction and protecting the interests of human beings against the selfishness of accumulators. While, in short, formerly, constitution and law had a care only for the property of the rich, now they deem the property of all classes worthy of protection. And since the year 1832, hardly a session of Parliament has passed which has not contributed something toward the development of humanitarian principles, and which has not been a step forward in civilization.

This advance, too, has been peaceful, conservative, with due regard for all reasonable acquired rights, and is at the same time not only a proof that popular sovereignty is a requisite of civil liberty, but also an earnest of what may be expected of it, as it becomes daily better understood and better trusted.

Third. The definition of civil liberty.

As the result of our investigations we are now able to formulate a definition of civil liberty; a definition embodying a principle that may serve as a guide in the enactment of laws and furnish a canon of criticism for laws already enacted. It is this:

Civil liberty is the result of the restraint exercised by the sovereign people on the more powerful individuals and classes of the community, preventing them from availing themselves of the excess of their power to the detriment of the other classes.

It may be necessary to call attention to the fact that in this definition the word classes is not used in the sense of caste, so that each person is not considered as confined to a single class; on the contrary it is assumed that every person actually belongs to several classes, in one of which indeed he may act as oppressor, while in the others he may be himself oppressed. It is also to be remarked that the same class may be at the same time oppressor and oppressed; thus the manufacturing classes may suffer from the encroachment of monopolies, and as such be oppressed, while at the same time they themselves may be oppressors of their workmen.

In the second place I must call attention to the fact that the principle contained in the definition, far from being in conflict with the rights of private property, is, on the contrary, their very safeguard and maintenance.

A person has no more right to use his property for the purpose of encroaching on others, than he has to commit a nuisance by means of it. And just as he is restrained from the latter in the very interests of private property, so he may be in the former case. In fact, the encroachments of monopolies, such as railway corporations, on the rights of others, are nothing less than purprestures,—nuisances, by encroachment on public rights,—and their restraint is absolutely necessary to liberty. For we must ever remember that liberty is not characterized by absence of restraint, that, indeed, restraint is its very life and being; but by absence of oppression.

Nor does any danger arise from carrying out this principle to its extreme consequence, as it carries its own limitation within it. So far as the government interferes in private concerns in order to prevent encroachments of the more powerful classes—so far, and only so far, the interference is justifiable and necessary to liberty. But the moment it steps beyond this limit, it becomes itself oppressive, for then its action will be in itself a wrongful encroachment and subversive of liberty.

In the third place, the principle we have reached furnishes a conclusive answer to those who decry all governmental interferences for the purpose of counteracting oppression as " paternal," and unfit for a free people, who should rely on self-help; for this principle points to governmental interference as the essential feature of civil liberty. Moreover, a government by the people can in no case become a paternal government, since its law-makers are its mandatories and servants, carrying out its will, and not its fathers or its masters. I admit that the self-protecting organization of classes in arms against each other, culminating in lock-outs on the one side and strikes on the other, with selfishness, hatred, discord, oppression, brutality, attended by general demoralization and harrowing suffering, may be considered self-help, but it is the self-help of feudalism, and savors strongly of barbarism.

I contend, however, at the same time, that the action of a people through its elected agents, organized as a government, is equally entitled to be called self-help, and that it is a self-help just as manly, nay, far more manly, if we use this word in its highest sense; for it is productive of regard for law, of deference to the common weal, and of an harmonious and peaceful development of the resources of individuals and the State.

And this I consider to be the self-help of liberty, progress and civilization, the ideal of democratic institutions.

RECOLLECTIONS OF ABRAHAM LINCOLN AND THE CIVIL WAR

HAMILTON BUSBEY

WHEN the Hungarian patriot, Kossuth, came to the United States in the latter part of December, 1851, he found a responsive soul in William T. Coggshell, at one time editor of the *Ohio State Journal*, but who died of fever when United States Minister to Ecuador. Mr. Coggshell toured the country with Kossuth and introduced him in Kentucky to James F. Robinson, a slave-holder, who was proud of his Revolutionary ancestors, and in Illinois to Abraham Lincoln, who was made to feel by his conditions of birth and boyhood in Kentucky, that all men are not equal in opportunity at the threshold of life. Change of environment added to the stature of Lincoln. North of the Ohio River there was more freedom for him than in the State of his nativity, and he became the standard bearer of those who were opposed to the domination of slavery. He was moved to action by the same liberty-loving spirit which lifted Kossuth above his fellow men. Attempts to disrupt the Union after he had been elected President of the United States, saddened Lincoln, but did not undermine his courage. At a reception given to him by Governor Dennison of Ohio, the bright-eyed young daughter of Mr. Coggshell attracted his attention, and taking her by the hand he stooped and kissed her on the left cheek. The child blushed and asked:

"Mr. President, what shall you do when you get to Washington?"

Placing his hand on the head of the girl he slowly and pathetically said:

"What shall I do? Ask God. He knows best. But you, little one, can say when you grow up, that Abraham Lincoln bent half way to meet you."

The South American fever which proved fatal to William T. Coggshell, ended the life of his brilliant daughter; but the mother of the girl, a slender, gray-haired, dignified woman, is still with us, and it was from her that I recently heard the story.

When the Southern States began to secede and it looked as if the Republic of Washington and Jefferson was doomed, James F. Robinson, listening to the call of fellow citizens, left his law office, his banking interests and his stock farm at Georgetown, to become Governor of Kentucky. The fact that he had worn ruffled shirts when Lincoln was wearing cheap hickory shirts, made him more acceptable to powerful factions than a radical from the mountain districts, and he preserved to the Stars and Stripes the autonomy of the State.

The only daughter of Robinson, a woman of rare beauty and tact, presided over the executive mansion at Frankfort, and checked to a marked degree development of the spirit of bitterness. The Governor had the respect of leading Kentuckians who wore the Gray and the Blue, and used his persuasive powers upon both. His daughter made more than one urgent plea to the military authorities for the pardon of young men, mere boys, fired by Southern enthusiasm, who were captured in Confederate uniforms and lodged in Federal prisons.

Recently, in Washington, I stood with uncovered head in the unpretentious room in which Abraham Lincoln died, and brushed the dust and cobwebs from the tablets of memory. I was eighteen years old when Lincoln and Douglas canvassed Illinois for the senatorship of that State, and the speeches which commanded the attention of the nation profoundly impressed me.

In my uncle's house at Tuscola I met an industrious lawyer whose fame now covers two hemispheres,—the Hon. Joseph G. Cannon, Speaker of the House of Representatives. Although not born in the breezy West, he adapted himself to the customs of the country, and his strong face and direct speech commanded respect. The rapid rise of Illinois to power and greatness in the sisterhood of States was due to the sterling virtues of men like Mr. Cannon. Abraham Lincoln had been nominated by his party for President of the United States, and the enthusiasm of the plain people swept Illinois like a prairie fire. I remember a drive of thirty odd miles to hear one of the Lincoln supporters, Owen Lovejoy, speak. The bed of the farm wagon was thickly strewn with hay and straw, and I went to sleep with the stars blinking at the moon. The dreams of youth were optimistic and the fragrance of flowers came to us with the breeze, which heralded the crimson glow of morning. In the throng which heard the speaking there were hundreds who had driven more miles across the prairie than we had done, and they remained for the torchlight procession. It was a wonderful campaign, and it is not strange that the figure of Abraham Lincoln towered high in youthful imagination.

The ballots of November were counted, and Lincoln succeeded James Buchanan as the sixteenth President of the United States. The result was a bitter disappointment to the slave-holding States and the land was convulsed with strife. The issue as to whether one flag or two flags should float over the territory embraced in the government founded by Washington and his compatriots was long in doubt, and on more than one field I saw the smoke and heard the roar of battle. There were days and months and years of anxiety and blood-letting, and the timid who watched from afar the strife which paralyzed industry, made desolate the homes of peace and plenty, and turned sweet valleys and romantic hillsides into cemeteries, asked if it was not a fearful price to pay for an advance step in civilization.

The fortitude and hopeful patience of Lincoln in dark hours compelled admiration, and his words in his 1858 debate with Douglas were recalled: " I believe this Government cannot endure permanently half slave and half free. I do not expect the Union to be dissolved —I do not expect the house to fall—but I do expect it will cease to be divided. It will become all one thing or the other. Either the opponents of slavery will arrest the further spread of it, and place it where the public mind shall rest in the belief that it is in the course of ultimate extinction; or its advocates will push it forward till it shall become alike lawful in all the States, old as well as new, North as well as South." A year after these words had been spoken, the John Brown tragedy at Harper's Ferry took place, and twelve months after the execution of Brown, December 20th, 1860, South Carolina declared its secession from the Union. President Lincoln and Vice-President Hamlin were inaugurated March 4th, 1861, and wise men hesitated to predict the end. With Georgia, Mississippi, Florida, Louisiana and Texas rapidly following the lead of South Carolina, there was grave cause for anxiety. The hesitating border States, Virginia, Kentucky and Missouri, became the camping ground of hostile armies and suffered most from the very beginning of civil war.

As Kentucky was the birthplace of Lincoln and the home of relatives of his wife, he was particularly anxious to silence, as far as possible, opposition to his administration in that commonwealth. Through the influence of Robert J. Breckenridge, and James F. Robinson, who succeeded McGoffin as Governor at Frankfort, Kentucky was saved to the Union, but her gallant sons were conspicuous in both armies.

Soon after the fall of Fort Sumter, General William T. Sherman expressed the opinion that the war would prove something more than a three months' picnic, and Northern radicals bitterly assailed him. He was even denounced as crazy, but Governor Robinson and Mr. Prentice, of the *Louisville Journal*, vigorously protested against his removal. General Sherman was so grateful to Mr. Prentice for his journalistic support that he always made it easy for a representative of the *Journal* to obtain information for publication. I was a member of the *Journal* staff in later years of the war, and was the medium through which the information was conveyed to the type-setters. In the performance of my duties I had ready access to such officers as General W. T. Sherman, General D. C. Buell, General John A. Logan, General George H. Thomas, General John M. Palmer and General Stanley.

The people of the State of South Carolina in convention assembled December 20th, 1860, reasserted their objection to " the election of a man to the high office of President of the United States whose opinions and purposes are hostile to slavery," and, " appealing to the Supreme Judge of the world for the rectitude of our intentions, have solemnly declared that the Union heretofore existing between this State and the other States of North America, is dissolved, and that the State of South Carolina has resumed her position among the nations of the world, as a separate and independent State." This solemn declaration met with applause in the South and was received with grim determination in the North. The voice of Alexander H. Stephens rang clear before the legislature of Georgia and awoke responsive echoes in millions of hearts. " The President of the United States is no emperor, no dictator—he is clothed with no absolute power. He can do nothing unless he is backed by power in Congress. The House of Representatives is largely in a majority against him. . . . Is this the time, then, to apprehend that Mr. Lincoln, with this large majority in the House against him, can carry out any of his unconstitutional principles in that body? . . . Why, then, I say, should we disrupt the ties of this Union when his hands are tied—when he can do nothing against us?" President Lincoln in his inaugural address attempted to allay the fears of the slave-holding section: "Apprehension seems to exist among the people of the Southern States, that, by the accession of a republican administration, their property and their peace and personal security are to be endangered. There has never been any reasonable cause for such apprehension. Indeed, the most ample evidence to the contrary has all the while existed and been open to their inspection. It is found in nearly all the published speeches of him who now addresses you."

I was young and sanguine at the time, and I could not see how the pathetic closing words could fall on deaf ears: "You can have no conflict without being yourselves the aggressors. You have no oath registered in heaven to destroy the Government, while I shall have the most solemn one to preserve, protect and defend it. I am loth to close. We are not enemies, but friends. We must not be enemies. Though passion may have strained, it must not break, our bonds of affection. The mystic cords of memory, stretching from every battlefield and patriot-grave to every living heart and hearth-stone all over the broad land, will yet swell the chorus of the Union, when again touched, as surely they will be, by the better angels of our nature."

The North uprose in response to Lincoln's call to arms in April, 1861, and for four years the conflict raged. Valor was displayed on both sides, and tears were shed upon myriads of graves. Only those who lived at the front can properly estimate the ruin wrought. The severest possible strain was put upon the manhood and the womanhood of the country. March 4th, 1865, President Lincoln delivered his second inaugural address, and the storm had then spent its force. Andrew Johnson had succeeded to the Vice-President's chair, and he represented the strong Union sent.. .ent of the mountain districts of Tennessee. An end had been put to drafting and recruiting for the Federal army and to the purchase of munitions of war, and reconstruction was the subject of profound thought. The President was kindly disposed to the vanquished, and his life was never more valuable to the people at large.

Often I had to wait for late dispatches, and the time from 9:30 to 11 P. M. was spent in one of the theatres. Louisville was then a general headquarters, a big camp of wonderful activity, and the theatres did a rushing business. John Wilkes Booth, a striking personality of twenty-six years, played a short engagement, and I saw him in every act, little dreaming that in a comparatively brief spell he would fill an important part in the great drama of the century. I also formed at Louisville the acquaintance of Edwin Adams, and he was playing with Laura Keene in Ford's Theatre, Washington, the night that President Lincoln received his death wound. It was the 14th of April, 1865, and having had a strenuous day, I had gone to bed earlier than usual. A room had been fitted up for me in the office of the *Journal* so that I could promptly respond to any emergency call during the night. I was roused from a deep slumber by the foreman of the composing room, who stood over me with blanched face. It was midnight and I was informed that confused reports from Washington were to the effect that the President and all of his Cabinet had been murdered. Orders were sent to the press room to hold the forms for the latest information. Scores of dispatches were brought to me and I edited them at a little table in the composing room. It was after three o'clock in the morning when threads were untangled and woven into a coherent story.

The rabid zeal of John Wilkes Booth to help the Southern people deeply injured them. Among the members of his fanatical coterie were Lewis Powell, George Atzerodt, David E. Herold, Samuel Arnold, Michael O'Laughlin and John H. Surratt. At noon on Friday, April 14th, Booth was informed that President Lincoln would occupy a box at Ford's Theatre that night, and he quickly planned for the assassination of Lincoln, Vice-President Johnson, and Secretary of State Seward. It is an old story of how Booth obtained access to the President's box, fired the fatal shot and then made a sensational escape. The President was carried to the little house opposite the theatre, 516 Tenth Street, N. W., and at twenty-two minutes past seven o'clock on Saturday morning, April 15th, he drew his last breath.

On the day after the assassination, Andrew Johnson took the oath as President of the United States, and to one of the delegation that waited upon him he said: " I know it is easy, gentlemen, for anyone who is so disposed to acquire a reputation for clemency and mercy. But the public good imperatively requires a just discrimination in the exercise of these qualities."

Andrew Johnson was as variable in temperament as George D. Prentice claimed him to be, and his administration was sadly disappointing to many of his best friends.

The declaration of Secretary of War Stanton, when the heart of Lincoln ceased to beat,—" Now he belongs to the ages,"—has been verified by the lapse of time. The greatness of the man is recognized even by those who wore the Confederate gray.

At nine o'clock on Saturday morning, April 15th, the body of Mr. Lincoln was taken to the White House, where it remained until the 19th, and then was exposed to public view in the Capitol. On the 21st the journey to the tomb in Springfield, Illinois, commenced.

Mr. Prentice said that he would like to have me represent the *Journal* at Springfield, and on the advice of Mr. Osborne I went to Frankfort and conferred with Governor Bramlette. After a short talk the Governor went to his desk and handed me a commission to represent the State of Kentucky at the funeral of Abraham Lincoln. It was an unsought honor and I greatly appreciated it. Lincoln was born in a cabin in Kentucky, and an adopted Kentuckian from Ohio was sent by the State of Kentucky to pay a final tribute to the remains of the murdered President. I know of no other Kentuckian who held a like commission.

General John M. Palmer, who was a close friend of Lincoln, was in command of the post at Louisville, and he gave me warm letters of commendation to his friends and the friends of Lincoln in Springfield. My reception in the Capital of Illinois was all that could be desired, and as I was there in advance of the funeral, I picked up plenty of gossip.

One of the stories was that Mrs. Lincoln had threatened to bury her husband elsewhere than in Springfield unless the plans were changed so as to make a double tomb. She wanted to sleep through the ages by the side of the martyr and to catch the reflected glow of his fame. It was a natural wish, but there was objection to it, and the strife threatened to mar the solemnity of the funeral pageant. The demand was conceded and the wife and husband rest side by side in Oak Ridge Cemetery.

I shall never forget the hours that I stood as a guard of honor over the casket, or the reverence of the host which filed past the face of the dead. My youthful imagination was stirred and I stretched forth my hands hoping to imprison a sunbeam from the shores of immortality. It was May 4th when the remains of the distinguished dead were placed in the receiving vault, and when I recall the imposing ceremony, I feel that it sometimes is worth while to bear the troubles of a nation and to suffer martyrdom.

The words which President Lincoln spoke at Gettysburg in November, 1863, often ring in my ears: " We are met on a great battle-field of that war. We have come to dedicate a portion of that field as a final resting-place for those who here gave their lives that that nation might live. It is altogether fitting and proper that we should do this. But, in a larger sense, we cannot dedicate—we cannot hal-low—this ground. The brave men, living and dead, who struggled here, have consecrated it far above our poor power to add or detract. The world will little note, nor long remember, what we say here; but it can never forget what they did here. It is for the living, rather, to be dedicated here to the unfinished work which they who fought here have thus far so nobly advanced. It is rather for us to be dedicated here to the great task remaining before us—that from these honored dead we take increased devotion to that cause for which they gave the last full measure of devotion—that we here highly resolve that these dead shall not have died in vain—that this nation, under God, shall have a new birth of freedom—and that government of the people, by the people, for the people, shall not perish from the earth." The words will live as long as the Republic endures.

The great tragedy of April 14th left President Lincoln's family rather poorly provided for. Mrs. Lincoln, embittered by her sudden removal from the White House, the atmosphere of which was pleasant to her, took the radical step of putting personal effects on exhibition in New York and announcing that they were for sale. The loyal friends of the dead President were startled by this proceeding. The sad, careworn face of Abraham Lincoln was not wholly due to perplexing questions of State. In 1866, a book, *Behind the Scenes*, was published, and it produced a sensation. It was from the pen of Elizabeth Keckley, a bright-eyed, thin-lipped, regular-featured colored woman, who in the early part of the war was the confidential maid of Mrs. Jefferson Davis in Richmond, and in the closing years of strife was the confidential maid of Mrs. Lincoln in Washington. She had taken advantage of her position in each family to preserve personal letters on social and other topics in Government circles, and the extracts given from the letters excited public curiosity and created a large sale for the book. I saw the letters and know that they were genuine. It is difficult to say what would have happened had they fallen into the hands of a modern muckraker.

Mary Todd, who was brought up in the aristocratic atmosphere of Lexington, Kentucky, would never have become the wife of Lincoln had both remained in the State in which they were born. Social barriers were too strong for that. The poor boy of the cabin could not have found an opportunity to meet on equal terms the girl reared in a home of culture with slaves to wait upon her. But change of environment opened the door of opportunity, and there was a marriage in which the fires of affection often burned low. The first love of Abraham Lincoln, as is generally known, was buried in the grave of Ann Rutledge. I gained the impression from my frequent talks with General John M. Palmer that President Lincoln was more anxious to preserve Kentucky to the Union than any other of the border States, for the reason that it was the birthplace of himself and of the mother of his children.

One had to live in debatable territory to understand thoroughly the emotional fluctuations of those strenuous times.

ENIGMA

DOROTHY LANDERS BEALL

WITH her pale finger pointing delicately,
She wrote upon the sand. We sat alone
On a wide beach that sloped down evenly
To meet the little gaily-lilting waves.
Before us, moved the sea, and all around
Earth-fiends had tossed up cliff and broken rock,
And cruel mountain-reefs!
      She stooped.   She wrote.
And round her slender finger glowed a light,
Silver upon the sand-floor.
       One short word
She traced, one little and mysterious word,
Then fled before me to the silent land!
And lo, while yet I pondered on that name,
An eager wave leaped in and stamped it out—
And that is all I know of my Beloved!

FRAGMENTS

ATKINSON KIMBALL

THE Sanborns left the cemetery before the grave was filled in. The master of ceremonies had whispered to Sanborn that it would be easier for his wife if she didn't see the grave filled in. It was no longer customary, he said, for the mourners to stay after the pine-boughs had been placed on the box; and he had led the way to their carriage while two burly men with shovels waited impatiently beside the pile of fresh-turned earth. John Sanborn, in his anguish, felt a rebellion against all these formalities of death with which mankind tried to soften the terrible fact. It seemed to him that it would be a relief to fill the grave in, himself; to hear the earth strike and re-sound on the box below.

The numbness possessing him ever since he had known that his little daughter was going to die, had passed away, and he had a desire to express the bitterness that filled his heart. He had an impulse to stop the undertaker at the carriage door, and say, " Do you think, because I haven't seen my child covered up in that hole, I shall not realize she is in it? " In these first moments of realization, the one thing he couldn't bear was any attempt to comfort him for his loss. The only comfort was to turn the knife in the wound.

Sanborn looked at his wife on the seat opposite. Her slight figure seemed slighter than ever in the folds of the crêpe veil which billowed about her. Her face behind it was a grayish blur. He hated the symbols of mourning, but he felt an inconsistent jealousy that custom permitted women deeper signs of grief than it allowed men. He had an impulse to throw the veil back from her face; and then, with a quick motion, he pulled down the curtain on the carriage door. Two workmen, in one of the thousand of plots which lined the streets of the great cemetery, had stopped their indolent pruning of some budding shrubs to gaze curiously into the carriage; and it seemed to Sanborn that his stricken face was as bare as a wall beneath the narrow brim of his hat. His wife, at his action, gave a little cry.

" Is it going back with us? " she asked, and he knew that she meant the white hearse. On the way out, she had looked through the window to see how near they were to their lot, and had seen the little white hearse going on ahead, and Sanborn had pulled down the curtain so that she wouldn't see it again.

At her cry and question, he moved to the seat beside her, and took her in his arms. The crêpe veil was stiff and slippery, and faintly creaked as he crushed its fresh folds. His wife, within his hold, was very quiet. It made him think of the night they had driven away from the church together; and he had felt the delicate crispness of her white veil melt beneath his touch as he drew her to him in an ecstasy of possession and joy.

The possession had lasted; the ecstasy and the joy had gone long ago. He possessed her, and she possessed him; and the years of this bondage stretched into the future, arid, irritating, trivial. It had seemed to him when he married her that he had found the one other being whose mind and heart were attuned to his own, whose aspirations soared beside his and above his. Later, he came to believe that he had merely attributed to her his own emotions, projected as images in a mirage against the luminous, distorting atmosphere his love had thrown about her. She hadn't turned out to be the woman he thought she was; and, if he had asked himself whether he had turned out to be the man she thought *he* was, he would have answered that he didn't believe she had ever thought what he was or what he wasn't. She didn't think, she only felt. Her convictions were prejudices; her analyses, intuitions; her abstractions, superstitions.

When Alice and he became engaged, the world appeared suddenly peopled with engaged couples like themselves, except for the difference that the other couples weren't so happy as they were; when the dream had vanished, he saw about him only other dreary married couples, except that the others weren't so dreary as Alice and himself. John Sanborn wondered what it was that made them less dreary. Perhaps they hadn't demanded as much of life as he had. In his heart, he was proud of how much he had demanded, and of how little he would compromise with what he had received. And then, he had received his child, and understood what it was that made the other couples contented, and even, in a way, happy.

Sanborn had thought very little what it might mean to be a father. He did not care much for children, and he had an idea that his interest in his own child would be an intellectual concern for its development rather than an emotion. The night little Louise was born, beneath his anxiety for his wife, there was a restlessness, an excitement, a sort of inexplicable dumb elation that he explained by the fact that he felt nearer Alice than he had since the early months of their marriage. Toward morning, the house had become very quiet, and then suddenly there broke upon the ears of the waiting man, above the scurrying of feet, a faint, high, queer cry; and he realized in that moment that, if he hadn't cared for other people's children, he should care for his own with an intense absorption.

From that time, his wife and he had a common interest, a mutual emotion in their love for little Louise. This love manifested itself in ways that were as divergent as their characters. Alice spent herself in a passion of motherhood. She thought of nothing, talked of nothing except her baby; but this thought did not, like Sanborn's, project itself into the future of their child. She didn't wonder what talents Louise might possess; she didn't develop these talents with the particularity of a fond imagination; she didn't choose a college for her while she was still in the cradle; she didn't graduate her with all the honors. She thought only of her baby's daily needs; it seemed to her husband that her thought was largely worry. She would have kept her a baby forever if she could. When she put her into short clothes, she wept as she laid away the long, tiny, first dresses; and when the baby began to toddle alone, she used to catch her up from the floor, and hold the strong, struggling, little body close to her heart in a jealous embrace.

The child developed rapidly. She was fair-haired and rosy-cheeked, with pretty, affectionate ways and a high, sweet voice in which she talked a great deal as soon as she learned to talk at all. There were one or two letters she couldn't pronounce, and Sanborn had found this defect so bewitching that he knew he should miss it when she outgrew it.

And then she had died.

Sanborn felt his wife stir within his arm. It had been a long time since he had sat thus encircling her. The impulse to do so had been involuntary; it wasn't the expression of a conscious emotion, and at the first sign from her, he released his hold.

"I think we have got back," she said, and Sanborn became aware that the carriage had stopped at the station of the railroad which would carry them home to New York.

The door of their apartment was opened by the Swedish maid before Sanborn had time to get the key out of his pocket. It was evident that the girl had been watching for their return. Her thick features were swollen with crying, and her eyes overflowed as she let her employers into the narrow private hallway. This show of grief irritated Sanborn. It seemed to him merely the expression of the morbid interest in death of an ignorant mind, but his wife gave a little sob beneath her veil as she saw the girl's face. The maid's reluctant feet went on down the hall to the kitchen as the Sanborns entered the living-room. In their absence, she had worked hard to make the room look as it had before the funeral, and she would have liked to linger to receive a word of praise for her efforts. In spite of these efforts, however, a faint odor of flowers was still in the air; and although the table with its reading-lamp had been brought back to its place between the two windows, Sanborn continued to see there, instead, the white casket with its pitiful burden.

He went to one of the windows, and stood with his back to the room, looking out over Morningside Park that their apartment faced to the heights from which it descended with such irregular abruptness. The sun hung low in the heavens, and the rosy-colored air enveloped the great empty arch of the new cathedral which was building on the heights. The light softened the unfinished edges and gave it the appealing beauty of a ruin. Little Louise had pretended that this cathedral was a palace; through that arch had come and gone all the princes and princesses of the fairy tales he had read to her. He lowered his eyes. He couldn't bear to look behind him at the room so eloquent of her death, nor out at the park and the terrace so filled with memories of her life. He heard his wife go out of the room. She was gone some moments, and when she returned, he faced about and looked at her.

She had removed her bonnet and veil; her black dress, trimmed heavily with crêpe, gave out the peculiar, sweet, acrid smell of that material. It seemed to Sanborn that, in facing her, he faced a personification of the rest of their lives together. What had they left?

What was each for the other except a constant reminder of the loss of their child? If only he could be free of it all, free of all his old associations; if only he could plunge into a new, untrammeled life! Yet he must go on as he was until the end. The bond might be broken if Alice shared his disillusion; but she had never given a sign that their marriage had not fulfilled her expectations: she seemed contented with the unemotional, humdrum level of their life.

The laughter and the shouts of children playing in the park came in through the open window. Her eyes slowly filled with tears.

"It seems as if she must be over there playing with the other children," she said.

"I can't stand it," broke from Sanborn; "I can't stand living on here where everything is a reminder of her."

"But don't you want to be reminded of her?" his wife asked, her blue eyes, which showed large in spite of being swollen with weeping, growing wider with surprise. "It's such a comfort to me to find reminders of her everywhere. It makes her seem so near. When I am in one room, it seems as if I only had to go into the next room to find her there."

"I don't want to be reminded of her," Sanborn cried fiercely. "I want to forget her. It's this continual, ceaseless memory that is enough to kill a man. If I could forget her, I shouldn't feel that I had lost her."

"But, John, don't you see that if you didn't feel her loss, it would be as if you had never had her?" She made her explanation with a tender pity, and, coming near him, laid her hand tentatively on his arm. "Try to be thankful that you *have* had her."

"Why thankful?" he demanded, turning away abruptly as if to free himself from her touch and her pity. "If she'd never been born, I wouldn't be suffering as I suffer now. What will the thought of her ever bring me except regret and anguish? What was the good of her short life? What was the meaning of it?"

"Oh, John, don't say such things! *I* felt that way at first, and it seemed to me that if I didn't believe that it was somehow for the best that Louise should die, I couldn't live. I felt angry with God; and it wasn't until that young minister came to see me, and talked with me about death and the hereafter, that I began to understand

and be comforted. I wish, John, that you had let him talk with you."

"I heard what he had to say," Sanborn said impatiently. "You forget that I was present at the funeral services."

"And didn't it comfort you? Didn't you feel he was right; that everything that happens *is* for the best, if we only believe that it is?"

"Perhaps I should be capable of such a general optimism," he said, "if I could make out the specific purpose in this case. I suppose *you've* made it out?"

A faint color came into Mrs. Sanborn's cheeks. She had a round, pretty face that a pointed chin kept from looking babyish without, however, keeping it from looking weak. She went near her husband as she had before, and laid her hand on his arm.

"I believe," she said softly, "that I *do* see why Louise was taken from us. We haven't seemed to care for each other," she went on, "as much as we used to when we were first married, have we, John?" Her manner had a sort of girlish shyness as if she were affirming the growth of their love rather than its waning. "We haven't been as happy as we ought to have been, have we?"

Sanborn stared at her. After all, she hadn't been contented; their marriage had disillusioned her, too! Under this revelation, some of the blame shifted to his shoulders; and he was not of a nature to bear such a burden with patience.

"Is it your idea, then," he said, "that Louise was taken from us because we weren't as happy as we ought to be? Isn't it the more generally accepted theory that we get punished for being *too* happy?"

She was so intent on what was in her mind that she didn't notice his irony.

"I believe," she said, "that the baby was taken away to bring us nearer, to make us happy."

"To make us *happy!*" Sanborn echoed.

"To make us care for each other the way we used to, to bring back our old love. I saw it like a vision there in the carriage, in the cemetery, when you had your arm around me."

Nothing of the pathos of this, nothing of her need, pierced to her husband's heart. He was conscious only of the monstrousness of her idea, born, it seemed to him, of a preposterous egotism. It filled him with a spiritual abhorrence so strong that it was like a physical repugnance for his wife. He drew away from her touch.

"It would be as easy to bring back our child from the dead as to bring back our old love," he said brutally.

She tottered, and looked at him with bewildered horror.

"Then you don't love me any more?" she half whispered.

Sanborn started toward her, fearing she might faint; but it was she who now drew away from his touch.

"You know that I care more for you than for anyone else in the world," he said doggedly.

"You don't love me," she affirmed with a certain stubbornness.

"Did you really believe, Alice, that we could feel for each other as we used to? Don't you know that that time is buried as irrevoeably as our child is buried?"

His wife's head drooped, and, turning, she walked slowly toward the door of the adjoining room.

Sanborn took a step or two after her.

"Alice," he said, "I don't want to be cruel. I suppose I am, but it's better that we should face the truth at once. I couldn't endure pretending that I believed that Louise had been taken away to make us happy. Now, we can live the rest of our life together without illusion."

His wife made no answer to this, but went on out of the room. He did not follow her. It would do her good to have her cry out; but when an hour had passed, and it was beginning to get dusk, he went in search of her.

He found her in the little room off their bedroom where their child had slept. She was sitting on the floor before the bureau, the drawers of which were open, surrounded by neat piles of their child's clothing. He stood beside her, looking down without speaking, while she went on with her sorting and folding, without looking up. The sight of the little garments was like a searching finger on a wound. He knew how she must be suffering, too, and he pitied her; but he felt angry, that at such a time she should give them both so unnecessary an access of grief.

"For Heaven's sake, Alice," he broke out, "why do you do this now?"

"It has to be done," she answered, going steadily on with her work, "and this is the only time I have to do it."

"The only time?" he asked with vague alarm. "What do you mean?"

"I am going away. I want to take the baby's things with me."

"Going away!"

"I am going to Cousin Sarah's," she said.

Sanborn was relieved. Cousin Sarah was Alice's only near relative, a maiden lady living in Tarrytown whom his wife and child visited every summer.

"I am glad you are going; the change will do you good," he said. "And don't hurry back on my account," he added.

"I am not coming back."

Her hands trembled, and she folded them in her lap; but there was no hint of faltering in the white face she raised toward her husband.

The separation had not had, at first, for Sanborn, the air of finality; it was as if Alice were merely visiting her cousin; and when he had established himself in the Harvard Club where he had lived for a time before his marriage, there was a blessed interval when it seemed to him that his child was with Alice.

Even during the two days which Alice and he spent in their old home while she was getting ready to leave him, it did not seem as if she were preparing to carry out her resolution. He thought that it would be easier for her to leave the dismantling of their home to the men from the storage warehouse; but she insisted upon doing it herself and she covered the furniture with sheets and packed the brie-à-brac as carefully as though she had been going to unpack it in some new home. Sanborn wondered at the love for inanimate objects which women feel, and considerately refrained from suggesting that it would be wiser to sell their furniture than to store it. He did suggest, however, that she stay on in the apartment, and not go to her cousin's; she liked to have her own things about her, he said, and he could afford to keep it up for her if she wished it; but she had replied that if she lived there without him, the other people in the house would find out about the separation. Of course, they would find it out in Tarrytown, but that couldn't be helped.

The ceaseless, practical concerns of those two days were an undoubted help to both of them. Every moment was filled with exter-
nalities; and even their ride down town to the Grand Central Station
was robbed of its true significance by the countless commissions and
cautions that she gave him, scarcely fewer, now that she was going
away forever, than those she always gave him when she went away
for a week or so. She had packed his trunks, and she told him just
where to look for the various articles, and she made him stop at a
drug-store near the station to get something for a slight cold he had
caught. This errand caused them nearly to miss the train, and there
was only time to make sure that she had her tickets and checks and
bag before she was hurried through the gate by the commuters behind. He stood at the iron grating, and tried to see whether she got
on the right train; but he couldn't make her out in the crowd that
had to walk almost to the end of the great shed to reach its train.

As he turned away, it flashed across his mind that in the confusion at the gate, he hadn't kissed her good-bye. When they were
first married, they never used to kiss each other in welcome or farewell before people, but later they used to kiss each other at such times
as a matter of course. He smiled bitterly at the essential ridiculousness of kissing her at all when she was separating from him, and then
he was struck by the essential ridiculousness of everything they had
done during the last two days. The separation of a married couple
ought to take place upon a plane of intense emotion, either of anger
or sorrow or hatred. He tried to imagine how Alice and he would
have parted when they were first married, and he saw that they would
have felt the situation so deeply that they would have ended by not
parting at all. The fact that Alice and he could spend their last
moments together over the thousand and one little, practical concerns
around which their mutual life had crystallized was a measure of
what that life had become; although her thought was all for him and
his thought largely for her, it was entirely a matter of habit.

Late that afternoon, as he unpacked his trunks in the room that
was henceforth to be his home, he experienced that sense of freedom
which husbands and wives feel when they are temporarily separated,
in which they seem to regain a lost individuality and, at the same
time, to lose half their being.

Sanborn told himself that he would take up his life where he had dropped it before he married; he would renew his acquaintance with the men who used to frequent the club; but when he went down to dinner, he recognized none of the men who were dining by twos or threes at the little tables in the vast baronial dining-hall. He was very lonely at his own little table.

Of course, as the days passed, some of his old acquaintances occasionally drifted into the club; but Sanborn found that their lives and his no longer had the numerous points of contact that had formerly kindled a warm comradeship. It was as if their lives were confined within a constantly narrowing circle which crowded out everything except the issues of personal success and happiness.

On the other hand, when he came to make new acquaintances among men younger than himself and usually unmarried, he found that now he had slight interest in the things that so absorbed their interest, although they settled the problems of the universe as enthusiastically as he had once settled them. These young men went to the theatre a great deal, and though the performances, in most cases, fell short of their high standard of dramatic art, their disapproval of a play took nothing from their pleasure in discussing it; and Sanborn began to go to the theatre in the hope of catching some of this critical interest. In the past, his pleasure had been marred by the impossibility of sharing his critical enthusiasm with his wife, who was always enthusiastic enough, but her enthusiasm was for the wrong thing. Now, however, he found that the theatre awakened no interest of any kind in him.

He began to spend his evenings in his room, reading; but books had lost their savor. He got to going earlier to his office and staying later, poring over his briefs, not because his cases absorbed him, but because he preferred the office to his room at the club. It struck him as grimly humorous to work so hard when he no longer had child or wife to work for. Of course, in a sense, he still worked for Alice, and he sent her, each month, a check for a scrupulous half of his income. After receiving the first check, she wrote asking him not to give her so much as she didn't need it; but he continued to send the same amount.

The Sanborns' social life had had the meagreness only possible, perhaps, in a great city. Mrs. Sanborn had not lived in New York before her marriage, so that she did not have her girlhood friends as a social asset; and the separation effectually sundered the few social ties they had formed. Sanborn was thus spared the condolences and the curiosity he dreaded. He told none of the men at the club that his child had died or that he had ever had a child, but in spite of all these attempts to foster forgetfulness, time, supposedly the universal healer, pressed hard upon his wound with a hand that lingered without soothing. Alice, he knew, would draw comfort from a hundred sources that would only augment his suffering; she would keep the memory of Louise green with a hundred observances which it made him shrink to think of. He knew that it would be a source of comfort to her to visit Louise's grave and a source of anguish to him, but, on a Sunday, which was always his loneliest day, he had himself gone up to Woodlawn Cemetery. The vast place was thronged with a Sunday crowd that found a mild sort of recreation in looking at the various monuments and at the decorations on the graves, especially the new graves where the display of the florists' art was most triumphant; but Sanborn, when he came to the narrow street where his child was buried, saw that her grave was as covered with flowers as though it had been made that day, and he turned away marveling at the illogical process of mind by which people could believe in the immortality of the spirit, but still seem to find their greatest comfort in an apparent denial of the mortality of the body.

As the hot weather came on, a number of the men who lived at the club went out of the city; but Sanborn remained during the whole summer. In August, when the club was almost deserted, a young man came to stay there, or, as he phrased it, " blew in from Kansas City to stir things up in New York "; and Sanborn decided that Winson Treslow was, indeed, like a fresh, animating breeze. He had come to New York, he said, to be a journalist; not to tie himself to any particular paper, but to be a free lance searching the great city for phases of life which could never come under the eye of the routine reporter. When he unearthed one of these mysterious phases, he used to ask Sanborn to go with him to have a look at it; and very often Sanborn went, not because he had much interest in the discovery, but because he liked to be with the young man. Most of these discoveries Sanborn had seen discovered a dozen times before in the Sunday newspapers, but he didn't tell Treslow this; and a Sunday paper sometimes printed Treslow's account of his find. Treslow was of a very happy nature; and in this happiness lay, perhaps, the reason of Sanborn's liking for him.

Sanborn dined with him at queer restaurants; together, they went to Ellis Island to see the immigrants land; they inspected a college settlement; they attended a Russian wedding feast; they tracked the wild animals in Bronx Park. Sanborn got into the habit of staying away from the office on Saturday afternoons to go about with Treslow.

One Saturday in September, as Sanborn sat in the dining-room of the club waiting for Treslow to join him at lunch, he felt that he had got to the end of his rope. His grief at the loss of his child was apparently as keen as on the day she died; and added to it, was a loneliness constantly augmented. He had come, of late, to yearn for some recognition of his loss.

When Treslow arrived, he wore the ecstatic expression which showed Sanborn that he was on the scent of a fresh mystery.

"I say," he began when he had seated himself and given his order to the waiter, "have you ever thought what it would mean to a man to have some one he had cared for come back from the dead?" He went on without waiting for an answer. "Just imagine that a man has lost some one he loves, his wife, say, or his child. Just imagine how he'd feel! He'd feel that he hadn't a thing left to live for, but the greatest trouble would be that he couldn't be sure that he had a thing left to *die* for,—I mean that he couldn't be sure that when he died he'd find his loved one in the other world. Catch my idea?" he asked as he paused to squeeze some lemon juice on the clams the waiter set before him.

"Yes," Sanborn answered laconically.

"Well, then," Treslow continued, "just imagine that this man receives proof that his wife or child has, as they say, only ' passed beyond,' and is waiting for him in the next world. Wouldn't it sort of solve the riddle of the universe for him? Just imagine it!"

"I don't have to imagine it," Sanborn answered. He was on the point of telling Treslow of Louise's death; but when the young man looked over at him and asked eagerly, "Do you mean that *you've* ever had such a proof?" Sanborn found that he couldn't tell him.

"I mean that you have enough imagination for both of us."

"Oh," Treslow laughed, "I have to draw on my imagination when it comes to a case like that, for I never had a single soul I cared for die. I always thought I was to be congratulated on that fact; but this afternoon I'm in need of a few dead friends." He laughed again, and looked at Sanborn, enjoying his bewilderment. "I need a few dead friends to make some well-authenticated ghosts. Ever been to a spiritualistic séance?"

"No, I haven't," Sanborn said.

"Well, I haven't either, but I'm going to one this afternoon, and you're going too. Graham says—Graham's the man who put me on to it—that Mrs. Nicholson is the real thing in mediums. Graham says that through her friends of his have talked with him from the other world. By George, if only I'd have the luck to see a ghost this afternoon! It would make a great story." He sighed with energetic envy.

"There needs no ghost come from the grave to make a great story for *you*," Sanborn said, pushing his chair from the table and standing up.

In the light of what did happen, Sanborn was never able to determine what he had expected would happen, or whether he had expected anything.

The preliminaries of the séance were already over when Treslow and he arrived at Mrs. Nicholson's house on Eightieth Street. The back parlor was shrouded in the artificial night of curtained windows and closed doors, through which the two men stumbled to their seats in one of the rows of camp-chairs. At first, the room seemed to be in total darkness; presently, Sanborn could make out the shadowy outlines of the persons nearest him and the indistinct bulk of a cabinet between the two rear windows, and he saw that a faint light was glimmering in a translucent square of glass placed on a side wall near the ceiling.

Sanborn would once have said that any one who attended a séance except in a spirit of scoffing curiosity was a fool; but the loss of his child made him understand how one might go with a hopeful credulity.

He believed that he was neither hopeful nor credulous, but he had said to Treslow, on their way uptown, that man undeniably possessed some psychic faculty as yet so undeveloped in the race at large that the sporadic manifestations of it were naturally attributed to an agency not human; and, as he sat in the twilight, surrounded by persons thinking of their dead, yearning for some sign of their continued existence, he felt both oppressed and excited. He found himself thinking of his child with an intensity that brought up visual images of her as distinct and involuntary as those mental pictures which sometimes precede the first sleep of a weary brain. He tried not to think of her. He smiled at himself for being fearful of Mrs. Nicholson's power, whatever it was, but the fact remained that he was fearful. It was not that he was afraid of any possible evocation of his dead child; but the idea that any such evocation should become part of a public entertainment in a setting of contrived mystery filled him with repulsion.

Suddenly, something white, like a pallid, non-luminous flame, flickered up from the floor before the cabinet, wavered in the air an instant, sank down, disappeared.

The suspended breath of the assemblage was exhaled in a soft "Ah!"

Above the cabinet, a tenuous white hand floated out over the heads of the people, floated back and vanished.

"Harriet is here," said a voice behind the curtains of the cabinet. "Is anyone present who wishes to speak with Harriet?" ·

A man in the front row cleared his throat, and got noisily to his feet.

He held a whispered conversation with the voice, and sat down with a deep sigh of satisfaction.

Again, something white flickered in front of the audience. This time it was broader; it rose higher; but it disappeared without assuming definite shape. As before, it was the herald of the dead. They now crowded fast, one upon the other, with their messages to the living. Before each new visitant, the white flame rose and fell; with its recurrence, it grew in size and substance until, at length, it did not vanish but remained, the vague but undeniable semblance of a shrouded human form.

" It's Winston," proclaimed the voice.

A woman, sitting in front of Sanborn, stood up.

" My darling son!" she murmured. The white shape beckoned her to come nearer. She made her way between the chairs. For an instant she was enveloped in a mist of flowing white; then she was alone before the cabinet. She came back to her seat, weeping with joy.

These reunions filled Sanborn with nostalgia and, at the same time, with repugnance. The images of his child persisted, and he tried persistently to shut them out until the dim, crowded room, surcharged with emotion, pervaded continually by some floating white form, became merely a background for the struggle within him; and the high childish voice that rang out suddenly, stumbling bewitchingly over certain letters, was for him, at first, only part of this inner vision; but the childish shape which appeared, vague and white, above the cabinet was very different from the clear, bright image in his brain.

For an instant, Sanborn sat motionless while the voice appealed for recognition in the name of his child. Then he sprang to his feet; he pushed his way between the chairs; he reached out his arms to the tiny figure. At the touch, he gave a quick cry. There was a low imprecation, the sound of a scuffle.

" Treslow! Light the gas! Open the door!"

Immediately, the light in the square of glass went out; but, even in the darkness, Treslow with reportorial agility managed to find the chandelier.

One glance laid bare Mrs. Nicholson's mysteries and miracles, all the ridiculous simplicity of her devices; and Mrs. Nicholson, herself, struggling to get free from Sanborn's grasp, was her own best example of ridiculous simplicity. Her large person, almost grossly fat, but buoyant and agile, was clad in a black union suit which made her look as vulnerable in the light as it had made her invisible in the dark. At her feet, lay the white-clothed doll which, held aloft by her black arm, had appeared to float through the air.

What Sanborn intended to do, he didn't know. His one thought was to keep that woman from getting away until those people whom she had duped could take in her outrageous trickery. He looked around to see what had become of Treslow. Close at his side, staring at him as though he were a spirit, stood his wife.

His grasp on Mrs. Nicholson loosened. With a jerk she was free; with a bound she was behind the curtains of the cabinet; there was the sound of a banging door, a thrust bolt, as she made her escape.

Treslow sprang forward to prevent this.

"Let her go," Sanborn called to him. "Get me a carriage." He had drawn his wife's arm through his. Pale, bewildered, she seemed about to faint. "I must get Mrs. Sanborn out of this."

Treslow looked as if he had found his great story, but one too great for him to cope with. He pushed his way out of the room. The people who had seen Mrs. Nicholson exposed had the sheepish, resentful expression of having themselves suffered exposure; and they hurried into their wraps with a panic eagerness to avoid getting mixed up in unpleasant publicity.

"Drive around anywhere," Sanborn said to the man on the hansom which Treslow had managed to find for him. "Go to the park," he added as he helped his wife into the cab and got in after her.

Shivering with the excitement of the scene through which she had passed, Mrs. Sanborn sank back in a corner of the cab.

"Are you cold?" he asked.

She shook her head. Behind the veil with a heavy black border which she had let down over her face, he saw that her lips were trembling. He closed the apron of the cab. They drove in silence for several blocks through the early dusk of the September day.

"Alice," he asked as they turned into Central Park, "have you gone to that woman's often?"

"Quite often," she answered faintly.

Disgust and shame at his own credulity made him break out bitterly against her credulity. "And each time, I suppose, she has exploited our child? Each time, for the edification of the audience, you have embraced a doll?"

"No, to-day was the first time she appeared. I'd only had messages before. Oh, you might have let me go on thinking it was Louise!" she cried, his bitterness calling forth her bitterness. "It was all you had left me!"

Sanborn saw that she had no idea he had been as credulous as herself, and he was touched by her forlorn protest.

"I didn't know you were there," he said. "I didn't know you

ever went there. For a moment, I believed, too, that Louise had come back."

His confession left her speechless. She stared at him in amazement; then her face softened with understanding and pity.

"And *you* were as lonely as *that?*"

"Yes."

For Sanborn, who had isolated himself among strangers as ignorant of his child's life as of her death, and who had come to desire even the perfunctory sympathy of these acquaintances, the realization that his loneliness had been felt equally, similarly, by his wife flooded his heart with comfort. He had thought of her as finding a kind of happiness in a hundred sentimental observances; and he saw, with the larger comprehension his suffering had brought him, that she had thought of him as stoically calm with the suppression of all memories. He turned toward her; she was looking straight ahead; he saw her pretty profile, the small, pointed chin. He experienced the odd sensation he always experienced when he saw her after an absence. In beholding her features, even more familiar to him than his own, and in which, as in a mirror, he had seen reflected, year after year, his own joys and sorrows, it was as if he came suddenly face to face with himself; and the part of his being that he lost when he left her, he found when he was with her again. To be sitting there beside her was the only natural thing he had done since they parted; perhaps it seemed natural because they had formed the habit of being together; but it was a habit so rooted in mutual need that it had become more instinct than custom.

This lifting of his loneliness was like the cessation of physical pain. He felt grateful to her, he felt very near her; and, as in the early days of their marriage, he desired to share his thoughts, his emotions, with her.

"Alice," he said, "don't you feel that it is better Louise didn't come back to us this afternoon? Don't you feel that our memory gives her to us more completely than she could give herself to us as an embodied spirit? I can shut my eyes and see her and hear her voice. Can't you?"

"Yes," she answered softly.

Their eyes met and lingered, and they exchanged that smile of fond pride with which parents turn to each other for recognition of the charm of their child.

"Just because she *has* lived, she never *can* die," he added. "That's a sort of immortality."

Under the arching trees of the roadway it was growing dark. The driver pulled up his horse and opened the little door in the top of the cab.

"Where to now, sir?" he asked.

Mrs. Sanborn started nervously. "Tell him to go to the station. I didn't know it was so late. Cousin Sarah will be worried."

"Drive around the park until I tell you to stop," Sanborn said.

The little door in the cab roof shut with a bang.

"I don't know how to tell you what I want to say," Sanborn began. "I didn't know I wanted to say it until a minute ago when you wished the cabman to drive to the station. It seemed so natural to be with you that I hadn't thought how unnatural it was in the circumstances." He paused, and then broke out, "I can't stand living as I have been living for the last six months. I thought I could go back and be the man I used to be, but I couldn't. I've been utterly miserable."

His wife in her corner of the cab made no sign.

"When I asked you to marry me, I thought I couldn't live without you. I know now that I *can* live without you, but I need you much more than I needed you then. Alice, I want you. Will you come back to me?"

He put out his hand and found hers.

"But you don't love me," she said tremulously.

"I don't know whether I love you or not," he answered. "I don't feel for you as I did when we were engaged, and I can't, any more than I could go back and be the man I used to be when I was just out of college, or any more than our child could come back to us this afternoon. But that I need you, I know. Will you come back to me?"

For answer his wife let him draw her to him. It was Mrs. Sanborn who broke the silence.

"It's queer, but I feel as I did when we drove away from the church together after being married. It seems as though we were starting out to live our life all over again. Don't you feel that way, John?"

For an instant, Sanborn had an impulse to remind his wife that he had just told her that a renascence of their early love was impossible; but the patience and toleration his suffering had taught him caused him to hold his tongue. He saw that death and sorrow had not made her more logical or more capable of taking his viewpoint than she had been before they parted; but was it any more possible for him to take her viewpoint? Yet, in spite of these ineradicable differences, their lives were united as merely similar tastes could never have united them. They were bound together by the innumerable ties of mutual experiences, by all their shared dreams and their lonely disillusions. Doubtless Alice did feel as she said—romantic love seemed to spring eternal in a woman's heart—and, after all, didn't he himself feel that love was eternal? Because it had been, it always would be; it had the immortality of all mortal experiences, the immortality that had given him his child again.

The impatient cabman had brought them to the entrance of the park. The lights of the Plaza and the great hotels facing it glowed softly through the September haze.

Sanborn drew his wife closer to him and kissed her. His heart was filled with the peace that comes of the acceptance of life as it is, of the belief that all things work together for some large, inexplicable purpose.

THE PRICE OF PRUDERY

C. W. SALEEBY, M.D.

ADDRESSING a meeting of clergymen some time ago, the present writer endeavored to trace back to the beginning the main cause of infant mortality, and endeavored to show that that lay in the natural ignorance of the human mother. In the discussion which followed, an elderly clergyman insisted that the causes had not been traced far enough back, maternal ignorance being itself permitted in consequence of our national prudery.

Ever since that day one has come to see more and more clearly that the criticism was just. Maternal ignorance is a natural fact of human kind, and destroys infant life everywhere, though prudery be or be not a local phenomenon. But where vast organizations exist for the remedying of ignorance, prudery indeed is responsible for the neglect of ignorance on the most important of all subjects. Let it not be supposed for a moment that in this protest one desires, even for the highest ends, to impart such knowledge as would involve sullying the bloom of youth. It is not necessary to destroy the charm of innocence in order to remedy certain kinds of ignorance; nor are prudery and modesty identical. Whatever prudery may be when analyzed, it seems perfectly fair to charge it as the substantial cause of the ignorance in which the young generation grows up, as to matters which vitally concern its health and that of future generations. Let us now observe in brief the price of prudery thus arraigned.

There is, first, that large proportion of infant mortality which is due to maternal ignorance. The nation has had the young mother at school for many years; much devotion and money have been spent upon her. Yet it is necessary to pass an Act ensuring, if possible, that when she is confronted with the great business of her life—which is the care of a baby—within thirty-six hours the fact shall be made known to some one who, racing for life against time, may haply reach her soon enough to remedy the ignorance which would otherwise very likely bury her baby. Prudery has decreed that while at school she should learn nothing of such matters. For the matter of that she may even have attended a three-year course in science or technology, and be a miracle of information on the keeping of accounts, the testing of drains, and the principles of child psychology; but it has not been thought suitable to discuss with her the care of a baby. How could any nice-minded teacher care to put such ideas into a girl's head? Never having noticed a child with a doll, we have somehow failed to realize that Nature, her Ancient Mother and ours, is not above putting into her head, when she can scarcely toddle, the ideas at which we pretend to blush. Prudery on this topic, and with such consequences, is not much less than blasphemy against life and the most splendid purposes towards which the individual, " but a wave of the wild sea," can be consecrated.

This question of the care of babies offers us much less excuse for its neglect than do questions concerned with the circumstances antecedent to the babies' appearance. Yet we are blameworthy, and disastrously so, here also. Prudery insists that boys and girls shall be left to learn anyhow. That is not what it says, but that is what it does. It feebly supposes not merely that ignorance and innocence are identical, but that, failing the parent, the doctor, the teacher, and the clergyman—and probably all these do fail—ignorance will remain ignorant. There are others, however, who always lie in wait, whether by word of mouth or the printed word, and since youth will in any case learn—except in the case of a few rare and pure souls—we have to ask ourselves whether we prefer that these matters shall be associated in its mind with the cad round the corner or the groom or the chauffeur who instructs the boy, the domestic servant who instructs the girl, and with all those notions of guilty secrecy and of misplaced levity which are entailed; or with the idea that it is right and wise to understand these matters in due measure because their concerns are the greatest in human life.

After puberty, and during early adolescence, when a certain amount of knowledge has been acquired, we leave youth free to learn lies from advertisements, carefully calculated to foster the tendency to hypochondria, which is often associated with such matters.

It is the ignorance conditioned by prudery that is responsible later on for many criminal marriages; contracted, it may be, with the blind blessing of Church and State, which, however, the laws of heredity and infection rudely ignore. Parents cannot bring themselves to inquire into matters which profoundly concern the welfare of the daughter for whom they propose to make what appears to be a good marriage. They desire, of course, that her children shall be healthy and whole-minded; they do not desire that marriage should be for her the beginning of disease, from the disastrous effects of which she may never recover. But these are delicate matters, and prudery forbids that they should be inquired into; yet every father who permits his daughter to marry without having satisfied himself on these points is guilty, at the least, of grave delinquency of duty, and may, in effect, be conniving at disasters and desolations of which he will not live to see the end.

Society, from the highest to the lowest of its strata, is afflicted with certain forms of understood and eminently preventable disease, any public mention of which by mouth or pen involves serious risk of various kinds. Prudery, again, is largely responsible for the continuance of these evils at a time when we have so much precise knowledge regarding their nature and the possibility of their prevention. Medical science cannot make distinctions between one disease and another, nor between one sin and another, as prudery does. Prudery says that such and such is vice, that its consequences in the form of disease are the penalties imposed by its inexorable god upon the guilty and the innocent, the living and the unborn alike, and that therefore our ordinary attitude towards disease cannot here be maintained. Physiological science, however, knowing what it knows regarding food and alcohol, and air and exercise and diet, can readily demonstrate that the gout from which Mrs. Grundy suffers is also a penalty for sin; none the less because it is not so hideously disproportionate, in its measure and in its incidence, to the gravity of the offence. These moral distinctions between one disease and another have little or no meaning for medical science, and are more often than not immoral.

It would be none too easy to show that the medical profession in any country has yet used its tremendous power in this direction. Professions, of course, do not move as a whole, and we must not expect the universal laws of institutions to find an exception here. But though they do not move, they can be moved. It is when the public has been educated in the elements of these matters, and has been taught to see what the consequences of prudery are, that the necessary forces will be brought into action. Meanwhile, what we call the social evil is almost entirely left to the efforts made in Rescue Homes and the like. It is much more than doubtful whether Rescue Homes—the only method which Mrs. Grundy will tolerate—are the best way of dealing with this problem, even if the people who worked in them had the right kind of outlook upon the matter, and even if their numbers were indefinitely multiplied. Everyone who has devoted a moment's thought to the question knows perfectly well that this is merely beginning at the end, and therefore all but futile. I mention the matter here to make the point that the one measure which prudery permits is just the most useless, ill-devised, and literally preposterous with which this tremendous problem can be mocked.

The two forms of disease to which we must refer are appalling in their consequences, both for the individual and the future. In technical language they are called contagious; meaning that the infection is conveyed not through the air as, say, in the case of measles or small-pox, but by means of contact with some infected surface—it may be a lip in the act of kissing, a cup in drinking, a towel in washing, and so forth. Of both these terrible diseases this is true. They therefore rank, like leprosy, as amongst the most eminently preventable diseases. Leprosy has in consequence been completely exterminated in Anglo-Saxon countries, but though venereal disease—the name of the two contagions considered together—diminishes, it is still abundant everywhere and in all classes of society. I declare with all the force of which I am capable that, many and daily as are the abominations for which posterity will hold us up to execration, there is none more abominable in its immediate and remote consequences, none less capable of apology than the daily destruction of healthy and happy womanhood, whether in marriage or outside it, by means of these diseases. At all times this is horrible, and it is more especially horrible when the helpless victim is destroyed with the blessing of the Church and the State, parents and friends; everyone of whom should ever after go in sackcloth and ashes for being privy to such a deed.

The present writer, for one, being a private individual, the servant of the public, and responsible to no body smaller than the public, has long declined and will continue to decline to join the hateful conspiracy of silence, in virtue of which these daily horrors lie at the door of the most honored and respected individuals and professions in the community. More especially at the doors of the Church and the medical profession there lies the burden of shame that, as great organized bodies having vast power, they should concern themselves, as they daily do, with their own interests and honor, without realizing that where things like these are permitted by their silence, their honor is smirched beyond repair in whatever Eyes there be that regard.

I propose therefore to say that which at the least cannot but have the effect of saving at any rate a few girls somewhere throughout the English-speaking world from one or other or both of these diseases, and their consequences. Let those only who have ever saved a single human being from such horrors dare to utter a word against the plain speaking which may save one woman now.

Something is known by the general public of the individual consequences of the first disease. It is known by many, also, that there are babies being born alive but rotted through for life. Further, it is not at all generally known, though the fact is established, that of the comparatively few survivors to adult life from amongst such babies, some may transmit the disease even to the third generation. There is a school of so-called moralists who regard all this as the legitimate and providential punishment for vice, even though ten innocent be destroyed for one guilty. Such moralists, more loathsome than the disease itself, may be left in the gathering gloom to the company of their ghastly creed.

The public knowledge of the first of these diseases, though far short of the truth, is not nearly so inadequate as that of the second. "No worse than a bad cold" is the kind of lie with which youth is fooled. The disease may sometimes be little worse than a bad cold in men, though very often it is far more serious; it may kill, may cause lasting damage to the coverings of the heart and to the joints, and often may prevent all possibility of future fatherhood.

These evils sink almost into insignificance when compared with the far graver consequences in women. Our knowledge of this subject is comparatively recent, being necessarily based upon the discovery of the microbe that causes the disease. Now that it can be identified, we learn that a vast proportion of the illnesses and disorders peculiar to women have this cause, and it constantly leads to the operations, now daily carried out in all parts of the world, which involve opening the body, and all that that may entail. Curable in its early stages in men, it is scarcely curable in women except by means of a grave abdominal operation, involving much risk to life and only to be undertaken after much suffering has failed to be met by less drastic means. The various consequences in other parts of the body may and do occur in women as in men. Perhaps the most characteristic consequence of the disease in both sexes is sterility; this being much more conspicuously the case in women, and being the more cruel in their case.

Of course large numbers of women are infected with these diseases before marriage and apart from it, but one or both of them constitute the most important of the bridegroom's wedding presents, in countless cases every year, all over the world. The unfortunate bride falls ill after marriage; she may be speedily cured; very often she is ill for life, though major surgery may relieve her; and in a large number of cases she goes forever without children. One need scarcely refer to the remoter consequences to the nervous system, including such diseases as locomotor ataxia, and general paralysis of the insane; the latter of which is known to be increasing amongst women. Even in these few words, which convey to the layman no idea whatever of the pains and horrors, the shocking erosion of beauty, the deformities, the insanities, incurable blindness of infants, and so forth, that follow these diseases, enough will yet have been said to indicate the supreme importance of publicity.

There is no need to horrify or scandalize or disgust young womanhood, but it is perfectly possible in the right way and at the right time to give instruction as to certain facts, and whilst quite admitting that there are hosts of other things which we must desire to teach, I maintain that this also must we do and not leave the others undone. It is untrue that it is necessary to excite morbid curiosity, that there is the slightest occasion to give nauseous or suggestive details, or that the most scrupulous reticence in handling the matter is incompatible with complete efficiency. Such assertions will certainly be made by those who have done nothing, never will do anything, and desire that nothing shall be done; they are nothing, let them be treated as nothing.

It is supposed by some that instruction in these matters must be useless because, in point of fact, imperious instincts will have their way. It is nonsense. Here, as in so many other cases, the words of Burke are true—Fear is the mother of safety. It is always the tempter's business to suggest to his victim that there is no danger. Often and often, if convinced there is danger, and danger of another kind than any he refers to, she will be saved. This may be less true of young men. In them the racial instinct is stronger, and perhaps a smaller number will be protected by fear, but no one can seriously doubt that the fear born of knowledge would certainly protect many young women.

There is also the possible criticism, made by a school of moralists for whom I have nothing but contempt so entire that I will not attempt to disguise it, who maintain that these are unworthy motives to which to appeal, and that the good act or the refraining from an evil one, effected by means of fear, is of no value to God. In the same breath, however, these moralists will preach the doctrine of hell. We reply that we merely substitute for their doctrine of hell—which used to be somewhere under the earth, but is now who knows where—the doctrine of a hell upon the earth, which we wish youth of both sexes to fear; and that if the life of this world, both present and to come, be thereby served, we bow the knee to no deity whom that service does not please.

How then, should we proceed?

It seems to me that instruction in this matter may well be delayed until the danger is near at hand. This is not really education for parenthood in the more general sense. That, on sane eugenic principles, can scarcely begin too soon; it is, further, something vastly more than mere instruction, though instruction is one of its instruments. But here what we require is simply definite instruction to a definite end and in relation to a definite danger. At some stage or other, before emerging into danger, youth of both sexes must learn the elements of the physiology of sex, and must be made acquainted with the existence and the possible results of venereal disease. A

father or a teacher may very likely find it almost impossible to speak
to a boy; even though he has screwed his courage up almost to the
sticking place, the boy's bright and innocent eyes disarm him. Unfortunately boys are often less innocent than they look. There exists far more information among youth of both sexes than we suppose; only it is all colored by pernicious and dangerous elements, the
fruit of our cowardice and neglect. Let us confine ourselves to the
case of the girl.

Before a girl of the more fortunate classes goes out into society,
she must be protected in some way or another. If she be, for instance, convent bred, or if she come from an ideal home, it may very
well be and often is that she needs no instruction whatever, because
she is in fact already made unapproachable by the tempter. Fortunate indeed is such a girl. But those forming this well-guarded class
are few, and parents and guardians may often be deceived and assume
more than they are entitled to. At any rate, for the vast majority of
girls some positive instruction is necessary. It is the mother who
must undertake this responsible and difficult task before she admits
the girl to the perils of the world. Further, by some means or other,
instruction must be afforded for the ever-increasing army of girls who
go out to business. It is to me a never ceasing marvel that loving
parents, devoted to their daughters' welfare, should fail in this cardinal and critical point of duty, so constantly as they do.

This paper may be read not by the girl who is contemplating
marriage, but by one or both of her parents. If the reader be such
an one I here charge him or her with the solemn responsibility which is
theirs whether they realize it or not. You desire your daughter's
welfare; you wish her to be healthy and happy in her married life;
perhaps your heart rejoices at the thought of grand-children; you
concern yourself with your prospective son-in-law's character, with
his income and prospects; you wish him to be steady and sober; you
would rather that he came of a family not conspicuous for morbid
tendencies. All this is well and as it should be; yet there is that to
be considered which, whilst it is only negative, and should not have
to be considered at all, yet takes precedence of all these other questions. No combination of advantages is worth the dust in the balance when weighed against either of these diseases in a prospective

son-in-law: infection is not a matter of chance but of certainty or little short of it. Everything may seem fair and full of promise, yet there may be that in the case which will wreck all.

It follows, therefore, that parents or guardians are guilty of a grave dereliction of duty if they neglect to satisfy themselves in time on this point. Doubtless, in the great majority of cases no harm will be done. But in the rest irreparable harm is often done, and the innocent, ignorant girl who has been betrayed by father and mother and husband alike, may turn upon you all, perhaps on her death-bed, perhaps with the blasted future in her arms, and say "This is *your* doing: behold your deed."

It is just because public opinion is so potent, and, like all other powers, so potent either for good or for evil, that its present disastrous workings are the more deplorable. The power is there, and it means well, though it does disastrously ill. Public opinion ought to be decided upon these matters; it ought to be powerful and effective. We shall never come out into the daylight until it is; we shall not be saved by laws, nor by medical knowledge, nor by the admonitions of the Churches. Our salvation lies only in a healthy public opinion, not less effective and not more well-meaning than public opinion is at present, but informed where it is now ignorant, and profoundly impressed with the importance of realities as it now is with the importance of appearances.

ANTI-CLERICALISM IN FRANCE

KENNETH BELL

A dialogue between Mr. Cuthbert, *an English country gentle-man, and his guests,* M. Gustave Flambert, *Deputy and Member of the Moderate Left in the French Chamber; and* M. le Comte de Brissac, *formerly Deputy and Member of the Right: lately resigned.*

I

The French Revolution

Mr. Cuthbert. It would be interesting to discover exactly why it is that though France is a Republic and the French the most intelligent people in Europe, there is so little freedom of thought and so little civil liberty there.

M. Flambert. The reason is that France is still in bondage to the Catholic Church.

M. de Brissac. The reason is that France is still under the tyranny of the Revolution.

Mr. Cuthbert. But in England we have had at least two revolutions and we still have an established Church.

M. Flambert. In England you have forgotten your revolutions because their results have been achieved. In 1641 you disposed once for all of the attempt of Laud to introduce uniformity in Religion. Since then the Anglican Church has maintained a precarious position checked on the one side by Parliamentary control, on the other by innumerable rival sects. There is no parallel between your established Church and our recently disestablished one. Again in the century following 1688 you disposed once for all of the chances of the Stuart dynasty in England. Since 1760 you have had no Jacobites. The successors of George III have had no serious rivals for their throne. All Englishmen are agreed in the comfortable faith that their form of government is the best in the world. There is no such moral unity in France. The Catholics have never whole-heartedly accepted the Revolution.

M. de Brissac. No: because to do so in your sense would be to be false to France. The Revolution was, and is, a purely destructive movement. It swept away the ancient civilization, the old corporate life which French history had slowly created, and put in their place —what? The childish and self-contradictory formula: Liberty, Equality and Fraternity—liberty to the informer, equality before the guillotine, fraternity in the tumbril. This was the motto of the men who cut up our provinces into departments, desecrated Notre Dame, destroyed our educational system, had our judges elected by popular vote, shattered the throne, the nobility and the Church, and replaced them by the most grinding of all forms of tyranny, the tyranny of universal suffrage, the tyranny of the ignorant, of the unbalanced, of the undisciplined. It was, I repeat, a purely destructive movement. France may well envy England where it is still true that " orders and degrees jar not with liberty but well consist," where the liberties of the parent, of the churchman, of the lawyer, of the schoolmaster, of the professor, even of the soldier, are still respected, where some institutions, at any rate, are still safe from the leveling zeal of the popular nominee.

Mr. Cuthbert. Well, there are some people, landowners especially, who would not agree with you. Vested interests are not quite so reverently treated here as they once were.

M. Flambert. Exactly: what M. de Brissac calls liberties, I call privileges. The Revolution was destructive, I grant, but destructive of injustice, of monopoly, of tyranny, and of privilege. The liberty of the noblesse and the clergy not to pay taxes, the liberty of the censor to throw an author into prison for telling the truth, the liberty of the rich to oppress the poor, of the educated to keep the uneducated in ignorance, are liberties which are, indeed, contradictory to equality and fraternity. The Revolution destroyed them in the name of the right of all men equally to be free. Its work will not be done till the privileges of the few have finally ceased to conflict with the freedom of all but themselves.

Mr. Cuthbert. Then the Revolution is still in progress in France?

M. Flambert. Yes. That is the point. We must not be false to our history. In 1789 France came forward in Europe as the apostle of Democracy. The Renaissance was Italian, the Reformation was

German, the third great impetus to the emancipation of humanity was preëminently French. The Sovereignty of the People, proclaimed by Rousseau, must be worked out to its logical conclusion by France. Hitherto there have been innumerable difficulties in the way, for every advance has had its accompanying reaction. All depends— for the future—on how we carry forward the work of our great predecessors.

M. de Brissac. Yet I too can invoke history. Only I go further back. French history does not begin for me in 1789. It is not only since then that France has given the lead to Europe. Since the days of Charlemagne she has stood for civilization, for intelligence and for chivalry. She fought the Crusades. She created Gothic archi·tecture. St. Bernard, St. Louis and St. Jeanne d'Arc are her national heroes. Pascal, Bossuet and Fénelon were Frenchmen. Voltaire was not our first writer any more than Dumouriez was our first general. The French tongue, the most perfect vehicle of luminous thought since Greek became a dead language, was moulded in the service of the Church. French art, still supreme in Europe, was never so spontaneous or so eloquent of national endeavor as when it was devoted to the same service; the chivalry of French arms won its spurs at the head of United Christendom. France is *la fille aînée de l'église.* The old ordered life, the simple faith, the traditional education of Catholicism made France great. She will never be great again till she returns to the belief of her fathers. It is not we who are false to her history.

Mr. Cuthbert. Still, the Middle Ages are a long way away now. France cannot be blamed for looking to the future.

M. de Brissac. Agreed. But that is exactly what the friends of M. Flambert will not do. It is he who is the real reactionary, for he wishes to preserve the atmosphere of the Revolution, whereas we wish France to advance, as she has always done on the traditional lines of her policy. It is the object of the Radicals to keep up in French life the bitterness, the heated passions, the murderous antagonisms which are inevitable in a revolutionary era. It is as if Walpole should have treated his political opponents as Cromwell treated his. This constant invocation of the rancors of the past, this insistence on the logical working out of the destructive principles of a long-past upheaval, are a fatal obstacle in the way of Progress. " *Le Cléricalisme, voilà l'ennemi!* " What a motto to carry into public life!

Mr. Cuthbert. It has certainly seemed to me that it is one of the misfortunes of France that she can forget nothing of her history. It is less intelligent, no doubt, but also safer to do as we do here—and let bygones be bygones. A long memory is a dangerous thing in politics.

II

The Atmosphere of Public Life

M. Flambert. That may be so. But it is perhaps in part responsible for what seems to me the fault in England and the vice in American public life—the lack of real principles dividing the parties. All are opportunists anxious only to catch votes. The Conservatives in office calmly take over the programme of the outgoing Liberals. There is no consistency in party programmes, nor in the careers of public men. In many ways Disraeli was more of a Radical than Gladstone. The Liberals seem to devote themselves to proving that they are more Conservative than Radical, the Conservatives that they are rather Liberals than Tories. The Socialists alone have a definitely thought-out programme based on logical principles. They alone cannot be accused of timidity and opportunism.

Mr. Cuthbert. Well, but in England we are apt to think that the only justification of the party system is that it leads to compromise. Nothing frightens us more than an outburst of party spirit, which we take to indicate a tendency to sacrifice the national welfare on the altars of personal convictions. The Opposition exists to act as a brake on the Government. We rely on a black and white party between them to produce a gray policy.

M. de Brissac. That is certainly not the atmosphere of French public life. There the object of debate is not to arrive at a compromise, but to inflame passions, to vindicate principles, to arouse opposition and enthusiasm. The atmosphere of the British House of Commons when a bill is in committee would bore us all to extinction. We must have oratory, we must have drama, we must have logic. It is for this reason that I am convinced at heart that the form of government invented by you is unsuited for us. I agree with you, Mr.

Cuthbert, that great national interests ought not to be discussed or settled in a fever of passion. The Latin races are too excitable, too passionate, and too logical for Parliamentary government. Hence the disease of French public life. France is too intellectual and too feminine to govern herself. She requires to rule her a man, and a man of action.

III

Foreign Policy

M. Flambert. In other words M. de Brissac's party is not wholeheartedly Republican. In spite of the efforts of Leo XIII, it is obvious that a convinced Catholic cannot genuinely rally to the Republic. There is a complete opposition of principle between the two. In the sphere of foreign policy, to take one example, the Catholic is preoccupied with other interests than those of France. Undeterred by the ghastly failure of Napoleon III, in the face of the fact that even Spain is breaking with the Vatican, that Italy, Germany, and now Portugal, have refused to acknowledge the right of the Pope to intervene in State affairs, he would have the most intelligent people in Europe come forward as the champions of a mediæval theory and defend the temporal power. France is to refuse to treat with ordinary courtesy the Government of Italy, because the Pope is foolish enough to continue to quarrel with the masters of Rome. In memory of the Crusades, the country of Danton and Victor Hugo is to insult the country of Garibaldi. Once already the French Republic has soiled its honor by destroying the Republic of Rome and restoring a mediæval despotism. It will never do so again.

M. de Brissac. I am as jealous of the honor of France as anyone, but I do not see that it is safe in the hands of either the Socialist agitators or the Jewish financiers who between them direct your foreign policy. Patriotism is certainly not a strong point with either. The Socialist is the enemy, whether he avows it or not, of the Army, and any day prefers a British or German workingman on strike to the honest bourgeois who is the backbone of his own country. Because of the internal difficulties of Russia, he opposed the alliance, the conclusion of which was a vital step forward in the recovery of France after 1870. The Jewish capitalists who negotiate our loans are equally cosmopolitan, for to them France is one only among innumerable lands of exile, all to be exploited for the advantage of their race. The Jews' control of the Freemasons, who in their turn have the allegiance of the workingman, makes possible an unholy alliance between capital and labor which, so it seems to me, agree only in a conspiracy against the honor of France. At least you will allow that one may prefer the dictation of the head of the Catholic Church, to that of the Director of the Jewish Syndicate?

Mr. Cuthbert. Then you really think there was something at the back of the Dreyfus case?

M. de Brissac. The Dreyfus case was a bad pretext for a thoroughly justifiable outbreak. Dreyfus was innocent. But the accusations which were concentrated on him were thoroughly earned by those whose policy he was taken to typify. The subsequent history of France shows only too clearly that the anti-Catholic organizations were determined to dispose once for all of Catholicism, and make France stand at home and abroad for militant atheism. The Army, which was loyal to the Church, has been betrayed by this policy: the Dreyfus case was a blind struggle on the part of both to defend themselves against the enemies of their God. It was unfortunate that they found so bad a pretext.

M. Flambert. It was indeed: for the honor of France and of the French Army which they claimed to defend came out of the Dreyfus case besmirched in the eyes of Europe. The Catholics did not improve their prestige by standing up in the name of Christianity against the defence by a free-thinker of obvious justice. The Dreyfus case alone is enough to justify the subsequent policy of the Republic.

M. de Brissac. Yes, unfortunately for us and for France, the Republic which cannot forgive us for using the guilt of Dreyfus to defend our cause, has gone on to use his innocence as a pretext for the proscription of the ancient religion of France.

IV

The Concordat

Mr. Cuthbert. But surely Catholicism has not been proscribed? The Church has merely been disestablished and facilities have been granted by which the resources of the Church, apart from the State endowment, can still be held by voluntary associations of the faithful, though they cannot be increased.

M. Flambert. In fact, the Republic, being anxious to avoid any future interference of the Vatican in its home or foreign policy, has simply set free the Church from its ill-assorted union with the State. Henceforth each is free to go its own way.

M. de Brissac. No, that is not so. The State is now free to attack the Church. The last barrier has been thrown down which protected the Church from the hostility of the Republic. The Concordat was one of the great pieces of constructive work by which Napoleon repaired the ravages of the Revolution. At least it gave to Bishops and Curés a legal status, and though the State was forever trying to undermine that status, still it could not openly flout the Concordat. The Bishop was at least a functionary. The Revolution has destroyed the religious orders, it can now go on to destroy the secular clergy.

Mr. Cuthbert. Well, but is a bishop any freer for being a State functionary? I should have said that nothing could have been more trying to him than the constant effort to reconcile his position as a Government official with his allegiance to the Pope. At once a Frenchman loyal to the Pope and in the pay of the Government, he must surely have despaired of being simultaneously a good patriot, a good Catholic, and a good official. Especially as the Government was, I gather, only too anxious to bring out the incompatibilities of his position.

M. de Brissac. I know that many good Catholics are disposed to welcome the Separation. Still I cannot but feel that, in the first place, it makes us even more defenceless against anti-clericalism, and secondly, that it is now even less possible for us than it was before to fight against the blasphemous and disloyal policy which would make France stand for atheism—the Godless School and the Godless State.

Mr. Cuthbert. Would you not do well, then, to accept the law of associations?

M. de Brissac. No, because that law maintains all the disadvantages of the Concordat with none of its advantages. It still leaves the State with a handle against the Church, which has no legal position against the State. For who decides what constitutes a legal association? Not the ecclesiastical authorities, but the civil. Two rival associations form in the same parish. Both demand the possession of the parish church and its resources. It is the State court which decides between them. And can we trust the State to decide in the interests of the Church? No one who knows French conditions will say that we can. Better abandon all our material resources and throw ourselves on the generosity of the faithful than allow an atheistic State to pronounce upon the orthodoxy of a Catholic association.

M. Flambert. Nevertheless the law of associations represents an attempt on the part of the Government to disregard its extreme supporters' views and to come to terms with the Church. The responsibility for declining this offer of conciliation lies on you—or rather on the Vatican, whose intransigeant policy is not approved by many of the more moderate bishops.

M. de Brissac. We resent this attempt to separate us from our head. We distrust the law of associations because we are convinced that it would be the pretext for endless petty interference with our Church. *Timemus Danaos et dona ferentes.* We cannot trust the Republicans, for it is clear that their object is our extermination. The justice and clemency of which they talk are mere words. Look at their educational campaign.

Mr. Cuthbert. There certainly the intransigeance seems to be on the other side.

V

Education

M. Flambert. The reason is that to which I referred just now. As in foreign politics, so in education, there can be no compromise with the Catholic Church. The spirit of Laud which you exorcised in 1641, lives on in the Church. Its aim is two-fold. First, as I have said, to control the foreign policy of France in the interests of a foreign potentate. Secondly, by establishing a monopoly of education to control the national mind in the interests of a reactionary policy. The social degradation of the masses, whom we aspire to rouse to intellectual life, to elevate to true citizenship, to fire with public spirit, is to be perpetuated under the bondage of a degrading superstition. The poor are to be solaced, or rather drugged, in this life by illusory promises for the next. The progress of Science, the betterment of social conditions, are as impossible, so long as clericalism remains, as the political independence of France. Then again, we have not even Napoleon's motive for suffering all this. He supported Catholicism because he could rely on it to inculcate loyalty to himself. As I have said, the result of Catholic teaching is to undermine the Republic. Any régime, says Rome, except that of Universal Suffrage!

M. de Brissac. My answer is that the very offences of which you accuse us are those which you yourselves commit. You accuse us of aiming at an educational monopoly. You have captured an educational monopoly. You have closed Catholic schools, proscribed Catholic teaching. In its place you have put what you consider to be the teaching of Truth. In our view it is as pernicious a system of error as in your view is our faith. You teach dogmatic atheism. You ignore God. You deny immortality, we affirm it. You give a materialistic explanation of the universe, we a spiritual. Why should you be right and we wrong? Your science gives as little certainty as does our faith. If we have not solved the problem of existence, neither have you. You may say that we claim to have done so and you do not. But you are just as dogmatic in your rejection of our explanation as we are in its affirmation. Again, you accuse us of degrading and deceiving the masses. You take away from them what we offer —the hope of Heaven. What do you give them instead? The promise, of which you offer no guarantee, of an earthly millennium. We face the facts—there will always be misery, inequality and injustice in human life: it can never fulfil its own purpose. You refuse to face the facts—instead of teaching patience and endurance and discipline, you teach false hopes and a false ideal. They carry out your teaching—there is a Railway strike, and what do you do? "You take a firm grip of the situation "—in other words, you postpone your millennium indefinitely and call out the soldiers. The result is that your First Minister goes about for months in fear of his life from the overzealous attentions of his former friends, the anarchists. So much for Liberty, Equality, Fraternity, Free Thought and State Education! We may felicitate Portugal on following our example.

VI

The Right of Minorities

M. Flambert. Indeed we may. For these agitations are only the inconveniences of progress, not its goal. It is better that the workingman should be discontented than that he should suffer in silence. Moreover, the weathering of such storms as these are all testimonies to the Republic. Backed by the vast majority of the people, it can defy at once its too extreme supporters and its treacherous enemies. It is true that, as Victor Hugo prophesied, the advent of Universal Suffrage has ended the epoch of the Barricades. Liberty need no longer have recourse to Revolution to obtain her demands.

M. de Brissac. No, for the simple reason that her oppressors are now too strong for her. Yours is a despotism not even tempered by assassination. You accuse us of being false to the régime of Universal Suffrage. But to disregard the rights of the minority is the worst offence of which Democracy can be capable, for thereby it becomes the worst of all tyrannies. In the name of Liberty, Equality and Fraternity you, like your model Robespierre, like your prophet Rousseau, believe in liberty only for those who agree with you. Even the *Ancien Régime* was not a Reign of Terror, and that is what you have set up in France.

M. Flambert. If that be so, which, of course, I deny, it is that we, like Robespierre, have been forced to it, by your attempts to maintain a worse one. It was the *émigrés* who made the September massacres necessary. It is the reactionary ultramontanism, the insane violence of the clergy, which makes it necessary to shatter their authority in France. If our régime is a tyranny, what did you make of the reign of Charles X, what would you have made of the rule of Napoleon III?

VII

Church and State

Mr. Cuthbert. It would seem that either Church or State, or both, are putting forward excessive claims, thereby endangering civil liberty.

M. Flambert. But the State is French and modern, and the Church is Roman and mediæval. Can modern France really allow herself to be dedicated to the Sacred Heart? Can she sit by and watch all the antiquated machinery of miracle-working being used to enslave the intelligence of a free people? Can she allow her women, with their vast personal and political influence—far greater than in Teutonic countries—to receive in the confessional the *mot d'ordre* which may determine the future of French families, French husbands, even of ministries and of France itself? We are bound, in the name of Liberty, to fight this mysterious, sinister and treacherous influence which is sapping our homes and our politics.

M. de Brissac. The priest, however, you forget to mention is a Frenchman. The Freemason is possibly a Jew, certainly a cosmopolitan. Liberty and toleration are alike at the mercy of his machinations. His influence is at least as sinister, at least as mysterious as that of the Jesuit. Might not these two bogeys be allowed to cancel one another out?

Mr. Cuthbert. Both in fact seem to an Englishman rather like children's bogeys.

MM. Flambert and de Brissac (together). You do not understand the Latin temperament, nor the situation in France.

M. Flambert. At any rate, you will acknowledge that Democracy implies Education. You must, as your own Sir Robert Lowe said, " Educate your masters." Voters must be educated in order to vote freely. Bonapartism was based on the manipulation of the ignorant voter. Only the educated man can appreciate or defend the priceless benefits of self-government. That moral unity, that universal conviction that political liberty is a national inheritance, which you have in England, we are striving for in France.

Mr. Cuthbert. But is not your method rather hasty and violent? Lloyd George would like to have moral unity on the subject of the taxation of land values. But he does not at once expel all Tory schoolmasters, shut up Eton and Winchester, and bring out a new series of elementary school text-books in which Dukes are convicted of every crime and he himself given semi-divine honors.

M. de Brissac. No, because England is a free country. Everyone from the anarchist in Hyde Park to the university professor can teach what he likes up to a point which is decided not by the State, but by the Law. In France the State is everywhere, it can leave no one and nothing alone. Before its influence the Law is as powerless as is public opinion. A long course of centralization, the steady dispersal of all the influences or corporations which could stand out against the action of the State, has finally destroyed civil liberty in France. " What an Englishman asks of a lawyer," it has been said, " a Frenchman asks of an official." Such a habit of mind is fatal to liberty, for it means that there is no longer the possibility of resistance to the tyranny of an omnipotent Government. Napoleon I heard of a successful private schoolmaster. " Who is this man," he said, " who keeps three hundred people in his house without my knowledge? "— and he made him a Professor in the University of France and drafted all his boys into the State schools. This is still the spirit of French government. The State must do everything; and the suppression of minorities is its special duty. No wonder my co-religionists in Canada prefer the Union Jack to the Tricolor.

M. Flambert. That is all very well. But is Canada a nation? No, and never will be till someone or something brings it about that its people can all speak a common tongue. Why did Great Britain fight the South African War? To settle the racial question. They have not done it. South Africa will be cursed with racialism indefinitely. You can leave too much outside the sphere of State action.

Mr. Cuthbert. We are content to leave the solution of such problems as these to time.

M. Flambert. *We* cannot wait on a process. The great disaster of 1870, the still threatening power of Germany, makes national reconstruction imperative. In England your national homogeneity is already secure. Yet even you do not grant Home Rule to Ireland. We have an Ireland in our very midst.

M. de Brissac. And your treatment of us will have the same results as the English treatment of Ireland. The oppressor of freedom of thought is always made to pay in kind for his oppression. You refuse to the Church its most elementary rights. You trample on the rights of parents to choose the form of their children's education. You forbid men and women to choose for themselves the vocation of monasticism, which is always harmless and which is often as a means

of charitable work immensely valuable. The Church asks her rights
from you in the name of Liberty, and it is your cynical disregard of
your own basic principles which will bring your system to the ground.

M. Flambert. You will acknowledge, however, that the whole
history of the Church is an illustration of the difficulties in the way
of granting complete liberty of thought. The Catholic Church,
which has always persecuted the heretic, is surely able to sympathize
with our difficulties in dealing with a heresy which, we maintain, is as
fatal in the world of Democracy as Manichæism in the bosom of the
Church. The only foundation of a sane Democracy is in the free
judgment of the elector. Universal Suffrage becomes the merest
sham if a large proportion of the electors have ceased to be citizens
of the State, and have transferred their allegiance to another body.
The whole design of the Church is to undermine private judgment.
You say monks and nuns are harmless. They certainly are not citizens. They are bound by vows of poverty, obedience and chastity.
That is to say, economically, politically, and socially they have ceased
to exist as independent beings. Again, one of the great features of
your religion is the exaltation of the priesthood. The priest is for the
layman the representative of God. He has the keys of Heaven and
Hell, the whole of the believer's future welfare is in his hands. Can
you pretend that when he becomes an electioneering agent, his influence is legitimate in a Democracy? The claims of the Church are so
vast, its influence so far-reaching, that its existence in any but a
purely spiritual sphere is incompatible with Democracy. What more
daring defiance of the spirit of the age was ever made than the declaration in 1870 of Papal infallibility?

M. de Brissac. Personally I see little to choose as representing the
spirit of the age between the infallibility of the Pope and that of the
Democratic majority. It is no longer that *vox populi* is *vox dei*, for
you have abolished God. The Pope only claims to be the Divine representative—the modern State has made itself its own Divinity. To
Universal Suffrage, it seems to me that the menace from the State
is just as dangerous as that from the Church. In France at any rate,
where to be a *fonctionnaire* is the ambition of everyone who is not so
already, the number of voters who are not amenable to Government
influence is small indeed. You say that the priest from the pulpit

can threaten the indocile voter with the pains of Hell. What of the illicit influence brought to bear by the Government through fear of dismissal? Do you think the Deputies on the Right are the only men who are returned as a result of unduly influenced votes? No: there is an inherent vice in your system,—the exaltation of mere numbers. For the majority consists of those who are most easily influenced. At present it is the State which is pulling the wires. It would certainly be no worse if they were pulled by the Church.

Mr. Cuthbert. The fault with France would seem to be that the wire-pullers are too few. In England we have so many that they cancel one another out. Churches, schools, universities, women, politicians, pamphleteers and poster-makers are so busy influencing the voter that there is just a chance that he may disregard them all.

M. Flambert. To reach that result in France, we must just root out the political influence of the Church.

M. de Brissac. To reach that result in France, we must vindicate the right of the individual against the all-absorbing influence of the State.

BERNARD SHAW: THE REALIZER OF IDEALS

TEMPLE SCOTT

It is a matter for pathetic amusement when we reflect for a moment on the peculiar reputation Mr. Bernard Shaw has acquired, either by his own gallant efforts, or by our inane simplicity and Podsnappian superiority. The pathos in the amusement lies in the fact that it is we and not Mr. Shaw who are the sufferers by it. Mr. Shaw, perhaps, even welcomes it; for our inordinate conceited superiority may supply him with further materials for use in his work of showing us up. He goes on his airy way rejoicing; while we, heavily encumbered with the weight of our self-esteem, which is truly colossal, plod wearily in the Slough of Misunderstanding and arrive anywhere or nowhere utterly worn out and totally unfit for the appreciation of the fine thought offered us. I will not say a word about the injustice we do Mr. Shaw by our attitude toward him; but I do think we are spilling the wine of life and letting slip many things that are most good for us to know. We have a very bad habit of labeling things with catch-names. It is a bad habit because it causes us to throw the unique product into the same general heap on to which we cast the things for which we have no use. Of course, to discriminate requires thought, and to think is an apparently profitless labor if we can get others to do the thinking for us. We are, probably, too lazy or incompetent to estimate for ourselves each piece of work as it is offered us. We prefer to accept a superficial criticism provided it saves us trouble, and especially if it supplies us with a catch-phrase that shall pass current as the gold of thought. So that when one exclaims questioningly, " Shaw? ", and he is answered, " Pshaw! ", we think the reply brilliantly satisfying.

Now in treating Mr. Shaw in this fashion we have not treated him any less sensibly or less courteously than we have treated other men of even greater genius. We have never distinguished ourselves in our conduct toward contemporary genius. Yet, so far as Shaw is concerned we can say that we have not neglected him as we have the men of greater genius. We have not neglected him, because Mr. Shaw will not allow us to neglect him; and because he does not mind our misunderstanding him. He has the rare attribute of temper which is the crowning mark of the up-to-date salesman—an imperturbability which will not be disturbed and which will never recognize an insult. He is so anxious for our welfare that he cannot afford to feel insulted by our reception of him. And he is so convinced of the value of the article he has to sell that even when he does feel the injustice we are meting out to him, he comes up smiling the next day hoping to find us in a better mood. Mr. Shaw has undoubtedly learned the profound wisdom of the maxim of the Gentlemen of the Road: If a customer insult you, the best way to get back on him is to sell him a bill of goods.

But if we have not neglected Shaw we have done far worse—we have made him a fashion. And this is the bitterest pill Shaw has to swallow. I do not quite know how he will meet this line of treatment, though meet it he will, I am sure. Perhaps he will follow Ibsen's example and write his own *The Wild Duck* and make his astonished victims think he is satirizing himself. If our fashion-making methods with Shaw were intended by us as a retort courteous it is a consummate example of it. But it does not redeem us. To make a teacher, or a preacher, or a humorist fashionable is to bury him instanter beneath the faded rags of our complacent misunderstanding. We have the laugh on him now, of course, because he cannot do or say anything that will upset us. We simply will not let him. We calmly go on smiling and smiling with truly villainous cunning. When Mr. Shaw is most serious everybody says he is joking; when he is laying bare his heart and speaking burning words we think he is amusing us at his own expense; when he tries to show us how foolish we are we laugh back all the more and applaud him for his clever fun-making. We will not take him seriously because we say that to do this would be to miss his humor; and his humor is too good to be wasted. Oh, but we are extremely clever! So clever, indeed, that we are become enamored of our " smartness." And just here we make the great mistake. Like all " smart " people who are convinced they " know it all," we become obsessed. We see things as we have made up our minds to see them. When a simple man comes along and tells us quietly we are myopic, we call him by all the bad names in our vocabulary. Where ninety per cent. are purblind,

it is the clear-sighted man who is abnormal. Where ninety per cent.
are crooked, it is the upright man who has fallen from grace. Now,
believing as I do that Shaw is the straight-visioned man and the man
of rectitude, I say it is a matter for pathetic amusement that we have
given him the peculiar reputation he has. And it is more—it is a
matter for serious and profound self-examination. For if Shaw be
the man I say he is, then it is time to find the adjustable spectacles
that will enable us to see straight, and it is time that we determined
upon a new standard of uprightness.

Sometimes, indeed, Shaw himself will not let us take him seriously.
At those times he asks us, as it were, to accept him as the privileged
royal jester who may say to King Demos the most unpleasant truths
so long as he makes that worthy monarch laugh at the way these are
put. The sting is deadened by the livelier sensation of the enjoyment of the humor. This is, perhaps, unfortunate for Shaw, because
the humor has served its own purpose and not Shaw's. Like the terribly tragic ending of Ibsen's *Ghosts*, where the dénouement over-
powers the real intent of the dramatist, Shaw's humor is too much for
his lesson. I am sure, however, that Shaw is, at those times, aware
of this counter-effect and is content to wait until the laughter shall
have died away, when, it may be, we shall begin to reflect and ask ourselves why we laughed. In the meantime, the jester will go on jesting, sure by this means of obtaining a hearing.

But may it not be that Punchinello also has a heart that knows
sorrow and responds to pity? Is it not possible, not to say probable,
that this man is more than a merely amused and amusing observer of
life's little ironies? If we ever ask ourselves these questions we, probably, answer them as lightly as we ask them. The public's jester,
we say in effect, is the public's servant; it must suffice him that we
buy his books and enjoy his jokes and enable him to gather in his
royalties. What more can he need? And so it comes about that a
new book by Mr. Bernard Shaw is as eagerly looked for as a new song
by Harry Lauder or a new monologue by Nat Wills.

Still, laughter is a good thing, and perhaps even the price of our
misunderstanding is not too high to pay for it. The habit of laughing is worth acquiring even if we wear it unintelligently and awkwardly. It opens minds by opening hearts and is therefore the best

of educators, the educator of the feelings.   Some day we shall know what we were laughing at.   When that day comes we shall have to pray that we become not too serious.   For otherwise the jester's work must be done all over again.   We are such vain puppets that we jump to the other extreme when pulled up by the shock of a conscious realization of having made ourselves ridiculous, and we then do things at the other end just as ridiculous as those we laughed ourselves out of.   Thus it is that we go on affording sport for the gods.   Was it not Heine who conceived mankind as the puppets of an Aristophanes in Heaven?

Now it is one thing to laugh with and quite another thing to laugh at.   To laugh with a humorist means that he has made us understand him; whereas even empty minds can give vent to a loud noise at a humorous remark.   In order that a humorist shall be able to make us laugh with him he must see the very heart of the thing purely as humor.   There shall be no opposite to it in his mind.   Its whole essence shall be laughter-moving.   He is making us dance for the sheer joy of dancing, not for the sake of the exercise.   This is what Molière did, and we laughed the ridiculous and silly people of his day into hiding their heads in the desert places of their own self-complacency.

Now Shaw also makes us laugh at silly and ridiculous things, though not so often at silly and ridiculous people—an important difference, to be explained later.   Shaw makes us dance to his own tune that the bee in his bonnet is all the time humming.   He is compelling us to laugh *at* things.   He does not make us laugh with him, because at bottom he is not laughing himself.   He is terribly in earnest.   His laughter is but a literary method used by him because he is craftsman enough to know the value of the method, and because the Irishman in him gives him a natural power of expressing himself in this laughter-provoking way.   The Frenchman had the advantage of Shaw in this respect, because Molière was more interested in the joy of life than in its problems.   If Shaw were not serious he would not be a Socialist; if he were not heartily in earnest he would not have permitted himself to be elected a vestryman of St. Pancras, and he might not be a Vegetarian wearing Jaeger clothes.   Shaw began his public career by speaking from the back of a cart in Hyde Park.

I cannot conceive Molière doing any one of these or similar things. These are the marks of the moral reformer, the social reformer, the Salvationist, the enthusiastic worker in the cause of humanity, the man ever anxious for the welfare of human souls. They are not the marks of the artist and the maker and giver of joy. Shaw can no more help himself in these matters than can most Englishmen whose " sweetest songs are those which tell of saddest thought." He may laugh at the moral Englishman as Swift laughed at him, but the same nurse suckled both Irishman and Englishman. If the genius of Stevenson were depressed, as Henley said it was, by the spirit of the Shorter Catechism, the genius of Shaw is drabbed through and through by the heavy atmosphere of English middle-class life. His very opposition to this life proves the fact. As an Irishman, he was born with a grievance against it, and the grievance remains even when the smaller stage of English social life has been transformed by him into the larger stage of the world's social life. As an Irishman, he may be gifted with a satirical wit; but even as an Irishman he remains the Englishman for whom abstract ideals are the object of his efforts and their worship the glory of his devotion.

It is because of this that Shaw uses abstractions and not individuals as the objects of his fun-making. When Molière made people ridiculous they became ridiculous in their own eyes, and if they laughed with him it was with a bitter laugh. They took good care afterwards to change their ways. Shaw, however, laughs at principles, institutions, dogmas; which means that he is not so much a humorist as he is a satirist. It is well to hold up to ridicule conventions that are no longer fitting for human requirements; but to expeet us to reform our ways for fear of being ridiculous because of those conventions is to expect too much of human nature. Where all are ridiculous no one is any the wiser or foolisher. To change a convention which is become rooted as an institution is to accomplish a revolution, and revolutions are not easily brought about—at any rate, not by the satirical method. Satire is founded on thought processes and to think a revolution into existence is a matter of centuries, not decades; and even then the final accomplishment is not so much the result of thought, as it is the expression of the emotions— of the personal emotions. Molière knew this instinctively. He attacked not the convention but the individual who personified the convention. Shaw knows this also, but his attack is only indirect at the individual and directly against the conventions. The result is a moral object lesson or a social tract in a dramatic form. And as we do not go to theatres to listen to sermons or political speeches, but in order to enjoy ourselves, we go to see Shaw's plays for the fun he makes. When, as is the case with Shaw, the fun is really good, we are so amused that we ignore the lesson. The fun being at the expense of no one in particular, we hide ourselves behind the convention and are free to laugh at each other, which we do most good-naturedly. No one is hurt by the ridicule. Were one of us, either as a class or as a profession, to be made really ridiculous, the emotions would be aroused and something would happen. That very thing would happen which the humorist intended should happen; the individual would sneak away and take good care he did not again make himself so ridiculous. What you can do with an individual you cannot do with Society. Society will not be insulted or hurt however ridiculous you make it appear. Society is not a person; it is an abstraction. It is not even a thing. So that what is everybody's business is here, as in other matters, nobody's business. We can afford to laugh as much as the humorist wishes us to laugh, and that's all we do. That is another reason why Shaw's fun is so much enjoyed and his preaching so little heeded. The fun that hurts nobody can be enjoyed by everybody.

Are we, therefore, to conclude that Shaw has failed? By no means. In the first place he has not had, as yet, the time in which to make his efforts tell. He has undertaken a giant's labor, and a giant's labor is not accomplished in a generation even by a giant. To give Shaw a fair field he should have the theatre of edification and not the theatre of amusement. He is aiming to get that. He has pleaded for it with all the power of his keen satire in his preface to the *Three Plays for Puritans*. When people go to theatres to be educated and uplifted Shaw will have his real chance. We might argue that a great dramatic genius would have worked his way with existing limitations, and we should argue with reason. But we must take Shaw as we find him and give him his chance. In the second place we do not understand Shaw; and it is our business first to un-

derstand him before we dare pass judgment upon him.   In pointing
out his weakness as a dramatic artist I have done so in order that
proper justice shall be done him.   If he has permitted his reforming
spirit to get the better of his dramatic genius; if he has allowed the
fountains of his exuberant satirical wit to overflow the fields of his
splendid tillage, let us make due allowance for his energizing will and
call these defects the faults of his virtues.   For Shaw's is a genius the
artistic expression of which best finds itself in freedom from conventions.   Because of this I call Shaw a great moral force.   He is,
perhaps, the most virtuous man of his age.   With him virtue is a
passion.   Until we understand that we do not understand Shaw.

This may appear to be but a poor attempt at an amusing paradox.   That Shaw, the man whom we scorn as Socialist, Free-thinker,
Anti-Vivisectionist, Revolutionist, Free Lover, etc., and only tolerate
because he is amusing; that this man should be a virtuous man is,
on the face of it, simply ridiculous.   Why, we exclaim, he transgresses all the virtues!   Yes, he does transgress all the virtues, and
yet it is not in his nature to be other than virtuous.   It is because
he transgresses " the virtues " that he is a man of virtue.   He must
do it or he would not be true to himself.   For what are " the virtues "
that Shaw transgresses?   Let us ask ourselves that question before
we condemn the man.   Do we mean by " the virtues," telling the
truth, respecting the property of our neighbors, respecting our
neighbor's good name and wife, and life; acting kindly, generously
and justly to each other?   I am sure we do not mean these by " the
virtues."   If we did then Shaw the transgressor would long ago have
been either ostracized as a liar or enthusiastically welcomed as a phil-
anthropical captain of industry, or imprisoned as a thief or a murderer or wife-stealer.   As Shaw is still a free man and far from being
a millionaire (thank God for both!), he cannot have transgressed
" the virtues."   Then the phrase " the virtues " must mean something else.   Of course it does.   It means what we sum up in the word
convention, or the word orthodoxy.   Now when I agree and say that
Shaw transgresses all the virtues I mean that he is unconventional
and unorthodox; and everybody surely must agree with me.   But still
they will feel that there is a flaw in my way of putting it.   But,
really, there is not.   What we do feel is not a flaw but that our *amour*

propre has been hurt; we feel insulted that a man like Shaw should come along and tell us, in effect, that we are blind sheep, or amiable asses.   Now why is Shaw unconventional and unorthodox? He is unconventional and unorthodox because he is a man of virtue, because existing conventions, institutions and dogmas no longer permit men and women to be virtuous.   Existing conventions, institutions and dogmas prevent human happiness, interfere with man's freedom to assert his best self, and asphyxiate the finer emotions in humanity, and as such they are not virtues but damnable vices.   Under such conditions the virtuous man must be a rebel, because he asks for conditions that shall be favorable for the exercise of his virtue, which means that he asks to be a strong man, an upright man and a free man.   Under conventions that weaken, bend and enslave him he cannot be virtuous.   Shaw asks for life as against death; for freedom as against slavery; for assertion as against negation.   He is against present institutions and present morality because these do not make for life and freedom and happiness, but for misery, poverty, sorrow, disease and death.   That is one reason why Shaw is what he is.

Another reason why Shaw is the man of virtue is that he is not a worshiper of idols.   The man of virtue is the strong, straight man. An idolater must be weak and crooked.   The more sincere he is in his worship the more feeble and crooked he must necessarily be.   He is for ever bending, bowing, begging, relying on a strength other than his own.   We are all of us idolaters, even the most enlightened of us.   It is true that we no longer set up actual brazen or wooden images to worship; but we do what is just as stupid.   We set up what we are pleased to term Ideals.   We precipitate the best we know and feel, and objectify the abstractions, making them seem as if they were real entities.   These we personify by some such fine-sounding names, with capital letters, as Truth, Society, Morality, Property, Public Opinion, Democracy, The State, and we cry out: " These be your gods, O Israel! "   Having done this we sit down in contented abjectness and carry on the usual ceremonial of idol-worshiping. In other words we have changed a living thought into a dead convention.   Then we stop thinking, stop feeling, and stop progressing. We have become the creatures of a Frankenstein who will not permit us to do other than he wishes.   We despise those who refuse to obey him and do as we are doing; so that the unconventional man is reviled as a mocker and scoffer, and the unorthodox man ostracized as an insulter and denier. No opprobrium is too harsh for him; no treatment too bad for him. When he becomes too obstreperous we cast him into dungeons or burn him at the stake. And we do all these things in absolute good faith. We are unable to do otherwise, because we know no better.

The time comes, however, when these idols of ours do not answer to the demands we are making on them. Society is deaf to our prayers; Property is robbing us of our own; Morality is crippling our individuality; Democracy is feeding us with stones instead of bread; The State is denying us our freedom with its tyranny; Truth is found out to be falsehood, for we are very unhappy. When that time comes we are no longer upright, strong, and joyous. We have lost faith in the ideals and with the loss of faith we have lost our virtue. We begin to exercise the baser qualities in our natures and become crooked, cunning, cruel, hypocritical, self-seeking at the expense of others. We do this in order to circumvent those who have taken advantage of our good faith. We are not yet ready for the manlier part of knocking down our idols, and so we play the coward's part and try to get the better of them in underhand ways. When this happens it means that a change is imminent. It means that conditions are so rotten that the entire social fabric is threatened with disintegration. Once upon a time, when this point was reached, a revolution followed, and new conditions were brought about at a terrible cost—the cost of lives and the cost of hope. Nowadays we try to avoid such revolutions. We find out, if we can, where the trouble really is. We ask why is it that we are no longer upright, no longer strong, no longer happy? Here is the opportunity the one man of virtue left among us has been waiting for. This is the moment for his revelation, for his re-inspiring hope that shall keep us straight and strong and open-eyed. When he comes we may be certain he is wanted; that the age has been in labor with him. That is the kind of man Shaw is. I do not ask you to take my word for this. I can but say that is how I see him. But read his books for yourselves; and read them twice. Once, in order that you may enjoy the fun and get rid of the laugh. A second time, so that you may see what a wise friend this jester really is.

Here is a new book by him—*The Doctor's Dilemma, Getting Married and The Shewing-Up of Blanco Posnet**—three short plays with three long prefaces.   Most of us will like the plays, because they amuse us.   I advise you to read the plays first and have your laugh out.   Then will be the time for the prefaces.   Shaw's prefaces were never meant to be read first; they were intended to speak for him with those who may never have an opportunity to see the plays acted, and to recall to himself those who, having seen the plays, have missed their meaning.   Shaw thinks his method of writing plays with prefaces an improvement on Shakespeare's, and I agree with him in being willing to give up half a dozen of the plays Shakespeare wrote for one of the prefaces he ought to have written.

The dilemma in which the doctor of the first play finds himself is brought about by his falling in love with the wife of a man who is a consumptive and whom he is called upon to save from death.   The doctor can save the man's life because he has discovered a " culture " which, when injected at the right time into the veins of a person afflicted with tuberculosis, will so strengthen the phagocytes in the blood that these will eat up the tubercle bacilli.   The consumptive husband is a marvelous artist, but utterly lacking in a sense of honor. Any decent person would call him a selfish scoundrel who did not deserve to live.   But he is a great artist and his wife loves him devotedly.   Her life is given up to aiding him to achieve the fame which she believes should be his by right.   She begs the doctor to give her husband life so that he may fulfil his great genius.   The doctor has room in his hospital for but one more patient.   An old fellow medical student of his is suffering from consumption also.   This friend is a fine, noble, great-hearted man, but a failure in life.   What shall he do?   Which of these two lives shall he save?   That is his dilemma. He chooses to save the life of the unselfish friend who is a failure rather than the selfish scoundrel who is a genius.   The latter he leaves in the care of a famous king's physician, knowing that this physician while employing the same culture will kill the patient through ignorance of the method.   The expected happens.   The friend's life is saved and the artist is killed by the ignorant royal physician.   But where is the dilemma? we ask.   The doctor's duty

* Published by Brentano's, New York.

was plain; he could not do otherwise than he did. But how, if the doctor, knowing what would happen to the artist, deliberately chose that he should be killed in order to marry the widow? There is the tragedy of the situation. And there Shaw leaves it.

Now read the preface and you will find, what is not at all made straightly plain in the play, that the cause for the tragedy must be laid at our doors. It is we, the idol-makers, who are to blame for placing the doctor in such an awful situation. We have raised the Medical Profession to an ideal position, attributing to its members not only infallibility of judgment, but a positively god-like dispassionateness. We utterly forget that these men are human beings like ourselves and, therefore, liable to be weak, ignorant and susceptible. Our ideal Medical Profession is not at all like the real, living members. It is an abstraction with a capital letter which we have ideally manufactured and then accepted as if it were the real thing. It is not the truth of the medical profession; it is untrue because it does not harmonize with the facts of experience. Not that medical men themselves think they are what we have idealized them to be; but our idealization of them compels them to assume the virtues they do not have, and to undertake tasks for which they are not fit. They are not found out because we have also made them the judges of their own work. So that our ideal Medical Profession is become petrified as a convention under the laws and dogmas of which we, the ideal (idol) worshipers, take our place as abject and fearful conformers. Have we not here a living illustration of the evil of idealotry?

Thus it is that we make kinglets—the doctor, the lawyer, the priest—to rule over us in their several ways. Now Shaw does not object to our making kinglets, though he does not like the name. What, in effect, he says to us is: " If you must have them, then in the name of common sense don't idealize them. They have not changed into a different order of being in taking office. They are still human as we all are. You have asked them and entrusted them and are paying them to do a certain work. See to it that they do that work. Don't have them bamboozle you and make you believe they know it all because they spout words of learned length and thundering sound. You didn't put them there to talk but to work; and if they can't or won't or don't work, send them about their own business; they are not fit for yours. What's the matter with the doctor is not that he can't or won't do his business, but that you won't let him do it. You expect the doctor to cure diseases; that is your ideal of a doctor. But a doctor can't cure diseases; he can try to prevent them. And because you expect him to do what he can't do he has to pretend to do what you expect him to do. You expect him to give you a bottle of medicine that shall be endowed with magic powers, and he gives it knowing that the stuff is not endowed with magic powers; but if he's an honest doctor he'll tell you to do things in addition to swallowing the nostrum. Be sensible, good people, be sensible." If you ask Shaw what you ought to do, he tells you in the following fourteen pieces of advice:—

" 1. Nothing is more dangerous than a poor doctor: not even a poor employer or a poor landlord.

2. Of all the anti-social vested interests the worst is the vested interest in ill-health.

3. Remember that an illness is a misdemeanor; and treat the doctor as an accessory unless he notifies every case to the Public Health authority.

4. Treat every death as a possible and under our present system a probable murder, by making it the subject of a reasonably conducted inquest; and execute the doctor, if necessary, *as* a doctor, by striking him off the register.

5. Make up your mind how many doctors the community needs to keep it well. Do not register more or less than this number; and let registration constitute the doctor a civil servant with a dignified living wage paid out of public funds.

6. Municipalize Harley Street.*

7. Treat the private operator exactly as you would treat a private executioner.

8. Treat persons who profess to be able to cure disease as you treat fortune tellers.

9. Keep the public carefully informed, by special statistics and announcements of individual cases, of all illnesses of doctors or in their families.

10. Make it compulsory for a doctor using a brass plate to have inscribed on it, in addition to the letters indicating his qualifications, the words ' Remember that I too am mortal.'

11. In legislation and social organization, proceed on the prin-

* Harley Street in London is the residential quarter of doctors of high reputation.

ciple that invalids, meaning persons who cannot keep themselves alive by their own activities, cannot, beyond reason, expect to be kept alive by the activity of others. There is a point at which the most energetic policeman or doctor, when called upon to deal with an apparently drowned person, gives up artificial respiration, although it is never possible to declare with certainty, at any point short of decomposition, that another five minutes of the exercise would not effect resuscitation. The theory that every individual alive is of infinite value is legislatively impracticable. No doubt the higher the life we secure to the individual by wise social organization, the greater his value is to the community, and the more pains we shall take to pull him through any temporary danger or disablement. But the man who costs more than he is worth is doomed by sound hygiene as inexorably as by sound economics.

12. Do not try to live for ever. You will not succeed.

13. Use your health, even to the point of wearing it out. That is what it is for. Spend all you have before you die; and do not outlive yourself.

14. Take the utmost care to get well born and well brought up. This means that your mother must have a good doctor. Be careful to go to a school where there is what they call a school clinic, where your nutrition and teeth and eyesight and other matters of importance to you will be attended to. Be particularly careful to have all this done at the expense of the nation, as otherwise it will not be done at all, the chances being about forty to one against your being able to pay for it directly yourself, even if you know how to set about it. Otherwise you will be what most people are at present: an unsound citizen of an unsound nation, without sense enough to be ashamed or unhappy about it."

Getting Married is a dramatic situation in which the whole subject of marriage as it is understood and practised at present is exemplified in several ways and discussed and turned into ridicule. Here is another instance of the evils of idealotry; perhaps as glaring an instance of our stupidity as could be found even among the many stupid things we have done. Our marriage law is become " inhuman and unreasonable to the point of downright abomination." The convention established no longer permits either the freedom of the individual or his happiness. On the contrary, it binds him in bonds from which there is no escape except at the price of reputation and social position. The result is that we have lost our respect for it. Those who have a reputation to maintain evade it by every trickery and subterfuge, and those who have not, openly disregard it.

How has this come about? Simply by the idealization process. We began with the natural attraction of the two sexes for each other and idealized this power in the abstract term, Love. It was then an easy step to the second idealization, namely, that of marriage. The ideal marriage became then a life-long cohabitation (or living together) of two individuals of different sexes in the ideal state of Love. This was the priest's part of the work. But there was work here for the lawyer also. Woman being but a chattel with the rest of the man's property she must be protected as such. Therefore her marriage with the man she is supposed to love and who is supposed to love her must be recognized by the State. When this is done she is bound absolutely, for better for worse, and the two are left to live happily ever after. The trouble began when the real thing did not fit the ideal; and the trouble has grown to such a size that we are actually beginning to believe there must be something wrong. That should be a sign of sanity in us. But we do not act as if we were sane. We do not ask if the ideal has anything the matter with it. To do that would be sacrilege. The idol we have created must be right or we would not all believe in it. So we blame ourselves for not being other than we are, and as we must be of the faith at any price, we do as our human nature prompts us to do surreptitiously. That is to say, we keep the idol for ornament and make beasts of ourselves. We hang up the framed marriage certificate over the head of the bed, give it an occasional approving nod, and then proceed stealthily to fill our cities with prostitutes.

This sounds amusing; but it isn't. It is anything but amusing. It is tear-compelling to contemplate. This pitiable idealotry business is making hypocrites and sneaks and charlatans and humbugs of us all. We have lost our faith in our ideals and the loss of faith has bereft us of our virtue, our strength of character, our uprightness, our well-being.

Well, we have one thing to be thankful for; the more civilized among us no longer tolerate the marriage for better for worse. Indissoluble marriage is an academic figment, for even a Roman Catholic marriage can be annulled by the Pope. And we have really formulated the problem which the rotten conditions have forced upon us.

No one questions the necessity for the recognition of marriage as a proper relation between men and women. So long as Society is constituted as it is at present marriage is inevitable, and the sooner people acknowledge this the sooner shall we set to work to make it decent and reasonable. But what shall we understand by marriage? There are so many different kinds of marriage even in English-speaking countries that a satisfactory definition is almost impossible. "In the British Empire," says Shaw, "we have unlimited Kulin polygamy, Muslin polygamy limited to four wives, child marriages and marriages of first cousins: all of them abominations in the eyes of many worthy persons." The average respectable citizen often means by marriage monogamy, fidelity, chastity, and other things that have no real connection with marriage. But, perhaps, we would all agree if we said that a union for the purpose of establishing a family and registered and regulated by the State is marriage. Now there is no question of abolishing this marriage; but there is a very pressing question of improving its conditions. How are we to improve them? Shaw answers this question in a sentence: "Make divorce as easy, as cheap and as private as marriage." . . "A thousand indissoluble marriages mean a thousand marriages and no more. A thousand divorces means two thousand marriages; for the couples may marry again. Divorce only reassorts the couples; a very desirable thing when they are ill-assorted. Also, it makes people much more willing to marry, especially prudent and proud people with a high sense of self-respect. Further, the fact that a divorce is possible often prevents its being petitioned for, not only because it puts married couples on their good behavior towards one another, but because, as no room feels like a prison when the door is left open, the removal of the sense of bondage would at once make marriage much happier than it is now. Also, if the door were always open, there would be no need to rush through it as there is now when it opens for one moment in a lifetime, and may never open again."

What shall we do with the children then, we ask, if we make divorce easy and cheap? What do we do with them now when we imprison or hang the parents or consider them unfit for the custody of children? What do we do with them when we grant divorce decrees now? The question is really no argument against divorce. As a rule children are a bond uniting in a common interest those who might separate if they were childless. In these cases the marriage law is superfluous, and this is proven by the fact that the proportion of childless divorces is much larger than the proportion of divorces from all other causes.

But the question of the children is really a most powerful argument for divorce. " An unhappy household is a bad nursery." Children are as much the property of the State, nay, more so, than they are the property of the parents. When this is recognized and acted upon, parental bondage will disappear with conjugal bondage. And we already do recognize it in other ways. We compel children to be educated; we compel them to be vaccinated; we compel them to be doctored and bathed and nursed; we take them from the care of abandoned and disgraceful parents; and we do these things whether the father or the mother does or does not approve. We shall do better some day when the parents fit themselves for the work of parentage. But as this day can come only when we abolish poverty it is not possible to push rational measures of any kind very far at present.

" As long as people are too poor to be good parents or good anything else except beasts of burden, it is no use requiring much more from them but hewing of wood and drawing of water. . . But however we settle the question, we must make the parent justify his custody of the child exactly as we should make a stranger justify it. If a family is not achieving the purpose of a family, it should be dissolved just as a marriage should when it, too, is not achieving the purposes of marriage. The notion that there is or ever can be anything magical and inviolable in the legal relationship of domesticity, and the curious confusion of ideas which makes some of our bishops imagine that in the phrase ' Whom God hath joined,' the word God means the district registrar or the Reverend John Smith or William Jones, must be got rid of. Means of breaking up undesirable families are as necessary to the preservation of the family as means of dissolving undesirable marriages are to the preservation of marriage. If our domestic laws are kept so inhuman that they at last provoke a furious general insurrection against them as they already provoke many private ones, we shall in a very literal sense empty the baby out with the bath by abolishing an institution which needs nothing more than a little obvious and easy rationalizing to make it not only harmless but comfortable, honorable, and useful."

Is it not time we set to work cleaning up and thinning out our Pantheon? Is it not time we ceased from ascribing ideal virtues to our gods and rulers and began cultivating them ourselves? Give us Truth, we cried and still cry, as if Truth were a divine existence outside us. We have had the living truth with us in our midst every day of our lives, since summer first was leafy. For Truth is nothing but the fitness of our ideals to the needs of living. It is not the same to-day as it was yesterday. It is the ever-changing Proteus who becomes what our will makes him. That is the answer to the Riddle of the Sphinx. We have so long raised our eyes to heavens that existed in our imaginations only, that we have forgotten the ways of the jocund earth, where Truth has been all the time smiling and waiting for us. The noblest ideal is useless if it cannot walk with us by the roadside and be our friend. Let us take heart again in a new vision, a new commandment, and a new song; the vision of an earthly paradise, the commandment of human happiness, and the song of joyous workers.

In the two plays so far dealt with Shaw has been trying to answer the question: What is man doing with the world? In *The Shewing-Up of Blanco Posnet* he asks, in effect, What is God doing with man? The play was forbidden by the censor in England because it was considered blasphemous and immoral. It took God's name in vain. Posnet, in his mental agony, cries aloud against God whom he accuses of getting the better of him in an underhand way. The tremendous spiritual agony of Posnet was missed by the moral censor, who could see nothing in the man but an immoral and cursing blasphemer. Shaw also, in making Blanco say what he did, is an immoral and cursing blasphemer. The play was therefore prohibited. I agree with the censor that Shaw's writings are immoral. He would not be the man he is if they were not. He believes that it is our morality that is immoral and that it is his immorality that is sanity and health. But is not the best way to find out if he is right or wrong to listen to what he has to say, not to close his mouth and prevent him speaking? It may be we shall learn something for our good. I do not agree with the censor that Shaw is a cursing blasphemer. I confess I cannot help coming to the conclusion that the censor knows very little either about morality or blasphemy or God. And I cannot help believing that Shaw knows a great deal about God. Indeed, I have come to the conclusion that Shaw is a man after God's own heart. I think

that he has grown with God's help and God's grace in him, and that
he is doing God's work. I believe it because I do not see how otherwise he could have written *The Shewing-Up of Blanco Posnet* and
the other plays in this volume.

The play of *Blanco Posnet* is a tragi-comedy with the soul of
Blanco as protagonist. Blanco does not get on very well with God.
There is a misunderstanding between them, and the man is terribly
puzzled. We are brought face to face with him while he is still in the
struggling process of his soul's development, trying to understand
what God is doing with him—the strong, self-willed, daring man. He
has been in a situation out of which any man worth the name would
have come with flying colors and with an added conviction of his man-
liness. Blanco lost his head and his nerve and, in his opinion, made
a mess of it and himself. He had stolen or taken a horse which he
thought belonged to his brother to compensate himself for the legacy
their mother had left him which his pious brother would not give up.
It turned out that the horse was not his brother's property, but belonged to the Sheriff of the town who had loaned it to the brother,
Elder Daniels, as he was known. When Blanco left the town he
did not know this, or he would have hesitated courting the death sentence which was the fate of all horse-stealers in that Western place.
He blamed himself afterwards for not suspecting his brother, who,
he knew, was a " rotten man " ready to do a mean act even against
a brother and then call on the Lord to bear him out. In the mountains, thirty miles from the town, he meets a woman carrying a child.
The child is at death's door with the croup. She must get to a
doctor quickly or the child will not live through the day, and the nearest doctor is in the town Blanco had just left behind him. She begs
Blanco for the loan of the horse. He curses and blasphemes in the
manlike fashion of his nature, but ends by giving her the horse and
sending her off to the town. As the woman rides away with her child
Blanco remains in a trance looking at a rainbow, utterly beside himself. While in this state he is captured by the Sheriff's brother and
brought back to town to stand his trial and receive his death sentence.
When he realizes what he did and what is about to happen to him he
curses God for stealing a march on him by sending the woman to
make him " a softy." All his life he had been acting like a real bad

man, not caring for either God or his fellows. Now, suddenly, in a moment of " softness," he yields to the influence and gets caught like a hare in a trap. He can't make it out. What's God doing with him? That's what he doesn't understand. He understands well enough what man is doing with him. But he laughs at man. Man's a " rotten " thing; his kings, his judges and his priests are no better. He is not afraid of them. He can tell them to go to hell even if they hang him and fill him with lead after. He can be as bad as they are, and often is. What troubles him is that just when he ought to have been as bad as they are, God wouldn't let him. " Am I a miserable sinner? " he cries to the boys in the court-house; " No: I'm a fraud and a failure. I started in to be a bad man like the rest of you. You all started in to be bad men or you wouldn't be in this jumped-up, hospital-turned-out camp that calls itself a town. I took the broad path because I thought I was a man and not a sniveling canting turning-the-other-cheek apprentice angel serving his time in a vale of tears." He didn't keep to the broad path. He couldn't be a real bad man " that does what he likes and goes over or through people to his own gain." He is " a sniveling cry-baby that let a horse his life depended on be took from him by a woman, and then sat on the grass looking at the rainbow, and let himself be took like a hare in a trap. . . I'm a rottener fraud than the Elder here," he cries; " and you're all as rotten as me, or you'd have lynched me."

They didn't hang Blanco, because the woman to whom he gave the horse brought the animal back and testified that he was not the man. They let him go free though they knew he had taken the horse. They " went soft," as Blanco put it. And that is just what he cannot understand. Why did the child die, after all? he asks. If God wanted to kill the child why did He bring Blanco into his trouble? And " why did He make me go soft on the child if He was going hard on it Himself? Why should He go hard on the innocent kid and go soft on a rotten thing like me? Why did I go soft myself? What's this game that upsets our game? For it seems to me there's two games bein' played. Our game is a rotten game that makes me feel that I'm dirt and that you're all as rotten dirt as me."

And the other game? A revelatory thought, as it were, seems to flash through Blanco's tired and excited brain, as he cries out:

" T'other game may be a silly game; but it ain't rotten. . . When I
played it I cursed myself for a fool; but I lost the rotten feel all the
same."   And yet the question still remains: What is God doing with
man?   Why did He kill the child, if he meant Blanco to save it?
Why did He let Blanco be caught napping for doing what He wanted
him to do?   Elder Daniels answers the last question from his point of
view: " It was the Lord speaking to your soul, Blanco."   It must
indeed have been the Lord speaking to his soul that inspired Blanco to
make the reply he did to his brother's canting phrase:—

" Oh, yes: you know all about the Lord, don't you?   You're in
the Lord's confidence.   He wouldn't for the world do anything to
shock you, would He, Boozy dear?   Yah!   What about the croup?
It was early days when He made the croup, I guess.   It was the
best He could think of then; but when it turned out wrong on His
hands He made you and me to fight the croup for Him.   You bet He
didn't make us for nothing; and He wouldn't have made us at all
if He could have done His work without us.   By Gum," he cries, and
Blanco here rises to prophetic power, " that must be what we're for!
He'd never have made us to be rotten drunken blackguards like me,
and good-for-nothing rips like Feeny.   He made me because He had
a job for me.   He let me run loose till the job was ready; and then I
had to come along and do it, hanging or no hanging.   And I tell you
it didn't feel rotten: it felt *bully,* just bully.   Anyhow, I got the
rotten feel off me for a minute of my life; and I'll go through fire
to get it off me again."

Blanco comes to himself at last.   It was worth being a fraud and
a failure to experience this new sensation.   God, then, was really
doing something worth while with man.   What He did was to open
Blanco's eyes in a way they had never been opened before, in a way
that only suffering could have opened them.   He saw things in their
real light now.   " No more broad paths " for him, and no more narrow paths, either.   And no more of the canting talk about morality
and immorality.   These had been ideals but they had become conventionalized and degraded as idols.   The morality of to-day is the
immorality of to-morrow.   The passing through this furnace of fire
had purified Blanco's soul so that he could say with the gods themselves, " There's no good and bad."   If there is no good and no bad,
what then is there?   Blanco has the answer straight, for Blanco

knows now: "But by Jiminy, gents, there's a rotten game, and there's a great game. I played the rotten game; but the great game was played on me; and now I'm for the great game every time. Amen."

Can any of us think anything better than that to say? When we come right down to it what is there in life finer than living the best we know—playing the great game? But if we believe this, then, for God's sake, as well as our own, do not let us make the awful mistake of thinking we know better than God. Do not let us fix our ideals so that they can no longer grow. Let them be as free as we believe God Himself is free; bound only by our ignorance, our selfishness, our blindness. We are climbing, step by step, the Stairway of Truth, of which each stair is a Truth, and yet each stair but a landing-place from which to take the next step to a new Truth. The great game is climbing the Stairway of Truth with God's help. That is what God is doing with man.

Thus have we come to the solution of the ancient Riddle of the Sphinx. "There is no good and no bad but thinking makes it so." To set up the idol Truth is to cease thinking. It is to cease living. It is to commit the unforgivable sin, because it is to deny the splendid, ever-evolving procession of God's being that must be made manifest in us. The Truth that is ever flowing, ever living, ever growing, that alone is the Truth that shall make us free; for in that Truth we and the Ideal are one.

MYRTIS OF MYTILENE

BLISS CARMAN

THERE is a pink upon the almond trees,
The sunlight is grown warm, the south-west wind
Makes a soft music in the soughing pines;
And where the blue seas break more gently now
On all the shores of Hellas it is spring.

And yesterday I saw a swallow flash
Across the azure noon to wheel and drop
To her old nest by thy deserted door.
O Myrtis, why wilt thou not also come
Back with the spring to Mytilene now?

The pear tree in the garden is in bud,
The vines once more are full of twitterings,
And in the woods the violets unfold.
All these return, why not the only one
That ever could enhance the year's rebirth?

Men buy and sell, folk gossip at their work,
Children make noise at play, black ships come in
To the gray wharves; but where thy beauteous head
Was wont to pass is only empty air,
With silence where thy laughter used to ring.

Even the little street looks poor and mean
That used to wear such glory. Loneliness
Is heavy on the doorsill where last year
The lightest feet in Lesbos came and went.
There is no welcome in the twilight now.

Sadly the starlight comes to visit there;
The soft spring winds sigh at the latch in vain;
In their Pandean chorus the green frogs
Cry from the marsh and there is none to hear;
The rain beats down and there is none to heed.

O Myrtis, to what country art thou gone?
And is there golden sunlight in that land,
And kindly air and love and joy and peace?
Is the new day more wonderful than ours,
And are the loving fortunate and wise?

Men say there is a country of the dead,
But I know only that thou art not here,
That something dims the sunlight on the sea,
And makes the wind among the grasses sigh
A mournful music at the heart of spring.

Some prophesy we shall return in time
And wear this earth's mortality again.
If that were so, how easily I could dream
Of a far country, Myrtis, where the spring
Should come with fresh and unassuaged desire,

Among the wild dark mountains full of snow,
Where the strong sun should melt the icy brooks
And unloose mighty rivers to the sea,
And all men's hearts should be renewed and glad
In that fair time of blossoms and great joy.

Beyond the golden sunset who can tell
What undiscovered continents may lie,
Where life might find a happier trend than here,
And mortals learn a love without alloy
Of cruelty, untruth, or late regret,

Where bitterness of heart could be no more,
With all misunderstanding done away!
There on a soft still day I would go down
Among the beech trees on a warm hillside
With white upspringing windflowers underfoot,

And find thee watching with the patient smile
Of joy made perfect past the reach of pain,
And take thy hand and travel down the pass
Into the valley with its twinkling lights,
By our own sign the new moon in the firs.

EDITORIAL NOTES

I⊤ is a platitude—and therefore worth repeating—that the whole course of history may be changed by an apparent detail. If General Bonaparte had accepted one of the bullets which were offered to him on the Bridge of Arcole, it is conceivable that the affairs of Europe might have been conducted very differently for a generation, and even—to pursue a remoter consequence—that Louisiana might not now be associated so closely with this Republic. There have been occasions when the mere turning of an individual to the right hand or the left has influenced the destinies of empires. It will be a matter of general concern at the present time, and of the gravest importance in the future, whether those who can make or mar the reciprocity agreement with Canada will turn to the right—or the wrong.

* * *

Whatever may have been the feeling, from time to time, in this country and in Canada, with regard to annexation, the question is not now considered seriously. The Republic does not covet its neighbor's autonomy; the Dominion has no desire to change its present status. But it is impossible not to realize that the problem of reciprocity has far-reaching implications. Tariff Reform in England has been occluded by what appeared to be more pressing issues. To a large extent, it has been popularly discredited. A leader of more aggressive personality than Mr. Balfour, and of more intense convictions, was needed to conduct a propaganda which appeals to patriotism and promises prosperity, but offers no guarantees. Yet it was the dream of Mr. Chamberlain and his disciples to rectify the casual colonial policy which had prepared the way for the dissolution of the empire, and to invoke a new spirit and a new phenomenon—a world-wide Federation, linked by Preference and the glamour of the Crown. It was a big dream: the tenacity of a Bismarck and the enthusiasm of a Garibaldi, combined, might have achieved its consummation. But Preference, though obscured, is not yet a dead issue; and British statesmen cannot regard with indifference any arrangement which would seriously menace the possibility of an imperial zollverein in the future. The progress of the reciprocity negotiations

358

has been watched with concern by the Unionist leaders, though not by the Government; and some degree of popular agitation may be attempted. This is legitimate, and cannot be caviled at. But it is well that it should be understood clearly, and not misinterpreted. To the United States, the question is one merely of economics; not of politics, in the broader sense, or of sentiment. It remains to be seen what will be the final resultant of the varying pressures of public and private interest and self-interest.

On March 4th, 1861, Abraham Lincoln was inaugurated for the first time as President of the United States. Fifty years have passed, and the fame of the strong, unpretentious man has become a national heritage, inspiring effort and moulding character. In another place in this issue is told the simple story of his answer to a child who had asked what he would do when he got to Washington.

" 'What shall I do? Ask God. He knows best. But you, little one, can say when you grow up, that Abraham Lincoln bent half way to meet you.' "

We know now what he did at Washington. If only some of our public men and so-called leaders at the present time could reach half way to the stature of Abraham Lincoln, then indeed this nation should have " a new birth of freedom."

It is too early to suggest that party government is outmoded; for the spirit of partisanship is tenacious and the majority of men will still continue to attach themselves, ignorantly or determinedly, by chance or by choice, to one of the greater political organizations. But it is not too early to suggest that parties are a means, not an end; that the object of their existence is supposed to be the welfare of the nation, not the exploitation of private interests. Patriotism and civic duty are rightly inculcated in our schools: they are scarcely conspicuous in the actual administration of affairs—municipal, state or federal. Government of the people, by a party, for the party, seems but a poor travesty of democracy—unless the party is justly entitled to use the prefix " national." Perhaps the time is not far distant when such a party, based on a coalition of the sincere and far-sighted, will change the whole outlook and spirit of politics in this country.

In England, the greatest constitutional change of the century is impending. No sympathy need be wasted on the House of Lords. The Peers have had their opportunity, and ignored it. Comprised, on the whole, of men who should have been set apart by their condition from the littlenesses of life and the graver faults of partisanship; wealthy, with traditional influence and with exceptional opportunities of public service and consequent prestige; it seems strange that as a body they should have fallen so far short of the standards set by many individuals amongst them. By legitimate methods, they could have established themselves impregnably—in an English environment —as a strong Second House. Instead, they assumed an attitude of subserviency to each Conservative Premier, of ill-regulated and unremitting hostility to every Liberal Administration. The result, sooner or later, was inevitable. Yet it is regrettable that effective reform could not have been initiated within the House itself, as suggested by Lord Rosebery, rather than imposed upon it from without. For however high political feeling may run, it can scarcely be maintained that the close voting of the last two elections—complicated by so many side-issues—formed such an effective mandate of the people as would justify Mr. Asquith in his menacing attitude.

＊　＊　＊

The recent controversy between George Bernard Shaw and Frank Harris, in which the latter rather impetuously brought forward the charge of plagiarism, is interesting because it draws attention to the widely divergent views of two brilliant men with regard to a personality which both have studied faithfully. If it be true, as Mr. Harris maintains, that a great artist inevitably reveals himself in his work, and that he can be " reconstructed " by careful consideration of the dominant characters, with their recurrent traits, it would seem that competent criticism by two such experts would result at least in some general form of agreement, and that further inquiry would lead gradually to the elimination of differences and the emergence from obscurity to clearness of a portrait accepted as distinctive by both. Mr. Shaw, in *The Dark Lady of the Sonnets,* and Mr. Harris, in *Shakespeare and His Love,* have both presented Shakespeare as they see him; yet the figures in the two plays are in polar opposition. Mr. Shaw's Shakespeare is a snob, a coxcomb and a philanderer; big intellectually, little emotionally; hard and self-centred. Mr. Harris sees him as a very human, tragic figure; gentle and generous, yet jealous and love-racked; with weaknesses, but with transcendent compensations; transmuting his pain into golden gifts for posterity; and in the end, world-worn, passion-weary, immortal. Mr. Harris has found Shakespeare in his plays; and perhaps there is a good deal of Mr. Harris in his Shakespeare. With regard to Mr. Shaw's Shakespeare there can be no doubt. He is necessarily Shavian.

Courage, especially in our over-refined time, is perhaps more valuable than style. To the quality of courage, indeed, that of style has still a chance to come. It is this that is likely to keep in remembrance the name of David Graham Phillips as an American novelist. In a time when, despite the greater number of writers and the higher average of technical skill, our novelists were not so adequately depicting their time and place as did, say, the two Edgars, Fawcett and Saltus, or even the earliest efforts of Henry James and Mr. Howells, Phillips came up out of the journalistic ranks conspicuously determined to write, as forthrightly as possible, a candid chronicle of the world he lived in. Candor and courage remained, to the end, his distinguishing virtues. He discovered the sinister side to our conduct of affairs political and financial; having done that, he moved on to what took still greater courage: to discover to herself, and the world in general, the shortcomings of the American woman, whom so many artists in pen and pencil conspire to figure as humanity's supreme development in our time. He did this, realizing that woman dominates America's taste for fiction as for all the other arts. Devoid of charm in manner, he so honestly was telling the truth as he saw it, that—like England in some of her campaigns—he " blundered through somehow " to a secure position among the best-sellers. While there was no advance in craft between his first novel, *The Great God Success,* and the last, *The Husband's Story*, he was obviously coming constantly to a larger outlook upon life, though he had not yet sloughed off a certain jingoistic parochialism permitting him to utter some essentially journalistic commonplaces about foreign aristocracies. More balance, and a greater concern for English, might still have come to him. It seems never too late for that; we need only to remember the case of Joseph Conrad.

In the latest Report of the United States Bureau of Education, instructive reference is made to the conditions of progress in Germany. The work is not consistent; much is left to the initiative, or lack of initiative, of the local authorities. But the general trend is excellent. Details are given with regard to 468 cities with a population exceeding 10,000, and with a total of more than 3,000,000 pupils in 4,500 graded elementary schools. There are valuable points in the following quotations, which cannot fail to interest school authorities here, whether for purposes of comparison, imitation or rejection.

" Gymnastic exercises in the open air, during recesses and after school hours, were held in the lower schools of 193 cities, while the sessions were interrupted by calisthenic exercises in the schools of 236 cities and breathing exercises by open windows in the schools of 160 cities. Orthopedic gymnastics for children suffering from curvature of the spine are arranged in 22 cities. In 205 cities the school authorities offer opportunities for swimming baths in pools with constantly changing water.

" Gymnastic school excursions on free afternoons (Wednesdays and Saturdays) are made in 163 cities; games for children in the open air on playgrounds and in neighboring groves are arranged in 357 cities; and in 382 the teachers are obliged to take their classes out walking through woods and fields. Four cities have arranged rowing matches; skating on ice is promoted in 174 cities; 226 cities have play afternoons as regular school lessons. In 36 cities forest sanitariums are maintained, 3 have forest homes for sickly children, and 8 have forest schools.

" As many as 443 cities offered instruction in the upper grades of school on the evil effects of alcohol. In 20 cities school dental clinics are established, and in 15 other cities such clinics were planned, the authorities merely waiting for the required appropriation; 53 cities attend in other ways to the teeth of their school children; and in 163 an examination of the children's teeth takes place at regular stated intervals. In 274 cities a careful examination of children's eyes is made at intervals, and records are kept; three cities have appointed professional oculists for that purpose; and 215 furnish glasses at the city's expense. For children with defective hearing 131 cities have appointed experts, but only 24 have arranged special schools for such children.

" In 196 cities courses of instruction for teachers for curing defects of speech are arranged; in 171 cities special treatment of throat and nose diseases and for children suffering from impediments in their speech is arranged. Also for children with nervous troubles and for weak-minded children, 103 auxiliary classes in fully graded schools and 169 independent auxiliary schools are established. In 238 communities special physicians are appointed to determine the existence of tuberculosis among the school children; 109 cities merely exclude such children from attendance at school; in 139 other cities such children are sent to appropriate institutions at the city's expense.

" This brief review shows what schools can do in a practical way in the field of hygiene. Physical health deserves fully as much attention in school as do mental and moral health. The question of organizing the department of physical development and health, so as to do the most good without seriously interfering with the intellectual school work, is of great importance.

" To all the efforts mentioned in the foregoing may be added the duty of feeding hungry children, which is done in 201 cities. This is not done in Germany from charitable motives; free breakfasts or lunches are not given or taken as alms, but the whole movement is prompted by pedagogical motives, since instruction to hungry children is about as useless as it is to sick children. It may be stated that the appointment of school physicians is to-day almost universal in Germany, and that in consequence of the work of these men, as well as of school nurses, new ideas have been developed, and improvements have been introduced, so that the foregoing report is in some of its statements already antiquated."

THE NEW MACHIAVELLI

H. G. WELLS

CHAPTER THE SECOND

SEEKING ASSOCIATES

IX

OF course, when Evesham talked of this ideal of the organized State becoming so finely true to practicability and so clearly stated as to have the compelling conviction of physical science, he spoke quite after my heart. Had he really embodied the attempt to realize that, I could have done no more than follow him blindly. But neither he nor I embodied that, and there lies the gist of my story. And when it came to a study of others among the leading Tories and Imperialists the doubt increased, until with some at last it was possible to question whether they had any imaginative conception of constructive statecraft at all; whether they didn't opaquely accept the world for what it was, and set themselves single-mindedly to make a place for themselves and cut a figure in it.

There were some very fine personalities among them: there were the great peers who had administered Egypt, India, South Africa, Framboya—Cromer, Kitchener, Curzon, Milner, Gane, for example. So far as that easier task of holding sword and scales had gone, they had shown the finest qualities, but they had returned to the perplexing and exacting problem of the home country, a little glorious, a little too simply bold. They wanted to arm and they wanted to educate, but the habit of immediate necessity made them far more eager to arm than to educate, and their experience of heterogeneous controls made them overrate the need for obedience in a homogeneous country. They didn't understand raw men, ill-trained men, uncertain minds, and intelligent women; and these are the things that matter in England. . . . There were also the great business adventurers, from Cranber to Cossington (who was now Lord Paddockhurst). My mind remained unsettled, and went up and down the scale between a belief in their far-sighted purpose and the perception of crude vanities, coarse ambitions, vulgar competitiveness, and a mere habitual persistence in the pursuit of gain. For a time I saw a good deal of Cossington—I wish I had kept a diary of his talk and gestures, to mark how he could vary from day to day between a *poseur*, a smart tradesman, and a very bold and wide-thinking political schemer. He had a vanity of sweeping actions, motor car pounces, Napoleonic rushes, that led to violent ineffectual changes in the policy of his papers, and a haunting pursuit by parallel columns in the liberal press that never abashed him in the slightest degree. By an accident I plumbed the folly in him—but I feel I never plumbed his wisdom. I remember him one day after a lunch at the Barhams' saying suddenly, out of a profound meditation over the end ·ᶜ a cigar, one of those sentences that seem to light the whole interior being of a man. "Some day," he said softly, rather to himself than to me, and *à propos* of nothing—" some day I will raise the country."

"Why not?" I said, after a pause, and leant across him for the little silver spiritlamp, to light my cigarette. . . .

Then the Tories had for another section the ancient creations, and again there were the financial peers, men accustomed to reserve, and their big lawyers, accustomed to—well, qualified statement. And below the giant personalities of the party were the young bloods, young, adventurous men of the type of Lord Tarvrille, who had seen service in South Africa, who had traveled and hunted; explorers, keen motorists, interested in· aviation, active in army organization. Good, brown-faced stuff they were, but impervious to ideas outside the range of their activities, more ignorant of science than their chauffeurs, and of the quality of English people than welt-politicians; contemptuous of school and university by reason of the Gateses and Flacks and Codgers who had come their way, witty, light-hearted, patriotic at the Kipling level, with a certain aptitude for bullying. They varied in insensible gradations between the noble sportsmen on the one hand, and men like Gane and the Tories of our Pentagram club on the other. You perceive how a man might exercise his mind in the attempt to strike an average of public serviceability in this miscellany! And mixed up with these, mixed up sometimes in the same man, was the pure reactionary, whose predominant idea was that the village schools should confine themselves to teaching the catechism, hat-touching and curtseying, and be given a holiday whenever beaters were in request. . . .

I find now in my mind as a sort of counterpoise to Evesham the figure of old Lord Wardingham, asleep in the largest armchair in the library of Stamford Court after lunch. One foot rested on one of those things—I think they are called gout stools. He had been playing golf all the morning and wearied a weak instep; at lunch he had sat at my table and talked in the overbearing manner permitted to irascible important men whose insteps are painful. Among other things he had flouted the idea that women would ever understand statecraft or be more than a nuisance in politics, denied flatly that Hindoos were capable of anything whatever except excesses in population, regretted he could not censor picture galleries and circulating libraries, and declared that dissenters were people who pretended to take theology seriously with the express purpose of upsetting the entirely satisfactory compromise of the Established Church. " No sensible people, with anything to gain or lose, argue about religion," he said. " They mean mischief." Having delivered his soul upon these points, and silenced the little conversation to the left of him from which they had arisen, he became, after an appreciative encounter with a sanguinary woodcock, more amiable, responded to some respectful initiatives of Crupp's, and related a number of classical anecdotes of those blighting snubs, vindictive retorts and scandalous miscarriages of justice that are so dear to the forensic mind. Now he reposed. He was breathing heavily with his mouth a little open and his head on one side. One whisker was turned back against the comfortable padding. His plump strong hands gripped the arms of his chair, and his frown was a little assuaged. How tremendously fed up he looked! Honors, wealth, influence, respect, he had them all. How scornful and hard it had made his unguarded expression!

I note without comment that it didn't even occur to me then to wake him up and ask him what *he* was up to with mankind.

X

One countervailing influence to my drift to Toryism in those days was Margaret's quite religious faith in the Liberals. I realized that slowly and with a mild astonishment. It set me, indeed, even then questioning my own change of opinion. We came at last incidentally, as our way was, to an exchange of views. It was as nearly a quarrel as we had before I came over to the Conservative side. It was at Champneys, and I think during the same visit that witnessed my exploration of Lady Forthundred. It arose indirectly, I think, out of some comments of mine upon our fellow-guests, but it is one of those memories of which the scene and quality remain more vivid than the things said, a memory without any very definite beginning or end. It was afternoon, in the pause between tea and the dressing bell, and we were in Margaret's big silver-adorned, chintz-bright room, looking out on the trim Italian garden. . . . Yes, the beginning of it has escaped me altogether, but I remember it as an odd, exceptional little wrangle.

At first we seem to have split upon the moral quality of the aristocracy, and I had an odd sense that in some way too feminine for me to understand our hostess had aggrieved her. She said, I know, that Champneys distressed her; made her "eager for work and reality again." ·

"But aren't these people real?"

"They're so superficial, so extravagant!"

I said I was not shocked by their unreality. They seemed the least affected people I had ever met. "And are they really so extravagant?" I asked, and put it to her that her dresses cost quite as much as any other woman's in the house.

"It's not only their dresses," Margaret parried. "It's the scale and spirit of things."

I questioned that. "They're cynical," said Margaret, staring before her out of the window.

I challenged her, and she quoted the Brabants, about whom there had been an ancient scandal. She'd heard of it from Altiora, and it was also Altiora who'd given her a horror of Lord Carnaby, who was also with us. "You know his reputation," said Margaret. "That Normandy girl. Every one knows about it. I shiver when I look at him. He seems—oh! like something not of *our* civilization. He *will* come and say little things to me."

"Offensive things?"

"No, politenesses and things. Of course his manners are—quite right. That only makes it worse, I think. It shows he might have helped—all that happened. I do all I can to make him see I don't like him. But none of the others make the slightest objection to him."

"Perhaps these people imagine something might be said for him."

"That's just it," said Margaret.

"Charity," I suggested.

"I don't like that sort of toleration."

I was oddly annoyed. "Like eating with publicans and sinners," I said. "No! . . ."

But scandals, and the contempt for rigid standards their condonation displayed, weren't more than the sharp edge of the trouble. "It's their whole position, their selfish predominance, their class conspiracy against the mass of people," said Margaret. "When I sit at dinner in that splendid room, with its glitter and white reflections and candlelight, and its flowers and its wonderful service, and its candelabra of solid gold, I seem to feel the slums and the mines and the overcrowded cottages stuffed away under the table."

I reminded Margaret that she was not altogether innocent of unearned increment.

"But aren't we doing our best to give it back?" she said.

I was moved to question her. "Do you really think," I asked, "that the Tories and peers and rich people are to blame for social injustice as we have it to-day? Do you really see politics as a struggle of light on the Liberal side against darkness on the Tory?"

"They *must* know," said Margaret.

I found myself questioning that. I see now that to Margaret it must have seemed the perversest carping against manifest things, but at the time I was concentrated simply upon the elucidation of her view and my own; I wanted to get her conception in the sharpest, hardest lines that were possible. It was perfectly clear that she saw Toryism as the diabolical element in affairs. The thing showed in its hopeless untruth all the clearer for the fine, clean emotion with which she gave it out to me. My sleeping peer in the library at Stamford Court and Evesham talking luminously behind the Hartstein flowers embodied the devil, and my replete citizen sucking at his cigar in the National Liberal Club, Willie Crampton discussing the care and management of the stomach over a specially hygienic lemonade, and Dr. Tumpany in his aggressive frock-coat pegging out a sort of copyright in Socialism, were the centre and wings of the angelic side. It was nonsense. But how was I to put the truth to her?

"I don't see things at all as you do," I said. "I don't see things in the same way."

"Think of the poor," said Margaret, going off at a tangent.

"Think of every one," I said. "We Liberals have done more mischief through well-intentioned benevolence than all the selfishness in the world could have done. We built up the liquor interest."

"We!" cried Margaret. "How can you say that? It's against us."

"Naturally. But we made it a monopoly in our clumsy efforts to prevent people drinking what they liked, because it interfered with industrial regularity—— "

"Oh!" cried Margaret, stung; and I could see she thought I was talking mere wickedness.

"That's it," I said.

"But would you have people drink whatever they pleased?"

"Certainly. What right have I to dictate to other men and women?"

"But think of the children!"

"Ah! there you have the folly of modern Liberalism, its half-cunning, half-silly way of getting at everything in a roundabout fashion. If neglecting children is an offence, and it *is* an offence, then deal with it as such, but don't go badgering and restricting people who sell something that may possibly in some cases lead to a neglect of children. If drunkenness is an offence, punish it, but don't punish a man for selling honest drink that perhaps after all won't make any one drunk at all. Don't intensify the viciousness of the public-house by assuming the place isn't fit for women and children. That's either spite or folly. Make the public-house *fit* for women and children. Make it a real public-house. If we Liberals go on as we are going, we shall presently want to stop the sale of ink and paper because those things tempt men to forgery. We do already threaten the privacy of the post because of betting touts' letters. The drift of all that kind of thing is narrow, unimaginative, mischievous, stupid. . . ."

I stopped short and walked to the window and surveyed a pretty fountain, facsimile of one in Verona, amidst trim-cut borderings of yew. Beyond, and seen between the stems of ilex trees, was a great blaze of yellow flowers. . . .

"But prevention," I heard Margaret behind me, "is the essence of our work!"

I turned. "There's no prevention but education. There's no antiseptics in life but love and fine thinking. Make people fine, make fine people. Don't be afraid. These Tory leaders are better people individually than the average; why cast them for the villains of the piece? The real villain in the piece—in the whole human drama—is the muddle-headedness, and it matters very little if it's virtuous-minded or wicked. I want to get at muddle-headedness. If I could do that I could let all that you call wickedness in the world run about and do what it jolly-well pleased. It would matter about as much as a slightly neglected dog—in an otherwise well-managed home."

My thoughts had run away with me.

"I can't understand you," said Margaret, in the profoundest distress. "I can't understand how it is you are coming to see things like this."

XI

The moods of a thinking man in politics are curiously evasive and difficult to describe. Neither the public nor the historian will permit the statesman moods. He has from the first to assume he has an Aim, a definite Aim, and to pretend to an absolute consistency with that. Those subtle questionings about the very fundamentals of life which plague us all so relentlessly nowadays are supposed to be silenced. He lifts his chin and pursues his Aim explicitly in the sight of all men. Those who have no real political experience can scarcely imagine the immense mental and moral strain there is between one's everyday acts and utterances on the one hand and the "thinking-out" process on the other. It is perplexingly difficult to keep in your mind, fixed and firm, a scheme essentially complex, to keep balancing a swaying possibility while at the same time under jealous, hostile, and stupid observation you tread your part in the platitudinous, quarrelsome, ill-presented march of affairs. . . .

The most impossible of all autobiographies is an intellectual autobiography. I have thrown.together in the crudest way the elements of the problem I struggled with, but I can give no record of the subtle details; I can tell nothing of the long vacillations between Protean values, the talks and re-talks, the meditations, the bleak lucidities of sleepless nights. . . .

And yet these things I have struggled with must be thought out, and, to begin with, they must be thought out in this muddled, experimenting way. To go into a study to think about statecraft is to turn your back on the realities you are constantly needing to feel and test and sound if your thinking is to remain vital; to choose an aim and pursue it in despite of all subsequent questionings is to bury the talent of your mind. It is no use dealing with the intricate as though it were simple, to leap haphazard at the first course of action that presents itself; the whole world of politicians is far too like a man who snatches a poker to a failing watch. It is easy to say he wants to "get something done," but the only sane thing to do for the moment is to put aside that poker and take thought and get a better implement. . . .

One of the results of these fundamental pre-occupations of mine was a curious irritability towards Margaret that I found it difficult to conceal. It was one of the incidental cruelties of our position that this should happen. I was in such doubt myself, that I had no power to phrase things for her in a form she could use. Hitherto I had stage-managed our "serious" conversations. Now I was too much in earnest and too uncertain to go on doing this. I avoided talk with her. Her serene, sustained confidence in vague formulæ and sentimental aspirations exasperated me; her want of sympathetic apprehension made my few efforts to indicate my changing attitude distressing and futile. It wasn't that I was always thinking right, and that she was always saying wrong. It was that I was struggling to get hold of a difficult thing that was, at any rate, half true, —I could not gauge how true—and that Margaret's habitual phrasing ignored these elusive elements of truth, and without premeditation fitted into the weaknesses of my new intimations, as though they had nothing but weaknesses. It was, for example, obvious that these big people, who were the backbone of Imperialism and Conservatism, were temperamentally lax, much more indolent, much more sensuous, than our deliberately virtuous Young Liberals. I didn't want to be reminded of that, just when I was in full effort to realize the finer elements in their composition. Margaret classed them and disposed of them. It was our incurable differences in habits and gestures of thought coming between us again.

The desert of misunderstanding widened. I was forced back upon myself and my own secret councils. For a time I went my way alone; an unmixed evil for both of us. Except for that Pentagram evening, a series of talks with Isabel Rivers, who was now becoming more and more important in my intellectual life, and the arguments I maintained with Crupp, I never really opened my mind at all during that period of indecisions, slow abandonments, and slow acquisitions.

CHAPTER THE THIRD

SECESSSION

I

At last, out of a vast accumulation of impressions, decision distilled quite suddenly. I succumbed to Evesham and that dream of the right thing triumphant through expression. I determined I would go over to the Conservatives, and use my every gift and power on the side of such forces on that side as made for educational reorganization, scientific research, literature, criticism, and intellectual development. That was in 1909. I judged the Tories were driving straight at a conflict with the country, and I thought them bound to incur an electoral defeat. I under-estimated their strength in the counties. There would follow, I calculated, a period of profound reconstruction in method and policy alike. I was entirely at one with Crupp in perceiving in this an immense opportunity for the things we desired. An aristocracy quickened by conflict and on the defensive, and full of the idea of justification by reconstruction, might prove altogether more apt for thought and high professions than Mrs. Redmondson's spoilt children. Behind the now inevitable struggle for a reform of the House of Lords, there would be great heart searchings and educational endeavor. On that we reckoned. . . .

At last we talked it out to the practical pitch, and Crupp and Shoesmith, and I and Gane, made our definite agreement together. . . .

I emerged from enormous silences upon Margaret one evening.

She was just back from the display of some new musicians at the **Hartsteins.** I remember she wore a dress of golden satin, very rich-looking and splendid. About her slender neck there was a rope of gold-set amber beads. Her hair caught up and echoed and returned these golden notes. I, too, was in evening dress, but where I had been escapes me,—some forgotten dinner, I suppose. I went into her room. I remember I didn't speak for some moments. I went across to the window and pulled the blind aside, and looked out upon the railed garden of the square, with its shrubs and shadowed turf gleaming pallidly and irregularly in the light of the big electric standard in the corner.

"Margaret," I said, "I think I shall break with the party."

She made no answer. I turned presently, a movement of inquiry.

"I was afraid you meant to do that," she said.

"I'm out of touch," I explained. "Altogether."

"Oh! I know."

"It places me in a difficult position," I said.

Margaret stood at her dressing-table, looking steadfastly at herself in the glass, and with her fingers playing with a litter of stopper bottles of tinted glass. "I was afraid it was coming to this," she said.

"In a way," I said, "we've been allies. I owe my seat to you. I couldn't have gone into parliament. . . ."

"I don't want considerations like that to affect us," she interrupted.

There was a pause. She sat down in a chair by her dressing-table, lifted an ivory hand-glass, and put it down again.

"I wish," she said, with something like a sob in her voice, "it were possible that you shouldn't do this." She stopped abruptly, and I did not look at her, because I could feel the effort she was making to control herself.

"I thought," she began again, "when you came into parliament——"

There came another silence. "It's all gone so differently," she said. "Everything has gone so differently."

I had a sudden memory of her, shining triumphant after the Kinghampstead election, and for the first time I realized just how perplexing and disappointing my subsequent career must have been to her.

"I'm not doing this without consideration," I said.

"I know," she said, in a voice of despair, "I've seen it coming. But—I still don't understand it. I don't understand how you can go over."

" My ideas have changed and developed," I said.

I walked across to her bearskin hearthrug, and stood by the mantel.

" To think that you," she said; " you who might have been leader —— " She could not finish it. " All the forces of reaction," she threw out.

" I don't think they are the forces of reaction," I said. " I think I can find work to do—better work on that side."

" Against us! " she said. " As if progress wasn't hard enough! As if it didn't call upon every able man! "

" I don't think Liberalism has a monopoly of progress."

She did not answer that. She sat quite still looking in front of her. " *Why* have you gone over? " she asked abruptly as though I had said nothing.

There came a silence that I was impelled to end. I began a stiff dissertation from the hearthrug. " I am going over, because I think I may join in an intellectual renascence on the Conservative side. I think that in the coming struggle there will be a partial and altogether confused and demoralizing victory for democracy, that will stir the classes which now dominate the Conservative party into an energetic revival. They will set out to win back, and win back. Even if my estimate of contemporary forces is wrong and they win, they will still be forced to reconstruct their outlook. A war abroad will supply the chastening if home politics fail. The effort of renascence is bound to come by either alternative. I believe I can do more in relation to that effort than in any other connection in the world of politics at the present time. That's my case, Margaret."

She certainly did not grasp what I said. " And so you will throw aside all the beginnings, all the beliefs and pledges—— " Again her sentence remained incomplete. " I doubt if even, once you have gone over, they will welcome you."

" That hardly matters."

I made an effort to resume my speech.

" I came into parliament, Margaret," I said, " a little prematurely. Still—I suppose it was only by coming into parliament that I could see things as I do now in terms of personality and imaginative range. . . ." I stopped. Her stiff, unhappy, unlistening silence broke up my disquisition.

" After all," I remarked, " most of this has been implicit in my writings."

She made no sign of admission.

" What are you going to do? " she asked.

" Keep my seat for a time and make the reasons of my breach clear. Then either I must resign or—probably this new Budget will lead to a General Election. It's evidently meant to strain the Lords and provoke a quarrel."

" You might, I think, have stayed to fight for the Budget."

" I'm not," I said, " so keen against the Lords."

On that we halted.

" But what are you going to do? " she asked.

" I shall make my quarrel over some points in the Budget. I can't quite tell you yet where my chance will come. Then I shall either resign my seat—or if things drift to a dissolution I shan't stand again."

" It's political suicide."

" Not altogether."

" I can't imagine you out of parliament again. It's just like—like undoing all we have done. What will you do? "

" Write. Make a new, more definite place for myself. You know, of course, there's already a sort of group about Crupp and Gane."

Margaret seemed lost for a time in painful thought.

" For me," she said at last, " our political work has been a religion—it has been more than a religion."

I heard in silence. I had no form of protest available against the implications of that.

" And then I find you turning against all we aimed to do—talking of going over, almost lightly—to those others." . . .

She was white-lipped as she spoke. In the most curious way she had captured the moral values of the situation. I found myself protesting ineffectually against her fixed conviction. " It's because I think my duty lies in this change that I make it," I said.

" I don't see how you can say that," she replied quietly.

There was another pause between us.

" Oh! " she said and clenched her hand upon the table. " That it should have come to this! "

She was extraordinarily dignified and extraordinarily absurd. She was hurt and thwarted beyond measure. She had no place in her ideas, I thought, for me. I could see how it appeared to her, but I could not make her see anything of the intricate process that had brought me to this divergence. The opposition of our intellectual temperaments was like a gag in my mouth. What was there for me to say? A flash of intuition told me that behind her white dignity was a passionate disappointment, a shattering of dreams that needed before everything else the relief of weeping.

" I've told you," I said awkwardly, " as soon as I could."

There was another long silence. " So that is how we stand," I said with an air of having things defined. I walked slowly to the door.

She had risen and stood now staring in front of her.

"Good night," I said, making no movement towards our habitual kiss.

"Good night," she answered in a tragic note. . . .

I closed the door softly. I remained for a moment or so on the big landing, hesitating between my bedroom and my study. As I did so I heard the soft rustle of her movement and the click of the key in her bedroom door. Then everything was still. . . .

She hid her tears from me. Something gripped my heart at the thought.

"Damnation!" I said wincing. "Why the devil can't people at least *think* in the same manner?"

- . .

II

And that insufficient colloquy was the beginning of a prolonged estrangement between us. It was characteristic of our relations that we never reopened the discussion. The thing had been in the air for some time; we had recognized it now; the widening breach between us was confessed. My own feelings were curiously divided. It is remarkable that my very real affection for Margaret only became evident to me with this quarrel. The changes of the heart are very subtle changes. I am quite unaware how or when my early romantic love for her purity and beauty and high-principled devotion evaporated from my life; but I do know that quite early in my parliamentary days there had come a vague, unconfessed resentment at the tie that seemed to hold me in servitude to her standards of private living and public act. I felt I was caught, and none the less so because it had been my own act to rivet on my shackles. So long as I still held myself bound to her that resentment grew. Now, since I had broken my bonds and taken my line it withered again, and I could think of Margaret with a returning kindliness.

But I still felt embarrassments with her. I felt myself dependent upon her for house room and food and social support, as it were under false pretences. I would have liked to have separated our financial affairs altogether. But I knew that to raise the issue would have seemed a last brutal indelicacy. So I tried almost furtively to keep my personal expenditure within the scope of the private income I made by writing, and we went out together in her motor brougham, dined and made appearances, met politely at breakfast—parted at night with a kiss upon her cheek. The locking of her door upon me, which at that time I quite understood, which I understand now, became for a time in my mind, through some obscure process of the soul, an offence. I never crossed the landing to her room again.

In all this matter, and, indeed, in all my relations with Margaret, I perceive now I behaved badly and foolishly. My manifest blunder is that I, who was several years older than she, much subtler and in many ways wiser, never in any measure sought to guide and control her. After our marriage I treated her always as an equal, and let her go her way; held her responsible for all the weak and ineffective and unfortunate things she said and did to me. She wasn't clever enough to justify that. It wasn't fair to expect her to sympathize, anticipate, and understand. I ought to have taken care of her, roped her to me when it came to crossing the difficult places. If I had loved her more, and wiselier and more tenderly, if there had not been the consciousness of my financial dependence on her always stiffening my pride, I think she would have moved with me from the outset, and left the Liberals with me. But she did not get any inkling of the ends I sought in my change of sides. It must have seemed to her inexplicable perversity. She had, I knew—for surely I knew it then!—an immense capacity for loyalty and devotion. There she was with these treasures untouched, neglected and perplexed. A woman who loves wants to give. It is the duty and business of the man she has married for love to help her to help and give. But I was stupid. My eyes had never been opened. I was stiff with her and difficult to her, because even on my wedding morning there had been, deep down in my soul, voiceless though present, something weakly protesting, a faint perception of wrong-doing, the infinitesimally small, slow-multiplying germs of shame.

III

I made my breach with the party on the Budget.

In many ways I was disposed to regard the 1909 Budget as a fine piece of statecraft. Its production was certainly a very unexpected display of vigor on the Liberal side. But, on the whole, this movement towards collectivist organization on the part of the Liberals rather strengthened than weakened my resolve to cross the floor of the House. It made it more necessary, I thought, to leaven the purely obstructive and reactionary elements that were at once manifest in the opposition. I assailed the land taxation proposals in one main speech, and a series of minor speeches in committee. The line of attack I chose was that the land was a great public service that needed to be controlled on broad and far-sighted lines. I had no objection to its nationalization, but I did object most strenuously to the idea of leaving it in private hands, and attempting to produce beneficial social results through the pressure of taxation upon the land-owning class. That might break it up in an utterly disastrous way. The drift of the Government proposals was all in the direction of sweating the landowner to get immediate values from his property, and such a course of action was bound to give us an irritated and vindictive landowning class, the class upon which we had hitherto relied—not unjustifiably—for certain broad, patriotic services and an influence upon our collective judgments that no other class seemed prepared to exercise. Abolish landlordism if you will, I said, buy it out, but do not drive it to a defensive fight, and leave it still sufficiently strong and wealthy to become a malcontent element in your State. You have taxed and controlled the brewer and the publican until the outraged Liquor Interest has become a national danger. You now propose to do the same thing on a larger scale. You turn a class which has many fine and truly aristocratic traditions towards revolt, and there is nothing in these or any other of your proposals that shows any sense of the need for leadership to replace these traditional leaders you are ousting. This was the substance of my case, and I hammered at it not only in the House, but in the press. . . .

The Kinghampstead division remained for some time insensitive to my defection.

Then it woke up suddenly, and began, in the columns of the *Kinghampstead Guardian,* an indignant, confused outcry. I was treated to an open letter, signed " Junius Secundus," and I replied in provocative terms. There were two thinly attended public meetings at different ends of the constituency, and then I had a correspondence with my old friend Parvill, the photographer, which ended in my seeing a deputation.

My impression is that it consisted of about eighteen or twenty people. They had had to come upstairs to me and they were manifestly full of indignation and a little short of breath. There was Parvill himself, J.P., dressed wholly in black—I think to mark his sense of the occasion—and curiously suggestive in his respect for my character and his concern for the honorableness of the *Kinghampstead Guardian* editor, of Mark Antony, at the funeral of Cæsar. There was Mrs. Bulger, also in mourning; she had never abandoned the widow's streamers since the death of her husband ten years ago, and her loyalty to Liberalism of the severest type was part as it were of her weeds. There was a nephew of Sir Roderick Newton, a bright young Hebrew of the graver type, and a couple of dissenting ministers in high collars and hats that stopped halfway between the bowler of this world and the shovel-hat of heaven.

There was also a young solicitor from Lurky done in the horsey style, and there was a very little nervous man with a high brow and a face contracting below as though the jawbones and teeth had been taken out and the features compressed. The rest of the deputation, which included two other public-spirited ladies and several ministers of religion, might have been raked out of any omnibus going Strand-ward during the May meetings. They thrust Parvill forward as spokesman, and manifested a strong disposition to say "Hear, hear!" to his more strenuous protests provided my eye wasn't upon them at the time.

I regarded this appalling deputation as Parvill's apologetic but quite definite utterances drew to an end. I had a moment of vision. Behind them I saw the wonderful array of skeleton forces that stand for public opinion, that are as much public opinion as exists indeed at the present time. The whole process of politics which bulks so solidly in history seemed for that clairvoyant instant but a froth of petty motives above abysms of indifference. . . .

Some one had finished. I perceived I had to speak.

"Very well," I said, "I won't keep you long in replying. I'll resign if there isn't a dissolution before next February, and if there is I shan't stand again. You don't want the bother and expense of a by-election (approving murmurs) if it can be avoided. But I may tell you plainly now that I don't think it will be necessary for me to resign, and the sooner you find my successor the better for the party. The Lords are in a corner; they've got to fight now or never, and I think they will throw out the Budget. Then they will go on fighting. It is a fight that will last for years. They have a sort of Social discipline, and you haven't. You Liberals will find yourselves with a country behind you, vaguely indignant perhaps, but totally unprepared with any ideas whatever in the matter, face to face with the problem of bringing the British constitution up-to-date. Anything may happen, provided only that it is sufficiently absurd. If the King backs the Lords—and I don't see why he shouldn't—you have no Republican movement whatever to fall back upon. You lost it during the Era of Good Taste. The country, I say, is destitute of ideas, and you have no ideas to give it. I don't see what you will do. . . . For my own part, I mean to spend a year or so between a window and my writing-desk."

I paused. "I think, gentlemen," began Parvill, "that we hear all this with very great regret. . . ."

IV

My estrangement from Margaret stands in my memory now as something that played itself out within the four walls of our house in Radnor Square, which was, indeed, confined to those limits. I went to and fro between my house and the House of Commons, and the dining-rooms and clubs and offices in which we were preparing our new developments, in a state of aggressive and energetic dissociation, in the nascent state, as a chemist would say. I was free now, and greedy for fresh combination. I had a tremendous sense of released energies. I had got back to the sort of thing I could do, and to the work that had been shaping itself for so long in my imagination. Our purpose now was plain, bold, and extraordinarily congenial. We meant no less than to organize a new movement in English thought and life, to resuscitate a Public Opinion and prepare the ground for a revised and renovated ruling culture.

For a time I seemed quite wonderfully able to do whatever I wanted to do. Shoesmith responded to my first advances. We decided to create a weekly paper as our nucleus, and Crupp and I set to work forthwith to collect a group of writers and speakers, including Esmeer, Britten, Lord Gane, Neal, and one or two younger men, which should constitute a more or less definite editorial council about me, and meet at a weekly lunch on Tuesday to sustain our general coöperations. We marked our claim upon Toryism even in the color of our wrapper, and spoke of ourselves collectively as the Blue Weeklies. But our lunches were open to all sorts of-guests, and our deliberations were never of a character to control me effectively in my editorial decisions. My only influential councillor at first was old Britten, who became my sub-editor. It was curious how we two had picked up our ancient intimacy again and resumed the easy give and take of our speculative dreaming schoolboy days.

For a time my life centred altogether upon this journalistic work. Britten was an experienced journalist, and I had most of the necessary instincts for the business. We meant to make the paper right and good down to the smallest detail, and we set ourselves at this with extraordinary zeal. It wasn't our intention to show our political motives too markedly at first, and through all the dust storm and tumult and stress of the political struggle of 1910, we made a little intellectual oasis of good art criticism and good writing. It was the firm belief of nearly all of us that the Lords were destined to be beaten badly in 1910, and our game was the longer game of reconstruction that would begin when the shouting and tumult of that immediate conflict were over. Meanwhile we had to get into touch with just as many good minds as possible.

As we felt our feet, I developed slowly and carefully a broadly conceived and consistent political attitude. As I will explain later, we were feminist from the outset, though that caused Shoesmith and Gane great searchings of heart; we developed Esmeer's House of Lords reform scheme into a general cult of the aristocratic virtues, and we did much to humanize and liberalize the narrow excellencies of that Break-up of the Poor Law agitation, which had been organized originally by Beatrice and Sidney Webb. In addition, without any very definite explanation to any one but Esmeer and Isabel Rivers, and as if it was quite a small matter, I set myself to secure a uniform philosophical quality in our columns.

That, indeed, was the peculiar virtue and characteristic of the *Blue Weekly*. I was now very definitely convinced that much of the confusion and futility of contemporary thought was due to the general need of metaphysical training. . . . The great mass of people—and not simply common people, but people active and influential in intellectual things—are still quite untrained in the methods of thought and absolutely innocent of any criticism of method; it is scarcely a caricature to call their thinking a crazy patchwork, discontinuous and chaotic. They arrive at conclusions by a kind of accident, and do not suspect any other way may be found to their attainment. A stage above this general condition stands that minority of people who have at some time or other discovered general terms and a certain use for generalizations. They are—to fall back on the ancient technicality—Realists of a crude sort. (When I say Realist, of course I mean Realist as opposed to Nominalist, and not Realist in the almost diametrically different sense of opposition to Idealist.) Such are the Baileys; such, to take their great prototype, was Herbert Spencer (who couldn't read Kant); such are whole regiments of prominent and entirely self-satisfied contemporaries. They go through queer little processes of definition and generalization and deduction with the completest belief in the validity of the intellectual instrument they are using. They are Realists—Cocksurists—in matters of fact; sentimentalists in behavior. The Baileys having got to this glorious stage in mental development —it is glorious because it has no doubts—were always talking about training "Experts" to apply the same simple process to all the affairs of mankind. Well, Realism isn't the last word of human wisdom. Modest-minded people, doubtful people, subtle people, and the like—the kind of people William James writes of as "tough-minded," go on beyond this methodical happiness, and are forever after critical of premises and terms. They are truer—and less confident. They have reached scepticism and the artistic method. They have emerged into the new Nominalism.

Both Isabel and I believe firmly that these differences of intellectual method matter profoundly in the affairs of mankind, that the collective mind of this intricate complex modern State can only function properly upon neo-Nominalist lines. This has always been her side of our mental coöperation rather than mine. Her mind has the light movement that goes so often with natural mental power;

she has a wonderful art in illustration, and, as the reader probably knows already, she writes of metaphysical matters with a rare charm and vividness. So far there has been no collection of her papers published, but they are to be found not only in the *Blue Weekly* columns but scattered about the monthlies; many people must be familiar with her style. It was an intention we did much to realize before our private downfall, that we would use the *Blue Weekly* to maintain a stream of suggestion against crude thinking, and at last scarcely a week passed, but some popular distinction, some large imposing generalization, was touched to flaccidity by her pen or mine. . . .

I was at great pains to give my philosophical, political, and social matter the best literary and critical backing we could get in London. I hunted sedulously for good descriptive writing and good criticism; I was indefatigable in my readiness to hear and consider, if not to accept advice; I watched every corner of the paper, and had a dozen men alert to get me special matter of the sort that draws in the unattached reader. The chief danger on the literary side of a weekly is that it should fall into the hands of some particular school, and this I watched for closely. It seems almost impossible to get vividness of apprehension and breadth of view together in the same critic. So it falls to the wise editor to secure the first and impose the second. Directly I detected the shrill partisan note in our criticism, the attempt to puff a poor thing because it was " in the right direction," or damn a vigorous piece of work because it wasn't, I tackled the man and had it out with him. Our pay was good enough for that to matter a good deal. . . .

Our distinctive little blue and white poster kept up its neat persistent appeal to the public eye, and before 1911 was out, the *Blue Weekly* was printing twenty pages of publishers' advertisements, and went into all the clubs in London and three-quarters of the country houses where week-end parties gather together. Its sale by newsagents and bookstalls grew steadily. One got more and more the reassuring sense of being discussed, and influencing discussion.

CHAPTER THE FOURTH

THE BESETTING OF SEX

I

ART is selection and so is most autobiography. But I am concerned with a more tangled business than selection, I want to show a contemporary man in relation to the State and social usage, and the social organism in relation to that man. To tell my story at all I have to simplify. I have given now the broad lines of my political development, and how I passed from my initial liberal-socialism to the conception of a constructive aristocracy. I have tried to set that out in the form of a man discovering himself. Incidentally that self-development led to a profound breach with my wife. One has read stories before of husband and wife speaking severally two different languages and coming to an understanding. But Margaret and I began in her dialect, and, as I came more and more to use my own, diverged.

I had thought when I married that the matter of womankind had ended for me. I have tried to tell all that sex and women had been to me up to my married life with Margaret and our fatal entanglement, tried to show the queer, crippled, embarrassed and limited way in which these interests break upon the life of a young man under contemporary conditions. I do not think my lot was a very exceptional one. I missed the chance of sisters and girl playmates, but that is not an uncommon misadventure in an age of small families; I never came to know any woman at all intimately until I was married to Margaret. My earlier love affairs were encounters of sex, under conditions of furtiveness and adventure that made them things in themselves, restricted and unilluminating. From a boyish disposition to be mystical and worshiping towards women I had passed into a disregardful attitude, as though women were things inferior or irrelevant, disturbers in great affairs. For a time Margaret had blotted out all other women; she was so different and so near; she was like a person who stands suddenly in front of a little window through which one has been surveying a crowd. She didn't become womankind for me so much as eliminate womankind from my world. ... And then came this secret separation. . . .

Until this estrangement and the rapid and uncontrollable development of my relations with Isabel which chanced to follow it, I seemed to have solved the problem of women by marriage and disregard. I thought these things were over. I went about my career with Margaret beside me, her brow slightly knit; her manner faintly strenuous, helping, helping; and if we had not altogether abolished sex we had at least so circumscribed and isolated it that it would not have affected the general tenor of our lives in the slightest degree if we had.

And then, clothing itself more and more in the form of Isabel and her problems, this old, this fundamental obsession of my life returned. The thing stole upon my mind so that I was unaware of its invasion and how it was changing our long intimacy. I have already compared the lot of the modern publicist to Machiavelli writing in his study: in his day women and sex were as disregarded in these high matters as, let us say, the chemistry of air or the will of the beasts in the fields; in ours the case has altogether changed, and woman has come now to stand beside the tall candles, half in the light, half in the mystery of the shadows, besetting, interrupting, demanding unrelentingly an altogether unprecedented attention. I feel that in these matters my life has been almost typical of my time. Woman insists upon her presence. She is no longer a mere physical need, an æsthetic by-play, a sentimental background; she is a moral and intellectual necessity in a man's life. She comes to the politician and demands, Is she a child or a citizen? Is she a thing or a soul? She comes to the individual man, as she came to me, and asks, Is she a cherished weakling or an equal mate, an unavoidable helper? Is she to be tried and trusted or guarded and controlled, bond or free? For if she is a mate, one must at once trust more and exact more, exacting toil, courage, and the hardest, most necessary thing of all, the clearest, most shameless, explicitness of understanding. . . .

II

In all my earlier imaginings of statecraft I had tacitly assumed either that the relations of the sexes were all right or that anyhow they didn't concern the State. It was a matter they, whoever "they" were, had to settle among themselves. That sort of disregard was possible then. But even before 1906 there were endless intimations that the dams holding back great reservoirs of discussion were crumbling. We political schemers were ploughing wider than any one had ploughed before in the field of social reconstruction. We had also, we realized, to plough deeper. We had to plough down at last to the passionate elements of sexual relationship and examine and decide upon them.

The signs multiplied. In a year or so half the police of the metropolis were scarce sufficient to protect the House from one clamorous aspect of the new problem. The members went about Westminster with an odd, new sense of being beset. A good proportion of us kept up the pretence that the Vote for Women was an isolated fad, and the agitation an epidemic madness that would presently pass. But it was manifest to any one who sought more than comfort in the matter that the streams of women and sympathizers and money forthcoming marked far deeper and wider things than an idle fancy for the franchise. The existing laws and conventions of relationship between Man and Woman were just as unsatisfactory a disorder as anything else in our tumbled confusion of a world, and that also was coming to bear upon statecraft.

My first parliament was the parliament of the Suffragettes. I don't propose to tell here of that amazing campaign, with its absurdities and follies, its courage and devotion. There were aspects of that unquenchable agitation that were absolutely heroic and aspects that were absolutely pitiful. It was unreasonable, unwise, and, except for its one central insistence, astonishingly incoherent. It was also amazingly effective. The very incoherence of the demand witnessed, I think, to the forces that lay behind it. It wasn't a simple argument based on a simple assumption; it was the first crude expression of a great mass and mingling of convergent feelings, of a widespread, confused persuasion among modern educated women that the conditions of their relations with men were oppressive, ugly, dishonoring, and had to be altered. They had not merely adopted the Vote as a symbol of equality; it was fairly manifest to me that, given it, they meant to use it, and to use it perhaps even vindictively and blindly, as a weapon against many things they had every reason to hate. . . .

I remember, with exceptional vividness, that great night early in the session of 1909, when—I think it was—fifty or sixty women went to prison. I had been dining at the Brahams', and Lord Braham and I came down from the direction of St. James's Park into a crowd and a confusion outside the Caxton Hall. We found ourselves drifting with an immense multitude towards Parliament Square and parallel with a silent, close-packed column of girls and women, for the most part white-faced and intent. I still remember the effect of their faces upon me. It was quite different from the general effect of staring about and divided attention one gets in a political procession of men. There was an expression of heroic tension.

There had been a pretty deliberate appeal on the part of the women's organizers to the Unemployed, who had been demonstrating throughout that winter, to join forces with the movement, and the result was shown in the quality of the crowd upon the pavement. It was an ugly, dangerous-looking crowd, but as yet good-tempered and sympathetic. When at last we got within sight of the House the square was a seething sea of excited people, and the array of police on horse and on foot might have been assembled for a revolutionary outbreak. There were dense masses of people up Whitehall, and right on to Westminster Bridge. The scuffle that ended in the arrests was the poorest explosion to follow such stupendous preparations. . . .

(To be continued.)

THE FORUM
FOR APRIL 1911

A NATIONAL CONSTITUTIONAL CONVENTION

Do the Existing Public Conditions Favor a Second Constitutional Convention?

EDWARD L. ANDREWS

The present age when it comes to be appraised in history will be described as the age which in the face of innumerable discouragements and undeterred by the jibes and mockery of a great many clever and fastidious people, set itself to getting the democratic ideal or idea of human liberty, really started as a practical working condition.—*Edinburgh Reviewer.*

HE suggestion of a Federal Convention may sound unfamiliar and even unwelcome. We are somewhat accustomed to the process of amending the instrument of national government; but the assemblage of a special parliament, convoked for the purpose of effecting general and systematic changes in our political system, involves far deeper and broader considerations. So much sentiment has gathered about the Constitution of the United States that the mere idea of convening a body of men with the object of revising and remoulding our national Magna Carta produces moral as well as mental friction.

To justify resort to this greatest constituent power known to our system of government, it is incumbent to demonstrate that its requirement is urgent—that it is demanded by practical as well as theoretical forces. We will endeavor to show that compliance with this requirement is evidenced by the organic changes already in course of consummation—that the effort to reconcile our political system and our economic situation has already entailed illegitimate demands upon the judicial power—that we have invoked that department to perform constructive instead of interpretative labors. By this indirect process, we are effecting changes in the Constitution which should more readily and more overtly be accomplished through the appointed medium of a constituent council. It is not, therefore, a question whether we shall effect changes in our political organization. The problem is really limited to an election between the methods for effecting such changes. Shall we continue to drift along, seeking solutions of an originative nature from the judicial department—solutions which it is not instituted to furnish? Or shall we resort to the highway of action which the framers of the Constitution have themselves provided, in a National Convention?

While the adjustment of our economic and our governmental systems is the more concrete phase of this entire subject matter, a Constitutional Convention would necessarily be called upon to consider political and social questions which the lapse of a century and a quarter have developed. Within an allowable compass, the merest outline of this great theme, in its historic causes and its present demands, is now permissible.

In approaching this question of modernizing the Constitution, we are confronted by this paradox. If the Federal Government had been left to the limited activities for which it was designed, many of the influences which are now operating to mould the body politic would not have any points of contact with the central authority. But the general Government has been promoted into so many phases of common law authority, that it has been subjected to the prevailing changes of public opinion in that direction. Inherently, in respect to the mere Federal machinery, a Convention might not be needed. It is the United States, transformed by the erosion of new opinion and practice, which requires regularizing, which demands that a changed Constitution shall formulate the new Americanism.

To array more clearly the bearing of these organic influences upon the Constitution of 1789, its spirit and salient note should be recalled. There is a popular misconception of the Constitution, as a charter of fundamental liberties. In fact, it was not concerned with any declaration of the rights of man, and it scarcely originates or ordains a single public principle. Its reference to them is purely negative—prohibiting their violation by the United States.

After the arrangement of the mechanism of the organization, the dominating feature in the construction of the Government consists in the enumeration of the Federal powers. Their restriction to the purposes of domestic harmony and foreign relations was foremost in the minds of the founders. Taxation, borrowing, and coining; army, navy, militia, fortification, admiralty, and diplomacy; the control of the seat of government and the territories; the judicial settlement of certain controversies—these topics of power form practically the main subjects permitted to national legislation. The power to regulate commerce with foreign nations and among the several States likewise belongs to a similar category of international and internal freedom and pacification. The provisions for compulsory interstate relations impinged more effectively upon the internal affairs of the States than did the direct Federal powers—notably, the faith and credit, the privilege and immunity, and the extradition clauses. Postal service, copyright, and bankruptcy are the only subjects of power conferred on the general Government which may be estimated as non-essential to its operations. The crowning functions of the Union—to guarantee a republican form of government to every State, to protect each of them against invasion, and on their application against domestic violence—are in the nature of duties toward the States rather than powers affecting them. Upon these features of this particular association, the legislative, judicial, and executive departments were designed to operate.

When it came to express itself specifically with reference to the States, the Federal Convention moved on opposite lines of construction. Instead of seeking to enumerate the powers which the States should possess in the entire system, it confined the instrument to a declaration of the powers which the States should not possess. They relate mainly to the exclusion of the States from the exercise of powers similar to those conferred on the Federal Government—diplomatic, military, and certain financial functions—thereby avoiding conflict between the Union and the States. The Ten Amendments are designed to protect the individual from legislative, executive, or judicial tyranny by Federal officials; and to prevent the national Government from trespassing beyond the boundaries assigned. If such arbitrary power could have been implied in the new republican Government, these amendments are proper restrictions; otherwise they were unnecessary, as Hamilton insisted. In either event they exhibit the jealous maintenance of the limitations on the newly-installed central authority. Probably the most important substantive provisions of the Constitution, in their bearing upon the affairs of the States respectively, are the prohibition against the passage of laws impairing the obligation of contracts, and the Fourteenth Amendment—" nor shall any State deprive any person of life, liberty or property without due process of law, nor deny to any person within its jurisdiction the equal protection of the laws."

This transcript of the main lines of the Constitution indicates the existing material upon which a Convention would predicate its labors. It carries conviction that the Constitution is mainly concerned with the arrangements necessary to evolve harmony from the pending political conflicts. While all plenitude pertains to the Federal powers and their exercise, it teems with evidence that the principle of special agency was applied to that authority—in the sense that the territory of its substantive powers was not to be extended by any implication. It does not authorize any constructive legislation concerning life, liberty, property, or contract: it merely protects against hostile action relating to these subjects. In respect to the ordinary relations between citizens and their Government, or between man and man, there are no lines of national endowment. On the contrary, the reservations of power to the States and the people must be deemed plenary in reference to all those matters. The proposed Convention would be called upon to contrast this circumscribed orbit with the mass of new relations demanding vigorous national authority.

It may seem anomalous that an instrument of government, with its limitations so outlined and with its historic character so clearly illustrated, should become the subject of radical change in the period of four generations. On the other hand, it should be remembered that the mutations in human affairs since 1789 exceed the changes of all the previous years of modern civilization. These transformations have been multiplied in our receptive country, have concentrated their demands for practical application, and are crowding those demands upon the central agency of government.

However, it is useless to emphasize the truth that the prescriptions of 1789 are not perennial. The founders have taken that question out of our hands. They foresaw that the lapse of time or the course of events would necessitate comprehensive and fundamental revision. Therefore the Constitution provides in effect for a new Constitution. While two-thirds of both Houses of Congress may propose amendments, the Constitution contemplates more comprehensive and radical changes in the framework of the Federal system. This purpose is evidenced by the provision requiring Congress " *to call a Convention for proposing amendments*," upon the application of the Legislatures of two-thirds of the States. Ordinary amendments may originate in Congress, but the source of a National Constitutional Convention is located in the States.

Upon this call from the States, it becomes mandatory upon Congress to convene such a Body. A constituent assembly, specially convoked and representing the people of the United States, may thus be brought into being in an orderly manner and in accordance with constitutional directions. In the last decade of the eighteenth century our Government was probably unique in providing for its own reorganization. By these prescient arrangements, the Convention of 1789 intended to obviate the difficulties that had surrounded its own inception. Significantly it recognized the transitory nature of its own labors, and desired that the proper reconstruction should be regularly effected through the representation of the American people in one organic Council. We are thus provided with the civic machinery for effecting general as well as fundamental changes in our system of government.

It may be assumed that this provision for a National Constitutional Convention was not intended to remain dormant at all times. Undoubtedly the constituent power of the nation should ordinarily be directed to concrete objects as they arise. It should not be invoked for the consummation of theoretical changes, except in the maturity of a political situation, when the organization of public authority no longer responds to essential requirements. When such a critical point in national affairs has been encountered, resort to this ultimate solvent is the logical sequence.

Has the period in our history been reached when the machinery of a National Convention should be utilized—when the general review of our public organization may justifiably be considered? As all institutes of government should, in our political philosophy, reflect the requirements of the governed, the solution of this question depends upon the moral and material changes that have transpired in this country during the past century and a quarter. If this test establishes essential alterations in the public consciousness and thought, as well as in the practical conditions of the American people, then we should act upon the Convention Clause of the Constitution with the same confidence that we are daily reposing upon other warrants in that benign instrument. In summing up the influences that have wrought modifications in our body politic, they may be assigned to political, economic, and social causes. It is now possible to present merely an outline of these phenomena. They all tend, however, to sustain the theme that these forces are making for a stronger and more efficient national power, exercising more diversified activities.

In the contrast between the origin and character of the present American electorate and its composition after the treaty of 1783, we may trace the source of some requisite political changes. Our eighteenth century Constitution was the first attempt at Anglo-Saxon federalism since the Heptarchy. The Constitution that may be framed in the twentieth century must take account of a novel and less homogeneous constituency, with efficient adaptation to these new Americans. Indeed by reason of the abolition of limitations on the suffrage, these alien elements have themselves become factors in the making of changes that may transpire in our political organization. These newcomers, not being identified with any particular State, take cognizance solely of the United States. All their sentiment associated with their adopted nationality is confined to the general Government. They are natural advocates for its increased powers.

Our recent political history has maximized the prestige of the Union at the expense of State authority. The assertion of the physical power of a Union dominant over States was followed by Amendments which incorporated considerable progress in its legal dominance. Our late foreign conflicts, with the subsequent increase of territory entirely subject to national control, and the incidental diplomatic relations, have increasingly constituted the general Government the magnet of political interest.

The development of facilities for transportation and communication has influenced our mental attitude toward our public authorities. It is a mere truism to say that the natural effect of these modern improvements is to strengthen the national element in our government —by making public opinion all over the land responsive with the central organization at Washington. If the nation's agents are under the surveillance of San Francisco just as effectively as of New York, certainly a serious objection to the increasing potency of the general Government in a Federal republic is fairly removed. Is it not reasonable to believe that the existence in 1789 of the metamorphic conditions produced by steam and electricity would have resulted in a more Hamiltonian Constitution?

Still more important in its effect upon our institutions is the great intellectual change which has supervened in the public attitude toward some of the objects and subjects of government. The *rights* of person and of property were the corner stones of our government in the eighteenth century; we sought to protect those elements of the social fabric against arbitrary power, whether that power was called a monarchy or a democracy. As the progress of mechanical invention has steadily and forcibly dedicated a large proportion of our accumulated wealth to the appointed service of the public, the legend has been reversed: the rights of the public and the *duties* of person and of property have become the watchwords which we are seeking to reflect in contemporary legislation. Subject to this impulsion, we have reached that stage in our development when the American constituency has undertaken to assert its suzerain claims over certain classes of property, specifically over property conditioned as natural or artificial monopolies. Upon this principle, investments in public utilities have been logically the first objects of the new scrutiny. Production by concentrated control has attained such large proportions, and the public has become so dependent on a few individuals for the requisite service, that it is becoming chargeable with the disabilities of monopoly, with subjection to official regulation. As the extent of these industrial operations is nation-wide, a single legal power over equal territory has become the desideratum vigorously evoked.

From an agricultural and maritime community we have been transformed into a commercial and manufacturing nation, subject to a universal diffusion of political power. The patriarchal and ecclesiastical strata in our public structure are rapidly disintegrating, and we have become dominantly an industrial empire, normally controlled by purely economic forces. In these conditions, the rights and duties of labor have likewise approached the orbit of public regulation. Concurrently the extensive organizations of workingmen are drifting this supervision beyond State lines toward Federal jurisdiction. The platonic stage of voluntary executive administration over these conflicts is passing to the field of Congressional action.

These motors in our public life are evolved more distinctly from our internal organism. In addition we belong to the great intellectual world-family of thinkers, and the great social family of progressive nations. The institutional changes taking place in Europe through the rapid media of parliamentary systems are reflected across the Atlantic to the American constituency like a political kaleidoscope. They evidence that the modern world is seeking the most powerful machinery that it can discover—for social support, and improvement. In surveying the field of human endeavor to find this instrumentality, it can perceive nothing more adequate, nothing more potent than the mechanism of government itself. This is the common voice of humanity from the Baltic to the Pacific. It claims the adaptation of our governmental agencies to more socialized requirements.

These material and moral transformations are represented and transfused in a powerful force of American opinion. It has gathered strength from the concentration in the cities, the extension of the elective franchise, and the increased power of the press. While these considerations intensify the demand for constituent changes, they also amplify their field of action—they involve the passage from a government designed for specific Federal purposes to a régime of activity by the general authority beyond the existing province of States in the Union. They are magnified by a deep feeling that the political power of our democracy has not subserved its plenary usefulness. Side by side with our gigantic increase of wealth, an enormous proportion of material values arising from the general development properly belongs to the body politic itself. Through abuse of franchises, through the incidence of the tariff, and through avoidance of taxation, a judgment has been reached that these resources have been diverted from the public credit.

Concurrently with this popular impression, there is a demand that an equation be reached concerning the status of the man dependent on his daily labor, concerning the position of his organizations in the eyes of the law. Because of the great hope held out by our new world democracy, the disappointment has been proportionate—that we have not settled more satisfactorily the juridical situation on these topics.

From these widely-separated sources of material and moral power, a National Convention derives its impulse. They outline a field of discussion which is broader than the sum total of State and Federal legislation—broader than our traditions have included in the domain of government. But the contemporary point of view of the scope of government is favorable to reposing additional activities in all public authority; to coördinating the collective action of the community with the exertion of individuals. And the logical course of these accessions of public power in modern times is to strengthen the largest unit of government; under a Federal system to reinforce the national authority. We have all instinctively felt the influence of these conditions, and this slight analysis may subserve their application to the question at bar—the bearing of these signs of the times upon the opportuneness of a National Convention.

These great civic and social changes are seeking translation from our current life into our juristic institutions. Through what governmental channels are these new conceptions to take effect in this country? In a true political sense the natural field inviting their operation is the common law territory of the States—less trammeled in the theory of its powers and therefore logically more receptive to new developments. On the other hand the specific character of our Federal system renders it inimical to radical changes, unless they are preceded by alterations in the Federal system itself. That system is essentially non-idealistic, and publicists agree that it is not designed for the facile reflection of great economic and social changes. Therefore, from the institutional side, it is anomalous that the new convictions concerning the functions of government should become tangent with our central machinery as now constituted.

Nevertheless, concrete forces—principally the continental extent of enterprises and industries—have been working toward the allotment of the economic side of this great governmental adjustment to Federal mediation. The conclusion must therefore be accepted that these changes in our government, almost in its philosophy, are to assume legal forms in the national organizations. They have already been struggling for expression in various methods—through Congressional enactments and through judicial interpretation, as well as through combined action of the States. The selection among these modes of action, or the choice of a more effective alternative for the introduction into the central body politic of the great changes apparently contemplated by the citizens of this republic, is self-presented for examination.

Broadly speaking, the settlement of this new nationalism must be reached through the test of its conformity with the United States Constitution as it stands; or by effecting changes in the Constitution itself. The former method, by successive legislative and judicial action, is the process now in vogue. Its operation consists in the enactment of aleatory measures which Congress surmises to be within its constitutional powers. Whether it be correct in this legislative anticipation is sooner or later tested in the judicial alembic.

In the ultimate resort, this is the department of government on which we are now relying for the final adjustments of our public affairs. It is therefore essential that we should realize the nature and limitations of the judicial organism in the body politic, particularly its province in a government based on a written Constitution.

This question has been somewhat obscured by sentiment. The rightful respect which we entertain for the judicial element as the great peace-making factor in the affairs of life has misled us into maximizing its scope. We have appealed to it in various extralegal eventualities, until the public mind has become impressed with the belief that any governmental as well as forensic question can be satisfactorily determined by judicial arbitrament.

This attitude of opinion toward the judiciary is indeed a natural outcome of its extended field of action under our Constitution. As it existed in England and in this country before the formation of the Federal Constitution, it was mainly a civic provision for determining disputes affecting individuals. In that capacity it is revered as the great arbiter over the right or wrong, crudely speaking, of individual controversies. When it was invoked to assign the position of legislative acts in reference to the organic law, it entered upon a novel field for the exercise of its faculties. Through this assignment of action it has seemed to overrule the other departments. Hence it has come to be looked upon as a dominant authority, capable of adjusting all our public difficulties.

More definitely speaking the true theory of the labors of the judiciary consists in the ascertainment of the meaning of our written instruments of government. To appreciate the obstacles in the way of obtaining practical results from this source, it is important to realize the general conception which presided over the formation of the Constitution and which now affects the labors involved in its interpretation. This pervading spirit is illustrated by the historic dialogue between Talleyrand and Sieyès, during a discussion concerning a proposed French Constitution. Sieyès remarked: " Above all it should be definite." Talleyrand replied: " Above all it should be obscure." Even a modern student of the subject would agree that an organic law should not tie too closely the hands of the legislature, should therefore be somewhat vague. The history of our Constitutional Convention, with its conflict between the National and Federal principles, furnishes an eminent example of resulting compromises in matters of substance—which in turn involve intended vagueness or latent conflict in expression.

Therefore when an Act of Congress comes before the Courts for alignment within constitutional boundaries, it cannot be adjudged by any standard approaching exactitude in its delineations of power. The most tentative methods of judicial interpretation are alone applicable to an instrument which is largely a political adjustment. If we can trace the working of these factors, we shall be enabled to ascertain the limitations of this interpretative method, and the extent to which its product in adjudications furnishes an efficient instrument of government.

For many years the Federal Courts were engaged in adjudging whether certain processes adopted by Congress were legitimate exercises of its general powers. For example, they were called upon to determine whether Congress could effectuate granted Federal powers by establishing corporations, though specific authority to create corporations was not conferred. In this category of decision—resulting in the doctrine of implied powers, or more properly processes—the Courts were acting in the appropriate exercise of their power of interpretation.

But government by interpretation has its inherent limitations. The judicial power is not germane to certain classes of controversy. It is not adequate to effect many of the potential adjustments of democracy and economics. Above all, when questions which are essentially political in their nature are forced upon the judicial department for attempted solution, an anomalous public situation is created, attended by incidents calculated to retard prosperity. Conceding these premises, we are still confronted with this elusive problem —to ascertain when the legitimate functions of the Federal Courts cease and determine, and when the originative powers of a National Convention properly begin. Denoted in its length and breadth, no more important query is presented to American opinion.

In one sense the Supreme Court has traced some segment of this disputed territory—by refusing to pass upon occurrences which it deemed to be solely within the purview of executive or legislative discretion. But that is not the phase of this broad question which is immediately at bar. We are seeking to ascertain whether the Federal Courts, in determining the limits of Federal and State powers, may not trespass upon the great reserve of political power which the Constitution refers " to the people."

Probably the most effective means for tracing the boundary between the interpretative and the organic powers under our system is to present some concrete question—to test the appropriateness of its solution by judicial or by constituent methods. For that purpose it is pertinent to select some prevailing problems and to cast them in legal form: What is the extent of Congressional power over corporations engaged in interstate commerce? Does it include the control of the prices which they may charge for transportation? Or the amounts of bonds and stocks which they may embody in corporate issues? By what public authority known to our system are these problems to be solved? If they are judicial questions, in their true and essential nature, then the Courts should be the arbiters. But if these controversies do not possess the necessary judicial content—if the factors of opinion involved are really political—then their determination should not be imposed on the Courts. In that event Congressional action over these subjects should be authorized or prohibited by constituent authority.

While the power to regulate commerce among the several States is conferred on Congress, the power to establish and regulate property rights is reserved to the States, no less effectively reserved because that reservation is not specifically expressed. As long as the exercise of the commerce power reacted only in an incidental way upon certain uses of property (The Northern Securities Case) conflict between these two political authorities was not so apparent. But the legislation directly affecting the titles and values of property—encumbrances, and rates of carriage—enacted or proposed under the claim to regulate commerce, brings these two public ordinances into direct conflict. The regulation of commerce is said to require the establishment of the legal status of the personalities and the property engaged therein. The incidents of ownership and devolution of such property demand their control by the State authorities, the powers that ordain all similar rights within their borders. If we interpret the regulative power in the light of its historical surroundings, it would not be difficult to eliminate the legislation referred to. But the pronouncements of the Courts already indicate a more extensive outlook for the commerce power; notably is this condition emphasized by the manner in which effect was given to some of the Commodities Clauses—that a corporation cannot transport its own property.

In this exigency, by what standard are the Courts to measure the validity of these statutes? Observe that there is no question of interpretation remaining—the factors for forensic judgment and reconcilement have been eviscerated—the commerce power is being baldly made dominant. We have proximately reached the point of a judicial postulate—that these powers overlap each other—that Federal regulation cannot be plenarily exercised except by constituting property relations. There is simply an irrepressible conflict between the two powers, as they are now aligned. In respect to these subjects, the Federal and State Governments are in a legal sense very much on the level of the old proposition in scholastics: When an irresistible force meets an impregnable body, which shall give way? And so it is with the regulation power meeting the property power. Juridically speaking, their conflict is so irreconcilable that resort to antecedent political theories of our government is the sole test of opinion. As neither of the traditional theories of our institutions wholly prevails in the formation of the United States Government, each judicial officer seeks support in the school of political thought in which he was educated.

It follows that in the last analysis these controversies have become political. They may be cast in the form of judicial theses, but they are subject to decision according to the political theories that the judges may entertain concerning our dual system. As the normal elements of forensic judgment are lacking, the Judges are necessarily relegated to their political philosophy. If they are Hamiltonians, they will hold that regulation empowers Congress to resort to any assertion of power that may be deemed to exert a direct or indirect economic influence upon commerce, even if it ordains personal or property rights. If they are Jeffersonians, they will maintain that power over the course of commerce does not warrant ordinances instituting the revenues from investments in railroad estates, or the marshaling of their encumbrances—that the States never surrendered such powers over any part of the realty within their borders, differentiating it from other property because it became engaged in interstate commerce.

We have now reached a point where decisions nominally judicial are really predetermined by a political conviction; and upon this basis it is to be settled whether a Federal or a State power shall prevail. Be it remembered that there is no arbitrator provided by the

Constitution for questions of this character. Through the importation of such alien components into the interpretative function, the judiciary will be denatured as an appropriate instrumentality of government. Under these extraordinary calls, the Judges are not merely invited to legislate, but in effect to institute novel constitutional relations. Per contra, if the Federal and State relations insolubly conflict—if new conditions of an economic or historical character have produced this conflict—the constitutional resort is to the source of all political power in this country.

Another phase of this broad subject arises under the Fourteenth Amendment. The circumstances that brought forth this post-bellum provision are familiar: suffice to add that its extended application was not imagined. Theoretically it has resulted in a radical change in our political system, and practically it is difficult to assign a boundary for its action on State institutions (Baker Shop Cases). It has placed the police powers of the States under guardianship—another word for control—of the Federal judiciary. It is true that Congress cannot enact affirmative legislation concerning the ordinary relations of citizens—their employments or any of their domestic concerns. But the United States Courts can annul the State laws on these subjects if they are deemed violative of the requirements of this amendment. In their essence due process and the equal bearing of all law are indisputable requirements. But the care for those principles had been reposed in the States. In erecting this visitatorial power in the Federal authority, we have advanced ten leagues toward changing the structure of our government. When we consider the thousand incidents of daily life to which this new power extends, it may be safely affirmed that the work of a Constitutional Convention would not more completely remove the landmarks of 1789. Indeed it may be instrumental in restoring some of them.

Passing from the theoretical objections to the attempted solution by judicial interpretation, let us glance at the practical infirmities of this method. It is clearly the most disastrous method for an industrial country; because uncertainty and delay are its essential concomitants. It is demoralizing for the judiciary because it invokes their action upon a class of questions which are really more of a political or economic character than they are of a legal nature. It divides the Judges in continuous array between the opposing schools of thought in reference to our political fabric. Therefore it results in a mere struggle of dialectics. The American people should not impose such a burden on their judiciary—should not transform them from the interpretating department to the creating department of the government. The electorate should accept the responsibilities which a democratic republic imposes. It should proceed to express in some positive and literal form the new ideas which it is seeking to incorporate in its political system. If it awaits the outcome of the existing process of legal opinion, what will be the epilogue? The Courts may decide that the indicated class of enactments made or proposed at Washington affecting corporate property is not within the powers ceded to the Federal agency. In that case, and after these protracted delays, no recourse for effecting national control of these instrumentalities will remain, except the amendatory relief provided by the organizers of the Federal institutions. After more decades, a National Convention must be convoked to perform the constructive work which could be less frictionally performed at the present time.

In another constructive era in our history, we shall be compelled to ordain the relations between the governing powers and the country's industries. Before we can make such ordinances upon a broad, practical and efficient basis, we must readjust the powers of the Nation and the States. The Nation is the sole political power which can exercise physical control over these extensive agencies: but the Constitution does not confer upon the Federal Government the legal control over them as properties.. The States possess the property powers, but they have not the physical control over the entireties of these corporate estates. If normal relations are to be established between these nation-wide enterprises and public authority, the powers of the general Government must be constitutionally extended over such property and its incidents—over property which from natural or artificial causes has assumed a quasi-dedication to public uses.

Can it be doubted that the calling of a Federal Convention some years ago, to trace the frontiers of power for the general Government over public utilities and monopolies, would have been preferable to the prevailing conditions? During that time Congress and the Courts

have expended their efforts in trying to adjust the limited powers of
our Federal system to more or less novel fundamental relations of person and property, relations entirely novel to the Federal authority.

Can a practical people long remain insensible to the erroneous
plan by which they are trying to subject the body politic to these new
conditions? It is inevitable that they will substitute the direct, prompt
and effective action of the organizing deliberative body, provided by
the Constitution itself, to express their judgment upon pending controversies.

Accepting this machinery of organic legislation, the selection of
subjects for its action looms portentously. Our scope is confined to
a mere statement of the topics which could appropriately be placed on
the calendar of such an assembly. In presenting these formative provisions, we will sacrifice their logical sequence to their immediate practical importance. From this point of view, the status of business activities engaged in commerce among the States presents the foremost
subject of adjustment. After the attrition of the past quarter of a
century, we should at last be in the presence of an organizing body
endowed with all the necessary constructive powers—enabled to lay
the legal foundation of all material activities. For this purpose it
may regard or disregard State lines, according to the requirements of
the industrial situation. To adapt the law to the fact, the instruments of transportation, communication, and production that require
interstate expanse for their operation, may be placed under the sole
dominion of the Federal Government. From the time of the adoption
of the Convention's plan, their organization would be compulsorily
effected under the corporate system of the general Government. The
origin, nature and amount of their security issues would be ordained
—the limitation of their earnings and all the relations of the donor
and donees of franchises would be outlined. The position of employees
as a part of this interstate organism would also fall within the purview of this fundamental establishment. In compelling this transfer
of creative power and the unlimited regulation that pertains thereto,
the United States will subject the future development of industry that
is not confined to intra-State boundaries. The proposed demarcation
may be set on these lines: The inclusion of a portion of intra-State
business among its activities should not debar a corporation from Fed-

eral incorporation. All purely local or municipal industries would be left under the sole control of their present domestic régime. Without venturing upon more than an adumbration of the new American corporate system, it may be cast on this basis:

All corporations conducting business among the several States must be organized under Federal statutes. The Congress shall have power to except from the provisions of this article such classes of corporations as it may prescribe.

The term business is employed as more comprehensive than commerce—as inclusive of production as well as transportation and communication. Besides excluding public utility enterprises of a mere municipal scope, the design of this draft is to avoid Federal control over production—manufacturing, and mining companies—which is mainly confined within the limits of any State. In view of the diffusion of business, and of the extra-State shipments by small manufacturing enterprises, the percentage of corporations engaged in State domestic business solely must be comparatively slight. It would, therefore, cause less public friction if the Federal provision were made inclusive, leaving to Congress the relegation to State authority of organizations having only a slight interstate business. An analogy to this course exists where non-exercised Federal powers are now exercised by the States.

Even the above tentative verbiage would eliminate many troublesome questions now embarrassing the legislative and judicial departments. Undoubtedly the subjection of the indicated species of property to Federal control, while the derivation of other titles would remain in the States, might seem anomalous; although we have the same principle now prevailing in reference to the Federal proprietorship for civil and military purposes.

Such a constitutional amendment would produce a finality of all contests for regulation, with the advent of a single regulator. And the extent of the regulation by Federal power would cease to be debatable—it would include all the power over this subject which the States and the Nation now possess—the common law power over the estates dedicated to interstate business, as well as the power to regulate the conduct of commerce among the States.

There are some corollaries which should follow this extension of Federal commercial power. The new Constitution so amended should recognize another species of public power which the complication of modern industry has developed. It is commonly designated as the Administrative power, and has recently enhanced sufficiently to be entitled to its place by the side of the three coördinate branches of our Government. It does not strictly belong to the legislative, executive, or judicial department; yet it partakes of the nature of all of them. It is the arm of that newly organized function which consists in the supervision or regulation of quasi-public activities, in which private resources are invested. It is the instrumentality by which the public protects itself through its own Commissions. The absence of any distinct place for it in our juridical system has hampered its usefulness. The necessity for its defined status among our recognized institutions would be redoubled in view of the enlarged field of its activity.

These Constitutional changes should form a solvent of the questions of monopoly and restraint of trade and their remedial appliances in the Anti-Trust laws. As every corporation engaged in interstate business would derive its vitality from the general Government, the supervision of its business would form an essential part of the statutory and administrative machinery of the United States. The latter resource would supplant to a great extent the resort to judicial proceedings.

Passing from the economic phases, let us consider the work of the Convention in its more strictly political aspect. Primarily, what would be the area of power of a National Convention? While the Constitution has been sparing of any absolute limitations, it would be practically subject to certain implications. As it could not deprive a State without its consent of its equal representation in the Senate, this limitation involves some other restrictions on the power of Conventional action. Whatever changes may be wrought, the bicameral construction of the Congress must be maintained, as a Senate implies the continuance of a House of Representatives. With these exceptions the Convention could deal with a *tabula rasa*. It could practically create a new government in all its relations to political power and administration, to proprietary and economic matters, to personal and quasi-social relations.

The theory of construction on which the remodeled instrument may be based is a foremost consideration. Are all the powers not specially assigned to the States to be deemed vested in the general Government? This is the presumption incorporated in some modern types of federal government, notably in the case of Australia. Or is our present constitutional presumption to be repeated—that all powers not conferred on the central authority are reserved to the States or the people? While it may be difficult to give specific expression to the common law powers which will be retained by the States, some definite substitute for their present negative and unexpressed condition should really increase their vitality.

Whenever the exercise of any Federal power is suggested, the first aspect presented is its bearing on the theory of relations between the National and State Governments. Contemporaneous history emphasizes this problem. If the second Constitutional Convention in our annals is to subserve a useful purpose it must deal effectually with this permeating political relation. The spirit in which these relations should be approached is a primary consideration. Under the present Constitution, the general Government is in effect treated as an aggregation of political units, each unit surrendering a share of its political authority. But the Second Constitutional Convention may proceed upon the theory of distributing from a sum total of political power the proportions which may, for the public weal, be best exercised by the Nation and the States respectively. Under this doctrine, it is perceptible that a wider scope of action would be vested in the Convention, and quite a different organism would naturally result. The spectre of guarantees against Federal powers should be dissipated. It was originally a survival of the antagonism to the general authority personified in a monarchy. Changed conditions have by themselves eliminated all sanction for this apprehension. Governmental systems on this continent are to be gauged purely by their response to utilitarian requirements.

Material and social conditions have made the States less and the Nation more, greater as a factor in government. The sequence of these conditions is the conversion of the States from political organizations into administrative bodies. With its preponderant powers, the Convention could mould these local Governments to new, and mayhap to reduced proportions. The field for this action would include both economic and political provinces.

The purely political aspect of its power would present many phases to the Convention. Does the provision of the present Constitution requiring the consent of a State to the deprivation of its equal suffrage in the Senate, prevent the admission of new States without such equal suffrage? If a negative reply be the true one, provision for such change would enable existing Territories to be admitted with one Senator.

Nor would the Convention be restricted in providing for alterations in the present category of States. While no new State can be formed, under the Constitution as it stands, out of existing States without the consent of their Legislatures, the Convention may change this provision without the consent of the States affected. In short its amendatory power in this particular is not restricted, as it is in the matter of equal representation in the Senate. The Convention may authorize the creation of a single State from New Jersey and Delaware; or it may provide for the formation of two States out of New York. Whether such changes would not properly obviate existing disparities in State representation in the Senate may form a proper subject of deliberation.

With the assignment of mainly administrative functions to the States there would no longer be any rationale for their immunity from suit by individuals. Irrespective of the payment of their debts, the eleventh amendment has developed an obstructive opposition to the enforcement of the Federal protection of property from deprivation without due process.

There are some political incidents of State power that are palpably relics of extreme particularism. They belong to the period of the Confederation rather than to the era of a Federal Union. The power of the States over the times, places, and manner of holding Congressional elections seems under present conditions to constitute an anomaly. The existing provision covers a lurking conception of sovereignties sending delegates. In the light of our national development, the qualified revisory power of Congress over State action concerning this subject-matter should be replaced by original and comprehensive national jurisdiction over the machinery for the choice of

Federal legislators. This should naturally lead to an educational requirement for the exercise of the elective franchise.

Whatever may be the extent accorded to Federal power over electoral affairs, the principle of unrestricted liberty of constituencies in selecting officials should be adopted as the law of the Union. All American citizens should be eligible everywhere for selection to any office in the gift of constituencies. This provision would eliminate much of the local and petty character of elections. Conjoined with State-wide tickets for Congressional officials, it should bring the leading men of the country into public life.

In view of the deterioration of State legislative bodies, the selection of Senators should no longer be restricted to their action. The eligible ages prescribed for Senators and Representatives should be abolished, and also the age limitation for the Presidency. The same principle applies in respect to the requirement of inhabitancy for Senators and Representatives. The House of Representatives should be so renewed that the period of its assemblage would be co-incident with the inauguration of a new President. The delay in responding to changes in policy, which the elections frequently demand, would be thereby avoided.

It would follow from the control of naturalization and cognate subjects that the general Government should control the qualifications for the elective franchise throughout the Union. The requirements for citizenship of the United States are ordained by Congress. That citizenship carries with it the citizenship of the State where the person resides. The power of the States has been further abridged by the prohibition against making any distinction on account of race, color, or previous servitude. In these conditions, it is logical that the general Government should prescribe the educational or other qualification for voting for all public offices throughout the country. Such power would properly result in uniform qualification.

There will hardly be a difference of opinion that some change would be acceptable in the manner of electing the President and Vice-President, though there may be much difference concerning the nature of such change. The more radical proposition would involve the abolition of the present fictitious system of electoral colleges and the substitution of direct popular votes. If this course be not adopted, the dangers involved in the present vague and indeterminate prescription for counting the electoral vote should be prevented by more specific constitutional directions. Another Electoral Commission should be avoided.

Original jurisdiction in the Supreme Court over constitutional questions would obviate the uncertainties and delays now incident to the progress of such controversies through the inferior courts. They are ultimately submitted to the tribunal of last resort, and indeed this result is now sought through fictitious proceedings. When John Marshall took his seat there were only twelve cases on the docket; now they are numbered by hundreds. This class of fundamental questions involves consequences too pervading to admit of the ordinary tardiness of adjudication.

The principle of the distribution of the subject-matter of taxation, between the Union and the States, should now prevail. As the wealth of the country was comparatively diminutive in 1789, the Philadelphia Convention apprehended fiscal weakness for the new Government unless all sources of taxation were thrown open to it. But now any single head of taxation would fulfil the requirements of our Governments. Such a scheme of distributive burdens would avoid the anomalies and duplications of taxing power, illustrated by the pending income tax amendment. This distribution of the taxing power, as between the general and local Governments, presents a field for the broadest differences. As duties upon exports are now prohibited, so may opponents of protective tariffs advocate the extinguishment of Congressional power to levy duties on imports. Strenuous efforts will certainly be made in such a representative body to secure unrestricted national power of taxation upon income and its extension to cover all the requirements of the general Government. On the other hand, the power of Congress to levy excise conflicts with the State authority over internal police matters and may therefore be abolished. Property and excise taxation could form the mainstays of the local Governments. The rule of tax apportionment among the States has lost its significance and should no longer limit the power of the general Government. Moreover, the several species of taxation may be defined, instead of resting upon antique and presumed economic distinctions.

The great increase in the number of Federal officials, entailed by the enlargement of Federal activities, should be counterbalanced by a constitutional system of civil service. Permanency, dissociation from politics, and increased efficiency would be subserved by removing office holding from the uncertainties of partisan action in Congress.

Ample authority may be conferred to establish any species of banking system. It should be an absolute and independent power legally unrelated to the necessities of the treasury. Whether assets banking or postal savings, it could be separated from governmental requirements, or the resort thereto for the basis of its legality.

The questions of forest and irrigation control demand some readjustment of public powers. Centring within the boundaries of the several States, their operative functions extend beyond those boundaries. The exercise of the appropriate agencies to manage this species of interstate utility was clearly not within the purview of the framers of the present instrument. But it now demands a place commensurate with its physical requirements, among the unquestionable prerogatives of an interstate authority.

The powers of Congress over copyrights and patents should be extended, so that these species of property may be placed upon a level with all other property. The present limitation upon this Federal power is the result of antiquated conditions and ill-reasoned judicial decisions existing in England at the time of our Revolution. These restrictions are unworthy of an enlightened people.

The relations of the United States to the States under the treaty power demand examination. Are the rights conferred upon aliens by treaty to be limited by the action of the States in respect to subjects of local authority? Or should the approval by two-thirds of the Senate be sufficient to make the most ample treaties legally current throughout the Union?

With the increased control by the general Government over corporate property, the control *pari passu* over the subject-matter of labor would be a logical result. That control under the present questionable national powers is already partly legislative and partly voluntary, and with the extension of the field of Federal power over the property relations of corporations engaged in interstate commerce and production, it is difficult to perceive how the legal control of labor engaged therein can be avoided.

The continuance of other police powers of the States has been challenged, under our changed conditions. The personal status of individuals, as affected by marriage and divorce, is foremost in subjection to special criticism under the present régime of State control. Even if it be not practicable to render the causes of divorce uniform, the " full faith and credit clauses " may be so extended that people shall not occupy differing marital status in different localities. Bills of exchange, bills of lading, and other commercial documents have become instrumentalities of interstate commerce. In fact the greater proportion of their usefulness is outside of intra-State business. These documents peculiarly require uniformity in their tenor and in the authority for controlling legislation.

Do not the present conditions require a national direction to the subject of education? The illiterateness among natives that still subsists in some sections, and the mass of uninstructed immigrants that has settled in other neighborhoods produce a certain exigency on this subject. The strong financial aid of the nation is the foremost need in this connection. This may be followed by a reduction of the academic element, and an increase of the practical features more peculiarly required in a system of free public education. This national supervision need not impair many of the local agencies, but it should secure the use of the English language as the medium of instruction. A new force is needed to educate our electorate.

Some minor questions, not involving matters of principle, naturally suggest themselves as subjects of deliberation: the extension of the President's term, with prohibition of reëlection or such probibitiou without change in the present term of office; fixing the constitutional day for the meeting of Congress in October instead of December; the settlement of a national quarantine power; the disposal of the accumulation of causes on the Supreme Court calendar, so that litigants may reach judgment within a reasonable time; the extension of Federal jurisdiction to the subject of insurance as a branch of interstate commerce.

Some of these results might, strictly speaking, be obtained by Congressional legislation, but they are of such an unaccustomed nature that they should preferably receive the sanction of constitutional endorsement. Probably many other subjects of legitimate action will present themselves, and perhaps some topics not so relevant may be eccentrically suggested.

There may be some aspects favorable to the enlargement of the State powers. Or rather those powers may on some points require reinstatement to the position they occupied before they had been legislated away, or interpreted away, by the Courts. It may be pertinently asked: What would be the residuum of State power after these labors of a Convention? The reply is that the legal power of the States would be retained over the vast field of individual rights, both personal and proprietary; it would include all private enterprises affected with public uses whose extent was confined exclusively within State boundaries, and it would cover the administration of all local affairs. In administering their powers they would be uncontrolled by any agencies of the general Government, thereby contrasting with centralized republics on the European continent.

The method by which the labors of the Convention may be sanctioned obviates objection to their extent and diverse character. In calling the Convention, Congress should provide that the amendments proposed be ratified by Conventions in the States. As we know from the history of the present Constitution, these State Conventions will, in all likelihood, contribute a valuable share to the scrutiny of the principles incorporated in the new instrument.

The amendatory power itself should, in the light of modern exigencies, be rendered more flexible. The intention in drafting this power was to render its exercise somewhat difficult, in order that additions to Federal authority should not be facilitated. With the Atlantic States alone constituting the Union, there was a comparative equality among them, so that the number of States required to effect amendments corresponded more nearly than at present to their wealth and population. But we have super-added to the difficulty of amendment by the admission as new States of communities grossly unequal to the original thirteen. As the result, twenty-eight State Legislatures count twenty-eight votes against New York's single vote in all matters of constitutional amendment, though the total population of these twenty-eight States is not equal to that of New York. To remedy this anomaly there would seem to be no valid objection to the efficiency of a majority of both Houses as proposers of amendments, and the same proportion of the State Legislatures as ratifiers thereof. The same proportions should apply to the call for national conventions and the ratification of their action.

Contrasted with other countries, we have changed our structure of government very slightly in the whole course of the nineteenth century. We may complacently declare that it needed few changes, and from the standpoint of 1789, it is agreed that there was a marvelous prevision of our political future. But our governmental changes have not in modern times been commensurate with those effected under unitary systems. It was no doubt expected that the States would respond to these progressive demands, the ordinary topics of human experience being within their province. But the inertia of the States has been compulsory—their geographical boundaries presenting the anomaly of being less extensive than the range of territory covered by modern enterprises. In respect to many phases of modern legislation, particularly of a quasi-social nature, we still remain par excellence the conservative nation. In extending the field of Federal action, our Government would be merely following the course of the great historical confederations. Recently this cohesive tendency has been intensified. Even in the most centrifugal of republics, the legalized Swiss democracy, the directive centre has become more masterful, as recent modifications of its system have developed.

The moral supremacy of the general Government is shown by the fact that it has become the political compass for the guidance of State Governments. In the administration of current economic and social questions, example is sought at Washington. Not estimated by positive authority alone but by ethical considerations, Washington has become the civic centre of the nation. On the other hand the considerable withdrawals of intelligence and merit from State officialdom have been contributing causes from the opposite direction. The contrast between the character of State legislative bodies at the time of the formation of the Constitution and their present subsidence is amply suggestive on this score. Legal power should follow this centre of political gravity.

Much will depend upon the personnel of the Convention. The delegates to the Philadelphia Convention were selected by the Legislatures. Under our changed conditions, this electorate would not be

suitable. When Congress provides for the proposed Convention, it
may specify the method of selection of delegates. An appropriate
basis for their choice may consist in a special election in each State,
all the candidates to represent the State at large, and to be chosen
without reference to residence—by some method conducive as far
as possible to the assemblage of the best material in the Nation.

Is this presentation to be regarded from a mere academic point of
view? Observation of current affairs furnishes a negative reply.
Upon one ground alone, the method of electing Senators, the complement of Legislatures required for the call of a National Convention is now nearly attained.

If this cohesion results from the desire for a single constitutional
change, it would seem that the demand for other developments in our
public affairs would produce proximate unanimity in the call of the
State Legislatures.

In pursuing this purpose, the State Conference now organized
to bring about a Constitutional Convention, may well take courage
from this language of Washington's Farewell Address:

" If, in the opinion of the people, the distribution or modification of the constitutional powers be, in any particular, wrong, let it
be corrected by an amendment in the way which the Constitution
designates. But let there be no change by usurpation; for though
this in one instance may be the instrument of good, it is the customary weapon by which free Governments are destroyed. The
precedent must always greatly overbalance in permanent evil any
partial or transient benefit which the use can at any time yield."

CONSCIENCE

MARIAN COX

THE gaiety of criminals upon their way to the scaffold has often struck, amazed, bewildered their observers. None have understood it. Most have fancied it a mask adopted by the lost soul in a final defiance flung at mankind: defiance which is the pride of the fallen. But I— a criminal condemned to death to-morrow—am experiencing this gaiety, and will reveal how it has come to me.

And why do I do this? Why trouble myself to give anything to a world whose laws I have always despised?

Because my experience has been so unique, unparalleled, incredible, that I, in my pride of defiance, desire to fling in the face of the world its ignorance of the human heart.

I have won a victory. My gaiety tells me so.

The whole world is in quest of gaiety. It hates the gray. It hates its aches. Fallen into the shadow, it squirms to reach the light. It denies its pain and wants to laugh like a drunkard: idiot laughter that comes not from the gaiety but from the ache of the heart. For the soul is not gay until it has opened and filled with all the suffering and sin the world can bestow upon it. Its gaiety is its fearlessness. This I shall prove.

I do not pretend to understand the cause or rationale of my deeds, but I do understand the thoughts and feelings that have prompted them; and I shall relate them faithfully, completely, shamelessly, so that those whose minds are curious about the human heart can peer into these hitherto unlit corners before they make their sweeping synthesis of man.

I will show them where their research has never probed. I will open a vista of surmise to them which will wither their conceit of understanding. It fattens my gaiety to think that, some day, they —the thinkers—will say of me: " This, too, was a man."

To begin at the beginning.

I had the good or the ill fortune (who can ever say which?) to be born into a family distinguished for its piety and held in the highest regard by the community in which its members had always dwelt. I remember that I sometimes wondered if the cold and rigid armor of their respectability did not weigh upon them. It seemed to me that they lived in a perpetual vigil against any infringement of the laws of man, and that the importance of their self-guardianship and of their neighbors' jurisdiction made them featureless and sad. What made them so anxious to march with the world in its lockstep of safety? Had they something in their hearts to conceal? Unfortunately, so far, the world has never been given the confessions of the virtuous. Only the evil confess; and the virtuous are always dull and the evil are often gay.

I had the advantage of an excellent education under the ægis of a college whose curriculum embodied instruction in morals, ethics, and the dogmas of its faith, far in excess of the usual scholasticism to be gleaned in an American academy. Yet what knowledge I gained was merely engrafted, superficially, upon me; for, being without mental desire or curiosity, it soon fell away, a thing without foothold.

An indifferent student, I dragged through college, often escaping severe punishment and even expulsion, merely because of the seeming willingness, patience and affability of my nature; qualities which I learned to cultivate, to an excessive degree, as soon as I discovered their value in placating or diverting the ire of the authorities.

Yes, I early learned the value of being a gentleman. If one be endowed with the appearance of a gentleman (upon my high bred looks I have always prided myself, even in my lowest degradation) and adds to it suave manners, soft tones, gentle, deprecating ways and words,—one can frustrate the suspicion and hostility of the world. But these qualities can only be developed and utilized by those who are sufficiently *indifferent* to do so; for from the profound indifference of mind and heart, they spring.

. Through my childhood, youth and early manhood, the one thing that characterized me and stands in my memory as the very color, in fact, of my inner natural self, was—indifference.

Beware of the indifferent. Of those who seem devoid of ambition and appetite, of those whose eyes never sparkle with a lust of success, of love, of work, of knowledge, of gold, of those who never have a rash impetuous youth nor make the mistakes of passion, which are after all but the expansiveness of a warm humanity within, unable to form itself into strength and value until bruised into shape by the iron of the outer world. Beware of the indifferent; for indifference is not strength; it is not stoicism nor self-sufficiency and mastery—for which it is so generally mistaken: no; it is the swamp of the spirit. Like a bog it hangs upon the nature, destroys all springing and sound growths to throw its succulent shade over the breeding of glazed unvital things, laggard serpentine things, mucous, swollen, stinging things. Beneath indifference grows the ill health, the abnormality and the wickedness of the human soul.

But the world likes, admires, trusts and follows those who are indifferent to it—as they must be indifferent to all else. The prizes of life are for those who do not prize them. And to this alone do I attribute my early success in life.

I cannot deny that I was singularly fortunate in gaining the esteem of men and the material weal of life, up to the time of—well, it is difficult to say just when it began, but as a distinctive epoch which marked my career, I will say—my marriage.

I had left college, several years, and was filling a position that was a subordinate one, to be sure, and not very remunerative, but was one of public trust with inevitable opportunities for advancement, when I decided to entrench myself still further into settlement in life through marriage.

Naturally the idea of a home allured me more than that of a wife. Men of the indifferent temperament invariably do marry for a home. If they possess any ideal at all it is that of peace, quiet and the shelter from all foreign things, which somehow has come to be associated with the idea of home.

Love was nothing to me. To this day I neither know nor care if my wife ever loved me. But although I did not harbor any of those bemeaning feelings, politely termed sentiment, I must admit that my choice of her for a wife was actuated by the charm she exercised over me through her possession of a pair of extraordinarily beautiful hands.

Never have I seen anything so beautiful as Nellie's hands. And I am a man singularly unsusceptible to beauty in any of its forms.

Her hands were similar to those one sees in Sir Peter Lely's portraits of the 17th century *grandes dames*. They looked as though solely made to languish amidst silken splendors, to "trail fringes and embroidery through meadows and purling streams," to caress the creamy wool of a lamb, emblem of innocence, to toy with nothing heavier than a shepherdess's crook or the chain of a pet falcon. Aristocratic, slender, exquisitely white hands, from whose shell-tinted palms branched five pointed fingers, as nervous, flexible, vital, all feeling, as though they were the very antennæ of her soul. Ah, most rarely lovely, once were Nellie's hands!

During the days of our courtship they fascinated and absorbed me completely. I never extended to her any caress beyond holding one of them, and losing myself in long studious contemplation of its flowerlike charm.

She, too, may have been cold and indifferent. I know little about her even after I have lived with her these past eight years. She never exacted or seemed to expect from me any form of endearment. But often she smiled at me and her pale blue eyes seemed tender when she consented to become my wife.

Our home was in the suburbs of a large town. All around it ranged little plots of similar homes, small, simple, commonplace as our own.

I believe that at first Nellie was happy. At least I heard her sometimes singing at her work. She had insisted upon performing without assistance all the household duties of our little *ménage;* and this in spite of the fact that I could have afforded a servant for her and that all our neighbors could boast of one. But her ambition never took the form of display or of emulation with others; ambitious though she was in her own way. Her ambition, as she said, was to save sufficient money to secure us against any possibility of future want; and from the very start she was solicitous about every dollar of my earnings, and unnecessarily denied herself various comforts, in order to manipulate as many of both as possible into that visionary armory of protection which she was constantly building against some mysterious attack of the future.

At first I experienced much satisfaction in my home. It afforded such a tranquilizing contrast to the tumultuous city wherein I spent the entire day, that I looked forward to my return in the evenings with a real pleasure. The little house was embedded amidst a nest of trees from whose bosky darkness it threw forth the beacon of its evening light to greet me immediately upon my descent from the train. To that genial harborage I always hastened, to spend the ensuing hour in the relaxing comfort of smoking and watching Nellie as she moved about the kitchen in preparation of our supper. .

I found it singularly pleasing to watch her deft and dainty hands perform those homely rites. At first it seemed so incongruous: those hands of a seventeenth century great lady, solely fashioned to be idle, pensive and frivolous, grasping wooden and iron ladles, holding the sputtering grill over the boisterous fire, plunging into hectic ovens, gripping their little pink nails into the greasy scour-cloths with which she wiped out the black pots or pans, and burying themselves beyond their slim blue-veined wrists within the leaden water that filled the sink as they searched in its depths for the slippery china.

It was indeed fascinating to watch her hands. It formed my sole diversion, and seemed for awhile to fill my life with the charm of a beauty to which I was strangely insensible and unappreciative, and yet vaguely held by it alone within the inviolate precincts of this home.

As I say, I do not know whether she ever loved me or I loved her. Those sentimentalities, which so slavishly preoccupy the minds of others, never assumed any importance to me. In fact it has always appeared absurd to me that a man should name as sentiment that which is but the trickery of an unacknowledged instinct, and seek to exalt his own life by means of a passion so cunningly devised to diminish it in making him share or bestow it upon others. But this is a subject upon which I must not dwell, for it does not materially concern the subsequent events of my fate.

My wife was always thinking of the future. Whatever emotions or thoughts she was capable of, seemed to be wholly expended upon it. She was always solicitous, cautious and anxious about it; and in those days never mentioned or discussed anything else. She was constantly forecasting it and planning and worrying. Yes, whatever individual life she possessed appeared to be wholly projected into the morrow.

The morrow!

He who said, " Take no heed of the morrow," was the one who understood the beginning of all evil.

Because of this—her fear of the future—she became exacting and wearisome to me. I, the unaspiring, the peace-lover, the unmoved, was incessantly told what I ought to do, what I must do, what I was failing to do, wherein was my duty and my neglect. She pointed out to me the possibility of losing my position, the probability of being unable to secure another, and the dire disasters which would then befall us because of the insufficiency of our little bank fund. In anticipation she experienced every ill of poverty; and her constant endeavor was to impart to me the same meticulous frame of mind. My stolid sense of security seemed to distress her more than anything else; and she fought against it with a relentless persistency. She tried to undermine it like some little hoarding mole who burrows hither and thither beneath a flower bed, until all suddenly collapses in rents like wrinkles upon a careworn face. She begrudged me a sense of security even in my food, and whenever I appeared to be particularly relishing some dish, would invariably speak of its expensiveness, and the unlikelihood of our being able to procure it in the future. Thus in countless petty and ingenious ways she added to the Persecution of the Future. Always she spoke of *our* future, but it soon appeared to me as solely her own welfare of which she was so obsessed.

An obsession it certainly was. But it did not define itself into any explicit desire or want until one day when a neighbor's wife happened to come in and mention to Nellie a life insurance policy which her husband had just taken out for her benefit in one of the big companies.

From that moment my wife fixed upon her desire. Like a lightning flash the words of the visitor had illumined the chaos of her anxiety. Immediately upon her departure, I was told that I, too, must do as this woman's husband had done and insure my life for her. She seized upon the idea with the avid tenacity for which her long groping had evidently prepared her. At last she knew exactly what she wanted, and from that moment I had no rest.

I was not then an ill-tempered or impatient man and I endured her besetting with an equanimity at which I afterwards marveled.

Not a day of respite would she give me. She sent for circulars and particulars from all the insurance companies, both large and small, and soon we were deluged with mail that she would read aloud to me over the breakfast table. And in the evenings the exclusive topic of her discourse became comparisons between the statements and annual reports of the various companies, and comparisons between the respective merits of the different kinds of policies. The more she learned of the subject, the more enthusiastic and urgent she became. Now impatient as well as persistent she harped upon it, she nagged, petitioned, harassed me, until, all of a sudden, I became—suspicious!

Yes, suddenly from its long sleep, my inertia stirred and from it sprang forth a dark, a sinister, a terrible suspicion.

What good could my insurance do her unless with it came my *death?* Was it then for my death that she was thus planning and hankering?

From the moment the suspicion seized upon me I lost my sluggish peace forever.

The law of self-preservation, deep hidden beneath the indifference within my breast, was aroused and armed against this parasitic thing that demanded of me—its future.

Then I could contain myself no longer. Although I did not accuse her of her design against my life nor allow her to suspect my growing conviction of it, I accused her of the basest selfishness in thus and always thinking of her future, her security, her own well-being, even at the expense of my peace of mind.

"What good would my insurance do *me?*" I demanded of her. And then, for the first time, presented to her my point of view: the arrant selfishness of her request, when to comply with it meant for me to expend a considerable portion of my income in a way that could be of no benefit to me whatsoever, with the still more disagreeable condition it would possess of reminding me of my death every time I should be constrained to make one of the quarterly, bi-annual, or annual payments. This latter phase appeared particularly obnoxious, burdensome, insupportable to me; and as I realized how she was attempting to inflict it upon me, she became in my sight more and more culpable and offensive. Did she then desire to rob me of my peace of mind forever? If I were to be forced thus to contemplate and prepare for death, periodically, systematically, compulsorily, throughout the year, I should be assigning my entire life to a compact with the Arch-Destroyer, which would take from it all the lightness of an irresponsible existence—all the blithe sense of freedom in mind and heart—forevermore.

And I waxed wroth the longer I dwelt upon it, and began to censure her so harshly and bitterly for her flagrant egoism, and with an anger and evident animosity, to which she was so unaccustomed from me, that it surprised her into a spell of alarmed nerves and she broke down and cried for the first time since our marriage.

She cried, while I observed with disgust how weak, foolish and homely she was. Then she suddenly gained some control over her sobs, and told me, in a breaking voice, of how cruelly I was wronging her, of how unjust I was to accuse and upbraid her for selfishness, when it was not for herself at all that she had been thus importunate. It was for another, for our child, our unborn child, which she was carrying and feeling at that very moment as it beat like a bird in the encagement of her womb.

"It worries me, it worries me," she whispered between her sobs. "It makes my heart ache with the responsibility of its life, its future." And she placed both her hands upon my arm and looked up at me with that dreadful wistfulness of woman which asks and asks so much from man that he cannot give nor even understand.

Silently, in return, my gaze swept over her figure and noted its dawning deformity, then was recalled to those clinging hands which I felt, with an exaggerated consciousness, upon my arm. At first I observed them with curiosity, then, with a startled wonder, then with sheer consternation, as, abruptly, I realized how they had changed.

Changed, completely changed; that there was no mistaking. How unfamiliar they seemed in their new guise! How incredible and shocking in their transformation!

They, the erstwhile ensigns of beauty, had been replaced by strange members that dazed and daunted me with their ugliness, their unmitigated eldritch ugliness.

And I, who had always prided myself on being unmoved by beauty, became shudderingly alive to the horror of the ugliness of those hands.

I studied them in a sickening fascination. Red, coarsened, uncouth, their pores harsh as the bark on some uncanny carnivorous tree, their nails broken and spotted with white bruises,—*these* were the things that had once exercised upon me such a different fascination, that fatal fascination which had made me choose them for a lifelong affiliation. And now they had turned against me and were revealing their true character; they were mocking me with their malific ugliness, maddening me with their ominous secrets, terrifying me with their baleful powers and threats. Cheated and betrayed by them, I was their dupe, and the dupe of this woman who was peering up into my face with such unanswerable demands, with such a tragic wistfulness.

In that poignant second of lucidity, I lost all trace of my past self. A vague wave of hostility swept through me that rendered me a stranger to myself. She, too, was suddenly a stranger, and in her new aspect was revealed as the Enemy of Man. I feared her but loathed her more than I feared. She desired my death; of this I was now convinced, and whether her desire was for her own benefit or that of the child did not change, augment, or detract in any way from the enormity of her offence. She desired my death! That was the one and only thing that mattered. She represented that woman's lust of life which will sacrifice everything, all beauty, love, peace, man, herself, for merely another embodiment of life, even though it be a wretched life; life being the monomania of woman. Strange mystery of human existence that covenants alone with woman and yet penalizes her for her consecration!

Suddenly I felt my brain swell as with a viper's poison, and in the dizziness of a whirling second, transported beyond my own conscious powers of volition—my arm shook itself free from the repugnance of her hands and dashed its fist in full vigor against her mouth.

Never, never can I forget her cry; nor her look of bleeding horror as she fell back against a table standing in the centre of the floor. Her arms strained backwards upon it, she gazed at me with fixed dilated eyes.

Trembling, both, we gazed at each other in silence, during moments which were marked off by the ticking of the clock upon the cupboard, marked off in some punctilious greed as though they were being lapped up slowly, carefully, voluptuously by an Eternity of Hell.

Then—I know not why, it was not shame, she was too abhorrent to me to cause shame—but I lowered my burning face and slunk away from the house with the sense that it was I who had been struck, and not she.

During the ensuing months our eyes never met. Neither did I, during that period, ever gaze at her freely and fully again. No longer did I watch her at her work, as of yore, but when at home sat smoking in morose silence or in gloomy idleness and brooding. She, too, became silent, she who had once been so loquacious. Like a pall silence enwrapped our home.

In justice to myself I must confess that, during those interminable months whilst she awaited the newcomer into our home, I was frequently tempted to speak to her and break that pall of silence. There was something about it that ached and weighed upon me like a nightmare. Formerly I had fancied that silence was peculiarly congenial to me, but during that prolonged immemorial spell of it, I learned how awful it is, how implacable and ghastly and crushing in its unreachability—which yet reaches one in a closeness from which there is no escape. Silence is a mirror of Eternity held before the shrinking face of man. Is that not why we hate it? Is there aught more terrifying than its blankness which yet glassily magnifies us to ourselves?

Again and again I was tempted to exorcise that fatal silence from our home, but when upon the very verge of words was invariably restrained by pride. I felt that my words would have to consist of some overture or apology to her. Because of my one act of brutality, an act I could justify to myself through the abnormal excitedness of the moment, I would have to ask, perhaps sue for pardon, and to this my jealous pride would not permit me to stoop. It would be a weakness. The man of strength must never explain himself. He must be his own tribunal. Above all woman must not be led to believe that she can judge man.

I knew that my views regarding this subject were correct, and they seemed to justify my conduct of stubbornly maintained silence, until I began to feel that she owed me the initial advance, and that I, and not she, was being daily wronged by the continuation of our silence. Yes, she might have broken it as well as I. In fact it was her duty more than mine; for she, as woman, was imbued with the greater responsibility toward the unborn, and had she been worthy of the trust, would have expected nothing from me, but herself would have done everything to secure that household harmony which, like a holy amulet, would have averted from us the fell curse.

With my footsteps upon the very border of the Styx, with my last breath panting from beneath the black muffles of justice, this, I can solemnly swear: for that damnable silence which blighted our home *she* must be held chiefly to blame.

Finally the child was born.

I had been sitting alone a long time listening to the strange sounds overhead from the chamber where she lay in travail.

At last the silence of the house was broken. For deathless moments I heard her moaning; and then a havoc of cries resounded through the sepulchral walls. It seemed as though they ripped away the vampirish grip of silence upon that dwelling to leave it forever full of bleeding noise. But, no; after one culminate shriek that seemed wrung from some bottomless pit of torture, all sound subsided; and silence again reigned in that doleful domain.

I shivered in it as though from a deadly chill; I buried my face in my unstrung hands until, hours later as it seemed, someone came for me and summoned me to the chamber above wherein lay the mother and our child.

With a stupendous effort to comport myself with a natural demeanor, I accompanied the nurse, and ascended to the chamber above. On tiptoe I approached the bed, as though fearful of again uncovering those raw wounds of cries, hidden beneath the silence; and saw her as she lay ensconced amidst the pillows, holding something small and breathing within the curve of her arm.

For the first time since months my wife and I steadily met each other's eyes. I looked down at her and she looked up at me. Her lips were quivering, and her eyes were humid as though with incipient tears: not hard covetous eyes as they had seemed to me before I struck her, nor hurt malign eyes as they had been after my blow, but, shy and benign, they looked up at me as though they might, as though they were preparing to—forgive.

But she said nothing and still seemed as though waiting for me to break the silence between us.

And why did I then recoil? Why have I always been incapacitated for a performance as soon as I have perceived it expected and awaited from me? What bane of perversity has been the taint in my blood?

For now when I saw how easy it would be to stretch forth my hand and span the chasm between us, when I was even aware that something within me was bent upon this deed and ached for its enactment —I was unable to do so; and turned away, abruptly, in silence, and left the room to spend many hours thereafter in restless aimless wandering upon the country roads and suburban streets.

While I had stood at the bedside, and turned away, it was with the clear understanding that I was hurting myself far worse than her. And yet if it had instantaneously cost me my life I could not have refrained from the act. That act had caused in me a sort of taloned gloat of the mind, as it held fast some guiltless slave, some unknown foe in my soul, which ached and gasped for liberation from the execrated thraldom. And I feared to liberate It, that aching thing, more than I feared any deed, however heinous.

Thereafter, on to the end, I lived solely to suppress and deaden it. When it churned in my heart with its unbearable pangs, I took long prostrating walks, or concentrated my thoughts feverishly upon my daily commercial tasks; but above all I resolutely avoided that darkened chamber where they lay. I never reëntered it during the weeks of her convalescence. But while in the house, I found myself listening, constantly listening to catch some sound from overhead which would betoken the presence of the little stranger within its walls.

But nothing ever reached my strained ears, save the occasional footfall of the old woman who daily came to serve their needs. And I marveled at this as I recalled that babies with their inveterate crying were said to be utterly devastating to all domestic quiet.

Evidently my child did not cry; and as finally I realized this, it was with a peculiar thrill. The fact seemed to establish its difference, aye, its superiority, to the children of others, and made me, for the first time, aware of my paternity in this thrill of anomalous relief and pride. Then at least the child would not make this atmosphere more discordant.

At last the old woman visited the house no more, and the mother and child came down to the lower floor.

My wife gradually resumed the household tasks while the child remained most of the time in its cradle with its little muslin canopy trailing on either side like broken wings.

I took more interest in them than I would acknowledge even to myself. And when Nellie was occupied or unobservant, I would slyly look at her and note how weak and thin she seemed at first and how she regained her strength and elasticity, unslackeningly, every day.

Our child appeared to be incredibly good and asserted its existence only in little kicks and flutters of arms amidst its soft bedding, and in the periods of nursing when the sound of its sucking mouth filled the room.

But what chiefly interested, thrilled, amazed me was that she— my wife—seemed to be content, aye, positively content, even gay, during those early days after the advent of the new life.

Thus she completed my alienation. Her attitude confirmed all my harbored suspicions. For one thing, did it not prove that I counted for less than nothing in these two lives? It was only too apparent that she was endeavoring to obliterate the very consciousness of my existence from this household and was solely occupied with the thought of herself and of her child; perhaps was dreaming of their future, as a future from which the old anxiety seemed now to have been strangely abolished. Otherwise how could she look so opulent in content?

Concluding thus, I again felt fully justified in my silence; and determined to prolong it indefinitely as her merited punishment. No longer remained the vestige of a doubt within my mind that if I had been such a fool, during those days of her haranguing, as to have acceded to her desire to insure my life for her,—by this time she would have contrived for me—death!

And as I brooded I endeavored to exult in the triumphant sense of self-preservation, but no effort of will seemed adequate to cast off the fearful spell which, like a vise, still clamped down my spirits; and I can honestly declare that never in my life have I exulted in the sense of a secure freedom, until I found myself behind the hopelessness and the fearlessness of these prison bars.

The days sped by, in tongueless unmeasured hours, until there came the time when I noticed that Nellie did not move about so lightly or glibly as at first. Had the old ailment of fret again fastened upon her? Was her content but a fallacious reaction gathering itself together for fresh ravages of worry?

For I noticed her as she bent over the cradle, during long intervals, and saw that a puzzled anxiety was darkening upon her brow. Then I watched her poring in close absorption over the infant's face as she held it in her arms, sometimes crushing it to her bosom as if to absorb its identity within her own, and again extending it in her grasp, arm-length, for her singular steadfast scrutiny; then, I became suddenly aware that the mysterious wild intensity of her gaze and mien was deepening, incessantly deepening, until at last I recognized fully that she was in the petrifying throes of some terrible inscrutable fear. Ah, fear indeed; benumbed and shaken in the teeth of some ghastly, incommunicable fear—which whitened her lips and made her eyes one great, fixed, glittering stare.

That day, the doctor was summoned again to the house.

Without a word to me the three remained together in the upper chamber—an endless while.

The doctor descended alone.

And I recall how the heavy clack of his heels upon the uncarpeted stairs irritated my morbid nerves, so long habituated to no step more onerous than the slippered one of Nellie.

He asked to speak with me, but scarcely had he terminated the request before he followed it with the unspeakable, the diabolical revelation!

Almighty God of the Accursed—hast Thou centuries wide enough to bury one mortal memory!

Our child was deaf, dumb and blind!

Without another word he was gone; and I found myself alone.

Alone in the clamoring silence of those unchanged walls, alone with the haunted silence of my cowering soul, alone with a bloodless heart, a breathless body, stunned senses—all dead or dying save for the quick brute-like consciousness that I, and naught, could ever die. Horror of horrors!—to live forever in a death that could never die, alone, forever alone, in the silence of a death which no prayer or curse can ever touch or lift. Was this to be *my* curse?

In those hideous moments treading fast upon one another after the juggernaut of the revelation, my shattered will clung only to one intention—to contemplate my own curse—to face my own hell rather than, for one unwary second, to realize that of the others, of the two beings in the chamber above. Far better all solitudes of hell than one peopled with accusing eyes and fingers!

With the tenacity of despair I clung to my intent and thought only of *my* anguish, of *my* nerves as they strove to steady themselves after the shock. What hot torrents can fall into the heart while seemingly withered in cold? And why does it tick like a clock? Is it the timepiece of some eternity which marks off its minute pangs as the only realities?

Unsparingly, I held my attention fast upon the poignant centre of self, until suddenly the door opened and a frenzied creature rushed in. Was this Nellie? Was this the silent wife, the tranquil mother who once had looked up at me from the bed of nativity, so gently, as if she might forgive?

She was unrecognizable in this crazed witch-like woman who burst into the room and fell shrieking upon me, striking me wildly with her small fists, raining mad random blows over my head and chest.

I submitted to them, bowing my head to her attack, and hearkened to her half-strangled words as to a malediction.

"You—you have made her thus. You have cursed my child. Your treatment of me has destroyed her. You have given her this death in life. I hate you, despise you, could kill you for your crime, you—*worse* than murderer!"

Exhausted by her paroxysm of fury, she fell upon the floor and wailed.

Crumpled and motionless, her arms limply outstretched cruciform fashion, she lay and wailed. Wailed and wailed as though she would never end; as though she were filling the cosmos with all its lugubrious notes for the wailing of seas and winds. Ah, blessed is silence, even though the silence of a hell, after the ears have quaked beneath the wails of woman or probed the meaning in the wails of the seas and winds!

That wailing made the ache in my heart unbearable; it, too, seemed to wail and lament with her; and I slunk from the house and roamed the countryside, blindly seeking the remotest vicinities.

The night grew on as I wandered, and from the confusion of its

duskiness there sprang forth myriad lights which revealed to my
dazed senses the fact that my purposeless steps had brought me to
the city.

From the gloom of the nightfall its lights leapt forth and winked
like bubbles, beads, spangles, toy-balloons, everything light, festive,
heart-free and gay—and smote my soul with a more wretched sense
of its own inexorable darkness. Could nothing relieve its cimmerian
shade? As I saw the flamed globes broidering the night scene, I began to hanker, desperately hanker for something to lighten my own
inner weltering ache of darkness. Wildly I wondered if I too might
not find some illuminant to falsify its night. What artifice was pro-
curable to festoon the human gloom? What nepenthe could be
wrested from the world to mitigate the heart's most hideous hurt?
Would not even a devil grant something to assuage such transcendent
anguish as mine?

Like a lurid rift in the smothering pall of my misery—I thought
of drink. And in that flashing second before a drop of liquor had
ever touched my lips I became a drunkard.

I was soon an habitué of the haunts of the god, Alcohol. It did
not deceive my hope, but held out to me its all-consuming arms, in
whose embrace I found I could—forget. To forget became my sole
aim. I feared nothing now but thought and memory; and as soon
as I found how the new god granted draughts of oblivion to its vo-
taries, I voraciously accepted its tyranny; believing no yoke could
be so unbearable as that which shackled me in the *self-conscience* hell.

With those transfiguring draughts I found I could dishevel my
self-consciousness from its aching knot of lucidity, and could glut my
heart into stupors that kept it swimming within the smug orbit of
illusions. The illusion that came to be the one most plied by me was
that I had done nothing in my life which might not have been committed by any strong character under the flagellations of Fate.
With the new springs of fire teeming through my veins, I gained the
assurance that I was indeed a man of strength whom superabundance
of life's forces imbued with the right of might.

Of course there came implacable hours when I was forced to face
my old accursed self, and in a wrecked frame of nerves, inflammation
and unutterable debility. These hours were so exquisite in their tor-

ture that I could never have borne them, suicide would have been the inevitable resort, had I not found I could relieve their extremity by heaping abuse, insults, even blows upon my wife.

I was forced to this by my own pain. Often it gave me a positive delectation of relief to see her cower and pale at my approach. But what never failed to astound me was that she never resisted nor complained at anything after that one everlasting day when she had lain upon the floor and wailed out her soul.

Had she then broken the inner springs that respond to suffering? How otherwise explain her imperviousness to my brutality? Or might it not be that it afforded a counterpoise to some profoundly hidden agony within her own breast? At times when my ill treatment of her surpassed itself, I surprised strange eager gleams in her eyes, as though she, too, in this way welcomed the outrages to self which disheveled it from the curse of too lucid thought and memory.

The child was no longer in the house. As soon as I had girded myself within the cuirass of gin, I had commanded that it be removed forever from our home and placed in one of those asylums dedicated to the care of creatures thus afflicted. My wife had complied without protest. Someone had told her that in such an institution her little one's fingers could be taught to serve for its eyes, ears and tongue; and this may have comforted her, and accounted for the patience which ever afterwards characterized her life.

The subsequent years are confused and indeterminate to me. I seemed to be in some vague sphere detached from all surroundings and contacts, alone with a self that lived like a moribund, solely in its own exaggerated pulse: either speeding softly through my body like a heart-cleaving patter of ghosts or galloping in the glorious deadening paces of sin.

I vaguely remember moving away from the place whose walls had shadowed so dire a drama—and that afterwards we fell so low in the worldly scale that the very memory of the time when I had held a position of trust or of work of any kind, became a grotesque mockery.

I made no attempt to avert the devastation of poverty as it fell fully upon us, but she—yes, shamed as I should be to confess it— she worked; and from the meagre earnings of those humble, marred hands, which now were continually plunged into sud-filled tubs or were pressing out with heavy irons the curled linen of the urbans, from those fateful hands I extracted what portion I required for my unspeakable indulgences.

This lasted for many years. Our life became a routine of poverty and degradation which it seemed no fresh adversity could have power to disturb, when, late one afternoon, I entered our one room, filled with victualled air and the acrid stench of soap, to behold my wife sitting upon the floor, and beside her—our child!

Seven years had now passed since I had last seen her. I had nourished the hope that I was rid of her sight forever. I had forbidden her mother—with unnameable threats—ever to bring her again within the shadow of our shelter; and now her defiance of me transfixed me in speechless amazement.

My wife was sitting upon the floor, one arm around the child's shoulders, and she was talking to this creature who could neither see, nor hear, nor speak, and upon her moving lips there rested its little fingers, lightly, deftly, strangely.

Upon the child's face, protruded in an intentness as though she were listening, hovered the wan, subtle, disturbing smile one sees upon the faces of the blind, upon the faces of all the living dead.

And the mother, too, smiled: smiled as she had done in the days of our courtship, and in the early days after the child was born, before she had learned—the ultimate of calamity. And I noticed how old she had grown since then. Never have I seen anyone age so swiftly as she. Her skull showed through her colorless hair, and breaking over some odd lasting youthfulness of her face were a multitude of puny wrinkles.

In that moment, as I stood there, I remember wondering if the child's fingers were going to touch those wrinkles as they were touching the mouth. And would they find them little graves to be filled with its touch? What was that weird touch seeking? Why did those strange hands do this inexplicable, unheard-of thing?

How did they dare—how did these two confederates against my peace —dare afflict me with such a harrowing sight?

At this I started from my stupor of surprise. That vision before me aimed arrows of agony straight at my heart that cut it in a thousand intricacies of smarting pain; the old burning pain which I fancied was buried deep beneath the poison flora of drink. I started from my stupor of surprise and demanded, hoarsely:

"What does this mean?"

My wife looked at me. And I saw that there was no vestige of fear in her, only a consummate calm that faced me in redoubtability as she replied.

"Richard, I have brought her home to stay. She is blessed with the strangest gift. She can understand one's words by feeling the mouth as it utters them."

And in her loss of all fear of me—she even seemed oblivious to my presence—she smiled and talked again to the child, whose hands —so like those of Nellie before our marriage—hovered, fleetingly, searchingly, wooingly, upon her lips.

The affront to my authority was inexpiable. I paled and trembled in the blood-curdling intensity of my indignation. My tongue thickened and clove in dry inarticulation to the palate before I could free its rage of speech. Then I swore, I raved, I paced the floor in violent steps, back and forth, near the doorway; for somehow, even though I was lost to all reason, I could not approach nearer to those two as they sat together, in protective enfoldment, beneath the window whence the livid skies shone in, stamped with the dim pearl crescent of the evening.

As I stormed and raved my wife held the child tightly to her bosom; but she, who could neither see, nor hear, nor speak, seemed suddenly to become aware of my presence, for if ever a face expressed inquiry, hers did, as suddenly she raised it and approached it close to her mother's in a heartrending interrogativeness.

"Yes, darling," the mother said, as if she understood her, "there is someone here. It is your father."

At this some curious guttural sound burst from the throat of the little thing and she sprang from her mother's arms and came running toward me, her smile brightening as though it sought to greet and welcome.

Yes, that child fled to me gladly as I cursed her; and when she reached me, I stood instantly motionless and mute in some freezing horror of surprise.

For she reached me as directly and swiftly as if she could *see* exactly where I stood, and then tiptoeing up to me, she placed her fingers upon my lips and waited.

Waited!

Oh, God, for *what?*

With those chill fingers upon my lips every demon in my being was unloosened to fight for life. My flesh armed itself in a cold ferocity, my spirit empoisoned itself with the malevolence of mortal dread. To make them drop their touch from off my lips, my mouth filled with imprecations and the lust to bite them; but they *waited*, with an expectant suspensive touch, which rendered me helpless to speak, or bite, or move.

"Richard, say something to her," said my wife, and her eyes were streaming. "I beg of you to say something kind to her. She will understand it. Treat me as you like but do not hurt her. Take it all out on me later—if you must!"

But I could say nothing with those fingers upon my lips. They choked me, they racked me in every fibre with the old damnation of silence. They threatened to extinguish my very life with their stifling touch—and drawing backwards from them, stealthily, by infinite degrees, lest they arrest my intent, I turned and fled madly from the house.

Until that day my life had been wretched and wicked, but from now on it became appalling. I plunged deeper and deeper into the paradisic-perdition of drink, for now I had new fears to drown, fears far more terrible than those of thought and memory. Fears of the future, fears of the supernatural, fears which the touch of those fingers had driven into my life, and from now on made it—mere *life*— unutterably tortured and despairing though it was, by far preferable to the things that waited, to the influences of the Superearthly, to those awful unknowable Elements which meet and claim us *inescapably* in death!

Earth holds no persecution which cannot be escaped in the respites found in drink. But what of the persecutions *after* death! Ah, from them there could be found no respite. Therefore I must live.

So I lived; and lived in fear.

Constant fear of those child fingers which had pressed upon me, that one ineffaceable moment, and repeated their atrocious ordeal every time I was compelled to return to the place wherein it dwelt.

Yes, inconceivable as it seems, upon my every entrance there the creature fled to me and pressed its fingers upon my lips, to paralyze me with terror, to craze me with the unfathomable mystery of its haunting, expectant, waiting touch. Never could I speak or move with it upon me; and it greeted me without fail every time I returned to that place. For the creature who could neither see nor hear nor speak, yet *knew*, unerringly, of my presence the instant I entered the door.

And why did I return there? Why did I subject myself to this torture, more frightful than was ever devised by arch-fiend of hell?

Because I was now thoroughly incapacitated for procuring through any means or labor of my arms, the wherewithal by which I could secure the oblivion of drink. Without drink I could not live. And I must live.

Hence I was forced to return there, forced to resort to her for what I required. And dearly did I pay for it, well was virtue venged, when my funds were exhausted and I was compelled to go to that spot where *it* waited and ran to meet me upon my every entrance.

One night I was in one of my familiar haunts, sitting alone in a corner of the lurid, noisy room, when I observed a stranger enter who was sufficiently under the influence of drink to become at once jocose and intimate in his address as he leaned over the bar and conversed with one of the attendants. After he had emptied his glass he became still more profuse in his manner and while confiding something to the man, with an affectation of surreptitiousness, he pulled from his coat pocket a thick roll of bills and displayed it to him, chuckling.

The sight of this instantaneously aroused and electrified me; for it suggested an idea which clutched my mind in the fierceness of its first hope.

" If I could get that from him, it would purchase me freedom, a lengthy freedom for months, perhaps for years, from the necessity of returning to that abhorrent place wherein awaits *its* persecution."

Ah, impossible to describe how this hope appealed to my despair ravaged mind! No sooner had it presented itself than I resolved upon it. By fair means or foul I determined to secure possession of that magic roll.

With no method of procedure resolved upon save this grimly unshakable intent, I approached the stranger and made his acquaintance, with a resumption of all my old suave, ingratiating manners of the past.

Soon we were in that precipitate intimacy achieved by drink. But I—with an acumen and will force of which I would not have previously believed myself capable—refrained from taking any more that night, but plied him cleverly. He said that he had recognized me as a friend the moment he had seen me and knew that I was one to be trusted implicitly. Therefore I perceived with satisfaction how easy it was going to be to attain my object.

I permitted him to confide to me various intimacies of his life whilst the hours wore on beyond midnight, and he at last reached the precise stage of semi-helplessness I desired.

Then we went out together, arm-in-arm, into the moist dappled blackness of the night.

I waited until we were far from the last house, straggling on the environs of the town, and were upon the margin of the river, thickly ambushed in trees, before I insinuated my hand deftly into his pocket —as he laughed at one of his own jokes, he was a merry trusting soul!—and extracted the roll there.

My dexterity blundered or he was not so drunk as I had believed; for no sooner had I the roll in my hand than he became aware of what I had done, and dropping his clasp on my arm, open-mouthed in his alarm, he balanced himself, as he eyed me and then began to plead. He pleaded between hiccoughs for his money as though he were pleading for his life. I started to run from him, but had taken but a few steps when he began to yell. Simultaneously I realized the doom upon me if his clamor were heard and so I was forced to return to him, to hold him and struggle until I succeeded in plunging my pocket knife deep into his throat, and then drew it, nauseatingly, from ear to ear.

When it was all over I found that the front of my shirt, over which the coat had been open, was badly saturated and that during the scuffle—he had prolonged it with a convulsive force unbelievable in one so soft and fat and drunk—I had lost my hat and dared not return to seek where it lay. I could not return even though it seemed I ought to drag that body to the waterside and throw it in; for I feared to saturate myself still more incriminatingly in that copious blood.

Already the lambent flood of the dawn was falling from the red-rimmed horizon and sickling over the landscape with its disenshroudments. Wisps of vapor hung here and there over the ground like crusts from the whitening skies. From afar the long-drawn note of a train whistle punctured the vast monotony of the air.

I buttoned my coat high over my wet bosom, and for a brief spell I felt *quiet*, in that sense of accomplishment, that instinctive sense of having consummated a *law*, which every supreme deed, whether good or evil, creates in the human heart.

Then the thought of the penalty of murder darted into my mind. Death! *Again* death threatened me.

Always I had placed an inordinate value upon life—and now after I had taken that of another, it appeared still more inestimably of value. Does the love of life fatten upon that of which it robs others? I believe so. No human being loves life so intensely as the one who destroys it in others; thus a murderer represents the triumph of that passion which is fostered by maternity.

As I realized that I was a murderer, I realized how precious to me my life had become, and with what a delirious lust I was determined to protect myself against any mete of justice. I recollected that murderers had invariably been detected by trifling things which could have been avoided so easily had they used acumen and foresight and not been so fatally transported by excitement, haste or panic. This I must avoid. Every move must be reasoned out: every possibility foreseen.

There was nothing upon the scene of the murder which could possibly connect me with it except the hat. When it fell from my head I was not conscious of it, and it might have rolled into the river, we were so near. But even if found it could not present any real danger, as no mark of identification was on it and it was the facsimile of the hats of many men who moved in the circles I frequented. Therefore I concluded it could furnish no clue of any kind and I could safely leave it wherever it lay.

The only circumstance which could possibly attract attention to me was the fact that I was hatless and might be seen thus in the early

morning by someone who would later supply the suspicious incident to the scavengers of crime. I must not be seen until I had procured another hat and as there was no shop within too great a distance to reach safely, there was no alternative but to return to my
home where I remembered there was some sort of an old discarded
headgear. To avert all risk of observation, I decided to take a circuitous route, avoiding the highways and pursuing the most desolated
pathways over fields and hills until I arrived at my destination.

With this single idea of being unseen, and concentrated wholly
upon every safeguarding precaution, I set forth on my way in a
stealthy, darting pilgrimage through the dew-drenched lands and
silver-tipped trees, once or twice breathlessly startled by the looming
head of a cow or horse through foliage or over a fence—and never
once remembered *what* was awaiting me there at the end of my
journey.

Had the thought of *it* occurred clearly to my mind, I believe that,
even then, I would have retraced my steps and undertaken to seek my
hat *there*, near the dreadful corpse, rather than have gone to that
other haunted spot wherein awaited the thing that had crazed me.

But possessed wholly by the alarmed passion of self-preservation
—it actually did not occur to my mind until I was at the doorway;
too late, alas, to retreat when life was the forfeit.

When I entered I saw that the creature was playing upon the
floor with some bits of kindling wood and—for the first time since
it abode with us—it seemed unaware of my entrance.

My wife was making the fire in the stove and took no notice of
me; so long accustomed was she to the wildness and irregularity of
my habits.

Very softly and noiselessly, I began to search for my hat. I
could not recall exactly where I had left it, since it had not been
worn for a long while—and I rummaged among the encumbered
closets and cupboards during what seemed an interminable length of
time, before I found it.

Pulling it down hastily upon my head, I drew a deep breath of
relief and felt excited almost ungovernably, for the first time since
the deed.

I plunged for the door, when simultaneously I was stopped by a
trampling sound outside, and then a knocking.

My wife opened the door and there stepped in two men and an officer.

Immediately I knew *why* they were there and saw that their attitude was one of uncertainty. Cunningly I divined it behind their pretentious pose of authority.

They presented no warrant. There was no threat or suspicion in their manner. They merely stated, quietly and simply, that I had been seen leaving a saloon with a man who had been found murdered an hour ago and that I was to be called upon to give an account of my movements since the time I was seen with the murdered man.

Wild beasts when caged can be mastered by those who enter their cage with perfect certitude. They cower and abdicate to those in whom they sense an imperative certainty. But let them falter ever so little from it, let them weaken the merest trifle in their mental grip, and the beasts sense it—through what mysterious power God only knows—and instantaneously will spring and rend. Like a caged beast, I perceived their uncertainty and at once realized that I was master of the situation.

Indeed I felt a veritable braggadocio of courage as I thought of my weapon, the old ingratiating ways of my college days which were wont to conquer the ire and suspicion of its authorities—and summoning them now to my aid, with my gentlest, most high-bred air, I prepared to launch forth upon an ingenious explanation that came to me in one of those flashes of genius which dart through the night of danger and which I felt convinced—with a fixed insensate conviction—could not fail to establish an irrefutable alibi, when——

Suddenly, without warning, without hint of its intent, the little creature upon the floor—the thing that could neither see, nor hear, nor speak—sprang up with light feet and ran to me and placed her fluttering fingers upon my lips.

My words froze down into the marrow of my bones and made all silent. My blood forsook its channels. My brain dizzied from the abrupt cessation of its train of thought, and mute, stricken, aghast, held in the talons of unearthly Fear, I was solely conscious of those monstrous fingers pressing, pressing down and down, deeper and deeper, until at last they reached and unlocked the foe in my breast.

I was lost. I shouted:

" Yes, it was I who killed him. I will lie no more. Take me. Slay me. I am many times a murderer!"

As the words burst from my lips, *Its* hands fell away from them as if at last satisfied, in fulfilment. They had gained their end.

And I—delivering myself to the foe, to death, found that instead —*I was free!*

Free from fear of them; free from all Fear.

And as the minions of the law fell upon and manacled me, I could have laughed aloud in the victory of my fearlessness. For those fingers had wrenched open my soul but to brand upon it this message:

" *He who admits suffering and punishment into his heart has nothing to fear.*"

Thus have I procured my gaiety.

Good-bye, sad world; I pity you. For I, alone of men, know how you could exchange the wild pain of your gloom for the fantastic lightness of my gaiety!

THE PROBLEM OF RABIES

F. C. WALSH, M.D.

THE State of New York has been battling with an epidemic of rabies for the past three years, with varying success. During that period, one hundred and five persons were bitten by animals that were known positively to be mad. Thousands of other persons were bitten, whether or not by mad animals, was unknown at the time; but—and this is an important point—these thousands suffered just as much in mental anguish, until they knew all danger was past, as did those one hundred and five who were known absolutely to have been infected by the terrible poison. Of the one hundred and five actual victims, twelve died in agonies, the devilish tortures of which surpass anything ever conceived in the dark annals of man's inhumanity to man. And the shame written large in these figures, taken from official statistics; the pity of the condition existing behind these cold facts; looms painfully before our civic consciousness, when the truth is borne home to us that all this actual suffering and mental fear, is wholly preventable and unnecessary. Any tragic happening which is preventable, is deplorable.

The average person is in the habit of thinking that the subject of madness in animals is something to be considered only in the months of July and August, and then to be put aside and entirely ignored for the remaining months, particularly the winter ones. The New York figures, taken alone, show the folly of this belief. They show that in that State there were as many victims as a result of rabies in the months of January and February, as there were in the hot " dog days " of July and August. The New York figures, alone, should show the importance of instituting a continuous, radical policy, with the determined object of stamping out, forever, the ravages of such a terror,—terror at least to the individual affected. Good government in public policy, aims to strike at all evils which are a menace to even one single individual. But epidemics of rabies,— serious ones,—are ravaging other of our States at this very moment, giving to the subject an interest of more than local importance, and not permitting us to cast unfavorable reflections on the State of New York alone.

The human mortality is of paramount importance. But of some interest in its bearing on the animal industries, and as a further means of conveying a better idea of the number of rabid animals at large, it must be stated that, in addition to the one hundred and five human victims already mentioned, the incomplete records of New York show that ten horses were bitten by mad animals, of which number, five horses died; sixty-eight cattle were attacked, of which thirty-eight died; while eleven swine were bitten, ten of these dying.

As a matter of fairness in assigning whatever degree of credit or discredit may be due, let it be said that New York State has been making spasmodic efforts to stamp out the epidemic, and has, during the three years of its continuance, put under quarantine two villages, seven cities, and fifty-one townships. Not a very drastic perform-ance, to be sure; but let us hope that it has not been entirely useless in preventing, to even a slight extent, the further spread of the dis-ease, and that it has lessened, in some measure, the rate of human mortality.

Indiana is another State, remote enough from New York to have problems of its own, in which rabies has been rampant for a longer time than in New York, namely, four years. Since 1906, its ravages have held sway almost unchecked, causing some anxious nights, if not sleepless ones, to those whose lot it is to solve such problems, and devise ways and means for the prevention of further havoc. During this four years' epidemic in Indiana, the number of persons bitten by animals that were known to be mad, was one hundred and sixty-five. These figures take no account of the hundreds of persons who were bitten by animals merely suspected of madness. As in the case of New York, vast numbers of live stock, hundreds of which were never reported, also suffered heavily. As an instance of the great amount of loss and damage that can be done by one single mad animal, it is a matter of State record that one lone mad dog put to death no less than fourteen of a herd of choice dairy cows, the property of a dairy-man at Richmond, Indiana. The disease is fast spreading to all parts of the State, and the outlook for its suppression is at present very unpromising.

Rabies is a disease of the lower animals, and is properly termed hydrophobia when present in man. The disease itself is identical in either case. It has held the interest of the popular mind from the beginnings of history. From the days of Aristotle to the present, it has been considered one of the most strange and peculiar of diseases. It has always been of special interest to the scientific world. As is generally known, one of the greatest savants of all time, Louis Pasteur, devoted some of the best years of an arduous life to its study.

Until recently, the exact nature of the poison transmitted from a mad animal to another, when bitten, baffled all investigation. To-day, it is widely conceded, with little or no contradiction, that the infectious poison, thus transmitted, belongs to the group of microscopical parasites known as protozoa,—the minutest forms of animal life,—and spoken of specifically as Negri " bodies," after Negri, who discovered them. These malicious " bodies " attack from choice, and perhaps necessity, the nervous tissues of the animal economy, and hence are always found, when present, in the brain or spinal cord of their victim. Parasites of a similar nature, but of quite another species, are well, but unfavorably, known as the cause of malarial fever, and are always present in the blood stream of those who are afflicted with " fever and ague." In a case of the latter, it is an easy matter to take a drop of blood from the patient, and after examination with the microscope, state definitely whether malaria is present, or not.

In the case of an animal which gives cause to suspect the presence of madness, or rabies, the only recourse which would justify one in making a positive statement, is in killing the animal, and making a thorough examination of the brain, in a search for the essential Negri " bodies." Only after such a rigid examination, can it be safely predicted that a human being, bitten by a suspectedly mad animal, will be safe, or otherwise, from the consequences of possible infection caused by the bite.

It is of the utmost importance, in every instance, to make sure as to whether the animal that does the biting really has rabies, as the consequences from the mere fear of the disease, a condition known as " false rabies," or pseudo-hydrophobia, are almost as pitiful, and probably, in a small number of high-strung, nervous individuals, even as fatal, as in the instances of true rabies. No one is comfortable with the possibility of madness hanging over him. There is one redeeming feature, which offsets, to a slight extent, this excessive fear, when one has been bitten by some animal, supposedly mad. It may be said, truthfully, that all persons bitten by a mad animal, do not necessarily suffer from the affliction, as the resources of the human system are sometimes sufficient to produce from its own blood an antidote powerful enough to overcome the poisonous influence of the infection. This is not intended to justify the least neglect in finding out as early as possible whether in any instance the animal suspected were mad or not.

Of all domestic animals, our friend the dog is oftenest afflicted with madness, and therefore the most to be feared, and safeguarded against. He commits enough serious and fatal ravages, in the aggregate, to warrant the most careful watching. In Paris, France, of a list of nineteen hundred and three of all kinds of animals which had bitten people, and which were suspected of being afflicted with rabies, there were as many as eight hundred and thirty-three dogs; of the remaining animals in this official list, there were two hundred and forty-seven horses, six cats, and seven others of the various domestic animals. It will be seen from this, that the dog is not the only offender, though he leads all others by a large plurality. In Prussia, that country of statistical delight, there are numerous instances, officially listed, of bites from rabid cattle, and even from that mildest of animals, ordinarily, the deer. As regards Russia, one would naturally suppose that wolves would figure largely, as a source of danger, in biting other animals and man. Russian statistics substantiate the correctness of this supposition, In our own country, as any western ranchman will verify, the depredations of rabid wolves among colts and young cattle afford a noticeable number of instances as a cause of death. It is of interest to note that young colts seem to be especially susceptible to the poisonous effects of wolf bites, probably because there is some element lacking in their blood, from which the blood itself forms an antidote to the poison, which is nature's own defence against this and all other diseases of an infeetious character.

This fact brings us to one of the most fascinating chapters in science and discovery,—that pertaining to Pasteur's studies in rabies, and his preparation of a serum to prevent fatal consequences after a person has been so unfortunate as to be bitten by some rabid animal. His discovery is especially noteworthy, inasmuch as it opened the way for the discovery of special serums for the treatment of other infectious diseases, the most brilliant achievement being that which gave us a sure weapon to combat successfully that formerly most dreaded disease of childhood,—diphtheria.

Like many great and beneficent discoveries, that of Pasteur has had one bad effect, through no fault of the discovery itself. It seems to be a common law of human nature, that when we once have succeeded in finding a certain cure for any given disease, we at once relax our vigilance in guarding ourselves against any possible contraction of that disease; in other words, we are too apt to cast all preventive policies to the winds, feeling a security, oftentimes false, in the very fact that we have a safe and efficient remedy at hand. This attitude, in both public and private life, is only mentioned to be condemned.

It is quite true that in most instances the early use of the Pasteur treatment gives apparently brilliant results; but of three hundred and seventy-four persons who received the treatment in Berlin and Breslau, according to figures recently published, eight died in spite of the treatment; of thirty-two persons who were not inoculated against the disease, but two died. The conclusion to be drawn from these series of cases is, that where the Pasteur treatment was used, the number of fatalities was lowered by about two per cent. Not a flattering inducement to encourage one to expose oneself heedlessly to a possible contraction of the disease; nor sufficiently brilliant to justify our casting to the winds any practical policy of prevention.

There are greater evils and problems than that of rabies, but in attacking the greater, we cannot, in justice to ourselves, afford to forget the lesser ones. A glance at the figures quoted, in the case of New York, Indiana, Breslau and Berlin, will be sufficient to demonstrate that the problem is one that requires serious attention; at least two of our sovereign States have been contending with continuous epidemics of the disease for the past three and four years. What is the trouble? Why have they failed in suppressing the disease and its devastations? What is there to offer that will aid in solving the problem?

In the first place, the whole problem is not a medical, but a sociopolitical one. It is well enough for the medical men to handle the individual cases that have been bitten by a rabid animal, but if the disease is to be prevented and suppressed, it will not be done by the medical profession. The medical man is a poor executive, and proverbially a poor politician. Individually, he is well able to suggest ways and means, but in any movement demanding harmonious, organized effort, the rank and file of the profession are an absolute failure. Clearly, then, actual accomplishment will have to come from without. The suggestion of a way once given, the people will have to act for themselves. This they can and will do, once they rightly understand the means of action, and its necessity.

Any average person, even when he possesses no scientific information whatever, is naturally interested in anything pertaining to his personal welfare, or his property interests, and ready to act on any information gained. If he can be shown by a plain, unvarnished statement, his own responsibility in the prevention of an ever menacing peril, all the better for himself and his citizenship. Impending perils, like the poor, we have with us always, and though many are of lesser importance, these must also be constantly borne in mind, and their dangers pointed out, lest we forget that the prevention of disease, all disease, is better than a cure. A public conscience, once aroused and rightly informed, is the first step toward the eradication of all preventable diseases.

If we can rid the dog of rabies, the greatest source of danger to the human being, as regards this particular disease, is forever removed. Eternal vigilance, and the continuous pursuance of a definite policy, day after day, year in and year out, are absolutely essential to this end. From figures just compiled by the French governmental authorities, it is clearly demonstrated that whenever their rigid crusade against unmuzzled and stray dogs was to the slightest degree relaxed, rabies amongst animals, and their human victims, instantly increased at a most alarming rate. Whenever the crusade was again resumed at its full vigor, the number of victims immediately decreased. In other words, the rise or fall in the number of victims afforded a most accurate index to the degree of vigilance evinced, in the campaign against the undesirables of the canine race. But, thanks to a continuous crusade on the part of the

French authorities, Doctor Letulle, of Paris, has shown in a series of very exact statistics that from four hundred and seventy-four cases of rabies in 1902, the number had fallen to only thirteen cases in 1909, truly an instance in which figures speak most eloquently for themselves. Paris has succeeded in reducing its number of fatalities from rabies, by impounding and destroying from twelve thousand to fourteen thousand unmuzzled and vagrant dogs each year. Our mistake, or one of our mistakes, has been in not continuously persisting in a selected course, when once we have found it to be a correct one.

Other countries have succeeded in reducing to a minimum the number of cases of rabies in both animals and man. One country, in particular, has exterminated the pest completely. We ourselves have been primarily on the right road; our start was good, but we have handled the problem too half-heartedly, and have either lost interest, or expected results too soon. That is our weakness.

Foremost of all methods in dealing with the question of the suppression of rabies is the one so successfully advocated and employed in France. To advocate is one thing; to do is quite another. We are too much addicted to the former in so many things relating to public sanitary policies. But let us not mince matters further. We must come to the point. Every dog without an owner, every stray dog, and every unmuzzled dog, regardless of ownership, must be rounded up and painlessly put out of the way; not merely during the mid-summer months, but during all the winter months as well, for our vigilance cannot safely be relaxed for one single hour, in any one month, week or day of the entire year. That is, if we wish to exterminate the terrorizing, destructive nuisance. Unless the policy suggested, or a better one, be carried into effect, and especially in those States already mentioned where rabies is epidemic, we may expect its ravages to increase, or forever go on unnecessarily.

There is no room for sentiment in any discussion of the matter; the stray, ownerless dog must go. It will be doing the homeless canine a kind turn, anyway. There is another thing which would be a useful pleasure to see accomplished: that is, the enactment of a law making the owner criminally responsible for any overt act on the part of his dog, particularly when that dog goes mad. This would have sufficient force to make the owner exceedingly careful in seeing to it that his dog was muzzled, or cause him to get rid of the animal altogether. In either case, the public would receive the benefit. This course would apply very aptly to the country districts, where it is often a difficult matter to enforce rigidly the law which requires all dogs to be muzzled.

The entire question is a social one, and the means for its solution lie near at hand, within grasp of the people. A momentary consideration of the figures already presented as regards conditions in New York and Indiana should give cause for serious thought and early drastic action. But let any policy, once decided on, be persistently prosecuted in every detail, until the bark of the mad dog shall no longer be heard in the land. England has succeeded in stamping out the disease completely. There is no longer any rabies in any part of England, and the chances of its ever implanting itself there are very small, as no dog is allowed to be taken into the country without undergoing a lengthy quarantine. So let New York State and Indiana take notice, and courage; to the other States which may congratulate themselves on being free from such a vexatious pest, there is one word of warning: " in time of peace prepare for war," whether the prospective foe be a man-o'-war or a microbe.

NOTES ON VERNON LEE

VAN WYCK BROOKS

THE modern conception of criticism as an art implies, I think, a changing conception of art itself. Criticism, as embodying the theory of art, peers ahead in the darkness and suggests the direction it shall take, surveys the land for it. Now creative criticism if it means anything means the treatment of works and intellects and periods not in relation to themselves and each other, but in relation to universal life. How far then will the creative critic confine himself to a certain branch of art, or a certain period, or to art exclusively at all? Only so far as the accidents of a momentary inclination or training lay the stress upon this or that detail: for being admitted into the family of artists he has taken all life as his province.

Now the central fact of life, to which all its forces tend, is conduct. And I should like in passing to glance at the two most considerable modern critics who have concerned themselves wholly with art, and to ask why it is that the one found while the other failed to find a synthesis of his ideas. . . . From the study of æsthetics Pater arrived at some such conclusion as this: the object of life is to find out the kind of situation that calls out our own special hidden fire; to unite those scattered moments for which we have spent our lives experimenting and in which we seem to have realized ourselves; to remember the circumstances in which they arose, to demand them ever afresh. Now this conclusion might of course have been reached through the study of biology or geology or the history of religions, because all syntheses imply a counsel on conduct. In Pater we find a conclusion which is consistent with every stage in the development that led up to it. In a word Pater never lost himself in his themes, never failed to draw them in—as illustrations essentially—of his own growing view of life.

In the case of J. A. Symonds we have a result quite different. Symonds's life was entirely occupied in writing round himself, catching now at this mind, now at that, apprehending everywhere the fragments of general ideas. He wrote lives or studies of Michelangelo,

Ben Jonson, Sidney, Boccaccio, Dante—of whom not?—eagerly going out in all directions: a disorderly gathering of information suggesting the pressure of a facile gift and an eager delight in ideas
too readily accepted. Symonds had in fact no gift for conclusions.
Those of whom he wrote were to him conclusions in themselves, or if
links in a chain the chain was that of a world of speculation which left
him without a sense of having in some way and for his individual set
of circumstances formed the latest link of it. He knew that the world
of thought had not intended him to be one of its points of crystallization. What central place in his work then is there which may
prove to have the power of expressing him into immortality? Well,
the fragments of an autobiography and a diary—not yet, I think,
wholly published—in which we find a soul struggling and baffled.
And the final value of his other books will be perhaps that through
them he became conscious of this agitation. In the diary he writes:
" To emulate others nobler than myself is my desire,—but I cannot
get beyond."

Pater's theory of art accepts art substantially as it is and is
occupied with its use in stimulating us to the expression of ourselves
in terms not of art but of life. But the artist himself—why is he
forced to resort to a secondary medium? The artist desires above
all things to be normal—all his work is a straining to right himself,
to become normal. And the normal man finds it possible to express
himself simply through life. Every moment in which one is really
conscious of oneself is an idea, and art expresses these moments in
the form of ideas. Now an idea is before all an incentive to live,
an assurance of the wonderful importance of being alive: yet in
order to be expressed in terms of life it has to be practicable, to
have the conditions of life around it. The tragedy in the lives of
almost all men of ideas has been that they were unable to live their
ideas. An idea essentially compels expression, and if it cannot be
expressed through life it has to be expressed through some other
medium; and men of ideas whose ideas are not practicable and who
have had a gift for sensuous forms have expressed their ideas
through those forms. Properly an idea has neither beginning nor
end. Expressed through the natural channels of life in conduct it
develops out of one idea and into another: it has no sharp edges;

it appears and passes.   To express it in terms of art is to call a halt
to its natural expansion, to urge upon it a temporary reckoning.
So that all art has been a kind of Limbo in which all the ideas that
have not been able to fit themselves for life have had a dim unearthly
incarnation.

Upon what assumption has all art been based?   That life itself
is insufficiently expressive.   In what manner is art to be made to
contribute to conduct?   How are the types of experience that have
hitherto found expression only through art to be drawn into the
service of life, to be given the chance of expressing themselves in
conduct?   Under what conditions, to be attained how, can the artist
reach normality?   How, in brief, is the pulse of the world to be made
to beat as fast as the pulse of the artist?   These, I think, are the
questions with which creative criticism will have to occupy itself.
And to these questions Vernon Lee seems to me to have offered an
interesting response.

II

Two points connect Vernon Lee immediately with both Pater and
Symonds.   She was at first, as they were always, occupied with pure
æsthetics.   Her equipment in facts too was much the same as theirs,
although in her study of the Renaissance the emphasis fell rather
upon its aftermath.   In her early books one observes that the eighteenth century obsessed her less for its lookings-forward than as
the last age in which the Renaissance mood remained authentic,—
remaining so remote from its original springs that its manifestations were highly tenuous, complex and subtle.   From the first she
wrote with authority.   Her impulse came from the study of facts,
facts accepted and half-forgotten and fertilized with fresh facts
until her mind was unable to generate a barren or a superficial
thought or a thought not hung about and garlanded with associations.   With her the process gave birth not to opinions but to radia-
tions, sudden risings to the surface and the sunlight of strange fragments of human experience bearing with them odors and evanescent
hues and curious forms that belong to the depths whence they have
come: fragments really of those wraithlike existences we call race,
history, tradition, which in the hands of art become nations and

periods. For without art there is no such thing as a nation or a period: without art the past is as formless, as essentially non-existing, as the future.

Vernon Lee gave herself at first entirely to the creating of nations and periods. And one of the charming examples of her early gifts, interests, and theories is *The Prince of the Hundred Soups* (1883), a "puppet-show in narrative," in which the traditional Italian mask comedy with all its type characters is written out into a tale as delicate and whimsical as *The Rose and the Ring*.

. . . It is the year 1695 in the pompous little principality of Bobbio, all of whose twenty-four cannons are celebrating the accession of the Magnificent Pantalone Busdrago I. These acclamations are not grateful to the ears of the aristocratic Generalissimo Scappino Scappini because Pantalone's great-grandfather was a sausage-maker. Nevertheless Leandro and Giacinta, son and daughter of the rival houses, are madly in love with each other. Now the doge's chief function is to consume during his hundred days of office a hundred soups, prepared after a secret recipe by the ducal cook. . . . How shall the blackhearted Scappino reduce the upstart rival? —by concocting of course a false and altogether abominable recipe which he browbeats the miserable cook into serving out for the unsuspecting doge. . . . Presently the latter finds that his dinner grows more and more unpalatable until a point comes when, like Chubby Augustus, he simply cannot, cannot eat his soup at all. Driven into forgetfulness of the results of treason, he has a little box of sandwiches smuggled in to him each day: Scappino entraps him and will have wrought his ruin—but for a certain lady. . . . This is the lovely Signora Olimpia Fantastici, the celebrated singer who has finally agreed, upon receiving the sum of a five years' tax upon the entire principality, to come to Bobbio, sing for at least an hour, and thus confer perpetual lustre upon the reign of Doge Pantalone. . . . But when she finds that Bobbio has a secret, the recipe of the state soup, she utterly refuses to sing a note until she has been told the secret. Of course Olimpia has her way—but she gets the false recipe. Thus she holds in her hands the fate of the rivals. . . . The final day has come. Pantalone is to be condemned. All Bobbio is in the square. . . . Has anyone a word to say for Pantalone? . . . A coach dashes up. Olimpia steps out. In a word she sets all things right. . . . "Good!" cries Olimpia. "And now I will sing!"

Who can doubt that this little romance exists for the last sentence? that this little world has been set in motion to listen to an hour's song? . . . In this, too, the world of art is offered as existing for its own sake. One detects in it no searchings of conscience.

III

I fancy that when for once a writer turns aside into an unaccustomed medium—writes a novel as we now know that Taine did, and Renan, and Samuel Butler—

"Puts to proof art alien to the artist's
Once, and only once,"—

I fancy that in such a case the second line of these two forms an essential part of the desire expressed in the first: that a unique need suggests the wish, a need for the discovery of a medium that offers none of the familiar rewards but will share in the desperate intention. In 1883 Vernon Lee published a novel, *Miss Brown*, which is I suppose the most colossal piece of amateurishness that can still rightly be claimed for literature. (As a detail, one feels in reading this novel that the writer is never quite certain whether a character should be made to *remark* or *observe*.) Now the only figure in this book that entirely fails to exist is Miss Brown's brother, Richard Brown, who is offered as a great labor-leader, formerly a miner. Inadvertently he is made to quote Pater and to be familiar with far too many other unlaborlike things to serve in true fiction. (In Vernon Lee one sees that the trappings of the mind are not always portable baggage for a traveling spirit.) But this laborman *does* throw a black shadow over the languorous twilight of those very small pre-Raphaelite satellites of his sister: and she, like a great slumbering Titan, awfully pure, stirs in her dream. She has all noble traits except receptiveness, all effectual traits except adaptiveness. She opens her eyes upon two worlds: on the one side her husband, the Priors, old Saunders,—the world, for better or worse, of art; and on the other Richard Brown. . . . Three facts in the story are significant. These are: the character of Miss Brown, the failure of Richard Brown to assume a form approaching in coherence the figures who stand for the world of art, and the fact that Richard Brown, inchoate as he is, forms a disquieting element in the story.

In perspective one sees that this novel is a symbolical expression of Vernon Lee's transitional period.

In the opening of *Juvenilia* (1887), she tells of a kind of conversion through which she has been led to put away childish things:

" For do what we will, devote ourselves exclusively to the pleasant and certain things of this life, shut our eyes and ears resolutely to the unpleasant and uncertain, we shall be made, none the less, to take part in the movement that alters the world. . . . The question therefore is, in which direction our grain of dust's weight shall be thrown? "

This new light shines upon two collections of dialogues, which deal as their sub-titles say with " duties and aspirations." These books are *Baldwin*, issued in the same year with *Juvenilia*, and *Althea* (1893). In these dialogues a number of shadowy, half-allegorical but modern men and women take part, wandering in lovely scenes at sunset or after dawn: little pictures of the world about them are set here and there as a kind of refrain, as if nature in the arrangement of some cloud-group or the uncertain waving of an ilex-tree were glad to give a universal application to each of these conflicting turns of the human mind.

In *Baldwin* we observe an effort to throw the grain of dust's weight decisively in a certain direction. Baldwin is intended to picture the perfect positivist, cheerful, sane, well-organized, convinced of the self-sufficiency of the world. His mission is to clear the ground, to rid his friends of sentiment, superstition, or faith in any but the useful issues of morality. . . . We discover that he is however but a cloudy symbol. . . . He himself offers a doubt as to whether science, in its ultimate elimination of pain, will not thus take away part of the steel upon which character sharpens itself. Thus in the end he becomes non-committal.

We are told that Althea is naturally the pupil of Baldwin. From him certainly she has learned that there is a certain futility in attempting to cast one's grain of dust's weight in any rigid direction. Althea is described as "one of those rare natures so strangely balanced that they recognize truth as soon as they see it . . . natures which know spontaneously what the rest of us learn by experience and reflection; fortunate samples of what we may perhaps all become but, for that very reason, incapable of serving as guides in the difficult way of becoming it." . . . Here at last assertion is thrown to the winds and we have a personality (Miss Brown again really) so entirely in solution, so inherently intelligent and pure, that we recognize in her the achieved human soul, in whom the serenity of perfect intuition has succeeded the battles of thought and in whom progress has arrived at its destination. . . . In Althea we contemplate the ideal of a future in which character will have taken the place of thought.

Althea urges nothing, but she offers above all, as the wind and the stars offer it, a silent reproof to all propaganda. And the more we come to identify her with Vernon Lee's view of life, evolving but always essentially the same, we discover a reason for the failure of Baldwin to justify his apparent assertiveness and for the incoherency of the propagandist Brown amid a group of clearly-conceived artists who in all their insignificance are at least passive.

It is Althea who speaks in the collection of essays, *Gospels of Anarchy* (1908), which are devoted to Tolstoy and Nietzsche, Emerson, Whitman, and Ruskin, Professor James and H. G. Wells. Here we find that Vernon Lee has passed into a fully developed quietism in which however the world has taken the place of heaven. You may if you like—I understand her to say—expect the world to live after a pattern that seems to you the best; but the fact is that the individual has no more than enough energy to get through the day all by himself. Man really has no gift for organization, no room for the vicarious experience of other men's ideas. Therefore why be urgent? Why plan out elaborate utopias that have no power to illuminate each passing hour in the solitary growth of a human life? . . . So Pascal said, "I have discovered that all human misfortune comes from one thing, which is not knowing how to remain quietly in one room." . . . But I should like to give what seems to me the central passage in this book:

" To be able to face *fact* as *fact*, as something transcending all momentary convenience and pleasantness; yet at the same time to preserve our human preferences, to exercise our human selection all the more rigidly because we know that it is *our* selection, reality offering more but we accepting what we choose; such a double attitude would surely be the best. . . . It would be more respectful both to our own nature and to the nature which transcends ours, to recognize that what mankind wants it wants because it is mankind; and to leave off claiming from the universe conformity to human ideals and methods. . . . The sense of this (however vague) has been furthered by occasional fortunate conditions of civilization, and it is, most probably, constitutional in certain happily balanced natures. It is what gives the high serenity to men of the stamp of Plato and Goethe and Browning; they can touch everything, discuss everything, understand the reason of everything, yet remain with preferences unaltered. Perhaps we may all some day attain, by employing equally our tendencies to doubt and our tendencies to believe, to such a fearless, yet modest, recognition of what is, and also of what we wish it to be."

IV

The conception of this perfect apprehension of fact in a state which implies also the full expression of personality is the conception of a perfect intuition. And it is Vernon Lee's conception of the future. It is a kind of quietism that has got rid of heaven and become sublunized. Now the reason we got rid of heaven was because we discovered that we could have all the really good things of heaven without waiting so long for them. The dream of man has always been for a state of perfect intuition. The ideal of love has been simply the ideal of a relationship in which our natures would be to someone so transparent that we should not have to explain anything. Just as we know that to express a care alleviates it, so we have dreamed of a relationship in which care would be expelled in the mere act of being divined. Thus if we stood in this relation to the conscious universe we should be without care: we should be at peace in all things. The idea of heaven was simply the projection of this ideal from a world which of itself could not respond to it; and the idea of heaven centred in a God capable of divining our cares even before we became conscious of them, through faith in whom we could have the benefits of this intuitive understanding.

Althea represents quite literally the idea of heaven expressing itself in human society. And in this society the artist having regained his normality would cease to exist, while art, exactly as in some celestial scene of Fra Angelico's, springing up everywhere as a kind of exultation would

"Float and run
Like an unbodied joy, whose race is just begun."

V

So now I have built up a little tower, as orderly as I could build it, and have called it Vernon Lee. It may be Vernon Lee, but it probably is not: and I want now to add a fifth story and topple it all down. How is it possible to order our thoughts about anyone who interests us? We gather together an army of facts, of impressions, and go through them with a sword. And we try to find the one curve that passes through them all, makes them a unique combination, appears to result in a personality. Then we learn one fact more, gain one more impression, and the curve has to be drawn afresh. . . . For in truth a human soul does not periodically add to itself like a coral reef and become, so to speak, bigger and redder and solider. It becomes, on the contrary and if it has grown at all, more and more vapory, inconsistent, inapprehensible, incapable of being pigeon-holed. Just in proportion as it approaches the state of wisdom it casts behind it the memories of all that mental warfare, those battles of opinion, of conviction—half-sights struggling with half-sights—in the pauses of which one is able to shout the words of command or counsel or defiance which are the only quite articulate words. Wisdom, like innocence, is apt to be inarticulate because its language is too universal for any immediate application. I suppose that is what is meant in the saying that we must become like little children before we can enter the kingdom of heaven. We must have passed through organization—which is merely a convenient thing —back into the disorganization which is the only human attitude, considering the whole universe, that is not positively impudent.

Not only, as it seems to me, has some such conception of growth come to be with Vernon Lee the central theme, but she herself has grown in this kind of way. . . . The best we can do is to act the photographer and stand our subject up and snap the record of its momentary setting, realizing that a leaf more or less in the tree through which the sun drifts down upon it will cast a shadow on the hand, the eyes, the hair, which will never repeat itself.

In considering a writer we ask ourselves first of all, What has been the development of his ideas? In which of his works do the succeeding stages of this development take form? For we understand that work is important in the degree in which it possesses personality. It is true that these alone or chiefly are the books by which a writer is remembered. Now certain it is that the books which tell us the most about Vernon Lee are those of hers that are least known. As a figure, as one who has attained to a distinguished view of life, she has never assumed popularly a clear-cut form. I can think of three reasons for this. For one, she has kept herself as a human being sedulously unknown. For another, her views are so free from the stress and prejudice of propaganda that they have never lent themselves to combat, refutation, discipleship, or that exaggeration which implants an idea in the popular mind. But a third reason is, I think, the most responsible. She has won a reputation, too considerable to be called secondary, as an occasional writer. Almost every pleasant thing in the lives of cultivated men and women she has touched with a happy phrase. Her gift has been so gracious that she seems not to have asked for austere consideration.

THE PROTECTION OF OUR "INFANT INDUSTRY"

HARRY ALBERT AUSTIN

For some time past the Administration at Washington has been endeavoring to get Congress to enact legislation providing for the establishing of a Children's Bureau in the Department of Commerce and Labor, which, to use an apt paraphrase, would have for its objcet the "protection of our infant industry." This proposed legislation presents a phase of the "protective policy" which members of all parties and shades of political faith could support with credit to themselves and to their parties. The benefits to be derived from the creation of such a bureau would not only affect the present generation, but extend far into the future.

In the establishment of this Children's Bureau the main object sought to be accomplished is the investigation of all matters pertaining to the welfare of children and child life. It would be especially charged with the investigation of questions relating to infant mortality, the birth rate, physical, mental and moral degeneracy, dangerous occupations, accidents and diseases of children, and to report upon legislation affecting children in the various States and Territories.

No matter from what standpoint—economic, eleemosynary or moral—we view this question, it presents an interesting subject for study and consideration.

It is well to state at the outset that this bureau would in no way encroach upon the prerogatives, rights or police powers of the individual States. It would be in the nature of what may be termed an intelligence bureau. It would not aim to spread any legislation on the statute books, but by expert investigations and the systematic formulation and publication of the results of such investigations, would furnish to the States authoritative and unbiased information on the subjects affecting child life upon which the several legislatures could act intelligently in passing laws relative thereto. In addition to this, it would multiply the efficiency of philanthropic societies and agencies in the distribution of millions of dollars annually expended in the work in which they are engaged.

To understand more clearly the character and scope of the work of this bureau, it may be well to refer briefly to somewhat analogous bureaus now existing in the Department of Agriculture, such as the Bureaus of Animal Industry, of Plant Industry, of Soils, of Chemistry, and the like. Millions of dollars are annually spent through these bureaus for the investigation of diseases of animals, for the inspection of cattle, for the eradication of diseases among sheep, and so forth, and the information secured and results obtained by capable experts and published to the farmers and stock-raisers of the country have been the means of saving untold millions of dollars and much wasted effort in the several industries to which they pertain.

And yet, during all these years, with the good results accomplished by the Department of Agriculture in respect to purely agricultural products of the country as an example for emulation, there has never been any attempt on the part of the Federal Government, except in a limited way, to gather and disseminate in a systematic manner that information in regard to the " child crop " of the country which could be used to the betterment of the physical, moral and financial welfare of our posterity.

There are born every year in this country over two million children—boys and girls who will constitute the future citizenship of the nation. The value of this " crop " as compared with the cereal and meat products of the country cannot be estimated; but in view of its effect upon the future destiny of the nation, it is certainly entitled to as much consideration, to say the least, as the wheat, corn or cattle crops.

To illustrate this phase of the question, suppose that the Census report for 1910 shows that the wheat crop of Iowa has decreased twenty-five per cent. in production as compared with 1900, or that the production of cattle in Nebraska has fallen off thirty per cent. in the same time. It would be the duty of the Department of Agriculture to take cognizance of this fact, and experts of the Department would at once be sent out to investigate and report upon the causes of this decrease, and if the causes could be ascertained and a remedy suggested, bulletins would be published and freely circulated among the farmers and cattle-raisers of the respective States which would be of great value as a guide in raising the next year's crop. Now suppose that the Census report shows that in Iowa the rate of infant mortality had increased twenty-five per cent. in 1910 as compared with 1900, or that the proportional increase in injuries to children in factories or mines of a certain State was thirty per cent.: there is no bureau under the Federal Government, and in fact under but few State Governments, whose duty it would be to investigate and report upon the causes of those increases. Just one other illustration in this connection. If an epidemic should break out among the live stock of a certain State or community, the Agricultural Department would at once send out agents to investigate the causes and report upon a remedy, or should some agricultural crop be damaged by insects—as in the case of the boll weevil in the cotton crop of the South—an investigation would be made and bulletins published suggesting certain steps to be taken—based on the opinions of agricultural experts—to eradicate the evil. But should an epidemic break out among the children of a certain State or community, there is no bureau under the Federal Government which would be charged with the investigation of the subject, and while the State authorities if they had the proper organizations and facilities for doing so, would probably make some sort of an investigation, yet the reports of the results of the investigation might not be available to other States at some future time when a similar epidemic might occur therein. In other words, there is no centralization in the work of investigating matters relating to the welfare of the children as there is in the investigation of matters relating to farm products, and without this centralization no systematic work is possible and much valuable effort must be wasted.

As stated before, there are born in this country every year over two million children. A certain portion of these children will grow into healthy, useful, industrious citizens, while another portion will become physically weak or morally degenerate men and women who will be a blot upon the society of our nation. What percentage of these two million children will become members of the former or latter class it is impossible to foretell, but if any means can be taken or remedy suggested whereby the one class will be increased and the other decreased, it is certainly the duty of an altruistic nation like ours to put forth every effort to accomplish the desired result.

Considering another phase of the question, it is estimated that out of these two million children born every year, 300,000 under one year of age die annually, and that one-half of these deaths are preventable by the knowledge and application of the proper remedies or preventive measures. In other words, it may be said that over one million American-born children are lost to the country every ten years through lack of proper information. Of course it cannot be claimed that all these children could be saved by the dissemination of information by the Federal Government, but a general diffusion of sanitary knowledge and instructions as to the proper care of children would undoubtedly save the lives of many children in years to come.

In this connection it is interesting to note that recently a certain philanthropic society in the city of Washington made an investigation into the physical condition of the children attending the public schools of that city. The results of this investigation have been published in pamphlet form, together with certain simple remedies for children's diseases and sanitary rules to be followed. Sixty thousand copies of this pamphlet were distributed among the school children and each child was requested to have its parents read it over to him or her at home.

As a result of the investigation it was discovered that out of 43,000 pupils attending the public schools in Washington, an amazingly large number had physical defects which should give the parents serious concern. For instance, one in each twenty pupils had defective eyesight. One in thirty was affected with defective hearing. Nearly seven thousand had defective teeth which needed attention and which affected the health of the child. Over two thousand were " mouth breathers " suffering from adenoids, enlarged tonsils, etc., in such aggravated form as to impair the health and mind of the child; 703 were under size; 727 were ill-nourished, and 923 were anæmic.

After setting forth these facts, the bulletin discusses in a general and simple way the questions of proper food and drink, need of fresh air in the school room and at home, the importance of personal cleanliness, care of the teeth, eyes, ears and nose, the matter of proper clothing, the quantities of work, rest and play required by children, curable diseases of childhood, and so forth. As stated above, the pamphlet is prepared in simple language, devoid of all technical and medical phraseology, and is easily understood by both the parents and the children themselves, where the latter are far enough advanced to be able to read. It is just such work as this, only covering a much wider scope of subjects, that would be accomplished by the proposed National Children's Bureau.

There are other just as important subjects with which the bureau would have to deal. For instance, it is stated that one-quarter of the blind children now in schools for the blind are unnecessarily so afflicted, such affliction being easily preventable by the application of a simple remedy soon after birth. An authoritative publication of the Government setting forth this fact and suggesting the remedy therefor would undoubtedly greatly decrease the number of children suffering from blindness.

Another problem which would be considered by the bureau is that relating to dependent children. The whole question of the institutional care of the orphans and the work of home-placing societies needs authoritative investigation. It is estimated that there are 90,000 children now living in these institutions and that the cost of supporting them is between fifteen and twenty million dollars a year. Besides this, there are probably fifty thousand orphans being taken care of by other charitable agencies of various kinds. At present no authoritative data are available to the general public showing how these children are being cared for, or how they turn out after leaving these institutions or their adopted homes, and hence no systematic effort can be made to remedy any evils or defects that may exist.

Again, the subject of child labor, embracing the question of accidents to children and the minimum age at which children should be allowed to enter the ranks of the wage-earners, is another question upon which a comprehensive report of conditions would enable the Legislatures of the various States to base remedial legislation. Such information as would be furnished by a national bureau would be authoritative and would, of course, be devoid of any biased opinions in regard to the subject-matter.

The question of juvenile delinquency has only recently been given serious study in this country, and many States and communities are still without knowledge upon which they would act if it were available. What are the best methods of treating delinquent children, the various problems arising in juvenile courts and the best methods of meeting these problems—all these questions need to be investigated and the information, secured by experts, given to the people of the country in the form of governmental bulletins, speaking with authority. In this connection, Thomas Nelson Page has said: " If you go into any juvenile court in the country and sit in there some morning, you cannot help seeing that there is something needed in addition to the agencies we now have at work." Many cities and communities have no juvenile courts at all and are without knowledge of the character and scope of their work.

Philanthropic societies in this country have all been handicapped by their inability, under existing agencies, to secure reliable information upon the subjects relating to children, and especially the unfortunate ones. The action of the several States in providing for these children could be guided without waste of energy and money, and the efforts of the various philanthropic societies, which are spending millions for the welfare of the children, would, with the character of information furnished by the proposed bureau, avoid useless expenditure of money and would profit by the experience of others who are working along the same lines of endeavor.

While the Census Bureau, the Bureau of Education, and the Bureau of Labor, publish bulletins relating to certain subjects affecting the children of the country, the information so published is simply in the nature of general statistics and is not of such a character that measures can be taken to remedy the evils which may be found to exist. Thus, the Census Bureau might report that the infant mortality rate in one city was twice as great as that in another city of the same size and apparently the same general conditions, but the facts thus ascertained would be of no practical value unless the reason for the excessive death rate in the one city should be found. These statistics, in order to be of value, should be made the basis of a careful study and the more unfortunate city be given the necessary information for remedying the evil conditions. This the Census Bureau is not organized or equipped to do.

There does not now exist in any of the States, as far as known, any such bureau as the one contemplated, although some of the facts desired are collected by a few of the States through bureaus of education, labor and health. There are other States without vital statistics of any kind and these States would be stimulated to investigations of their own by the aid of the proposed Children's Bureau. However, if several of the States did have the means of collecting such data and of reaching conclusions, it would be of no special benefit to the other States unless some person in those States happened to know to whom to apply for the information, and even then it might not be applicable to the particular conditions existing in the State to which it was furnished. With a national bureau, all data and statistics collected, and all expert conclusions drawn therefrom, could be coördinated and systematized, and the results of a general character published to the country at large, and those affecting particular States or communities circulated in the respective localities.

Other nations have already organized government agencies for researches of this character. Germany, for example, has a very complete and thorough system of research and publicity concerning all the facts relating to child life. The British Parliament has passed what is known as the " Children's Act," with the double function of investigation and administration. The different sections relate to the protection of the lives of infants, prevention of cruelty to children, reformatory and industrial schools, juvenile offenders, and the health, safety and welfare of the children in general. Of course under our form of government, such a national bureau would have no administrative authority that would interfere with the rights or police powers of the States. But if the several States had authoritative information emanating from a Federal bureau composed of experts, they could act upon it as the best judgment of their executive officers or legislatures might dictate.

If our Government is to inaugurate a systematic effort to conserve our natural resources in order to prevent the great waste now going on, no better field for research can be found than the millions of American-born children, one of the greatest of our natural resources, and one which will be an important factor in the future uplift or degeneration of American society and a potent element in the political and economic policies of the Government for years to come.

THE TRANSPORT

LOUIS HOW

THITHER we came, and there we sat us down
  In the exuberant hushes of the night,
And from the hill-side looked across the town
To where the river motionless moved down,
  Burnished beneath the pallor of the night.

Not listening, we knew how leaf brushed leaf,
  Not noticing, we felt the smell of earth;
The world grew simple, sleeping out its grief.
And superhuman, softly as a leaf,
  Peace fell upon us, raising us from earth.

Softly we talked, not knowing all we said,
  And, on our voices, floated as in space,—
One in accord with heaven overhead,
One with the earth; our hearts commingled said
  All: we were one, we occupied one space.

Time ceased: and yet the moon across the sky
  Wore on, the dipper sought his resting-place;
And we, unsated, knew that heaven is high,
But founded on our earth:—having scaled the sky,
  Moved thence, and set a stone to mark the place.

THE DISINTEGRATION OF THE THEATRE *

MONTROSE J. MOSES

THE theatre in America is passing through its newspaper phase; in every department it is being influenced by those economic forces which try to inflate the market without improving the product, and which measure the product as a commodity rather than as an art. Every industry is subject to the laws of profit and loss, and the theatre is an ever-increasing industry, since the amusement territory is increasing. There is no concentration which would make New York the theatrical centre in the way that London is the hub of the United Kingdom.

Only by the combining of theatrical interests in the hands of a few dictators has the theatre settled into some orderly adjustment, exchanging independence of selection on the part of the small manager and of the actor, for certain salaried assurance. The theatrical interests have largely been held in New York, although Chicago is increasing in importance, while the road has accepted what it could get, the local manager being only a dependent, with no incentive or means to give his public what they want other than what the syndicate might allow them.

The history of the theatrical trust is hardly different from the growth of any other trust, save in respect to the personalities of the men behind the combination. The magnates who govern Wall Street know their trade down to the smallest detail; they know the men with whom they have to deal, and they are quick to measure the risk. The same may be said for the theatrical manager. But the extraordinary business man exceeds the exceptional theatre man in this large respect: he understands the way the country is going; he has his hand on the pulse of business conditions at their greatest energy; he knows how the people are thinking on public affairs. The theatre manager has no such penetration; he launches his individual enterprises as a gamble, and depends upon the physical resources of theatricalism to " boost " his product.

* _The Regeneration of the Theatre,_ by the same author, will appear in the next issue.

The history of the men who constitute the trust is the same in each case. Their one claim to serious consideration, outside of the sphere of menace to an art, is the fact that, having seen an opportunity to place art upon a sound commercial basis, they combined with sufficient foresight to corner the theatrical market. What they were not able to observe was that however sound the commercial basis, art was still art, and that while *les affaires sont les affaires*, human nature is human nature. This fact alone would assuredly betray them in the end.

We have heard much of the commercial theatre, but if we stop to think, why should not a theatre be commercial? For the play which does not draw is not acceptable to the people, and while the box office should not limit the art, at least the art should not hold the box office in contempt, since herein is worldly measure of its own excellence. The weak spot in the theatrical situation is not the commercial theatre, but the business methods of those behind it; and the business methods proclaim the man.

Judged by all business, large enterprises must be organized, and organization is either scrupulous or not scrupulous. The men behind the trust were in it for profits, and having launched enterprises, they had to make these enterprises sell. To do this, they found it necessary to control the amusement arteries of the country. Thus, audiences either had to take the food they found or else go without. This blockading system was reached through a booking agency whereby time assignments were distributed for attractions at the pleasure of the dictators on the payment of certain fees. Once under operation, this group of men, known as the Theatre Trust, practically became inquisitorial in its policy, tampering even with the independent opinion of the press.

Now was the time to prove the personality of the men, to measure their attitude toward art, to realize their unfitness to the full. They found the theatre business precarious, and after a fashion they placed the finances on a basis of equilibrium. But in return the drama had to sacrifice all that conduced to the maintenance of its health as an art and as a civic force. These men were " in " for the money, and so skilful was their generalship that they told the North, South, East, and West what they must have, whether they would or no.

Salaries were assured, but voices were silenced, and there was no say in the theatrical world save that of the trust.

Then arose an opposition, the chief significance of which was that it did oppose. Cut of the same stuff, yet dissatisfied with its stock, this new combination grew because the time was ripe, and because there was enough public opinion in the air to father its growth. Factions kept coming its way, from the South and from the West, while new theatres at significant stations in the theatrical territory began to fall away from the control of the octopus. Yet despite the disintegration brought about by this condition of affairs, we have yet to see whether or not we have on our hands more than one octopus. The meaning of this insurgency in the theatre was nevertheless health-giving, or at least held promises of renewed hope. For let it here be said that, after all, a manager's business is dependent upon the will of the people, however much he may dictate terms. They like what they like, and just as soon as they discriminate in their liking, the manager's standard will have to change. If good plays draw, the theatres will want good plays. Whether those at the head have sufficient judgment to know a good thing when they see it, is a matter of doubt. But the commercial theatre has a perfect right to vend mediocre musical comedies, if the people persist in wanting them.

As far as the trust is concerned, all this time, art, the supreme cause of the theatre, the life expression of the people, was languishing beneath an ignorance of its nature. Plays were manufactured for particular " stars," and these actors, instead of the drama, were featured as the drawing attractions. The dramatized novel and musical comedy monopolized the boards. Those who were not in the game, and those who refused subjection, suffered on the road. Mr. Belasco, booking through the trust, was refused time at St. Louis for *The Darling of the Gods* during the Exposition, while the opposition rushed its own *The Japanese Nightingale* into the breach. Mrs. Fiske, unwilling to come to terms, had to act in music halls and second-rate houses, while Mme. Bernhardt carried with her a stage and a circus tent. In the Southern circuit, the small manager was practically nothing more than a janitor who received no concessions and who could adopt no house policy. The situation was chaotic.

Actors like Richard Mansfield and Francis Wilson, who had been among the first to oppose strenuously the dictatorial policy, had, one by one, to come to terms.

Through publicity, ground was prepared for the opposition. The open door cry was an excellent slogan, and one in accord with popular sentiment. An independent policy was nothing more nor less than the right for any manager, irrespective of whether or not he was a member of a trust, to " book " his attraction in any town possessing an independent theatre. This free trade even admitted of the opposition party asking for " time " in its rival's houses. For a while, this will have the appearance of healthy competition, but as events are transpiring, there is every reason to believe that the two will coalesce, and become more powerful than ever.

Meanwhile, nevertheless, the theatre has been affected by changing conditions, mental and economic. The drama, as a subject of popular consideration, is being more sanely discussed, and the type of play, closely in touch with the newspaper, reflects a different order of interests. Public agitation against old methods of management has made opportune another slogan about an endowed theatre, a civic playhouse, a memorial auditorium, wherein might be perpetuated the real classics of dramatic art—away from the blighting touch of commercialism. But even here, the popular conception is wrong. Endowment on any basis whatsoever does not permit the manager to disregard popular demand; it only allows a certain margin of risk and does not require an immediate return on the investment. It does not say, " Lose "; but it assures the manager support where there has been failure in a judicious cause.

The one danger of independence, in the commercial sense, lies in the sudden appearance of numberless mushroom managers. Though we do not see it plainly at present, the actor will eventually find that salaries will decrease, and demands on his part will fail to possess their former value. There will come a general slump in the market of stipend, and while this may aid in the establishment of stock companies, it will not guarantee, as the trust did, that a company in its circuit through the country will not be left high and dry somewhere in the deserts of Arizona.

In other words, the disintegration of the theatre, in spite of the efficacy of free trade, will be attendant with dangers. It might degenerate into every playwright being his own manager, just as there is an economic possibility of every author having to pay for the publication of his own book. Mr. Charles Klein has affiliated himself in a business way with the Author's Producing Company; he prefers to have this organization present Charles Klein's play than to have announced Henry B. Harris's new play by Charles Klein (in small type). The open door affords an ample opportunity for the new playwright to procure a hearing; it widens the market, and increases the possibility of a production. But it lacks concentrated energy; it is wanting in the assurances of stability.

Nor has the open door policy prevented Mr. Charles Frohman from cornering the market in English playwrights, as Harper and Brothers have cornered certain authors and illustrators for their exclusive use. It is all in the game of business competition. Mr. Frohman, strange to say, now finds himself in a peculiar position; he has the plays and he has not sufficient theatres in which to present them. The Shuberts, by an almost phenomenal ability to procure realty support, and by their persistent policy of fighting through the medium of a newspaper which they founded for this express purpose, have weakened the territorial influence of the old theatrical trust. In return, they have not succeeded in inspiring confidence as to their own intentions.

This disintegration of the theatre, therefore, points to a step which is very evident to those most desirous of honest intent. The Syndicate faction assuredly placed the theatre on a business basis, as I have indicated; but they tampered with the vital organ of the corporation, and became dictatorial in their booking of time, demanding excessive terms wherever they wished commercially to make a production impracticable in a neighborhood they themselves desired. There is now an essential need for a dramatic clearing house, which will ensure for the theatre business the same confidence and the same stability which the New York Clearing House does for the banks. A man's business is his own, but when he undertakes to serve as middle man for another, then he subjects himself to ethical responsibility.

Another thing is to be said for the theatrical trust, however wrong it may have been in its business methods: there was an efficiency about its work that was due entirely to the experience of its theatre officials. The principle of its booking system is excellent; its advance agents keen and alive. Nor can there be much fault found with its railroad arrangements. Only when the theatre began to disintegrate did one detect a laxity in management, due very largely to the haste with which productions were thrown upon the road, and to the calibre of the man sent ahead of the " show." However ignorant the officials governing theatrical affairs, they were sufficiently wise to bring to their aid cleverness from the outside. They took newspaper men as their press agents and paid them large salaries to pursue a course that has well-nigh been the undoing of dramatic criticism in this country.

For the one corrective of the theatre is the publicity which is given to it in our papers. The theatre manager assures his press representative an authoritative position, from which vantage ground . he seeks to establish a chain of papers willing to print any news emanating from the theatre office. This eagerness to accept copy given freely, has been largely responsible for the attitude assumed by the manager in his demand that dramatic criticism in no way be allowed to conflict with the positive effect of his advertising.

This struggle is wrong, but it may be easily attributable to the unofficial character of the theatre critic's work. The papers are not careful in their appointment of well-trained men for the position. And we need such men in this period of disintegration . It is usually argued, and rightly, that the attractions of the " pass " are too great to confine the privilege to one person; the advantages of advertising are too evident to sacrifice them to the whim of one person's idea. The press agent's position is more sharply defined than that of the dramatic critic; he is not handicapped; he may go to the limit, and he does so cleverly.

Another aspect that has aided in the disintegration of the theatre is the character of the outside forces which have detracted from the resources of the legitimate theatre. First, the vaudeville houses have organized themselves into a trust as potent as that of the straight houses; second, the moving picture interests have combined so thoroughly as to threaten theatre business on the road; and finally, so many theatres are being erected in the large cities, notably in New York, that they cannot be guaranteed sufficient support by the assurance of adequate demand or of worthy supply. In other words, the economics of the theatre, having passed through the stage of experimentation and organization, need to be studied with wisdom and forethought.

I cannot see where the open door policy is productive of large and wholesome results *per se*. It is of course more honest by far to have all doors open than to work in the dark and with a cut-throat policy at hand. But there still remains the problem of personality, of manhood, in the theatrical business. The situation is quite similar to that of politics: a better class of men must be drawn into the business, even as they must be drawn into the civic life of the people. It is not enough that we have an organization; each man must be of the highest quality. It is not enough that plays be produced in order to fill the increasing number of theatres; the producer must be instinct with art. The theatrical trust gave us an excellent shell; the soul has yet to be supplied.

The disintegration of the theatre has shown us the imminent dangers of theatrical organization. There are two phases of the business: the ledger side and the art side. These should be separate in working process, and the former should not limit the latter, even though art should have regard for the box-office. The crying need of the theatre at present is for a dramatic clearing house, and for a different quality of art which flourishes upon a different spirit of organization. The outward form will be very much the same as it is now. We shall see that the theatre is disintegrating in order that it may be more closely and more soundly organized in the light of its excellences and of its failings.

THE TARIFF BOARD

JAMES BOYLE

THERE is a consensus of opinion that the recent political " land-slide " was caused mainly by the wide-spread belief that " the interests " had too much to do with the fixing of the schedules of the tariff law passed August 5th, 1909, and that that measure is responsible for the high prices of the necessaries of life. The question of the soundness or otherwise of this belief is not germane to the subject-matter of this article; still, it is but noting a fact to state that there is much to be said against the proposition that the present abnormal advanced cost of living is the result of the tariff law. No less an authority than Professor Taussig, of Harvard, the author of the standard work, *The History of the Tariff*, and certainly not a Protectionist, declared in a recent issue of the *Atlantic Monthly* that the reduction of duties would in most cases bring no lowering in prices and no advantage to consumers.

In 1882 a Commission was appointed to investigate the tariff question, and in its report to make recommendations to Congress. The functions of the Tariff Board appointed by President Taft are confined to investigation, but the scope of its inquiries and observations is much broader than that of the Commission of 1882. It should be kept clearly in mind that the present Tariff Board is simply a Bureau of Information, for the use of the President and of Congress.

The National Republican platform of 1908 declared that—

" in all tariff legislation the true principle of protection is best maintained by the imposition of such duties as will equal the difference between the cost of production at home and abroad, together with a reasonable profit to American industries."

It is generally conceded that Congress has neither time nor the facilities to find out the difference between the cost of production at home and abroad. In all the later tariff laws based on the protective principle, the theory of an equalization between the productive cost at home and abroad has been professedly kept in view, but it is

472

only within recent years—and specifically only since 1904—that the formula has been set forth in an axiomatic way as the true basis of a protective tariff; and it was not until 1908 that the last clause, that covering " a reasonable profit to American industries," was included, —although it is reasonable to claim that that feature was always intended to be part of the national policy.

The legal status and the scope of work of the new Tariff Board have been a development. The original authority is found in section 2 of the present Payne-Aldrich Tariff Law, passed August 5, 1909, in which the President is authorized to employ such persons as may be required to secure information to assist him in discharging the duties imposed upon him as to the minimum and maximum rates so as to secure equality of treatment by foreign nations in fiscal matters, and also to assist the officers of the Government in the administration of the customs laws. From the first, President Taft construed this provision as giving him a wide scope, and at the time of the passage of the tariff law he announced that he would assume that it gave him authority " to secure statistics covering the prices and costs of production of goods at home and abroad upon which scientific tariffs must be built," and he subsequently asked Congress to broaden the authority, extend the scope, and furnish additional funds. Accordingly, in the Sundry Appropriations Act, passed June 25, 1910, there was an appropriation made of a quarter of a million of dollars to enable the President to secure information to assist him in these matters, " including such investigations of the cost of production of commodities, covering cost of material, fabrication and every other element of such cost of production, . . . including the employment of such persons as may be required for those purposes." The President has expressed himself definitely and boldly as to the work of the Board and the possible outcome of its inquiries:—

" It is not unlikely that, in the light of accurate statistics, we may find that certain schedules in our tariff are too high. If we do, I shall at that time not hesitate immediately to recommend their revision. . . I believe that the work of a Tariff Board should be to secure and to present evidence, not to frame a tariff. With this evidence before it, Congress will act fairly and wisely, and the United States will have, under this method, a tariff established on a thoroughly scientific basis—as it should have had a quarter of a century ago."

The work of the original Board appointed under section 2 of the Tariff Act and the Sundry Appropriations Act of June, 1910, was rather restricted, according to the strict letter. After the work had progressed some months a movement took form, and was supported by many of the leading manufacturing and commercial organizations of the country, to make the Board a permanent body, and to widen its scope, by a specific law. So on January 5, 1911, Representative Longworth, of Ohio, introduced a bill to create a Commission of five persons, to be appointed by the President, not more than three to be of the same political party. Soon afterwards another bill was introduced by Representative Dalzell, of Pennsylvania. To the general surprise, the Ways and Means Committee of the House, after several disagreements, united unanimously upon a bill, which embodied features of both the Longworth and the Dalzell bills, and also incorporated the demand of the Democratic members of the Committee that the Board should be required to report to Congress direct when called upon to do so, as well as to the President and to the Ways and Means Committee of the House and the Finance Committee of the Senate.

Professor Taussig asks the question how far this proposed inquiry is " worth while." " No one," he says, " who stops to think will suppose that inquiries of this sort will be easy, or will lead to other than rough and approximate results." But he proceeds, after declaring that the " much paraded ' true principle ' is worthless," and that if applied with consistency it " would lead to the complete annihilation of foreign trade ":—

" And yet I believe that the proposed inquiries of the excellent Tariff Board selected by President Taft are worth while. I believe they will conduce to a better understanding of the tariff situation, and are likely to lead to considerable improvement in legislation. They may even pave the way to something like a settlement of the tariff question.

" In two directions the investigation of relative costs of production will be of advantage: as to undue gains in monopolistic or quasi-monopolistic industries; and as to the extent to which there are vested interests which must be respected in a future settlement of the tariff."

The New York *Independent* is still more emphatic. It thinks that " there must soon be another revision," but—

" The next revision, whether made for revenue only or in harmony with the protective policy, should be made upon a basis of facts ascertained by competent officers. We mean that they should be ascertained by a good tariff commission. They are needed as much by revenue-only Democrats as they are by protection Republicans. The reception of such facts from a commission by a Democratic House majority would not bind that majority to apply the protective policy in legislation. Such a commission as ought to be established at Washington would not report as to tariff policy; it would only procure and report the information without which neither the protective nor the revenue policy ought to be enforced."

Grave doubts have been expressed as to the practicability of the scheme for finding out the differences of the cost of production of commodities—these doubts applying both to the home and foreign field, but particularly to the latter. Professor Harrison S. Smalley, of the University of Michigan, in an article in last November's *North American Review*, gives a number of reasons why he arrives at the conclusion that the attempt will fail; but he admits that if it succeeds—

" We shall have a ' scientific ' tariff—a tariff based on and determined by a governing principle in place of the haphazard creations which have hitherto existed. And in the second place, the tariff will cease to furnish monopolies with a ready means of extortion. It is, therefore, evident that much will be gained if this new experiment succeeds."

In Professor Smalley's opinion, if the experiment succeeds it will be to the advantage of protection; while if it fails, it will advance the cause of free trade.

The American Protective Tariff League at its last annual meeting (in January), opposed " piece-meal " revision as " fraught with injustice and danger to the general body of industrial producers," and also set itself against the " continual tariff disturbance that must result from the activities of a Tariff Board of Commission sitting for the express purpose of continually changing the tariff."

Among the leading daily newspapers which look with dubious-

ness upon the plan is the ever-critical New York *Sun.* In its opinion
the most valuable provision of the Longworth Bill was that " for the
expansion of the Board's work." In speaking of " the uselessness
of production costs as a basis for rates," the *Sun* puts this query:—

" An army of investigators and accountants may be kept busy in
this country for an indefinite time, and another army in foreign
countries, but what practical value will their work have when it is
done ? "

Nevertheless, after making due allowance for the opposition and
criticisms stated above, it is beyond question that the overwhelming
sentiment of the country is in favor of the idea,—of giving the plan
a fair trial, at any rate.

The objections of the American Protective Tariff League are
purely from a high-tariff standpoint, and they do not come within
the scope of this article. The objections of most of the other critics,
including Professor Smalley and the New York *Sun,* lose much of
their force because of two reasons: 1. they are based mainly on the
fallacious assumption that the expected results of the inquiries as to
comparative cost of production will be *absolute,* or *exact,* enabling a
" scientific " tariff to be drafted, so far as equitable rates are concerned, in the same sense that insurance actuary tables can be framed,
or a mathematical demonstration can be made:—whereas the best that
can be hoped for is an *approximate average,* as to both domestic and
foreign commodities, and especially so as to the latter; and 2. a
failure to recognize that—whatever may be the merits or fallacies of
the protective principle, whether the tariff be high, low, or moderate
—in its application it must be *national,* that is, the country as a
whole must be taken as a unit; and this principle holds good though
the tariff system were based upon a free trade or revenue-only
theory. Whatever may have been the errors of the system of Fried-
rich List, he took an impregnable position in this regard in his famous German work, *National System of Political Economy,* and in
his American letters, written after he had become a resident of this
country.

The difficulties suggested as preventing the obtaining of the required information with regard to the comparative cost of products

at home and abroad, do not seem insuperable, upon examination, always subject to the inevitable condition that only approximate results need be expected; but these results can be made fairly accurate, and will be an immense improvement on the haphazard results now obtained by Congress. The work in detail will not be one-hundredth part as great as that successfully performed in obtaining the United States census, nor one-tenth that involved in collecting the British income tax. Difficulties which now seem insuperable will gradually disappear before well-organized, persistent and patient labor. It is probable that up to the present the Tariff Board have confined themselves mainly to the laying out of a plan of operations, and the creation of a staff, limited to the original scope of their inquiries, although it is understood that considerable " field work " has been undertaken at home, and some abroad, in respect to several schedules. The entire subject is new, and necessarily much of the labor of the Board has been in the nature of a general survey of the situation; time must be given to the Board to lay out a definite plan, and it is not improbable that for some months not a few of the undertakings will be of a tentative nature.

In regard to the furnishing of information to the Tariff Board, there would probably not be the same objection and spirit of evasion at home as confront the tax collector, for the intelligent American producer would readily appreciate that the information sought would not affect him separately, as an individual, injuriously, but would relate to and would be used in connection with the entire industry as a whole in which he was engaged,—fairly, impartially, and equally; and he would readily accept the assurance of the Federal official that the information would be treated as confidential so far as he was personally concerned. Even supposing that manufacturers refused to impart the necessary information, the Board would not be helpless, —it could go elsewhere for it. The problem is to find out what is the approximate cost of actual production; and naturally, the cost of the raw material would be the first factor to be inquired into. The prices paid for most raw material are not private confidential matters which can be hidden under a bushel; not only do the daily papers give quotations, but almost every branch of industry has its special trade journals, which generally go into details as to prices.

The next important item in the cost of production is that of labor, and as a rule that is not a very difficult matter to obtain: the many volumes of statistics on wages issued by the Governments of our own country, of Germany, and of England, being evidence of this fact. This phase of the investigation would be exceedingly interesting and important as helping to solve a much disputed question, namely, the relation of the comparatively high wages in America to the total cost of production. That high wages generally mean efficiency in labor, given certain other conditions, and that they do not *necessarily* mean an addition to the cost of production to the extent of the relative increase of wages, are not only dicta of political economy, but are accepted as facts borne out by observation and actual experience. It is now a favorite argument of free traders that the individual superior efficiency of the American workman, combined with the vast superiority of the plant and organization of the American manufacturer, fully compensates for the higher wages in this country as compared with competing countries, in many of the leading industries,—that is, that notwithstanding the higher wages paid in America, the total cost of production in many industries is no greater in America than in competing countries. On the other hand, it is argued that in most American industries wages would have to be lowered if the protection of a tariff equal to the difference between wages at home and abroad were withdrawn. Then would come in all the many other items which must be included in the total make-up of the cost of production:—the rent of the land or premises occupied, or interest on original cost of purchase; the cost and upkeep of plant, with allowance for depreciation; insurance; the " over-head " and administerial and managerial expenses; transportation, etc.

It is true that the problem is complicated by the fact that the cost differs in different parts of the country, owing to different conditions, environments, proximity to the raw materials, etc.; but, as before pointed out, only approximate results can be hoped for. The cost of production at a number of centres of any given industry can be ascertained, and an average be struck for the country at large;—for the whole industry under investigation,—as, indeed, the whole problem—must be considered from a *national* standpoint. As to the objection that the cost of production varies in different parts of the country because of differences in cost of transportation, that can be met by applying a general rule determined by charging a certain percentage for transportation by figuring the cost from a central point in the country to its confines. Anyway, this difference exists under the present system, and would exist under free trade, as pointed out with respect to another phase of the problem.

The cost of production of home commodities having been approximately ascertained, it is next necessary to find out the cost of like products abroad, and then to compare the two, and thus to find out the difference. Should the comparison show that a product can be produced cheaper abroad than at home, then, under the Republican doctrine of " the true principle of protection," the difference, plus " a reasonable profit to American industries," should be the basis of the duty on that particular product. But the Tariff Board will have nothing to do with the application of this principle; that is a matter which concerns Congress,—and of course, the President, as regards his right of recommendation to that body.

It will in all probability be much more difficult to find out the foreign cost of production than that at home; and there will in all likelihood have to be more generalization as to the foreign costs. The American Government cannot reach out its arm across the seas and compel the foreign manufacturer to show his books and methods and process to the agent of our Tariff Board. On the contrary, the American official will probably have all sorts of obstacles placed in his way. Consuls know,—and I have had personal experience—and they sometimes know to their personal humiliation, that their inquiries as to foreign trade and commerce are not infrequently treated as impertinences by the foreign manufacturer and merchant. This was especially the experience of a number of our Consuls when they endeavored to ascertain the cost of foreign products (by order of our Government) for the use of the Ways and Means Committee in framing the present Tariff Law. Therefore, in addition to statistical clerks and technical experts in particular lines of industry, other men of experience abroad and with some diplomatic training, may be required to be employed for the foreign field.

Some of the critics of the Tariff Board idea have pointed out an initial difficulty, viz.: that the cost of production differs in different countries. But this difference already exists under our present tariff, and the objection is merely an extension of that applied to the home situation. This acknowledged difficulty can be met—at least within reason—by finding out the approximate cost of production in each of the competing countries, and then striking an average. There would undoubtedly be some inequalities in the application of this rule: that is, some competing countries can produce a given article cheaper than others can, and the former would have an advantage over the other foreign competitors in the American market. But this inequality exists now, under the present haphazard, rough-and-ready method; and it would exist under a system of free trade or of a tariff-for-revenue. So, in our own country, there is an inequality as to foreign products. For instance, viewed from a protection standpoint, the States nearest the importing point are at a disadvantage as compared with those States at a considerable distance away. Again, take free raw materials, under free trade or reciprocity: the consumers near the importing point would be at an advantage as to cost as compared with those in a distant State. Such inequalities are inevitable under any tariff system, or even absence of any customs restrictions. It would be absolutely impossible to frame any fiscal system which would place all competing countries on an equality as between themselves in the American market. It would be practically impossible to have different rates for different countries according to the differing costs of production of those countries, quite apart from the obligations of treaties and of international law; and then, it would not be necessary. All that a Tariff Board can do, all that any " scientific " system can do, is to arrive at an approximation of the difference of cost of production in competing countries as a whole.

The objection that the Government, or the Tariff Board, cannot determine what is " a reasonable profit to American industries," has some apparent force in it; but, after all, the proposition is of such a general and indefinite nature, that no hard-and-fast rule can be applied. There would probably be a general agreement that American manufacturers, like American workmen, ought to obtain higher financial rewards than prevail in foreign countries. Exorbitant profits are absolutely opposed to the theory of the new method of tariff adjustment, if they be the result of high tariff rates to the detriment of " the ultimate consumer." Possibly a general standard of fair profits can be arrived at through the information which is now being obtained under the Federal law taxing the net incomes of corporations. But again, this is a matter for Congress itself to settle, and not for the Tariff Board.

It is objected that it would be necessary, under the proposed new system, to change the tariff rates whenever there was a change in the cost of production; and that this would mean frequent changes, the result being a frequent dislocation of business. This objection is based on the extreme and misleading assumption that the basis of the duty—namely, the difference in the cost of production at home and abroad—must be mathematically .exact, and must be automatically responsive to every relative change in the cost of production. This is absolutely impossible. This same objection, only much multiplied, applies to the present happy-go-lucky system. Changes could be made at indeterminate periods whenever conditions called for a change; but as a change would presumably not be made unless conditions justified action, the danger of causing business dislocation would be much less than is the case under the present system—or lack of system; and then, whatever slight disturbance would result would be confined chiefly to the particular item or items under consideration, and would not affect the entire range of industrialism, as now,—although, of course, there is always a mutual interrelation of one industry with others. Furthermore, whatever change would be made would be under a definite, well-known policy, without the operation of any secret influence of " the interests," and in consequence no harm would be done to any legitimate American interest, the application of the policy being in response to the natural demand of the American consumers, and being acceptable to those producers who were willing to compete with foreigners on the basis of a fair profit. Again it is pointed out that whatever changes were made would be made by Congress and not by the Tariff Board.

Both theoretically and practically, the whole matter resolves itself into this: At present all tariff legislation is haphazard, principally because of the lack of accurate information and a definite policy on the part of Congress; the Tariff Board has been established really only as a Bureau of Information, for the benefit of both the President and of Congress; and Congress will still, as in the past, be charged with the responsibility of passing tariff legislation; but now, for the first time, Congress will be able to act intelligently, with justice to both the American producer and the consumer,—whether on the assumption that the American people desire the protective principle to be maintained in our fiscal system, or that they desire to adopt a tariff-for-revenue policy.

But the inquiries of the Tariff Board, as broadened by the Longworth Bill, were not to be confined to statistics covering comparative costs of production. The Board were required to investigate " the condition of domestic and foreign markets affecting the American products, including detailed information with respect thereto, together with all other facts," etc.; and, on his direction, they were to " advise the President as to the state of the commerce of the United States with foreign countries."

These provisions of the bill probably commended themselves to general acceptance, even to those who criticised its main feature— that providing for an investigation of the comparative costs of production.

The bill creating a permanent Tariff Board had a remarkable career in Congress. After passing the House by a large majority, and also passing the Senate with several inconsequential amendments, it failed to become a law. During the throes of the dissolution on the Fourth of March, " filibustering " Democrats succeeded in preventing a vote on the Senate amendments, and the bill was thus killed " by default." But just before the adjournment of Congress a sum of $200,000 was voted for the use of the present Board—as it exists under the special clause in the Tariff Act and the Sundry Appropriations Act—to enable it to continue its work for another year. It must be said that the prospects of a continuance of the inquiries of the Board after the end of the fiscal year of 1912 are not encouraging. It is, however, very unsafe to make a political prophecy; and possibly the results of those inquiries will be so satisfactory as to lead to such a pronounced public demand for its establishment on a permanent basis that the legislators at Washington will feel constrained to pay heed.

EDITORIAL NOTES

ONE of the most regrettable features of modern American life is the indifference to ruffianism, in its various forms. It is inevitable that in a democratic country, constantly absorbing immigrants accustomed to different conditions, the principle of personal equality will lead at first to a lowering of the general standard of courtesy. It is not without cause that the word " vulgar " has acquired its special significance, so closely connected with its original meaning. It takes time for the average man to realize that liberty involves responsibility, and that freedom carries with it the obligation of fitness. But the one hundred and thirty-five years of our national history would seem a period not too brief for the development of a code of private conduct which should bear some adequate relation to our public professions. We have discarded the affectations of the old world; but our directness and naturalness are sometimes a little too direct and too natural. The prevalent tendency is to regard rudeness either as normal, or as an experience to be expected, and tolerated easily. This attitude has been reflected in the Press and in Congress: it was instructive to note the general absence of critical comment on the regrettable scenes which marked the adjournment of the Sixty-first Congress. The facts were recorded; but little surprise seemed to be felt at the exhibition of vulgar rowdyism in the National Legislature. The quotation which follows, from a daily paper, should be peculiarly gratifying to Representative Hughes, of New Jersey, and Representative Johnson, of New York.

" Three times Speaker Cannon, unable to control the militant democratic minority, intent upon preventing the passage of the measure in order that they might revise the tariff on their own information, ordered the Sergeant at Arms to bring forth the mace, the emblem of the authority of the House. But he was dealing with more than one hundred and fifty members, all of whom were determined to defeat the bill. They disregarded the mace as if it had been an ordinary stick of wood. On one occasion Representative Hughes, of New Jersey, stood defiantly in the centre aisle, glaring at the Sergeant at Arms, although Speaker Cannon had ordered every member to take his seat. Representative Johnson, of New York, threatened the Speaker with personal violence."

It is often assumed that it is impossible for a large body of men to discuss important and controversial questions without relapsing from time to time into some degree of rowdyism. This, of course,— like the statement that there are only 30,000 civilized people in Europe—is either not true, or it is a painful comment on the crude process that has long been mistaken for education. Earnestness is not measured by ebullience. Passion is rarely aroused by a desire for the public welfare or for the discovery of truth: thwarted personal interest and wounded personal conceit are more usual causes. There is something incongruous in the makers of our laws being also the makers of such exhibitions of themselves as Representative Hughes, of New Jersey, and Representative Johnson, of New York. In a national assembly, the dignity of debate should be an inviolable tradition. No man who is capable of losing his temper in the course of an argument should be in a position to lose it in the Capitol. The affairs of the nation should not be at the disposal of men who have not learnt the elements of self-control. Our actual transgressions may appear trivial when compared with those of other countries: but it is time that public opinion made itself felt decisively, in big and little matters; and this is a type of offence that cannot be regarded with complacency. The Latin temperament has its own modes of expression; the amenities of the French Chamber of Deputies and the Spanish Cortes are characteristic, if unfortunate. But America can dispense with such excitability: we do not wish to emulate, even remotely, the scene in the British House of Commons seventeen years ago, when the present Speaker of the House, Mr. Lowther, struggled in vain to prevent two hundred honorable members—including, of course, the combined Irish party—from indulging in a general free fight.

* * *

As was generally anticipated, the reciprocity agreement failed to secure the approval of the old Congress. Its fate in the new session will be carefully watched. There can be no doubt that the interests arrayed against the measure are formidable and far-reaching. Amongst the other subjects which will come up for consideration in a Democratic House are the Payne-Aldrich tariff law, the direct election of Senators, and the revival of the general age pension bill.

* * *

The situation in Great Britain remains complex and grave. It is one of the ironies of history that England, which has so long refused Home Rule to Ireland, should now be governed by the Irish party. Home Rule, of course, is inevitable in the near future; the principle is accepted, and the present electorate is unfamiliar with the bitterness of feeling which followed Mr. Gladstone's dissolution of Parliament in 1886 and caused the recasting of the great political parties. The opposition of Ulster is more formidable, but not insuperable; it is probably due as much to financial reasons as to religious or racial differences. The burden of taxation would affect her more seriously than any other part of Ireland, and the prospect is naturally not pleasing. The most striking personal feature of the situation is the inflexibility of Mr. Asquith—in his attitude, at least, toward the suffragettes and the House of Lords. The reconstruction of the Second Chamber is regarded without any sentimental reverence for the oldest Constitution in the world: the creation of five hundred new peers would scarcely come within the range of " slowly broadening from precedent to precedent," which is the natural and most satisfactory way of dealing with constitutional difficulties. Yet exceptional conditions require exceptional measures. England herself adopted them conspicuously in 1649 and 1688; and our own country has some need for drastic, though not violent, reform.

*   *   *

It is a pity that no clear and convincing picture of the Czar of Russia can be obtained; a true interpretation of his character would be curiously interesting. Here is a man of strange contradictions. His original pronouncement in favor of universal peace at the beginning of his reign came to Europe like sunshine in a cloudy sky— something beautiful, but leaving men doubtful as to its durability. Was this new autocrat an idle visionary or a strong idealist? Was the disarmament of the world to come from Tennyson's " o'ergrown barbarian in the East "? The High Priest of Brotherhood has since seen the war with Japan; he has permitted the massacre of Red Sunday and the long agony of the Jews; he has witnessed throughout his empire a carnival of courts-martial, of butchery and exile. And now again he comes forward with one of the big schemes of a generation: the serfs who were freed by Alexander are to be made free in reality, as well as in name. They are to have the means to live, as well as the right to live. If this be carried out, millions will bless the name of the man whom millions have cursed. It is a strange world.

*   *   *

In another place in this issue there is an article on Rabies and on the methods which must certainly be adopted to control it. Apart from the actual or possible prevalence of the disease, the question of general inconvenience and annoyance is involved. In many suburban districts this annoyance, with its risk of danger, is serious. There are places within twenty miles of New York where a commuter cannot walk from the station to his house after twilight, without being followed by some yapping, ill-trained cur. Not only the " stray, ownerless dog " must go; but unregulated, indiscriminate ownership must be prevented. The only condition on which dogs can be kept is that they be kept under complete control.

*   *   *

There are some subjects which it is difficult to discuss in a public review; some which it is undesirable to discuss. But the public opinion which approves or tolerates in many of our newspapers a perpetual saturnalia of sensationalism, can be guided, and must be guided, to realize that matters which affect the deepest welfare of the human race should be brought sanely and truthfully to the knowledge of those concerned. There is incredible ignorance or indifference with regard to vital matters—an indifference which the medical profession and the churches, to their shame, have made no organized effort to dissipate. It is often assumed that there is something immoral in morality; that it is unpleasant to face the fundamental facts of life intelligently. So we blunder on, more or less consciously hypocritical. Prejudice, stupidity, false shame, are the chief bulwarks of convention: our hospitals and cemeteries bear witness to the price which is paid for " respectability." The leaven of the old lies still lingers: there is one code for man, and another for woman; and it is impolite to ask why. Is it impolite to mention that there are fifty thousand men in New York City alone who are worse than leprous—a horror to themselves, and a festering, fatal sore to the community? And is it impolite to point out that this is due to ignorance, more than to viciousness; that the idea of the "double standard" of life has too often been absorbed by men because it permeated the atmosphere of their training and adolescence? A truer spirit is growing; but the solution depends upon the women. They could so influence the lives of their sons, and mould their characters, that there would be little need for this insistent demand for the vote which is to bring a finer spirit into public affairs and substitute sociology for politics. But what they have failed to do with their children, they can still attempt with their husbands, now that economic conditions are changing, and woman can resume more and more her original right of selection. It would be well if every woman in America could read and consider the following letter to the Editor of The Forum.

"I read with deep interest the article on 'The Problem of Divorce,' by Rheta Childe Dorr, which appeared in the January issue of The Forum.

"While Mrs. Dorr refers to 'The Double Standard of Morals,' she has not given it the emphasis which it deserves. If it were possible thoroughly to investigate divorce, I think statistics would confirm her in this belief.

"I believe the double standard of morals to be both the cause and occasion for the majority of divorces.

"Woman is emerging from slavery; she is no longer a plaything or at best a mere 'Haus-frau'—but is rapidly evolving into a thinking, volitional being. Is it possible to believe that she will continue to suffer the wrong she has borne through the centuries?

"She, trained for purity of living, chastity of thought, cleanness of body—honor and loyalty—is it *reasonable* to suppose that she will be satisfied with a mate wholly her inferior in these vital points?

"Take the average man of to-day: there is scarcely one who has maintained before marriage the personal purity demanded as a matter of course from women. In every city, thousands continually prostitute the most sacred function of their lives; hundreds of these thousands are infected with the foulest diseases known to the human race.

"I ask any rational being, can it be thought a possible thing that the women of this free land will suffer this outrage any longer? When they in their shame and humiliation seek to escape from the intolerable burden of this hideous mockery—for such is marriage under these conditions—shall they be martyrs—objects of condemnation and censure among intelligent, Christian people?

"Is it civilized that the law of the land should endeavor to make more difficult the divorce from one entirely unfit and unworthy to be husband and companion? However it is—whatever may be attempted —the time of woman's real emancipation is at hand: though actual suffrage may be delayed yet awhile, she will meet the situation bravely and fearlessly—she will know the man she is to marry and refuse to mate with one not her *moral equal;* she will refuse to become an accomplice in the conspiracy against coming generations.

" To some I may appear to have over-stated, or been unduly harsh in my statements, but I am sustained by *facts*, evil and tragic though they be.

" There is so much twaddle about marital unrest, destruction of the home, etc., so much apprehension over the *result*—why not frankly face the *cause?*

" When a chemist mixes an acid and an alkali, is he surprised at the fermentation that takes place? When society and individuals aid and abet a union of purity and corruption, should they exclaim with consternation at the psychic and physical ebullition that follows? Is not ' unrest '—tragedy—the natural sequence?

" The problem is one that women must solve. First as mothers they must educate their children in the matter of life's great truths— self-control, self-reverence, the sacredness of the racial function, the hideous wrongs and penalties of its abuse. Then as prospective wives they must *know* their lovers—as I have said before—not yielding to the sophistries of a mock-modesty; they must demand of them chastity of life as their right and the right of their unborn children.

" When this ideal is realized and prevails, marriage will be, indeed, a ' holy state,' and marriages contracted may endure in mutual happiness and honor."

THE NEW MACHIAVELLI

H. G. WELLS

CHAPTER THE FOURTH

THE BESETTING OF SEX

III

LATER on in that year the women began a new attack. Day and night, and all through the long nights of the Budget sittings, at all the piers of the gates of New Palace Yard and at St. Stephen's Porch, stood women pickets, and watched us silently and reproachfully as we went to and fro. They were women of all sorts, though, of course, the independent worker-class predominated. There were gray-headed old ladies standing there, sturdily charming in the rain; battered-looking, ambiguous women, with something of the desperate bitterness of battered women showing in their eyes; north-country factory girls; cheaply-dressed suburban women; trim, comfortable mothers of families; valiant-eyed girl graduates and undergraduates; lank, hungry-looking creatures, who stirred one's imagination; one very dainty little woman in deep mourning, I recall, grave and steadfast, with eyes fixed on distant things. Some of those women looked defiant, some timidly aggressive, some full of the stir of adventure, some drooping with cold and fatigue. The supply never ceased. I had a mortal fear that somehow the supply might halt or cease. I found that continual siege of the legislature extraordinarily impressive—infinitely more impressive than the feeble-forcible "ragging" of the more militant section. I thought of the appeal that must be going through the country, summoning the women from countless, scattered homes, rooms, colleges, to Westminster.

I remember too the petty little difficulty I felt, whether I should ignore these pickets altogether, or lift a hat as I hurried past with averted eyes, or look them in the face as I did so. Towards the end the House evolved an etiquette of salutation.

IV

There was a tendency, even on the part of its sympathizers, to treat the whole suffrage agitation as if it were a disconnected issue, irrelevant to all other broad developments of social and political life.

We struggled, all of us, to ignore the indicating finger it thrust out before us. "Your schemes, for all their bigness," it insisted to our reluctant, averted minds, "still don't go down to the essential things. . . ."

We have to plough deeper, or our inadequate children's insufficient children will starve amidst harvests of earless futility. That conservatism which works in every class to preserve in its essentials the habitual daily life is all against a profounder treatment of political issues. The politician, almost as absurdly as the philosopher, tends constantly, in spite of magnificent preludes, vast intimations, to specialize himself out of the reality he has so stupendously summoned— he bolts back to littleness. The world has to be moulded anew, he continues to admit, but without, he adds, any risk of upsetting his week-end visits, his morning cup of tea. . . .

The discussion of the relations of men and women disturbs every' one. It racks upon the innate life of every one who attempts it. And at any particular time only a small minority have a personal interest in changing the established state of affairs. Habit and interest are in a constantly recruited majority against conscious change and adjustment in these matters. Drift rules us. The great mass of people, and an overwhelming proportion of influential people, are people who have banished their dreams and made their compromise. Wonderful and beautiful possibilities are no longer to be thought about. They have given up any aspirations for intense love, for splendid offspring, for keen delights, have accepted a cultivated kindliness and an uncritical sense of righteousness as their compensation. It's a settled affair with them, a settled, dangerous affair. Most of them fear, and many hate, the slightest reminder of those abandoned dreams. As Dayton once said to the Pentagram Circle, when we were discussing the problem of a universal marriage and divorce law throughout the Empire, "I am for leaving all these things alone." And then, with a groan in his voice, "Leave them alone! Leave them all alone!"

That was his whole speech for the evening, in a note of suppressed passion, and presently, against all our etiquette, he got up and went out.

For some years after my marriage, I too was for leaving them alone. I developed a dread and dislike for romance, for emotional music, for the human figure in art—turning my heart to landscape. I wanted to sneer at lovers and their ecstasies, and was uncomfortable until I found the effective sneer. In matters of private morals these were my most uncharitable years. I didn't want to think of these things any more for ever. I hated the people whose talk or practice showed they were not of my opinion. I wanted to believe that their views were immoral and objectionable and contemptible, because I had decided to treat them as at that level. I was, in fact, falling into the attitude of the normal decent man.

And yet one cannot help thinking! The sensible moralized man finds it hard to escape the stream of suggestion that there are still dreams beyond these commonplace acquiescences,—the appeal of beauty suddenly shining upon one, the mothlike stirrings of serene summer nights, the sweetness of distant music. . . .

It is one of the paradoxical factors in our public life at the present time, which penalizes abandonment to love so abundantly and so heavily, that power and influence to control fall largely to unencumbered people and sterile people and people who have married for passionless purposes, people whose very deficiency in feeling has left them free to follow ambition, people beauty-blind, who don't understand what it is to fall in love, what it is to desire children or have them, what it is to feel in their blood and bodies the supreme claim of good births and selective births above all other affairs in life, people almost of necessity averse from this most fundamental aspect of existence. . . .

V

It wasn't, however, my deepening sympathy with and understanding of the position of women in general, or the change in my ideas about all these intimate things my fast friendship with Isabel was bringing about, that led me to the heretical view I have in the last five years dragged from the region of academic and timid discussion into the field of practical politics. Those influences, no doubt, have converged to the same end, and given me a powerful emotional push upon my road, but it was a broader and colder view of things that first determined me in my attempt to graft the Endowment of Motherhood in some form or other upon British Imperialism. Now that I am exiled from the political world, it is possible to estimate just how effectually that grafting has been done.

I have explained how the ideas of a trained aristocracy and a universal education grew to paramount importance in my political scheme. It is but a short step from this to the question of the quantity and quality of births in the community, and from that again to these forbidden and fear beset topics of marriage, divorce, and the family organization. A sporadic discussion of these aspeets had been going on for years, a Eugenic society existed, and articles on the Falling Birth Rate and the Rapid Multiplication of the Unfit were staples of the monthly magazines. But beyond an intermittent scolding of prosperous childless people in general—one never addressed them in particular—nothing was done towards arresting those adverse processes. Almost against my natural inclination, I found myself forced to go into these things. I came to the conclusion that under modern conditions the isolated private family, based on the existing marriage contract, was failing in its work. It wasn't producing enough children, and children good enough and well trained enough for the demands of the developing civilized State. Our civilization was growing outwardly, and decaying in its intimate substance, and unless it was presently to collapse, some very extensive and courageous reorganization was needed. The old haphazard system of pairing, qualified more and more by worldly discretions, no longer secures us a young population numerous enough or good enough for the growing needs and possibilities of our Empire. Statecraft sits weaving splendid garments, no doubt, but with a puny, ugly, insufficient baby in the cradle.

No one so far has dared to take up this problem as a present question for statecraft, but it comes unheralded, unadvocated, and sits at every legislative board. Every improvement is provisional except the improvement of the race, and it became more and more doubtful to me if we were improving the race at all! Splendid and beautiful and courageous people must come together and have children, women with their fine senses and glorious devotion must be freed from the net that compels them to be celibate, compels them to be childless and useless, or to bear children ignobly to men whom need and ignorance and the treacherous pressure of circumstances have forced upon them. We all know that, and so few dare even to whisper it for fear-that they should seem, in seeking to save the family, to threaten its existence. It is as if a party of pygmies in a not too capacious room had been joined by a carnivorous giant —and decided to go on living happily by cutting him dead. . . .

The problem the developing civilized State has to solve is how it can get the best possible increase under the best possible conditions. I became more and more convinced that the independent family unit of to-day, in which the man is master of the wife and owner of the children, in which all are dependent upon him, subordinated to his enterprises and liable to follow his fortunes up or down, does not supply anything like the best conceivable conditions. We want to modernize the family footing altogether. An enormous premium both in pleasure and competitive efficiency is put upon voluntary childlessness, and enormous inducements are held out to women to subordinate instinctive and selective preferences to social and material considerations.

The practical reaction of modern conditions upon the old tradition of the family is this; that beneath the pretence that nothing is changing, secretly and with all the unwholesomeness of secrecy everything is changed. Offspring fall away, the birth rate falls and falls most among just the most efficient and active and best adapted classes in the community. The species is recruited from among its failures and from among less civilized aliens. Contemporary civilizations are in effect burning the best of their possible babies in the furnaces that run the machinery. In the United States the native Anglo-American strain has scarcely increased at all since 1830, and in most Western European countries the same is probably true of the ablest and most energetic elements in the community. The women of these classes still remain legally and practically dependent and protected, with the only natural excuse for their dependence gone. . . .

The modern world becomes an immense spectacle of unsatisfactory groupings; here childless couples bored to death in the hopeless effort to sustain an incessant honeymoon, here homes in which a solitary child grows unsocially, here small two or three-child homes that do no more than continue the culture of the parents at a great social cost, here numbers of unhappy educated but childless married women, here careless, decivilized fecund homes, here orphanages and asylums for the heedlessly begotten. It is just the disorderly proliferation of Bromstead over again, in lives instead of in houses.

What is the good, what is the common sense, of rectifying boundaries, pushing research and discovery, building cities, improving all the facilities of life, making great fleets, waging wars, while this aimless decadence remains the quality of the biological outlook? . . .

It is difficult now to trace how I changed from my early aversion until I faced this mass of problems. But so far back as 1910 I had it clear in my mind that I would rather fail utterly than participate in all the surrenders of mind and body that are implied in Dayton's snarl of " Leave it alone; leave it all alone! " Marriage and the begetting and care of children, is the very ground substance in the life of the community. In a world in which everything changes, in which fresh methods, fresh adjustments and fresh ideas perpetually renew the circumstances of life, it is preposterous that we should not even examine into these matters, should rest content to be ruled by the uncriticised traditions of a barbaric age.

VI

Now, it seems to me that the solution of this problem is also the solution of the woman's individual problem. The two go together, are right and left of one question. The only conceivable way out from our *impasse* lies in the recognition of parentage, that is to say of adequate mothering, as no longer a chance product of individual passions but a service rendered to the State. Women must become less and less subordinated to individual men, since this works out in a more or less complete limitation, waste, and sterilization of their essentially social function; they must become more and more subordinated as individually independent citizens to the collective purpose. Or, to express the thing by a familiar phrase, the highly organized, scientific State we desire must, if it is to exist at all, base itself not upon the irresponsible man-ruled family, but upon the matriarchal family, the citizenship and freedom of women and the public endowment of motherhood.

After two generations of confused and experimental revolt it grows clear to modern women that a conscious, deliberate motherhood and mothering is their special function in the State, and that a personal subordination to an individual man with an unlimited power of control over this intimate and supreme duty is a degradation. No contemporary woman of education put to the test is willing to recognize any claim a man can make upon her but the claim of her freely-given devotion to him. She wants the reality of her choice and she means "family" while a man too often means only progression. This alters the spirit of the family relationships fundamentally. Their form remains just what it was when woman was esteemed a pretty, desirable, and incidentally a child-producing chattel. Against these time-honored ideas the new spirit of womanhood struggles in shame, astonishment, bitterness, and tears. . . .

I confess myself altogether feminist. I have no doubts in the matter. I want this coddling and brow-beating of women to cease. I want to see women come in, free and fearless, to a full participation in the collective purpose of mankind. Women, I am convinced, are as fine as men; they can be as wise as men; they are capable of far greater devotion than men. I want to see them citizens, with a marriage law framed primarily for them and for their protection and the good of the race, and not for men's satisfactions. I want to see them bearing and rearing good children in the State as a generously rewarded public duty and service, choosing their husbands freely and discerningly, and in no way enslaved by or subordinated to the men they have chosen. The social consciousness of women seems to me an unworked, an almost untouched mine of wealth for the constructive purpose of the world. I want to change the respective values of the family group altogether, and make the home indeed the women's kingdom and the mother the owner and responsible guardian of her children.

It is no use pretending that this is not novel and revolutionary;

it is. The Endowment of Motherhood implies a new method of social organization, a rearrangement of the social unit, untried in human experience—as untried as electric traction was or flying in 1800. Of course, it may work out to modify men's ideas of marriage profoundly. To me that is a secondary consideration. I do not believe that particular assertion myself, because I am convinced that a practical monogamy is a psychological necessity to the mass of civilized people. But even if I did believe it I should still keep to my present line, because it is the only line that will prevent a highly organized civilization from ending in biological decay. The public Endowment of Motherhood is the only possible way which will ensure the permanently developing civilized State at which all constructive minds are aiming. A point is reached in the life-history of a civilization when either this reconstruction must be effected or the quality and *morale* of the population prove insufficient for the needs of the developing organization. It is not so much moral decadence that will destroy us as moral inadaptability. The old code fails under the new needs. The only alternative to this profound reconstruction is a decay in human quality and social collapse. Either this unprecedented rearrangement must be achieved by our civilization, or it must presently come upon a phase of disorder and crumble and perish, as Rome perished, as France declines, as the strain of the Pilgrim Fathers dwindles out of America. Whatever hope there may be in the attempt therefore, there is no alternative to the attempt.

VII

I wanted political success now dearly enough, but not at the price of constructive realities. These questions were no doubt monstrously dangerous in the political world; there wasn't a politician alive who didn't look scared at the mention of " The Family," but if raising these issues were essential to the social reconstructions on which my life was set, that did not matter. It only implied that I should take them up with deliberate caution. There was no release because of risk or difficulty.

The question of whether I should commit myself to some open project in this direction was going on in my mind concurrently with my speculations about a change of party, like bass and treble in a complex piece of music. The two drew to a conclusion together. I would not only go over to Imperialism, but I would attempt to biologize Imperialism.

I thought at first that I was undertaking a monstrous uphill task. But as I came to look into the possibilities of the matter, a

strong persuasion grew up in my mind that this panic fear of legislative proposals affecting the family basis was excessive, that things
were much riper for development in this direction than old-experi-
enced people out of touch with the younger generation imagined,
that to phrase the thing in a parliamentary fashion, " something
might be done in the constituencies " with the Endowment of Motherhood forthwith provided only that it was made perfectly clear that
anything a sane person could possibly intend by " morality " was
left untouched by these proposals.

I went to work very carefully. I got Roper of the *Daily Telephone* and Burkett of the *Dial* to try over a silly-season discussion
of State Help for Mothers, and I put a series of articles on eugenics,
upon the fall in the birth-rate, and similar topics in the *Blue Weekly*,
leading up to a tentative and generalized advocacy of the public endowment of the nation's children. I was more and more struck by
the acceptance won by a sober and restrained presentation of this
suggestion.

And then, in the fourth year of the *Blue Weekly's* career, came
the Handitch election, and I was forced by the clamor of my antagonist, and very willingly forced, to put my convictions to the
test. I returned triumphantly to Westminster with the Public Endowment of Motherhood as part of my open profession and with the
full approval of the party press. Applauding benches of Imperialists cheered me on my way to the table between the whips.

That second time I took the oath I was not one of a crowd of
new members, but salient, an event, a symbol of profound changes
and new purposes in the national life.

VIII

Here it is my political book comes to an end, and in a sense my
book ends altogether. For the rest is but to tell how I was swept
out of this great world of political possibilities. I close this Third
Book as I opened it, with an admission of difficulties and complexities, but now with a pile of manuscript before me I have to confess
them unsurmounted and still entangled.

Yet my aim was a final simplicity. I have sought to show my
growing realization that the essential quality of all political and
social effort is the development of a great race mind behind the in-
terplay of individual lives. That is the collective human reality,
the basis of morality, the purpose of devotion. To that our lives
must be given, from that will come the perpetual fresh release and
further ennoblement of individual lives. . . .

I have wanted to make that idea of a collective mind play in this book the part United Italy plays in Machiavelli's *Prince*. I have called it the hinterland of reality, shown it accumulating a dominating truth and rightness which must force men's now sporadic motives more and more into a disciplined and understanding relation to a plan. And I have tried to indicate how I sought to serve this great clarification of our confusions. . . .

Now I come back to personality and the story of my self-betrayal, and how it is I have had to leave all that far-reaching scheme of mine, a mere project and beginning for other men to take or leave as it pleases them.

Book the Fourth

ISABEL

CHAPTER THE FIRST

LOVE AND SUCCESS

I

I COME to the most evasive and difficult part of my story, which is to tell how Isabel and I have made one common wreck of our joint lives.

It is not the telling of one simple disastrous accident. There was a vein in our natures that led to this collapse gradually and at that point and that it crept to the surface.

One may indeed see our destruction—for indeed politically we could not be more extinct if we had been shot dead—in the form of a catastrophe as disconnected and conclusive as a meteoric stone falling out of heaven upon two friends and crushing them both. But I do not think that is true to our situation or ourselves. We were not taken by surprise. The thing was in us and not from without, it was akin to our way of thinking and our habitual attitudes, it had, for all its impulsive effect, a certain necessity. We might have escaped no doubt, as two men at a hundred yards may shoot at each other with pistols for a considerable time and escape. But it isn't particularly reasonable to talk of the contrariety of fate if they both get hit.

Isabel and I were dangerous to each other for several years of friendship and not quite unwittingly so.

In writing this moreover there is a very great difficulty in steering my way between two equally undesirable tones in the telling. In the first place I do not want to seem to confess my sins with a penitence I am very doubtful if I feel. Now that I have got Isabel we can no doubt count the cost of it and feel unquenchable regrets, but I am not sure, if we could be put back now into such circumstances as we were in a year ago, or two years ago, whether with my eyes full open I should not do over again very much as I did. And on the other hand I do not want to justify the things we have done. We are two bad people—if there is to be any classification of good and bad at all—we have acted badly, and quite apart from any other considerations we've largely wasted our own very great possibilities. But it is part of a queer humor that underlies all this, that I find myself stepping again and again into a sentimental treatment of our case that is as unpremeditated as it is insincere. When I am a little tired after a morning's writing I find the faint suggestion getting into every other sentence, that our blunders and misdeeds embody after the fashion of the prophet Hosea profound moral truths. Indeed I feel so little confidence in my ability to keep this altogether out of my book that I warn the reader here that in spite of anything he may read elsewhere in the story intimating however shyly an esoteric and exalted virtue in our proceedings, the plain truth of the business is that Isabel and I wanted each other with a want entirely formless, inconsiderate and overwhelming. And though I could tell you countless delightful and beautiful things about Isabel, were this a book in her praise, I cannot either analyze that want or account for its extreme intensity.

I will confess that deep in my mind there is a belief in a sort of wild rightness about any love that is fraught with beauty, but that eludes me and vanishes again and is now I feel to be put with the real veracities and righteousnesses and virtues in the paddocks and menageries of human reason. . . .

We have already a child and Margaret was childless and I for myself strove to insist upon that, as if it was a justification. But indeed when we became lovers there was small thought of eugenics between us. Ours was a mutual trust or philo-progenitive passion. Old Nature behind us may have such purposes with us, but it is not for us to annex her intentions by a moralizing afterthought. There isn't in fact any decent justification for us whatever—at that the story must stand.

But if there is no justification there is at least a very effective excuse in the mental confusedness of our time. The evasion of that passionately thorough exposition of belief and of the grounds of morality, which is the outcome of the mercenary religious compromises of the late Victorian period, the stupid suppression of any but the most timid discussions of sexual morality in our literature and drama, the pervading cultivated and protected muddle-headedness, leaves mentally vigorous people with relatively enormous possibilities of destruction and little effective help.

They find themselves confronted by the habits and prejudices of manifestly commonplace people and by that extraordinary patched-up Christianity, the cult of a " Bromsteadized " deity, diffused, scattered and aimless, which hides from examination and any possibility of faith behind the plea of good taste. We are *forced* to be laws unto ourselves and to live experimentally. It is inevitable that a considerable fraction of just that bolder, more initiatory section of the intellectual community, the section that can least be spared from the collective life in a period of trust and change, will drift into such emotional crisis and such disaster as overtook us. Most perhaps will escape, but many will go down, many more than the world can spare. It is the unwritten law of all our public life, and the same holds true of America, that an honest open scandal ends a career. England in the last quarter of a century has wasted half a dozen statesmen on this score; she could, I believe, reject Nelson now if he sought to serve her. It is wonderful that to us fretting here in exile this should seem the cruelest as well as the most foolish elimination of a necessary social element. It destroys no vice; for vice hides by virtue. It not only rewards dullness as if it were positive virtue, but sets an economic premium upon hypocrisy. That is my case and that is why I am telling the sexual side of my story with so much explicitness.

II

Ever since the Kinghamstead election I had maintained what seemed a desultory friendship with Isabel. At first it was rather Isabel kept it up than I. Whenever Margaret and I went down to that villa, with its three or four acres of garden and shrubbery about it, which fulfilled our election promise to live at Kinghamstead, Isabel would turn up in a state of frank cheerfulness, rejoicing at us, and talk all she was reading and thinking to me, and stay for all the rest of the day. In her shameless liking for me she was as natural as a savage. She would exercise me vigorously at tennis, while Margaret lay and rested her back in the afternoon, or guide me for some long ramble that dodged the suburban and congested patches of the constituency with amazing skill. She took possession of me in that unabashed, straight-minded way a girl will sometimes adopt with a man, chose my path or criticised my game with a motherly solicitude for my welfare that was absurd and delightful. And we talked. We discussed and criticised the stories of novels, scraps of history, pictures, social questions, socialism, the policy of the Government. She was young and most unevenly informed, but she was amazingly sharp and quick and good. Never before in my life had I known a girl of her age, or a woman, of her quality. I had never dreamt there was such talk in the world. Kinghamstead became a lightless place when she went to Oxford. Heaven knows how much that may not have precipitated my abandonment of the seat!

She went to Ridout College, Oxford, and that certainly weighed with me when presently after my breach with the Liberals various little undergraduate societies began to ask for lectures and discussions. I favored Oxford. I declared openly I did so because of her. At that time I think we neither of us suspected the possibility of passion that lay like a coiled snake in the path before us. It seemed to us that we had the quaintest, most delightful friendship in the world; she was my pupil, and I was her guide, philosopher, and friend. People smiled indulgently—even Margaret smiled indulgently—at our attraction for one another.

Such friendships are not uncommon nowadays—among easygoing, liberal-minded people. For the most part, there's no sort of harm, as people say, in them. The two persons concerned are never supposed to think of the passionate love that hovers so close to the friendship, or if they do, then they banish the thought. I think we kept the thought as permanently in exile as any one could do. If it did in odd moments come into our heads we pretended elaborately it wasn't there.

Only we were both very easily jealous of each other's attention, and tremendously insistent upon each other's preference.

I remember once during the Oxford days an intimation that should have set me thinking, and I suppose discreetly disentangling myself. It was one Sunday afternoon, and it must have been about May, for the trees and shrubs of Ridout College were gay with blossom, and fresh with the new sharp greens of spring. I had walked talking with Isabel and a couple of other girls through the wide gardens of the place, seen and criticised the new brick pond, nodded to the daughter of this friend and that in the hammocks under the trees, and picked a way among the scattered tea-parties on the lawn to our own circle on the grass under a Siberian crab near the great bay window. There I sat and ate great quantities of cake, and discussed the tactics of the Suffragettes. I had made some comments upon the spirit of the movement in an address to the men in Pembroke, and it had got abroad, and a group of girls and women dons were now having it out with me.

I forget the drift of the conversation, or what it was made Isabel interrupt me. She did interrupt me. She had been lying prone on the ground at my right hand, chin on fists, listening thoughtfully, and I was sitting beside old Lady Evershead on a garden seat. I turned to Isabel's voice, and saw her face uplifted, and her dear cheeks and nose and forehead all splashed and barred with sunlight and the shadows of the twigs of the trees behind me. And something—an infinite tenderness—stabbed me. It was a keen physical feeling, like nothing I had ever felt before. It had a quality of tears in it. For the first time in my narrow and concentrated life another human being had really thrust into my being and gripped my very heart.

Our eyes met perplexed for an extraordinary moment. Then I turned back and addressed myself a little stiffly to the substance of her intervention. For some time I couldn't look at her again.

From that time forth I knew I loved Isabel beyond measure.

Yet it is curious that it never occurred to me for a year or so that this was likely to be a matter of passion between us. I have told how definitely I put my imagination into harness in those matters at my marriage, and I was living now in a world of big interests, where there is neither much time nor inclination for deliberate love-making.

Isabel was as unforeseeing as I to begin with, but sex marches into the life of an intelligent girl with demands and challenges far more urgent than the mere call of curiosity and satiable desire that comes to a young man. No woman yet has dared to tell the story of that unfolding. She attracted men, and she encouraged them, and watched them, and tested them, and dismissed them, and concealed the substance of her thoughts about them in the way that seems instinctive in a natural-minded girl. There was even an engagement—amidst the protests and disapproval of the college authorities. I never saw the man, though she gave me a long history of the affair, to which I listened with a forced and insincere sympathy. She struck me oddly as taking the relationship for a thing in itself, and regardless of its consequences. After a time she became silent about him, and then threw him over and by that time, I think, for all that she was so much my junior, she knew more about herself and me than I was to know for several years to come.

We didn't see each other for some months after my resignation, but we kept up a frequent correspondence. She said twice over that she wanted to talk to me, that letters didn't convey what one wanted to say, and I went up to Oxford pretty definitely to see her

—though I combined it with one or two other engagements—some-when in February. Insensibly she had become important enough for me to make journeys for her.

But we didn't see very much of one another on that occasion. There was something in the air between us that made a faint embarrassment; the mere fact, perhaps, that she had asked me to come up.

A year before she would have dashed off with me quite un-scrupulously to talk alone, carried me off to her room for an hour with a minute of chaperonage to satisfy the rules. Now there was always some one or other near us that it seemed impossible to ex-orcise.

We went for a walk on the Sunday afternoon with old Fortescue, K.C., who'd come up to see his two daughters, both great friends of Isabel's, and some mute inglorious don whose name I forget, but who was in a state of marked admiration for her. The six of us played a game of conversational entanglements throughout, and mostly I was impressing the Fortescue girls with the want of mental concentration possible in a rising politician. We went down Carfex, I remember, to Folly Bridge, and inspected the Barges, and then back by way of Merton to the Botanic Gardens and Magdalen Bridge. And in the Botanic Gardens she got almost her only chance with me.

" Last months of Oxford," she said.

" And then? " I asked.

" I'm coming to London," she said.

" To write? "

She was silent for a moment. Then she said abruptly, with that quick flush of hers and a sudden boldness in her eyes: " I'm going to work with you. Why shouldn't I? "

III

Here, again, I suppose I had a fair warning of the drift of things. I seem to remember myself in the train to Paddington, sitting with a handful of papers—galley proofs for the *Blue Weekly*, I suppose—on my lap, and thinking about her and that last sentence of hers, and all that it might mean to me.

It is very hard to recall even the main outline of anything so elusive as a meditation. I know that the idea of working with her gripped me, fascinated me. That my value in her life seemed grow-ing filled me with pride and a kind of gratitude. I was already in no doubt that her value in my life was tremendous. It made it none the less, that in those days I was obsessed by the idea that she was transitory, and bound to go out of my life again. It is no good trying to set too fine a face upon this complex business, there is gold and clay and sunlight and savagery in every love story, and a multitude of elvish elements peeped out beneath the fine rich curtain of affection that masked our future. I've never properly weighed how immensely my vanity was gratified by her clear preference for me. Nor can I for a moment determine how much deliberate intention I hide from myself in this affair.

If she had been only a beautiful girl in love with me, I think I could have managed the situation. Once or twice since my marriage and before Isabel became of any significance in my life, there had been incidents with other people, flashes of temptation—no telling is possible of the thing resisted. I think that mere beauty and passion would not have taken me. But between myself and Isabel things were incurably complicated by the intellectual sympathy we had, the jolly march of our minds together. That has always mattered enormously. I should have wanted her company nearly as badly if she had been some crippled old lady; we would have hunted shoulder to shoulder, as two men. Only two men would never have had the patience and readiness for one another we two had. I had never for years met any one with whom I could be so carelessly sure of understanding or to whom I could listen so easily and fully. She gave me, with an extraordinary completeness, that rare, precious effect of always saying something fresh, and yet saying it so that it filled into and folded about all the little recesses and corners of my mind with an infinite, soft familiarity. It is impossible to explain that. It is like trying to explain why her voice, her voice heard speaking to any one—heard speaking in another room—pleased my ears.

She was the only Oxford woman who took a first that year. She spent the summer in Scotland and Yorkshire, writing to me continually of all she now meant to do, and stirring my imagination. She came to London for the autumn session. For a time she stayed with old Lady Colbeck, but she fell out with her hostess when it became clear she wanted to write, not novels, but journalism, and then she set every one talking by taking a flat near Victoria and installing as her sole protector an elderly German governess she had engaged through a scholastic agency. She began writing, not in that copious flood the undisciplined young woman of gifts is apt to produce, but in exactly the manner of an able young man, experimenting with forms, developing the phrasing of opinions, taking a definite line. She was, of course, tremendously discussed. She was disapproved of, but she was invited out to dinner. She got rather a reputation for the management of elderly distinguished men. It was an odd experience to follow Margaret's soft rustle of silk into some big drawing-room and discover my snub-nosed girl in the blue sack transformed into a shining creature in the soft splendor of pearls and ivory-white and lace, and with a silver band about her dusky hair.

For a time we did not meet very frequently, though always she professed an unblushing preference for my company, and talked my views and sought me out. Then her usefulness upon the *Blue Weekly* began to link us closer. She would come up to the office, and sit by the window, and talk over the proofs of the next week's articles, going through my intentions with a keen investigatory scalpel. Her talk always puts me in mind of a steel blade. Her writing became rapidly very good; she had a wit and a turn of the phrase that was all her own. We seemed to have forgotten the little shadow of embarrassment that had fallen over our last meeting at Oxford. Everything seemed natural and easy between us in those days; a little unconventional, but that made it all the brighter.

We developed something like a custom of walks, about once a week or so, and letters and notes became frequent. I won't pretend things were not keenly personal between us, but they had an air of being innocently mental. She used to call me " Master " in our talks, a monstrous and engaging flattery, and I was inordinately proud to have her as my pupil. Who wouldn't have been? And we went on at that distance for a long time—until within a year of the Handitch election.

After Lady Colbeck threw her up as altogether too " intellectual " for comfortable control, Isabel was taken up by the Balfes in a less formal and compromising manner, and week-ended with them and their cousin Leonora Sparling, and spent large portions of her summer with them in Herefordshire. There was a lover or so in that time, men who came a little timidly at this brilliant young person with the frank manner and the Amazonian mind, and, she declared, received her kindly refusals with manifest relief. And Arnold Shoesmith struck up a sort of friendship that oddly imitated mine. She took a liking to him because he was clumsy and shy and inexpressive; she embarked upon the dangerous interest of helping him to find his soul. I had some twinges of jealousy about that. I didn't see the necessity of him. He invaded her time, and I thought that might interfere with her work. If their friendship stole some hours from Isabel's writing, it did not for a long while interfere with our walks or our talks, or the close intimacy we had together.

IV

Then suddenly Isabel and I found ourselves passionately in love. The change came so entirely without warning or intention that

I find it impossible now to tell the order of its phases. What disturbed pebble started the avalanche I cannot trace. Perhaps it was simply that the barriers between us and this masked aspect of life had been wearing down unperceived.

And there came a change in Isabel. It was like some change in the cycle of nature, like the onset of spring—a sharp brightness, an uneasiness. She became restless with her work; little encounters with men began to happen, encounters not quite in the quality of the earlier proposals; and then came an odd incident of which she told me, but somehow, I felt, didn't tell me completely. She told me all she was able to tell me. She had been at a dance at the Ropers', and a man, rather well known in London, had kissed her. The thing amazed her beyond measure. It was the sort of thing immediately possible between any man and any woman, that one never expects to happen until it happens. It had the surprising effect of a judge generally known to be bald suddenly whipping off his wig in court. No absolutely unexpected revelation could have quite the same quality of shock. She went through the whole thing to me with a remarkable detachment, told me how she had felt—and the odd things it seemed to open to her.

" I *want* to be kissed, and all that sort of thing," she avowed. " I suppose every woman does."

She added after a pause: " And I don't want any one to do it."

This struck me as queerly expressive of the woman's attitude to these things. " Some one presently will—solve that," I said.

" Some one will perhaps."

I was silent.

" Some one will," she said, almost viciously. " And then we'll have to stop these walks and talks of ours, dear Master. . . . I'll be sorry to give them up."

" It's part of the requirements of the situation," I said, " that he should be—oh, very interesting! He'll start, no doubt, all sorts of new topics, and open no end of attractive vistas. . . . You can't, you know, always go about in a state of pupilage."

" I don't think I can," said Isabel. " But it's only just recently I've begun to doubt about it."

I remember these things being said, but just how much we saw and understood, and just how far we were really keeping opaque to each other then, I cannot remember. But it must have been quite soon after this that we spent nearly a whole day together at Kew Gardens, with the curtains up and the barriers down, and the thing that had happened plain before our eyes. I don't remember we ever made any declaration. We just assumed the new footing. . . .

It was a day early in the year—I think in January, because there was thin, crisp snow on the grass, and we noted that only two people had been to the Pagoda that day. I've a curious impression of greenish color, hot, moist air and huge palm fronds about very much of our talk, as though we were nearly all the time in the Tropical House. But I also remember very vividly looking at certain orange and red spraylike flowers from Patagonia, which could not have been there. It is a curious thing that I do not remember we made any profession of passionate love for one another; we talked as though the fact of our intense love for each other had always been patent between us. There was so long and frank an intimacy between us that we talked far more like brother and sister or husband and wife than two people engaged in the war of sexes. We wanted to know what we were going to do, and whatever we did we meant to do in the most perfect concert. We both felt an extraordinary accession of friendship and tenderness then, and, what again is curious, very little passion. But there was also, in spite of the perplexities we faced, an immense satisfaction about that day. It was as if we had taken off something that had hindered our view of each other, like people who unvisored to talk more easily at a masked ball.

I've had since to view our relations from the standpoint of the ordinary observer. I find that vision in the most preposterous contrast with all that really went on between us. I suppose there I should figure as a wicked seducer, while an unprotected girl succumbed to my fascinations. As a matter of fact, it didn't occur to us that there was any personal inequality between us. I knew her for my equal mentally; in so many things she was beyond comparison cleverer than I; her courage outwent mine. The quick leap of her mind evoked a flash of joy in mine like the response of an induction wire; her way of thinking was like watching sunlight reflected from little waves upon the side of a boat, it was so bright, so mobile, so variously and easily true to its law. In the back of our minds we both had a very definite belief that making love is full of joyous, splendid, tender, and exciting possibilities, and we had to discuss why we shouldn't be to the last degree lovers.

Now, what I would like to print here, if it were possible, in all the screaming emphasis of red ink, is this: that the circumstances of my upbringing and the circumstances of Isabel's upbringing had left not a shadow of belief or feeling that the utmost passionate love between us was in itself intrinsically *wrong*. I've told with the fullest particularity just all that I was taught or found out for myself in these matters, and Isabel's reading and thinking, and the fierce silences of her governesses and the breathless warnings of teachers, and all the social and religious influences that had been brought to bear upon her, had worked out to the same void of conviction. The code had

failed with us altogether. We didn't for a moment consider anything but the expediency of what we both, for all our quiet faces and
steady eyes, wanted most passionately to do.

Well, here you have the state of mind of whole brigades of people,
and particularly of young people, nowadays. The current morality
hasn't gripped them; they don't really believe in it at all. They may
render it lip-service, but that is quite another thing. There are
scarcely any tolerable novels to justify its prohibitions; its prohibitions do, in fact, remain unjustified amongst these ugly suppressions.
You may, if you choose, silence the admission of this in literature and
current discussion; you will not prevent it working out in lives.
People come up to the great moments of passion crudely unaware,
astoundingly unprepared, as no really civilized and intelligently
planned community would let any one be unprepared. They find
themselves hedged about with customs that have no organic hold
upon them, and mere discretions all generous spirits are disposed to
despise.

Consider the infinite absurdities of it! Multitudes of us are trying to run this complex modern community on a basis of " Hush "
without explaining to our children or discussing with them anything
about love and marriage at all. Doubt and knowledge creep about
in enforced darknesses and silences. We are living upon an ancient
tradition which everybody doubts and nobody has ever analyzed. We
affect a tremendous and cultivated shyness and delicacy about im-
peratives of the most arbitrary appearance. What ensues? What
did ensue with us, for example? On the one hand was a great desire,
robbed of any appearance of shame and grossness by the power of
love, and on the other hand, the possible jealousy of so and so, the
disapproval of so and so, material risks and dangers. It is only in
the retrospect that we have been able to grasp something of the effectual case against us. The social prohibition lit by the intense glow
of our passion, presented itself as preposterous, irrational, arbitrary,
and ugly, a monster fit only for mockery. We might be ruined!
Well, there is a phase in every love affair, a sort of heroic hysteria,
when death and ruin are agreeable additions to the prospect. It
gives the business a gravity, a solemnity. Timid people may hesitate and draw back with a vague instinctive terror of the immensity
of the oppositions they challenge, but neither Isabel nor I are timid
people.

We weighed what was against us. We decided just exactly as
scores of thousands of people have decided in this very matter, that
if it were possible to keep this thing to ourselves, there was nothing
against it. And so we took our first step. With the hunger of love
in us, it was easy to conclude we might be lovers, and still keep every-

thing to ourselves. That cleared our minds of the one persistent obstacle that mattered to us—the haunting presence of Margaret.

And then we found, as all those scores of thousands of people scattered about us have found, that we could not keep it to ourselves. Love will out. All the rest of this story is the chronicle of that. Love with sustained secrecy cannot be love. It is just exactly the point people do not understand.

V

But before things came to that pass, some months and many phases and a sudden journey to America intervened.

" This thing spells disaster," I said. " You are too big and I am too big to attempt this secrecy. Think of the intolerable possibility of being found out! At any cost we have to stop—even at the cost of parting."

" Just because we may be found out! "

" Just because we may be found out."

" Master, I shouldn't in the least mind being found out with you. I'm afraid—I'd be proud."

" Wait till it happens."

There followed a struggle of immense insincerity between us. It is hard to tell who urged and who resisted.

She came to me one night to the editorial room of the *Blue Weekly,* and argued and kissed me with wet salt lips, and wept in my arms; she told me that now passionate longing for me and my intimate life possessed her, so that she could not work, could not think, could not endure other people for the love of me. . . .

I fled absurdly. That is the secret of the futile journey to America that puzzled all my friends.

I ran away from Isabel. I took hold of the situation with all my strength, put in Britten with sketchy, hasty instructions to edit the paper, and started headlong and with luggage, from which, among other things, my shaving things were omitted, upon a tour round the world.

Preposterous flight that was! I remember as a thing almost farcical my explanations to Margaret, and how frantically anxious I was to prevent the remote possibility of her coming with me, and how I crossed in the *Tuscan,* a bad, wet boat, and mixed seasickness and ungovernable sorrow. I wept—tears. It was inexpressibly queer and ridiculous—and, good God! how I hated my fellow-passengers!

New York inflamed and excited me for a time, and when things slackened, I whirled westward to Chicago—eating and drinking, I remember, in the train from shoals of little dishes, with a sort of desperate voracity. I did the queerest things to distract myself—no novelist would dare to invent my mental and emotional muddle. Chicago also held me at first, amazing lapse from civilization that the place is! and then abruptly, with hosts expecting me, and everything settled for some days in Denver, I found myself at the end of my renunciations, and turned and came back headlong to London.

Let me confess it wasn't any sense of perfect and incurable trust and confidence that brought me back, or any idea that now I had strength to refrain. It was a sudden realization that after all the separation might succeed; some careless phrasing in one of her jealously read letters set that idea going in my mind—the haunting perception that I might return to London and find it empty of the Isabel who had pervaded it. Honor, discretion, the careers of both of us, became nothing at the thought. I couldn't conceive my life resuming there without Isabel. I couldn't, in short, stand it.

I don't even excuse my return. It is inexcusable. I ought to have kept upon my way westward—and held out. I couldn't. I wanted Isabel, and I wanted her so badly now that everything else in the world was phantom-like until that want was satisfied. Perhaps you have never wanted anything like that. I went straight to her.

But here I come to untellable things. There is no describing the reality of love. The shapes of things are nothing, the actual happenings are nothing, except that somehow there falls a light upon them and a wonder. Of how we met, and the thrill of the adventure, the curious bright sense of defiance, the joy of having dared, I can't tell—I can but hint of just one aspect, of what an amazing *lark*—it's the only word—it seemed to us. The beauty which was the essence of it, which justifies it so far as it will bear justification, eludes statement.

What can a record of contrived meetings, of sundering difficulties evaded and overcome, signify here? Or what can it convey to say that one looked deep into two dear, steadfast eyes, or felt a heart throb and beat, or gripped soft hair softly in a trembling hand? Robbed of encompassing love, these things are of no more value than the taste of good wine or the sight of good pictures, or the hearing of music,—just sensuality and no more. No one can tell love—we can only tell the gross facts of love and its consequences. Given love —given mutuality, and one has effected a supreme synthesis and come to a new level of life—but only those who know can know. This business has brought me more bitterness and sorrow than I had ever expected to bear, but even now I will not say that I regret that wilful home-coming altogether. We loved—to the uttermost. Neither of us could have loved any one else as we did and do love one another. It was ours, that beauty; it existed only between us when we were close together, for no one in the world ever to know save ourselves.

My return to the office sticks out in my memory with an extreme vividness, because of the wild eagle of pride that screamed within me.

It was Tuesday morning, and though not a soul in London knew of it yet except Isabel, I had been back in England a week. I came in upon Britten and stood in the doorway.

"*God!*" he said at the sight of me.

"I'm back," I said.

He looked at my excited face with those red-brown eyes of his. Silently I defied him to speak his mind.

"Where did you turn back?" he said at last.

VI

I had to tell what were, so far as I can remember, my first positive lies to Margaret in explaining that return. I had written to her from Chicago and again from New York, saying that I felt I ought to be on the spot in England for the new session, and that I was coming back—presently. I concealed the name of my boat from her, and made a calculated prevarication when I announced my presence in London. I telephoned before I went back for my rooms to be prepared. She was, I knew, with the Bunting Harblows in Durham, and when she came back to Radnor Square I had been at home a day.

I remember her return so well.

My going away and the vivid secret of the present had wiped out from my mind much of our long estrangement. Something, too, had changed in her. I had had some hint of it in her letters, but now I saw it plainly. I came out of my study upon the landing when I heard the turmoil of her arrival below, and she came upstairs with a quickened gladness. It was a cold March, and she was dressed in unfamiliar dark furs that suited her extremely and reinforced the delicate flush of her sweet face. She held out both her hands to me, and drew me to her unhesitatingly and kissed me.

"So glad you are back, dear," she said: "Oh! so very glad you are back."

I returned her kiss with a queer feeling at my heart, too undifferentiated to be even a definite sense of guilt or meanness. I think it was chiefly amazement—at the universe—at myself.

"I never knew what it was to be away from you," she said.

I perceived suddenly that she had resolved to end our estrangement. She put herself so that my arm came caressingly about her.

"These are jolly furs," I said.

"I got them for you."

The parlormaid appeared below dealing with the maid and the luggage cab.

"Tell me all about America," said Margaret. "I feel as though you'd been away six years."

We went arm in arm into her little sitting-room, and I took off the furs for her and sat down upon the chintz-covered sofa by the fire. She had ordered tea, and came and sat by me. I don't know what I had expected, but of all things I had certainly not expected this sudden abolition of our distances.

"I want to know all about America," she repeated, with her eyes scrutinizing me. "Why did you come back?"

I repeated the substance of my letters rather lamely, and she sat listening.

"But why did you turn back—without going to Denver?"

"I wanted to come back. I was restless."

"Restlessness," she said, and thought. "You were restless in Venice. You said it was restlessness took you to America."

Again she studied me. She turned a little awkwardly to her tea things, and poured needless water from the silver kettle into the teapot. Then she sat still for some moments looking at the equipage with expressionless eyes. I saw her hand upon the edge of the table tremble slightly. I watched her closely. A vague uneasiness possessed me. What might she not know or guess?

She spoke at last with an effort. "I wish you were in Parliament again," she said. "Life doesn't give you events enough."

"If I was in Parliament again, I should be on the Conservative side."

"I know," she said, and was still more thoughtful.

"Lately," she began, and paused. "Lately I've been reading— you."

I didn't help her out with what she had to say. I waited.

"I didn't understand what you were after. I had misjudged. I didn't know. I think perhaps I was rather stupid." Her eyes were suddenly shining with tears. "You didn't give me much chance to understand."

She turned upon me suddenly with a voice full of tears.

"Husband," she said abruptly, holding her two hands out to me, "I want to begin over again!"

I took her hands, perplexed beyond measure. "My dear!" I said.

"I want to begin over again."

I bowed my head to hide my face, and found her hand in mine and kissed it.

"Ah!" she said, and slowly withdrew her hand. She leant forward with her arm on the sofa-back, and looked very intently into my face. I felt the most damnable scoundrel in the world as I returned her gaze. The thought of Isabel's darkly shining eyes seemed like a physical presence between us. . . .

"Tell me," I said presently, to break the intolerable tension, "tell me plainly what you mean by this."

I sat a little away from her, and then took my tea-cup in hand, with an odd effect of defending myself. " Have you been reading that old book of mine? " I asked.

" That and the paper. I took a complete set from the beginning down to Durham with me. I have read it over, thought it over. I didn't understand—what you were teaching."

There was a little pause.

" It all seems so plain to me now," she said, " and so true."

I was profoundly disconcerted. I put down my tea-cup, stood up in the middle of the hearthrug, and began talking. " I'm tremendously glad, Margaret, that you've come to see I'm not altogether perverse," I began. I launched out into a rather trite and windy exposition of my views, and she sat close to me on the sofa, looking up into my face, hanging on my words, a deliberate and invincible convert.

I had never doubted my new conceptions before; now I doubted them profoundly. But I went on talking. It's the grim irony in the lives of all politicians, writers, public teachers, that once the audience is at their feet, a new loyalty has gripped them. It isn't their business to admit doubts and imperfections. They have to go on talking. And I was now so accustomed to Isabel's vivid interruptions, qualifications, restatements, and confirmations. . . .

Margaret and I dined together at home. She made me open out my political projects to her. " I have been foolish," she said. " I want to help."

And by some excuse I have forgotten she made me come to her room. I think it was some book I had to take her, some American book I had brought back with me, and mentioned in our talk. I walked in with it, and put it down on the table and turned to go.

" Husband! " she cried, and held out her slender arms to me. I was compelled to go to her and kiss her, and she twined them softly about my neck and drew me to her and kissed me. I disentangled them very gently, and took each wrist and kissed it, and the backs of her hands.

" Good night," I said. There came a little pause. "Good night, Margaret," I repeated, and walked very deliberately and with a kind of sham preoccupation to the door.

I did not look at her, but I could feel her standing watching me. If I had looked up, she would, I knew, have held out her arms to me. . . .

At the very outset that secret, which was to touch no one but Isabel and myself, had reached out to stab another human being.

(To be continued)

WANTED—LEISURE

TEMPLE SCOTT

 MAKING a living is not living; making a living is only a means to living. We have not thought of this, of course. We are so tasked in the work that we have not the time in which to recover ourselves for reflection. We never do recover ourselves. Our selves are lost, drowned in the flood of labor and the waves of competition. We are so accustomed to spend the best years of our lives in efforts to keep alive that living is come to mean working in order to be able to go on working. The wage is not the stepping-stone to independence; it is the exchange value of the indispensable daily bread. So ingrained in us is this habit of work that we even count ourselves fortunate and think ourselves happy when we have secured a position which assures us the work. Like the negro laundress who thought herself lucky in the husband who saw to it that she did not want a day's washing, we also are grateful that each to-morrow finds the work ready for our hands to do. For work means food and shelter; and food and a shelter mean life. Life, quotha! God help us!

The day's work done we go home to rest, to regain the strength lost for the next day's work, if we can. Perhaps anxiety about the work prevents us from resting; then we lie awake disturbed and distressed. Perhaps the work absorbs our whole thoughts; then is every other interest excluded—self, friends, wife and family, home and the duties of social life. We are machines that are run down each evening, to be cranked up again each morning. And we are glad thus to labor. Thank God for work, we cry, when sorrow or affliction visits us. In work, at any rate, we can drown our troubles. Work is the sustainer of hope, the comforter and soother in times of despair; the one remedy for the thousand heart-ills which afflict us in this Vale of Tears. Great writers have penned vibrating dithyrambs in praise of work. "Blessed are the horny hands of toil"; "Yet toil on, toil on; thou art in thy duty, be out of it who may"; "To Labor is to pray"; "To Labor is the lot of man below"; "Labor is independent and proud." They write the word with a capital letter as if it were in itself a splendid and inspiring truth. They have raised a new idol for us to worship. Oh, idolatrous and Sabbathless Satans!

It is a melancholy *utinam*, as Sir Thomas Browne would say, this inhuman craving for work—the cry of the starving for food, the prayer of the lost for success, the petition of the condemned for respite. The will to live is so strong in us, and the way to live so narrow and crowded, that the market for labor is like a battlefield with the fight still going on. For we have found out but one means of living—killing the weaker and taking his place. And yet the work we get is not for the fulfilment of the spirit; it does not ennoble us. We grasp after it with the convulsive, passionate hands of the drowning man stretching for a spar that will float him to a haven; and when the haven is reached we find ourselves harnessed to a mortar-wheel. Like stupid oxen or blind horses we go, henceforward, round and round in a daily grind. And man's free spirit is killed. "Thou toilest for the altogether indispensable, for daily bread." What a satire on living is this making a living!

Is it not time we took thought a little on this business of work? I am not railing against the toil for the daily bread. I am ready to agree with all the fine things that have been and can be said of it. But I do denounce and stigmatize as contemptible and unmanly that attitude toward the work we are compelled to do, which accepts it as the be-all and the end-all of human aspiration. This is not work, it is drudgery, and as such it is degrading and enslaving. As it is practised and understood to-day in the thousands of centres of modern civilization, this drudgery is one of the most pernicious influences that can afflict mankind. There is nothing sacred in it, nothing beautiful, nothing worthy. Go through a modern department store and tell me if the work done there by the hundreds of young men and young women is either worthy or beautiful or sacred. Examine the factories, the coal mines, the railroads, the offices of merchants and newspapers and shop-keepers, and show me there the sanctity and the beauty of labor. Oh, yes, all these creatures are earning their living. Some of them have, perhaps, found the work fitted for them and have made inventions and improvements in the enterprises with which they are associated. Some have even progressed in position and have themselves become employers. What of it all? Have they done anything more than make a living? And if they have saved money, if even they have become millionaires, have they done anything more than work? Do they do anything more than go on working? If they do—then for what? For doing more work, and more work? For making more money and more money? And this is living!

I hear you! You are telling me that it is through work that these United States have become the leading country in the commerce of the globe; that it is through work America is richer and more powerful than any other country. I do not doubt it. But have these United States become a country in which men and women are freer, as they set out to be? Are the people of this country wiser, nobler, more sanely brotherly to each other, more intellectually honest and upright, more premeditatedly kindly and intelligently humane than the people of other civilized countries? I doubt it. Human nature is the same here as it is the world over. They had grafters in Rome and we have grafters in New York. They have vested interests in Europe and we have politicians and trusts in America. They have debilitating armies and navies in the old world, and we have their like in the new. We have not changed much by taking a voyage across the Atlantic and founding a new republic. This new English republic is not such an advance on the old English monarchy that we need boast much about it. We had the chance to make it an advance, but we did not use it. We did not use it because we did not know how. And we did not know how because we did not understand that the difference between a republic and a monarchy is profounder than the mere superficial difference in government; we did not realize that a democracy meant not only political and legal freedom but economic freedom also.

The old feudal system was a military system. The basic assumption of the system was that men were not equal. Under it the monarch flourished as a kind of commander-in-chief of the nation as an army, and he had his generals and captains in his barons and overlords. It developed an aristocracy and class divisions. The workingman took his place among the lower classes. He worked for his superior because he was a unit in an army in which the employer was his captain or lord or baron—he was his vassal, serf or slave. He is still in these lower classes, to-day, in monarchical countries. He is still there because the feudal system is still the system of business and the employment of labor. The wage-earner is part of a militariat exactly similar to any military organization. As an individual he does not count. He counts only as a fraction of a larger unit—the factory, the brewery, the railway corporation, the mining enterprise, the store, the mercantile office. It is these larger units that are considered in estimating the power and prosperity of a nation. But so considered a nation is not rich and not powerful, but poverty-stricken, crime-infested and unstable as water. It cannot be otherwise when the few are enriched at the expense of the many.

The American Declaration of Independence rejected monarchy and its attendant aristocracy and class distinctions. It declared as truth—that all men are created equal. It left no room for an aristocracy or class distinctions in government. But it did not reject the militariat system in business. That system is still in vogue in this country as it is in every country of the world. Under it the wage-earner is relegated to a class subservient to the employer in business and to the plutocrat in social life. So that the laborer is now in the same position, economically and socially, as the vassal and serf were under the old military feudal system. In other words the laborer is the wage-slave. It is true, he is now free to remonstrate and combat by means of unions, but his remonstrance and opposition avail him little so long as the system under which he works compels him to devote the major part of his daily life to making a living. No wage-earner can be free in any real sense if he must labor for a wage from eight in the morning until six in the evening.

I have said that the difference between a monarchy and a democracy is profounder than the superficial difference in government. I mean by that that government, whether by a king or a president, is the same at bottom, so far as it affects the people governed. In republics as in monarchies the people are governed by officials; and it matters little whether these be elected by the people or selected by the king. Indeed, it is quite conceivable that a dictator would choose more wisely than the voters. The real difference between a democracy and a monarchy is in what I might call the soul attitude of the individuals governed, and that attitude is altogether different in a democracy from what it is in a monarchy. It is different in that in a democracy the unit, for the first time, counts. He is not merely a member of a social organization; he is not only one individual in a nation; he is not simply a number in a regiment of soldiers; he is all these, but he is also a man. It was to preserve him and his individuality; it was to safeguard him and his rights; it was to assert him and his soul that the democracy of the United States of America was founded. Otherwise the words of the Declaration of Independence are blasphemy. "We hold these truths to be self-evident,—that all men are created equal; that they are endowed by their Creator with certain unalienable rights; that among these are life, liberty, and the pursuit of happiness."

"Life, liberty, and the pursuit of happiness"!

Buried in foul basements and bereft of sunlight and air, hundreds of thousands of young men and young women are daily occupied in a deadly routine of employment at tasks that concern them only in so far as their accomplishment brings them a weekly wage. They are stitching garments, treading sewing-machines, pounding typewriters, inserting meaningless figures in ponderous ledgers, packing parcels, turning cranks. And they are doing these tasks from early morn till dewy eve. Without, the blue sky is effulgent in golden sunlight, and trees are blossoming, birds singing, clouds sailing and gentle breezes blowing. But the toilers see nothing and feel nothing of what is doing without. They have not the time; they are too busy asserting their God-given rights to "life, liberty, and the pursuit of happiness." "Blessed are the horny hands of toil"!

Enclosed in the storeyed lofts of department-stores are other hundreds of thousands, standing through the livelong day, serving customers, waiting on exacting and irritating women, scribbling bills, displaying articles for sale, anxiously glancing the while at the task-

master who walks the lofts with the threat of punishment in his
eye. Some of them catch glimpses through the windows of a gleaming river and purple hills; but they have no time to look long. They
dream of these beautiful things on their way home in the evening when
they are tired and worn out. Not for them are these pleasant
places; they are too busy proving their rights to "life, liberty, and
the pursuit of happiness." "To labor is the lot of man below"!

In stuffy little shops are thousands of others—husbands and wives
and children—smirking, genuflexing, tricking, flattering, deceiving,
begging customers into buying the wares they are offering for sale.
From seven or eight in the morning until seven, eight, nine and even
ten o'clock at night, they are engaged in this degrading labor. They
have no time for anything else; for if they took the time their neighbor store-keeper might take customers away from them. Moreover,
they must, at any cost, make good their unalienable rights to "life,
liberty, and the pursuit of happiness." "Toil on, toil on; thou art
in thy duty, be out of it who may"!

Digging in mines, delving the earth, spinning in mills, forging
and hammering in factories are hundreds of thousands of others, face-
begrimed, callous-handed, narrow-chested creatures who may be men
and women, but they look like parchment-stretched skeletons. These
have never even tasted joy; they are only ravenous for existence.
They are the slaves of captains of industry. Their pleasures are
debilitating excitements, body-racking indulgence, and soul-destroy-
ing satisfactions. And these too are God-endowed with rights to
"life, liberty, and the pursuit of happiness." "Labor is independent
and proud"!

Ask any one of these millions of wage-slaves if he is happy; ask
him what he is doing and why he is doing it. This will be his best
answer, even when he has succeeded; in the words of the shop-keeper,
Madame Bernin, in Brieux' play, *Maternité*, he will say:

"No; we have not been happy, because we have used ourselves up
with hunting for happiness. We meant to 'get there'; we have 'got
there', but at what a price? Oh, I know the road to fortune. At
first, miserable sordid economy, passionate greed; then the fierce
struggle of trickery and deceit, always flattering your customers,
always living in terror of failure. Tears, lies, envy, contempt, suf-

fering for yourself and for everyone round you. I've been through it and a bitter experience it was. We're determined that our children shan't. Our children! We have only two, but we meant to have only one. That extra one meant double toil and hardship. Instead of being a husband and wife, helping one another, we have been two business partners, watching each other like enemies, perpetually quarreling, even on our very pillow, over our expenditure and our mistakes. Finally we succeeded; and now we can't enjoy our wealth because we don't know how to use it, and because our later years are poisoned by memories of the hateful past of suffering and rancor."

"Life, liberty, and the pursuit of happiness"!

Go into the millions of city homes, or what we may call homes as a pathetic compliment to those who live in them, and see how they fare there, these asserters of divine rights. What are these places, when they are not just bearable? The breeding grounds of crime and the farms of prostitution—poisonous weeds that spring up in a night from the soil of poverty. Ask them what God is doing for them; and if they understand your question, they will answer: "God gives us eyes—to cry with." They compel themselves to forget their state when they can weep no more. These are the women whose lives have been broken on the wheel of competition and crushed beneath the Juggernaut car of the militariat system. And they always carry with them an added source of suffering—the corpse of the woman they had hoped to be. "Yet toil on, toil on, thou art in thy duty, be out of it who may"!

Watch the farmer at his work and his family at their daily tasks. The pageant of landscape and of sky passes by them unseen. They are bowed and bent earthward. For a brief moment they look up; but their eyes are blind. For a short space they plod homeward a weary way and leave the world to darkness and themselves to brutish sleep. He is his own taskmaster, with the whip of anxiety to spur him on to effort after effort. His wife scarce knows what it is not to work; for there are "chores" to do every day, Sundays as well as week days. The grind of their toil has worn their faces to unlovely lines. They live on hope—the hope that marries the daughter, and educates the son for the ministry or fits him for the labor of the cities. They suck sustenance out of the earth with life-spending gasps. Each day's labor is a crucifixion of Love on the market cross. Yet they are told that "To labor is to pray"!

See the employer at his office desk, tricking, cajoling, swindling, haggling, directing, smiling, desiring, and doing the many other worthy and unworthy acts that he calls business. He also is harnessed to the mortar-wheel. He is the blind leading the blind. He is the slave of his enterprise, the creature of his success. Listen to him, in his hours of ease, at the restaurant, in the theatre, or at his own dining-table, and he is saying "Dollars, dollars, dollars!" If other words fall from his lips they have reference to dollars; if he talks of art, it is in terms of dollars; if he descants of pleasure, it is in the language of the marketplace; if he speaks of love it is with synonyms for money. He knows no God but the Golden Calf and no joy but the fever of desire. And he is oppressed with worry and depressed by anxiety. He makes thousands in a day and loses them in a night. He is the gambler offspring of competition and the militariat system. He is Time's slave; he is the chained driver of the competition car, doomed for life to cross and re-cross the Bridge of Sighs. And in his wake follow the groans of the hungry and the moans of the stricken. Yet he cannot help them because he is himself stricken; he is the slave of the system which compels him to do what he does. Deep in his heart he is moved to compassion and charity, but he can only talk in the language of dollars, and he knows no other mediator. His wealth has ruined his manhood and his home is a sepulchre of stillborn hopes and frustrated happiness. He also may pray for grace, but it is too late to be redeemed from the passion of his low ambition. He has sold himself for wealth, and he must remain a slave to the most terrible of all taskmasters—"Yet toil on, toil on; thou art in thy duty, be out of it who may"!

And these are they who have asserted and fought for their rights to "life, liberty, and the pursuit of happiness"!

I am not here picturing the lives of the people of a tyrannous autocracy. The people I have described are the people of an enlightened democracy, of the splendid United States. They bear the standard of freedom, "Old Glory" they proudly and rightly call it. They chant the Battle Hymn of the Republic; they devoutly honor their brave who died for liberty and emancipation; they teach their children to lisp the uplifting words of their epoch-making Declaration; they have the power to choose their own leaders and the right of a great nation's might. And yet they have allowed themselves to be enslaved by an economic Shibboleth. They have deified Competition as a Law of Nature and have become worshipers of a heartless, hopeless idol. Even if this idol were a living god, a true ideal, what are we doing that we do not compel it to answer our demands? We compel gravitation to irrigate our deserts; we imprison the fire of heaven to move our railways; we command the force of expansion to alleviate our suffering, and employ the lightning to bear our messages round the globe. Why have we failed to subjugate this so-called Economic Law of Competition? Why? Because it is not a Law of Nature at all. It is a false god set up by our ignorance, and enthroned by our greed. We ask it for bread and it gives us a stone; we beg it for work and it tells us the labor-market is overstocked; we pray to it for leisure and it imprisons us in cells; we petition it for freedom and it sends us to get it for ourselves; we cry to it for life and it is deaf to our cry; we plead to it for happiness and it spurns us to misery; we demand of it our rights and it calls us "wage-slaves." And this is the Ideal we have idolized! Natural Law! If ever a law were unnatural this is that law.

I am not now attempting a detailed examination of competition. I am concerned here with one outcome of it, namely, over-production, for over-production is the immediate cause of the wage-slave's condition. Capital has an eager eye. When it sees profits it will immediately engage itself. It can, however, only see profits when the market has already been supplied; but it is too jealous to allow one or two or three to make the profits, so it rushes into this profit-making enterprise, with the result that the market becomes over-supplied. Prices then go down and profits decrease. On the decrease the capitalists take a rest. The capitalists' rest means either the reduction of the wage-earner's wage or his discharge. Evil number one. The reduction in prices does not much help the wage-earner who is unemployed and has no money with which to buy. If he is fortunate enough not to be discharged and has only had his wage lowered he is yet the first to feel the pinch of the situation; and if he goes on strike for higher wages, both employer and employed are sufferers. Evil number two. Perhaps the surplus product is sold in foreign markets at below cost; then a new situation of danger is brought about by a retaliating tariff from the foreign country that has its own economic troubles. Evil number three. When the foreign market is closed to the over-producer he becomes a Jingo, an Imperialist, an advocate for colonization and conquest in order to find a new market for his produce; he is the first to cry "Fight." Evil number four.

To contend that over-production balances itself and that the period of depression is followed by a period of rise, only adds insult to the injury. Is this a Law of Nature that breaks down just when it ought to work? Surely, this is but speculating with the market and taking a chance to win the race for the profit. Why should we be content to go hungry to-day, when an industrial panic is on, because we may get a meal next week when the panic shall have quieted down? Why are we to permit ourselves to be thus gambled with? We object most strongly to the gambler in industries (for the average capitalist is nothing but a gambler) staking our lives in the game of chance he is playing. We refuse to be cast on the green table as "chips." And there is danger to the gambler in this protest; for the protest is the protest of a proletariat army that will grow in solidarity very rapidly in the coming years. And if the idol of Competition be not quietly hidden away in some lumber room of discarded faiths, there will be trouble for the capitalist-gambler.

The wily capitalist, seeing the evils of over-production, set to work and elaborated a way for himself by which he could avoid them. He combined with other capitalists in the same industry, and formed the trust. He formed it peaceably where he could, but when he met with resistance he used drastic methods, strange and weird methods, that take us back to the middle ages for their like in cold-blooded implacability. What the trust is we all know. I call it evil number five of over-production, and the worst evil of them all.

To resist the tyranny of the capitalists, and to save himself from utter slavery, the wage-earner combined with his fellow wage-earners and founded the Trade-Union. So that now we have the two armies of capitalists and wage-earners opposed to each other, and hating each other, and only working together in what is in reality a state of armed peace because each cannot do without the other. And the wage-earner has become the creature of his tyrant union. Evil number six of over-production.

Yet out of all these evils good is certain to come. The evil of the unemployed has already opened the eyes of the unemployed, and a discontent is ripening into an awareness of injustice. The evil of strikes has produced the Labor Commissions and Arbitration Boards; the evil of the retaliating tariff leads to Reciprocity and will eventually bring us to Free Trade; the evil of the Jingo fighter will make good blood in a juster and more righteous cause; the evil of the trusts will be transfigured when their public utility corporations shall have been municipalized and their magnificent organizations of industries nationalized and socialized. And with the transformation of these evils the wage-earner will no longer be the wage-slave at the mercy of capital and the competition system. He will break free from the tyranny of his unions by abolishing them, for the day of their need will have passed away. And he will give his strength to a coöperative commonwealth which, assuring him of his life and liberty, will enable him to devote his free spirit to the pursuit of his happiness.

The ruins of over-production being the result of the blind cataclysmic force of competition, it might be well to study this blind force and see how it can be prevented or directed. This has been done; but as the result of investigations points to a *bouleversement*, to an entire reversal of present economic methods, it is too dangerous an experiment to engage the wage-earner in it, and he is not yet fit for the undertaking. It is certainly asking of the employer more than he will consent to. It will be wise for us to take a seemingly more circuitous road, especially if we desire to bring about the final result peaceably and intelligently. This road is the road of Leisure.

A signal victory over the capitalist was won by the skilled wage-earner when he secured the eight-hour day. But the advantage gained is only partial; and it is not all along the line of labor. The skilled wage-earner will have done better when he has secured the four-hour working-day; and labor will have done better still when its unskilled shall be as happily conditioned as its skilled. A four-hour working-day will mean the employment of more labor and give more leisure to the laborer. Prices will, of course, go up; but there is a limit to the rise, and when that limit is reached capital will find that it does not pay to engage itself too insistently in competitive markets, and labor will discover its proper place in the changed economic conditions that will follow. And if capital attempt to ignore the limit, it may find its very existence threatened. Competition will decrease and over-production cease. Wages will, of course, go down; but there is a limit to the fall, for the capitalist, in an uncompeting market, will find his profits settling to a satisfactory level, or to a level that he must eventually content himself with. The capital that is unengaged will find other fields for enterprises, which over-production has not made barren. If it does not, it will not matter, for capital is not wealth; it becomes wealth only when transmuted by labor.

But the skilled laborer forms only a small body of the industrial population of this country. There are thirty odd millions of clerks, domestics, petty tradesmen, shop-assistants, and other unskilled workers, who are still subjected to their employers' will in the matter of the length of the working-day. Whether through indifference or incapacity, these have not organized themselves into unions, with the result that they are the flotsam and jetsam on the ocean of labor. They live in continual fear of being supplanted by a great army of unemployed always ready to take their places. Well, little good will be accomplished until these also combine and obtain the shorter working-day. Elements for strong associations undoubtedly exist among clerks, typists and shop-assistants, and these must be welded for a common purpose. Public sentiment will help them, for public sentiment is easily enlisted on the side of injustice done to the unprotected. They must, if they are to live decently, obtain, at any rate, the eight-hour working-day. No store should be open after four o'clock in the summer and five o'clock in the winter; and there should be a mid-week half holiday as well as the Saturday half day. We need not be afraid of the results of these changes. Capital can stand this strain, and it will be afraid to resist a united and determined opposition. Dislocation in business is a thing more to be dreaded than the shortening of the working-day. A definite and reasonable demand and a solidarity of f ont are the first requisites to an alleviation of hard-pressing conditi ns. Unity of purpose and solidarity of effort will, in the end, overcome every economic difficulty. And if to ask these of the unskilled wage-earner is to ask too much of him, then is he lost. It is because I think I am not asking too much of him, and it is because I believe he must be saved, that I am appealing to him to take heart and be up and doing. He has not so much to lose that he should be fearful of risking it; and he has much to gain. He has his life, his liberty, his happiness to gain, and the lives, liberties and happiness of his wife and children. He has the love of country to recover; he has his pride in his citizenship to reëstablish; he has the dignity of his manhood to maintain. And he can do none of these things so long as he permits the hours of his conscious life to be at the call of a master who has no interest in him except as a possibility for profit, and so long as he accepts the wages of a slave for his life as a man.

Why do I insist so much on leisure? Because leisure is time, and time is life. Leisure alone means liberty, freedom for the assertion of self; leisure is the first requisite for making possible for us the pursuit of happiness. Give a poor man time and you enrich him. Give him time and you will empower him so that he will move mountains by taking thought. In time he will rejuvenate the earth and make it, indeed, a jocund earth. I ask for leisure because with leisure a man can recover himself and find his right place in the society which should dignify him and he it. He can grow in understanding and grow in wisdom, with leisure. He has the time in which to be a father, a lover, a friend, and a comrade. The fine sap of his humanity can mount and nourish the tender branches of his family tree. The Home will realize his dreams of Home, for it will be the joyous place where character is made, and with the making of character will be born nobler fathers and willing mothers.

Give a man leisure and you re-create him. We may not then be able to hoodwink him with our economic shibboleths, but we shall be glad that we are not thus able. His eyes will have been opened, and he will open our eyes in turn. We shall realize our past foolishness in the splendid coöperation of this new-born friendly helper. Work will be no longer the hateful necessity it is now; it will be acceptable, and accomplished as the expression of the workers' sincerity. It will be honest work, giving in labor done one hundred cents for every dollar of wage received. It will be this because the worker will be fit, and willing, and bound in honor. He will give then more in four hours than he gives now in fourteen.

This time for which I ask would not be missed by the employer. Were we to-day to collect the time wasted in our many business enterprises and present it to the workers we should find we had lost nothing by the gift, and the gift would be no less than one-fourth of a present working-day. As a matter of fact, few human beings can possibly be equally efficient during every hour of the ten or twelve hours of a laboring day. Time is wasted in make-believe at work, in fussing and moving to and fro, in lifting and putting back what need not have been moved. Especially is time wasted in talk—the talk of the foreman, the talk of the manager, the talk of the employer, the talk of the schemer, the talk of the incompetent and hesitating and feeble and vain. It is a rare business that is really efficient. Indeed, much of the distaste for work is not so much due to the work itself as it is to the compulsory waste of time and consequent prolonged confinement imposed on the worker by incompetent employers and supervisors. We grudge the wage-earner a dollar rise in his wages, but we lose a dollar a day by our waste of his time. The shorter working-day will compel a wiser supervision, a more concentrated effort, a closer application and a more definite attention. Time wasted is money wasted, opportunity lost, enthusiasm dampened and the working spirit demoralized.

There has never been a time in the history of the world so stirred by social discontent as the present; and never before, not even during the years immediately prior to the French Revolution, was the discontent so deep-rooted and so fraught with danger to the community. Increase in population, overcrowding in cities, competition in the labor-market, over-production, higher cost of living, the stupidity and the selfishness of the capitalist, the vicious remedy of labor strikes, all these have contributed to the sowing of discontent. How to allay it; how to bring about juster conditions for the mass of the population, are questions which have occupied and are occupying the minds of the best thinkers. Solutions without number, from Utopias to Coöperative Societies, have been propounded and tested, and yet the situation remains unaltered. No solution is, however, possible without the active sympathy and intelligent coöperation of the people to be satisfied. The solution must come from them and not from the academic philosopher, be he never so well-meaning, and they cannot as yet know what is best for them. Their sympathies are too easily engaged, because of the stress of their conditions, for any seemingly helpful schemes; and their coöperation cannot be intelligent because their outlook is narrowed by their immediate wants. Unintelligent sympathy is a terribly dangerous emotion to experiment with. Our first business is to refine their sympathy to the fineness of discretion, and cultivate their intelligence to the point of enthusiasm. It is not possible to produce either of these qualities so long as the wage-earner is the slave of his work, and so long as he is compelled to give to it the greater part of his day's life. It is to rationalize his emotion and to emotionalize his intelligence that I ask for Leisure. When he acquires an intelligent enthusiasm for service, then will his service be a vital contribution; the patient will then help the doctor. Perhaps, indeed, he will not need the doctor.

Leisure makes for health, and health is an absolute necessity to the education of intelligence. The unintelligence displayed by the average labor voter is largely due to bad health brought on by drink. Drink is the solace of the tired laborer who takes it in the first instance as a spur to his jaded body. The leisured workingman will have no need for this spur. With the decrease in drunkenness the health of the community is assured.

Leisure makes for character; not the character of the poverty-smitten creature of the competitive labor-market, but the character of the free man, the democratic citizen, the gentleman in the best sense of the word. He will have time for social intercourse, for study, for invigorating and inspiriting exercise. He will recapture his flown youth in play with his children, and regain his lost hopes, and re-live the joyous days of his early love.

Leisure is no respecter of class distinction; it is a splendid democrat. It has been made to symbolize aristocracy, but its nature is not aristocratic; its nature is humanitarian. Ignorance on the one hand, and sentimentality on the other, have accorded it aristocratic honors;

but ignorance and sentimentality are responsible for most of the mistakes we make, not the least of which is the abuse of Leisure by the so-called leisured class.

Leisure is a re-distributor of power. When leisure shall be a common enjoyment and over-production ceases, wealth will be more evenly divided, and with the more even division of wealth will follow a redistribution of power. Moreover, the leisured man is thrown on his own resources and he will have the chance to make good. If he fails he will only have himself to blame. What he is to do with leisure so that he shall make good I must leave for a future consideration.

This being to be born of Leisure, and he alone, is the man we want for our revolutionary purpose. We want him because without him all our efforts at betterment are mere patching and tinkering. He, and he alone, will have the insight that we lack; and he alone can help us to a happy practical issue out of all the afflictions which beset us to-day. When the leisured workingman comes he will show us how to do away with sweat-shops, how to clean slums and wash streets, and drain cities. He himself will reform our schools, regulate our traffic, reject our faithless servants. He will rebuild our cities, remake our homes, reform our parliaments. He will remodel our armies and reëstablish our navies. He will reëlect our officials and redeem their broken pledges. He will plant gardens and people desert places and grow vineyards. He will do all these things with the enthusiasm of knowledge, and he will accomplish all these things because he will have the seeing power—the tremendous power secretly stored in the ballot-box. Look out for the workingman who shall say every day at four o'clock with Charles Lamb, "I am Retired Leisure." You will find him in libraries and art galleries, at times; and at other times he will be resting on the grassy banks of murmuring brooks, or walking smilingly in trim gardens. *Otium cum dignitate.* He will not be the Superannuated Man who was once doggedly content to waste his soul at the wooden desk of drudgery and is now presented with the bonus of a few twilit years in which to sun his silvered body. He is the Superlaborated Man who cannot live without his soul. He never can be superannuated because he is always wanted; and he will be a long time growing old because he has a long time in which to be young.

AMERICA'S NAVAL POLICY

HARRY D. BRANDYCE

In these days of mad scramble among the nations of the world for sea power as expressed in terms of Dreadnoughts, we constantly hear the wish expressed that the United States might use her prestige for putting an end to such a ruinous and un-Christian competition. The good people who live in hopes of seeing the millennium firmly believe that this desirable consummation is to be obtained through universal disarmament, and they are convinced that if America were to cease building men-of-war the other great nations would be only too glad to follow our example.

Of course it is incontestable that if we might be assured of the other powers following our lead we should be in duty bound to set the example. But can we feel sure that such would be the result? Decidedly no! If Germany were willing to curtail her naval expenditure, it is reasonable to suppose that she would long since have made overtures to England for a reciprocal diminution of shipbuilding programmes; whereas not only has she not done so, but she has even repulsed England's suggestions to that effect. Germany has committed herself to a definite naval policy—no doubt after having carefully weighed the cost—and apparently nothing can swerve her from her chosen course. England, who depends for her very existence upon the invincibility of her navy, cannot choose but build Dreadnoughts at such a rate as may be necessary to maintain her ancient supremacy upon the sea. The fact that she is entirely dependent upon transoceanic countries for her food supply is reason enough why she must keep open the lines of communication between herself and the great agricultural colonies, Canada and Australia, as well as the United States.

Germany's motives for suddenly deciding to quadruple the power of her fleet are by no means self-evident. The Germans are not dependent on over-sea nations for their food supply—it would be possible in time of war for them to draw on Russia and Austria for their grain; they have no colonies worthy of the name which must be protected; and their merchant shipping is only about one-fourth that of

England. Neither do they stand in fear of invasion from the sea; their only potential enemies—France and Russia—have other and more convenient means of ingress into their territory. In seeking the answer to this question we must review the history of the Fatherland for the last twenty years.

The population of the German Empire in 1890 was about 50,000,000. It was an agricultural nation for the most part, ruled by a young, impulsive Kaiser whose great ambition was to make Germany the dominant power in Europe. His grandfather, ably seconded by Bismarck and Moltke, had already taken from Austria and France a great part of their prestige, and there remained only Russia and England to contend with Germany for the leadership of Europe. Wilhelm II saw at a glance that the next great contest would be a commercial one, and he realized that national greatness in the nineteenth century was to be measured by manufacturing industry rather than by agriculture. So he determined that Germany should become one of the foremost manufacturing nations, and bent all his tremendous energy toward furthering that end. Having succeeded in stimulating industrial growth throughout the Empire by a highly paternal policy of governmental aid to factories, railroads, canals, etc., he inaugurated a system of ship subsidies which have made it possible for German ships to capture a large part of the world's water-borne traffic, mostly at the expense of England. Two little steamship lines, the Hamburg-American and the North German Lloyd, have thus grown to be the greatest and most powerful ship-owning corporations in the world. Their ships ply in all the seven seas, and their prosperity is enormous.

While all this was going on the Empire was growing rapidly in population. The census just completed shows that Germany now numbers nearly 70,000,000 inhabitants—an increase of 20,000,000 in twenty years. The country is fast becoming overcrowded, and for many years Germans have been emigrating to foreign countries where competition is not so keen and a man can earn enough to keep his family in comfort. Until about the end of the last century the major part of this outflow was directed toward the United States, where the emigrants found conditions so much to their liking that they settled down and eventually became citizens. In the last ten years, however, a goodly proportion of the wanderers have found their way into the Argentine and Southern Brazil, in which latter country several of the more temperate States are now preponderantly German.

This did not altogether meet with the Kaiser's approval. He could not bear to see good German farmers and workmen—all potential soldiers—seeking homes where they would become denationalized and thus lost to the Fatherland, and he has sought by every possible device to divert some of these homeseekers into the German colonies in South Africa, China and Polynesia, but with conspicuous lack of success. Whether on account of the unfavorable climate obtaining in those colonies or for political reasons, certain it is that the German emigrant seems to prefer to settle under an alien flag. Wilhelm II, noting this regrettable state of affairs, has long desired to acquire some over-sea possessions which will prove attractive to his own people. Everywhere he sees himself thwarted either by Great Britain or by the American Monroe Doctrine. He cannot hope to found any new Deutschland on the South American continent so long as the United States stands pledged to uphold that doctrine of autonomy for the South American republics. The only way that remains open to him if he is to achieve his ambition is the way of force. He must seize what he wants if he is to get it at all.

Up to the year 1906 the idea of Germany's attempting to rival England's power on the sea would have been laughed to scorn. But in that year England completed the original "Dreadnought"—a battleship so much more powerful than any yet built that all earlier battleships were from that moment rendered practically obsolete. That gave Germany her chance, and the Kaiser did not hesitate to make the most of it. He forced the Reichstag to adopt a new and more vigorous naval policy which stupefied the world with its scope. This programme, which is fixed (except that in 1908 it was increased somewhat), calls for the completion by 1917 of no less than 38 battleships, 20 large armored cruisers, and 144 torpedo-boat-destroyers, besides numerous smaller cruisers, submarines and auxiliaries. To accommodate this immense fleet great sums must be spent on enlarging the Kiel Canal ($50,000,000), which provides a safe inland waterway between the Baltic and the North Seas; docks and shipyards must be increased in size and number; new and better facilities provided for the manufacture of armor-plate and structural steel. All this is being done, though it bids fair to overwhelm the country with its frightful expense. The naval budget has increased from $55,000,000 in 1905 to over $110,000,000 in 1910. And this does not include the extraordinary expenses of widening and deepening the Kiel Canal, nor the building of the great naval depot at Wilhelmshaven.

This sudden activity in Germany has had a deplorable effect upon other nations. England, feeling that it was directed particularly at her, has not yet recovered from the panic it caused, and has strained her utmost to outdo Germany in the number and power of her Dreadnoughts. She had every advantage at first in the matter of experience and shipbuilding facilities, but these have by now been set at naught by the thoroughness of German preparation and organization. The sole advantage remaining to Britain is the size of her purse, and in this she is, and long will be, supreme. Her colonies, too, have rallied to her aid, the practical fruits of their patriotism being a Dreadnought each from Canada, Australia and New Zealand.

All the other great nations of the earth have taken up the burden and are building as many battleships as they can afford; all save the United States, which has lately contented itself with but two a year. Though at present we rank second only to England in naval strength, another year will see Germany usurp our place; but we seem definitely committed to a passive policy, which is perhaps allowable in view of the security which we owe to our isolated position. Yet there are many who think it unwise for us to remain content with third place, and their opinions are certainly worthy of attention.

It has been said* that "America must either require a much more powerful navy than she has to-day or she has no vital need of any navy at all." This somewhat categorical statement arouses the following questions in our minds: 1. How much more powerful a navy does she require than the one she already possesses?—and 2. Why, on the other hand, does she need no navy at all? The answer to the former question is one for experts to decide. As to abolishing our navy altogether, that would be tantamount to inviting an attack upon us by any nation which desired that which it could only obtain from us by going to war.

* See Mr. A. G. McLellan's article in the January (1911) *Atlantic Monthly*.

Assuming, for the sake of argument, that we shall have done away with our fleet, what would be the result? Germany would at once see the way clear to achieving one of the Kaiser's most cherished ambitions—a German colony on American territory—probably along the south-east shore of Brazil. Who would stop her? Certainly the Brazilians themselves, even if aided by the Argentines and the Uruguayans, could not hope to repel an invasion by so mighty a nation as Germany. England? Possibly—and yet it would seem as if, with the United States acquiescent toward so flagrant a breach of the Monroe Doctrine, Great Britain could hardly be expected to involve herself in a war which did not directly affect the integrity of the British Empire. If we should protest too strongly, or seek to render aid to the South Americans, we should find ourselves at war with Germany, and our coasts at the mercy of her fleets. She might even attempt to invade the United States and obtain by force that which she has long coveted—the abrogation of the Monroe Doctrine.

Could we defend ourselves against such a dire calamity as invasion by a hostile army? If we are to have no navy we must entrust the integrity of our shores to our coast defences and our land forces. We have some 14,000 miles of seaboard, with innumerable harbors, almost any one of which would prove useful to an attacking army for the landing of troops. To fortify every harbor along our coasts sufficiently heavily to ensure their immunity from seizure by an attacking fleet would entail not only a stupendous outlay for guns and emplacements, with their accessory searchlights, rangefinders, ammunition, etc., but an immense force of Coast Artillery troops to man them. In the past twenty years we have spent scores of millions on such fortifications as were found indispensable by the Endicott Board, and still there remain dozens of harbors entirely unprotected by a single gun. Our Coast Artillery Corps now numbers about 20,000 officers and men; yet experts declare that this force is only about one-third of the number required completely to man the guns already mounted.

Now coast artillery alone is not sufficient to prevent an enemy from landing an army on our shores. The forts may be quite impregnable from the sea, and yet require a strong force of mobile troops—with cavalry and field artillery—to guard them against seizure from the flank or rear. (This was proved to be the case last summer when a small force of Rhode Island Volunteers attacked with success Fort Greble in Narragansett Bay, though that fortress is a veritable Gibraltar from the water side.) In the matter of protection to her coasts Germany has two tremendous advantages over America—her coast line is comparatively short; and she has a standing army of over 500,000 men constantly under arms with which to guard the land approaches to her fortifications.

Some foreign critics are fond of assuming that an enemy which tried to force an entrance into this country would choose one of our great ports—New York or Boston—for assault, and they prophesy certain failure for the fleet that attempts to join issue with our 16-inch or 14-inch guns. Yet they must know that we possess exactly one 16-inch gun, and that one not mounted (experience having shown that results did not justify the tremendous expense of building and firing ordnance of such great calibre). We are at present constructing rifles of 14-inch bore, but these cost money and take time to build, and it will probably be many years before any considerable number have been erected in their emplacements. Therefore a foreign fleet would have nothing more formidable to contend with than 12-inch rifles and mortars, although past history has shown that in a hypothetical duel between ships and land batteries the latter have the better of the argument.

Now, if America is to have no navy at all, what is to prevent a nation like Germany, for instance, sending an army over here convoyed by her fleet and attempting a landing *near* some fortified harbor *out of range* of its guns? Does it seem impossible that she could land a preliminary strong force of bluejackets in small boats under the protection of the guns of her fleet? And could not these bluejackets—supported by marines with field guns—very probably effect a quick and successful assault on the adjacent fortifications which are confessedly vulnerable from their land sides? Remember, we are supposed to be without any navy, so that there would be nothing to prevent the enemy's ships—men-of-war and transports—lying in safety while awaiting the outcome of the land attack on the forts. If these fall, the harbor may readily be cleared of mines and other obstructions, and the hostile fleet may land its men and supplies unimpeded. I have assumed that in their assault on the rear of the fortifications the naval brigade was not opposed by mobile troops of the United States Army. These, few as they are, could not expect to be everywhere at once, and we may rely on the enemy's having, by feint attacks and other deceptive ruses, adequately obscured the scene of their intended attack. Without a fleet of fast scout cruisers to spy upon them this would prove a simple matter, and by the time our army had reached the beleaguered city it would have already been seized and newly fortified by the just-landed hostile troops.

Once having obtained a foothold on our soil, and with the ocean providing an unrestricted means of communication with their base of supplies, the invading army could sit tight and await reinforcements from home. To oppose it we could bring our meagre Regular Army of 60,000 men backed by a larger number of volunteer troops. But the enemy's forces would consist of trained men, with trained officers in command, and the new levies from home would only be more of the same kind, whereas we should have to depend for reinforcements upon utterly untrained newly enlisted volunteers. That Germany— or, for that matter, Japan—has the merchant fleet sufficient to keep an army of several hundred thousand men adequately supplied with ammunition, food and other necessities is undeniable, and a war waged under such conditions would be very protracted and expensive, even though we might ultimately be successful in defeating and expelling the invaders.

Let us now assume that we have a navy. Would such an attack be possible? Certainly not until every important vessel should have been captured or sunk, for no nation would risk a fleet of transports, poorly armed and entirely unarmored, in waters infested by hostile battleships or armored cruisers. Even if the enemy's own fleet were still in battle trim the transports would yet be a prey to fast American cruisers or torpedo-boat-destroyers. Admiral Mahan, who is recognized as one of the foremost naval strategists of the day, has said that the best defence for a nation's coasts is a militant battle fleet cruising in the enemy's waters. Nor would it be possible for any country in these days of 26-knot scouts and practicable wireless communication to make a sudden landing at any point on our shores unheralded; and if the warning came in time—as it doubtless would —we could hurry our regular troops to the proper spot to contest the landing of men in small boats, and to defend the fortifications from attack on flank or rear. The truth of this statement was demonstrated only a few weeks ago when a squadron of seven fast vessels under Rear Admiral Staunton, U. S. N., easily discovered the whereabouts of Rear Admiral Schroeder's returning battle fleet when it was still over 1,300 knots from our shores.

It need not be an overwhelmingly powerful navy, but it must be of such size and strength as to preclude the possibility of its being completely destroyed or captured in battle; for not until every considerable unit had been overcome could a hostile fleet of transports venture to approach close to our shores. The Japanese, in their late war, did not risk throwing an army into Korea—only 100 miles from their home port of Sasebo—until they were assured that every Russian war-vessel was either sunk or bottled up in Port Arthur and Vladivostock. They did lose several transports and men-of-war by floating contact mines, it is true; but that is an attendant risk which must be run in cases of this sort.

Our navy at the beginning of the year 1911 consists of 31 battleships (of which six are Dreadnoughts), 13 armored cruisers, a score of smaller cruisers, and 31 destroyers, beside 20 or more submarines. This fleet will be increased annually by two Dreadnoughts and half-a-dozen destroyers,—just enough to replace the older vessels as they become obsolete from year to year. We have no desire to enter the race for sea power, but at the same time we dare not lag too far behind; for a weak navy is in itself an invitation to aggression on the part of others, and we continue unwilling to increase the size and strength of our land forces as the European nations are constantly doing.

The main objection to the building of Dreadnoughts for the navies of the world is the frightful cost of these leviathans. A battleship costs to-day between ten and twelve millions of dollars. Five years ago it was but little more than half of this. The "Wyoming," of 26,000 tons is, however, just three times as powerful as the 16,000-ton "Connecticut," but will have cost considerably less than twice as much; and her complement of officers and men will be only 25 per cent. more than that of the older ship. In answer to those who decry the maintenance of our navy on the ground of expense I shall give a few figures which, I think, will show that we are really very moderate in our outlay compared with England and Germany. In 1907 (before she had entered the list of Dreadnought-builders) Germany's naval budget was $65,000,000; England spent $156,-000,000, and the United States $105,000,000. In 1910 these figures had increased to $110,000,000, $200,000,000 and $122,000,000 respectively. Germany is now spending almost as much on new construction alone ($55,000,000) as she authorized in 1907 for her entire naval appropriation, while we have only increased our budget by 15 per cent. And a great part of this increase may be attributed to the increased rate of pay which our officers and men have received since 1909. Indeed, almost one-third of our whole outlay is for the pay of the navy and the Marine Corps, while England's appropriation for pay is but 22 per cent., and Germany's only 9 per cent. of their respective totals.

The wealth of the United States has been estimated as $120,-000,000,000; and our foreign trade—exports and imports—amounts to some $3,500,000,000 annually. If we choose to consider our navy as insurance against foreign aggression we find that we are paying for it at the rate of one-tenth of one per cent. on our total wealth, and are affording protection to our foreign commerce at a premium of but three-and-a-half per cent. per annum. Taking a purely business view of the situation I cannot see that there is anything so very ruinous about it, nor do I share the feelings of those alarmists who affect to see general bankruptcy staring us in the face.

Those who argue that we have no real need of a navy because we have no merchant marine are mistaken in assuming that the only need of a fleet emanates from the necessity for giving protection to water-borne commerce. We have colonies and outlying dependencies to protect—the Philippines, Hawaii, Tutuila, Guam in the Pacific; and Porto Rico and the Panama Strip in the Atlantic. Furthermore, we stand sponsor for the integrity of the Monroe Doctrine, and the Policy of the Open Door in China. Would the United States attempt to insist on the maintenance of the *status quo* in South America and in China if she had no navy to lend force to her arguments?

Ever since the Spanish War we have found in England a friend

and ally in the matter of upholding the doctrine enunciated by Secretary John Hay. He stated at the outbreak of hostilities between
Japan and Russia that the United States could not allow those or any
other nations to make the war an excuse for seizing Chinese territory.
After England had accepted this doctrine—a daring example of the
"new diplomacy"—the continental nations reluctantly followed her
lead, and the geographical aspect of China is now practically the same
as it was in 1904. It was probably only England's prompt endorsement of Mr. Hay's note that prevented the other powers from object-
ing strenuously to the dictation of the United States. But England
had the navy to enforce the observation of the pact, and no one dared
challenge her ultimate control of the situation.

If America is to maintain, and if necessary enforce, her avowed
principles, a strong navy is as indispensable to her as to England.
We must keep our fleet keyed up to the highest practicable standard
of efficiency; and we must see to it that our coast defences shall be of
such strength that they may safeguard the territorial integrity of
the United States at such times as the exigencies of war may make it
desirable for the fleet to absent itself from home waters. Neither of
these desiderata will cost much money, and there is no reason why
Congress should display other than a generous policy with regard
to them. We must hasten to complete the fortifications at Manila
so as to protect that city from possible attack. Pearl Harbor,
Hawaii, should be made a great naval base and strongly protected by
14-inch and 12-inch guns; for Hawaii is strategically the vital point
in the defence of our Pacific Coast. And thirdly, the Panama Canal
must be fortified with strong land works at either end, so that our control may be absolute in war as in peace. The Harbor of Guantanamo,
Cuba, should be transformed into an important naval station, with
dry-docks and repair-shops for the maintenance and repair of our
fleet; and strong forts should crown the surrounding hills.

When all these necessary enterprises shall have been brought to
completion, and with the Canal open to provide a means of quick passage for our fleet from one ocean to the other, we may consider that
we have done our duty.

FINANCIAL FEUDALISM AND A CENTRAL BANK

EDMUND D. FISHER

THE simple system followed by the great clearing houses of the country is so successful in its operation that it is surprising the principle has not been given wider application. Clearing is the essence of good business in individual transactions as well as in the larger operations which involve national and international finance, and the difficulties which for so long have prevented an orderly march of business in this country have grown largely out of a lack of its proper use.

Prior to the organization of the New York Clearing House it was necessary for a messenger from each bank every day to present all current items for payment to the various other banks where they were payable. This occasioned much confusion, loss of time, labor and the constant danger of the loss of money. This custom, in effect, still prevails among the banks of the country in the collection of out-of-town items, although the maximum degree of efficiency and economy would result if the clearing function was performed by a central organization. In other words, if every bank in the United States had an account in a central bank, or its convenient branch, all banking items would be cleared within twenty-four hours through the facilities of the mails, or by telegraphic transfer. Such a system would prevent the manufacture of temporary credits, which now unduly increase deposits during the lengthy period of collection and deceive the banker into believing the volume of his business to be greater than it really is. The best evidence of this dangerous condition appeared in 1907, when a temporary cessation in the manufacture of new credits from continuing business emphasized the fact that a large amount of deposits always is canceled automatically through payments of outstanding items presented for redemption.

The check is but an instrument used to effect a transfer of credit or cash and the bank note performs a similar function. The bank note, therefore, after performing its service, should also be subject to cancellation, as is the check. The restrictive regulations governing the issue and redemption of bank note currency, based on Government bonds rather than on business needs, constitute one of the most adverse elements in American finance and tend to periods of inflation with which we unfortunately are familiar. A central banking organization having the power to clear the currency of the country as well as the checks would remove this weak feature in our system of finance.

Credit is mainly the basis for both the check and the note and best serves its purposes when it is properly cleared. The banker who accepts a four months' note covering a business transaction does so upon the supposition that it will be paid at maturity, and his business is on a bad basis if his assets are encumbered by notes that cannot be properly cleared by prompt payment. It is, of course, entirely proper for different kinds of banking institutions to include in their assets a reasonable amount of credits which, because of their very nature, cannot be promptly cleared, such as mortgages, bonds and other investment securities. The lack of definite regulations covering the relative proportion of such securities held by banking institutions, however, gives too wide a scope of operation to the average banker. A distinct line should be drawn between such non-liquid assets and those based upon legitimate business transactions which may be readily cleared.

The conditions which precede a panic usually grow out of fundamental errors committed by both banking and commercial interests in the diversion of credit to assets which cannot be promptly liquidated, or which never can be liquidated, and have to be charged to " profit and loss " in the process of rehabilitation.

Through the standardization of credit which a central banking organization would eventually develop, banking methods would be placed on a sounder basis than at present and the business of the country would be more promptly cleared. The slower credits should be held chiefly by the investor, who desires income rather than a banking basis for his investments.

The prompt clearing of our international financial and commercial credits is equally important as the clearing of those of our own country. While this function is now voluntarily performed by bankers of great ability, yet they act as individual units and for their own purposes. Hence, our need for a greater and more unselfish power, working for the entire nation. A central bank, therefore, thoroughly representative of the whole country and with agencies abroad, would be most valuable as an international clearing agent. It would also, in a large way, anticipate and prevent business difficulty, growing out of domestic as well as foreign relations.

The truth is that the United States is yet in the feudal age of its financial history. The weaker banker serves and is dependent upon the stronger, and, through lack of some central governing power with lawful authority, alignments of various interests necessarily are made by those who usually can work in harmony. But the entire fabric too frequently is threatened in times of financial crises. At such times the " robber baron " is a source of great damage through the exposure of his attempts to capture the spoils of his profession under the guise of legitimate banking.

We are accustomed, in a crisis, to look to the city clearing houses as the last resort, and they never have failed us. Why? Because through their medium bankers are compelled to get together and apply their united reserves for the benefit of all. But for some it is too late. Much then has been lost and the financial disease is acute. Why not get together in advance of difficulty and establish the national clearing house, or central bank, well equipped at all times to perform all the essential clearing and banking functions? It matters not what it may be called, but it should be a bank for bankers that will be a help; that will not compete with bankers but serve them; that will not destroy clearing houses but coöperate with them; that will not weaken our national reserves but systematically conserve or distribute them.

The crystallization of the best thought on this subject is undoubtedly the suggested plan for monetary legislation submitted to the National Monetary Commission by its chairman, the Hon. Nelson W. Aldrich (see appendix). It is not expedient, within the limits of this article, to criticise this plan. It merely has been suggested for general consideration and doubtless will be modified before final legislation is had with regard to several important particulars. In general, however, it may be said that its adoption would materially cure many of the financial ills which have grown out of our present confused financial system.

The country has been long fearful of a centralized banking power. Such a power exists to-day, but in the inefficient archaic and feudal form. Why not then accept the principle of centralization as expressed by the central bank, but applied under a control based upon a fair representation of the commercial and financial interests of the entire country?

Analysis of "Suggested Plan for Monetary Legislation" submitted to the National Monetary Commission by Hon. Nelson W. Aldrich

I. RESERVE ASSOCIATION OF AMERICA (CENTRAL BANK).

ORGANIZATION:

Authorized Capital $300,000,000.

Paid in, say, $150,000,000.

Stock held by subscribing national banks to extent of one-fifth of their capital.

Charter, fifty (50) years.

Headquarters, Washington.

Branches, fifteen.

Officers: Governor, who shall be chairman of board and selected by President of United States from list submitted by board;

Two Deputy Governors, appointed in like manner; terms seven years (commencing four and seven, respectively).

Secretary.

Other officers to be provided for in by-laws.

Directors: 3 Officers of bank (*ex officio*)—Governor, two Deputy Governors;

3 Officers of Government (*ex officio*)—Secretary of Treasury, Secretary of Commerce and Labor, Comptroller of Currency;

15 Elected by branch boards (1 each);

12 Elected by voting representatives of each branch district, based on proportionate stock ownership;

33

> 12 Representing business interests to be elected by preceding thirty-three, who shall not be bank officers;

> ———

> 45 Total board.

Board shall be classified in three year terms.

Those holding National or State legislative office not eligible.

EXECUTIVE COMMITTEE:

> Governor; two Deputy Governors.
>
> Six other members elected annually by the directors.
>
> POWERS: All that are vested in board except what may be delegated to officers or other committees.

BOARD OF SUPERVISION:

> Chairman,
>
> Secretary of Treasury (*ex officio*),
>
> Members elected by board of directors.

POWERS AND FUNCTIONS OF CENTRAL BANK:

> *a.* Prescribe powers and duties of branch officers and committees and establish branches in foreign countries;
>
> *b.* Act as depositary for Government of United States and for subscribing institutions;
>
> *c.* Buy and sell: Government and State securities, securities of foreign Governments, gold coin and bullion; 90 day "prime" bills with endorsement of depositary banks, short-time Government obligations with not more than year to run; depositors' checks or bills of exchange, 90 days, with three signatures, payable in foreign countries; 90 day foreign "prime" bills with two endorsements;
>
> *d.* Make loans and contract for loans on gold coin and bullion;
>
> *e.* Fix rate of discount, which shall be uniform at all branches;
>
> *f.* Discount: Notes of depositary banks with guarantee

of local association, if secured, and with approval
of Governor, Executive Committee and Secretary of
the Treasury.

g. Rediscount: 28 day paper with endorsement of depositary bank made at least 30 days prior (total amount not to exceed capital of offering bank, and aggregate of one concern not to exceed 10 per cent. of capital of bank); also paper running more than 28 days and not more than 4 months, if guaranteed by local association;

h. Confine domestic banking transactions to Government and subscribing banks;

i. Make Government disbursements, transfer balances on books and between branches; open accounts in foreign countries.

REPORTS:

Weekly, public, to Comptroller of Currency; full reports to said Comptroller coincident with reports of national banks.

NOTE ISSUE:

Central Bank shall,

a. Offer to purchase from national banks Government 2's, for one year;

b. May exchange 2's for 3's if issued by Government;

c. Hold Government bonds ten years, but may, after two years, sell $50,000,000 annually to Government or postal savings bank;

d. Have currency privilege attached to 2's, and so issue new currency and assume responsibility for redemption of outstanding notes; issue additional circulation as follows: The whole or any part of the first $100,000,000 of such additional notes shall pay to the Government an annual tax of 3 per cent.; above $100,000,000 and not more than $200,000,000 may be issued at an annual tax of 4 per cent.; above $200,000,000 and not more than $300,000,000 may be issued at an annual tax of 5 per cent.; all above $300,000,000 shall pay an annual tax of 6 per cent;

> *e.* Note issues must have reserve—one-third gold or other
> lawful money; two-thirds United States bonds or
> bankable commercial paper;
>
> *f.* Notes shall be first lien on assets; shall be redeemed
> in lawful money;
>
> *g.* Shall be received at par, except as to Government ob-
> ligations specifically payable in gold;
>
> *h.* Shall be sent on application to depositary bank,
> against credit balance, without charge.
>
> (No further note issues by national banks.)

GENERAL PROVISIONS:

> Dividends: first, 4 per cent. cumulative;
> > Of excess ½ to surplus;
> > > ¼ to Government;
> > > ¼ to stockholders;
> > Maximum dividend, 5 per cent.;
> > Maximum surplus, 20 per cent. of paid in
> > capital;
> > Final excess to Government.
>
> All privileges of bank to be equitably extended to sub-
> scribing banks.
>
> No interest paid on deposits.

II. BRANCHES (CENTRAL BANK) RESERVE ASSOCIATION OF
AMERICA:

> Officers: Manager and Deputy Manager, both appointed by
> Governor of bank with approval of executive com-
> mittee of Central Bank board.

BOARD OF DIRECTORS:

> *a.* One representing each local association;
>
> *b.* A number equal to two-thirds of local associations,
> whose election is based on proportionate stock
> ownership in Central Bank;
>
> *c.* One-third elected by branch board from representative
> business interests;
>
> *d.* Manager of branch to be *ex officio* member and chair-

man of board. (Members of board divided at first
into 1, 2 and 3 year classes, respectively; thereafter
3 year terms.) None of final third shall be officers
of a bank or members of a legislative body.

POWERS OF BRANCH BOARDS:

Elect one member of board of Central Bank; also, to
elect one voting representative to choose, with others,
twelve members of Central Bank board based on proportionate ownership of stock;
Exercise locally the banking powers and functions of
Central Bank.

III. LOCAL ASSOCIATION OF NATIONAL BANKS:

(Composed of ten or more banks having a total capital and surplus
of not less than $5,000,000, and subscribing to stock of Central
Bank.)

ORGANIZATION:

LOCAL BOARD OF DIRECTORS:

Number determined by by-laws.
Elected *a.* three-fifths by member banks, irrespective of
size;
b. two-fifths by member banks, proportionate to
share ownership in Central Bank.

POWERS OF LOCAL BOARD:

a. To elect one director of branch board of own district
and one voting representative to vote for additional
directors equal in number to two-thirds of those
previously chosen; vote to be based on proportionate ownership of stock in Central Bank.

b. To guarantee commercial paper for a commission, to
member banks, for rediscount at branch;

c. Fix rate of commission for guarantee;

d. Require security to cover guarantee or decline paper.

GENERAL PROVISIONS:

    a. Banks shall be grouped into fifteen districts. There shall be a branch of Central Bank in each district.

    b. Losses from guarantee of commercial paper shall be met proportionately by member banks.

    c. Profits from guarantee shall be distributed *pro rata* after payment of losses.

    d. Total amount of guarantee at no time shall exceed aggregate capital and surplus of member banks.

IV. ADDITIONAL POWERS AND FUNCTIONS GRANTED TO NATIONAL BANKS:

    a. Accept 90 day commercial paper properly secured (amount not to exceed one-half of capital and surplus of accepting bank);

    b. Hold stock in banks authorized to do a foreign business, which shall not compete for domestic business;

    c. Count balances in Central Bank as part of legal reserve;

    d. File duplicate reports to Comptroller of Currency with Central Bank (five annually);

    e. Make weekly reports of principal items to Comptroller of Currency.

    (No further note issues by national banks.)

V. NEW CLASS OF NATIONAL BANKS:

May have savings department;
May make real estate loans to cover portion of savings accounts;
Maintain minimum reserve against savings and time deposits.

VI. ORGANIZATION OF NATIONAL TRUST COMPANIES:

POWERS:

    Similar to State trust companies;
    Subject to Government inspection.

HIC JACET

WITTER BYNNER

She who could not bear dispute
Nor unquiet, now is mute;
She who could not leave unsaid
Perfect silence, now is dead.

AT THE HEIGHT

B. RUSSELL HERTS

Yes, my story must be told to you calmly, line by line, just as it occurs to me, for it is happening now, at this very moment, and it will stretch on, I suppose, right through the few remaining hours. It is, indeed, nothing more nor less than my actual life that I am going to tell you, or just these few last hours of it, at any rate. I am giving my life into this writing, and I feel that it is giving me life in return, new, more vital, more ecstatic life than I have ever felt before. Never has my accustomed art given me the thrills that come to me with the penning of these lines. This is what makes it all worth while, and perhaps it is worth while also because it will leave something of me to all the rest of you in the world, something more imperishable even than the great marble monument which I had hoped to rear where I now stand, and which another, I suppose, will finish as his own. It is no longer possible for the written word to die. That is a bit of consolation, at any rate. But I must be calm and quiet, and start at the beginning, or as near the beginning as need be, for your enjoyment of this document. Enjoyment? How strange the word seems! It is a thought quite outside of anything I can conceive. It is no longer of the least importance to me. I think only of all the little things that have gone into the past, and of all the great hopes that went with them, and of the one thing that still remains for me to do. But the minutes are speeding, and I must begin, calmly, line by line, just as it occurs to me. . . .

I left the office at about two o'clock in the afternoon, intending to catch the four o'clock train at the Grand Central, but my valise proved too heavy for a walk up Fifth Avenue. Having boarded one of the automobile stages, I found myself at Forty-second Street long before three o'clock, and could not resist the temptation to walk round to my "great marble monster," as I called the huge hotel I was putting up on Broadway. It occurred to me that my wife might have a final parting word to say (I was to be gone at least a week); so I went and checked my valise, and called her up on the 'phone. Dear, good woman! She was sweet and lovely, as I found her every day of our life together. She was dearer to me than anything in the world, save only my great marble giant, my giant-child, the mass of beauty that I had borne out of my soul, and that, as a last bit of self-gratification, I was going to see before leaving town. She knew that she was second to it; she herself loved it almost as I did; for all the vast, undefined yearning that every woman feels had gripped her great mother's heart and opened it to this big being of iron and stone, which was warm as the dearest infant to me, but must have been cold and dreary, in spite of all, to one who might have borne a child.

I walked down Broadway, filled with the joy of labor and of conquest. Beside me clanged the street cars, and wagons and trucks rattled by. Newsboys offered the latest evening editions, and when I was unresponsive begged for a cent or two in charity. The hotel frequenters were just beginning to assemble, with newspapers and canes in one hand, and their overcoats tucked under their arms. It was long before the factories or department stores farther down would send home their dreadful herds of pale, anæmic men and girls; even too early for the four o'clock departers from professional service. There were only the well-groomed men with their beautifully bonneted women going to tea in the up-town restaurants; the errand-boys with their various parcels and messages; and the frightful old women with their torn shawls and toothless simperings, as they squatted at the street corners in the gradually lessening sunlight, their tin cups clutched in work-distorted hands. But these were only picturesque to me on that May afternoon. My spirit floated high among the topmost beams of my splendid monster, where the brave workmen hammered away at the last steel rivets of the framework. Even at this stage it was beautiful, and half a dozen others had stopped to look at the white marble façade that already had been built up at the Broadway corner. I knew well that behind this there was nothing but the bare beams; but my fancy hid the fact from me as effectively as it was hidden from the most ignorant observer. It pictured to me the complete building, stretching twenty mighty storeys toward the stars that would soon twinkle above its almost completed roof.

My heart was singing in my breast as the lift took me upward through the very centre of my great structure. I felt like a giant myself, or perhaps like a creating god capable of all things. I was in the heart of my most perfect piece of craftsmanship, about which, as I only then realized, I had been dreaming through all the years, laying out the construction, modeling the decoration, imagining the supreme glory of the completed building, while my actual consciousness was busied with small things.

Slater, the foreman, greeted me on the roof.

"She's great! She's wonderful!" I cried, though I had always thought of my child in the masculine gender when I was alone.

Slater had a mind for the actual, and he drawled between his puffs.

"Yes, all except the seventh storey, to the west of the court. Looks to me like some trouble with the engineering. I can't help thinking the beams don't hitch right."

"What! Casper's the best man in America at this sort of thing!" I was back on the job again, mind, heart and all, as ready to deal in actualities as Slater, who spent his life in nothing else.

"Yes," he drawled; "but Fitzgerald says it won't go, and ought to be examined. It's hard to tell, because it's a difficult place to get at."

"Have you a lift near it?" I asked. He had. I looked at my watch, and found myself with fifty minutes before train time. "I am going down," I announced.

"Better have the plans examined before you bother."

"No, I'm going to Boston to-day, and you never can tell what will happen with the unions in their present condition. It looks as if we might have a strike any morning."

"Matter of fact," he said, taking out his pipe at last with what looked like almost a twinkle in his eye, but quite as unperturbed as ever, "we've got it already."

"What?"

"They're goin' out to-morrow morning."

"The combined trades?"

"Just so."

"Damn!"

This was blasting news, fearful news, though the men could scarcely be blamed with the advantages conditions generally afforded them just at this time. . . . (I must pause now in my narration. I am weak and weary. I wonder, shall I ever continue?)

I begin again at the end of what seems to be an hour.

I determined to spend my half hour as profitably as I could; as enjoyably, as a matter of fact, for nothing in the world could have given me greater pleasure than actually working on this building of mine, on the real solid framework. It was the first time I had had a hand in more than the dreaming of it, it seemed to me. We stood above the great inner court, the largest in America in a building of the sort—there were few owners who would have allotted this large piece of land, so close to the greatest thoroughfare in the world, and worth so many millions, to this purpose. But we were to have a hotel worthy for the world to visit, one beside which all the gorgeous forerunners would seem cramped and crowded.

We were standing among the huge, bare steel beams. Not a single stone had as yet been laid on what would be the most sumptuous court outside of Italy, the birthplace of this architectural delight. Where palms and rare stunted trees were to bloom a year hence, if all went well, were masses of sand and dirt, among which some of the men were getting their things together.

" How long has the news been out? " I asked Slater.

" Half an hour, I should say. We're not supposed to know nothin' about it. They'll all be gone before the hour's up. Can't keep 'em here; they're too excited to work, anyway."

Indeed, the men were already gathering in little groups, or leaning toward each other across the beams, even where they were working on the building. Some seemed filled with repressed exultation, while others were desolate, seeming to see before them the weeks or months of privation that the strike was almost certain to entail. All of them wanted but an excuse to leave. Many waited for some diverting miracle to turn their minds away from sorrow and distress. None seemed anxious to carry the fateful news into the dingy little tenements, where wives, or children, or parents were waiting.

Slater directed a man below to raise the lift to the roof. It hung on a double rope attached to the roof and manipulated from the ground floor of the building. The lift itself had been put up for examination purposes, and was just about big enough to accommodate one man comfortably. I got in, pulled the bell rope, and was hoisted down to what was to be the seventh storey.

"Just where is it, Slater?" I cried.

He leaned a little over the roof.

"The man on the eighth can show you exactly."

"There's no man on the eighth, or anywhere else," I called back. Looking down I saw the workman who had been taking charge of my lift standing still, waiting for me to finish. Almost all the rest of the men were also below. There was no help to be expected from down there, and I surveyed the scene at hand.

"It's all right. I have it. You've got it marked."

"All right, sir. I may not be here when you come up. Will you leave in spite of the strike?"

"I can't do any good here," I answered. "What time have you?"

"Three-twenty-five," he called.

"I can give just twenty minutes to it, then," I said, and set to work.

(Again a kind of palsy overcomes me. I cannot go on. I must, I must! There can be no end to my life until I have completed this account. Strength, O God, strength! Ah, once more. . . .)

Leaving the lift, I stepped out on one of the horizontal beams. The trouble lay with the pivot connecting this with one of the vertical ones. As I looked up and down the lines of heavy iron-work, I wondered whether the men who toiled hour by hour on this vast network felt anything of my thrill at the growing-up and filling-out of this mighty creature. It was like a human thing to me—superhuman; and yet the work of my brain. Could they also feel the breath-catching joy of creation in what they did with their hands?

I looked down into the court, without the slightest dizziness, at the men grouped together in a corner below already waiting for the gong to sound. Then I realized that my time would be up before theirs, and that there were only a few minutes left to take my measurements.

A gong seemed to sound, I heard it dimly, half consciously, just as I heard the shuffling below, and the men clearing out. I paid very little attention to it for the moment. Then I realized that it could not yet be time to quit work; and at·that moment the bell of the fire-chief's runabout interpreted the gong I had dimly heard before. The men followed it. The court was empty. This didn't worry me particularly, and I went back to work. After working for a little while I looked at my watch, saw that my time was up, and stepped back into the lift. A minute may have passed while I was thinking of my train and other business. Then again I looked up sharply, impatiently. The lift was motionless. I raised my hand and pulled the rope, signaling by the proper number of bells to the man who had let me down. No response. I looked. There was no man.

"H'm-m. How annoying, when I have only a few minutes," I remember thinking aloud. I called down to the men below, twice, I believe, and then once, more loudly. No response. I looked. There were no men below. "All gone to the fire," I said to myself. "Damn! They have no right to do this. They don't care what they do, as long as they've got to go out to-morrow, anyway."

My only hope of catching my train was to get out within five minutes. It would have been worse than hopeless to try to climb down the iron-work, and I couldn't raise the lift while I was in it. I did the only sane thing, and sat down and waited, even starting a cigarette, to take only three puffs, and then throw it away. The silence began to be oppressive. It was getting dark. Then I could hear cars clanging by. Once or twice a policeman's whistle cut the silence, and a whole gamut of automobile horns, clarions, sirens and the rest. I almost thought I heard the moving of feet—thousands, it seemed. There must have been thousands passing me in the street below at that moment. It was annoying to realize that I was seated not two minutes' walk from the greatest thoroughfare in the world, tantalizing.

I grew restless, apprehensive, frantic. I called out. Just noises at first. Then halloos. I remember using an Indian call I had learned in the Maine woods. At last, unnerved, I resorted to the inevitable "Help! Help! Help!" again and again, alternating with less coherent things. I exerted myself. My tone became shrill. Then, by an exercise of will, I kept it low and resounding for a while. . . . A few moments of silence. Absolute silence. Deafening silence. I was feeling a kind of nausea. Again my voice insisted on going forth, and I strained every muscle. My throat was sore. I was getting hoarse. My neck became taut, and my face was perspiring. Half an hour of this, and I sank down, exhausted and giddy, almost losing my balance as I did so.

Not two minutes from the greatest thoroughfare in the world! I was alone, entirely and utterly alone. I might as well have been on an uninhabited planet. All my plans upset! Everything disarranged. It was frightfully irritating. I swore. I called out helplessly, hardly above a whisper this time. I cried tears of vexation. Then, in a heap, I must have fallen asleep.

It was scarcely daylight, when I awoke, surprised and dazed. Again I almost lost my balance. At first I thought I was dreaming. I had not dreamt during the night. I had been simply exhausted, utterly worn out. What I saw with blinking eyes seemed like a vision of my aspiration. It was unbelievable. I was actually in the building itself. As I grew more awake I tried to convince myself that I was not so. But hunger and weakness told me that I had wasted time and energy and was still in my quandary. However, an hour or two would put things right and I might get the ten o'clock for Boston and still have time for a good breakfast beforehand. Then I remembered the strike.

That was all right. Someone would be coming back at any rate. There was a twitch of misgiving in my assurance, but I smothered it. Again I went to my examination of the beams, trying to work up an enthusiasm, as I contemplated my immense structure. I was too weak and had to go back to the lift, where I could be more or less comfortable. The morning passed by, occupied with thoughts, which were interrupted now and then by the rhythmic noises on the avenue. My wife would expect a telegram from me; perhaps she was even now wondering why it hadn't arrived. I asked myself if I should ever see her again; and then laughed, rather nervously, I guess. Why, it was quite possible I might have to stay here interminably.

I have been here interminably. My mind, as if of its own volition, grew reminiscent. I remembered things, first incidents that had happened recently; and then events from long ago, from childhood, some of them. My marriage to the girl who had been so sweet and good—and unsatisfying; who had given me all she could, and from whom I had asked more than I suppose any woman could give. I remembered the strivings at school, and the wonderful exhilaration of the *concours* in Paris. The names and faces of long-forgotten friends came back to me vividly. A life of search and struggle mine had been, a life full of the joy of accomplishment, a joy to which many minor pleasures had been sacrificed. Here I was, likely to die in the midst of the last achievement of my ambition. To die! Ha! ha! The thought had an element of the ridiculous in it. How I had soared to the stars, in thinking of this life-work of mine! There was no child of our marriage, but here was a child of my very own that should whisper my name in the ear of eternity; here was a child whose life might be a hundred years, sure to be famed throughout the world. For would not this be the greatest and most gorgeous of all buildings of its sort? Another would finish my task, another would gather the glory of my endeavor! My name would remain in the memory of only a few of those now living. There was nothing, absolutely nothing through which my name could live. The few trifles for which I had been responsible since my return to America had never satisfied me, even in the exaggerated moments of creation. They were worse than nothing. To be without any recognition, without any memory in the world, that would be terrible for me who had given my life to accomplishment, who had spurned the offer of a hundred joys. Here was a thought to die with! And it might be weeks before anyone knew that I had died. For now I looked the fact squarely in the face, and I realized that the strike might be long, and that perhaps no one would return until it was settled. I realized too that someone might come to my relief at any moment. I was not distraught; but I had simply come not to care. In a rather impersonal way I wondered how long a man could live without food. I felt I could scarcely stand present conditions very much longer. I was cramped and weak and dizzy. . . . Then darkness came again, and semi-consciousness. I had watched the sun circle the square opening of the court above me. I had prayed for darkness and rest. . . .

Suddenly, in the midst of coma, a happy, strengthening thought came to me. Involuntarily I felt for the plans in my pocket, and for the pencil beside them. I had never tried to write before. I had bothered very little about correspondence. But now I feel I must write. Instinctively, unreasonably, I feel I must write this memoir. I began with seventeen sheets of paper. Now only two remain, and I have torn up most of the others and rewritten them. All that is with me now I have done since this morning. It is the fourth day of my solitude. I am not so absolutely alone any more. I have cried out only once since my first frantic calling. I am busy, and almost satisfied.

But now I feel myself drifting again, just beginning to drift, and not to care. It is becoming really hopeless now. I know that these papers are all that I shall leave of myself. I feel sure of it. It seems so trifling; of so little worth. I, who might have done so much, am reduced to a few scraps of paper for my accomplishment here in the world. I wonder do authors think of the littleness of their work? I suppose they think of the thousands over the world, and throughout the ages, who may read them. All this seems so far away! Thousands might have seen and felt and lived in the work that I did. I cannot think that this scrawl is worth while. I continue it. There is nothing else. I suppose I might throw myself from the lift. That, too, seems scarcely worth the trouble; I am so weak. I suppose I shall do so if the pain is great. I wonder shall I know? Shall I write about it here? I have wondered about so many things. That is all I have strength left to do. Soon, soon, just the silence.

I can scarcely see. I think I may hear the clanging of the outside, but perhaps it is only the clanging in my own ears. If it were closer I should know. Now there is silence. Perfect quiet. Perhaps this is the end. . . . I shall write no more. . . . This one thought yet, true or false. . . . Just an idea, I guess, but . . . *I hear footsteps of a man below,* and he calls! *God!*

THE AMERICAN FARMER AND RECIPROCITY
WITH CANADA

WILLIAM J. TRIMBLE

MOST sensible men, the bulk of the farmers among them, recognize the advantage of freer trade relations with our great neighbor to the north. Yet, though we admit that reciprocity is sound in principle, does it follow, therefore, that the proposed treaty is equitable and wise? Ought not very mature deliberation to be given it on its own worth?

If it be objected to deliberate action that "now or never" is the time for reciprocity, we may observe that that is an argument ill-suited to large ends and real statesmanship. When such an argument is advanced in private business, a prudent man wants all the more to think a proposition over for a night or two. The currents drawing the two countries together are so strong that some form of reciprocity seems inevitable; but just because these currents are strong is all the more reason for making certain that adjustments are not unwisely forced.

The proposed agreement, in fact, is not that of an ordinary treaty or law, but initiates a new national policy. Even in reciprocity itself it would seem to strike out on a new principle, since the reciprocity of Blaine and McKinley was mainly directed to exchange of non-competitive products. In ultimate effects, however, this new kind of reciprocity simply does for the United States what the repeal of the corn laws did for England; it places agriculture in this country upon a basis of free trade.

The repeal of the English corn laws was determined upon after discussion for a dozen years; are the farmers of the United States not entitled to a dozen months for consideration of this far-reaching policy? For even yet the wisdom of the English policy is questioned. To be sure the full effects of that policy were not at once apparent after these laws were passed in 1846. But in the two decades from 1875-1895 when the new wheat fields of the United States were being opened up by improved machinery and better transportation facilities, under their competition the value of farm lands in England decreased one-half and the number of her agricultural laborers fell off almost one-half. The lessened sturdiness of her population was revealed in the enfeebled soldiery of the Boer War and is now manifest in the appalling problem of destitution which confronts her. Might not England have bought prosperity for her manufacturers at a less cost?

It can scarcely be denied that there is at least the possibility that the treaty with Canada, on the present terms, may depress American agriculture; but just to what extent no one can now forecast. The effect of this treaty may not be measured in a year, but in a decade or a generation.

No one knows the possibilities of the Canadian North-West better than the farmer of our North-West, for his relatives and old neighbors are already there in large numbers and he himself may have journeyed through it. He knows that it will take him thirty-six hours to ride from Winnipeg to Edmonton, and thence twenty hours to Calgary, and then thirty hours back to Winnipeg; and that all the way he rides over soil as fertile as his own was when it was new, and that only a fraction of that vast area is under cultivation. He takes down his year book of the Department of Agriculture and notes that the wheat crop of Saskatchewan rose from 34,742,000 bushels in 1908 to 85,197,000 in 1909 and its barley crop for the same year from 1,952,000 bushels to 4,493,000. (Just here he may pause to wonder what Mr. McCall meant in his report on reciprocity when he speaks of saving the Canadians the bother of hauling barley from Ontario to Western Canada. 61st Cong., 3d Session, Report No. 2150, p. 5.) At any rate he naturally tries to forecast future production, especially when he thinks of the new machinery that is on the market this spring. Time was when he thought a two-bottom gang plow and five horses a great improvement on old methods, but here are gas and steam engines, almost as powerful as locomotives, which will drag behind them plow, harrow and drill in the spring, or half a dozen binders in the fall. Moreover, they are equipped with lights and can be worked all night by using relays of men. Add to this the fact that the great railway systems are spiking down hundreds of miles of new lines into all parts of the Canadian West, and you see that this frontier region will be developed at a rate surpassing even our own marvelous achievements, and that a veritable flood of grain may be turned upon our boundaries in the next few years.

Then what? Any thoughtful student of American history or of American agriculture knows that the farmers on old soils cannot profitably compete with the farmers on new soils, even though freight be against the latter. On new soil a farmer sows less seed, with less expensive methods, has no weeds to fight and gets bigger returns; he has no interest charges (or very low) on the cost of his land, and he has little invested in buildings. The worst of it is, from the point of view of the older farmer, he is ordinarily without capital and must let his crop go to the speculators in the fall for what he can get.

But, we are told by a host of well-meaning friends, "If you cannot raise wheat profitably, you can raise other things." Undoubtedly there is much reason for rotation of crops, but its adoption is a slow and expensive processs, and a man must make a living while he is adopting it. One thing is certain and that is that the farmers of the hard wheat States cannot turn to corn as do the farmers of Kansas and Nebraska. Moreover, if you increase the corn crop you tend to lower the price. True, this treaty puts corn on the free list and Canada may take some corn, but in general any decided and long continued lowering of the price of wheat will cause a general lowering in the price level of other related products.

But we are assured complacently by even our most thoughtful magazines that the price of wheat is on a world basis and that therefore the wheat farmer cannot be injured. This phase of the matter is so complicated that a final determination could be made only by such an expert study as a tariff commission could make. In the lack of such authoritative pronouncement, we would venture some observations from our own study:

1. In the past it was generally true that the price to the American farmer was regulated by world conditions.

2. During the past two years the average price has been above the export level, until about the middle of February last.

3. In the future the last condition will be likely gradually to become permanent.

Now, the farmer dreads being forced back upon the world basis. The past few years have brought to him fair prices, which have begun to give him a measure of the comfort and respect that other Americans enjoy; but he can look back only a little while when the world basis forced him to sell his wheat for fifty cents or less. Cheap wheat means for him toil repaid by deprivation, means that his daughters must do without new clothes, that the boys must be kept out of school, or that no help can be allowed to the worn wife or mother in the kitchen. Thousands of farmers in the United States to-day can look back to the time when, the crop being required for the debts, the mother worked far into the night to make butter which sold for ten or twelve cents a pound. Do you wonder at the indignation that deepens and broadens daily through our farming population at the effort to force us back upon the world basis?

It is true that the world basis will possibly never again bring fifty cent wheat, but seventy-five would be as disastrous under present expenses of production. It is urged that world consumption is increasing faster than production, and that prices on the world basis must go higher. This will probably be true ultimately if over-stimulation of city growth continues. But who can assure the farmers of this generation that Argentine, Russia and Siberia cannot enormously increase their production during the next decade, while Canada in the same time is adding to the world's stock a half billion or more bushels?

But, we are indignantly told, would you keep up the cost of living by taxing the poor man's bread? Right here I want to present a dilemma to the advocates of this treaty. If the treaty is going to lower the cost of living, how are you going to accomplish that lowering without lessening prices and damaging to that extent producers? If you do not lower prices to the producers, how are you going to reduce the cost of living? . But let us look squarely at this contention. Suppose that the price of wheat on the average is lowered ten cents per bushel, how much will the price of bread be lowered? The answer to that question was carefully worked out in the masterly speech of Senator McCumber on reciprocity, in which he demonstrates that the price of a loaf of bread would be lowered one-thirty-seventh of one cent and then pertinently asks whether the consumer will get the reduction or the baker or miller! Moreover, in proportion as you injure the prosperity of the farmer, you injure the best market in America for the products of manufacturing labor, and thus the consumer may lose far more than his one-thirty-seventh of one cent.

On the other hand, consider the farmer's side. If the price of wheat is reduced ten cents, the profits of the farmer are reduced out of all proportion to any possible gain to the consumer. How many city people pause to think that what the farmer gets is not all profit? When he has figured all expenses, the margin of profit is often very small. It is safe to say that, year in and year out, a reduction of ten cents in the price of wheat in the United States means a loss of not far from one-half of the farmers' net profits in wheat.

Furthermore, remember that the farmer shares the high cost of living. Labor, clothing, machinery, magazines—everything that he buys is higher. And of course he is not content, and rightly so, with the old mode of living that drove from the farms our brainiest and our best. He now wants telephones and proper clothing and better schooling for his children, and all of these things cost money. On the other hand, salaries and wages of city dwellers are on the average higher than ten years ago. Will they wish to revert to the old scale of income and the old plane of living, if the farmer is forced to do so?

It is true that some farm products may find markets in Canada, but the benefit here is small compared with the possible detriment. Free cotton seed and cotton-seed oil may benefit our Southern brethren somewhat, but Canada must buy these from us any way, and in 1910 did buy 15,458,774 pounds of the first and 2,092,732 gallons of the latter. Fruits may pass back and forth over the line in small quantities, but Canada can produce the kinds that go on the free list about as well as we can. The net gain to the United States in this treaty cannot accrue to the agricultural interest.

It is urged, however, that the farmer will be benefited in other ways. For example, it is said lumber will be cheaper. But this treaty provides not for free lumber, but merely for free rough lumber; and rough lumber cannot be shipped to advantage in competition with dressed lumber because the freight is proportionately much higher on account of weight. Certainly the giant lumber combines of the Pacific North-West have little to fear from British Columbia on the basis of protected reciprocity.

In fact, this treaty in the main from one end to the other bears hard on the small, individual, ill-organized producer from Maine to Washington and leaves untouched or actually benefits the large combinations. What trust article will be cheapened by this treaty? On the contrary, several trusts will be directly benefited, as for example the great meat companies, the coal barons and the International Harvester Company; but the man who fishes, or farms, or cuts a few posts or ties for a living is exposed to the competition from which the great concerns are carefully shielded.

We are told that these reductions are only a beginning and that matters will be equalized by the revision of other schedules. What assurance have small producers that this will be so? Some of them recall the effort made at the time of the Wilson bill and what came of it. Suppose the House takes up schedules for making further reductions; will the Senate countenance them and the President endorse them?

Advocates of this treaty have charged the farmers with being narrow and sectional in their views, while they have urged broad national considerations. Put on that ground, is it certain that this policy is wise? Its tendency is to accentuate and perpetuate certain movements which are admittedly menacing to our nation's welfare. On the one hand it tends to continue, perhaps to accelerate, the movement away from the farms to the cities; on the other it stimulates the growth of cities and aggravates their problems. It tends further to fatten the fortunes of the few and to deepen the congestion and with it the destitution of the masses, who will continue to pour in from Italy and Hungary and Russia. If this treaty passes, we trade our sturdy farmers of the North-West, whose exodus even now is preparing, for the lower types who mass in New England towns. Are numbers of population to be preferred to stamina and character?

We recognize that the policy proposed to be initiated by this reciprocity agreement is national in scope. On full consideration we may see that we are wrong in our views and that in the long run we shall be benefited with the rest of the country. But we do claim for ourselves and for the nation just and mature deliberation. We claim that we are as much entitled to patient hearings before Congressional committees as representatives of other interests were accorded before the passage of the present tariff bill. We doubt whether rules of closure, executive pressure and extra sessions are wise and just methods of arriving at right decisions of momentous policies. And, finally, we are coming more and more to believe that the only sane and healthful treatment of the tariff lies in the creation of a tariff commission, with powers and procedure analogous to those of the Interstate Commerce Commission.

Since, however, a permanent commission seems at present impossible, why not refer this reciprocity matter to a special commission as in the case of postal rates on magazines? If the President has promised to use his utmost exertions in favor of early action, there may be all the more need for Congress to temper urgency with counsel. We cannot see that anything would be lost to postpone the final decision until next December. Or is this grave question to be decided on partisan grounds, by high pressure methods, and amid the vociferations of a host of interested individuals who are crying pity for the consumer and advantage for the nation to their own gain? Give the farmers, along with all Americans, justice in reciprocity. With time and patient thought and fair-minded consideration of all interests, we think that it would be possible to work out a more equitable measure than the one now proposed.

THE IBSEN MYTH *

EDWIN BJÖRKMAN

I

Ibsen is being read more to-day than he was ever before, particularly in this country, where he remained overlooked or scorned longer than in Europe. He is even finding a foothold on the American stage at last. And I believe that he will be more read and played to-morrow than he is to-day. Yet I fear that the understanding of his work has not moved abreast with the spreading fame of his genius. Where you find one person speaking intelligently and sanely of his dramas, you meet ten who claim an insight they do not possess, and hundreds who openly profess themselves baffled or repelled. The very men who feel most keenly that he has a message in store for them are often heard to remark that " he never said just what he meant."

To one familiar with the man's genuine spirit such words are fraught with a horrible irony. For fond as Ibsen was of clothing his sallies against sham and humbug and shallow indifference in the guise of subtlest sarcasm, this inclination was always subordinate to a sincerity that could rest satisfied with no expression falling short of the greatest attainable clearness. Above all other motives or tendencies actuating him stood his unrelenting sense of duty as an artist. And the logical outgrowth of his attitude was a passionate craving for understanding as the highest reward that could be reaped by the artist. Success, praise, renown, these were to him little more than the obvious dues of his endeavor. In a sympathetic comprehension, making a complete fellowship of soul between artist and reader, he saw the one truly satisfactory compensation for the labors of creative genius. In the lack of it he saw supreme misfortune.

In public Ibsen was wont to assume the same attitude of proud indifference that Whitman voiced in his defiant, " I do not trouble

* Thankfully dedicated to Minnie Maddern Fiske as the artist who has done most for the faithful interpretation of Ibsen in this country.

my spirit to indicate itself or to be understood." And once, when planning to tell how some of his plays had come into being, he hastened to declare: "Of course, I shall undertake no interpretation of my works—it is better that the public and the critics be left to disport themselves at their own sweet pleasure in that field."

But in his correspondence with personal friends he showed repeatedly how he suffered from misunderstanding, misconstruction and, above all, from the insistency of friend and foe alike to read esoteric profundities into passages of unmistakable clearness or utter insignificance: as when a Swedish critic discovered deep meaning in the fact that Nora gives a whole "crown" instead of a half to the man who carries home her Christmas presents. After reading some reviews of *Peer Gynt*, Ibsen was moved to exclaim that, "by the employment of such methods, he could turn the works of any man into allegory from beginning to end."

Now he can protest no more, nor suffer from the futility of his protests. But still the critics are disporting themselves as when he lived. And still there stands like a wall between the man and the mass of his readers what I might call the Ibsen Myth—a fictitious, sphinx-like figure, surrounded by a world-wide and assiduously supported reputation for inherent, wilful obscurity of language and thought. In the false light of this myth the study of his work has come to be looked upon as an awesome task, a forbidding and largely fruitless pursuit of evasive paradoxes through mazes of ambiguous and disguised and impishly distorted utterances.

Much of this general misconception has, of course, sprung from incompatibility of temperament, from hopelessly divergent attitudes toward life, from honest differences of opinion. But far too much of it has originated with the very men who, in the last forty years, have worked hardest and most disinterestedly to proclaim the worth of Ibsen's achievement to the whole world: men who, in more cases than one, stood near enough to the poet during his lifetime to receive, from his own lips or pen, passionate proclamations of the fundamental directness and clearness of his spirit. Of unwillingness to comprehend his meaning such men cannot be suspected. The trouble must be sought in some other direction. And as I see it, the responsibility lies primarily with the traditions and conventions of the critical profession, by which even men of great originality and uuquestioned sincerity have hitherto been governed and hampered.

From the days of Aristotle to those of Brunetière, literary criticism has had its face turned backward, its glance inward. It has judged the living poetry of the current day by the dead poetry of days long gone by—and by nothing else. It has rightly accepted certain works of supreme merit as models, as " classics "; but it has also sought to establish these models as insurpassable types binding on all the future. Furthermore—and as a logical consequence of its retrospective attitude—criticism has judged books by books in a manner tending to diverge further and further from real life. And finally, in its judgments and classifications of art-works and art-currents, it has unduly accentuated form at the expense of feeling and thought.

Even critics like Taine and Brunetière were too prone to forget that, after all, the main purpose of tradition is to serve as a firm starting point for new progress. And though both of those men realized that, beyond its indispensable perfection of form, all artistic creation, to be truly great, must evidence emotional and intellectual perfection as well, they failed in their efforts to find criteria for the appraisement of this inner and higher perfection. And they failed chiefly because they turned to the past rather than to the future for guidance.

Not only in his work, intuitively, but also consciously and apart from it, Ibsen saw the truth and expressed it thus: " That man is right who stands closest to the future." For in order to reach greatness and to live beyond his own little hour, a poet must depart from the past without losing his hold on it; he must embody not only the best life of his own day but something above it; he must be in advance of his time, and consequently the effect of his work must lie largely in the future. If he fill these conditions, one may, naturally enough, expect nothing but miserable failure when those set to appraise him on behalf of his own time relate him only to what has been, and not— as Ibsen suggested—to what will come; when, in fact, they condemn him, or, at the best, apologize for him, in so far as he differs from the past and renders it obsolete.

If it be asked how an artist's originality may be tested, I answer once more: comparisons with the past, and with related forms of artistic expression, will always prove helpful and needful, but they will never suffice. Like everything else, art springs from life and must return its dues to that origin. For this reason the power and endurance of its appeal must, in the last instance, be decided by its proximity to life itself. In form art may touch life by being merely imitative. In feeling and thought it must go further—it must interpret. And it must do so because feeling and thought are, in themselves, more or less close-fitting interpretations of life's methods and meanings.

. Matthew Arnold defined poetry as " criticism of life." Rightly understood, his dictum tells most of the truth. For poetry, like everything else, gives its dues to the life from which it has sprung only in so far as its critical interpretations of that very life prove a means toward better and higher and more effective living. And in the same way as life reaches its highest efficiency not by standing still, but by pressing constantly onward, so art, too, must take its place with the forces that make for progress the moment it aspires at anything above mere amusement.

And now we are getting near the basis of the Ibsen myth. The man who did more than anybody else to create the modern prose drama was far ahead of his time and generation, as all true poets must be; and he kept constantly ahead by pressing closer and closer to life. Nor did he content himself with the faithful portrayal of mere surface appearances. Like the miner in his own famous poem of that name, he was ever swinging his hammer " to break a way into the heart of what is hidden." And he perceived things that were still so deeply secreted from the rest of his kind that at times he seemed to them like a man talking of another world.

Until he appeared, the drama was like a letter written with an eye to publication—or like the memoirs of a man with a long and dubious public career to defend. The figures on the stage said and did not what their own natures and the premised situation made inevitable, but what the author needed for the furtherance of his plot, or what he thought might impress the public. Ibsen placed life itself on the stage. He swept aside the arbitrary and artificial conventions that formed the playwright's main stock in trade—traditional makeshifts that were still used and defended even by men like Augier, the younger Dumas and Henri Becque. He banished the clever phrase, and he made his characters address each other instead of the audience. He built actable, intense dramas with a dialogue as natural as the talk of two men in the street. And if some readers doubt this final assertion, I must tell them that there is not yet a translation that gives an English equivalent of Ibsen's wonderfully keen and vital prose.

For years his formal innovations did as much as anything else to arouse antagonism. But those days are past. Long ago the leading critics admitted the validity of Ibsen's leadership in this respect. To-day his demands for greater verisimilitude of form have become accepted parts of the new dramatic technique. Similarly, though more slowly, we are lessening his lead in social and moral attitude. And I am not referring to mere political radicalism now. That sort of thing, needful as it be, meant very little to Ibsen. Political reforms were important to him only in so far as they prepared or reflected individual reform.

But it was he who taught us to be ourselves without being selfish as the trolls. It was he who made us acknowledge that woman has a soul and a right to use it in accordance with her own needs and inclinations. It was he who threw the sharp light of the stage on the responsibility owed by one generation toward the next. It was he who had the courage to question the redeeming value of deeds done in grudging surrender to " duty." It was he, finally, who pointed the way toward a higher kind of individualism by making his superman not an end in himself, as had Nietzsche, but an instrument for the ennobling of all mankind—a hand reached out by the race for its own uplifting.

But even when leading us along these new moral paths—toward his " third kingdom," where poetry, philosophy and religion were to be merged into a new synthesis, and where " good " and " evil " would once for all be translated into " true " and " false "—even then he never reached quite out of sight of the host plodding in the rear. This happened only when he glimpsed and mirrored truths touching closer still on the core of all existence.

" I have often thought of what you wrote to me once," he said of himself in a letter to Brandes; "that I have not acquired the present-day scientific viewpoint. How could I get over this handicap? But then, is not every generation born with the qualifications of its own time? Have you ever, in a collection of portraits from some bygone century, noticed a peculiar family resemblance between the different individuals belonging to the same period? That is just what happens to us spiritually. What we laymen do not possess as knowledge, that, I think, we have in a certain degree as presentiment and instinct."

It was just this intuitive power that enabled him to see, first of all, the radical error underlying the popular assumption that "the past is what it is." He perceived that, on the contrary, the past is changing constantly; that it is revealed in new light by every passing moment; that what seems an unmitigated evil to-day may be changed into a great blessing by the unexpected event of to-morrow; that, in a word, the past is ever unfolding out of the present, just as is the future. This double process of simultaneous unfoldment he illustrated beautifully in some of his later plays, while in some of the earlier ones, as in *Lady Inger of Östråt*, he carried it to excess.

The same power brought Ibsen to realize the secret value which the seemingly insignificant has in life's economy. It made him divine the symbolism that underlies very simple things and every-day events because of their deep-hidden connection with the mysterious workings of our own souls. None knew better than he the artist's duty —as Millet formulated it—of "using the trivial to express the sublime." Witness, for instance, the manner in which he employed the keys in *The Lady from the Sea* to denote Ellida's changing relationship to the Wangel household. And the fact that Nora gives an excessive tip has meaning, indeed, as throwing light both on her character and her momentary mood—but not as a "key" to any cleverly construed allegory, which has to be solved as a mathematical problem and furnished with a triumphant "Q. E. D." at the end.

With equal force, however, Ibsen felt the truth of Dostoievsky's assertion that "what people call fantastic is often the very essence of the real." Typical of this side of his art is Hedda Gabler's use of the phrase "with vine leaves in the hair" to embody all the things that her existence lacked and craved for its normal development.

The phrase is indisputably symbolical, but only in the manner of life itself. If we analyze it in the light furnished by modern psychology, we find in it nothing esoteric or illegitimately mystical. The human mind is constantly taking hold of some striking term or fact and making it stand for a whole group of associated ideas. The use of such " shorthand talk," as it might be called, forms one of the standard labor-saving devices of the human brain, and language itself is full of it. What it all comes to is that Ibsen saw, and saw through, many of the things that still elude and puzzle us. And no matter how "fantastic" or "mystical" his words and dramatic devices may appear to us, we may rest assured that—with but very few exceptions—they indicate a firmer grip on life's deepest realities than we dare call our own.

He saw likewise that life, as a rule, is not direct and simple and palpable in the weaving of its all-including web of cause and effect— that, on the contrary, it is prevailingly complex and ambiguous, so that we are almost incapable of an act that may not be traced to some alternative of motives. And Ibsen built the shadow-life of his dramas accordingly. Wherever he indicated a motive as the probable explanation of some act or attitude, he held another one ready in the background as a possible factor. The behavior of Hedda may be the logical expression of nothing but her inborn nature plus early environmental influences, but it may also be prompted by the erratic impulses of impending motherhood. As the average man is a born absolutist, full of hearty hatred for all uncertainties and equivocalities that require additional mental alertness, it is not to be wondered that this feature of Ibsen's dramatic construction has served particularly to provoke the accusation that he was weaving riddles for the mere pleasure of puzzling the rest of mankind.

But the most remarkable and most far-reaching expression of his extraordinary grasp on life's mainsprings must be sought in his discovery and application of certain forces which, though always present within and about us, had to remain partly submerged and largely overlooked until modern social and economic conditions brought their inherent possibilities into full light—forces whose share in the shaping of life's course was barely suspected until the concerted labors of latter-day biology and psychology revealed it. In Ibsen's prophetic recognition of the increasingly important part played by these forces as rulers of man's destiny lies undoubtedly, even now, the one serious obstacle to a clear and full understanding of his work by any reader of ordinary intelligence. And for this reason, though it may seem a digression, I must attempt a brief outline of what modern science tells us concerning the nature and operation of those forces. Science alone holds the key to the mighty, deep-running currents that make all life one. And it is advancing science that has done, and is doing, most toward the lasting disposal of the Ibsen myth.

II

The ultimate discoverable aims of life seem to be its own preservation and perfection. Everything wants to be and to grow. But everything is at once a unit, an entity, fighting as such against everything else for its own individuality; and an integral part of some larger whole, sharing every phase of its existence with innumerable other units. Thus we find that, wherever life makes itself felt— that is, everywhere—the forces employed on its errands group themselves under four heads, as static (anabolic) or kinetic (katabolic), as centripetal or centrifugal. These four universal principles represent the cardinal points on life's compass. They are not identical with any known forces. They are in themselves merely directions or tendencies, by which all forces known to us are oriented, so to speak. In every form of energy two of those principles are embodied. Each such form makes at once for stability or change, and for conformation or variation. For life demands existence and improvement in each part as well as in the whole.

Turning to man, we see that everything he does and suffers has meaning to him only in so far as it helps him to keep alive or to improve his existence—or in so far as it hinders him in the pursuit of these two objects. And from cradle to grave—without any choice on his part—his life is intimately, inalienably bound up with the lives of other men, and with these he must needs share both past and future, both heritage and ideals. At every moment of his life he craves, consciously or unconsciously, to be and to grow both individually and racially. He demands self-expansion no less than self-expression. Thus we reach the four main motives of his entire active and passive being—the all-pervading motives of self-preservation and self-perfection, of race-preservation and race-perfection.

These are the ruling passions of all mankind, speaking no less plainly in the race than in the individual. For purposes of easy identification I have ventured to name them the WILL TO LIVE, the WILL TO LOVE, the WILL TO DO, and the WILL TO RULE. And collectively I shall speak of them as the LIFE FORCES. Characterizing them roughly, it may be said that the Will to Live stands for self-preservation, or conflicting order; the Will to Love for race-preservation, or associative order; the Will to Do for self-perfection, or conflicting progress; and the Will to Rule for race-perfection, or associative progress.

The two preservative instincts have long been recognized, and it is common among scientists and philosophers to lead our entire being, with all its crudest and subtlest activities, back to hunger and desire. But when life has been secured and love has had its hour, there remains in a wholesome organism, under normal conditions, a surplus of unspent energy. The higher up an organism stands on the ladder of life, the greater is that surplus, and the more striking is the use made of it. To me it represents life's most precious asset. For out of it comes the energy which the perfective instincts transform into growth, progress, evolution. It is principally for the sake of that surplus and what life can do with it that man has to live and love.

The Will to Do and the Will to Rule lead at once to individual innovations and to the racial assimilation of these through imitation. And this notwithstanding the fact that one of their main characteristics is their identification with apparently purposeless exertions. Actual uselessness has no place whatever in life's economy, but life has a way of leading us blindfolded to our goal by making us accept its means as ends in themselves. This it accomplishes mainly through a system of rewards and punishments designed at once to tempt and to scare us into obeying the urge of the life forces. Commonly we speak of these coaxings and goadings as pleasure and pain, comfort and discomfort, happiness and unhappiness. Through the long ages that lie behind him, man has not eaten with the conscious purpose of safeguarding life, but to escape the sharp pangs of hunger and to enjoy the sweet taste of food. Nor has he mated to prolong the life of the race, but merely to assuage the carpings of passion and to drain its ecstasy.

Thus we find the Will to Do served, on one side, by a keen sense of discomfort that accompanies all overstocking of energy. This we speak of as ennui or boredom or restlessness. The first thing we need to learn about it is, that it is not an emotion but a physical condition, a " need," which gives birth to all sorts of disquieting feelings. On the other side there is to be noted a strangely acute and gratifying sense of increased vitality that goes with all expenditure of energy under normal conditions, and particularly with all such expenditure that seems to be its own warrant and reward. In the same way the biddings of the Will to Rule are enforced by a fear of isolation, a burning fever of loneliness, that at times seems worse than death, and also by the pleasure that inheres in every form of companionship. For the Will to Rule is, in the widest sense, a group-instinct. It is life's instrument for securing to the race whatever is gained by the individual.

The universal process of evolution embraces faculties and ideas no less than organisms and races. Thus the perfective instincts have grown wonderfully in scope and depth and meaning since that dawn when they were actually nursed on scraps of leisure time and energy left over by the more imperative claims of the preservative forces. What began as a mere hankering for diversion has since grown into a resolve to comprehend all creation; and what started as play has blossomed into heaven-aspiring efforts at the reconstruction of the whole world to suit our own ideals.

We want first of all to raise our being to its utmost potency of bodily and mental vigor. We want to have the triumphant sense of being alive in a higher, more complete, more satisfying manner. This feeling we want to increase still further both by sharing it with others and by stamping our own selves on everything and everybody that comes within the reach of our influence. But above all else we want to escape ennui and loneliness—that gouging sense of emptiness, of death-in-life, which we are coming to know as one of man's worst torments as well as one of the strongest factors among those that impel him to action.

Exercise for the mere pleasure of exercising; sports and pastimes of every description; games, whether physical or intellectual; dancing and chess-playing—these are some of the palpable manifestations of the Will to Do. But pursuits and proclivities of much subtler and higher order may be traced to it. The miser's greed and the collector's hobby have their origin in it. The student, the explorer and the inventor are inspired by it. Our sense of beauty is based mainly on the pleasurable stimulation of sight and hearing; and the artist is moved by a craving to exercise senses and muscles and brain long before he dreams of aspiring toward any ideals. Wherever man is seeking new paths and new light, there this ubiquitous, never-resting impulse may be found at work.

Our emotional faculties require exercise in the same way as do our muscles and senses, our memory and imagination. For the mere existence within us of a machinery for the production of a certain effect is in itself an impulse toward a search for just that effect. We are looking for pity, horror, awe—at the centre of a suddenly collected street crowd, or back of the curtain that parts the world of fact from the world of illusion—first because we have been made capable of experiencing those emotions; and next, because, through their " play-practice," we are trained into avoiding what is life-destroying and into seeking what is life-promoting.

The fundamental characteristic of the Will to Rule is beyond doubt a passion for power, and as such it was recognized by Nietzsche. But it seeks a power that presupposes combination and therefore leads inevitably to reciprocity. In its broadest aspect this instinct is a craving for the expansion of our own lives by their reflection in the lives of others. While partly responsible, at least, for vanity and pretension, for arrogance and intolerance, the Will to Rule breeds ultimately ambition, loyalty, patriotism and a fellow-feeling for all humanity. Among those inspired by it are the moralist, the true statesman, and the martyr-pioneers of every great cause. To understand how it wields its influence, we must remember that a reformer first of all is a man wanting to press his own feelings and ideas on his fellow-men—one determined that other men shall do things to which they are not in themselves inclined. Of this force it may be said that it teaches us to rule in order that we may obey, and to lead in order that we may serve.

If we consider mankind everywhere and in all ages, it may safely be asserted that, until recently, all but an insignificant minority used to be completely engrossed with the mere protection of life. And their efforts took the natural shape of fighting in one fashion or another. At first this perennial conflict was waged with all nature. By degrees it became directed principally against other men. Relief from it was found only in coarse material pleasures and in love—which was then little more than another kind of war. The perfective forces could not assert themselves except in their most primitive forms, by making men more fit to fight and to love. In a word, they had to serve the earlier instincts.

Modern times have brought law-guarded peace, machine-made prosperity, nation-wide coöperation, popular education and democratic ideas. Physical fighting is becoming less and less needful. The craving for it will one day be regarded as distinctly " atavistic." Fighting in other forms leads insidiously to combination and coöperation. The number of those not having to exert themselves at all for a living has been steadily increasing from age to age. And for all but a very few among men called " civilized " the struggle for mere self-preservation has been greatly ameliorated.

To a minority these changes have merely meant less to do with more time to do it in. But on the whole it may be said that the growing store of leisure and surplus energy available to most men has tended to give the perfective instincts their supreme opportunity. Within the last century they have assumed an importance often equalling and sometimes surpassing that of the primary instincts as life-compelling motives. Not only through the artist, the student, or the reformer, but through thousands upon thousands of comparatively commonplace human beings, these forces have been heard to speak with the commanding voice of passion. More and more, civilized man has come to feel that the one object warranting any and every sacrifice is the pure joy of " being himself "—as Ibsen termed the full and free expression of our natural tendencies.

One result of this development has been a rapid and radical

change in our understanding of work, as well as in our attitude toward it. Once it stood juxtaposed to fighting and was recognized chiefly by its implication of hateful and degrading effort. Then it became antithetical to playing, as forced drudgery is to free pleasure. Now we are beginning to see that it can and should embrace the life-promoting elements of both fighting and playing. In the light of this new conception, we may define work as " useful effort leading to normal functional self-expression."

In this new kind of work our own day is inclined to seek the most imperative motive of all. The dread of ennui is acquiring the same power—and the same dramatic validity—as that of hunger or a hurt to our vanity. Hereafter, as Professor Höffding has aptly put it, " we will not work to live; we will not live to work; but in work we will find life."

III

The main cause of Ibsen's supposed obscurity lies then, as I see it, in his intuitive realization of an evolutionary trend from mere preservation to increasing perfection as life's more essential purpose. He felt that a change had come over mankind, and he concluded that neither the primary instincts nor the more primitive forms of the perfective forces would remain capable of engrossing man's whole existence. And because he saw and pictured the struggle of the Will to Do and the Will to Rule to establish themselves on an equal basis with the preservative instincts as compelling motives in human life, he made his men and women say and do things which to many readers, if not to most, could only seem preposterously unreal.

Even at this late day the average man fears whatever is new. And he remains self-centred to the extent of expecting everybody else to be like himself in everything. To an overwhelming degree he is still moved and checked by the earlier and less subtle instincts. For this reason he expects to see people—on the stage as well as in reality —care most of all for life itself. Secondly, he expects to see them fighting ruthlessly for the male or female they want—just as the lion is pursuing the lioness, and as the bucks are fighting among themselves for the does. He has learned that, under some circumstances, the Will to Love may overshadow the Will to Live—that when people have been " driven beyond themselves " by being " crossed in love," they grow capable of many strange doings, such as the risking and taking of their own lives.

This average man of ours is at a loss to understand Ibsen's characters because he is a stranger to the motives that impel them— motives that have become clearly potent only under the pressure of recent conditions, and that are still decidedly potent only to a far advanced minority. It will be all but impossible to convince him that the ultimate reason behind Hedda's desperate act is not her hopeless love for Eilert Lövborg. And the possibility of her departing voluntarily from life just to escape unbearable boredom would to him seem unspeakably ridiculous, could such a possibility enter his mind at all. For ennui, to quote Jean Marie Guyau, " is in man a sign of superiority—of fecundity of will."

I have already indicated that Ibsen's grip on the perfective instincts was, on the whole, intuitive rather than reasoned—that he saw and pictured the results of their activities rather than those activities themselves. But the secret of art's power to move and to change us lies just in the fact that it presents ideas and truths and tendencies in their application to concrete being—that it shows them At Work, so to speak. Outside of poetry, we have to deal with them as pale, bloodless phantoms, created by our minds in forms little more tangible than our dreams. In art we find them clothed in flesh and blood; we find them wearing the faces and using the voices of our dearest and nearest; and thus we are able to See them. And seeing, we realize what they imply and lead to, in the future as well as in the present. It was thus that Ibsen pictured the motives and impulses on which modern man's everyday life is more and more beginning to hinge; and it was for this reason that he was able to picture them with a fidelity and power which could not have been surpassed by any scientific formulation.

In so far as Ibsen reached a reasoned consciousness of the new part played by work, for instance—as a blessing rather than a curse —this seems to have come to him only late in life. In a letter dated 1890, written when he was sixty-two and had just finished *Hedda Gabler*, we find him saying to a friend in business: " You learned early in life to love work. The joy of working was not grasped by me until later. But then I learned most effectively to treasure it." And it is only in the plays from his final period, beginning with *Rosmersholm*, that the need of soul-satisfying work as a human motive is given full and clear emphasis. That such should be the case is significant as illustrating the manner and order in which the life forces have made their appearance in literature as well as in life. Poetry is, in the last instance, nothing but a reflection of life, an experimental re-combination of elements entering into all life. It has to follow the general course of organic development like any other form of vital activity. Just as the life-history of the individual recapitulates that of the race, so the evolution of literature has repeated that of life itself. Just as the preservative instincts took precedence of the perfective ones in life, so they had to assume priority of birth and rank in poetry also. And in poetry as in life, the evolution of the instincts had to be mirrored in exact order, so that their more primitive forms preceded and antagonized the later and subtler and more "unselfish" ones. As the result of this order, we note the successive appearance in poetry of certain THEMES, in which we find close-fitting symbolizations not only of the life forces in their broadest aspect, but of their different evolutionary stages.

First of all came the Fight Theme—the singing of man's struggle to maintain himself in the face of a hostile fate—and it passed through a long progression of stages before the next one, or the Love Theme, could assume more than subordinate importance. The *Antigone* of Sophocles reaches the 568th of its 1,353 lines (Campbell's translation) before any reference at all is made to the love that binds the heroine to the son of the man who has just condemned her to death for burying the corpse of her rebellious brother—that is, for serving the Will to Live in a very subtle and far advanced form.

For ages the two primary themes held almost undisputed sway. And those are still in a majority who deem them indispensable as "central interests" of the drama. But at an early stage there appeared, though confined to the background, what might be called the Prowess Theme and the Honor Theme, being, respectively, equivalent to man's inner sense of superiority and his desire to see

that sense reflected in other men.   Here we encounter the Will to Do
and the Will to Rule in their most primitive forms—as a craving to
excel and to be admired for excelling.   We have here both fact and
appearance—both ambition and vanity.   Much later appeared the
Work Theme and the Service Theme, wherein we have to recognize
the highest known manifestations of the two perfective instincts.

Ibsen was not the first one who gave artistic expression to the
worth and power of work, or to functional self-expression as a life-
ruling motive.   There is Goethe's *Faust*, for instance, of which
Professor Höffding says that its most important aspect is represented
by " the idea of incessant endeavor."   But up to the time when Ibsen
became wholly himself, it may be said that modern literature was
overwhelmingly preoccupied with the Will to Love—with that " all-
subduing erotic yearning " which the Romanticists had proclaimed
as life's supremest expression.   Even the great French play-builders
of the mid-century failed, as a rule, to break away from this life-
perverting attitude.

Love's Comedy was the first play in which Ibsen's real genius asserted itself, and the first one in which he gave clear recognition to
the new importance gained by the perfective forces through the development of modern life.   It constitutes an impetuous onslaught on
love's power to fill up life to the exclusion of all other factors.   It
is a direct challenge to that sentimental side of Romanticism in
which Ibsen's own nature was rooted so deeply that, in order to rid
himself of it, he was forced to react antipathetically against it
throughout the greater part of his career as playwright.   To this
day it is mentioned as one of his worst " puzzle plays," and why this
should be so may be understood if we recall how a majority of current plays continue to accept love-making as man's chief claim to
attention at the hands of the poet.

From that first negative embodiment of the forces pressing forward everywhere, Ibsen passed by degrees to a more and more positive one.   For a while—in writing *Brand, Peer Gynt,* and *Emperor
and Galilean*—his mind wrestled with the problem of the human will
in its relation to the great world-will rather than to other human
wills.   But beginning with *Pillars of Society,* he accepted the condition of our will as one of " freedom within necessity."   Without

ceasing to hold man responsible to society for the RESULTS of his acts, he agreed with the " deterministic " position of modern science as to the origin of those acts. He cared no longer to sit in judgment on man for not using his will, as he had done in *Brand;* or to ask whether man's willing be of any avail at all, as he had done in *Emperor and Galilean.* Instead he strove to unravel the strands woven into that instrument we call will. He dealt no longer with it as an " immortal soul " bound for heaven or hell, but as a link in life's endless chain of cause and effect. He saw that wrong willing and no willing at all might equally be the result of inherited or suggested influences. He came to see man's salvation not in willing but in working—not in arrogant defiance of life, but in patient adaptation to its purposes and methods. He came, finally, to recognize work of the right kind as a vital necessity to normal man, and social service as the most soul-satisfying form of energetic expenditure.

The scope of this essay will not permit me to give detailed illustration of the manner in which Ibsen's increasing recognition of the perfective forces and their mission in life shows itself in his plays. All I can do here is to point out a few striking and typical instances.

In *An Enemy of the People* we meet a man of thought strongly moved by the Will to Do in a very refined stage. While following out his natural bent, he is brought to realize his fundamental antagonism to the emotional mass, which is still moved almost wholly by the primitive instincts and by the earliest forms of the perfective forces. In that play Ibsen had not yet reached his highest plane of thought, and he was content to let it end with the defiant resignation of an individualist who has not yet grasped the true relationship of his own fate to that of the race. As it stands, however, the play may be called the tragedy of all intellectual leadership.

Of *Rosmersholm* Ibsen himself wrote: " The craving for work makes itself felt throughout the play." But it goes farther. Rebecca came to Rosmersholm full of crude lust for power. There she met Rosmer, a man moved by her own life-governing instinct, the Will to Rule, but in so high a state of development that it should be called a Will to Serve. Thus we have set before us the clashing of an early and a late phase of the same instinct—we are made to watch the working of that instinct on two different planes of life—and the point of the play is that the mere contact with a higher form of life tends to impel the lower one upwards. And in her renunciation, first of love and then of life itself, Rebecca proves unconsciously that, in life's total scheme, the preservative instincts are means to an end, not ends in themselves.

Hedda Gabler might be called the drama of ennui. By birth and rearing led into circumstances where all her natural promptings to vigorous use of soul and body are either wholly thwarted or else dwarfed into dawdling over mere futilities, a strong-natured and strong-willed woman is led on step by step through petty naughtiness to error and death. Born in a more fortunate time and place, she might at least have caught the zest of life through the kind of political intriguing said to be found in so many Parisian salons. But she might also have become envied and admired, as more than one successful woman of to-day, because of her capacity for hard, well-applied work. *Little Eyolf* may be called the positive complement to the negative lesson conveyed by *Hedda Gabler*. It seems to proclaim that, if the Will to Do be satisfied in a supreme degree, the defeat suffered by the Will to Love may be outlived. But the play also foreshadows a possible interpenetration of the two perfective forces and the upbuilding of a higher and more effective Will to Grow.

In *The Master Builder, Borkman,* and *The Epilogue,* finally, Ibsen seems to have dealt mainly with the necessity of harmonious as well as free development. He shows how even that life force which is particularly our own must not be nursed at the expense of the other instincts; how a universal law of life commands the symmetrical exercise of all our faculties and makes it punishable to stifle any one of them; how, in fact, a higher law than that of specialization is the harmonizing of all our faculties in common service of life.

Borkman and Rubek have trampled on the Will to Love in order to let their dominant impulse have full swing. Both go down to disaster for having violated the law of harmonious vital development. Rubek finds no happiness with Maja—with life as it is felt and desired by youth and primitive man. He reaps nothing but death when he and Irene make a belated attempt to live their lost lives over again. But worst of all to him is that his art misses its highest pos-

sible note and becomes mere " caricature "—interpretation of life un-
informed by that sympathy which springs from the normal expression of our racial instincts.

These are mere hints. But anyone who takes the trouble to read
Ibsen in the light furnished by the life forces, as these are now coming to be understood, will soon see that the myth of which I have
been talking never had any foundation in fact. Ibsen never purposely manufactured riddles. He never desired to be, or to be found,
obscure. But to reach the heart of his message, it will not suffice
that we spend our time brooding over his words or delving into his
personal life. Instead we must school ourselves in the comprehension of life—in the knowledge not only of its superficial aspects, but
of its deeper and deepest truths. To know Ibsen better, we must
know life itself better. That is all.

THE REGENERATION OF THE THEATRE *

MONTROSE J. MOSES

I BELIEVE that the theatre has much to contend with in the increasing disillusionment of its audiences. A large asset in the appreciation of a play consists in a naïve acceptance of its *papier maché* and of its convention. There was a time when this was very real to all of us; when we did not care whether thunder came from a tin sheet or the patter of rain from the rattle of peas in a pan. The press agent has at last waked himself up to his great sin of commission: that in his publicity work he has opened the doors of wonder too wide, and has shown the miracle in shirt sleeves. In the regeneration of the drama, one of the first things will be to bring back the old-fashioned curiosity of audiences.

This will mean that the keen virtue of imagination will have to be cultivated. When we criticise the paucity of the Elizabethan stage with its paper signs, or of the mystery play platform with its bowl of water for the sea, we discount the responsiveness of an audience, whose education may not have been as general as ours, but whose minds were more active and more sensitive to mere suggestion. So rapidly has illusion deserted us, and so surprisingly have the mechanical excellences of the theatre increased that, in order to retain the shadow of "make-believe," audiences demand settings which materially decrease the manager's chances for large profits.

Such expenditure is warranted in spectacular pieces like *Ben Hur* and *The Shepherd King*, where the plays themselves had attractive appeal. But scenery can no longer prop a weak drama, for the simple reason that the people are at last beginning to know something of the art of the theatre. To a certain degree, the press agent has been responsible for this. Not that his journalism has lost any of its advertising quality, but he is becoming more judicious in his statements, and more sparing of his credulous stories. There has even been a change, within recent years, as regards the wild hero-worship which traveled in the wake of the "star" system—a hero-worship

---

* *The Disintegration of the Theatre*, by the same author, appeared in the last issue.

largely fed by the bits of stage gossip furnished from the press department of every manager's office.

This condition is improving. Though the press agent is still primarily an advertiser for his "show," he is smart enough to understand that his audience is manifesting interest in the technique of the theatre. The education which is thus taking place is somewhat due to the yearly publication of popular books on the drama by men who have knowledge, yet are gifted with an unscholastic style. While these volumes expound no new principles, they at least familiarize the public with those fundamental characteristics which combine to make an excellent play. The critiques thus gathered together in no way boast of the literary distinction of the work of Hazlitt, Lamb, or Lewes; but in their journalistic stricture, they do accustom theatregoers to question technique in drama as they would demand balance in art. What is now needed in our criticism is a more rigid scrutiny of our right to enjoy certain amusements, and a more minute examination of the methods of the actor as a creative artist.

In other words, indirectly through the better class press agent; directly through the conscientious critic; and partly through the publication of plays,—the theatre is receiving an intellectual training which the commercial manager already finds himself bound to recognize. Audiences are becoming technicians, despite the old cry of the tired business man.

The unrest which marks general theatrical interests and the dearth of plays which strains the manager's ingenuity, are sufficient indication that no "open door" policy will bring immediate relief, even though it give the unheard playwright a hearing and a chance. The New Theatre in its first year examined two thousand manuscripts for probably six acceptances. We are all writing plays, but they have the demerits of imitation and lack the strength of the soil. The one school which we have in the drama is in the observation of American conditions—especially as they apply to business affairs. Once there was opportunity to do big work in the aspects of rural life, but even James A. Herne, sensing Ibsen before he knew Ibsen, was touched by a fast declining melodrama which soon went out of date, even as the sentiment peculiar to it did, despite its splendid odor of rosemary.

In the regeneration of the theatre, therefore, the playwright is growing to recognize that his own citizenship means something in the conception of his drama; that the one original opportunity of the outward drama, apart from the spiritual essence of it, lies in the locality of which Howells, Bret Harte, Octave Thanet, Page, and Cable have made so much in literature. The scenic idea has created a seeable American drama, but hardly a readable one or a preservable one. *Salomy Jane, The Girl of the Golden West, In Old Kentucky,* and such titles occur to everyone; in fact, it is not too rash to state that the theatre topographically has very well considered the local differences of the country. But as yet the activity of dramatic authorship has also become too diffuse—a characteristic of newspaper training and showing a want of set purpose other than to write something for the theatre which affords large returns upon the right thing.

Yet the widespread interest as I see it will mean that a man properly accustomed to exact technique, and well-trained in the professional and in the cultural phases of his trade, will at last experiment in drawing from the soil matter which is the essence of national life. This consciousness of the matter at hand is not cultivated by artificial means, but comes through necessity from within, through big conviction, through personal belief, through consuming interest in this condition and in that type. It is not a mere observational, reportorial drama, such as we have in *The Lion and the Mouse,* or in *The Gamblers.* Not one of our American dramatists can thus far boast of challenging public thought or rousing public interest, other than that of fictitious excitement.

Our theatre needs a body of ideas; it needs to reflect in better ways the undercurrent of American life. It lags behind the newspaper instead of leaping forward and making the newspaper keep up with it in civic pride and in common honesty. If we are given poetic drama, it has the scholastic idea that *Marlowe* and *Sappho and Phaon* are better than *Hiawatha* and an epic of the wheat, of hemp, or of the New England conscience. If the play is social, it simply dramatizes the newspaper, busying itself about the outward movement of life. The playwright knows that he is sure of sympathy from audiences whenever he places the warmth of American character in contrast with the artificiality of foreign social intrigue; hence the popularity of *The Man from Home*. He knows that a certain representation of the stress and strain of Wall Street will rouse curiosity; hence *The Pit*. But he is too prone to lose sight of the ethics of business in the noise of " buncoism "; hence *The Gamblers* and *Get-rich-quick Wallingford*. That is the usual inclination of the reporter after a story.

The lure of large profits has been responsible to a marked degree for the general weakness of our native drama. Writers without technique in this special field have identified the narrative conversation of fiction with the vital dialogue of the stage, not realizing that the structure in each is different. Yet one cannot help believing that the interest of the literary man in the theatre will affect the intellectual character of its future.

But the literary man is not a frequent theatre-goer; whenever he is detected in numbers in the auditorium, it is safe to reckon that he has been brought there by a promise, not of drama in the theatrical sense, but of ideas in the literary sense. If he likes the ideas, but finds that critically the drama fails to be drama, he condemns the theatre and hastens outside to deplore the decadence of the stage. Thomas Bailey Aldrich never could realize why *Judith of Bethulia* did not prove acceptable; he attributed it to the uncultivation of the theatre-going public rather than to his own failure to meet some of the essential requirements of drama. Percy Mackaye, understanding the theory of stagecraft, persists in clogging his dialogue with sentiments and allusions wholly unsuited to quick-moving minds.

Since this is the literary condition of the drama, it is safe to count the literary clientèle as a body in itself dedicated to the improvement of the theatre according to wrong methods. In fact, since the Puritan first lodged his diatribe against actor folk, there has been a persistent cry for the improvement of the stage. Societies have risen upon their own hopes and fallen because of their own mistakes. Conditions are altered, not by dilettantism, but by whole knowledge and sound conviction. Audiences may organize for the encouragement of particular plays, but the big public outside of cliques will have its' say, and will register its decisions at the box office. I have seen committees of various organizations at the theatre, sent to report on the relative merits of a play. I have seen the reports: trite, commonplace, sweepingly impertinent in approval or disapproval. The theatre is not harmed by such a show of false culture, and there is some humor in the fact that though the drama is little influenced by such ostentatious intellectuality, the cliques themselves are at least being made to take themselves and the drama seriously. Undoubtedly they would have much more pleasure if they were able, which they are not, to join the vulgar crowd in its enjoyment. By their superiority they are violating the very essential spirit of the theatre.

Yet I do not wish to convey the idea that I want this connection between literature and the theatre to be so close as to hinder the theatre. Drama is no handmaiden to literature; it is the highest type of literary expression and the most difficult in which to excel. The disintegration of the theatre, as we have examined it, indicates clearly that the methods of the trust have not kept the good play from its rightful public, for since the talk of the "open door," we have had no startling discoveries in the way of exceptional productions. The process of reorganization shows that intellectual improvement must be coincident with the higher and more honest standard of presentation. For when we speak of social and economic forces in the theatre, we speak of the drama as a commodity and as an art.

THE NEW ART OF INTERPRETING DREAMS

EDWARD M. WEYER, PH.D.

DATING from certain revelations as far back as the year 1880, Professor Sigmund Freud of the University of Vienna has been engaged in the work of extending the frontiers of our knowledge concerning the human mind. This statement is meant seriously and literally; the mind indeed comprises territory that psychologists have scarcely more than suspected, never adequately explored. Freud gains access to these uncharted regions through the medium of dreams. One must frankly admit that in every age and among every people a familiar character of doubtful repute has been the revealer of dreams. Science has grown instinctively skeptical of such pretensions. But of Professor Freud it may be said that he is the first investigator whose daily work for fifteen active years has brought him constantly face to face with the dream as a practical problem, and also, he is the first whose attack has brought any practical result. His adherents are using his method for the relief of suffering; his theory already stands upon evidence gained from fully fifty thousand dreams subjected to a rational analysis.

Under such scrutiny dreams have lost much of their mystery. They always prove significant, yet they cannot reveal the future, but only the past. They are always ego-centric and personal; no external agency foists them into our mental life; they develop within that life, and belong as an integral part to it. Freud's investigations have strengthened the scientific conviction that the law of causation operates in the realm of ideas as rigidly as in the world of material things. Every mental state is determined in all particulars by the mental states that precede it. " Suppose I try," writes Freud, " to allow a number to enter my thoughts in a perfectly arbitrary manner; it is not possible; the number which occurs to me is unmistakably and necessarily determined, though it may be far from my momentary concern." So, too, even in our dreams, however fantastic they may be, all the details are determined by thoughts that have preceded and underlie them.

Certain repressed memories which we cannot, or at least do not, in our waking hours spontaneously recall, are very commonly expressed through our dreams. This statement will seem strange until we realize that everyone is accustomed in his waking hours to exercise a sort of censorship over his thoughts and behavior. In fact, our educational system is, in large measure, a process for suppressing natural instincts in the child. Consequently, his later years are hedged about by an intricate tangle of conventionalities. Etiquette forbids us all to speak as we think or to act as we feel. Certain broad classes of topics are tabooed, others are discussed only in conventional ways. We learn to deport ourselves differently toward persons of different stations in life. In short, the entire behavior of everybody lies under this self-imposed censorship by which he protects himself from the adverse judgments of society.

It is not at first glance so evident that we seek protection in the same way from pernicious influences which otherwise would persist within the mind itself. Yet we know that reminiscences, if they are such as would produce unrelievedly distressful emotions, tend soon to drop out of consciousness. Just as an animal organism may build protecting walls against a foreign body that has become imbedded in its substance, so the mind may build walls around a harmful desire or fear or regret, an unfulfilled aspiration or a painful reminiscence, after which the offending experience loses the links of association that bind it to the rest of consciousness.

One means of restoring these repressed memories has been known to psychologists for a long time. Even the general public is aware that by hypnotizing a person, his normal restraint, or as we have called it, his censorship over thought and action, can be overcome. Then he may be induced not only to carry out absurd suggestions, but even to recall events that have vanished utterly from his waking thoughts, and especially to recall with astonishing minuteness his experiences on other occasions when the censorship was similarly relaxed. In delirium, or intoxication, or while one is recovering from an anæsthetic, the lid, so to speak, is lifted. Besides, as every one knows, the censorship is notoriously lax during our dreams. One of Freud's adherents, Ferenczi, goes so far as to remark: " There is not a single dream which cannot be shown by analysis to offend against some ethical or legal canon."

The bearing of these facts on the problem of dreams is now obvious, but to former investigators their purport was not so apparent. Freud's insight into the mystery of dreams came as a logical result of his novel mode of attacking them. He did not seek, like his predecessors, to read a meaning directly from that confused and oftentimes irrational mass of impressions that the dreamer retains upon waking. Rather he strove to lay bare and to decipher the sources of the dream. As a practising physician, he was impelled by a motive stronger than any abstract love of science, the very practical and urgent need of bringing relief to patients suffering from mental diseases. He devised a very ingenious method, but it is unlikely that he would have succeeded had he not been fortunate in encountering dreams of remarkable significance, the dreams of victims of that most singular and, to the physician, most tantalizing of maladies, hysteria.

The fact that Professor Freud's first experiments were made upon hysterical-subjects does not mar his general theory. Their dreams are really normal, if by that word we mean that they are like the dreams of ordinary people. No one will claim, of course, that hysterical minds are other than abnormal in some respect. We can well sympathize with the verdict of the Middle Ages, that these unfortunates are possessed of devils. The prosaic fact is, however, that our hystericals languish under a tyranny imposed by that very censorship which for the normal mind provides a salutary mode of defence. Their repressed experiences, after being banished from consciousness, may continue to torment them under strange disguises, either as pains or paralysis or loss of sensation, or as some serious functional disorder. The variety of these symptoms is legion; they rarely come singly, and they may attack almost any organ or member of the body, even though the part, physically speaking, be perfectly healthy. No single case can give an adequate notion of the disease in its myriad forms, but consider the following:

There was in the summer a time of intense heat, and the patient had suffered very much from thirst; for, without any apparent reason, she had suddenly become unable to drink. She would take a glass of water in her hand, but as soon as it touched her lips she would push it away as though suffering from hydrophobia. . . . She ate only fruit, melons and the like, in order to relieve this tormenting thirst. When this had been going on about six weeks, she was talking one day in hypnosis about her English governess, whom she disliked, and finally told, with every sign of disgust, how she had come into the room of the governess, and how that lady's little dog, that she abhorred, had drunk out of a glass. Out of respect for the conventions the patient had remained silent. Now, after she had given energetic expression to her restrained anger, she asked for a drink, drank a large quantity of water without trouble, and awoke from hypnosis with the glass at her lips. The symptom thereupon vanished permanently.*

It is the duty of the physician to endeavor to trace every symptom of this kind to its source, not in the body of the patient, but among the patient's lost memories. When the source is discovered, it very often happens that a mere recounting of the restored memories, provided that the sufferer gives rein to his natural emotions in the telling, will effect a seemingly miraculous " casting out of the devil." But these memories are exactly the ones that the patient cannot under ordinary conditions recall. Therefore, the physician may resort to hypnotism in order to create a favorable state of mental susceptibility. Hypnosis does not, however, automatically reveal the memories sought. Moreover, as Freud was free to confess, many hysterical patients cannot be hypnotized at all.

Alternate successes and failures with hypnotism finally led Freud to discard it. Then he made two notable discoveries: first, that by interrogating the personality as manifested through dreams, one is granted admittance to a mental storehouse where the causes of hysterical symptoms are kept; secondly, that these repressed memories can be approached with good success in a very simple way, which is virtually the old method with the hypnotizing left out.

Most of my patients [writes Freud] accomplish it after the first instruction. I can do it myself very perfectly, if I aid myself by writing down what occurs to my mind. . . . A certain mental preparation of the patient is needed. He is urged to acquire skill in two directions: to increase his attentiveness toward his psychical impres-

* See *The American Journal of Psychology*, April, 1910, p. 184. This number of the Journal contains articles by Freud, Jones, Ferenczi, Jung, and Stern. These papers, taken together, furnish the best general statement of the Freudian doctrines as yet obtainable in English.

sions, and to rule out the criticism with which he is accustomed to sift the thoughts that spring up in his mind. . . . It is advantageous for him to assume a restful position with the eyes closed. [He adds] We may not make the dream as a whole the object of attention, but only the separate fragments of its content. If I ask the patient who is not yet proficient, What does this dream suggest to your mind? as a rule he knows of nothing to lay hold upon in his field of mental vision. I must lay the dream before him piecemeal, then to each fragment he supplies me with a series of fancies which may be called the " afterthoughts " of that part of the dream. (*Die Traum-deutung*, 2nd ed., pages 71 and 73.)

The word here used by Dr. Freud is *hintergedanken;* I have trans-lated it " afterthoughts," but it may also signify " mental reserva-tions." Both meanings are appropriate, since these fancies are after-thoughts and at the same time revivals of experiences which return with a show of mental reserve, as if something—a censor, perhaps—were tending to keep them back. Success depends upon the dreamer's frankness; he should report every vagrant impression, omitting none on the ground that to him it seems absurd or irrelevant or compro-mising. If the dream is very obscure or confused, the obscurity hints at an extra effort to conceal some important meaning. If any feature of the dream especially resists investigation, its latent factors are apt to be significant. For these reasons several hours are sometimes required to draw the submerged content to the surface. This content is sometimes ten or even twenty times greater in bulk than the bare dream itself. However, when the content is exposed, the dream's meaning lies plainly revealed. Freud, basing his judgment upon a great many such revelations, has become convinced that *every dream is a wish, the typical dream is the disguised fulfilment of some re-pressed wish.*

If the reader doubts the presence of repressed reminiscences in his own mind, he should submit a few of his own dreams to the test. He may verify for himself many of Freud's assertions, if he will keep a dream-diary, and will adopt the habit of picking the skeletons of his dreams immediately upon waking in the morning. The wealth of his own dream-life will probably astonish him at first; then he will come to know himself as the proprietor of a busy theatre—owner, spectator, and critic in one. The dreams he witnesses may seem like nothing that ever happened on land or sea, yet by psycho-analysis he will be able to resolve them into a mosaic of details, all borrowed from his past experiences, though assembled seemingly by the four winds of heaven. He will find that no dream-actor is ever a new creation; all are fabrications made up of old stage properties from out the mental storehouse of the dreamer. A face may be that of an acquaintance; or it may be a combination of separate features of different real persons, so that there lurk under one disguise several real characters; or again, it may be composed like the photographs produced by taking the portraits of several persons, one over another, on the same photographic plate. Add to this, that one actor may be replaced by another in the twinkling of an eye, the second continuing the action begun by the first. Then, too, the scraps of dream-conversations may be identified, frequently word for word, although in the dream they may be spoken by a character that did not originally utter them, and although their meaning may be strangely twisted by the context of the dream to signify something wholly different from that which they meant in waking life.

In general, dreams as they make their appearance before us are composed of fragments that are preferably either very recent in origin or else old and very familiar. The old often emerge from out our early childhood; the familiar are derived from that common fund of experiences whence come our proverbs, myths, legends, and such other symbolism as each succeeding generation inherits from its forebears. Always, on the other hand, the dream contains some element or other taken from among the events of the waking interval preceding the sleep in which the dream occurs—some trivial incident usually, that has formed no close bond of association with other factors in consciousness. This one element, however, often serves as a sort of peg on which the entire dream hangs. Also, when several dreams occur in the same period of sleep, we may safely assume that one main thought runs through them all.

Freud has made us realize how marvelous is the play of forces whereby a dream gains access to the stage of consciousness. In order to be presented, the dream must conform to principles similar to those that govern all dramatic art. Much detail must be compressed within small compass; must occupy a brief interval of time; past and future must be given in terms of the present, or else timelessly. The hurry of events, the bewildering confusion and the kaleidoscopic shifts of scenes and characters, are necessary in order to fulfil some definite purpose. Its import is further hampered by the fact that it must work through sensuous forms such as in waking life appeal to the ear and eye. Only feebly, therefore, can the dream convey logical relations such as we express by the connectives " if," " because," " although," " either—or." Yet all the details of the dream, notwithstanding these hindrances, are planned before the action commences. As if in preparation for a regular stage-performance, actors seem to know their parts, and the order of events seems predetermined. There is, thinks Freud, no evidence of any intellectual labor or direction during the conscious presentation of a dream; it comes into consciousness as a finished product, a creation of impersonal forces that bring it forth from regions lying beyond the dreamer's ken. Even when exceedingly elaborate, dreams may transpire within an incredibly brief interval of time. Veritable mushrooms they are, long in forming, but springing up in numbers in a single night.

As if to make the feat the more wonderful, the dream as it is dreamed is always a disguise. Its meaning invariably remains hidden beneath the threshold of consciousness; not in subconsciousness perhaps, for there may be no such state, but rather in a " fore-consciousness," that is, among mental experiences that were once conscious before the dream occurred. The latent memories which form the basis of a dream are frequently those that have no connection with the main body of our remembered experiences; in order to resuscitate them the mind must flash back along those paths by which the dream entered the little circle of light that we call consciousness. Freud's method enables it to make these excursions.

Let us next inquire how so great a mass of latent content gains representation within the narrow limits of the dream. You know how a playwright, while in the act of composing a drama, must hold in mind a bewildering confusion of details, many more than he can possibly introduce bodily into the written play. His success depends on giving virtual expression to everything that is in his mind. The dream accomplishes its task in much the same way as the playwright, not by judicious selection but by a general condensation. In ordinary waking life the mind rarely works in this way. Usually our thoughts follow one another either by some connection of time or place, or by linking effect to cause, means to end, or by suggestions arising from contrasts or differences. In dream-forming, the ideas are combined and associated according to similarity or analogy. A classic example of this mode, taken from waking life, is the case of Newton, who observed an apple fall from a tree, and was led thence to consider the fall of the moon toward the earth in the course of their joint revolution round the sun. His brilliant deductions on gravitation are supposed to have arisen from this unusual combination of ideas. Many psychologists have seen in the frequency of such combinations by similarity the essential difference that marks the mental processes in the mind of genius as compared with minds of ordinary intelligence.

We must regard, then, each element of any dream as a chosen representative, standing in the place of a whole group of analogous elements, none of which are present with it in the momentary scope of consciousness, but which form a series of related experiences extending downward through successive strata of mental content. Employing a metaphor, we may say it is as if certain latent memories and desires, long repressed and finding no other means of utterance, seize an opportunity while the vigilance of their jailer is relaxed, to struggle upward into the light. But even while we sleep the vigilance of the jailer is only relaxed, never suspended. Each group of struggling dream-thoughts, therefore, in order to evade his scrutiny, selects a substitute that represents them all, but under a disguise sufficiently disfiguring to pass muster.

For complete analyses of actual dreams, I must refer the reader to the examples supplied by Professor Freud in his work, *Traumdeutung*. However, from a group reported by Dr. Ernest Jones of the University of Toronto, I am kindly permitted to exhibit one that seems to be especially rich in interesting features, all of which are common enough to be met with in any serious study of dreams by psycho-analysis. Dr. Jones, in a letter, writes: " You will doubtless remember that I recorded them as *illustrations* of certain mechanisms, not in any sense as examples of dream analyses. I mention this because, in spite of my statements, some people have conceived the

idea that I merely heard the dreams and then read my own interpre
tation into them, whereas in fact the analysis of each took several
hours."

Absolutely, there is no way to test the new theory but by following minutely Freud's method. Much adverse criticism comes from
persons who have never attempted to investigate the latent content,
but have blindly sought for some repressed wish in the conscious part
of the dream, where it certainly cannot be found.

The account of the dream is as follows:

A patient, a woman of thirty-seven, dreamt that *she was sitting in
a grand stand as though to watch some spectacle. A military band
approached, playing a gay martial air. It was at the head of
a funeral, which seemed to be of a Mr. X; the casket rested on a
draped gun-carriage. She had a lively feeling of astonishment at
the absurdity of making such an ado about the death of so insignificant a person. Behind followed the dead man's brother and one of
his sisters, and behind them his other two sisters; they were incon-
gruously dressed in a bright gray check. The brother advanced
"like a savage," dancing and waving his arms; on his back was a
yucca tree with a number of young blossoms.*

. . . The true meaning of it, however, became only too clear on
analysis. The figure of Mr. X veiled that of her husband. Both
men had promised much when they were young, but the hopes their
friends had built on them had not been fulfilled; the one had ruined
his health and career by his addiction to morphia, the other by his
addiction to alcohol. Under the greatest stress of emotion the patient related that her husband's alcoholic habits had completely
alienated her wifely feeling for him, and that in his drunken moments
he even inspired her with an intense physical loathing. In the dream
her repressed wish that he would die was realized by picturing the
funeral of a third person whose career resembled that of her husband's, and who, like her husband, had one brother and three sisters.
Further than this, her almost savage contempt for her husband, which
arose from his lack of ambition and other more intimate circumstances, came to expression in the dream by her reflecting how absurd
it was that any one should make an ado over the death of such a
nonentity, and by the gaiety shown at his funeral not only by all the
world (the gay air of the band; her husband is, by the way, an officer
in the volunteers, while Mr. X has no connection with the army), but
even by his nearest relative (the brother's dancing, the bright
clothes). It is noteworthy that no wife appeared in the dream,

though Mr. X is married, a fact that illustrates the frequent projection on to others of sentiments that the subject himself experiences but repudiates.

In real life Mr. X, who is still alive, is an indifferent acquaintance, but his brother had been engaged to be married to the patient, and they were deeply attached to each other. Her parents, however, manœuvred to bring about a misunderstanding between the two, and at their instigation, in a fit of pique she married her present husband, to her enduring regret. Mr. X's brother was furiously jealous at this, and the pæan of joy he raised in the dream does not appear so incongruous when we relate it to the idea of the death of the patient's husband as it does in reference to his own brother's death. His exuberant movements and "dancing like a savage" reminded the patient of native ceremonies she had seen, particularly marriage ceremonies. The yucca tree (a sturdy shrub indigenous to the Western States) proved to be a phallic symbol, and the young blossoms represented offspring. The patient bitterly regrets never having had any children, a circumstance she ascribes to her husband's vices. In the dream, therefore, her husband dies unregretted by any one; she marries her lover and has many children.

This account lays before us a dream, with a part of its latent content and some pertinent facts from the life of the dreamer: it illumines an entire mental situation. But let us return to the bare dream (as printed in italics). The dreamer, looking back upon her vision and accepting it at its face value, would certainly fail to observe that it combines the features both of a funeral and of a wedding. She would be impressed by the definite event, which is a funeral, and by the display of gaiety with which the ceremony is conducted. Between the idea so dramatically enacted and the emotions which accompany it, there is a total lack of harmony. The lively music, the bright gray checks, and the savage dancing, as well as the vaguely triumphant attitude of herself as she sat in the grand stand, would give to the dream an appearance of fantastic unreality. This incongruity between idea and emotion makes a large proportion of our dreams seem foreign and grotesque. The ideas we may regard as imaginary, for often they are substitutions for something more rational or they are at least distorted. But the emotions we cannot deny are as real as any we ever feel; they are genuine, having undergone no alteration in quality by being conveyed into the dream. They are feelings that belong to the latent content in the dreamer's mind. To the dreamer in the case before us, the latent content was pleasing, however horrifying this may seem from a conventional point of view.

We have not shown why the conscious part of the dream is a sort of riddle, and why its meaning invariably lies hidden. Let us consider this reverse side of the problem, this effort at concealment, for, in fact, a counter-influence is continually at work, hindering the dream-forming process by dictating what it shall, and what it shall not, produce. The formative process operates in a rather mechanical way, but this force that opposes it appears to work with conscious intent, and I take the liberty of personifying it by calling it, the censor. If we regard this censor as a somewhat satanic influence, we shall be justified in applying to him the old adage, " the Devil is an ass." His wiles are numerous and peculiar, but he perpetrates all his pranks as if he were drowsy, and as a rule his ruses are fairly transparent. It is his habit, for example, to conceal important things under the cloaks of unimportant ones suggested by superficial resemblances. This is plainly seen in the substitution of Mr. X instead of the dreamer's dissolute husband. The men resemble one another in at least five accidental particulars; they differ in the one essential. Still, if we do not concede that Mr. X impersonates the husband, it will be difficult to explain why his funeral is conducted with military honors as befits the husband, " an officer in the volunteers, while Mr. X has no connection with the army." Another instance of the kind is the use made of the yucca tree; the censor delights in the employment of such a symbol.

In general, upon the materials that go to form the dream, the censorship rests lightly. When poor judgment has been displayed, the censor can cover the mistake by displacing the natural centre of interest in the conscious dream; he can relegate significant but too obvious features to the background, thus forcing trivial details to the front. Or, he will weaken the intensity of the emotions and shift them about, thus endowing with a sham emphasis some feature of no moment to the main issue. If, in his complacency, he allows the dream to go altogether too far toward clearness, he may introduce the notion often experienced while dreaming, that " anyhow, it is only a dream." His besetting desire is to put us off the scent, and the solicitude he has for a dream he carries over even into waking life. Whenever we attempt to recall a dream, we shall find him on the watch.

All have observed how a dream that is remembered vividly at breakfast may become confused and vague by noon. Now, it is Freud's belief that none of our experiences are ever quite forgotten, and dreams are remembered as distinctly as any waking experience of like vividness would be. Their rapid fading must be accounted for as a spell cast by the censor. We do not forget them, but, to serve his private ends, the censor instils into our minds doubts and hesitations.

By such ruses, however, the censor may defeat his own purpose. The wise interpreter will naturally select as the starting points for his investigation these stupidly emphasized weak spots in the disguise. Where, in the second telling of a dream, the story differs, where something is left out, or changes are introduced, or new but trivial details are added, where in fact there is any suspicion of " secondary elaboration," the investigator will do well to search with special diligence.

Little was known in this country concerning this entire scientific movement before the coming of Professor Freud and some of his coworkers to participate in the meetings held in September of 1909 to celebrate the twentieth anniversary of the founding of Clark University. It is not possible in a short article to follow all the threads of the discussions that took place on that occasion. Suffice it to say that the information derived from dreams has thrown light upon the proper training of children, and has led to a new theory of sex. The latent content has revealed facts that point the way toward a method for the detecting of crime, as well as toward a method for the treatment of mental diseases. The principles that govern dreams explain also our day-dreamings, and bear a striking resemblance to those that lie at the base of wit and humor. They seem to account in part for the growth of myths and superstitions, and they are found to operate throughout broad ranges of mental phenomena extending from the practical affairs of everyday life in health and disease to the rare manifestations of genius in literature and art. A rough sketch of the dream theory is as much as could here be attempted, but it should be remembered that it is largely owing to Freud's theory of dreams that a new movement in psychology, if not indeed a new psychology, has begun.

EDITORIAL NOTES

The controlling force in America to-day, as a hundred years ago, is supposed to be the People. They make, and unmake. They bind, and loose. They create their own conditions, and mould their own lives. Wherever there is wrong, they can right it. Whatever they want, they can have. The voice of the People is the voice of Power. Unfortunately, the People do not know this. They have been told; but they have forgotten. They easily forget. For though you cannot fool *all* the People *all* the time, you can fool the majority of the People for the greater part of the time. And that, naturally, is quite sufficient for the purposes of those who are specialists in exploiting the folly of the People, for their own personal profit, and with their own personal shamelessness.

* * *

One of the most signal features of this folly is the comparative indifference of the American public to *causes*, and its excitability over *effects*—if the effects are sufficiently sensational. For in this vast country, small tragedies are dwarfed. We have no interest in the regular toll exacted day by day—in the child crushed to death in the streets, because the city has no other place for children; in the victim of foul air, overcrowded tenements, vicious surroundings; in the consumptive, the degenerate, the unclassed; in the life flicked out on the railway, in the mine, in the factory; or in the slower but sure devitalizing of myriads born with " unalienable rights " to " life, liberty, and the pursuit of happiness." We imagine, perhaps, that we are interested. The subjects are mentioned from time to time. We have little agencies here, and little agencies there, to nibble at the problems. But public opinion needs something big, catastrophic, spectacular, to awaken it from its normal repose. It requires excitement on a large scale, whether in politics, finance or fire-calamities— in measures, millions or murders. But even then, when it is roused at last, it is concerned more with punishment than with prevention. It sees the effects, because they are big; and it demands a scapegoat. But it has forgotten, among so many other things, what a scapegoat really is—*a victim to carry the sins of the People.*

The Washington Place fire was an inevitable result of deplorable conditions—a result which could be foretold, as it *was* foretold, with mathematical certainty. There was the usual scramble on the part of the local authorities to disclaim responsibility, to pass it on from one department to another, and if possible bury it in a maze of denials, circumlocutions, excuses. But so far as can be seen at present, there has been unusual earnestness and thoroughness in the different investigations, and something of good can scarcely fail to result. If the powers of the local officials have been inadequate, or the regulations faulty, or their enforcement negligent and unfaithful, wider powers will be obtained, wiser regulations framed, and better men employed to see that they are observed. If there has been legal—as there has assuredly been virtual—criminality, someone, no doubt, will be punished. And this will have a certain valuable, deterrent effect—for a little while. But so long as punishment remains problematical, and is not rigorously inevitable, there will always be men who will take the risk—and compel thousands of others to take a greater one. But beyond the individual culprit, whoever he may be—capitalist or grafter—there is the real criminal. It is not the self-seeking politician, the dishonest or incompetent official, who has to be considered primarily. He is an effect. The cause is in the indifference and folly of the People—the People who remain satisfied with a corrupt, lax and vicious system of administration; who will tolerate and put into power organizations which deliberately and notoriously demoralize the public service. Day by day, throughout the country, there are countless " probes " and investigations; scandal follows scandal; the entire system of municipal and State government is honeycombed with abuses. We congratulate ourselves on these " probes "; they are a sign of a higher public ideal, a demand for honor and faithfulness. So might the eruptions of scrofula be taken as a sign of the vigor of the body, the purity of the blood. We have graft, incompetence, dishonesty, feeble administrations and inadequate laws, because the People choose to have them, because they tolerate and encourage a system that leads to inefficiency in every department of public affairs. It was the People who were responsible for the Asch Building fire—the People, of whom seventy-five thousand marched in the drenching rain, mourning their dead.

Wise and far-seeing statesmanship has been responsible for the proposal for a permanent arbitration treaty between the United States and the United Kingdom, and the reception of the proposal on both sides of the Atlantic has been impressive in its sincerity. This will be more than one of the decisive battles of the world: it will be *the* decisive peace. For it will be the precursor of other treaties, which other nations are even now anxious to negotiate; and it is impossible to forecast the ultimate results. The optimistic will see in it the beginning of the disarmament of the world, of the federation of nations, of universal brotherhood. But the worst pessimist can see in it nothing but a force for good, a long step forward for civilization. Posterity may link the names of President Taft and Sir Edward Grey with this achievement, when their other deeds and endeavors have perhaps little significance.

* * *

The Mayor of New York City has both enemies and friends, accusers and apologists. But no one who holds high public office can be judged by *ex parte* statements. His appeal is to the unprejudiced and unfettered, to those who place public before private interest, the State before the Party—not, as Governor Dix so naïvely expressed himself in his congratulations to Senator O'Gorman upon his election, the Party before the State. Much of the criticism directed against Mr. Gaynor has been vitiated by political and personal animus; yet there would seem cause for grave disquiet as to his fitness for public service, and especially for the position he now occupies. Correctly or incorrectly, Magistrate Corrigan made definite charges with regard to the prevalence of crime and vice in the city. The Mayor is reported to have dismissed the matter with the following comments:

"Do not persist in asking me about Corrigan. He is one of those in this city whose heads are filled with vice and crime. How did their heads get so filled with vice and crime? You only have to follow them around at night to find that out. Let those who want to befoul this city and picture it as a shameless and vicious place go right on. Those of us who have to deal with the city intend to go right on with the large things which confront us."

This is puerile—so puerile that it is impossible not to doubt the accuracy of the report. Yet, with the omission of the regrettable

personal innuendoes, a somewhat similar statement expressed the
Mayor's views with regard to the disclosures of Mr. John Purroy
Mitchel, when the latter was Acting Mayor of the city. Does Mr.
Gaynor really think that virtue lies in concealment; that dishonor
is not in vice, but in the public knowledge and condemnation of vice?
He speaks of " befouling " the city. If the alleged conditions exist,
it is their existence which " befouls " the city, not the public exposure and demand for remedial measures. Perhaps Mr. Gaynor
meant to suggest that a certain amount of vice is inevitable in a
large city; that the social evil, for example, must be, to some extent,
" winked at " by the authorities; and that New York is neither better nor worse than other huge centres of population. This, at least,
is a point of view—false, and terrible in its consequences; but often
held by the irresolute, by those who try to compromise. We cannot
compromise with a cancerous growth. We eradicate it, or are destroyed. If Mr. Gaynor believes that New York is better than it
has been, that there is less open display of vicious conditions, he is
possibly right. He is in a position to know the facts. Yet the public
can place little reliance upon the judgment of one who also believes
—or believed—that all the saloons in Manhattan are duly closed on
Sundays, because it has been made compulsory to leave a clear view
for the police, that they may see that the bar-rooms are empty—and
that the bartenders are busily engaged in supplying the customers
in the rear room. It is not without significance in this connection
that the streets of New York are universally in a disgraceful condition, and that the civic policy generally appears to be one of indifference and drift. And the men who stand for indifference and
drift are the men whom America can no longer tolerate. It is time
that Mr. Gaynor made his attitude clear.

*   *   *

It should be of some interest to the advocates of woman suffrage,
both here and in England, to study the political conditions in New
Zealand, which has long tried the experiment of votes for women.
The statistics show that the women do not neglect the responsibilities of the ballot, as more than three-quarters of those entitled to
vote actually do so—a slightly larger percentage than that of the

men. Yet the results of their activity have been unimportant. The no-license movement has been strengthened a little, perhaps; but not conspicuously. The general tendency of politics has undoubtedly been downward; the "boss" and the "machine," with their inevitable corruption, are now as strongly intrenched as in this country. It would be illogical to blame the women for this deterioration; yet, at the best, their voting power seems to have been singularly profitless.

* * *

The publication in English of Professor Henri Bergson's *Creative Evolution* (Henry Holt), *Matter and Memory* (The Macmillan Co.), and *Time and Free Will* (The Macmillan Co.), is, perhaps, one of the most noteworthy events in the history of modern thought. Three years ago the late Professor William James, in the sixth of his Hibbert Lectures delivered at Oxford, England, first awakened the popular interest in this remarkable thinker of our time. He expressed so large a personal debt to the works of this comparatively young writer, that his words of appreciation and acknowledgment have become the standard phrases of introduction with which other writers have brought Bergson before the reading public. "Open Bergson," he then said, "and new horizons loom on every page you read." And in another passage he confesses, "If I had not read Bergson I should probably still be blackening endless pages of paper privately, in the hope of making ends meet that were never meant to meet." A tribute of this nature by such a man should make us pause to inquire who the recipient of the tribute is, and what it is that he has done to merit it. Henri Louis Bergson was born in Paris on October 18th, 1859. He entered the École normale in 1878, and received his degree of docteur ès lettres in 1889. In 1897 he was appointed maitre de conférences at the École normale supérieure, but in 1900 became professor at the Collège de France, where he is still. In 1901 he was elected a member of the Institute of France. Such are the bare outlines of a career which has been passed quietly and unostentatiously in study and writing. But the man who wrote *L'Évolution Créatrice* could no longer remain unknown and unrecognized, for that work revolutionizes the whole of our philosophical thought. It approaches the problem of existence from a point of view altogether different from that of the great thinkers of the past, from Plato to Hegel, and, while it does not present us with a closed system, it does so illumine the fields of reasoning that future adventurers into those fields can nevermore mistake the roads. But Bergson is not only a philosopher, he is a great artist, a poet. His books are built up as splendid cathedrals are built. Stone is laid upon stone; column rises after column, arch grows out of arch, and all when completed tower into the sky, the masterpiece of expression of a great architeet's genius. France may indeed be proud of this great son of hers.

*　　*　　*

'Much has been written lately, and much has been heard, of Mexico, the country in which the Government has for many years saved the citizens the trouble of exercising their constitutional right to vote. But more remarkable than the history of President Diaz, the long maintenance of his autocracy, and the political incompetency of the people, is the strange national custom of courtesy in all ordinary relations. Impoliteness is so rare that it actually attracts attention in this curious republic. Civilizing influences will no doubt gradually remedy this weakness; but it will be a long time before any city in Mexico can hope to reach the high standard so easily maintained in New York.

*　　*　　*

The common failure to understand the work of Ibsen properly has its main reason not in any inherent obscurity or artificial mysticism, but in his intuitive grasp of the new importance given by modern conditions to some of the forces that dominate and direct human existence. Through the study of these forces and the part they have come to play in the life of modern man leads the only road to an intelligent reading of Ibsen's work. Mr. Edwin Björkman's article along these lines in the present issue of THE FORUM—*The Ibsen Myth*—is a remarkable literary achievement. In the opinion of *The New Age*, this writer is one of the coming men, not only of New York, but of all English-speaking countries. Those who read his contribution will not dispute this judgment.

WERE all the women of the world to come
  And droop their languorous hair about my heart
    They could not hold it in those nets so fine;
And pleading with lips lyrical or dumb,
  And howsoever an alluring art,
    They could not win the kisses that are thine.

If Helen came, her white limbs hung with gold,
  And Deirdre with dim visionary eyes,
    And Grania, flame-haired, fiery with command;
If Hero came—reluctant once of old—
  And she who all too long with Romeo lies,
    And she who led Dante heavenward by the hand,

They could not make me fain of their fair lips,
  Nor lure me to the languor of warm breasts
    With any soft compulsion of white arms;
And delicate dim touch of finger tips
  And fire that flames from eyes and fire that rests
    Would leave me cold and lose the name of charms.

Nay, Solomon's Love and Anthony's Desire,
  Héloïse, and frail Francesca, and their queen,
    Immortal Aphrodite, whom I praise,
And all her passionate daughters veined with fire,
  Might pass like old bent hags, for I have seen
    Beauty within thy beauty for all days.

THE NEW MACHIAVELLI

H. G. WELLS

CHAPTER THE FIRST

LOVE AND SUCCESS

VII

THE whole world had changed for Isabel and me; and we tried to pretend that nothing had changed except a small matter between us. We believed quite honestly at that time that it was possible to keep this thing that had happened from any reaction at all, save perhaps through some magically enhanced vigor in our work, upon the world about us! Seen in retrospect, one can realize the absurdity of this belief; within a week I realized it; but that does not alter the fact that we did believe as much, and that people who are deeply in love and unable to marry will continue to believe so to the very end of time. They will continue to believe out of existence every consideration that separates them until they have come together. Then they will count the cost, as we two had to do.

I am telling a story, and not propounding theories in this book; and chiefly I am telling of the ideas and influences and emotions that have happened to me—me as a sort of sounding board for my world. The moralist is at liberty to go over my conduct with his measure and say, " At this point or at that you went wrong, and you ought to have done "—so-and-so. The point of interest to the statesman is that it didn't for a moment occur to us to do so-and-so when the time for doing it came. It amazes me now to think how little either of us troubled about the established rights or wrongs of the situation. We hadn't an atom of respect for them, innate or acquired. The guardians of public morals will say we were very bad people; I submit in defence that they are very bad guardians—provocative guardians. . . . And when at last there came a claim against us that had an effective validity for us, we were in the full tide of passionate intimacy.

I had a night of nearly sleepless perplexity after Margaret's return. She had suddenly presented herself to me like something dramatically recalled, fine, generous, infinitely. capable of feeling. I was amazed how much I had forgotten her. In my contempt for vulgarized and conventionalized honor I had forgotten that for me there was such a reality as honor. And here it was, warm and near to me, living, breathing, unsuspecting. Margaret's pride was my honor, that I had had no right even to imperil.

I do not now remember if I thought at that time of going to Isabel and putting this new aspect of the case before her. Perhaps I did. Perhaps I may have considered even then the possibility of ending what had so freshly and passionately begun. If I did, it vanished next day at the sight of her. Whatever regrets came in the darkness, the daylight brought an obstinate confidence in our resolution again. We would, we declared, "pull the thing off." Margaret must not know. Margaret should not know. If Margaret did not know, then no harm whatever would be done. We tried to sustain that. . . .

For a brief time we had been like two people in a magic cell, magically cut off from the world and full of a light of its own, and then we began to realize that we were not in the least cut off, that the world was all about us and pressing in upon us, limiting us, threatening us, resuming possession of us. I tried to ignore the injury to Margaret of her unreciprocated advances. I tried to maintain to myself that this hidden love made no difference to the now irreparable breach between husband and wife. But I never spoke of it to Isabel or let her see that aspect of our case. How could I? The time for that had gone. . . .

Then in new shapes and relations came trouble. Distressful elements crept in by reason of our unavoidable furtiveness; we ignored them, hid them from each other, and attempted to hide them from ourselves. Successful love is a thing of abounding pride, and we had to be secret. It was delightful at first to be secret, a whispering, warm conspiracy; then presently it became irksome and a little shameful. Her essential frankness of soul was all against the masks and falsehoods that many women would have enjoyed. Together in our secrecy we relaxed, then in the presence of other people again it was tiresome to have to watch for the careless, too easy phrase, to snatch back one's hand from the limitless betrayal of a light, familiar touch.

Love becomes a poor thing, at best a poor beautiful thing, if it develops no continuing and habitual intimacy. We were always meeting, and most gloriously loving and beginning—and then we had to snatch at remorselessly ticking watches, hurry to catch trains, and go back to this or that. That is all very well for the intrigues of idle people perhaps, but not for an intense personal relationship. It is like lighting a candle for the sake of lighting it, over and over again, and each time blowing it out. That, no doubt, must be very amusing to children playing with the matches, but not to people who love warm light, and want it in order to do fine and honorable things together.

Perhaps we might at this stage have given it up. I think if we could have seen ahead and around us we might have done so. But the glow of our cell blinded us. . . . I wonder what might have happened if at that time we had given it up. . . . We propounded it, we met again in secret to discuss it, and our overpowering passion for one another reduced that meeting to absurdity. . .

Presently the idea of children crept between us. It came in from all our conceptions of life and public service; it was, we found, in the quality of our minds that physical love without children is a little weak, timorous, more than a little shameful. With imaginative people there very speedily comes a time when that realization is inevitable. We hadn't thought of that before—it isn't natural to think of that before. We hadn't known. There is no literature in English dealing with such things. . . .

There is a necessary sequence of phases in love. These came in their order, and with them, unanticipated tarnishings on the first bright perfection of our relations. For a time these developing phases were no more than a secret and private trouble between us, little shadows spreading by imperceptible degrees across that vivid and luminous cell.

VIII

The Handitch election flung me suddenly into prominence.

It is still only two years since that struggle, and I will not trouble the reader with a detailed history of events that must be quite sufficiently present in his mind for my purpose already. Huge stacks of journalism have dealt with Handitch and its significance. For the reader very probably, as for most people outside a comparatively small circle, it meant my emergence from obscurity. We obtruded no editor's name in the *Blue Weekly;* I had never as yet been on the London hoardings. Before Handitch I was a journalist and writer of no great public standing; after Handitch, I was definitely a person, in the little group of persons who stood for the Imperialist movement. Handitch was, to a very large extent, my affair. I realized then, as a man comes to do, how much one can still grow after seven and twenty. In the second election I was a man taking hold of things; at Kinghamstead I had been simply a young candidate, a party unit, led about the constituency, told to do this and that, and finally washed in by the great Anti-Imperialist flood, like a starfish rolling up a beach.

My feminist views had earnt the mistrust of the party, and I do not think I should have got the chance of Handitch or indeed any chance at all of Parliament for a long time, if it had not been that the seat with its long record of Liberal victories and its Liberal majority of 3642 at the last election, offered a hopeless contest. The Liberal dissensions and the belated but by no means contemptible Socialist candidate were providential interpositions. I think, however, the conduct of Gane, Crupp, and Tarville in coming down to fight for me, did count tremendously in my favor. "We aren't going to win, perhaps," said Crupp, "but we are going to talk." And until the very eve of victory, we treated Handitch not so much as a battlefield as a hoarding. And so it was the Endowment of Motherhood as a practical form of Eugenics got into English politics.

Plutus, our agent, was scared out of his wits when the thing began.

"They're ascribing all sorts of queer ideas to you about the Family," he said.

"I think the Family exists for the good of the children," I said; "is that queer?"

"Not when you explain it—but they don't let you explain it. And about marriage——?"

"I'm all right about marriage—trust me."

"Of course, if *you* had children," said Plutus, rather inconsiderately. . . .

They opened fire upon me in a little electioneering rag called the *Handitch Sentinel*, with a string of garbled quotations and misrepresentations that gave me an admirable text for a speech. I spoke for an hour and ten minutes with a more and more crumpled copy of the *Sentinel* in my hand, and I made the fullest and completest exposition of the idea of endowing motherhood that I think had ever been made up to the time in England. Its effect on the press was extraordinary. The Liberal papers gave me quite unprecedented space under the impression that I had only to be given rope to hang myself; the Conservatives cut me down or tried to justify me; the whole country was talking. I had had a pamphlet in type upon the subject, and I revised this carefully and put it on the bookstalls within three days. It sold enormously and brought me bushels of letters. We issued over three thousand in Handitch alone. At meeting after meeting I was heckled upon nothing else. Long before polling day Plutus was converted.

"It's catching on like old age pensions," he said. "We've dished the Liberals! To think that such a project should come from our side!"

But it was only with the declaration of the poll that my battle was won.   No one expected more than a snatch victory, and I was in by over fifteen hundred.   At one bound Cossington's papers passed from apologetics varied by repudiation to triumphant praise.   "A renascent England, breeding men," said the leader in his chief daily on the morning after the polling, and claimed that the Conservatives had been ever the pioneers in sanely bold constructive projects.

I came up to London with a weary but rejoicing Margaret by the night train.

CHAPTER THE SECOND

THE IMPOSSIBLE POSITION

I

To any one who did not know of that glowing secret between Isabel and myself, I might well have appeared at that time the most successful and enviable of men.   I had recovered rapidly from an uncongenial start in political life; I had become a considerable force through the *Blue Weekly*, and was shaping an increasingly influential body of opinion; I had reëntered Parliament with quite dramatic distinction, and in spite of a certain faltering on the part of the orthodox Conservatives towards the bolder elements in our propaganda, I had loyal and unenvious associates who were making me a power in the party.   People were coming to our group, understandings were developing.   It was clear we should play a prominent part in the next general election, and that, given a Conservative victory, I should be assured of office.   The world opened out to me brightly and invitingly.   Great schemes took shape in my mind, always more concrete, always more practicable; the years ahead seemed falling into order, shining with the credible promise of immense achievement.

And at the heart of it all, unseen and unsuspected, was the secret of my relations with Isabel—like a seed that germinates and thrusts, thrusts relentlessly.

From the onset of the Handitch contest onward, my meetings with her had been more and more pervaded by the discussion of our situation.   It had innumerable aspects.   It was very present to us that we wanted to be together as much as possible—we were beginning to long very much for actual living together, in the same house, so that one could come as it were carelessly—unawares—upon the other, busy perhaps about some trivial thing.   We wanted to feel each other in the daily atmosphere.   Preceding our imperatively sterile passion, you must remember, outside it, altogether greater than it so far as our individual lives were concerned, there had grown and still grew an enormous affection and intellectual sympathy between us. We brought all our impressions and all our ideas to each other, to see them in each other's light. It is hard to convey that quality of intellectual unison to any one who has not experienced it. I thought more and more in terms of conversation with Isabel; her possible comments upon things would flash into my mind, oh!—with the very sound of her voice.

I remember, too, the odd effect of seeing her in the distance going about Handitch, like any stranger canvasser; the queer emotion of her approach along the street, the greeting as she passed. The morning of the polling she vanished from the constituency. I saw her for an instant in the passage behind our Committee rooms.

"Going?" said I.

She nodded.

"Stay it out. I want you to see the fun. I remember—the other time."

She didn't answer for a moment or so, and stood with face averted.

"It's Margaret's show," she said abruptly. "If, I see her smiling there like a queen by your side——! She did—last time. I remember." She caught at a sob and dashed her hand across her face impatiently. "Jealous fool, mean and petty, jealous fool! . . . Good luck, old man, to you! You're going to win. But I don't want to see the end of it all the same. . . ."

"Good-bye!" said I, clasping her hand as some supporter appeared in the passage. . . .

I came back to London victorious, and a little flushed and coarse with victory; and so soon as I could break away I went to Isabel's flat and found her white and worn, with the stain of secret weeping about her eyes. I came into the room to her and shut the door.

"You said I'd win," I said, and held out my arms.

She hugged me closely for a moment.

"My dear," I whispered, "it's nothing—without you—nothing!"

We didn't speak for some seconds. Then she slipped from my hold. "Look!" she said, smiling like winter sunshine. "I've had in all the morning papers—the pile of them, and you—resounding."

"It's more than I dared hope."

"Or I."

She stood for a moment still smiling bravely, and then she was sobbing in my arms. "The bigger you are—the more you show," she said—"the more we are parted. I know, I know——"

I held her close to me, making no answer.

Presently she became still. "Oh, well," she said, and wiped her eyes and sat down on the little sofa by the fire; and I sat down beside her.

"I didn't know all there was in love," she said, staring at the coals, "when we went love-making."

I put my arm behind her and took a handful of her dear soft hair in my hand and kissed it.

"You've done a great thing this time," she said. "Handitch will make you."

"It opens big chances," I said. "But why are you weeping, dear one?"

"Envy," she said, "and love."

"You're not lonely?"

"I've plenty to do—and lots of people."

"Well?"

"I want you."

"You've got me."

She put her arm about me and kissed me. "I want you," she said, "just as if I had nothing of you. You don't understand—how a woman wants a man. I thought once if I just gave myself to you it would be enough. It was nothing—it was just a step across the threshold. My dear, every moment you are away I ache for you—ache! I want to be about when it isn't love-making or talk. I want to be doing things for you, and watching you when you're not thinking of me. All those safe, careless, intimate things. And something else——" She stopped. "Dear, I don't want to bother you. I just want you to know I love you. . . ."

She caught my head in her hands and kissed it, then stood up abruptly.

I looked up at her, a little perplexed.

"Dear heart," said I, "isn't this enough? You're my councillor, my colleague, my right hand, the secret soul of my life——"

"And I want to darn your socks," she said, smiling back at me. "You're insatiable."

She smiled. "No," she said. "I'm not insatiable, Master. But I'm a woman in love. And I'm finding out what I want, and what is necessary to me—and what I can't have. That's all."

"We get a lot."

"We want a lot. You and I are greedy people for the things we like, Master. It's very evident we've got nearly all we can ever have of one another—and I'm not satisfied."

"What more is there?"

"For you—very little. I wonder. For me—everything. Yes —everything. You didn't mean it, Master; you didn't know any more than I did when I began, but love between a man and a woman is sometimes very one-sided. Fearfully one-sided! That's all. . ."

" Don't *you* ever want children? " she said abruptly.

" I suppose I do."

" You don't! "

" I haven't thought of them."

" A man doesn't, perhaps. But I have. . . . I want them—like hunger. *Your* children, and home with you. Really, continually you! That's the trouble. . . . I can't have 'em, Master, and I can't have you."

She was crying, and through her tears she laughed.

" I'm going to make a scene," she said, " and get this over. I'm so discontented and miserable; I've got to tell you. It would come between us if I didn't. I'm in love with you, with everything—with all my brains. I'll pull through all right. I'll be good, Master, never you fear. But to-day I'm crying out with all my being. This election—— You're going up; you're going on. In these papers —you're a great big fact. It's suddenly come home to me. At the back of my mind I've always had the idea I was going to have you somewhere presently for myself—I mean to have you to go long tramps with, to keep house for, to get meals for, to watch for of an evening. It's a sort of habitual background to my thought of you. And it's nonsense—utter nonsense! " She stopped. She was crying and choking. " And the child, you know—the child! "

I was troubled beyond measure, but Handitch and its intimations were clear and strong.

" We can't have that," I said.

" No," she said, " we can't have that."

" We've got our own things to do."

" *Your* things," she said.

" Aren't they yours too? "

" Because of you," she said.

" Aren't they your very own things? "

" Women don't have that sort of very own thing. Indeed, it's true! And think! You've been down there preaching the goodness of children, telling them the only good thing in a state is happy, hopeful children, working to free mothers and children——"

" And we give our own children to do it? " I said.

" Yes," she said. " And sometimes I think it's too much to give— too much altogether. . . . Children get into a woman's brain—when she mustn't have them, especially when she must never hope for them. Think of the child we might have now!—the little creature with soft, tender skin, and little hands and little feet! At times it haunts me. It comes and says, Why wasn't I given life? I can hear it in the night. . . . The world is full of such little ghosts, dear lover—little things that asked for life and were refused. They clamor to me. It's like a little fist beating at my heart. Love children, beautiful children. Little cold hands that tear at my heart! Oh, my heart and my lord!" She was holding my arm with both her hands and weeping against it, and now she drew herself to my shoulder and wept and sobbed in my embrace. "I shall never sit with your child on my knee and you beside me—never, and I am a woman and your lover! . . ."

II

But the profound impossibility of our relation was now becoming more and more apparent to us. We found ourselves seeking justification, clinging passionately to a situation that was coldly, pitilessly, impossible and fated. We wanted quite intensely to live together and have a child, but also we wanted very many other things that were incompatible with these desires. It was extraordinarily difficult to weigh our political and intellectual ambitions against those intimate wishes. The weights kept altering according as one found oneself grasping this valued thing or that. It wasn't as if we could throw everything aside for our love, and have that as we wanted it. Love such as we bore one another isn't altogether, or even chiefly, a thing in itself—it is for the most part a value set upon things. Our love was interwoven with all our other interests; to go out of the world and live in isolation seemed to us like killing the best parts of each other; we loved the sight of each other engaged finely and characteristically, we knew each other best as activities. We had no delusions about material facts; we didn't want each other alive or dead, we wanted each other fully alive. We wanted to do big things together, and for us to take each other openly and desperately would leave us nothing in the world to do. We wanted children indeed passionately, but children with every helpful chance in the world, and children born in scandal would be handicapped at every turn. We wanted to share a home, and not a solitude.

And when we were at this stage of realization, began the intimations that we were found out, and that scandal was afoot against us. . . .

I heard of it first from Esmeer, who deliberately mentioned it, with that steady gray eye of his watching me, as an instance of the preposterous falsehoods people will circulate. It came to Isabel almost simultaneously through a married college friend, who made it her business to demand either confirmation or denial. It filled us both with consternation. In the surprise of the moment Isabel admitted her secret and her friend went off " reserving her freedom of action."

Discovery broke out in every direction. Friends with grave faces and an atmosphere of infinite tact invaded us both. Other friends ceased to invade either of us. It was manifest we had become—we knew not how—a private scandal, a subject for duologues, an amazement, a perplexity, a vivid interest. In a few brief weeks it seemed London passed from absolute unsuspiciousness to a chattering exaggeration of its knowledge of our relations.

It was just the most inappropriate time for that disclosure. The long smouldering antagonism to my endowment of motherhood ideas had flared up into an active campaign in the *Expurgator,* and it would be altogether disastrous to us if I should be convicted of any personal irregularity. It was just because of the manifest and challenging respectability of my position that I had been able to carry the thing as far as I had done. Now suddenly my fortunes had sprung a leak, and scandal was pouring in. . . . It chanced, too, that a wave of moral intolerance was sweeping through London, one of those waves in which the bitterness of the consciously just finds an ally in the panic of the undiscovered. A certain Father Blodgett had been preaching against social corruption with extraordinary force, and had roused the Church of England people to a kind of competition in denunciation. The old methods of the Anti-Socialist campaign had been renewed, and had offered far too wide a scope and too tempting an opportunity for private animosity, to be restricted to the private affairs of the Socialists. I had intimations of an extensive circulation of " private and confidential " letters. . . .

I think there can be nothing else in life quite like the unnerving realization that rumor and scandal are afoot about one. Abruptly one's confidence in the solidity of the universe disappears. One walks silenced through a world that one feels to be full of inaudible accusations. One cannot challenge the assault, get it out into the open, separate truth and falsehood. It slinks from you, turns aside its face. Old acquaintances suddenly evaded me, made extraordinary excuses; men who had presumed on the verge of my world and pestered me with an intrusive enterprise, now took the bold step of flat repudiation. I became doubtful about the return of a nod, retracted all those tentacles of easy civility that I had hitherto spread to the world. I still grow warm with amazed indignation when I recall that Edward Crampton, meeting me full on the steps of the Climax Club, cut me dead. " By God! " I cried, and came near catching him by the throat and wringing out of him what of all good deeds and bad, could hearten him, a younger man than I, and empty beyond comparison, to dare to play the judge to me. And then I had an open slight from Mrs. Millingham, whom I had counted on as one counts upon the sunrise. I had not expected things of that sort; they were disconcerting beyond measure; it was as if the world were giving way beneath my feet, as though something failed in the essential confidence of life, as though a hand of wet ice had touched my heart. Similar things were happening to Isabel. Yet we went on for a time, working, visiting, meeting, trying to ignore this gathering of implacable forces against us.

For a time I was perplexed beyond measure to account for this campaign. Then I got a clue. The centre of diffusion was the Bailey household. The Baileys had never forgiven me my abandonment of the young Liberal group they had done so much to inspire and organize; their dinner-table had long been a scene of hostile depreciation of the *Blue Weekly* and all its allies; week after week Altiora proclaimed that I was " doing nothing," and found other causes for our by-election triumphs; I counted Chambers Street a dangerous place for me. Yet, nevertheless, I was astonished to find them using a private scandal against me. They did. I think Handitch had filled up the measure of their bitterness, for I had not only abandoned them, but I was succeeding beyond even their power of misrepresentation. Always I had been a wasp in their spider's web, difficult to claim as a tool, critical, antagonistic. I admired their work and devotion enormously, but I had never concealed my contempt for a certain childish vanity they displayed, and for the frequent puerility of their political intrigues. I suppose contempt galls more than injuries, and anyhow they had me now. They had me. Bailey, I found, was warning fathers of girls against me as a " reckless libertine," and Altiora, flushed, roguish, and disheveled, was sitting on her fender curb after dinner, and pledging little parties of five or six women at a time with infinite gusto not to let the matter go further. Our cell was open to the world, and a bleak, distressful daylight streaming in.

I had a gleam of a more intimate motive in Altiora from the reports that came to me. Isabel had been doing a series of five or six articles in the *Political Review* in support of our campaign, the *Political Review* which had hitherto been loyally Baileyite. Quite her best writing up to the present, at any rate, is in those papers, and no doubt Altiora had had not only to read her in those invaded columns, but listen to her praises in the mouths of the tactless influential. Altiora, like so many people who rely on gesture and vocal insistence in conversation, writes a poor and slovenly prose and handles an argument badly; Isabel has her University training behind her and wrote from the first with the stark power of a clear-headed man. " Now we know," said Altiora, with just a gleam of malice showing through her brightness, " now we know who helps with the writing!"

She revealed astonishing knowledge.

For a time I couldn't for the life of me discover her sources. I had, indeed, a desperate intention of challenging her, and then I bethought me of a youngster named Curmain, who had been my supplementary typist and secretary for a time, and whom I had sent on to her before the days of our breach. "Of course!" said I, "Curmain!" He was a tall, drooping, sidelong youth with sandy hair, a little forward head, and a long thin neck. He stole stamps, and, I suspected, rifled my private letter drawer, and I found him one day on a turn of the stairs looking guilty and ruffled with a pretty Irish housemaid of Margaret's manifestly in a state of hot indignation. I saw nothing, but I felt everything in the air between them. I hate this pestering of servants, but at the same time I didn't want Curmain wiped out of existence, so I had packed him off without unnecessary discussion to Altiora. He was quick and cheap anyhow, and I thought her general austerity ought to redeem him if anything could; the Chambers Street housemaid wasn't for any man's kissing and showed it, and the stamps and private letters were looked after with an efficiency altogether surpassing mine. And Altiora, I've no doubt left now whatever, pumped this young undesirable about me, and scenting a story, had him to dinner alone one evening to get to the bottom of the matter. She got quite to the bottom of it,—it must have been a queer duologue. She read Isabel's careless, intimate letters to me, so to speak, by this proxy, and she wasn't ashamed to use this information in the service of the bitterness that had sprung up in her since our political breach. It was essentially a personal bitterness; it helped no public purpose of theirs to get rid of me. My downfall in any public sense was sheer waste,—the loss of a man. She knew she was behaving badly, and so, when it came to remonstrance, she behaved worse. She'd got names and dates and places; the efficiency of her information was irresistible. And she set to work at it marvelously. Never before, in all her pursuit of efficient ideals, had Altiora achieved such levels of efficiency. I wrote a protest that was perhaps ill-advised and angry, I went to her and tried to stop her. She wouldn't listen, she wouldn't think, she denied and lied, she behaved like a naughty child of six years old which has made up its mind to be hurtful. It wasn't only, I think, that she couldn't bear our political and social influence; she also—I realized at that interview—couldn't bear our loving. It seemed to her the sickliest thing,—a thing quite unendurable. While such things were, the virtue had gone out of her world.

I've the vividest memory of that call of mine. She'd just come in and taken off her hat, and she was gray and disheveled and tired, and in a business-like dress of black and crimson that didn't suit her and was muddy about the skirts; she'd a cold in her head and sniffed penetratingly, she avoided my eye as she talked and interrupted everything I had to say; she kept stabbing fiercely at the cushions of her sofa with a long hat-pin and pretending she was overwhelmed with grief at the *débâcle* she was deliberately organizing.

"Then part," she cried, "part. If you don't want a smashing up,—part! You two have got to be parted. You've got never to see each other ever, never to speak." There was a zest in her voice. "We're not circulating stories," she denied. "No! And Curmain never told us anything—Curmain is an *excellent* young man; oh! a quite excellent young man. You misjudged him altogether. . . ."

I was equally unsuccessful with Bailey. I caught the little wretch in the League Club, and he wriggled and lied. He wouldn't say where he had got his facts, he wouldn't admit he had told any one. When I gave him the names of two men who had come to me astonished and incredulous, he attempted absurdly to make me think they had told *him*. He did his horrible little best to suggest that honest old Quackett, who had just left England for the Cape, was the real scandalmonger. That struck me as mean, even for Bailey. I've still the odd vivid impression of his fluting voice, excusing the inexcusable, his big, shifty face evading me, his perspiration-beaded forehead, the shrugging shoulders, and the would-be exculpatory gestures—Houndsditch gestures—of his enormous ugly hands

"I can assure you, my dear fellow," he said, "I can assure you we've done everything to shield you—everything. . . ."

III

Isabel came after dinner one evening and talked in the office. She made a white-robed, dusky figure against the deep blues of my big window. I sat at my desk and tore a quill pen to pieces as I talked.

"The Baileys don't intend to let this drop," I said. "They mean that everyone in London is to know about it."

"I know."

"Well!" I said.

"Dear heart," said Isabel, facing it, "it's no good waiting for things to overtake us; we're at the parting of the ways."

"What are we to do?"

"They won't let us go on."

"Damn them!"

"They are *organizing* scandal."

"It's no good waiting for things to overtake us," I echoed; "they have overtaken us." I turned on her. "What do you want to do?"

"Everything," she said. "Keep you and have our work. Aren't we Mates?"

"We can't."

"And we can't!"

"I've got to tell Margaret," I said.

"Margaret!"

"I can't bear the idea of any one else getting in front with it. I've been wincing about Margaret secretly——"

"I know. You'll have to tell her—and make your peace with her." She leant back against the bookcases under the window.

"We've had some good times, Master," she said, with a sigh in her voice.

And then for a long time we stared at one another in silence.

"We haven't much time left," she said.

"Shall we bolt?" I said.

"And leave all this?" she asked, with her eyes going round the room. "And that?" And her head indicated Westminster. "No!"

I said no more of bolting.

"We've got to screw ourselves up to surrender," she said.

"Something."

"A lot."

"Master," she said, "it isn't all sex and stuff between us?"

"No!"

"I can't give up the work. Our work's my life."

We came upon another long pause.

"No one will believe we've ceased to be lovers—if we simply do," she said.

"We shouldn't."

"We've got to do something more parting than that."

I nodded, and again we paused. She was coming to something.

"I could marry Shoesmith," she said abruptly.

"But——" I objected.

"He knows. It wasn't fair. I told him."

"Oh, that explains," I said. "There's been a kind of sulkiness—— But—you told him?"

She nodded. "He's rather badly hurt," she said. "He's been a good friend to me. He's curiously loyal. But something, something he said one day—forced me to let him know. . . . That's been the beastliness of all this secrecy. That's the beastliness of all secrecy. You have to spring surprises on people. But he keeps on. He's steadfast. He'd already suspected. He wants me very badly to marry him. . . ."

"But you don't want to marry him?"

"I'm forced to think of it."

"But does he want to marry you at that? Take you as a present from the world at large?—against your will and desire? . . . I don't understand him."

"He cares for me."

"How?"

"He thinks this is a fearful mess for me. He wants to pull it straight."

We sat for a time in silence, with imaginations that obstinately refused to take up the realities of this proposition.

"I don't want you to marry Shoesmth," I said at last.

"Don't you like him?"

"Not as your husband."

"He's a very clever and sturdy person—and very generous and devoted to me."

"And me?"

"You can't expect that. He thinks you are wonderful—and, naturally, that you ought not to have started this."

"I've a curious dislike to any one thinking that but myself. I'm quite ready to think it myself."

"He'd let us be friends—and meet."

"Let us be friends!" I cried, after a long pause. "You and I!"

"He wants me to be engaged soon. Then, he says, he can go round fighting these rumors, defending us both—and force a quarrel on the Baileys."

"I don't understand him," I said, and added, "I don't understand you."

I was staring at her face. It seemed white and set in the dimness.

"Do you really mean this, Isabel?" I asked.

"What else is there to do, my dear?—what else is there to do at all? I've been thinking day and night. You can't go away with me. You can't smash yourself suddenly in the sight of all men. I'd rather die than that should happen. Look what you are becoming in the country! Look at all you've built up!—me helping. I wouldn't let you do it if you could. I wouldn't let you—if it were only for Margaret's sake. *This* . . . closes the scandal, closes everything."

"It closes all our life together," I cried.

She was silent.

"It never ought to have begun," I said.

She winced. Then abruptly she was on her knees before me, with her hands upon my shoulder and her eyes meeting mine.

"My dear," she said very earnestly, "don't misunderstand me!

Don't think I'm retreating from the things we've done! Our love is the best thing I could ever have had from life. Nothing can ever equal it; nothing could ever equal the beauty and delight you and I have had together. Never! You have loved me; you do love me. . . .

"No one could ever know how to love you as I have loved you; no one could ever love me as you have loved me, my king. And it's just because it's been so splendid, dear; it's just because I'd die rather than have a tithe of all this wiped out of my life again—for it's made me, it's all I am—dear, it's years since I began loving you— it's just because of its goodness that I want not to end in wreckage now, not to end in the smashing up of all the big things I understand in you and love in you. . . .

"What is there for us if we keep on and go away?" she went on. "All the big interests in our lives will vanish—everything. We shall become specialized people—people overshadowed by a situation. We shall be an elopement, a romance—all our breadth and meaning gone! People will always think of it first when they think of us; all our work and aims will be warped by it and subordinated to it. Is it good enough, dear? Just to specialize. . . . I think of you. We've got a case, a passionate case, the best of cases, but do we want to spend all our lives defending it and justifying it? And there's that other life. I know now you care for Margaret—you care more than you think you do. You have said fine things of her. I've watched you about her. Little things have dropped from you. She's given her life for you; she's nothing without you. You feel that to your marrow all the time you are thinking about these things. Oh, I'm not jealous, dear. I love you for loving her. I love you in relation to her. But there it is, an added weight against us, another thing worth saving."

Presently, I remember, she sat back on her heels and looked up into my face. "We've done wrong—and parting's paying. It's time to pay. We needn't have paid, if we'd kept to the track. . . . You and I, Master, we've got to be men."

"Yes," I said; "we've got to be men."

IV

I was driven to tell Margaret about our situation by my intolerable dread that otherwise the thing might come to her through some stupid and clumsy informant. She might even meet Altiora, and have it from her.

I can still recall the feeling of sitting at my desk that night in that large study of mine in Radnor Square, waiting for Margaret to come home. It was oddly like the feeling of a dentist's reception-room; only it was for me to do the dentistry with clumsy, cruel hands. I had left the door open so that she would come in to me.

I heard her silken rustle on the stairs at last, and then she was in the doorway. " May I come in? " she said.

" Do," I said, and turned round to her.

" Working? " she said.

" Hard," I answered. " Where have *you* been? "

" At the Vallerys'. Mr. Evesham was talking about you. They were all talking. I don't think everybody knew who I was. Just Mrs. Mumble I'd been to them. Lord Wardenham doesn't like you."

" He doesn't."

" But they feel you're rather big, anyhow. Then I went on to Park Lane to hear a new pianist and some other music at Eva's."

" Yes."

" Then I looked in at the Brabants' for some midnight tea before I came on here. They'd got some writers—and Grant was there."

" You *have* been flying round. . . ."

There was a little pause between us.

I looked at her pretty, unsuspecting face, and at the slender grace of her golden-robed body. What gulfs there were between us! " You've been amused," I said.

" It's been amusing! You've been at the House? "

" The Medical Education Bill kept me. . . ."

After all, why should I tell her? She'd got to a way of living that fulfilled her requirements. Perhaps she'd never hear. But all that day and the day before I'd been making up my mind to do the thing.

" I want to tell you something," I said. " I wish you'd sit down for a moment or so. . . ."

Once I had begun, it seemed to me I had to go through with it.

Something in the quality of my voice gave her an intimation of unusual gravity. She looked at me steadily for a moment and sat down slowly in my armchair. " What is it? " she said.

I went on awkwardly. " I've got to tell you—something extraordinarily distressing," I said.

She was manifestly altogether unaware.

" There seems to be a good deal of scandal abroad—I've only recently heard of it—about myself—and Isabel."

" Isabel! "

I nodded.

" What do they say? " she asked.

It was difficult, I found, to speak.

" They say she's my mistress."

" Oh! How abominable! "

She spoke with the most natural indignation. Our eyes met.

" We've been great friends," I said.

" Yes. And to make *that* of it. My poor dear! But how can they? " She paused and looked at me. " It's so incredible. How can any one believe it? I couldn't."

She stopped, with her distressed eyes regarding me. Her expression changed to dread. There was a tense stillness for a second, perhaps.

I turned my face toward the desk, and took up and dropped a handful of paper fasteners.

" Margaret," I said, " I'm afraid you'll have to believe it."

V

Margaret sat very still. When I looked at her again, her face was very white, and her distressed eyes scrutinized me. Her lips quivered as she spoke. " You really mean—*that?* " she said.

I nodded.

" I never dreamt."

" I never meant you to dream."

" And that is why—we've been apart? "

I thought. " I suppose it is."

" Why have you told me now? "

" Those rumors. I didn't want any one else to tell you."

" Or else it wouldn't have mattered? "

" No."

She turned her eyes from me to the fire. Then for a moment she looked about the room she had made for me, and then quite silently, with a childish quivering of her lips, with a sort of dismayed distress upon her face, she was weeping. She sat weeping in her dress of cloth of gold, with her bare slender arms dropped limp over the arms of her chair, and her eyes averted from me, making no effort to stay or staunch her tears. " I am sorry, Margaret," I said. " I was in love. . . . I did not understand. . . ."

Presently she asked: " What are you going to do? "

" You see, Margaret, now it's come to be your affair—I want to know what you—what you want."

" You want to leave me? "

" If you want me to, I must."

" Leave Parliament—leave all the things you are doing—all this fine movement of yours? "

" No." I spoke sullenly. " I don't want to leave anything. I want to stay on. I've told you, because I think we—Isabel and I, I mean—have got to drive through a storm of scandal anyhow. I don't know how far things may go, how much people may feel, and I can't, I can't have you unconscious, unarmed, open to any revelation——"

She made no answer.

"When the thing began—I knew it was stupid but I thought it was a thing that wouldn't change, wouldn't be anything but itself, wouldn't unfold—consequences. . . . People have got hold of these vague rumors. . . . Directly it reached any one else but—but us two—I saw it had to come to you."

I stopped. I had that distressful feeling I have always had with Margaret, of not being altogether sure she heard, of being doubtful if she understood. I perceived that once again I had struck at her and shattered a thousand unsubstantial pinnacles. And I couldn't get at her, to help her, or touch her mind! I stood up, and at my movement she moved. She produced a little dainty handkerchief, and made an effort to wipe her face with it, and held it to her eyes. "Oh, my Husband!" she sobbed.

"What do you mean?" she said, with her voice muffled by her handkerchief.

"We're going to end it," I said.

Something gripped me tormentingly as I said that. I drew a chair beside her and sat down. "You and I, Margaret, have been partners," I began. "We've built up this life of ours together; I couldn't have done it without you. We've made a position, created a work——"

She shook her head. "You," she said.

"You helping. I don't want to shatter it—if you don't want it shattered. I can't leave my work. I can't leave you. I want you to have—all that you have ever had. I've never meant to rob you. I've made an immense and tragic blunder. You don't know how things took us, how different they seemed! My character and accident have conspired—— We'll pay—in ourselves, not in our public service."

I halted again. Margaret remained very still.

"I want you to understand that the thing is at an end. It is definitely at an end. We—we talked—yesterday. We mean to end it altogether." I clenched my hands. "She's going to marry Arnold Shoesmith."

I wasn't looking now at Margaret any more, but I heard the rustle of her movement as she turned on me.

"It's all right," I said, clinging to my explanation. "We're doing nothing shabby. He knows. He will. It's all as right—as things can be now. We're not cheating any one, Margaret. We're doing things straight—now. Of course, you know. . . . We shall— we shall have to make sacrifices. Give things up pretty completely.

Very completely. . . . We shall have not to see each other for a time, you know. Perhaps not a long time. Two or three years. Or write—or just any of that sort of thing ever——"

Some subconscious barrier gave way in me. I found myself crying uncontrollably—as I have never cried since I was a little child. I was amazed and horrified at myself. And wonderfully, Margaret was on her knees beside me, with her arms about me, mingling her weeping with mine. "Oh, my Husband!" she cried, "my poor Husband! Does it hurt you so? I would do anything! Oh, the fool I am! Dear, I love you. I love you over and away and above all these jealous little things!"

She drew down my head to her as a mother might draw down the head of a son. She caressed me, weeping bitterly with me. "Oh! my dear," she sobbed, "my dear! I've never seen you cry! I've never seen you cry. Ever! I didn't know you could. Oh! my dear! Can't you have her, my dear, if you want her? I can't bear it! Let me help you, dear. Oh! my Husband! My Man! I can't bear to have you cry!" For a time she held me in silence. "I've thought this might happen, I dreamt it might happen. You two, I mean. It was dreaming put it into my head. When I've seen you together, so glad with each other. . . . Oh! Husband mine, believe me! believe me! I'm stupid, I'm cold, I'm only beginning to realize how stupid and cold, but all I want in all the world is to give my life to you. . . ."

VI

"We can't part in a room," said Isabel.

"We'll have one last talk together," I said, and planned that we should meet for half a day between Dover and Walmer and talk ourselves out. I still recall that day very well, recall even the curious exaltation of grief that made our mental atmosphere distinctive and memorable. We had seen so much of one another, had become so intimate, that we talked of parting even as we parted with a sense of incredible remoteness.

We went together up over the cliffs, and to a place where they fall toward the sea, past the white, quaint-lanterned lighthouses of the South Foreland. There, in a kind of niche below the crest, we sat talking. It was a spacious day, serenely blue and warm, and on the wrinkled water remotely below a black tender and six hooded submarines came presently, and engaged in mysterious manœuvres. Shrieking gulls and chattering jackdaws circled over us and below us, and dived and swooped; and a skerry of weedy, fallen chalk appeared, and gradually disappeared again, as the tide fell and rose.

We talked and thought that afternoon on every aspect of our relations. It seems to me now we talked so wide and far that scarcely
an issue in the life between man and woman can arise that we did
not at least touch upon. Lying there at Isabel's feet, I have become
for myself a symbol of all this world-wide problem between order and
conscious, passionate love the world has still to solve. Because it isn't
solved, there is a wrong in it either way. The sky, the wide horizon,
seemed to lift us out of ourselves until we were something representative and general. She was womanhood become articulate, talking to
her lover.

"I ought," I said, "never to have loved you."

"It wasn't a thing planned," she said.

"I ought never to have let our talk slip to that, never to have
turned back from America, never have thought for a moment of this
place."

"There were two in that."

"If I'd known——"

"I'm glad we did it," she said. "Don't think I repent."

I looked at her.

"I will never repent," she said. "Never!" as though she clung to
her life in saying it.

I remember we talked for a long time of divorce. It seemed to us
then and it seems to us still that it ought to have been possible for
Margaret to divorce me and for me to marry without the scandalous
and ugly publicity, the taint and ostracism that follow such a readjustment. We went on to the whole perplexing riddle of marriage.
We criticised the current code, how muddled and conventionalized it
had become, how modified by subterfuges and concealments and new
necessities, and the increasing freedom of women. "It's all like Bromstead when the building came," I said; for I had often talked to her
of that early impression of purpose dissolving again into chaotic
forces. "There is no clear right in the world any more. The world
is Byzantine. The justest man to-day must practise a tainted goodness."

These questions need discussion—a magnificent frankness of discussion—if any standards are again to establish an effective hold upon
educated people. Discretions, as I have said already, will never hold
any one worth holding—longer than they held us. Against every
"shalt not" there must be a "why not" plainly put,—the "why
not" largest and plainest, the law deduced from its purpose. "You
and I, Isabel," I said, "have always been a little disregardful of duty,
partly at least because the idea of duty comes to us so ill-clad. Oh!
I know there's an extravagant insubordinate strain in us, but that
wasn't all. I wish humbugs would leave duty alone. I wish all

duty wasn't covered with slime. That's where the real mischief comes in. Passion can always contrive to clothe itself in beauty, strips itself splendid. That carried us. But for all its mean associations there *is* this duty. . . ."

"Don't we come rather late to it?"

"Not so late that it won't be atrociously hard to do."

"It's queer to think of now," said Isabel. "Who could believe we did all we have done honestly? Well, in a manner honestly. Who could believe we thought this might be hidden? Who could trace it all step by step from the time when we found that a certain boldness in our talk was pleasing? We talked of love. . . . Master, there's not much for us to do in the way of Apologia that any one will credit. And yet if it were possible to tell the very heart of our story. . . .

"Does Margaret really want to go on with you?" she asked— "shield you—knowing of . . . *this?*"

"I'm certain. I don't understand—just as I don't understand Shoesmith, but she does. These people walk on solid ground which is just thin air to us. They've got something we haven't got. Assurances? I wonder . . . ."

Then it was, or later, we talked of Shoesmith, and what her life might be with him.

"He's good," she said; "he's kindly. He's everything but magic. He's the very image of the decent, sober, honorable life. You can't say a thing against him or I—except that something—something in his imagination, something in the tone of his voice—fails for me. Why don't I love him?—he's a better man than you! Why don't you? *Is* he a better man than you? He's usage, he's honor, he's the right thing, he's the breed and the tradition,—a gentleman. You're your erring, incalculable self. I suppose we women will trust his sort and love your sort to the very end of time. . . ." We lay side by side and nibbled at grass stalks as we talked. It seemed enormously unreasonable to us that two people who had come to the pitch of easy and confident affection and happiness that held between us should be obliged to part and shun one another, or murder half the substance of their lives. We felt ourselves crushed and beaten by an indiscriminating machine which destroys happiness in the service of jealousy. "The mass of people don't feel these things in quite the same manner as we feel them," she said. "Is it bcause we're different in grain, or educated out of some primitive instinct?"

"It's because we've explored love a little, and they know no more than the gateway," I said. "Lust and then jealousy; their simple conception—and we have gone past all that and wandered hand in hand. . . ."

I remember that for a time we watched two of that larger sort of gull, whose wings are brownish-white, circle and hover against the blue. And then we lay and looked at a band of water mirror clear far out to sea, and wondered why the breeze that rippled all the rest should leave it so serene.

"And in this State of ours," I resumed.

"Eh!" said Isabel, rolling over into a sitting posture and looking out at the horizon. "Let's talk no more of things we can never see. Talk to me of the work you are doing and all we shall do—after we have parted. We've said too little of that. We've had our red life, and it's over. Thank Heaven!—though we stole it! Talk about your work, dear, and the things we'll go on doing—just as though we were still together. We'll still be together in a sense—through all these things we have in common."

And so we talked about politics and our outlook. We were interested to the pitch of self-forgetfulness. We weighed persons and forces, discussed the probabilities of the next general election, the steady drift of public opinion in the north and west away from Liberalism toward us. It was very manifest that in spite of Wardenham and the *Expurgator*, we should come into the new Government strongly. The party had no one else, all the young men were formally and informally with us; Esmeer would have office, Lord Tarvrille, I . . . and very probably there would be something for Shoesmith. "And for my own part," I said, "I count on a backing on the Liberal side. For the last two years we've been forcing competition in constructive legislation between the parties. The Liberals have not been long in following up our Endowment of Motherhood lead. They'll have to give votes and lip service anyhow. Half the readers of the *Blue Weekly*, they say, are Liberals. . . .

"I remember talking about things of this sort with old Willersley," I said, "ever so many years ago. It was some place near Locarno, and we looked down the lake that shone weltering—just as now we look over the sea. And then we dreamt in an indistinct featureless way of all that you and I are doing now."

"I!" said Isabel, and laughed.

"Well, of some such thing," I said, and remained for awhile silent, thinking of Locarno.

I recalled once more the largeness, the release from small personal things that I had felt in my youth; statecraft became real and wonderful again with the memory, the gigantic handling of gigantic problems. I began to talk out my thoughts, sitting up beside her, as I could never talk of them to any one but Isabel; began to recover again the purpose that lay under all my political ambitions and adjustments and anticipations. I saw the State, splendid and wide as I had seen it in that first travel of mine, but now it was no mere distant prospect of spires and pinnacles, but populous with fine-trained, bold-thinking, bold-doing people. It was as if I had forgotten for a long time and now remembered with amazement.

At first, I told her, I had been altogether at a loss how I could do anything to battle against the aimless muddle of our world; I had wanted a clue—until she had come into my life questioning, suggesting, unconsciously illuminating. "But I have done nothing," she protested. I declared she had done everything in growing to education under my eyes, in reflecting again upon all the processes that had made myself, so that instead of abstractions and blue-books and bills and devices, I had realized the world of mankind as a crowd needing before all things fine women and men. We'd spoilt ourselves in learning that, but anyhow we had our lesson. Before her I was in a nineteenth-century darkness, dealing with the nation as if it were a crowd of selfish men, forgetful of women and children and that shy wild thing in the hearts of men, love, which must be drawn upon as it has never been drawn upon before, if the State is to live. I saw now how it is possible to bring the loose factors of a great realm together, to create a mind of literature and thought in it, and the expression of a purpose, to make it self-conscious and fine. I had it all clear before me, so that at a score of points I could presently begin. The *Blue Weekly* was a centre of force. Already we had given Imperialism a criticism, and leavened half the press from our columns. Our movement consolidated and spread. We should presently come into power. Everything moved towards our hands. We should be able to get at the schools, the services, the universities, the church; enormously increase the endowment of research, and organize what was sorely wanted, a criticism of research; contrive a closer contact between the press and creative intellectual life; foster literature, clarify, strengthen the public consciousness, develop social organization and a sense of the State. Men were coming to us every day, brilliant young peers like Lord Dentonhill, writers like Carnot and Cresswell. It filled me with pride to win such men. "We stand for so much more than we seem to stand for," I said. I opened my heart to her, so freely that I hesitate so to open my heart even to the reader, telling of projects and ambitions I cherished, of my consciousness of great powers and widening opportunities. . . .

Isabel watched me as I talked.

She too, I think, had forgotten these things for a while. For it is curious and I think a very significant thing that since we had become lovers, we had talked very little of the broader things that had once so strongly gripped our imaginations.

"It's good," I said, "to talk like this to you, to get back to youth and great ambitions with you. There have been times lately when politics has seemed the pettiest game played with mean tools for mean ends—and none the less so that the happiness of three hundred million people might be touched by our follies. I talk to no one else like this. . . . And now I think of parting, I think but of how much more I might have talked to you. . . ."

Things drew to an end at last, but after we had spoken of a thousand things.

"We've talked away our last half day," I said, staring over my shoulder at the blazing sunset sky behind us. "Dear, it's been the last day of our lives for us. . . . It doesn't seem like the last day of our lives. Or any day."

"I wonder how it will feel?" said Isabel.

"It will be very strange at first—not to be able to tell you things."

"I've a superstition that after—after we've parted—if ever I go into my room and talk, you'll hear. You'll be—somewhere."

"I shall be in the world—yes."

"I don't feel as though these days ahead were real. Here we are, here we remain."

"Yes, I feel that. As though you and I were two immortals, who didn't live in time and space at all, who never met, who couldn't part, and here we lie on Olympus. And those two poor creatures who did meet, poor little Richard Remington and Isabel Rivers, who met and loved too much and had to part, they part and go their ways, and we lie here and watch them, you and I. She'll cry, poor dear."

"She'll cry. She's crying now!"

"Poor little beasts! I think he'll cry too. He winces. He could—for tuppence. I didn't know he had lachrymal glands at all until a little while ago. I suppose all love is hysterical, and a little foolish. Poor mites! Silly little pitiful creatures! How we have blundered! Think how we must look to God! Well, we'll pity them, and then we'll inspire him to stiffen up again—and do as we've determined he shall do. We'll see it through,—we who lie here on the cliff. They'll be mean at times, and horrid at times; we know them! Do you see her, a poor little fine lady in a great house,—she sometimes goes to her room and writes."

"She writes for his *Blue Weekly* still."

"Yes. Sometimes—I hope. And he's there in the office with a bit of her copy in his hand."

"Is it as good as if she still talked it over with him before she wrote it? Is it?"

"Better, I think. Let's play it's better—anyhow. It may be that talking over was rather mixed with love-making. After all, love-making is joy rather than magic. Don't let's pretend about that even. . . . Let's go on watching him. I don't see why her writing shouldn't be better. Indeed I don't. See! There he goes down along the Embankment to Westminster just like a real man, for all that he's smaller than a grain of dust. What is running round inside that speck of a head of his? Look at him going past the policemen, specks too—selected large ones from the country. I think he's going to dinner with the Speaker—some old thing like that. Is his face harder or commoner or stronger?—I can't quite see. . . . And now he's up and speaking in the House. Hope he'll hold on to the thread. He'll have to plan his speeches to the very end of his days—and learn the headings."

"Isn't she up in the women's gallery to hear him?"

"No. Unless it's by accident."

"She's there," she said.

"Well, by accident it happens. Not too many accidents, Isabel. Never any more adventure for us, dear, now. . . . No! They play the game, you know. They've begun late, but now they've got to. You see it's not so very hard for them since you and I, my dear, are here, always faithfully here on this warm cliff of love, accomplished, watching and helping them under high heaven. It isn't so *very* hard. Rather good in some ways. Some people *have* to be broken a little. Can you see Altiora down there, by any chance?"

"She's too little to be seen," she said.

"Can you see the sins they once committed?"

"I can only see you here beside me, dear—for ever. For all my life, dear, till I die. Was that—the sin? . . ."

I took her to the station, and after she had gone I was to drive to Dover and cross to Calais by the night boat. I couldn't, I felt, return to London. We walked over the crest and down to the little station of Martin Mill side by side, talking at first in broken fragments, for the most part of unimportant things.

"None of this," she said abruptly, "seems in the slightest degree real to me. I've got no sense of things ending."

"We're parting," I said.

"We're parting—as people part in a play. It's distressing. But I don't feel as though you and I were really never to see each other again for years. Do you?"

I thought. "No," I said.

"After we've parted I shall look to talk it over with you."

"So shall I."

"That's absurd."

"Absurd."

"I feel as if you'd always be there, just about where you are now. Invisible perhaps, but there. We've spent so much of our lives joggling elbows. . . ."

" Yes. Yes. I don't in the least realize it. I suppose I shall begin to when the train goes out of the station. Are we wanting in imagination, Isabel? "

" I don't know. We've always assumed it was the other way about."

" Even when the train goes out of the station——! I've seen you into so many trains."

" I shall go on thinking of things to say to you—things to put in your letters. For years to come. How can I ever stop thinking in that way now? We've got into each other's brains."

" It isn't real," I said; " nothing is real. The world's no more than a fantastic dream. Why are we parting, Isabel? "

" I don't know. It seems now supremely silly. I suppose we have to. Can't we meet?—don't you think we shall meet even in dreams? "

" We'll meet a thousand times in dreams," I said.

" I wish we could dream at the same time," said Isabel. . . . " Dream walks. I can't believe, dear, I shall never have a walk with you again."

" If I'd stayed six months in America," I said, " we might have walked long walks and talked long talks for all our lives."

" Not in a world of Baileys," said Isabel. " And anyhow—— "
She stopped short. I looked interrogation.

" We've loved," she said. . . .

I took her ticket, saw to her luggage, and stood by the door of the compartment. " Good-bye," I said a little stiffly, conscious of the people upon the platform. She bent above me, white and dusky, looking at me very steadfastly.

" Come here," she whispered. " Never mind the porters. What can they know? Just one time more—I must.''

She rested her hand against the door of the carriage and bent down upon me, and put her cold, moist lips to mine.

CHAPTER THE THIRD

THE BREAKING POINT

I

AND then we broke down. We broke our faith with both Margaret and Shoesmith, fleeing career and duty and good lives, and went away together.

It is only now almost a year after these events that I can begin to see what happened to me. At the time it seemed to me I was a natural responsible creature, but indeed I had not parted from her two days before I became a monomaniac in whose world nothing mattered but Isabel. Every truth had to be squared to that obsession, every duty. It astounds me now to think how I forgot Margaret, forgot my work, forgot everything but that we two were parted. I still believe that with better chances we might have escaped the consequences of the emotional storm that presently seized us both. But we had no foresight of that, and no preparation for it and her circumstances betrayed us. It was partly Shoesmith's unwisdom in delaying his marriage until after the end of the session— partly my own amazing folly in returning within four days to Westminster. But we were all of us intent upon the defeat of scandal and the complete restoration of appearances. It seemed necessary that Shoesmith's marriage should not seem to be hurried, still more necessary that I should not vanish inexplicably. I had to be visible with Margaret in London just as much as possible; we went to restaurants, we visited the theatre; we could even contemplate the possibility of my presence at the wedding. For that, however, we had schemed a week-end visit to Wales, and a fictitious sprained ankle at the last moment which would justify my absence. . . .

I cannot convey to you the intolerable wretchedness and rebellion of my separation from Isabel. It seemed that in the past two years all my thoughts had spun commissures to Isabel's brain, and I could think of nothing that did not lead me surely to the need of the one intimate I had found in the world. I came back to the House and the office and my home, I filled all my days with appointments and duty, and it did not save me in the least from a lonely emptiness such as I had never felt before in all my life. I had little sleep. In the daytime I did a hundred things, I even spoke in the House on two occasions, and by my own low standards spoke well, and it seemed to me that I was going about in my own brain like a hushed survivor in a house whose owner lies dead upstairs.

I came to a crisis after that wild dinner of Tarvrille's. Something in that stripped my soul bare.

It was an occasion made absurd and strange by the odd accident that the house caught fire upstairs while we were dining below. It was a men's dinner—" A dinner of all sorts," said Tarvrille, when he invited me; " everything from Evesham and Gane to Wilkins the author, and Heaven knows what will happen!" I remember that afterwards Tarvrille was accused of having planned the fire to make his dinner a marvel and a memory. It was indeed a wonderful occasion, and I suppose if I had not been altogether drenched in misery, I should have found the same wild amusement in it that glowed in all the others. There were one or two university dons, Lord George Fester, the racing man, Panmure, the artist, two or three big City men, Weston Massinghay and another prominent Liberal whose name I can't remember, the three men Tarvrille had promised and Esmeer, Lord Wrassleton, Waulsort, the member for Monckton, Neal, and several others. We began a little coldly, with duologues, but the conversation was already becoming general—so far as such a long table permitted—when the fire asserted itself.

It asserted itself first as a penetrating and emphatic smell of burning rubber,—it was caused by the fusing of an electric wire. The reek forced its way into the discussion of the Peking massacres that had sprung up between Evesham, Waulsort, and the others at the end of the table. " Something burning," said the man next to me.

" Something must be burning," said Panmure.

Tarvrille hated undignified interruptions. He had a particularly imperturbable butler with a cadaverous set face and an eye of rigid disapproval. He spoke to this individual over his shoulder. " Just see, will you," he said, and caught up the pause in the talk to his left.

Wilkins was asking questions, and I, too, was curious. The story of the siege of the Legations in China in the year 1900 and all that followed upon that, is just one of those disturbing interludes in history that refuse to join on to that general schéme of protestation by which civilization is maintained. It is a break in the general flow of experience as disconcerting to statecraft as the robbery of my knife and the scuffle that followed it had been to me when I was a boy at Penge. It is like a tear in a curtain revealing quite unexpected backgrounds. I had never given the business a thought for years; now this talk brought back a string of pictures to my mind; how the reliefs arrived and the plundering began, how section after section of the International Army was drawn into murder and pillage, how the infection spread upward until the wives of Ministers were busy looting, and the very sentinels stripped and crawled like snakes into the Palace they were set to guard. It did not stop at robbery, men were murdered, women, being plundered, were outraged, children were butchered; strong men had found themselves with arms in a lawless, defenceless city, and this had followed. Now it was all recalled.

" Respectable ladies addicted to district visiting at home were as bad as any one," said Panmure. " Glazebrook told me of one— flushed like a woman at a bargain sale, he said—and when he pointed out to her that the silk she'd got was bloodstained, she just said, ' Oh, bother!' and threw it aside and went back. . . ."

We became aware that Tarvrille's butler had returned. We tried not to seem to listen.

"Beg pardon, m'lord," he said. "The house *is* on fire, m'lord."

"Upstairs, m'lord."

"Just overhead, m'lord."

"The maids are throwing water, m'lord, and I've telephoned *fire*."

"No, m'lord, no immediate danger."

"It's all right," said Tarvrille to the table generally. "Go on! It's not a general conflagration, and the fire brigade won't be five minutes. Don't see that it's our affair. The stuff's insured. They say old Lady Paskershortly was dreadful. Like a harpy. The Dowager Empress had shown her some little things of hers. Pet things—hidden away. Susan went straight for them—used to take an umbrella for the silks. Born shoplifter."

It was evident he didn't want his dinner spoilt, and we played up loyally.

"This is recorded history," said Wilkins,—"practically. It makes one wonder about unrecorded history. In India, for example."

But nobody touched that.

"Thompson," said Tarvrille to the imperturbable butler, and indicating the table generally, "champagne. Champagne. Keep it going."

"M'lord," and Thompson marshaled his assistants.

Some man I didn't know began to remember things about Mandalay. "It's queer," he said, "how people break out at times;" and told his story of an army doctor, brave, public-spirited, and, as it happened, deeply religious, who was caught one evening by the excitement of plundering—and stole and hid, twisted the wrist of a boy until it broke, and was afterwards overcome by wild remorse.

I watched Evesham listening intently. "Strange," he said, "very strange. We are such stuff as thieves are made of. And in China, too, they murdered people—for the sake of murdering. Apart, so to speak, from mercenary considerations. I'm afraid there's no doubt of it in certain cases. No doubt at all. Young soldiers—fresh from German high schools and English homes!"

"Did *our* people?" asked some patriot.

"Not so much. But I'm afraid there were cases. . . . Some of the Indian troops were pretty bad."

Gane picked up the tale with confirmations.

It is all printed in the vividest way as a picture upon my memory, so that were I a painter I think I could give the deep rich browns and warm grays beyond the brightly lit table, the various distinguished faces, strongly illuminated, interested and keen, above the black and white of evening dress, the alert men-servants with their heavier, clean-shaved faces indistinctly seen in the dimness behind. Then this was colored emotionally for me by my aching sense of loss and sacrifice, and by the chance trend of our talk to the breaches and unrealities of the civilized scheme. We seemed a little transitory circle of light in a universe of darkness and violence; an effect to which the diminishing smell of burning rubber, the trampling of feet overhead, the swish of water, added enormously. Everybody—unless, perhaps, it was Evesham—drank rather carelessly because of the suppressed excitement of our situation, and talked the louder and more freely.

"But what a flimsy thing our civilization is!" said Evesham; "a mere thin net of habits and associations!"

"I suppose those men came back," said Wilkins.

"Lady Paskershortly did!" chuckled Evesham.

"How do they fit it in with the rest of their lives?" Wilkins speculated. "I suppose there's Peking-stained police officers, Peking-stained J.P.'s—trying petty pilferers in the severest manner. . . ."

Then for a time things became preposterous. There was a sudden cascade of water by the fireplace, and then absurdly the ceiling began to rain upon us, first at this point and then that. "My new suit!" cried some one. "Perrrrrr-up pe-rr"—a new vertical line of blackened water would establish itself and form a spreading pool upon the gleaming cloth. The men nearest would arrange catchment areas of plates and flower bowls. "Draw up!" said Tarvrille, "draw up. That's the bad end of the table!" He turned to the imperturbable butler. "Take round bath towels," he said; and presently the men behind us were offering—with inflexible dignity— "Port wine, Sir. Bath towel, Sir!" Waulsort with streaks of blackened water on his forehead, was suddenly reminded of a wet year when he had followed the French army manœuvres. An animated dispute sprang up between him and Neal about the relative efficiency of the new French and German field guns. Wrassleton joined in and a little drunken shriveled Oxford don of some sort with a black-splashed shirt front who presently silenced them all by the immensity and particularity of his knowledge of field artillery. Then the talk drifted to Sedan and the effect of dead horses upon drinking-water, which brought Wrassleton and Weston Massinghay into a dispute of great vigor and emphasis. "The trouble in South Africa," said Weston Massinghay, "wasn't that we didn't boil our water. It was that we didn't boil our men. The Boers drank the same stuff we did. *They* didn't get dysentery."

That argument went on for some time. I was attacked across the table by a man named Burshort about my Endowment of Motherhood schemes, but in the gaps of that debate I could still hear Weston Massinghay at intervals repeat in a rather thickened voice: "*They* didn't get dysentery."

I think Evesham went early. The rest of us clustered more and more closely towards the drier end of the room, the table was pushed along, and the area beneath the extinguished conflagration abandoned to a tinkling, splashing company of pots and pans and bowls and baths. Everybody was now disposed to be hilarious and noisy, to say startling and aggressive things; we must have sounded a queer clamor to a listener in the next room. The devil inspired them to begin baiting me. "Ours isn't the Tory party any more," said Burshort. "Remington has made it the Obstetric party."

"That's good!" said Weston Massinghay, with all his teeth gleaming; "I shall use that against you in the House!"

"I shall denounce you for abusing private confidences if you do," said Tarvrille.

The little shriveled don who had been omniscient about guns joined in the baiting, and displayed himself a venomous creature. Something in his eye told me he knew of Isabel and hated me for it. "Love and fine thinking," he began, a little thickly, and knocking over a wineglass with a too easy gesture. "Love and fine thinking. Two things don't go together. No ph'losophy worth a damn ever came out of excesses of love. Salt Lake City—Piggott—Ag—Agapemone again—no works to matter."

Everybody laughed.

I made some remark, I forget what, but he overbore me.

"Real things we want are Hate—Hate and *coarse* think'n. I b'long to the school of Mr. F's Aunt——"

"What?" said some one, intent.

"In 'Little Dorrit,'" explained Tarvrille; "go on!"

"Hate a fool," said my assailant.

Tarvrille glanced at me. I smiled to conceal the loss of my temper.

"Hate," said the little man, emphasizing his point with a clumsy fist. "Hate's the driving force. What's m'rality?—hate of rotten goings on. What's patriotism?—hate of int'loping foreigners. What's Radicalism?—hate of lords. What's Toryism?—hate of disturbance. It's all hate—hate from top to bottom. Hate of a mess. Remington owned it the other day, said he hated a—mu'll. There you are! If you couldn't get hate into an election, damn it (hic) people wou'n't poll. Poll for love!—no' me!"

He paused, but before any one could speak he had resumed.

"Then this about fine thinking. Like going into a bear pit armed with a tagle—talgent—talgent galv'nometer. Like going to

fight a mad dog with Shasepear and the Bible. Fine thinking—
what we want is the thickes' thinking we can get. Thinking that
stands up alone. Taf Reforms means work for all,—thassort of
thing."

The gentleman from Cambridge paused. "*You* a flag!" he
said. "I'd as soon go to ba'ell und' wet tissue paper!"

My best answer on the spur of the moment was: "The Japanese
did." Which was absurd.

I went on to some other reply, I forget exactly what, and the talk
of the whole table drew round me. It was an extraordinary revelation to me. Every one was unusually careless and outspoken, and it
was amazing how manifestly they echoed the feeling of this old Tory
spokesman. They were quite friendly to me, they regarded me and
the *Blue Weekly* as valuable party assets for Toryism, but it was
clear they attached no more importance to what were my realities
then they did to the remarkable therapeutic claims of Mrs. Eddy.
They were flushed and amused, perhaps they went a little too far in
their resolves to draw me, but they left the impression on my mind of
men irrevocably set upon narrow and cynical views of political life.
For them the political struggle was a game, whose counters were
human hate and human credulity; their real aim was just every one's
aim, the preservation of the class and way of living to which their
lives were attuned. They did not know how tired I was, how exhausted
mentally and morally, nor how cruel their convergent attack on me
chanced to be. But my temper gave way, I became tart and fierce,
perhaps my replies were a trifle absurd, and Tarville, with that quick
eye and sympathy of his, came to the rescue. Then for a time I sat
silent and drank port wine while the others talked. The disorder of
the room, the still dripping ceiling, the noise, the displaced ties and
crumpled shirts of my companions, jarred on my tormented
nerves. . . .

It was long past midnight when we dispersed. I remember Tarville coming with me into the hall, and then suggesting we should
go upstairs to see the damage. A man-servant carried up two flickering candles for us. One end of the room was gutted, curtains,
hangings, several chairs and tables were completely burnt, the panel-
ing was scorched and warped, three smashed windows made the candles flare and gutter, and some scraps of broken china still lay on the
puddled floor.

As we surveyed this, Lady Tarville appeared, back from some
party, a slender, white-cloaked, satin-footed figure with amazed blue
eyes beneath her golden hair. I remember how stupidly we laughed
at her surprise.

(*To be concluded*)

THE FORUM
FOR JUNE 1911

ARBITRATION AND COMMON SENSE

CHARLES VALE

HERE is no more important question before the country than the Anglo-American Arbitration Agreement. It is not easy to change human nature, and men have too long been in the habit of regarding their ideals as vague and impracticable dreams, beyond the range of actual experience or effectiveness. It is time that they learned to consider them as normal, possible, realizable. Men have prayed for peace, from generation to generation; then gone forth valiantly to war—war, in ninety-nine cases out of a hundred, preventable even in this curious civilization of passion and prejudice. Now—not for the first time—comes a proposal rich in promise. Welcomed unmistakably by the enlightened public opinion of the two countries, and officially endorsed by their foremost representatives, the movement cannot be allowed to fail. There will be petty objections; but no spirit of littleness can prevail when the overwhelming sentiment of all reasonable men is in favor of an agreement conceived in the interest of humanity, and not of any individual man, or group of men. The treaty is to bind all English-speaking peoples to refrain forever from internecine war; but in its moral effects, not long delayed, it must lead to the peace of the world, or make war so strange, so repugnant and so difficult, that the nation which wantonly undertakes it will be regarded as outcast and self-condemned. Whatever practical difficulties may rise with regard to details, it is no small matter that five hundred millions of the world's inhabitants shall have solemnly agreed to stay their

hands from strife and submit all disputes to the arbitrament of reason. Let only those who know fully what war means, talk now of continuing the crude system of which all but the brutalized and decadent are wearied. That there would ever again have been war between the United States and Great Britain, with or without this agreement, is unbelievable. Yet the agreement is none the less valuable. It is the new Declaration of Independence, the declaration of man's freedom from the old shibboleths and the old barbaric creed— that the sword is mightier than the truth, that those who do not live under the same skies are natural enemies.

It should not be imagined that this is an isolated attempt toward progress. Good work has been done for many years past, notably by the American Conferences on International Arbitration which were held at Washington in 1896 and 1904. These two conferences, separated by an interval of eight years, were memorable gatherings, marked by profound feeling and clear and commanding purpose. They were called at critical times, they were attended by the ablest thinkers of the country, and they culminated in significant resolutions. Many will still recall the eloquent address of Carl Schurz in the earlier conference, calling upon the United States for brave leadership in the arbitration movement—the leadership that was naturally hers, through her peculiar position and strength, safely aloof from the feuds of the old world, with no dangerous neighbors threatening her borders, and no need of vast armaments on land and sea to maintain peace or protect her integrity.   .

"As an American citizen, I cannot contemplate this noble peace mission of my country without a thrill of pride; and I must confess that it touches me like an attack upon the dignity of this Republic when I hear Americans repudiate that peace mission upon the ground of supposed interests of the United States, requiring for their protection or furtherance preparation for warlike action and the incitement of a fighting spirit among our people. To judge from the utterances of some men having the public ear, we are constantly threatened by the evil designs of rival or secretly hostile powers that are eagerly watching every chance to humiliate us, to insult our flag, to balk our policies, to harass our commerce, putting us in imminent danger unless we stand with sword in hand in sleepless watch, and cover the seas with warships. What a poor idea those indulging in such talk have of the true position of their country among the nations of the world!"

And now, definitely and authoritatively, the work begun by these pioneers is being carried to its conclusion—one may well use here the trite phrase, *logical conclusion;* for there has been little logic before in the conduct of international discussions, with fleets and armies as the decisive arguments. But the spirit which made possible the Hague Tribunal, was bound to press on to further achievements. President Taft has used his influence in accordance with the highest traditions of his great office, and British statesmen, ignoring the exceptional bitterness of their own political situation, have responded whole-heartedly and without ambiguity. The attitude of the public has been unmistakable. There is a general sense that history is in the making—history of a rarer and finer kind than the usual records of quarrels and campaigns. A meeting was held in the famous Guildhall, attended, as the American Ambassador subsequently said, by " an extraordinarily representative body of British public men, the Prime Minister, the Leader of his Majesty's Opposition, the chief dignitary of the national Church, the English Head of the old Church that once was national, the Chief Rabbi, and the spokesmen for the great Nonconformist churches of the land." There were also representatives of every British colony. Mr. Whitelaw Reid continued:

" May that wonderful union at the Guildhall of all parties and all creeds prefigure the larger union of all branches of our race on the President's proposal that henceforth, as between English-speaking people, the settlement of differences by war shall be set aside at once and forever as immoral, unnatural and impossible."

At the meeting itself, Mr. Asquith, the Prime Minister, said:

" The unique situation which we have met to recognize and welcome has not been organized or engineered by the apparatus of diplomacy. The seed which the President of the United States cast fell on the ground prepared to receive it. That which a few years ago, even a few months ago, might have been regarded as the dream of idealists, has not only passed into the domain of practical statesmanship, but has become the settled purpose of two great democracies. The profound significance of the new departure is that between Great Britain and the United States, whatever the gravity of the issue and the magnitude of the interests involved, whatever the poignancy of the feelings it arouses ; there will be a definite abandonment of war as a possible solution, and the substitution of argument for force and the supersession by judicial methods of the old ordeal of battle."

After declaring that the Anglo-American irenicon involved no ulterior purpose and implied no menace to other nations, the Premier continued:

" But we may hope and believe that other things will follow. It is not for us to dictate or to preach to other nations, but if the United States and Great Britain renounce war, a step will be taken of immeasurable and incomparable significance in the onward progress of humanity."

Mr. Asquith then moved a resolution pledging support to the proposed agreement " as serving the highest interests of the two nations and as tending to promote the peace of the world." It was adopted enthusiastically and unanimously.

" That which a few years ago, even a few months ago, might have been regarded as the dream of idealists, has not only passed into the domain of practical statesmanship, but has become the settled purpose of two great democracies." It seems strange to realize that these are the words of the Prime Minister of one nation in effective reply to the President of another. " If the United States and Great Britain renounce war, a step will be taken of immeasurable significance in the onward progress of humanity." It is in this significance, and not merely in the actual scope of the proposed agreement, that those who believe in progress will find their incentive and their reward. A high responsibility rests upon all who can influence public opinion. The press has done much to inflame animosities, in the past. It can do more in the cause of peace, now and in the future.

POLITICAL INNOVATIONS

HON. ROBERT W. BONYNGE

No thoughtful citizen can fail to realize that great and far-reaching changes in the form of our government as originally established are impending and are in actual progress. After a century and a quarter of unprecedented national growth and development under the representative form of government, many of the States of the Union have in recent years adopted radical innovations in that system. If the movement now well under way continues to spread and finally reaches the National Government, the result must ultimately be the overthrow of the Republic and the substitution in its place of a pure democracy.

Our institutions were not hastily adopted; they should not be thoughtlessly discarded. Are we prepared to make the change?

In considering the issue thus raised, it is well to admit at the outset that there are defects in our present representative system of government which must be corrected. There can be no palliation for the corruption which unfortunately has too frequently characterized some sessions of the Legislatures of nearly every State in the Union. The connection between large private interests and public affairs has been thoroughly exploited in the magazines and press of the country. It is not at all necessary to our purpose to consider to what extent the writers of some of the sensational articles which have recently appeared have drawn upon their imaginations in order to make readable articles and saleable copies. The real problem is to find correct and adequate remedies for such defects as are known to exist in our present republican form of government. Can we correct those evils without destroying the system? Or must we, in the face of the fact that democracies have in all ages of the world's history led through anarchy to despotism, passively acquiesce in the destruction of the Republic and the substitution of a democracy? Will the impending innovations cure existing defects and remedy the evils complained of, or will they only augment and intensify them? These questions must soon be authoritatively decided by the American people. They will be briefly considered in this article in the inverse order from that in which they have been stated.

It may be advisable, first, to consider the changes that have taken place in the Federal and in many of the State Governments, and the effects, so far as apparent, of those changes. The form of the Federal Government has not been essentially modified. The most important change thus far made has been in the manner of selecting the President and Vice-President. They are no longer selected by the Electoral College as the result of the deliberations of its members. As is well understood the Electoral College simply acts as the registering body to record in an official way the choice theretofore made by the voters of the respective States between the candidates of the opposing political parties. It seems probable that before long an amendment to the Federal Constitution will be submitted to the States providing for the direct election of United States Senators by the people of the respective States. Indirectly this result has already been accomplished in many of the States through the adoption of the system of nominating candidates for the United States Senate at direct primaries, and in some of the States by voting directly for those candidates at popular elections. The Legislatures in those States perform practically the same functions in the election of United States Senators as the Electoral College does in the election of the President and Vice-President.

Already there are unmistakable signs that an agitation will soon be started for a Federal constitutional amendment providing for the election by popular vote of the Federal Judiciary for limited terms.

The changes in the Federal Government which have thus far been adopted have not been fundamental in their nature. While they tend indirectly to the creation of a democracy by permitting the people directly to choose their Executive and their Senators instead of doing so through some other body created by them, they do not immediately affect the character of the government. The Federal Government still remains a representative republic.

It is in our State Governments, and particularly in the newer States of the West, that fundamental innovations have been and are each year being made. When we entered upon our national career the total population of the country was less than 4,000,000 people, and it was practically homogeneous in its character. At that time there were restrictions upon manhood suffrage in each of the thirteen original States. Woodrow Wilson, in his *History of the American People,* states that probably not more than 120,000 people out of the 4,000,000 inhabitants, according to the census of 1790, had the right of suffrage. Gradually those restrictions were one by one removed, until about the time of Andrew Jackson's administration universal free manhood suffrage prevailed in all the States. At the close of the Civil War the right of suffrage was granted to the former slaves. Since then five States of the Union—Wyoming, Colorado, Utah, Idaho, and Washington—have given to women the right to vote.

While these changes have been taking place the population of the country has increased to more than 90,000,000 and every race and nationality on the face of the globe has contributed its quota to the heterogeneous total. Moreover, the duties imposed upon voters have been enormously increased. Instead of choosing a few of the principal officers at popular elections, as was formerly the rule, in most of the States the voters are now called upon to select at elections practically all important public officers. With the growth of population and with the necessary increase in all governmental functions, the number of officers has, as a consequence, multiplied many fold. It is not unusual now for an official ballot in some States to have as many as one hundred or more names of candidates for different offices printed on it.

It is manifestly impossible for ordinarily intelligent and busy citizens to know personally anything whatever about the qualifications of so many candidates. As a rule, they inform themselves in a general way regarding the candidates for the leading offices, and the balance of the ticket wins or loses in the great majority of elections according to the fate of the head of the ticket. There are some striking exceptions to the rule, such as the election of William Travers Jerome to the district attorneyship in New York City, and the election of Judge Ben B. Lindsey to the bench of the Juvenile Court in Denver. But those exceptions only serve to prove the general rule.

The result is, that owing to the hopeless confusion in which many voters find themselves, there has been a growing tendency on the part of a large number of busy and intelligent citizens to refrain from voting at all. Another considerable percentage of the people either vote at presidential elections only or vote for some candidate for the leading office to be filled at the election and do not vote at all for the candidates for the minor offices.

In addition to the general elections, the voters in a number of the States are now expected to select from the numerous aspirants at direct primaries the candidates of their political party for nominations for the many offices to be filled later by popular election. This method of nominating candidates, while having some advantages over the old method of selecting the candidates in party conventions, has not been in force long enough in any of the States to demonstrate fully its ultimate effects. It takes a long period of years for innovations in political methods to develop their true tendencies and effects. It does not seem unreasonable to expect that direct primaries applied to all offices at present elective will only add to the already great confusion of voters and finally result in fewer of the busy and intelligent people participating in the primaries.

In ten or a dozen States of the Union the initiative and referendum methods of legislation have been adopted. Oregon was the first State to adopt and put into practical operation " this instrument or tool of democracy," as it has been very correctly called. Colorado, at the election last fall, by a large majority of those citizens who were sufficiently interested in the question to vote upon it, adopted the Oregon initiative and referendum plan in all important respects except as to the manner of publishing the measures to be voted upon by the people. Ten other States and many municipalities all over the country have adopted the Oregon plan in some modified form. The other States in which it has been established in one form or another, or in which it is permissive, are South Dakota, Nevada, Montana, Illinois, Utah, Texas, Maine, Missouri, Oklahoma, and Arkansas, a sufficiently large number of the States to demonstrate that the question of its extension with the consequent change in our form of government has become a present-day problem which must be intelligently and seriously met. It is also being advocated in a number of other States, and recently a league composed, among others, of a number of United States Senators and Representatives, has been organized to conduct a campaign for its general adoption throughout the country. If the movement for its adoption proves successful and finally extends to the National Government, it must, we believe, as heretofore stated, lead to the overthrow of the Republic and the erection of an unrestrained democracy upon its ruins. It is true that representatives are still elected in those States that have adopted the initiative and referendum and the form of the legislative department of the government is still maintained; but it is only the form that remains. Augustus Cæsar was careful to maintain the forms of the republic after the establishment of the Roman Empire.

It cannot be expected that legislators will seriously discuss and divide upon contested questions when the easy method is presented to them of avoiding any responsibility or risk of unpopularity by referring all contested questions to the people under a referendum. The Legislature will then inevitably in the course of time become a mere registering body and not a deliberative assembly, in exactly the same way as the Electoral College has ceased to discharge its functions.

The constitutionality of the Oregon method of legislation was passed upon by the Oregon Supreme Court. That Court held that because the Legislature might repeal a law enacted by the people under an initiative petition the Oregon constitutional amendments for the establishment of the initiative and referendum did not infringe the Federal constitutional provision " that the United States shall guarantee to every State in this Union a republican form of government." It was admitted by the Court that a " republican form of government," within the meaning of the Constitution, was a representative form of government, consisting of three departments, the executive, legislative, and judicial. A careful study of the opinion of the Court would seem to indicate that the Court accepted the form for the substance of a republican government. While the Legislature may, as the Court held, repeal laws enacted by the people, it must also be remembered that under the referendum the people have the right to submit the repealing act to a vote of the people, and if a majority of the people voting on the proposition should declare against the repeal, the repealing act would become ineffective and the original law enacted by the people through the initiative proceeding would remain in force. Consequently, the legislative powers of the general assembly are practically destroyed and the people directly, and not

through their representatives, legislate. In other words, a government adopting the initiative and referendum method of legislating is
effectually changed from the republican form, which is a representative form of government, to a democracy in which the people directly
and not by their representatives legislate. Another case involving the
same question is now pending before the Supreme Court of the United
States, so that we may expect to have before long a final decision
from that tribunal upon the interesting constitutional problems involved. In the meantime, the people are having an opportunity to
demonstrate the practical workings of the system.

Under the Oregon and Colorado constitutions eight per cent. of
the voters may by petition have submitted to the people the full text
of any proposed statute or constitutional amendment, and if a majority of those voting thereon vote in the affirmative the measure, whether
a proposed law or a constitutional amendment, becomes a part of the
law or constitution of the State without any further action of any
kind by the Legislature, or the Governor, who is deprived of his veto
power over such measures.

This is known as the " initiative " method. In the same way, five
per cent. of the voters may cause any law passed by the Legislature to
be referred to the people or the Legislature may voluntarily cause any
bill passed by it to be referred to the people and they, by a majority
vote thereon of those voting on the proposition, may determine
whether or not the law shall continue in force. This method is known
as the " referendum."

It was in 1902 that Oregon amended its State constitution providing for the initiative and referendum methods of legislation. The
first year in which the system was put into practical operation was
1904. In that year two measures were submitted thereunder to the
people; in 1906, 11 measures; in 1908, 19; and in 1910, 32 measures,
consisting of 12 constitutional amendments and 20 statutes. The
pamphlet printed by the State, containing the text of these 32
measures, submitted in 1910, and a brief argument for and against
each measure, consisted of 202 closely printed pages. In South
Dakota, in which State the full text of the measures submitted to
the people is required to be printed on the official ballot, the
ballot at the last election was approximately seven feet long. Each

voter in Oregon was expected, first, to attend the direct party primary and select from numerous aspirants the nominees of his political party. Then, at the general election later held, he was expected intelligently to discriminate between the numerous candidates of all the political parties for all the elective offices and at the same time and on the same ballot, within a few minutes, to give his deliberate and well-considered judgment upon the merits of 20 statutes and 12 constitutional amendments. He had nothing but the title of the bill to guide him when he entered the polling booth. True, he had previously been furnished with a copy of the printed pamphlet containing the full text of the different measures to be voted upon, and it was therefore expected that from the title which was printed on the ballot he would be able to vote intelligently upon each measure. One of the constitutional amendments, it may be interesting to mention, comprised 36 sections. History does not record that any people at any time ever before undertook to legislate in that wholesale manner.

Every measure submitted, either by initiative or referendum petition, must be accepted or rejected in its entirety. In the case of the constitutional amendment submitted at the last election, which consisted of thirty-six sections, the people either had to vote for all the propositions contained in the amendment or against all. It bore the following title: " For an amendment of Article IV, Constitution of Oregon, increasing initiative, referendum, and recall powers of the people; restricting use of emergency clause and veto power on State and municipal legislation; requiring proportional election of members of Legislative Assembly from the State at large, annual sessions, increasing members' salaries and terms of office; providing for election of Speaker of the House and President of Senate, outside of members; restricting corporate franchises to twenty years; providing ten dollars penalty for unexcused absence from any roll-call, and changing form of oath of office to provide against so-called ' legislative logrolling.' " On this complicated set of questions each voter was expected to vote " yes " or " no."

There is no opportunity whatever afforded under the system for amendment or modification to any part of any measure submitted. The nearest approach to legislation in that manner is to be found in some special rules adopted by the House of Representatives of the

National Government, against which there has strangely enough been so much fulmination by many of the advocates of the initiative and referendum.

In the National House of Representatives bills are sometimes submitted under special rules, which provide that after a certain limited time for debate the measure shall be placed upon its final passage without intervening motion or amendment. Under such rules the members must either vote for the measure in the form in which it is submitted or reject it in its entirety. It must be remembered, however, that the rule cannot be effective unless a majority of the members vote for its adoption. It generally happens that the rule is not adopted unless there is a majority of the House in favor of the bill in the form in which it is later to be presented under the rule. Before the bill reaches that stage elaborate hearings have been had on the bill by the committee having it in charge and amendments have been made to it, frequently changing the entire character of the bill from what it was when originally introduced; members have expressed their views on the subject of the bill in speeches on the floor of the House, and as a result of those deliberations the bill has finally assumed a form which meets the views of a majority of the members. The time for action has then arrived. It is only at that stage that the rule can be adopted.

Under the initiative and referendum system there is no opportunity for deliberation and exchange of conflicting views. Usually the bills submitted are prepared by some interested parties. It is said in Oregon that petitions are frequently circulated among foreigners unfamiliar with our language, who are employed at some of the great construction camps in the State. They sign their names to the petition without any knowledge whatever of its contents. To correct this evil in Oregon it has been seriously proposed that a party signing an initiative or referendum petition shall be required to verify it, much in the same form as a party to a law suit is required to verify a pleading, by stating that he has read the bill to be submitted under an initiative petition, that he knows its contents, and that he is in favor of its adoption.

Even in the ancient democracies of Greece and Rome the measures upon which the people voted were discussed in their hearing and some opportunity was afforded them to understand the arguments for and against the proposition. To a limited extent a discussion can be had of measures submitted under the initiative and referendum method in public meetings and in the newspapers; but it is well understood that a political campaign, during which there are numerous candidates before the people for election and a great variety of complicated measures are at the same time submitted, is not a favorable time for calm and dispassionate deliberation of proposed legislation.

The method offers a great opportunity for the newspapers to extend their influence. They can frequently determine by the attitude they assume the fate of measures. They are impersonal and have no public responsibility. Ordinarily, the citizens do not know the writers of the articles that appear in the press. They cannot be held accountable by the public for the position that they may take on measures, except indirectly through possible loss of subscribers, and then they can readily change their positions. Naturally in many instances the newspapers seek to take the popular side regardless of the merits of the measure. There are all kinds of newspapers, as there are all kinds of people. There are great newspapers, whose managers and editors strive to present conscientiously and honestly their views on public questions, and to take the position on public measures which they believe to be for the best interests of the people. There was a time when editors of the press were great leaders of public opinion. There are a few of that class left, but their number, it is generally conceded, is rapidly diminishing. At the present time it is well understood that a very large number of managers and editors of newspapers regard the publication of a newspaper simply as a business enterprise. Entertaining this view, their course necessarily is dictated by what they believe to be for the best interests of their papers. It is not altogether uncommon to find editors writing strong editorials in favor of a particular party and voting the ticket of the opposing party at the polls.

If we are to turn the legislative department of the government over to the newspapers and make this a government " of the newspapers, for the newspapers, and by the newspapers," it will probably be found necessary to make the office of editor of a newspaper a public office to be filled at a popular election by the people of the community to be served. Indeed, the people of Oregon already recognize that something of that kind will have to be done. At their recent election one of the thirty-two measures submitted was a proposition to establish an Official Gazette to be published by the State and furnished free to the citizens, in which should be printed reports from a People's Board of Inspectors to be created, who should be charged with the duty of investigating the manner in which all other public officials discharged their duties. The bill was not adopted by the people, although nearly 30,000 people voted in its favor, and it is safe to predict that if the initiative and referendum methods are to prevail some similar plan will necessarily be eventually adopted.

Colonel Roosevelt expressed the same idea in a speech recently delivered before the Periodical Publishers of America, in which he is reported to have said: " I feel that a man who writes for the public press, either daily, weekly, or periodically, is just as much a public servant as the public office holder. He has as much power for the public good."

Another innovation which is also finding favor in many parts of the country is known as the " recall." It is a method by which some fixed percentage of the people, varying, as a rule, from five to twenty-five per cent., may by petition require a public officer who has been elected for a definite term to submit in effect to another election. Upon the filing of a petition with the requisite number of signers a special election is called and the people determine whether the officer originally elected shall continue for the term for which he was elected or whether some other candidate shall serve for the balance of the term.

In the constitution of the new State of Arizona the recall is made applicable to the judges of the Courts. Hereafter, in that State, it will not be necessary for the attorney for the unsuccessful litigant to go to the corner grocery to abuse the judge. He is to be furnished with a more effective weapon. He can circulate a petition for the recall of the judge! It is well known with what ease signers can be obtained to almost any petition. Recently in the city of Denver a petition was circulated for an amendment to the city charter to make Denver a " dry " city. It received about 27,000 signatures. The election was held shortly thereafter and there were about 14,000 people who voted for the amendment. It failed to carry. If the signers of the petition had all voted for its adoption it would only have been necessary to have had a few thousand more votes to secure its adoption. The instance is cited to show the ease with which signers to a petition may be secured. We may reasonably expect that with the " recall " applied to all elective offices election days will become so numerous that the average citizen will not have very much time left for his ordinary duties.

Neither is it a wild conjecture to assume, if the tendency shown by these laws is to prevail, that the referendum will finally be applied to the decisions of the courts. It might prove to be a very popular measure. A demagogue would have a splendid opportunity to expound its advantages. He could confidently ask, " Are you not willing to trust the people? " In the state of the feeling existing against the courts among many people all over the country, it would be useless to endeavor to answer the question. What a simple procedure it would be to appeal from the decision of the Court to the people and have the latter determine whether the judgment of the Court should stand as the judgment of the people! If answered in the negative a remedy would be immediately available. A petition could be circulated, which would find ready signers, to recall the judge. This is not a visionary or improbable development of the innovations now in progress. In Rome no Roman citizen could be condemned to capital punishment until he had an opportunity to submit his case to the people. It could be plausibly asked by those favoring the plan: " Are not the people as competent to judge of the merits of any case as a jury selected from the people? " A long array of cases could be cited in which juries have returned verdicts which have been set aside by the Court or which have not met public approval. Unfortunately, it is also true that juries have in some instances been corrupted. Therefore, according to the arguments which have led to the initiative and referendum as applied to the legislative department of the government, we should extend its operation for the same reasons to the judicial department.

This brief summary of some of the more important changes in the form of many of our State Governments is sufficient to demonstrate that the whole tendency of the times is toward the establishment of a pure democracy in which the people shall directly instead of through representatives chosen by them legislate and transact public business. However ideally perfect that form of government may theoretically be, we must determine whether it is a workable system for a country of our vast extent of territory, with its 90,000,000 (soon to become several hundred million) population.

Disregarding, as all the enthusiastic advocates of these reforms insist we should, the experiences of the different cities of Greece, of Rome, and of the mediæval times, because our modern conditions are so different from those which prevailed when the ancient democracies proved to be failures, we ask: " Is there any evidence in contemporaneous history which would justify us in believing that a democracy would be successfully administered by our people? "

In most of the States it has been found that as the duties of electors increase the total percentage of actual voters decreases, except on the most important occasions. Thus, in nearly every State there are a great many electors who only vote at presidential elections. Another large class who vote at State elections refuse to participate in local and municipal elections.

The returns of the recent elections show a large decrease in the number of voters in nearly every State of the Union as compared with the elections in 1908—the presidential election. The falling off in the total number of Republican votes has been accounted for in some States by dissatisfaction with the record of the party on the tariff question, in others, by antagonism to Colonel Roosevelt's activity in the campaign; and in others by different causes.

The fact seems to have been overlooked that there was also in most of the States a decrease in the Democratic vote. In New York State, for instance, John A. Dix, the Democratic candidate for governor in 1910, received 45,489 votes less than Lewis S. Chanler, the Democratic candidate for governor in 1908. In Ohio Governor Harmon received, in 1910, 75,492 votes less than he received as a candidate for governor in 1908. A somewhat similar falling off in Democratic votes occurred in many other States. The same tendency has been noticeable at nearly all the previous elections at which only State officers were to be elected.

It is well known that the number of people who vote on constitutional amendments in the various States is only a small percentage of the entire number of votes cast at the election. The number of people who participate in the old form of primary elections for the selection of delegates to political conventions has gradually decreased until, generally speaking, only those who actively participate in politics now attend the primaries.

The larger number of voters participating in direct primary elections may seem to furnish an argument against the proposition now being advanced. It is true that when direct primaries are first established in a State there is a great increase in the number of votes cast at the primary. All novelties are attractive. The number of people who have voted in Oregon on measures submitted under the initiative and referendum method of legislation has thus far been a very much larger percentage of the total number of votes cast than is generally cast in other States on constitutional amendments. But there have been only four elections in Oregon at which measures have thus been submitted to the people. The novelty has not worn off. Both the direct methods of making nominations and of legislating are in the experimental stage. If past experience proves anything it is that as the novelty wears off the number of voters under either of these methods will gradually decrease. In the course of time it will become evident that well-organized bodies can as effectually but perhaps with a little more difficulty control direct nominations. The fact that busy citizens cannot or will not give up the necessary time to attend the numerous primaries and elections, together with other causes, it may reasonably be assumed, will gradually lead to a decrease in the number of votes cast at direct primaries.

There certainly does not seem to be any good reason that can be assigned why a larger percentage of people would vote upon constitutional and statutory measures submitted under the initiative and referendum than under the old method of voting on constitutional amendments, which was in fact a referendum. It surely is much easier for voters to familiarize themselves with the general principles involved in a constitutional amendment than with the detailed provisions of the full text of numerous statutory and constitutional enactments. We, therefore, have a right, it seems, to conclude that in the course of time the number of people who will vote on measures submitted under the initiative and referendum, except on rare occasions, will be no greater than those who now vote on constitutional amendments.

It may be said the provisions of statutory enactments have a more direct interest for the people than the fundamental principles

involved in constitutional amendments. That is true as to some statutes; but some constitutional amendments, such as those that deal
with matters of taxation, sumptuary regulations, and franchise privileges, affect the people as directly as any legislative measures. It is
for this reason that upon measures of that character the largest total
number of votes have been cast in the States whether submitted under
the old method of amending constitutions or through the initiative
and referendum. At each election in Oregon since the adoption of
the initiative and referendum some measures of the character mentioned have been submitted and undoubtedly partially account for the
large number of votes cast, not only on those measures, but on all
others. Few complicated measures have yet been submitted to the
people of Oregon under the initiative and referendum. Most of
those that have been submitted have been brief measures dealing
with matters that have for many years been the subject of public
discussion, such as woman suffrage, regulation of the liquor traffic
and direct primaries, and a number of others have been for the creation of new counties and the establishment of branches of different
State institutions or kindred subjects.

In the past, elections have usually been determined by some one
great issue. Some popular demand expressed in a few words has frequently been more decisive of elections than any number of carefully
prepared and logical political discussions of pending issues. Our history is full of such instances, which will readily occur to everybody.
Under some popular clamor a whole ticket has frequently been carried to victory, although the people knew little or nothing about the
personnel of many of the candidates on the ticket or their views on
political questions.

These facts all seem to demonstrate that the American people are
too busy with their own personal affairs to give the necessary time and
study to the numerous political duties which would be demanded of
them in a pure democracy. Our own history conclusively proves that
the great mass of the voters will not or cannot give the necessary
time and study to the intricate details of legislation. They will decide
political policies, but they invariably expect some agents to work out
the details of the necessary legislation to make those principles effective.

The same disposition is shown in every private organization. At any large meeting of members of corporations or any social society or organization it is the invariable rule to appoint committees who are expected to work out the details of policies determined upon by the stockholders or members. A business corporation whose stockholders insisted upon having all business propositions submitted to a popular vote of the stockholders for their approval or rejection and who claimed the right to name all the minor officials of the company at each stockholders' meeting, together with the power to require any officer duly elected for a given term to submit the question of his continuance in office to all the stockholders every time a small percentage of their number filed a petition for a recall, would speedily be destroyed by its competitors who were more effectively organized for business.

It will not be seriously argued by anyone that all the stockholders of a company would take the time and trouble to study and become familiar with the details of the business of the company in which they have a financial interest. They select and pay officers and agents to do that work. How much less can we expect that all the voters of a State will thoroughly study the provisions of complicated laws submitted to them for their approval or rejection?

We are living in an age of specialization. Every business, every occupation and every profession has its specialists. The conditions which make specialists necessary in every branch of commercial and professional life are equally applicable to legislative affairs. Trained legislators are as necessary to secure good results in legislation as skilful lawyers are to obtain the best results in litigation.

The multiplication of duties imposed upon our citizens has thus far tended to increase rather than to diminish the evils of which we complain. A remedy for that condition certainly cannot be found in further increasing the duties of citizenship. The opposite course should be pursued. Instead of increasing the number of officers to be selected by the people at elections, it would be far better if our State Governments were to profit by the experience of the National Government and elect only a few of the important State officers and make all the other officers appointive. Our National Government unquestionably compares favorably in efficiency with any of the State Governments. The President, Vice-President, Senators and Representatives in Congress are the only Federal officials directly or indirectly elected by the people. All the other numerous Federal officers in all the branches of the service are appointed. If the people of the respective States were only called upon at State elections to elect their governor and senators and representatives every intelligent voter would be thoroughly posted upon the qualifications of the different candidates and their views on political questions. If the President of the United States can be trusted to select the heads of the great departments of the Federal Government, the Secretary of State, the Secretary of the Treasury, the Attorney General, and the heads of the other great national departments, there is no reason that can be assigned why a Governor of a State should not be equally capable of selecting from the citizens of his own State a Secretary of State, State Treasurer, and the Attorney General of the State.

With the increase of power and influence that would then attach to the office of Governor of a State, the office would become far more attractive to men of great ability and it would cease to be regarded, as it is in many of the States, merely as a means of securing a seat in the United States Senate. If candidates for the Legislature in each State were compelled to make their campaigns upon their own qualifications and upon their individual views of State questions instead of as candidates upon a general ticket containing the names of a hundred or more candidates, by reason of which the identity of individual candidates is lost, we would hear very much less about broken political pledges. Each voter would have an opportunity to scrutinize thoroughly the record of the candidates for his suffrage. The initiative and referendum, recall, and the elaborate and expensive machinery maintained in some of the States for the nomination and election of a host of candidates could all be dispensed with.

The adoption of the " short ballot " offers the simplest and most complete remedy for the defects in our present system of representative government. It does not involve any radical change in the form of the government, but, on the contrary, would be a return to a truly representative government. Its reinstatement would mean the application to political affairs of the methods that are so successfully employed by all the great industrial corporations of the country for the transaction of their business.

THE TRAGEDY OF THE WORLD

EDGAR SALTUS

BERNARD SHAW has complained that theosophy does not go far enough. One wonders what would please Mr. Shaw. The past is rather incoherent, the future equally vague. Theosophy elucidates both. It clarifies, foretells, gives the reason of things, the reason of everything, the reason even why you, Sir, or you, Madam, do us the honor to read these lines. This phenomenon it explains quite simply. It is your karma to read them, for karma is the destiny which you have made for yourself and in accordance with which are your present punishments and rewards.

Karma predicates reincarnation, which is perhaps the obvious resurrection of the dead and, in any event, the pivot of this creed in which you get history seen through the keyhole of folklore, surprised, too, at the casements of legend, yet history which you presently find to be demonstrable; history that is not fiction, but fact; not dry either, but colorful, enlightening, suggestive; in short, history as it should be instead of what it is; that is to say, the reason of things and not mere stupid recital.

The basis of it all is derived from the Book of Dyzan, the oldest book in the world, parts of which are said to be still older. Still older—a little enormity that again makes one wonder what might possibly please Mr. Shaw. Yet the statement, however extravagant, is almost negligible beside others that theosophy comports and which, while curious when not absurd to the many, are becoming foundlings that science adopts.

For instance, there is the fourth dimension. There is also the fact that the majority of us are like brutes. We believe but in the reality of things. Science, more hospitable, acknowledges the fourth dimension and with it the constant parade before our eyes of things and events ordinarily unseen. The phenomena of delirium tremens form a case in point. The shapes which the layman believes the patient only imagines are really seen and are rendered visible through the excitation of the pineal gland, which now is the rudimentary organ of what once was psychic vision. Alcohol stimulates this gland. The drunkard in his aftercups sees with it the hideousness of shapes which his own hideousness has attracted to him. For they are there, or rather they are here, about us in the fourth dimension, precisely as there are other shapes as gracious as these are revolting. Only, ordinarily, we do not see them. There are, though, those who can and do, and without being drunkards either.

Thinkers as sober as Jevons and Babbage go a bit further. They will, if you let them, tell you, that whatever occurs in the privacy of a room remains photographed in it. A mere extension of this enables occultists to say that nothing has ever occurred anywhere which is not also photographed, that in the ether above us is the great picture gallery of the world.

In India, at Adyar, the *chef lieu* of theosophy, this gallery is constantly being studied. The results, occasionally bizarre, are sometimes trivial. It has been found that Herbert Spencer was Aristotle; Gladstone, Cicero; Tennyson, Ovid. All of which is quite unimportant. But recently something more valuable has been obtained. It concerns Apollonios of Tyana.

Apollonios, as everyone knows, healed the sick, raised the dead, knew all things save the caresses of woman and spoke every language, including that of colors. His biographer, Philostratos, says of him that he came no one knew whence, went no one knew whither, that in these migrations he had beheld every form of ferocious beast except a tyrant, and that it was to see one, to see Nero, that he visited Rome.

The prefect there had a word with him. "What have you with you?" he asked. Apollonios answered: "Charity, Chastity, Temperance, Rectitude, and Justice." Said the prefect: "Your slaves, I presume? Make out a list of them." "They are not my slaves," Apollonios replied. "They are my masters."

Philostratos may have invented that reply. If not, he exaggerated. According to Adyar, Apollonios was the reincarnation of Jesus.

But not of the Christ. The Two are distinct. The Christ, or, theosophically, the Lord Maitreya, emanated, it is claimed, from a different evolution. The claim is specious, but not unique. It is advanced of other teachers and whether accepted or not it is suggestive. It is suggestive to think that from zeniths unknown to us, from planes perhaps where all beatitudes are as usual as all shames are common here, spirits commissioned to regenerate the hearts of man pass into the slums of space. Confident, with a crown of light they come, only to return with one of thorns.

This view, which is held of Orpheus and of Krishna, is held also of the Christ to whom, it is said, Jesus, in the last year of his physical life, surrendered his physical body. Jesus subsequently became Apollonios and later, Ramanujacharya, a Hindu reformer. According to Adyar, Jesus is now in Syria and to-day, in India, another physical body has been prepared for the second and approaching advent of the Lord.

Whether or not that will satisfy Mr. Shaw is a detail. Yet one may be sure that it would have singularly interested Renan, though chiefly perhaps because of addenda to the effect that Jesus was not crucified and preceded the present era by over a century.

This latter point is not perhaps entirely new, not new at least to those familiar with recent criticism. Bischoff in his *Geschichte Jesu* and Krauss in his *Leben* show that at best we have but uncertainties on the subject and that Pontius Pilate, through whom an approximate date might otherwise be obtained, is actually the most maligned of men. Pilate, it is asserted, had nothing whatever to do with Jesus, his pseudo-appearance in the Gospels being an intentional blind.

Jerome said of the Pentateuch that it contains as many secrets as it does words. The remark applies to the Gospels, which were not intended to be taken historically or even as written, but mainly as allegories, symbolic at that. Their basis, the higher criticism holds, was a common document and this protevangel was, according to Adyar, the work of a Palestine monk, who, about 100 A. D., wrote an essay on the Egyptian mysteries, in which he put a sketch of an ideal life, one derived partly from traditions of Jesus and partly from data concerning a minor Jewish reformer who, for some sedition in Jerusalem, was there stoned to death.

This story, written in Syro-Chaldaic, was sent to the abbot of an Alexandrine monastery to be recast for propaganda purposes into Greek. The abbot employed a number of young men on the work and a variety of recensions resulted. Of these four still endure and, though subsequently emended, still retain the names of their editors— Matthew, Mark, Luke and John.

One may assume that the primal and subsequent redactions incorporated more or less of the original document, together with such other legends and logia as individual taste suggested. In Alexandria, in the library of the monastery, in that of the Serapeion, were the treasures of nations, the gold, the frankincense, the myrrh of all the literature of the past. The editors had but to help themselves, which very commendably they did, to the felicities and paramitas of Hindu, Persian, Greek, Copt and Jew. The Avesta must have been suggestive, so also were Homer, Plato, the Tripitaka, the Talmud, the Law itself.

The opening passage in the fourth Gospel, the pronouncement: " In the beginning was the Word," comes from the Avesta and, previous to the Avesta, from the Book of Dyzan. Homer practically supplied the dictum: " Inasmuch as ye have done it unto the least of one of these my brethren, ye have done it unto me." Plato noted in the *Phædo* that many are called and few are chosen. The injunction to love one's enemies, the Talmud contained. Matthew's advice concerning thieves that break through and steal had been expressed in the Buddhist scriptures, as had also the Golden Rule which Luke advanced. In addition there was the Thorah. Moses fasted forty days. Elisha performed a miracle of the loaves. Job saw the Lord walking upon the sea.

In the effort to fill in a picture, of which the central figure had passed from the real to the ideal, these things, others as well, were probably useful. Yet that which perhaps inspired most was the protevangelist's account of initiation. According to Adyar, it is this that the allegory of the crucifixion is intended to convey.

The view may or may not be correct, yet there is a singular confirmation of it in occultism in which the letters I. N. R. I.—the legendary inscription on the Cross—represent the attainment of mastership. Another curiosity is the cry cited by Matthew and Mark, the " Eli, Eli, lama sabachthani," which it has been conjectured must be a misreading or a miswriting of " lamah azabvthnani "—how dost thou glorify me!—which were the words of thanksgiving uttered by the candidate when received initiate in the mysteries at last.

In Memphian crypts, before that thanksgiving could be expressed, the candidate was placed in a cross so hollowed that it could receive and support him. He was then entranced, lowered into a vault, put in a sarcophagus, where he remained for three days, after which he was raised again and ascended into the heaven of knowledge which the mysteries disclosed.

In these ceremonies, the hierophantic ritual, very archaic and equally suggestive, was as follows: The candidate shall be put upon the cross; he shall die, be buried, descend into the underworld and after the third day shall rise from the dead and ascend into heaven to be the right hand of Him from Whom he came.

Before the mysteries Isis stood, a finger to her lips. Yet the whispers from them that have reached us, while furtive perhaps, are clear. The candidate's death and burial symbolized the descent of the Logos into matter. The subsequent ascent and the attendant revelations changed his entire conception of things; they fractured the charm of illusion, disclosed the path that leads from the mansions of life which are death and enabled him to sunder the string of rebirths.

In what manner the ritual and epiphanies were tortured into scenarii of what was to be the tragedy of the world, the question, too, whether this drama was understandingly planned and then given as a glyph, or whether, as has been surmised, the symbolism of it may be due to esoteric teachings of the Christ—teachings which Valentinus said He confided only to the more spiritual of those about Him—these matters constitute an enigma so poignant, that the mistake regarding them, if mistake there be, is responsible for more wasted emotion, ennobling tears, idle hatreds and active love, than all the factors that have gone to the making of civilization.

One may wonder, though, if there be a mistake. In any case, there is a germ of truth in the gravest error, a residuum of error in the soundest truth. Between what really is and what is really not, those unable to function in the fourth dimension find it difficult to discriminate. On the other hand if, as theosophists hold, Adyar can discriminate, it is obvious that testimony from there cannot be intended to distress. It may amaze, yet always the beginning of truth is amazement, unless, as more often happens, it serves merely to annoy. But the one form of speech that the " Gita " permits is that which causes no annoyance, and theosophy, which primarily is a school of good manners, may seek perhaps to inform, but never to offend.

THE GHOSTLY BROTHER

JOHN G. NEIHARDT

BROTHER, Brother, calling me,
Like a distant surfy sea;
Like a wind that moans and grieves
All night long about the eaves—
Let me rest a little span:
Long I've followed, followed fast;
Now I wish to be a man,
Disconnected from the Vast!
Let me stop a little while,
Feel this snug world's pulses beat,
Glory in a baby's smile,
Hear it prattle round my feet;
Eat and sleep and love and live,
Thankful ever for the dawn;
Wanting what the world can give—
With the cosmic curtains drawn.

Brother, Brother, break the gyves!
Burst the prison, Son of Power!
Product of forgotten lives,
Seedling of the Final Flower!
What for you are nights and days,
Drifting snow or rainy flaw,
Love or hate or blame or praise,
Heir unto the Outer Awe?

I am breathless from the flight
Through the speed-cleft, awful Night!
Panting, let me rest awhile
In this pleasant æther-isle.
Here, content with little things,
How the witless dweller sings!

666

Rears his brood and steers his plow,
Nursing at the breasts of Now!
O, this little world is blest—
Brother, Brother, let me rest!

I am you and you are I!
When the world is cherished most,
You shall hear my haunting cry,
See me rising like a ghost!
I am all that you have been,
Are not now but soon shall be;
Thralled awhile by dust and din—
Brother, Brother, follow me!

'Tis a lonesome, endless quest;
I am weary; I would rest.
Though I seek to fly from you,
Like a shadow, you pursue.
Do I love?—you share the kiss,
Leaving only half the bliss.
Do I conquer?—you are there,
Claiming half the victor's share.
When the night-shades fray and lift,
'Tis your veiled face lights the rift.
In the sighing of the rain,
Your voice goads me like a pain.
Happy in a narrow trust,
Let me serve the lesser will:
One brief hour—and then to dust.
O, the dead are very still!

Brother, Brother, follow hence!
Ours the wild, unflagging speed!
Through the outer walls of sense,
Follow, follow where I lead!

Love and hate and grief and fear—
'Tis the geocentric dream:
Only shadows linger here,
Cast by the Eternal Gleam!
Follow, follow, follow fast!
Somewhere out of time and place,
You shall lift the veil at last,
You shall look upon my face.
Look upon my face and die,
Solver of the Mystery!
I am you and you are I—
Brother, Brother, follow me!

"THE CHILDREN'S BREAD"

FRANCES AYMAR MATHEWS

MRS. INGRAHAM was going out in her car. She came down the steps, splendidly attired in sables, velvets and plumes, all gray, with a bunch of violets pinned on her sleeve. Mimi was dressed in her blanket, embroidered with her name in jewels, and trimmed with silver fox fur. Mimi was further decked in her collar, with rubies and emeralds sparkling in their setting of gold; and the footman carried her on a cushion of satin stuffed with down, and placed her beside her mistress in the car.

"Come to mama, darling!" said Mrs. Ingraham; whereupon the footman lifted the animal to the lap of her mistress.

"Thank you, Joyce. Mimi is not well to-day. The fresh air may do her good. I hope so. Mama's pet!" She pressed her face against Mimi's. "To François', Joyce"—mentioning the name of her milliner. The footman sprang to his seat, and the car bowled down the avenue. But not far. At the first hold-up crossing, Mrs. Ingraham's car chanced to come right beside the car of one of her intimate friends.

"Ah, my dear, I am désolée, I assure you. Mimi's nose is warm! Mimi, whom I adore, for whom I paid a thousand dollars! If I should lose her!"

"Absurd, chérie! Look how happy she seems. As for my Prince Carl, he is tired, sleepy. We were up late last night, and his breakfast did not suit him."

"Too bad! There, we can move on now. These stops are so tiresome. Why are people allowed to walk where we want to drive, I wonder? Where do you go now?"

"Where? You really require to ask?" her friend laughed. "Where does one go in Lent but to one's dressmaker?"

"And after?" inquired Mrs. Ingraham.

"To Sherry's. Meet me for luncheon. Will you?"

"To be sure. And if I am a little late, for I am going to stop in at church——"

"Of course. I also!" interrupted her friend.

"Order a proper luncheon. No meats, remember. Broiled shad, eggs as you please, strawberries; a salad of fresh peaches, and Sauterne only, except a cordial."

"Yes! Yes! Don't fail me."

The two cars were starting.

"And, I almost forgot! a broiled chicken, please, for Mimi; well done, just the breast."

"To be sure; Prince Carl the same. With ice cream?"

"With ice cream, certainly. Au revoir."

One went to the dressmaker; the other to the milliner.

Over across the big city, in a street so filthy that it rivals the worst thoroughfares of the towns in China, in a sered and rickety tenement, up five flights, along a narrow, broken, dark corridor, a door, which hung on one hinge, gave entrance to the house of Elijah Sominsky.

It consisted of one room; in it were a thin mattress of straw, a stool, an empty shelf, a stove, a knife, a stew-pan and cover; two books on the box which served as a table; Elijah's wife, and Elijah's four children. There was no fire in the stove. Rags only covered their nakedness, the winter wind alone spoke, shrieking in seeming derision, at the tiny window, at the cracks in the walls, in the ceiling, and under the door.

Elijah himself had just come in.

His wife, Hanna, looked up.

He spread his hands out, empty; he turned inside out the pocket of his tattered cloak, empty also.

Hanna shook her head: some kinds of desperation are silent.

A footstep that was youthful, almost buoyant, came stumbling along the corridor. The door opened; the oldest son of Elijah jumped in with his thin arms full of sticks of wood and his tin pail brimming with cinders; on his white, pinched lips, the shadow of a smile.

"Now we shall be warm!" cried the boy, as his stiff fingers opened the stove and laid on the wood and cinders.

"Nay," muttered Elijah. "How can we be warm when we have no match to light the fire with?"

Hanna, holding the baby close and essaying to draw over its tiny form some of her own rags, said, " Our neighbors have already a fire, across the corridor; they will perhaps give us a flame with a scrap of paper. I will try."

She went out and presently came back hurriedly, panting, lest the precious spark should be killed by the cruel wind; and in a moment the bits of wood had caught and began to crackle, and the cinders to glow; and Elijah and Hanna and their children huddled over the scanty warmth.

" It is good to feel it, father," said the oldest girl as she took the empty pot from the top of the now hot stove.

Elijah nodded. " But it would also be good to eat."

And Hanna and her children all nodded as they spread their fingers to the stove, as Hanna held the baby to its blaze.

" It is three days since we have eaten," Elijah said, as he moved away from the fire, and pushed his oldest son in his place.

" Three days," echoed Hanna.

" Well, we can die," said Elijah.

" But the children?" Hanna answered.

" Yes, the children." Elijah took up the two greasy little books from the table in his trembling fingers.

" You can get a few pennies for the books, Elijah?" whispered Hanna.

" The ' Scriptures '?" cried Elijah in a frightful tone. " The bread that might be bought with the price of them would choke."

" But the other book?" Hanna urged, " the one you keep forever studying."

Elijah nodded again. " Look you, Hanna, and you, children, who have understanding; listen while I speak." And Hanna with the baby in her arms rose from the stool, weak as she was, and the children straightened themselves as well as they could, for the hand of their father lay upon the sacred book.

" I have been across the city to the west," he said. " I have passed in front of the palaces of the rich, the churches of the millionaires; the shops where those buy who live as princes live. I have seen the great women of those tribes arrayed in magnificence: I have seen many of them with dogs in their chariots; nay, in their arms,

nestling as children nestle. I have heard, yea, with these ears," and
the voice of Elijah rose and fell with weird impassionment born perhaps of the hectic fever that ran high in his veins, perhaps of the
sense of impotent injustice which burned in his soul. "With these
ears," he repeated, "have I heard their women call themselves the
mothers of these dogs! and about their brute necks hung priceless
jewels, and on top of their hairy skins were strapped blankets sparkling also with gems and gold; and lackeys served them as if they were
king's progeny. And they were fat and well liking, and luxurious
and happy, while ye, my children, and thou, my wife, starved!"

And Hanna sank upon her stool and the children crowded closer
to the stove staring at their father.

"It is not that I have not toiled," Elijah went on, "for I have,
until the fever of the tenements seized me. It is not that I would
not, and could not, toil now; but there is no work for me. They
turn me away: they turn me away." Elijah also now sank down,
upon his knees, for there was but one stool.

"Pawn the small book," murmured Hanna. "It will give us a
loaf of bread."

But Elijah, taking the small book up from the table, shook his
head.

"Listen to what it says." He turned the leaf and read: "'It is
not meet to take the children's bread and to cast it to dogs.'"

And Hanna bowed her head over the baby. "What manner of
man is it that says this?" she asked her husband.

"In the Book of the God of the Gentiles," answered Elijah;
"and, look you," for Hanna and her children had the sneer upon
their lips ready at his words: "Look you, sneer not, unless it be ye
sneer at me; for I have searched our Scriptures through and through,
yet have I not found words so comfortable to me as these of the
Prophet of the other tribes."

"A loaf of bread?" said the woman piteously, putting her wasted
hand upon the greasy book.

Elijah replaced the book on the table, shaking his head. "Once
more I go forth. When I come back, I will bring bread, yea, meat
for you and for our children." And he went forth and left them alone
by the stove.

Elijah went back to the west where he had been in the morning; it was now near one o'clock, and he stood at the curb of the steepled church and watched the great ladies come out in their lenten robes of gray and black, while the raw March air was sweet with the perfume of their violets, and the sun shone on their jewels and gold, and the gems of their pets who waited for them in their cars, tended by their lackeys.

Mrs. Ingraham stepped forth from the steepled church and her only word was: " Joyce, how is Mimi now?"

Before the lackey could reply, Mimi herself sprang out of the car and was barking to her mistress, when, amid the confusion of many cars and lackeys, and ladies and pedestrians, someone seized Mimi, and no one could even see her. It was as if the earth had opened and swallowed her.

Assuredly there was much excitement, of policemen, mounted, bicycle and foot; of friends, strangers, equals, servants, and the fringing crowd that always springs into being when an excitement occurs.

" My. Mimi! Mama's darling! Mama's darling! " wailed Mrs. Ingraham. " Two hundred dollars to anyone who will bring me back my Mimi. Her jeweled collar cost fifteen hundred dollars and I paid five hundred for her blanket. Oh, my Mimi!"

She entered her car and was driven at once to the Police Station, and detectives were put upon the case; then she was driven home, forgetting her engagement to luncheon with her friend.

Toward night word came to her: the jeweled collar had been found in the gutter on Third Avenue; a bearded, foreign-looking man had been seen with a ragged cloak around him,—evidently something, either human or animal, under it,—hurrying across further east. Indeed, even as the captain telephoned now, another detective came in to say that the man had been located, and, as Madam's orders were that she herself would go anywhere on earth to reclaim Mimi, well, the officer would come to her at once and conduct her to the abode of the thief.

Presently, then, Mrs. Ingraham and the detective were getting across the city as fast as the speed laws would permit. Also, presently, they were entering the tenement, climbing the stairs, opening the door of the room of Elijah Sominsky. He stood at the table near the narrow slit of a window; whatever was on the table was covered by his cloak. Hanna sat on the stool; at sight of the great lady she rose, holding the baby in her arms, wrapped as it was in the blanket of Mimi. The oldest girl hovered over the covered pot on the hot stove; the pot could be heard bubbling, boiling, and the close little room was steaming with the odor of meat being cooked. The other three children had their eyes fastened upon the bumping lid of the pot; they did not even move them when the door opened.

Mrs. Ingraham pushed in first. "Ah!" she said, spying at once the blanket of Mimi. "My darling is here! Don't deny it! That is her blanket. You have her hidden here, have you not?"

Elijah inclined his head. He took the dog's blanket off the baby: his wife Hanna caught the almost naked child closer to her breast. The baby was dead and the mother wailed.

"Bring her out," said Mrs. Ingraham. "Why are you silent? You are found out! You are a thief. It is useless to pretend. When she hears my voice she will bark and scratch. Come to Mama, darling!" While she listened impotently, Hanna wept in silence over the dead baby.

"Officer," Mrs. Ingraham's voice was now full of anger, "Officer, search this place."

While the detective made a motion as if to say, "there is nowhere to seek," the oldest girl held down the pot lid with a stick of wood, and the others crowded closer, eager, frantic for the food.

Mrs. Ingraham said frantically, too, "I will give you a reward; I will not arrest you."

Elijah shrugged his thin, stooping shoulders, but said nothing. He picked up the greasy little book.

"But my Mimi is here! Answer me!" Mrs. Ingraham stamped her velvet clad foot.

"Yes," replied Elijah, "that is so, here."

"Then call her out to me. I will throw you into prison! How can Mimi exist here!"

"Great lady," Elijah Sominsky handed to her the little greasy book, open at the page he had read aloud from to his family; his dirty finger pointed her the words. "Read," said Elijah, in a voice so far from fear that it sounded like a voice of thunder.

And she read.

Elijah lifted the lid from the pot, also the cloak from whatever was on the table.

"There is your dog." He uttered the words with a scorn so superb it savored of the prophets of old in their most mighty and righteous wrath. "And here are my children." He pointed to his family.

While Mrs. Ingraham shrieked and nearly swooned in the arms of the detective, Elijah picked up the dog's jeweled blanket and threw it over her face, and then he lifted the dead baby from the arms of his wife, and he said, "Let us eat."

POET MAKERS OF THE NEW ITALY

MARY W. ARMS

I

MAKING A NATION

" Victor Emanuel II, by the Grace of God and by the Will of the Nation, King of Italy."

Seldom, perhaps, has the proclamation of a new reign rung with more solemn feeling and significance than in the hush of that great hall at Turin where, on the 18th of February, 1861, the first Parliament of United Italy had assembled. The few formal words announced not only the accession of a king, but the birth of a nation; not only the sovereignty of Victor Emanuel, but the independence of Italy. They meant that the dream which had been carried through the centuries by poets and thinkers—changing often in form, not seldom darkened by personal passions, sometimes lost altogether for a moment in the strife of parties and the violence of nations—was at last made real. Reading them to-day, we recognize that they were a statement of one of the most interesting evolutions of modern times.

It has become almost a commonplace to speak of the present Italy as having been " made " within the short span of years covered by the active struggle for independence and unity known as the Risorgimento. In so far as the actual fact is concerned, this is of course true; but along with the history of fact goes always the history of emotion as sap in the tree of which facts are the fruit, and this history of emotion takes us back, for the roots of the Italian idea, to the dawn of the XIV Century and the mind of Dante. Dante's dream was that of the poet, the idealist. Cola di Rienzi, Arnaldo da Brescia, tried in vain to translate it into fact, each after his own fashion, each getting farther and farther away from Dante's conception as personal passions and political intrigues were brought into play. The years passed; and still, alone almost among the states of Europe, Italy had no aggregate existence but, split up into countless and inimical principalities, was constantly suffering from foreign invasions. Then came Machiavelli, the politician, the man of affairs, to pick up the thread of the thought and carry it on, modernizing it, adapting it, making of it finally almost a prophecy of what was actually to follow, although for three long centuries more Italy was to remain what she had been from the fall of the Roman Empire—the battleground of nations, the " woman country of the world," coveted for her beauty and an easy prey in her weakness. Even in those centuries, however, the old dream of national life never quite died, and when the French Revolution came to change the whole social fabric of civilization, its influence was nowhere more keenly felt than in Italy.

The overthrow of a long established monarchy, the evolution of " the people " as a new force having, in the words of an Italian writer, " the needs, the culture, the conscience, the dignity of men," could not fail to quicken tendencies and aspirations that had been for a long time obscurely germinating. This moral and intellectual influence of the Revolution, moreover, was further emphasized and brought into practical action by the Napoleonic invasion. Bonaparte descended upon Italy in 1796, and by the end of the following year he had overpowered the resistance of Vittorio Amedeo III, King of Sardinia and Piedmont, who was supported by Austria; had wrested Lombardy from the Austrian grasp; made himself master of Venetia; intimidated Pope Pius VI and King Ferdinand of Naples; and formed his conquests, with the exception of Venice,—ceded to Austria by the Treaty of Campoformio—into the so-called Cisalpine Republic under the protection of France. A few years later (in 1804) when the Republican General became Emperor of France, the Italian Republic was transformed into the Italian Kingdom. With the growth of Napoleon's power, the French possessions in Italy were continually enlarged. Naples was taken from the Bourbons and given first to Joseph Bonaparte and then to General Murat; the Papal States were annexed and the Pope exiled to Savona.

Upon what might have been Italy's future had the Bonapartist empire held, it is idle to speculate. Napoleon's overthrow necessarily carried with it that of the kingdom he had artificially created; and the Congress of Vienna in 1815 restored the Pope to Rome, the Bourbons to Naples, and most of the old rulers to their little states, with

Austria in possession of Lombardy and Venetia and exercising a certain lordship over the greater part of the peninsula. No such suppressive action, however, could do away with the real effect of the Napoleonic occupation. " The *Italian Republic* and the *Kingdom of Italy* had awakened in all Italians the national sentiment and the hope of being able to unite in a single and independent State." * Murat while he still clung to his seat on the Neapolitan throne had agitated a movement for a united Italy which, while rendered abortive by the unreadiness of the people and their lack of confidence in the would-be leader, nevertheless gave form and substance to what had before existed chiefly in vague aspirations and ill-defined ideals. Moreover, the tyranny which followed the restoration of the old order in Italy, was not without its share in the development of the national feeling. In the bond of a common suffering under the iron rule that crushed out every stir of political life, small differences and jealousies were gradually lost.

The workings of the popular mind began to make themselves felt in revolutionary outbreaks at various points through the peninsula— outbreaks promptly quelled by the authorities and followed by trials, condemnations, and renewed stringency. It was not until 1848 that anything like a simultaneous movement took place, and even then it was rather an effort to throw off the yoke of the foreigner than a conscious step toward unity. For this very reason it was foredoomed to fail. The King of Piedmont, Carlo Alberto, on whom the leadership of the movement devolved, was not fitted for a post requiring a more than common force and decision of character, and the union of a poet's enthusiasm with the grasp and executive ability of a statesman. The people of Italy, unversed in the principles or practice of organization, were not fitted to give him adequate support. After a struggle heroic in its personal manifestations, however weak in its general plan, Carlo Alberto was definitely defeated by the Austrians at Novara in March, 1849; and resigning his crown to his son went into voluntary exile, while Austria regained all she had momentarily lost in Lombardy and Venetia and the French restored the Pope at Rome. The history of the five days at Milan (March 18-22) when, with practically no organization and means utterly in-

---

* Ambrosoli: *Manuale della Letteratura Italiana.*

sufficient, the citizens succeeded in forcing the evacuation of the Austrian forces under Radetsky, is typical of the whole movement of '48· It shows the lack of cohesion, the *individualism* if one may so express it, which was its weakness; and it shows at the same time the heroism, the fine restraint, the courage not only under the stimulus of actual fighting but under the immeasurably more trying pressure of daily want and suffering that made its strength. Paolo Mantegazza, who himself fought, a boy of sixteen, on the barricades, says of it:

" It was a delirium of love of country, it was a transport which left the sky full of light and which made our soil fecund with the blood of the first martyrs."

For the time being it seemed that the heroic effort had been in vain and that Italy was doomed to sink back into the old servitude. In reality the first breath of the awakening had been drawn. Italians from the south had fought side by side with their brothers of the north; slowly out of the chaos of conflicting political tendencies, the idea of unity was being formed. In Piedmont Cavour was fostering, strengthening and making practicable such an idea by devoting all the energies of his far-seeing intellect and executive genius to the kingdom's internal affairs and its relations with foreign powers—to making it, in short, " a centre of attraction for Italy."

The war of '59 was the logical outcome of a ripened popular consciousness throughout the country. It was from its very beginnings as fortunate as previous struggles had been ill-fated, and not even the defection of Napoleon III and the forced Peace of Villafranca could stop the march of events. Lombardy by this treaty was ceded to Piedmont, and in 1860 a plébiscite added the whole of central Italy to what was now recognized as a coherent kingdom under the sovereignty of Victor Emanuel. Ten more years, and Garibaldi had given the Southern Kingdom and Sicily to the Crown; Venice had been gained by treaty with Austria; and the Italian troops (on September 20, 1870) were entering Rome to put an end forever to the temporal power of the Papacy and give the new state its natural capacity. Italy was free and one from the Alps to the extremest tip of Sicily, and from the Adriatic to the Mediterranean.

In his introduction to Countess Martinengo-Cesaresco's admirable book, *La Liberazione d' Italia*, Frederic Harrison speaks of the union of Italy as " a signal triumph of moral forces over physical and armed forces." It is this moral aspect and significance which gives to the Italian struggle its chief interest and value to-day. We have in its history something more than a mere shuffling of the political cards; we have the resurrection of a nation by the breathing into its people of certain vital principles of life—a belief in liberty and a consciousness of national responsibility. More, perhaps, than any other one manifestation of the XIX Century it showed the eternal survival in humanity of that divine enthusiasm which in the radiance of an ideal can utterly lose all selfish interest, and set at naught suffering and death. " The whole Italian people became for the moment an inspired and fecund poet . . . living and moving in the same enthusiasms." *

That at such a time the part taken by literature itself—and especially by poetic literature—would be an important one is self-evident. As a matter of fact its importance, both in its creative and interpretative aspects, can scarcely be overestimated. " From the beginning, about the rude altar of the God," say Professor Woodberry, in his recent book, *The Inspiration of Poetry*, " to the days of Goethe, of Leopardi, and of Victor Hugo, the poet is the leader in the dance of life." Apprehending with his clearer vision what should be in what is, he voices to the people their own vaguer yearnings, dissatisfactions, aspirations. His is the battle cry which can make triumph out of defeat and death—his the words that breathe new life into dying hopes, and incite to renewed effort with memories of past glories. The political Italy of to-day owes as deep a debt to Carducci as to Cavour, to Berchet as to Garibaldi. Nor does the value of the Risorgimento poetry end with the quickening influence it exerted in its own day. A country's truest history is to be found always in its literature which preserves the moving and universal idea free from the confusion, and often the misconception, attendant on actual facts. In the poetry of the XIX Century in Italy, there breathes every hope and fear, all the hatred, the love, the pity, and the faith, which, as we have seen, gave to the making of the nation its universal and lasting significance; and it is to this poetry the student

* Enrico Panzacchi: *La Poesia del '48·*

must turn who would feel again the very pulse of the time.   A volume would be required for the merest enumeration of the XIX Century writers who have place among the builders of Italy.   I have selected three only for consideration here, but three who would seem very fairly representative of different phases in the struggle.   Of these Leopardi may be called the forerunner since, himself often lost in a " dark wood " of doubts and discouragement, he was yet all unconsciously blazing a path; Berchet is the exile, one in the host of those who during the dark days, made " Proof how the bread of others savors of salt, and how hard a path is the descending and the mounting of another's stairs "; while in Carducci we find the very spirit and being of the new Italy.

II

LEOPARDI—THE FORERUNNER

It was at Recanati, a little town of the Umbrian Marches near Ancona, that Giacomo Leopardi was born in June of 1798.   In mediæval days Recanati had been a not unimposing example of the fortified burghs which made Italy practically an aggregation of tiny independent states, but at the time of the poet's birth it had already fallen into the quietude which broods over it to-day.   From the windows of the library in the grim old Palace of the Leopardi, Giacomo looked out at the guardian Apennines and the distant blue of the Adriatic—

> " the sky serene,
> Orchards and golden paths, and far away
> The line of sea here, and of mountains there." *

It was between this library, redolent of ancient bindings that held the garnered wisdom of bygone ages, and the luminous openness of the country without that the young poet spent his days.   The influence of both was to make itself felt throughout his life.   From earliest childhood, exceedingly frail physically, his mental development was extraordinarily rapid; and his ill health was undoubtedly aggravated and confirmed by his absorption in his studies.   After he

* A Sylvia.

was ten years old, he had no other teacher than himself and the books
with which he shut himself up in the library. At twenty, he was
master of Greek and Latin, a poet, a philosopher, and a writer of
prose that had been acclaimed by some of the most distinguished literary men of the day. He was also paying the penalty for the ill regulation of his life in bodily misery and a deep mental depression which
the years only increased, and which drove him out upon the hills to
solitary meditation at an age when most boys would still be indulging
in the pranks of the schoolroom and university. Those unaccompanied
wanderings and their setting live for us in much, especially of the
earlier, of Leopardi's poetry. We get an impression of lonely hills;
of wide spaces; of murmuring woods with a sense of sea beyond; of a
village, here and there, which with its surrounding orchards and cheerful sounds of life seems only to emphasize the note of remoteness
and melancholy.

Meanwhile, in the world without there was no lack of stir. The
turmoil of the French occupation, followed by Napoleon's downfall,
had brought about a chaotic condition in which stirrings of liberalism and the newly awakened, fierce desire of independence were tossed
up against the rocks of the old inertia. Count Leopardi, the
poet's father, was a narrow Catholic and unalterably opposed to any
movement that would mean change and expansion. Giacomo, his
blood on fire with the precepts and example of the seers and heroes
of the past, panted to offer himself on the altar of his country. The
two men, father and son, are types of the forces at work in the long
struggle between feudalism and modernism. Unable to live happily
at home, Leopardi, after his twentieth year, became a wanderer over
the face of Italy. He visited Rome, Florence, Pisa, Milan, Bologna
—making spasmodic returns to Recanati, but always driven forth
again by his father's intolerance and his own restless spirit. He felt
the pinch of poverty often—Count Leopardi refusing to support him
except in the paternal home—and the misery of ill health always.

In such circumstances, it would be natural to regard Leopardi
as the product rather of particular than of general conditions; yet
one who considers his life carefully, can scarcely fail to find a certain
correspondence between the two. Italy, likewise, was torn with the
struggle between social progress and an inherited feudalism, and in

her diseased condition—the result of long centuries of despotism—an easy prey to discouragement and melancholy. It was a day in which a hundred dissatisfactions, unappeased aspirations, yearnings too vague for concrete realization, were stirring obscurely; a day in which the leaven, as it were, of our modern life was just beginning to work. Rostand has expressed a very real phase of the early XIX Century in the few words between the Duke and the young Conspirator in *L'Aiglon*.

THE DUKE

An ill?

THE YOUNG MAN

A shuddering disgust—

THE DUKE

A weight

Hung on the soul—

THE YOUNG MAN

Quick impulses that die—

THE DUKE

A dull disquiet, and that falsest pride
In our own sufferings that makes us proud
To show the world the pallor of our brow—

THE YOUNG MAN

My lord!

THE DUKE

A fierce disdain for those who live,

Calm, satisfied—

THE YOUNG MAN

My lord!

THE DUKE

And always—doubt.

In Leopardi's work there is the same mingling of personal and national elements as in his life. Poetically, he was undoubtedly one of the most richly endowed of the singers of the Risorgimento, combining a trend of thought wholly modern with an expression classic in its dignity and reminiscent not seldom of Dante and Petrarch. In *Sylvia* we have an example of his art as a lyric poet; in *La Ginestra* of his intellectual power. The first shows at its best the delicate poetic sentiment and feeling for nature, the charm of descriptive touch, which are woven like a thread of moonlight through the blackness of his melancholy. Occasionally—in the description of the eruption of Vesuvius and the picture of Pompeü in *La Ginestra*, for instance,—you feel the intellectual force of the idea rather than the more poetic quality of atmospheric suggestion; but many of the minor poems like *Il Passero Solitario* and the fragment beginning

"The daily gleam extinguished in the west,"

with its contrast between the early peace of the evening and the later coming of the storm, show wonderful impressionistic touches.

It is probably in *La Ginestra* that Leopardi's philosophy is the most completely embodied. At first glance, this philosophy would seem merely negative; what is, is bad, says the poet, and yet gives no key by which better might be unlocked. The thesis which he here powerfully presents is that man is a helpless atom in the power of a destructive and cruel nature. He casts the keenest darts of his irony at the human vainglory which would make man the lord and chief end of all created things. Religion is only another form of this vainglory, since it teaches him to believe himself the special care of a personal God whose chastisements are to be received with submission as manifestations of divine interposition in human affairs. The brotherhood of man means to Leopardi simply the uniting of men against nature. Since all alike are born to struggle and suffer under nature's tyranny, why aggravate conditions by " fraternal wrath " ? Rather look upon your fellows as fellow-victims and conspire with them in the " common war " against natural forces. Immortality is an empty vaunt; the end of all things is nothingness, and all the joys and sweetness of life pass with youth. Old age is merely a waiting for the annihilation of death. Thus the Leopardian philosophy has no inspiration; it depresses instead of stimulating. I know few lines more spiritually tragic in their utter destruction of endeavor and aspiration than those in which, looking on the lava-covered fields at the base of Vesuvius, Leopardi ironically exclaims:

"Here pictured you may see of human kind
The glorious and progressive destiny."

Yet, notwithstanding the negative and hopeless tendency of his thought, Leopardi gave much to Italy. His feelings were often truer than his creed, and his love of country seems to have been made only the more intense by his scorn for prevailing conditions and his pessimism as to the future. The best example of his purely patriotic poetry is the famous ode *All' Italia*, which has been set down by some critics as a piece of rhetorical exercise pure and simple, but which to many must always seem much more. Voices of Italy breathe in its lines—the stir of things fundamental and vital in the Italian nature; an heroic and sincere aspiration; the weariness and melancholy that preceded the birth of a new life; scorn of the degradation, the vile servitude, into which the once glorious sons of Italy had fallen, a scorn which served as a powerful weapon to sting the fainting and discouraged spirits of his countrymen into renewed effort. In it we feel that subtler sense of country, that feeling of intimate attachment to the native soil in and for itself, which figures in so much Italian poetry both old and new. The beautiful pagan conception of the Earth Mother with humanity for her sons, has influenced the Italian mind with the same unconscious force that so much of ancient life and faith has done, and is not at all impossibly an element in Italian patriotism. The foreigner was not only a tyrant who crushed the Italian people; he was a violator of the maternal soil, into whose wide bosom had been gathered the generations of the Italian dead, great and humble alike. Here, too, in passages which have the fervor of a romanticism wholly modern combined with a certain antique massiveness and dignity in the sculpturing of the lines, we find evoked memories of the " ancient estate " and the glories of Greece—a " looking backward " very characteristic of the poets of the Risorgimento, especially of those who sang during the darker days of the struggle. Tracing their country's lineage through Rome to Greece, the Italian people to-day are probably more closely allied than any other nation with classic life. Its thought is their possession: its glories are a part of their inheritance. To call up before their mental vision, as Leopardi here does, the heroism of the defenders of Thermopylæ, is to stir their blood with the same personal pride, the same instinctive impulse toward active worthiness, that any one of us might feel in an act of daring or self-devotion performed by an ancestor of our own, and gives additional force to the idea which he brings out in closing—

that the tomb of heroes who died in defence of the ideal of liberty is an altar from the sacred fire of which the courage of the living may be kindled.

It is this same quickening influence which gives its value to *All' Italia*. Words from it were in the heart and on the lips of many an Italian patriot as he went to lay down his life for the " dear birthland "; and through it, even had he written nothing else, Leopardi would hold a place in the foremost ranks of those who prepared the way they did not live to see trodden. There is an hour which comes just before the dawn when a deeper blackness than that of the night seems to settle over the earth, and the watcher is pressed upon by a thousand doubts and forebodings the bustle of the day has kept at a distance. The history of the world shows such a dark hour before every great crisis in its social and spiritual evolution; and it is of that hour in the making of the new Italy Leopardi is peculiarly the poet. He died in 1837, when Italy's life seemed as broken in purpose and as hopeless as his own had been; but his last words as he lay in the arms of his friend Count Ranieri in the villa above plague-stricken Naples are a salutation to the new era.

" Apri quella finestra, lasciami vedere la luce "—*open that window, let me see the light.*

III

BERCHET—THE EXILE

A greater contrast could scarcely be imagined than that which exists between the life and personality of Leopardi and that of Giovanni Berchet, the Milanese. The one was of the nobility, his father a type of the rigid conservative bound by a thousand traditions and prejudices of caste and religion; the other the son of a merchant in close touch with all the practical activities and shrewd contemporary judgments of the bourgeoisie. Leopardi spent his early life within the four walls of a grim feudal palace or out in the solitude of the hills, and his later years in wandering restlessly from city to city, lonely in them all; Berchet was brought up amidst the stir of Milan, then a political and intellectual centre throbbing with the new influences set in motion by the French occupation and the literature of the French Revolution. Leopardi died at thirty-nine before the movement for freedom and unity in Italy had shown more than " flashes struck from midnights " ; Berchet lived to be nearly thirty years older and to see the sky streaked with dawn in 1848. Both men, differing as widely in genius as in the circumstances of their lives, nevertheless voice each a certain phase of the Italian struggle; both wielded a potent influence over the minds and spirits of their contemporaries.

Giovanni Berchet was born in Milan on December 23, 1783. His father intended him to pursue the same mercantile career he had himself adopted, and to this end encouraged him in the study of modern languages. All of Giovanni's tendencies, however, were toward the imaginative and intellectual; his knowledge of languages he promptly applied to the translation of poetry instead of to the pursuit of commercial information. Soon, indeed, it became manifest that literature was to be his chosen work. He secured an insignificant post as translator in the chancery of the Senate in Milan and a frugal living being thus assured, threw himself heart and soul into the intellectual battle then raging between the so-called classic and romantic schools. With the letter published under the name of *Grisostomo*, he ranged himself definitely on the side of the Romanticists, and from then on we find him contributing numerous articles and translations to *Il Conciliatore*—the paper which was the organ of the new school in Milan.

This warm espousal of what might be called the revolutionary movement in letters went hand-in-hand in Berchet, with an equally ardent sympathy for the Italian political movement. With the outbreak of 1821 he identified himself to such an extent that when the inevitable arrests and imprisonments followed its suppression his name was one of those listed, and it was only through a friend's timely warning that he was able to escape from Milan unmolested. He went to London, where he procured employment in an Italian commercial house and where he spent eight long years of exile, watching with a patriot's devotion every difficult breath drawn by his struggling country and serving her valiantly and constantly with his pen. In 1829, the Marchese Giuseppe Arconati, also a Milanese and an exile, took the poet into his household and gave him the advantages of prolonged travel through France, Belgium, and Germany. With the first flush of hope in 1848, however, he hastened back to Italy; nor could he make up his mind to leave the country again when Lombardy fell once more under Austrian dominion. Instead he sought and found refuge in Turin under the Piedmontese flag; and there he died on December 23, 1851.

The literary career of Berchet seems to fall naturally into four periods. In the first he was concerned chiefly with what might be called scholastic work—making translations from the English of Goldsmith and Gray, the German of Schiller and other romanticists, and feeling strongly the influence of Parini, Monti, and Foscolo, all exponents of the school of the new Italy. In the second—which may be called his Romantic Period—he was experiencing in its fullness the revolt against the old classic forms, and the enthusiasm for the ballads of Germany, which bore fruit in such of his poems as *I Visconti* and *Il Castello di Monforte*. The third period—and, poetically, by far the most important—was that in which his patriotism, roused to white heat by the events of '21, poured itself out in the poems which will keep his name alive because they have their root not in the intellect of one man but in the heart of a whole people. Of these are *I Profughi di Parga* (written just after he went into exile); *Il Rimorso; Clarina; Il Romito del Cenisio; Matilde; Giulia; Le Fantasie* (1829); *All' Armi! All' Armi!* (1830). It was in these nine years from 1821 to 1830 that Berchet's creative genius sprang up, as it were, over night, bore fruit, and faded away. After his return to Italy he became once more the man of letters rather than the poet, writing imitations of Spanish Romances and interesting himself in the collection and preservation of the folk songs of Italy.

Berchet has been called the Italian Chénier; certainly his genius in its exquisite sincerity and simplicity has a kinship with that of the poet of *La Jeune Captive*, with perhaps a note of even truer human feeling added—a note which must bring at once to the mind of every English reader a thought of the English ballads. In the simplest of words, with almost no use of figures but with a poignant reality of emotion which speaks straight to the heart, he voices the hopes, the tragedies, the bravery, the agony of the Italian struggle. His appeal is indirect. He rarely invokes the reader's sympathy with rhetorical addresses; he prefers to narrate an incident, to sketch a situation. The handful of poems on which his fame rests, is a handful of pictures, drawn from life, of the Italy of 1821, of 1830, of 1848. In *Clarina* we have the desolation of the girl whose lover, having raised his sword against the oppressors of their country, is wandering in exile and in danger of death while

> " seated at a royal board
> Laughs the wretch who has betrayed him."

In *Il Rimorso*, it is the humiliation of the Italian woman who has given herself in marriage to one of her country's tyrants; in *Giulia*, the agony of the mother whose son is torn from her side to fight in the Austrian ranks. Everywhere there breathes the deadliest hate against the stranger—the poet belongs to the period when the fundamental idea was not so much one of national unity as of freedom at any cost from the foreign yoke.

Perhaps one of the best examples of Berchet's chief characteristic, his ability to convey a vivid impresion of a situation, is to be found in *The Hermit of Mt. Cenis*. A traveler who has toiled up to the summit of the pass is described as pausing to look down with exultant joy on the smiling Italian plain spread beneath him and now so easy of attainment. His reverie is interrupted by a hermit who makes his home among the mountains, " difficult snows," and whose exclamation—

> " Accursèd he
> Who would, tearless, cross the threshold
> Of this land of misery "—

strikes the keynote of the poem. The stranger now remembers hearing, far off in the chill halls of his northern home, rumors of oppressions and discords in Italy—but surely these have been dispelled by royal assurances telling of peace restored and all Italy with glad applause swearing faith to the thrones? In the opening half dozen lines of the hermit's reply, there is gathered all the immense tragedy of the dark days when the struggle seemed hopeless, and the shadow of scaffolds and the Spielberg lay heavily over the entire land.

> " There is no gladness, but deep care;
> In the place of plaudits, silence;
> In the place of peace, a horror.
> Wide as the seas her shores that mirror,
> So wide the woes of Italy,
> So without end her agony."

The whole passage to which this is a prelude is masterly in the succession of sharply-incised vignettes it contains, and in the repressed emotion of its tone.   The treachery of the princes in whom the people had put their trust; the rule of iron under which

> " It is crime to love one's country,
> And a sigh is reckoned sin ";

the tyranny that made the peasant's labor as well as the soldier's strength serve a foreign lord, and that closed the lips of the wise and hung the feet of the just with chains; the heavy sadness that hushed the joy of youth and spread a pall over the life of the cities; the suspicion bred of repeated betrayals which closed every heart; the agony in households where sons were torn from their fathers and brother lamented the loss of brother; the slow torture of the years in foreign prisons, where the days dragged on reckoned only by the change of sentinels on guard—all that is even now a memory to play powerfully on the heart strings, and that was then a living and bleeding reality, passes before us in the poet's simple, poignant phrases.   At the end, the stranger feels his longing for the brightness and beauty of the Italian land die in his breast.

> " To the sunshine and the vineyards,
> Dimmed with tears by tyrants drawn,
> He preferred his sombre pine trees,
> And the fogs and winds unceasing
> Of his home by northern seas."

The Hermit of Mt. Cenis is among the masterpieces of Berchet. It appeals to the reader of to-day because of what has already been noted as giving its permanent value to all the best of his work—a quality of picturesqueness, an unrhetorical simplicity of expression, an emotional sincerity. The effect it must have produced at the time when it was written is easily imaginable. Literature then wielded a power it has largely lost with its wider dissemination; it was one of the strongest weapons of the workers for a New Italy. Settembrini, the Neapolitan professor and critic, tells how in his youth " each one of us treasured in secret a blank-book in which he set down the finest patriotic poems he could manage to copy, not being able to procure them in print; and these he learned by heart and recited among his companions." Poems by Berchet, by Rossetti, by all the ardent young poets of liberty passed thus from hand to hand among their contemporaries, giving form to their aspirations, courage on the battlefield, hope in exile and imprisonment, consolation even in the hour of death.

In studying the relation of Berchet to the Italian national movement, we find him standing between the phase Leopardi voices, when uncertainty and pessimism were the keynote, and the high noon of the new day. He realizes keenly the obstacles to freedom and unity presented by certain conditions of the age, by certain weaknesses in the people themselves. In *Le Fantasie*, after drawing glowing pictures of the heroes of the Lombard League, the Battle of Legnano, and the Peace of Constance, he gives in sharp contrast a biting analysis of the abject state into which their descendants had fallen. He does not, however, like Leopardi, stop here. Through all the seemingly abortive struggles, in the midst of confusion and doubt, he feels coursing the sap of a new endeavor; and in the *Call to Arms* in 1830, it is the triumphant cry of an emergent Italy which we hear.

> " From the Alps to the Straits now brothers are all!
> On boundaries broken, on thrones made to fall,
> Let us plant the three colors, our common delight.
> *Green*—for the hope through such long years sustained;
> *Red*—for the joy now at last we've attained;
> *White*—for pure faith and for brotherly love."

IV

CARDUCCI AND THE NEW ITALY

Berchet died in 1851. In that same year there was living in Florence a boy of sixteen whose pen was to be used in the cause of united Italy with a fervor as intense as Berchet's own and a poetic power much greater, and who was to live to see completed the triumph of the "three colors" predicted by the earlier writer. It is seldom given to a poet to have his life span so epic a period as did that of Giosue Carducci. Born in 1835 in Val di Castello, a tiny village of Tuscany, he was just at an age to receive deep and lasting impressions when the revolution of 1848 broke out. His father, a government physician, was an enthusiastic Manzonian and a man of strong character. He had been imprisoned as a *Carbonaro* after the movement of 1831, and at the first stirrings of life in '48 he allied himself afresh with the liberals and took so active a part in the ensuing insurrection that after its disastrous close he was deprived of his government position, moving to Florence with his family in consequence.

It is interesting to read the description of Giosue's earliest home by one who was familiar with it. " The humble house stands by a brook, whose waters murmur against obstructing stones, on the slope of one of the last outposts of the Apuan Alps. The Tuscan landscape assumes in this region an unaccustomed strength. Not here is the sweetness of the Florentine hills bathed in light where Dante composed the verses of *The New Life,* but a sterner beauty recalling rather the songs of Guido, of Alighieri, of Ariosto in their exile." Such a country as this, at once austere and beautiful, was of the type to appeal most strongly to a nature like Carducci's. Here he grew up to hate tyranny and to exalt the idea of country, learning Latin from his father, and devouring on his own account such books as the *Iliad,* the *Æneid,* Rollin's *History of Rome,* the *Gerusalemme Liberata,* and all the poetry and prose he could find which dealt with the French Revolution. One can picture the eager boy, seated in the shade of some gigantic pine-tree, with the sound of murmuring waters in his ears, immersed in the pages of his Virgil or his Tasso, and finding in the ringing words of those free spirits of the past the true voices of the solitude about him.

When the Carducci family moved to Florence, Giosue was sent to the Scolopi Fathers to school. Full of patriotic aspirations and revolutionary sentiments both political and religious he did not prove a tractable pupil; yet masters and students alike fell under the magnetism of his intellectual brilliance and originality, his impetuous enthusiasm and idealism. His studies in Florence finished, Giosue was sent to Pisa, where he took his Doctor's Degree in 1856, going soon after as teacher of rhetoric to the *Ginnasio* of San Miniato al Tedesco. It was while there that he published his first volume of verse, not—as he himself tells us—" with the haughty intention of opening a new road or re-opening an old road, not even with the modest hope of receiving encouragement from the Italian public, but solely with the very honest intention and intrepid hope" of paying the debt he had incurred at the café frequented by his friends and himself!

After the death of the elder Carducci in 1858, Giosue settled in Florence once more with his family, living sparely, studying and writing constantly, and following each fluctuation in Italy's progress toward freedom with all the absorbed eagerness of one to whom liberty was the supreme end of life. His name meanwhile was becoming known to those interested in the fine arts, and in 1860 he was given the Chair of Italian Literature at the University of Bologna. In 1871, he published a collection of his verses. The *New Poems*, which came out in 1873, secured for him more general recognition; and with the appearance of the first volume of *Odi Barbare* in 1877, his fame was firmly established. From then until his death, in February of 1907, he held the place of Italy's foremost living poet; it is perhaps not too much to say that time will give him place among the foremost of her poets of all ages.

One of the first things to impress a reader of Carducci, is likely to be his marvelous versatility. His pen ranges from the most graceful and delicate of lyrics, lovely, flowerlike things fresh with morning dew, to satires that eat like an acid into the weaknesses and hypocrisies of the age; from the grave music of odes classically restrained and dignified to the blood-stirring trumpet calls of such poems as *To the Cross of Savoy, The Plébiscite*, and a dozen others in which the new Italy lives and finds voice. Further study, however, reveals in him an underlying unity of philosophy, both as an artist and as a man. He himself in one of his noblest poems has given us his conception of the poet's work and of his mission to the world. He is no mere idle dreamer with his head always in the clouds; no gardener to raise crops of sonnets for fair ladies to wear and cast aside; no pensioner to repay his patrons with verses. He is a " great artisan," who faces the world proudly; into whose furnace go high thoughts and noble conceptions, memories of the past and prophecies of the future; who forges swords with which to smite tyranny and diadems with which to crown beauty—and who makes for himself a single golden arrow which he launches forth, asking no higher pay than to watch the gleam of its flight into the vast azure of the ideal.

It would hardly have been possible for any man gifted with so high a sense of the responsibility of genius, so quick a responsiveness to all idealism, to have lived through the forty years that saw a nation in the making without being deeply moved and influenced thereby. With Carducci the circumstances of his environment and his own temperament had made patriotism a religion. His verse vibrates with the longing, the agony, the exultancy, the dauntless endurance and heroism of Italy's birth-struggle. In the early poems we read the profound discouragement of the dark days when the country lay crushed beneath the Austrian heel, and every attempt to rise seemed only to end in deeper woe. " I do not live," the young poet writes—

> " I do not live—ah no! My spirit lies
> Weary and still, with follies vainly stung.
> For all that makes life dear away is flung
> When Liberty no longer is life's prize."

In many of these poems there sounds the weariness born of a deep and fastidious disgust—disgust with the pettiness, the sordidness, the intellectual and moral weakness of the age; disgust which prompts rather a proud retirement into self than a struggle amidst the world's din and dust. Always, however, there comes the imperious call of a higher duty, and as when, during his young manhood, there broke out a cholera epidemic where he was staying and he put books and studies aside to care for the sick and protect the well, so at the battle-summons, he turns from solitude to take his part in the fight, to sound his defiance against compromise, hypocrisy, all the littlenesses and artificialities that are stumbling blocks in the way of truth and liberty.

When Victor Emanuel drew his sword, the poet saw and welcomed in him the destined leader.

"Now, thou longed for of our dead,
Of our living love and joy—
O thou White Cross of Savoy,
Thou dost shine against our sky!"

And when the great plébiscite of 1860 united all the provinces of Central Italy with Piedmont, he cries exultantly to the Austrian power:

"Away! O'er the Italian towers
The ancient star dawns and grows bright;
Strike, stranger, your tents from our sight,
Your kingdom ends to-day."

Thus we follow, step by step, the making of Italy as the poet saw it. There is no event of political importance in the years from 1850 to the end of the century which is not reflected in his poems; more than that, we feel in them the essential spirit which animated those years, the varying currents of emotion which bore the events along. There is impatience at the political intrigues and calculations that followed the first monarchical success; there is burning indignation over the delay in seizing upon Rome, the natural capital of the newly formed kingdom; there is enthusiasm for Garibaldi and the Republicans— then as the republican ideals were lowered and its heroes disappeared, a return of allegiance to the monarchy sanctioned by the people's will. Always, tying the wide and varied body of his work into a homogeneous whole in its message to the world, there is a high, an almost stern devotion to the ideals of " truth and justice." One feels that the cause of Italy was sacred to Carducci most of all because it seemed to him in a large sense the cause of human development and progress—and it is this largeness of interpretation, joined to a wonderful mastery of poetic expression, which makes his greatness. The vision of Leopardi and Berchet was limited; they each interpret certain phases only of the Italian struggle. With the one we are taken into the dark, turbulent depths from which a nation was to be born; the other shows us vignettes of this and that element in the struggle. Then comes Carducci. He too puts before us the depths out of which truth rises, he too gives us pictures—such pictures as that of Garibaldi riding alone under the leaden sky while behind him sound—

> " The cadenced fall of footsteps, and the sighs
> Breathed from heroic breasts into the night."

He makes us share with him the ardent hopes of his early years;
the discouragements, rebuffs, disappointments of later ones; the final
triumph.   Then with the seer's vision, which passes through the mere
event, the historic fact, to the universal and spiritual significance at
its core, he interprets to later generations the true meaning and value
of Italy's Risorgimento.

> " A flower's shadow, Beauty—fluttered o'er
> By the white butterflies of poesy;
> A trumpet's echo, lost in distant vales,
>   Is Power.
> Only from out th' eternal flux of things,
> A light-house beacon through the ages' night,
> There rises, conquering violence and time,
>   The Ideal."

A MODERN SAINT FRANCIS

RICHARD LE GALLIENNE

WE were neither of us fox-hunting ourselves, but chanced both
to be out on our morning walk and to be crossing a breezy Surrey
common at the same moment, when the huntsmen and huntresses of
the Slumberfold Hunt were blithely congregating for a day's run.
A meet is always an attractive sight, and we had both come to a halt
within a yard or two of each other, and stood watching the gallant
company of fine ladies and gentlemen on their beautiful, impatient
mounts, keeping up a prancing conversation, till the exciting moment should arrive when the cry would go up that the fox had been
started, and the whole field would sweep away, a cataract of hounds,
red-coats, riding habits and dog-carts.

The moment came. The fox had been found in a spinney running down to Withy Brook, and his race for life had begun. With a
happy shout, the hunt was up and off in a twinkling, and the stranger and I were left alone on the broad common.

I had scanned him furtively as he stood near me; a tall, slightly
built man of about fifty, with perfectly white hair, and strangely
gentle blue eyes. There was a curious, sad distinction over him and
he had watched the scene with a smile of blended humor and pity.

Turning to me, as we were left alone, and speaking almost as
though to himself: "It is a strange sight," he said with a sigh. "I
wonder if it seems as strange to you? Think of all those grown-up,
so-called civilized, people being so ferociously intent on chasing one
poor little animal for its life—and feeling, when at last the huntsman
holds up his poor brush, with absurd pride (if indeed the fox is not
too sly for them), that they have really done something clever, in that
with so many horses and dogs and so much noise, they have actually
contrived to catch and kill one fox!"

"It is strange!" I said, for I had been thinking just that very
thing.

"Of course, they always tell you," he continued, as we took the
road together, "that the fox really enjoys being hunted, and that
he feels his occupation gone if there are no hounds to track him, and

finally to tear him to pieces. What wonderful stories human nature
will tell itself in its own justification! Can one imagine any created
thing *enjoying* being pursued for its life, with all that loud terror
of men and horses and savage dogs at its heels? No doubt—if we can
imagine even a fox so self-conscious—it would take a certain pride in
its own cunning and skill, if the whole thing were a game; but a race
with death is too deadly in earnest for a fox even to relish his own
stratagems. Happily for the fox, it is probable that he does not feel
so much for himself as some of us feel for him; but anyone who
knows the wild things knows too what terror they are capable of feeling, and how the fear of death is always with them. No! you may be
sure that a fox prefers a cosy hen-roost to the finest run with the
hounds ever made."

"But even if he should enjoy being hunted," I added, "the
even stranger thing to me is that civilized men and women should
enjoy hunting him."

"Isn't it strange?" answered my companion eagerly, his face
lighting up at finding a sympathizer. "When will people realize
that there is so much more fun in studying wild things than in killing
them! . . ."

He stopped suddenly in his walk, to gather a small weed which
had caught his quick eye by the roadside, and which he examined
for a moment through a little pocket microscope which I noticed,
hanging like an eyeglass round his neck, and which I learnt afterward
quite affectionately to associate with him. Then, as we walked on, he
remarked:

"But, of course, we are yet very imperfectly civilized. Humanity is a lesson learned very slowly by the human race. Yet we
are learning it by degrees, yes! we are learning it," and he threw out
his long stride more emphatically—the stride of one accustomed to
long daily tramps on the hills.

"Strange, that principle of cruelty in the universe!" he resumed,
after a pause in which he had walked on in silence. "Very strange.
To me it is the most mysterious of all things—though, I suppose,
after all, it is no more mysterious than pity. When, I wonder, did
pity begin? Who was the first human being to pity another? How
strange he must have seemed to the others, how incomprehensible and

ridiculous—not to say dangerous. There can be little doubt that he was promptly dispatched with stone axes as an enemy of a respectable murderous society."

"I expect," said I, "that our friends the fox-hunters would take a similar view of our remarks on their sport."

"No doubt—and perhaps turn their hounds on us! A man hunt! 'Give me the hunting of man!' as a brutal young poet, we know of, recently sang."

"How different was the spirit of Emerson's old verse," I said:

> "'Hast thou named all the birds without a gun?
> Loved the wood-rose, and left it on its stalk? . . .
> O be my friend, and teach me to be thine!'"

"That is one of my mottoes!" cried my companion with evident pleasure. "Let us go and quote it to our fox-hunters!"

"I wonder how the fox is getting on," I said.

"If he is any sort of fox, he is safe enough as yet, we may be sure. They are wonderful creatures. It is not surprising that mankind has always looked upon Reynard as almost a human being—if not more—for there is something quite uncanny in his instincts, and the cool, calculating way in which he uses them. He is come and gone like a ghost. One moment you were sure you saw him clearly close by and the next he is gone—who knows where? He can run almost as swiftly as light, and as softly as a shadow; and in his wildest dash, what a sure judgment he has for the lie of the ground, how unerringly—and at a moment when a mistake is death—he selects his cover. How learned, too, he is in his knowledge of the countryside! There is not a dry ditch, or a water-course, or an old drain, or a hole in a bank for miles around that is not mysteriously set down in the map he carries in his graceful, clever head; and one need hardly say that all the suitable hiding-places in and around farm-yards are equally well known to him. Then withal he is so brave. How splendidly, when wearied out, and hopelessly tracked down, with the game quite up, he will turn on his pursuers, and die with his teeth fast in his enemy's throat!"

"I believe you are a fox-hunter in disguise," I laughed.

"Well, I have hunted as a boy," he said, "and I know something of what those red-coated gentlemen are feeling. But soon I got more interested in studying nature than killing it, and when I became a naturalist I ceased to be a hunter. You get to love the things so that it seems like killing little children. They come so close to you, are so beautiful and so clever: and sometimes there seems such a curious pathos about them. How anyone can kill a deer with that woman's look in its eyes, I don't know. I should always expect the deer to change into a fairy princess, and die in my arms with the red blood running from her white breast. And pigeons, too, with their soft sunny coo all the summer afternoon, or the sudden lapping of sleepy wings round the chimneys—how can anyone trap or shoot them with blood-curdling rapidity, and not expect to see ghosts!"

"Of course, there is this difference about the fox," I said, "that it is really in a sense born to be hunted. For not only is it a fierce hunter itself, but it would not be allowed to exist at all, so to say, unless it consented to being hunted. Like a gladiator it accepts a comfortable living for a certain time, on condition of its providing at last a spirited exhibition of dying. In other words, it is preserved entirely for the purpose of being hunted. It must accept life on that condition or be extirpated as destructive vermin by the plundered farmer. Life is sweet, after all, and to be a kind of protected highwayman of the poultry-yard, for a few sweet toothsome years, taking one's chances of being surely brought to book at last, may perhaps seem worth while."

"Yes! but how does your image of the protected gladiator reflect on those who protect him? There, of course, is the point. The gladiator, as you say, is willing to take his chances in exchange for fat living and idleness, as long as he lives. You may even say that his profession is good for him, develops fine qualities of mind even as well as body—but what of the people who crowd with blood-thirsty eagerness to watch those qualities exhibited in so tragic a fashion for their amusement? Do they gain any of his qualities of skill and courage, and strength and fearlessness in the face of death? No, they are merely brutalized by cruel excitement—and while they applaud his skill and admire his courage, they long most to watch him die. So—is it not?—with our friend the fox. The huntsman invariably compliments him on his spirit and his cunning, but what he wants is—the brush. He wants the excitement of hunting the living thing to its death; and, let huntsmen say what they will about the exhilaration of the horse exercise across country as being the main thing, they know better—and, if it be true, why don't they take it without the fox?"

"They do in America, as, of course, you know. There a man walks across country trailing a stick, at the end of which is a piece of cloth impregnated with some pungent scent which hounds love and mistake for the real thing."

"Hard on the poor hounds!" smiled my friend. "Even worse than a red herring. You could hardly blame the dogs if they mistook the man for Actæon and tore him to pieces."

"And I suspect that the huntsmen are no better satisfied."

"Yet, as we were saying, if the secret spring of their sport is not the cruel delight of pursuing a living thing to its death, that Américan plan should serve all the purposes, and give all the satisfaction for which they claim to follow the hounds: the keen pleasure of a gallop across country, the excitement of its danger, the pluck and pride of taking a bad fence, and equally, too, the pleasure of watching the hounds cleverly at work with their mysterious gift of scent. All the same, I suspect there are few sportsmen who would not vote it a tame substitute. Without something being killed, the zest, the 'snap,' is gone. It is as depressing as a sham fight."

"Yes, that mysterious shedding of blood! what a part it has played in human history. Even religion countenances it, and war glorifies it. Men are never in higher spirits than when they are going to kill, or be killed themselves, or see something else killed. Tennyson's 'ape and tiger' die very hard in the tamest of us."

"Alas, indeed they do!" said my friend with a sigh. "But I do believe that they are dying none the less. Just of late there has been a reaction in favor of brute force, and people like you and me have been ridiculed as old-fashioned sentimentalists. But reaction is one of the laws of advance. Human progress always takes a step backwards after it has taken two forward. And so it must be here, too. In the end, it is the highest types among men and nations that count, and the highest types among both to-day are those which show most humanity, shrink most from the infliction of pain. When one thinks of the horrible cruelties that were the legal punishment of criminals, even within the last two hundred years, and not merely brutal criminals, but also political offenders or so-called heretics— how everyone thought it the natural and proper thing to break a man on the wheel for a difference of opinion, or torture him with hideous ingenuity into a better frame of mind, and how the pettiest larcenies were punished by death; it seems as if we of to-day, even the least sensitive of us, cannot belong to the same race—and it is impossible to deny that the heart of the world has grown softer and that pity is becoming more and more a natural instinct in human nature. I believe that some day it will have thrust out cruelty altogether, and that the voluntary infliction of pain upon another will be unknown. The idea of anyone killing for pleasure will seem too preposterous to be believed, and soldiers and fox-hunters and pigeon-shooters will be spoken of as nowadays we speak of cannibals. But, of course, I am a dreamer," he concluded, his face shining with his gentle dream, as though he had been a veritable saint of the calendar.

"Yes, a dream," he added presently, "and yet——"

In that "and yet" there was a world of invincible faith that made it impossible not to share his dream, even see it building before one's eyes—such is the magnetic power of a passionate personal conviction.

"Of course," he went on again, "we all know that 'nature is one with rapine, a harm no preacher can heal.' But because the fox runs off with the goose, or the hawk swoops down on the chicken, and 'yon whole little wood is a world of plunder and prey'—is that any reason why we should be content to plunder and prey, too? And after all, the cruelty of Nature is only one-sided. There is lots of pity in Nature, too. These strange little wild lives around us are not entirely bent on killing and eating each other. They know the tenderness of motherhood, the sweetness of building a home together, and I believe there is far more comradeship and mutual help amongst them than we know of. Yes, even in wild Nature there is a principle of love working no less than a principle of hate. Nature is not all-devouring and destroying. She is loving and building, too. Nature is more constructive than destructive, and she is ever at work evolving and evolving a higher dream. Surely it is not for man, to whom, so far as we know, Nature has entrusted the working out of her finest impulses, and whom she has endowed with all the fairy apparatus of the soul; it is not for him, whose eyes—of all her children—Nature has opened, the one child she has taken into her confidence and to whom she has whispered her secret hopes and purposes: surely it is not for man voluntarily to deny his higher lot, and, because the wolf and he have come from the same great mother, say: ' I am no better than the wolf. Why should I not live the life of a wolf—and kill and devour like my brother?' Surely it is not for the cruel things in Nature to teach man cruelty—rather, if it were possible," and the saint smiled at his fancy, " would it be the mission of man to teach them kindness: rather should he preach pity to the hawk and peace between the panther and the bear. It is not the bad lessons of Nature, but the good, that are meant for man—though, as you must have noticed, man seldom appeals to the precedents of Nature except to excuse that in him which is Nature at her worst. When we say, ' it is only natural,' we almost invariably refer to that in Nature of which Nature herself has entrusted the refinement or the elimination to man. It is Nature's bad we copy, not Nature's good; and always we forget that we ourselves are a part of Nature—Nature's vicegerent, so to say, upon the earth——"

As we talked, we had been approaching a house built high among the heather, with windows looking over all the surrounding country. Presently, the saint stopped in front of it.

" This is my house," he said. " Won't you come in and see me some time?—and, by the way, I am going to talk to some of the village children about the wild things, bird's nesting, and so forth, up at the school house on Thursday. I wish you'd come and help me. One's only hope is with the children. The grown-up are too far gone. Mind you come."

So we parted, and, as I walked across the hill homeward, haunted by that gentle face, I thought of Melampus, that old philosopher who loved the wild things so and had made such friends with them, that they had taught him their language and told him all their secrets:

" With love exceeding a simple love of the things
    That glide in grasses and rubble of woody wreck;
Or change their perch on a beat of quivering wings
    From branch to branch, only restful to pipe and peck;

Or, bridled, curl at a touch their snouts in a ball;
　Or cast their web between bramble and thorny hook;
The good physician, Melampus, loving them all,
　Among them walked, as a scholar who reads a book."

As I dipped into the little thick-set wood that surrounds my house, something stood for a second in one of the openings, then was gone like a shadow. I was glad to think how full of bracken and hollows, and mysterious holes and corners of mossed and lichened safety was our old wood—for the shadow was a fox. I like to think it was the very fox we had been talking about come to find shelter with me—and, if he stole a meal out of our hen-roost, I gave it him before he asked it, with all the will in the world. I hope he chose a good fat hen, and not one of your tough old capons that sometimes come to table.

SHELLEY'S SKYLARK

CHARLES HANSON TOWNE

IMMORTAL bird,
Whose song God's purest poet long since heard,
And caught within the golden chains of rhyme,
Our captive for all time!

O tender tones,
That none who, hearing, ever can forget,
Even when the city's thunder crashes and groans,
And the wood's whisper moans—
How wonderful that thou art with us yet!

High on the Hills of Song thy song is set,
Within the very blue where first thy voice
Made his young heart rejoice;
And from empyrean heights forever shall fall
Thy silver madrigal,
Drenching the world with thine enraptured stream,
Thy heavenly dream,
Cleansing us as in fires angelical,
Sweeping us to the mountain-peaks of morn
Where beauty and love were born.

He loved thee; and we love thee for his sake:
And sometimes when the heart is like to break
With ancient sorrows that wake
In the still darkness of some desolate night,
We hear thee too as he once heard thee sing
On a white morn of Spring;
And all our soul is flooded with the light
Thy melody, and thine alone, can bring.

We hear thee—yes; but only through his song!
Our ears were empty of thy fluted trills
Until he snatched thee from thy splendid hills,
And gave the wonder of thy joy to us,
O bird miraculous!

We hear thee now—through him;
And we rejoice that as thy date grows dim,
He, and not we, first heard that lovely sound
Which all his spirit drowned
In a wild ecstasy beyond our ken.
And if thy voice now fills heaven's leafiest glen,
Singing again,
Flinging its silver cataract of bliss
Down many a sheer abyss,
Be glad, O bird, that when thou eamest here,
Thy song fell on his ear,
And he was thy divine interpreter!

THE NEW DRAMA IN ENGLAND

H. Granville Barker

ARCHIBALD HENDERSON

MANY years ago, Matthew Arnold pleaded for the organization of the theatre in England—the irresistible theatre, as he so optimistically called it. For the past twenty years, tentative and groping steps, now this way, now that, have been directed toward this visionary goal. England may be the most conservative country in the world. Englishmen may be proud of their ability to " muddle through somehow." Once let a great creative and basically fruitful conception take shape in their minds, and then their perseverance and dogged determination brook no obstacle until their object is finally attained. By the year 1916 we may expect the consummation of that great project for a national theatre, in commemoration of William Shakespeare, which will place Great Britain abreast of the great nations of the world in the domain of the theatre. If the patient, arduous and unremitting efforts of the adherents and supporters of the drama, in its highest and most original forms, are taken as criteria, we may confidently look forward to a not far distant future when the repertory idea shall have found realization in stable practice, when the brilliant and original efforts of the dramatists of the new school shall have won the permanent support of the British public.

Whenever a creative movement, in no matter what field of human activity, is forward, and is triumphantly hailed as " New," the public is inclined to regard it with a certain amount of reserve, if not with suspicion and distrust. And when, besides, this " New " movement comes into existence as a form of revolt against existent conditions, the public is all the more inclined to say : " All right. Go ahead. But you must meet the tests of the commercial theatre. You must create your public, or at least show that there is a submerged public ready to support you. Make good if you can. But don't expect to achieve permanent results by counting solely on popular sympathy."

The New Drama in England to-day, with Bernard Shaw and

Granville Barker as its leading exponents, is essentially an experimental school. From the beginning, every effort has pointed toward fresh extensions of sense in the field of the drama. Freedom for the exercise of dramatic talents is posited as the fundamental pre-requisite for the healthy development of the drama. The exponents of the new school have sought above all things to free themselves from the confining restrictions of the drama, and to express themselves unreservedly—in idea, in form—regardless of whether the result seemed "dramatic" or not. These ideals brought them into conflict—an irrepressible conflict—with two established institutions—the commercial theatre, and the censorship. From the first, it was apparent that the long-run system of the commercial theatre was fatal to the chances of the new dramatist. His public was destined to be, not the "great public," but a "lesser public," in part composed of intelligent theatre-goers, in part of people who have ceased to encourage the banalities and falsities of the theatre of commerce, in part of a new quota of the human throng. Moreover, it soon became apparent that if the drama was to flourish, if new talent was to burgeon and blossom, if the path was to be made clear for the experimentalist—the first and most imperative necessity was the abolition, or at least radical modification, of the censorship. Not less essential—for it had nothing to do with mere institutional bars—was the desire to create, not simply strikingly new modes of stage entertainment, but works of art that would bear the test of publication. There was the thrust toward utter realism —the ambition to create a drama that would wear the drab, as well as the brilliant, garments of life itself.

It was Bernard Shaw who initiated the New Drama twenty years ago with *Widowers' Houses*. The Independent Theatre, inaugurated by Mr. J. T. Grein, failed in its effort, as did the New Century Theatre, to bring to the fore a group of budding dramatists. But it was the immediate cause of enticing Bernard Shaw into the field of dramatic authorship. Mr. Grein demanded evidence of the latent dramatic talent in England which only needed the offer of a field for its display. Shaw claimed to have manufactured the evidence; and that claim has been made good in the great capitals, and on the greatest stages, of the world. In *The Author's Apology*, prefixed to the *Dramatic Opinions and Essays* (English edition), Shaw especially insists that those dramatic criticisms were " not a series of judgments aiming at impartiality, but a siege laid to the theatre of the Nineteenth Century by an author who had to make his own way into it at the point of the pen, and throw some of its defenders into the moat." Shaw was accused of unfairness and intolerance as a critic of the drama, of the intent to stifle native dramatic talent with forcible condemnation. When Shaw vigorously charged Pinero, Jones and others with failure, he was simply charging them with failure to come his way and do what he wanted. " I postulated as desirable a certain kind of play in which I was destined ten years later to make my mark as a playwright (as I very well foreknew in the depth of my own unconsciousness) ; and I brought everybody, authors, actors, managers, to the one test: were they coming my way or staying in the old grooves? " He badly attempted " the institution of a new art," in which the dramatist could give the freest play to his originality ; and foresaw as result a new and hybrid drama—part narrative, part homily, part description, part dialogue, and part drama (in the conventional sense). In the days that have followed that pronouncement the English stage has been enriched by such original, such powerful, such unique plays as *Major Barbara, Getting Married, The Voysey Inheritance* and *The Madras House*—hybrids all perhaps, analytical and dialectical, strained and in some cases repellent—but marked by a mysterious novelty, the sign-manual of genius.

The next significant step in the glacially slow movement toward the creation of a native drama of spontaneous art and the establishment of a national theatre that would worthily represent the national genius, is found in the establishment of the Stage Society, of London. At first, its ambition was the very modest one of giving private performances, on Sunday afternoons, in studios and such other places as might prove available. The scheme found enthusiastic supporters among people of rather aimless intellectual tastes, who eagerly sought in the performance of the Stage Society a " refuge from the dullness of the English Sunday." As the society grew in strength and numbers, the performances came to be given in theatres—permissible when no admission fee was charged. After a time, the Sunday performance was generally followed by another performance on Monday afternoon. The Stage Society thus became the logical successor

of the Independent Theatre, founded some ten years before; and
while it has always remained a *théâtre à côté*, the importance of its
work in fostering latent dramatic genius cannot be too strongly emphasized. It was founded in 1899, and during the eleven seasons since,
has produced forty-six English plays, and twenty-nine plays by
continental dramatists. With seven exceptions, these plays were produced by the society for the first time on the English stage. In its
very first season it produced Bernard Shaw's *You Never Can Tell* and
Candida, Maeterlinck's *Intérieur* and *La Mort de Tintagiles*, Hauptmann's *Das Friedensfest* and Henrik Ibsen's *The League of Youth*.
In its second season, it produced Shaw's *Captain Brassbound's Conversion*, Hauptmann's *Einsame Menschen*, and Ibsen's *The Pillars of Society*. In its third season were produced *The Lady from the Sea*, and
The Marrying of Ann Leete, a remarkable play by a new dramatic
author, H. Granville Barker. It is needless for me to enumerate the
great modern dramas, chiefly dramas of thought and of purpose,
which have been produced by the Stage Society during the remaining
years up to to-day. Suffice it to say that the Stage Society has played
in England, though in a somewhat less conspicuous way, the rôle which
has been played on the continent by the Théâtre Libre, L'Œuvre, and
the Freie Bühne. From it came Bernard Shaw and Granville Barker—
soon to be united in an enterprise at the Court Theatre which is without a parallel in the history of the English stage. From that fecund
school of drama came also the late St. John Hankin, a dramatist of
rare promise, and Mr. John Galsworthy, the author of the original
and powerful dramas, *Strife* and *Justice*.

The Repertory Theatre idea has gained a firm footing in England; and to-day bids fair to go forward slowly to a more permanent
and enduring establishment. In 1898 was founded the Irish Literary
Theatre, under the auspices of the National Literary Society,
founded by Mr. W. B. Yeats seven years before. That energetic
woman who played the mysterious " angel " to the Avenue Theatre
production of Shaw's *Arms and the Man* in 1894, Miss A. E. F.
Horniman, may fitly be described as the mother of repertory in England. Largely through her efforts has come into being the Abbey
Theatre, the repertory theatre of Ireland—the only theatre in an
English-speaking country, said Mr. W. B. Yeats in 1908, " that is

free for a certain number of years to play what it thinks worth play-ing, and to whistle at the timid." The experiment of Mr. Barker and Mr. Shaw at the Court Theatre, of which I shall speak later, showed the way to the true repertory, of which it was,,technically, not a perfect example. At Manchester in 1907, the first true repertory theatre in Great Britain was established by Miss Horniman. The experimental theatres at Stockport, Glasgow, Edinburgh and Liver-pool are all healthy manifestations of the new movement towards Citizens' Theatres, on repertory lines, in modified forms. Mr. Charles Frohman's season of repertory at the Duke of York's Theatre (1909-1910), London, is the first sign, though of doubtful success, of the effort to plumb the commercial possibilities of the repertory system. In his recent book,* Mr. P. P. Howe says of Mr. Frohman's some-what inconclusive experiment:

"It is a step on the road. The seemly and requisite thing for the State to do is to elevate the drama above the chances of commerce, as Smollett in common with most thinking persons saw a century and a half ago, as nearly every European country has already done, and as this country will do in something much less than a century and a half. But the business of a National Theatre is primarily with the classical repertory of plays. Mr. Frohman's theatre, pointing as it does to endowment, points equally clearly along the path of individual experiment, which will always be the path of the advancing drama. The next step on this road is clear. A theatre combining convenience of site with a rent only moderately extortionate, forgoing the un-necessary complication of expensive stars, and keeping a clear eye on the public it would serve, may be set going in London to-morrow with satisfactory pecuniary profit. A certain definite public is now made familiar with the repertory idea, and to convert this public into a large, convinced, and permanent public for good drama is a mere matter of persistence. . . . The good playgoer will be created by good drama, but it is not to be forgotten that the good playgoer also exists and is awaiting a theatre worth his while."

The crown of the Stage Society's achievement, as Mr. William Archer once expressed it, was the presentation of Mr. H. Granville Barker to the world of dramatic art in England. Much has been written about Mr. Shaw, his genius, career, and influence upon con-temporary drama. Little enough, strange to say, has been written

* *The Repertory ₁Theatre.* Martin Secker, London, 1910.

about Mr. Barker, with his strange, austere talent, his anti-sentimental and chiseled art, his complicated simplicity in technique, his almost fierce contempt for the normal relations of average, everyday life. A few people nowadays are beginning eagerly to claim him as the one true dramatist—and English withal—of the movement. Though born (1877) in Kensington, the curiously complex strains in his ancestry are almost everything racial but English: Scotch, Welsh, Italian, Portuguese, and even a trace, perhaps, of the Jew.

Almost from birth, he seemed destined for the theatre. As Shaw learned from his mother, a well-known singer, the secrets of enunciation which so greatly aided him later as a platform speaker, so Barker learned from his mother, a well-known reciter, the art of speaking and reciting. At seven, he was already proficient in expression; and at the age of thirteen, though callow in the extreme, he was shot into the theatre—to hit or miss as fate, or his own genius, might decree. His education, in the conventional sense, then abruptly ceased; and to this circumstance perhaps is due his intolerance of the academic, and his conviction that the only great school of art is life. He served a rather severe apprenticeship to the stage between his thirteenth and seventeenth years; but he was not to attract public notice until several years later. Then he came into prominence in connection with the Stage Society—as actor, as producer, and as author. His own play, *The Marrying of Ann Leete*, which he produced, awoke the thoughtful attention and appreciative criticism of such men as Mr. Shaw, Mr. William Archer, and Mr. Arthur Symons. In Shaw's *Candida* he achieved a memorable effect in the part of Marchbanks; his impersonation of Richard II at an Elizabethan Stage Society performance helped also to mark him out as a brilliant actor. Much might be written about his art as an actor; for it is impossible to say how much his art as a dramatist owes to his skill as a player. It was in 1904 that Mr. Barker first came into association with the Court Theatre. Mr. J. H. Leigh, with Mr. J. E. Vedrenne as manager, was giving a series of creditable Shakespearean revivals at the Court Theatre; and he invited Mr. Barker to produce *The Two Gentlemen of Verona*. This production, in which Mr. Barker played the part of Launce, was a marked success; and the first result of his association with Mr. Vedrenne was a series of six matinée performances of *Can-*

dida. The final outcome was the Vedrenne-Barker management of the Court Theatre from 1904 to 1907.

Throughout this time, Mr. Barker took a leading part in a number of the plays which he produced; and this he continued to do in the subsequent productions at the Savoy Theatre. In 1904, Mr. Barker had produced for the New Century Theatre, under Mr. Vedrenne's management, Professor Gilbert Murray's "spiritual" translation of the *Hippolytus* of Euripides; and it was partly their association in this successful experiment that led to the Court Theatre enterprise. Had it not been for the "new" drama, Mr. Barker would probably, as he once told me, have left the stage much earlier—though he felt a strong sense of mastery in Shakespearean parts. His performances in his own and Shaw's plays, notably in *Waste, Man and Superman,* and *The Devil's Disciple,* were regarded as triumphs in the new style of acting. Had there been repertory in England, he would doubtless have remained on the stage. Despite the fact that he is still occasionally seen on the boards, he has definitely abandoned the actor's career. The close of the Vedrenne-Barker season at the Savoy marked his definitive severance from the stage as an actor, and his determination to devote himself wholly to the profession of writing plays.

To show the regard in which his work as an actor was held, I need only cite the words of the *Spectator* which appeared at the time of his retirement from the stage. The writer recognized Mr. Barker not only as an alert and subtle interpreter of character, a master in the art of suggestion, an intellectual actor dominating his audience by skill rather than by force. "One of the principal causes of his artistic success is that he can mingle intellect with fancy, and his acting is often at its sprightliest when it is most significant. He possesses in a high degree the indefinable quality of charm—a quality which he displays at its fullest perhaps in his rendering of Valentine in *You Never Can Tell,* and in the delightful third act of *The Doctor's Dilemma.* More than any other English actor, he can 'put the spirit of youth into everything,' so that the whole scene becomes charged with high spirits. . . . With Mr. Barker the art and the ingenuity are there, but they are softened and etherealized by a perpetual flow of English humor and English imagination."

Of that remarkable experiment at the Court Theatre, I would refer the reader in especial to its recorded history written by Mr. Desmond MacCarthy.* The companies trained by Mr. Barker, both at the Court Theatre and, subsequently; at the Savoy (September, 1907-March 14, 1908) wrought something very like a revolution in the art of dramatic production in England. The unity of tone, the subordination of the individual, the genuine striving for totality of effect, the constant changes of bill, the abolition of the " star " system—all were noteworthy features of these undertakings. There were given 985 performances of thirty-two plays by seventeen actors; 701 of these performances were of eleven plays by one author, Mr. Shaw. Plays of other authors were produced—and often with striking success; but in the main the whole undertaking may be regarded as a Shaw Festspiel, prolonged over three years. Mr. Galsworthy, Mr. Hankin, Mr. Masefield, Miss Elizabeth Robins, and Mr. Barker— all came strongly into public notice. The Court was not in the strict sense a repertory theatre; rather it furnished a tentative compromise between the *théâtre à côté* and the actor-managed theatre, backed by a syndicate of capitalists. As Mr. Barker said: " The first thing we did was to struggle against the long-run system, partly because we wanted to produce a lot of plays, and partly because we disagreed with it. It is bad for plays and bad for acting." In March, 1909, Mr. Barker produced a series of matinées of Mr. Galsworthy's *Strife* at the Duke of York's Theatre; and during the season of 1909-1910 we find him actively engaged for the repertory season of Mr. Charles Frohman at the same theatre—producing his own plays *The Madras House* and *Prunella*, among others. Mr. Barker was offered in 1907 the post of director of the New Theatre in New York—a convincing proof that he had made a great reputation as a producer; but his conception of the *théâtre intime* as the indispensable setting for the modern drama precluded his acceptance of the proffered directorship of the New Theatre, because of its grandiose proportions. The admirable book he wrote in collaboration with Mr. Archer, *Plans and Estimates for a National Theatre*, points forward to a future National Memorial to Shakespeare in the shape of a great theatre, supported by private endowment, and comprehensively representative in character.

* *The Court Theatre*, 1904-1907. A. H. Bullen, London.

In the face of these multifarious activities, and many that I have omitted to mention—as actor, as producer, as author, as builder and inspirer—Mr. Barker all the while was persisting in a strenuous course of straightforward drudgery in the effort to educate himself as a dramatist. In 1893, he began regularly to write plays; and in that year was produced his first drama—a play in which Mr. Barker and some amateur actors appeared before a "most select audience." Though the plays of this early period were amateurish and inexpert, they showed the genius of the natural dramatist. They were, as Mr. Barker expressed it, "stage-tight"—much as one would describe a box as water-tight: they played themselves, on the stage, before an audience. Shortly after turning dramatist, Mr. Barker began to write plays regularly in collaboration with Mr. Berte Thomas; and during the next six years these two wrote, in conjunction, some five or six plays. Only one of these plays, *The Weather-hen*, actually saw the light. The moderate success it enjoyed was well deserved. By this time Mr. Barker had worked free of derivative influences; and this play showed itself spontaneous in treatment, genuine in expression.

All these efforts can only be called promising tentatives. They have no significance for the public; and are merely important as successive links in the evolution of Mr. Barker's genius as a craftsman. In *The Marrying of Ann Leete*, produced by the Stage Society at the Royalty Theatre, January 26, 1902, Mr. Barker made his first serious bid for wide recognition. It registers, on his part, a serious and sincere effort to "find himself"—to discover an inevitable medium in dramatic expression which would remain permanently associated with his name. With all its peculiar originality, its almost unprecedented novelty of technique, it failed of its purpose, not for lack of meaning, but for excess of meanings.

If there is one outstanding feature of Mr. Barker's genius, which grows more evident with each new play, it is the scope, the social perspective, of his anecdote. This play, laid at the end of the eighteenth century, is not concerned merely with the fate and destiny of particular individuals: its theme is the moral, and physical, degeneration of a family. An air of languorous corruption, of polite blackguardism hangs, like a miasma, over the scene. Mr. Carnaby Leete, a brilliant but utterly unscrupulous politician, dextrously " stacking the cards " for his own advancement without regard to party fealty, personal loyalty or honor, is a remarkable figure—one of the most striking figures Mr. Barker has ever projected. There is one other remarkable feature of this play—the technique. Indeed it may be regarded as an unsuccessful experiment in technique. The action—if the static picture of a family in the final stages of polite corruption can be called " action "—is conveyed by a species of incoherent volubility, a sort of brilliant indirection, that is all but illuminating. The *disjecta membra* of vaguely significant conversations fall about us like hailstones; we experience a sense of suppressed excitement in tracking down some elusive secret to its hidden lair. But that is as far as Mr. Barker got—the suggestively cryptic. Already we see him ungallantly employing woman as the embodiment of an abstract idea—the woman boldly entangling the good-natured but dense philanderer in her carefully devised snare. The sense of grossness comes strongly upon one in the finale—this eugenic, but unnatural, solution of mating the over-civilized and devitalized woman with the coarse but pure-blooded man. It is that same oppressive and heavy atmosphere of sex communicated to us by James Lane Allen's *Butterflies—a Tale of Nature*. And we realize in the ending, not a natural nor even a morbid impulse—but a strictly sociologic motive which might have occurred to Westermarck, but never to Ann Leete! " Mr. Barker can write," said Mr. Arthur Symons in a contemporary account of the play. " . . . He brings his people on and off with an unconventionality which comes of knowing the resources of the theatre, and of being unfettered by the traditions of its technique. . . . Mr. Barker, in doing the right or the clever thing, does it just not quite strongly enough to carry it against opposition. . . . The artist, who is yet an imperfect artist, bewilders the world with what is novel in his art; the great artist convinces the world. Mr. Barker . . . will come to think with more depth and less tumult; he will come to work with less prodigality and more mastery of means. But he has energy already, and a sense of what is absurd and honest in the spectacle of this game, in which the pawns seem to move themselves."

Mr. Barker has recently said that, in his opinion, " the Theatre —with music—is marked out as the art of the immediate future, of the next hundred years." The prophecy called up to my mind an endless series of plays with *Prunella* as forerunner. That beautiful hybrid—in which collaborated a skilled technician and keen thinker, a poet, and a musician—is one of the most tender and gracefully conceived plays I can recall. With all its airy fancy, it contrives to embody a wealth of real meaning that creeps close to the heart of everyone. It is cut from the same pattern, and was doubtless influenced by, Rostand's *Les Romanesques*—that fanciful Watteau picture of love, life, disillusion and reconcilement, which takes place " anywhere so the scenery is attractive," in which the people dress as they please " provided the costumes are pretty." This Pierrot, with his rollicking, rackety band of gay mummers, is French in conception, but English in execution—lacking in the Gallic subtlety, but instinct with an *insouciance*, a playful *naïveté*, that is quaintly English. Through the eyes of his familiar, Scaramel, the *blasé* and the unilluded, we see Pierrot as the world's mad truant—lyrically in pursuit of a bright happiness that is all self-gratification. He is a graceful tyro in the poetic art of living—with no regret for the past, no thought for the morrow. Into Prunella's garden he trips with many a dextrous and insinuating pose, awakes love in her heart, and, as by a miracle of hallucination, transforms her into—Pierrette. The statue speaks to these twain its oracle of " Love whose feet shall outrun time "—and the lovers rapturously flee from this prim garden of the rectangular virtues out into a wide world of blue moonlight and many stars. A little space—and the once gay Pierrot, now in funereal black, returns to the garden, overgrown and choked with autumn leaves, to mourn for the lost Pierrette. Life has caught him in its snare; he forgot the little Pierrette when he was upon his travels, and when he returned he found her no more. In agonized accents, he calls despairingly beneath her window: " Are you there, little bird, are you there? " while Scaramel ever stands at his elbow like a symbol of world-weariness, of disillusion, of despair. In answer to his passionate petition, Love speaks, to show him his folly; and he drinks the bitter cup. But Pierrette, in tatters yet still tender and true, has found her way, also, back to the garden of true love. Life takes them by the hand, and re-unites them in the new bond of a perfected love.

From this time forward, Mr. Barker begins to " take his stride."
The Voysey Inheritance marks a new departure. We now recognize
in him a " new " dramatist in a very real sense—a dramatist with
original and clear-cut ideas, free of the " restrictions " of dramatic
art, and firm-poised in his conception of the limitless possibilities of
drama. He protests creatively against the professors of criticism and
the sophisticated playgoer, who are only too ready with the unthink-
ing and prejudiced: " Oh, yes, clever enough in its way. But not a
play." He deliberately sets himself to the arduous task of creating a
drama of " normal human interest "—not to capture the fancy of the
hardened playgoer or to tickle the palate of the professional critic,
but to win the intelligent interest of the normal man and woman.
" The English theatre, for heaven knows how many years," he said in
1908, " has diligently driven out everybody over the age of twenty-
five—I speak, at any rate, mentally, for there are plenty of people
with gray hairs who will never be more than twenty-five. And you
have got to get what you can call, in the strict sense of the word, an
intelligent and amusing entertainment, before you can get these people
back. When you've done that you've done all that you can do for the
English theatre." The professional playgoer wants the " same old
game " year after year—romantic love, thrills, *scènes à faire*, " curtains," dramatic tangles dextrously unwound, handsome men and
beautiful women, exquisite scenery, magnificent costumes. Mr. Barker
posits a drama of large humane concern, dealing sincerely and naturally with normal human life, which shall possess the indispensable
qualification of interesting an audience. It is this which he has given
us in the remarkable play, *The Voysey Inheritance*.

Here again, as in the case of *The Marrying of Ann Leete*, Mr.
Barker reveals a mastery in scope and perspective. It presents analogies to a novel of Balzac, rather than to a drama of Ibsen—is rather
more like a section of the *Comédie Humaine* laid on English soil, than
like a representation of such a bourgeois family episode as that of the
house of Bernick, or of Borkman. It goes to the root of a problem
which seems, somehow, peculiar to English life—the utter dependence
of a family upon a settled source of income from conservative investment. After the manner of his kind, Mr. Voysey has juggled with
the funds entrusted to his care in the conduct of a great business;

has robbed Peter to pay Paul; continues to do it, not simply to retrieve the losses, but latterly almost as a matter of course—his "right" as a shrewd financier. When he dies suddenly, his son Edward, upon whom the revelation of his father's and perhaps grandfather's peccadilloes has come with a devastating shock, finds that he must take up this loathly burden—the Voysey Inheritance. With an acute sense of honor, a set of high (as well as hard and fast) principles, he shrinks back in horror from the prospect of all the lying and shuffling, the trickery and deception that will be required of him. In solemn conclave the entire family is informed of the situation; and in one of the most remarkably natural scenes on the modern English stage, each character and personality standing out with cameo-like distinctness, the sensitive Edward finds that all, even Alice, the woman he loves, are against him. Character, individual temperament and prejudice, speak with entire clearness in the decision of each. And when Alice, with well-aimed words, brings his high-flown principles wounded and crippled to the ground, Edward begins to feel at last that fate has marked him out—for better or for worse, he must rid himself of "morality," "principle" and "duty," and sacrifice personal niceties of feeling in the sincere if Jesuitical effort to help to right, by questionable means, a great wrong. In the event, the grasping old Booth, a lifelong friend of the family, demands his money from the firm, for re-investment elsewhere, and—the secret is out! We are left in fine doubt as to the outcome—we only know that old Booth has revealed the secret, and suspect that the crash is inevitable. Edward, fortified at last by the consciousness that he has done all that was possible to set matters straight and to undo the things which his father did, faces the future with brave heart. The solution of a great ethical problem on terms that contravene conventional conceptions of morality, and the support of Alice, have made a man out of a coward. If he must go to prison, he will go proud and strong—in the consciousness that he has done the right, and that Alice will be proud of his stripes.

The Voysey Inheritance is a work of genius—original, deeply-conceived. It is a fine type of that bourgeois drama—what George Eliot called a "scene from private life"—which Ibsen, in play after play, brought to such a high pitch of technical perfection.

Its most remarkable feature, as Mr. Desmond MacCarthy has pointed out, " is the skill with which the interest in a single situation is maintained through four acts; that this is a sign of fertility and not poverty of imagination all who have ever tried to write know well." With such a situation, the successful playwright—who writes what the professional critic calls " plays "—in nine cases out of ten would have made an utter failure. Even Ibsen makes " heroes " out of Bernick and Borkman—throws about them a halo of daring chicanery or Napoleonic hazard. Mr. Barker delineates a financier without exaggeration or distortion, without even a trace of histrionism; and resolutely holds his protagonist down to the unheroic level of plain, soul-testing actuality. With his thesis, I cannot agree; for his treatment, I have the sincerest admiration. In many respects it is his most satisfying play—for its dynamic quality; the characters grow, enlarge, crystallize—or develop, narrow, harden: we mark the crucial changes successively wrought by circumstance on character. It ends, with artistic *finesse*, upon an unresolved cadence—imparting to the spectators, in the spectacle, a sense of " the strange irregular rhythm of life." It possesses a rare and memorable quality: we are left in the end with a haunting sense of actuality, the impression of life—of life still going on after the curtain falls.

In 1901, Mr. Barker was converted to Socialism. Socialism proved the most transforming influence of his life. His whole attitude toward the theatre underwent a change that can be described as nothing less than revolutionary. For the first time he became profoundly imbued with the necessity of organizing the theatre, of making it a great instrumentality in the social life of our time. He came to see in the repertory theatre the hope of the contemporary drama; and his notable undertaking at the Court Theatre, and afterwards at the Savoy, may be regarded as a direct outcome of Socialistic conviction. The National Theatre, in the shape of a Shakespeare Memorial, became, in his eyes, the inevitable instrumentality for the establishment of the English drama upon a great and permanent basis. His work in collaboration with Mr. William Archer * is the fruit of his studies in that intricate problem. His association with Mr. Shaw, Mr. Sidney Webb, and their *confrères* upon committees of the Fabian

---

* *Plans and Estimates for a National Theatre.* Duckworth & Co., London.

Society wrought a tremendous change in his methods of thought, teaching him to coördinate, to concentrate, to think in terms of reality and realizable fact. In *Waste*, his next drama, we observe the unmistakable signs of that influence.

The banning of *Waste* by the King's Reader of Plays created a tremendous sensation; the incident was a vitally contributory cause to the investigation of the censorship by a joint committee of the two Houses of Parliament in 1909. In many respects, it was a fortunate thing for Mr. Barker and for the future of the English drama. It focused public attention upon Mr. Barker and thrust him forward decisively as the most able of the " new " school of dramatists in England—a position which he might not have attained solely on the stage success of *Waste*. Moreover it tended to unite solidly the almost universal objection to the censorship—an opposition that finally burst forth when Shaw's *Press Cuttings* and *The Showing-up of Blanco Posnet* were banned in close succession. The report of the committee on the censorship * has brought the issues clearly before the English public; and there is strong reason to hope that a bill directed toward the improvement of the situation will be introduced before long in Parliament.

It is quite impossible to convey any adequate idea of *Waste* without narrating its story; and for that the reader is referred to the published play.† I have never read any play which evoked so many jarring and contradictory sensations. The theme—adultery, a consequent illegal medical operation, the death of the patient, the effect of her death upon the co-respondent, a brilliant politician, whose future is thereby ruined—is a theme from the mere mention of which one instinctively recoils. Once grant that the subject is a legitimate one for stage treatment, and the opposition of the censorship disappears. The topic is treated with earnestness and sincerity by Mr. Barker; but with an apparently needless insistence upon a certain phase. The ultimate meaning of the play would have remained unchanged had Mr. Barker treated this phase of the play with more delicacy and reserve. The treatment of great political, social and

* *Report of the Joint Select Committee of the House of Lords and the House of Commons on the Stage Plays (Censorship), etc.* Eyre and Spottiswoode.

† *Three Plays.* By Granville Barker. Sidgwick and Jackson, London.

religious questions in the play is the most powerful, most vitally interesting, and withal the most entirely true to life that I have ever encountered in any drama, with the single exception of *John Bull's Other Island;* of the two, Mr. Barker's play is superior to Shaw's in realistic detail and fidelity to actual life. From his contact with Mr. Webb and Mr. Shaw, Mr. Barker achieved a mastery of the political issues involved, and has presented them in impressive and convincing truthfulness. Trebell, the brilliant politician, is at once repellent and abnormal in temperament; a megalomaniac of the most virulent type. In his nature there is no spark of altruism; he has unbounded contempt for other people, sublime confidence in himself and his powers. His temperamental coldness—an inhuman coldness—takes the form, sincere though it be, of a sort of sensational cynicism. For the weak and vacuous victim of his passion he has not a spark of pity; he coldly argues with her at a moment when she needs and deserves sympathy and pity. There is nothing more gruesome or horrible in the whole play than the bond of union cemented between the adulterer and the betrayed husband—a fellow-feeling of sympathy in condemnation of the luckless woman. Trebell hates women; he hates with icy hatred this wretched victim because she will not abide the consequences—for the child's sake. He has always felt contempt for men and women because of his power over them; and he hates this woman all the more because he has given her the power to ruin him. The cabinet will be formed without him—people cannot work, even in politics, with a monster.

Trebell commits suicide—not because he has lost his chance for a place in the cabinet, but because by a strange twist of a kind of mystic psychology, he realizes his spiritual failure. This woman, to whom he has never given a passing thought, has shrunk instinctively from an ordeal, to endure which woman needs all the love and help that man can give. A dream-child of his morbid fancy has been slain—this spells his failure, his consciousness of his inability to cope with the vast human issues of creation and life.

Mr. Barker has publicly expressed his gratitude to Mr. Charles Frohman for proving the practicality of modern repertory. He has brought "Repertory from the regions of talk and agitation to be an accomplished fact." It was during the last season that Mr. Barker's new play *The Madras House* was produced by Mr. Frohman at the Duke of York's Theatre. Neither Mr. Shaw's *Misalliance* nor Mr. Barker's *The Madras House*, with eleven and ten performances respectively, proved to be " winning cards "; the audiences were small, and their size did not warrant the continuance of the performances. I recently read in proof *The Madras House*, now published; and once again was impressed with Mr. Barker's originality as a technician and the scope of his vision as an interpreter of life. Woman —her present status, her relation to marriage, her future—is the theme of the play; and this problem is viewed from a different angle in each successive act. Various types, all sharply delineated in personality, are brought upon the stage, not for their own sake, but solely for the light they may throw, by reason of their individual opinions and prejudices, upon the question of sex. In spite of the several incidents of the play, which vitally concern the characters, there is no real plot—the protagonist is Woman, and the play concerns itself with her destiny. We have, in succession, the attitude of the father of six marriageable, but unmarried, daughters; the oriental view-point of a man who has set up a harem in the East, after being separated from his English wife; a cheap American " hustler " with subtly gross ideas about the utility of sex in business, a rather heavy caricature of the P. T. Barnum type; a woman who has been " wronged," a woman whose husband is charged with infidelity, the shrill conventionalized figure of duty, and so on. And then there is the intimate trio—Philip Madras, his wife, and his friend Major Thomas, the " mean sensual man," who is always obsessed with the strange idea that if a woman evinces any interest in him, she must be secretly wanting him to kiss her!

As long as Mr. Barker is focusing a rapid fire from all corners of the stage upon the subject of woman, he holds our undivided interest. In this play I observe for the first time the clear influence of Mr. Shaw. For this is Mr. Shaw's method *par excellence*—to consider some theme of large human or social interest, and have everybody tell what they think about it. This is the technical basis of Mr. Barker's last play—save for this striking difference. Shaw's characters talk about countless things not germane to the theme; Barker's characters focus on the theme—as George Meredith would say, they " ramble concentrically." The last act, though still concerned with the theme, is in the nature of anti-climax. Woman has a hard innings; and never is she thought of as anything but a Shavian "mythological monster," unscrupulously using her personal charms for selfish gratification. Philip Madras, who seems to direct the entire play, rather inconsequentially comes to the conclusion—a conclusion inartistically unmotived—that the only career for a self-respecting man nowadays who wishes to help his fellow-man and fellow-woman, is to join the County Council and become a social reformer. As he says, "That's Public Life. That's Democracy. That's the Future." He is the self-satisfied young man who is coolly superior and always sure of himself—vastly irritating despite his large social views.

"In *The Madras House*," says Mr. Max Beerbohm, "there is only one character that does not stand forth vital and salient; and this is the character of Philip Madras, the wise and good young man who is always in the right—always perspicacious, unselfish and charitable by virtue of being himself so shadowy and cold. It is a note that pervades modern drama, this doctrine that human beings are always hopelessly in the wrong, and that only the inhuman ones can hope to be in the right. I don't say it is a false doctrine; but it certainly is a lugubrious one. And we must be pardoned for a certain measure of impatience with Philip Madras. Repressing our impulse to call him an impostor, and hailing him reverently as pope, we can't, even so, stand him—whether we feel we are in the right with him or in the wrong with the others."

Mr. Barker is a dramatist of marked power and strong originality, a master of the tools of his craft. He has freed himself from the restrictions of his art: instead of obeying its " laws," he experiments freely and successfully with any materials he chooses. He has taken the bold course of " leaving Aristotle out." His definition of a drama is a declaration of independence: " A play is anything that can be made effective upon the stage of a theatre by human agency." Perhaps his own words are prophetic—for he has already done great things, and will surely do greater: " We must go on breaking new ground, enlarging the boundaries of the drama, fitting it for every sort of expression. When we deserve it a new dramatic genius will arise. He will neither break laws nor obey them. He will make laws and there will happily be no questioning."

JAPANESE FICTION

SADAKICHI HARTMANN

THE prose composition of Japanese authors, in strange contrast to their poetry—so favorably known for its conciseness of form and expression—is lengthy, even intolerably lengthy. The *Genji Monegetari*, one of the classics, written like so many Japanese literary works by a lady of rank, runs to no less than 4234 pages. Novels exceeding one hundred volumes are frequently met with. Of course the volumes are thin and many of the pages devoted to illustrations, but even in modern reprints they would form four thick volumes of at least one thousand pages each.

The majority of prose compositions abound with endless descriptions of unnecessary details, long-drawn monologues, dismal enumerations and tedious displays of the author's erudition, which try the patience of the most indulgent reader. That we are less acquainted with the products of Japanese novel-writing than with those of any other country is largely due to their extreme length, which has always proved an insurmountable barrier to the translator.

Novel-writing pure and simple was unknown until the beginning of the eighteenth century. The prose literature of the preceding periods consisted largely of monegetari (*i.e.*, narratives), essays, fairy tales and so-called " pillow sketches." By " narratives " the Japanese understand descriptions of a journey or of the adventures of some imaginary hero or historical personality. They read very much like diaries. If bent on eulogy one might term them epics of real life or versions of Gulliver's travels. They bear at times a faint resemblance to the works of Richardson, Field and Swift. The style is simple and straightforward and often of rare elegance. The narrative flows on easily from one scene of life to another, giving varied and minutely detailed pictures of life and society. They give plenty of incident and are rarely dull; they have, however, no plot and no construction, and do not show the slightest knowledge of novel-writing as we understand it, a shortcoming that the Japanese novelist has not entirely overcome to this day.

The essays occupy an important position in literature, and some of them, written as early as the tenth century, have been handed down as the most esteemed models of prose composition. There is in them a perfection of apt phrase, which often enshrines minute but genuine pearls of wisdom and true sentiment. They are didactic, but their didacticism invariably finds expression in poetical metaphors, and rarely becomes wearisome. Even when the author criticises he remains metaphorical. He says, for instance: "Henjo excels in form, but substance is wanting. The emotion produced by his poetry is evanescent, and may be compared to that which we experience at the sight of a beautiful woman in painting. His verse is like a flower which, although withered and without bloom, yet retains its fragrance." The essay writers are loving admirers of nature, and have much to say (and say it well) of the sincerity of life, the folly of ambition and money-getting, and the necessity for casting aside the lusts of this wicked world and preparing betimes for eternity. But the old Adam is never far off, and the essays therefore read very much like the slightly cynical conversations of a polished man of the world. They have the appearance of simplicity and ease of expression which is in reality the result of consummate art.

The fairy tales have become familiar to Western readers through the medium of picture-books. They are dainty and yet highly imaginative creations which compare favorably with Grimm's and Andersen's best work. Their tendency, in motive as well as language, is to be as nearly as possibly purely Japanese. The supernatural machinery is either Buddhist or Taoist; many of the incidents, however, are borrowed from the copious fairy lore of China. The poetical element in them is strongly developed, and the commonest story is sure to contain some word-pictures of more than ordinary beauty.

The following synopsis of *The Shining Damsel* will give some idea of the general character of these stories.

An old man who earned a living by making bamboo, espied one day in the woods a bamboo with a shining stem. He split it open, and discovered in one of the joints a beautiful little maiden three inches in height. He took her home and adopted her as his daughter, giving her the name of "Shining Damsel." She speedily grew up to womanhood, when her beauty attracted numerous admirers.

To each of them she assigned a quest, promising that she would marry the suitor who successfully accomplished the task allotted to him. One lover was told to fetch Buddha's begging bowl of stone from India; another to bring her a branch of the tree with roots of silver, stem of gold, and fruits of jewels which grew on some fabulous island. A third was to procure the shining jewel of many hues of the Dragon's head. They all failed. The maiden was then wooed by the Mikado, but equally in vain, though they remained on friendly terms and kept up an exchange of sentimental poems. She was eventually taken up to heaven in a flying chariot, and dropped on the moon, where she is still supposed to be living.

A very peculiar form of literature is furnished by the *Pillow Sketches*. The title *Pillow Sketches* is supposed to mean that the author kept the manuscript by his pillow, and jotted down his thoughts and observations when going to bed or getting up in the morning. There is no sort of arrangement. The author simply " follows his pen " and sets down, upon the spur of the moment, anything which occurs to him: stories, anecdotes, descriptions, enumerations of incongruous things, lists of flowers, memoranda, sketches of social and domestic life, thoughts suggested by the contemplation of nature, quotations of conversations, etc. We have nothing like it in Western literature, unless it were Selden's *Table Talk* or Whitman's cataloguing of all sorts of subjects. The pillow sketches read very much like extracts from a traveler's note-book, but at times contain poetical illusions of true literary merit, as the following:

" In spring I love to watch the dawn grow gradually whiter and whiter, till a faint rosy tinge crowns the mountain's crest, while slender specks of purple clouds extend themselves above."

" In summer I love the night, not only when the moon is shining, also when it is dark and the fireflies cross each others' paths in their flight, or when the rain is falling."

" In autumn it is the beauty of the evening which most deeply moves me as I watch the crows seeking their roosting place in twos and threes and fours, and listen to the chirping of dicing insects or the sighing of the wind."

" In winter, how unspeakably beautiful is the snow! But I also love the dazzling whiteness of the hoar-frost, and the intense coldness that comes with it. Then it is meet quickly to fetch charcoal and kindle fires. And may not the gentle warmth of noon persuade us to allow the embers of the hearth to become a white heap of ashes?"

For centuries the Japanese reading public, consisting largely of the Daimyos (court nobles) and samurai (warrior) class, expressed no desire for a more elaborate style of prose literature. The bloody warfare which raged through the middle ages left but little time for reading. And the lower classes, the peasants, artisans, and traders, were satisfied with occasionally listening to a blind story-teller who first delivered his compositions in spoken form, in improvisatore fashion, and only later had them taken down by some admirer or pupil. They were really the first novelists, and one of their latter-day disciples by the name of Yencho is still plying his curious trade in the streets of Kyoto.

In the Yedo Period (1603-1867), when a "golden reign of peace" set in, literary taste changed considerably. The city populations enjoyed great material prosperity, and began to indulge in the luxury of art and literature. A want was created which had to be supplied. The writers of narratives addressed themselves for the first time to the people; and the result was a popular literature, the introduction of fiction.

The novel of the seventeenth and eighteenth century is a very peculiar phase of Japanese literature. The vital element of fiction was still lacking. We find in these works no real human beings depicted in such a way that we can follow their fortunes with interest and sympathize with their joys and sorrows. The power of delineating character is limited and reminds us very much of the way in which Japanese painters draw a portrait. Fiction was written to suit the taste of rustics, jugglers, ferry and jinrikisha men, and its principal aim was to excite wonder, amazement and horror. No wonder that everything seems unnatural, monstrous and improbable to the Western mind.

The novel of this period, as far as plot and construction is concerned, might be compared with our dime novel. Murders and homicides are described with an abundance of gruesome details, harakiri and other suicides, thefts and robberies, sales of women by their relations, terrific combats, hairbreadth escapes, tortures, strange meetings and suspicious recognitions follow each other in rapid succession. Each chapter has a special heading, and it is a most gruesome collection. I quote some at random: *The Danger by the Wayside Shrine, The Witchcraft of the Venomous Rats, Bloody Footprints on the Snow, The Village of Sinful Desires, The Drum of Hell*, etc.

The authors have not the least respect for truth and continually overleap the bounds of possibility. They do not hesitate to introduce monsters who have two pupils in their eyes and one arm longer than the other, and who after falling from a cliff many thousand feet high presently pick themselves up and walk home as if nothing had happened. The *deus ex machina*, in the shape of a ghost, demon or supernaturally gifted animal, is a far too frequent requisite.

The immoral tendency of the dialogue is another barrier to the just appreciation of Western readers. The language of frankness and Falstaff abounds in the majority of these novels and the government was repeatedly obliged to suppress publications. Their style, taken as a whole, however, is of true literary value; it is generally flowing, perspicuous and elegant, although sometimes distracted by the use of pivot words and similar rhetorical-like devices.

The talent that is wasted in artificialities and improbabilities is really deplorable. On rare occasions the Japanese author draws several degrees nearer to real humanity and shows that he can be graphic and simply picturesque. Of course every novel contains passages that we cannot help admiring for their wealth of metaphors, their subtlety and vagueness of expression. And yet there is less word-painting and description of scenery than one might expect, as the authors are in the habit of inditing a " tanka " (short poem) whenever they wish to give expression to a truly poetical sentiment.

Particularly striking is the way in which they frequently slur over the transition from one scene to another by the use of their device; something on the same principle as their artists in introducing a golden mist between different parts of the landscape to disguise defects of perspective.

Humor, wholesome and to the point, is often met with, and few books of the world's literature contain a more copious flow of rollicking fun than Ikka's *Hizakurige,* a work which occupies a somewhat similar position in Japan to that of the *Pickwick Papers* in English-speaking countries. Yet the quality which most strikes Western readers is the prodigious fertility of invention. The number and variety of incidents and exciting situations is simply astonishing. When these authors took up their pen, the flow of ideas seemed unlimited, a thousand words were quickly formed and long chapters fell from their hands, apparently without the slightest effort. Despite all their glaring faults and shortcomings, it is impossible to deny them a certain degree of merit in conception, as well as in the handling of their uncouth material. They handled comedy with the same ease as tragedy, intermixed poetry with prose, and in describing men and events changed their style with the change of subjects. Nearly all their personages speak the dialect proper to them.

Novel writing was no profession. Nearly all the well-known fiction writers had a vocation or plied some kind of trade. Kioden, who started novel-writing in Japan, was a tobacco dealer; Tanehiko was a samurai, Semba a bookseller, and Bakin, the greatest and most popular of all, was the principal of a private school. Although many of them were so popular that the school children and beggars in the street knew them by name, they received nothing for their manuscripts but an occasional invitation to supper from the publisher, or presents of trifling value, when their books sold well. They only gradually succeeded in receiving definite payment.

Both these disadvantages, however, did not hinder them from being extremely prolific. Bakin is said to have written not fewer than two hundred and ninety distinct works (of an average of two hundred pages each). The popularity of Bakin is difficult to explain. It is only too true that even Aristotle and Plato, far removed as they are from us in period of time, are immeasurably nearer to us in all their ideas, sentiments, and moral standards than the Japanese of fifty years ago. Bakin impresses us as being very learned, insufferably tedious and intensely moral. His writings alone were excluded from the sweeping prohibitive measure directed against light literature by the Shogun's Government in 1842. He used deep thought and intense reflection, giving careful attention to plot and construction. But nearly all his long novels prove wearisome reading; he has little or no humor, and his wit is mostly of the verbal kind. Nor can he always resist the temptation of irritating plainminded people with arrogant displays of his great learning and of introducing foreign or obsolete words not understood by even the most intelligent of his readers. Some of his shorter works, however, would appeal to us even to-day, as, for instance, his *Pawnbroker's Store*. A pawnbroker lies awake at night and hears a noise in his storehouse. He gets up, peeps into his warerooms and sees, to his great astonishment, the pledges deposited there assembled in conclave. Each tells its story, its various adventures, until it finally landed in the pawnbroker's store.

Some more realistic writers, among them Tanehiko, introduced the " dramatic story," which differs chiefly from other novels in the preponderance of dialogue over narrative, and in the choice of the ordinary spoken language for the speeches of the characters. They also vary less violently from actual living manners than the romantic novels. Sardou might have been very grateful to Tanehiko if he had known his *Faithful Daughter* some twenty-five years ago. It depicts a heroine of fifteen years who sets out to travel through Japan in quest of her father's murderer—a magician with the power of making himself invisible—with the intention of making love to him and then finding an opportunity for putting him to death.

But much as we at closer acquaintance may learn to admire in the Japanese fiction, it will never appeal to our sympathies like the works of our English novelists of the same period. The great defect of all Japanese novels is their want of interest. They carry unreal sentiment and conventional standards of morality to the extreme. Some of their character-delineations seem to us nothing short of travesties on human nature. They are too much occupied with sensational situations to study the human heart with its affections and passions. While they can describe the mischief produced by unlawful passion, and wifely fidelity and devotion are their frequent themes, such things as the gradual growth of sentiment in man and woman, the unwilling influence of a pure love, and all the more delicate shades of feeling are wholly neglected by them. Even Bakin shows us men and women as they might be constructed on principles derived from the Chinese sages and their Japanese expositors, and goes for his material rather to books than to real life.

This condition only began to change when translations of European novels made their appearance. They produced a profound sensation. The first of them was Bulwer-Lytton's *Ernest Maltravers,* which was followed by other works of fiction, morally English. More recently also French, German, and even Russian novelists have been laid under contribution, but there is no doubt that Bulwer-Lytton, Scott, Dickens, Rider Haggard, and perhaps Hugo and Jules Verne, have exercised the greatest influence in the change of style. The study of foreign literature was introduced at various institutes of learning, and at a recent examination at the Imperial University at Tokyo one of the students recited Schiller's *Die Glocke* in German, while several others performed a dramatization of Dickens' *Pickwick Papers* in English. (I must confess I would travel far to witness such a performance, as it must be ludicrous in the extreme.)

The Japanese authors at first made the serious mistake of simply imitating European fiction instead of adopting merely those elements which would improve their plot, interest and methods of construction. They even strayed away from oriental subjects, and tried themselves in historical novels of the Mühlbach style. In a few years hence works like *Appius and Virginia* and *Epaminondas, a Novel of Theban Life,* published in the early seventies, will be regarded merely as documents of a passing phase of the national development. For the time being it has the merit of acquainting Japanese readers with a more sober, common sense style of writing.

Tsubouchi, the leader of the new movement, made in *The Spirit of Fiction* an unsparing attack on the methods and principles of Bakin and his school, and proved that a Japanese novelist could present us with well and naturally drawn characters. His *Types of Students,* a collection of graphic and humorous sketches of modern student life, viewed from the seamy side, could just as well have some Scandinavian realist, some Strindberg or Knut Hamsun, as author. Human life is depicted by him with photographic accuracy, and with a verve and humor which no mere observation, however minute, could ever combat. It is a cleverly written *résumé* of personal experience.

The Ladies of the New Style, by Sudo Nausiu, is another noteworthy example of the modern style of novel writing, and we can express a feeling of regret that it has not yet been translated into English or some other European language. It introduces the Japanese reader into an entirely new world of wharves, docks, tramways and smoking factory chimneys. The heroine is a dairymaid—an up-to-date occupation, as formerly cow's milk was not used as food. This dairymaid's favorite reading is Herbert Spencer's treatise on education. She is a member of a ladies' club, where croquet and lawn tennis are played and woman's rights are discussed. The hero is an advanced politician, who is finally married to the dairymaid, at which occasion he wears a standing-up collar, a white silk necktie, white gloves, and a buttonhole bouquet of orange blossoms on his coat. Among the incidents we have a balloon ascent, a contested election, and a dynamite explosion.

The book, comical as it may seem to us in parts, has considerable literary merit. It has a coherent plot, and the characters converse in an easy natural fashion. And although there is hardly a page which does not bear traces of the author's studies of European literature, it is a faithful picture of new Japan in the eighties, depicted with an excellent command of language, more especially of the Chinese element in it, which is so prominent at the present time.

The social position of Japanese writers of fiction has of late been completely revolutionized. In Bacon's time they were *déclassés*, who were in constant trouble with the police, and were placed with actors, among the lowest of the people. Now they are respected members of society; some of them, like Tsubouchi, being graduates of the Imperial University. Notwithstanding the low prices at which their works are issued—a book of five hundred pages, well-illustrated, is published at about forty cents of our money—a popular novelist now commands a fair income from his works. Yano Fumio, out of the proceeds of the sale of one of his novels, was able to treat himself to a tour in Europe, and to build a fine house with the balance.

THE SEA-LANDS

ORRICK JOHNS

WOULD I were on the sea-lands,
  Where winds know how to sting;
And in the rocks at midnight
  The lost long murmurs sing.

Would I were with my first love
  To hear the rush and roar
Of spume below the doorstep
  And winds upon the door.

My first love was a fair girl
  With ways forever new;
And hair a sunlight yellow,
  And eyes a morning blue.

The roses, have they tarried,
  Or are they dun and frayed?
If we had stayed together,
  Would love, indeed, have stayed?

Ah, years are filled with learning,
  And days are leaves of change!
And I have met so many
  I knew . . . and found them strange.

But on the sea-lands, tumbled
  By winds that sting and blind,
The nights we watched, so silent,
  Come back, come back to mind . . .

I mind about my first love
  And hear the rush and roar
Of spume below the doorstep
  And winds upon the door.

734

EDITORIAL NOTES

An appeal to law, instead of an appeal to force, is the natural course for nations, as for individuals; and the nations are beginning to learn this. Public opinion has been moving; the number of arbitrations has been increasing; but the actual suggestion of permanent arbitration between the United States and Great Britain is a long step forward. In order to bring about changes so momentous and far-reaching, public opinion has to rise to a high plane, higher than it can rise to in ordinary times, and higher than many pessimists believe it ever can rise to. Yet when we look back we find there have been times with special conditions when public opinion has risen to heights which a generation previously would have been thought impossible. It was so when public opinion abolished slavery, with all its vested interests. There were occasions before that struggle when any person might have demonstrated, apparently, that public opinion in the United States could never rise to such a height. But it did, and without counting the cost in treasure, in blood, and in national danger. Surely it can rise to the present unequaled opportunity for advancing the cause of peace, until it becomes world-wide! The great nations of the world are now in bondage to their armies and navies—increasing bondage; and this growing and enormous burden of naval and military expenditure is coinciding not merely with friendly relations between the Powers, but with the growth of civilization as a whole. This is a curious paradox. Unless the incongruity and mischief of it are brought home, not only to men's heads generally, but to their feelings, so that they resent the inconsistency and realize the danger, the tremendous expenditure on armaments must sooner or later break down civilization. How long will it be before the nations realize that during all the time in which they have been in bondage to this expenditure, the prison door has been locked on the inside? Apparently, not very long, if the present rate of progress be maintained. More has been done for the cause of peace during the last three months, than during the previous thirty years.

There is something really heroic in the measures taken by the Chinese Government to eradicate the opium evil. The agreement with the British Government, by which both the native and the Indian supply were to be reduced one-tenth annually, has been loyally carried out, the decrease being considerably greater than had been stipulated. A new agreement has just been completed, by which the reform will be still further accelerated and total abolition will be effected in a much shorter period than the ten years originally contemplated. The conquest of the national curse has caused great suffering; temporary evils have sprung up. But there has been no wavering; utter extinction of the traffic is demanded and will soon be realized. It is a magnificent achievement. No one will grieve over the passing of the poppies; but many will ponder over this strange lesson from the Orient to the West, and wonder whether there are no evils at home that demand drastic treatment.

* * *

Dr. Walsh's article on rabies, in the April Forum, resulted in some interesting correspondence, emphasizing the conviction still prevailing among many friends of the " friend of man " that rabies is either an imaginary disease, or that its frequency and terrors have been grossly exaggerated. The average man does not question the newspaper accounts of fatalities, and regards hydrophobia as a disease of too frequent occurrence and of horrible significance. He has no prejudices on the subject; in the majority of cases he is a dog-lover; and he would be only too glad to be relieved from anxiety, and to be assured on indisputable authority that what he has been led to consider as a menacing risk is merely an idle and unwarranted invention. The subject is of such grave importance that thorough discussion is desirable; and to promote this it seems permissible to print one of the letters written to the Editor of THE FORUM.

" Before stating my objections to Dr. Walsh's article, I must explain to you that for the past twenty years or more, perhaps a thousand dogs, more or less, of all sorts and kinds, have passed through my hands. I have always had kennels and now have them as a means of livelihood. During this long period, I have been bitten repeatedly, well bitten, sometimes most painfully, from various reasons, such as fright, administration of medicine, fights, etc., so you must allow I have some interest in this so-called rabies. There have never been any evil results, and I know of no one more indifferent to dog bites than the very people who are continually with dogs.

I object to Dr. Walsh's article for these reasons:

First.—It is written upon ' Laboratory Knowledge,' not practical knowledge (such as mine).

Second.—He is an alarmist, evidently by temperament. It is a well-known fact that people die of imaginary fright; *vide* any cholera statistics.

Third.—As a humanitarian, not a sentimentalist, and a lover of the animal that is closer to the human than any other, I object to his suggestion that all dogs should be muzzled all the time. That alone shows his absolute lack of comprehension of animals, of the subject he attempts to write about.

Fourth.—He speaks of England as stamping out the so-called disease by quarantine. England, recognizing the low order of intelligence affected by this scare, used the tactics of the Christian Science Church, viz.: ' There are no mad dogs here, by reason of the quarantine, so it is impossible for you to have hydrophobia.'

Fifth.—He speaks of rabies in France. A poor example: the well-known inhumanity of the Latin races toward animals would in itself upset any animal's balance. If we adopted the same means of treatment for human beings in their pain, as we do for a dog, people would bite too, and no bite is more poisonous than a human bite. For humanity we have drugs, for hysteria, epilepsy, etc. etc.; but for an animal in pain we have stones, blows, brutality and various shots from a revolver. Is it any wonder an animal in agony should turn on these so-called civilized people? "

The letter concludes by quoting some medical testimony:

Dr. Charles K. Mills, University of Pennsylvania, a specialist in nervous diseases, says he " has never found a clear case of hydrophobia in a human subject."

President T. Parvin, National Academy of Medicine, says: " In forty-four years' practice, I have never seen a real case of hydrophobia, but many cases of hysteria that were wantonly called hydrophobia."

Dr. E. C. Spitzka " has made every effort to secure observation of rabies in man or dog; not a single opportunity has offered itself."

Dr. Dulles, University of Pennsylvania, an authority on this subject, says that " real rabies is more rare than any other disease."

Before considering the medical opinions, one may briefly review the five stated objections. The first need not be labored. Taken literally, it would require no consideration by anyone who knew what is implied by " laboratory " work and scientific investigation. Here, it is intended to contrast theoretical and practical knowledge. There is a distinction, and a difference; but Dr. Walsh's article was based on experience.

The second objection would seem to be answered by a quotation from the article itself. Dr. Walsh wrote:

" It is of the utmost importance, in every instance, to make sure as to whether the animal that does the biting really has rabies, as the consequences from the mere fear of the disease, a condition known as ' false rabies,' or pseudo-hydrophobia, are almost as pitiful, and probably, in a small number of high-strung, nervous individuals, even as fatal, as in the instances of true rabies."

The third objection is based on a misconception, due possibly to the wording not being quite clear. Dr. Walsh wrote:

" Every dog without an owner, every stray dog, and every un-muzzled dog, regardless of ownership, must be rounded up and painlessly put out of the way; not merely during the mid-summer months, but during all the winter months as well, for our vigilance cannot safely be relaxed for one single hour. . . ."

With regard to the fourth point, rabies was stamped out in England by a rigorous enforcement of the muzzling order, first adopted in 1889, when the number of rabid dogs officially reported was 312. This number fell to 129 in 1890, 79 in 1891, and 38 in 1892. Then, owing to persistent opposition, muzzling was stopped, and the effect was at once seen in the increase of rabies. In 1893 there were 93 cases; in 1894, 248; and in 1895, 672. At this point, owing to public alarm, muzzling was again enforced, reducing the number of cases in 1896 to 438, in 1897 to 151, in 1898 to 17, and in 1899 to 9. As no case was discovered during the next half year, it was believed that the disease had been eradicated in Great Britain.

The fifth objection raises some true and valid points. The treatment of animals, and especially of dogs, by the Latin races, is not always pleasant to witness.

An extract from a bulletin on *Rabies: Its Cause, Frequency, and Treatment*, issued by the United States Department of Agriculture, seems to deal conclusively with the general question, supported as it is by the statement (April 27th, 1911) of the Chief of the Bureau of Animal Industry that "the reality and nature of this disease have been well established by numerous competent scientific investigators and the disease occurs to a considerable extent in the United States. The bodies of dogs are frequently sent to the laboratories of this Bureau for diagnosis and many of these cases are found to be positive." The extract referred to follows:

"Numerous cases of rabies in the United States affecting the human subject have been reported from various parts of the country, and tests have been made by our most competent investigators. These tests show that the disease not only exists, but that it is far more common than has been generally admitted. . . . When the medical statistics of other countries are consulted, there are found in many of them the same conditions. In Austria, Belgium, France, Germany, and Russia the official reports show a large number of cases of rabies in dogs and other animals each year and a certain number in man. These are among the most enlightened countries of the world, where medical science has achieved its highest advancement, and where the theory of error on the part of the health authorities in regard to the nature of the disease is out of the question.

Such facts are met by the assertion that one prominent physician in Philadelphia has been endeavoring to find a case of rabies in man or in one of the lower animals for sixteen years without success; that another physician in New York has not been able to satisfy himself of the reality of the disease after many years of investigation, and that a neurologist in Washington City has publicly offered a reward of $100 for a case of rabies in man or dog. These assertions are plausible, and to those unacquainted with all the facts, they may be convincing. In reality they are deceptive and misleading. There have been numerous cases of rabies in dogs brought to the veterinary department of the University of Pennsylvania every year for many years, and any physician in Philadelphia could make arrangements with that institution to see and study the cases if he so desired. In the same manner any reputable physician in New York could have arranged with one of the veterinary schools or with the board of health in that city for a similar opportunity. There have been also rather frequent reports in the medical journals of patients at the hospitals in that city affected with this disease, and in some cases inoculation tests have demonstrated the correctness of the diagnosis. How can it be possible that a prominent physician living there and presumably well acquainted with the members of his profession has diligently searched for years for such cases and failed to find any?

As to the neurologist in Washington City, the writer publicly answered his advertisement, and proposed to produce a case of rabies,
the genuinenes of the disease to be decided by a committee appointed
by the Medical Society of the District of Columbia, and the reward,
if earned, to go to a charitable purpose. The·gentleman, however,
did not accept the proposition, but withdrew his advertisement, and
apparently had no further desire to see a case of the disease."

*   *   *

A good deal of excitement has been caused in England recently
with regard to Mormonism. Liverpool has long been the centre of
Mormon activity there, and the large industrial cities and towns have
been systematically and profitably exploited. According to official
figures, there are 82 Mormon churches in the Kingdom, with 80,000
members, while 300 missionaries carry on the work of securing converts. Nearly a thousand new members were baptized last year, of
whom almost 500 went to Utah—this number being considerably
augmented by recruits from other European countries. The Immigration Commissioner at Boston (Massachusetts) reports that over
700 Mormon converts entered that port in 1910 from Europe, the
majority being women. It would be interesting to know precisely
what happens to these women, and whether the law against polygamy
is still being flagrantly violated. This has been unequivocally denied
by the president of the Mormon Church; but there would seem to
be reasonable ground for further inquiry.

*   *   *

The New Machiavelli, which has been running serially in THE
FORUM, is concluded in this issue. The work has aroused, inevitably,
some opposition; for there will always be a difference of opinion as
to what is desirable in public discussion, both in regard to subject-
matter and the method of treatment. It is difficult to frame any
general rule: what one man may make vital and inspiring, another
will make prurient and repellent; while often it is not the author of
a book who should be arraigned, but the reader, who has measured
big work by his own littleness. *The New Machiavelli* belongs to a
type which may be both depreciated and deprecated by critics who
are thoroughly sincere; yet it must be placed in the category of
greatness. It has faults of carelessness, of sheer slovenliness; but it

is magnificent in its courage, its scope, and its comprehension of the conditions of life. The scheme of the book enables Mr. Wells to satisfy his "propaganda habit"; yet, whether we accept or reject his conclusions, there can be no doubt as to his consummate ability. Modern and pagan as Remington is, he stands for something immeasurably finer than the conventional, successful hypocrite. It may seem strange to select, as representing the crux of the book, the passage where the drunken little Oxford Don speaks out for his class —veritably, *in vino veritas;* sneering at "love and fine thinking," and demanding "hate and coarse thinking." And in that atmosphere where reticence and concealment have temporarily been discarded, those for whom he speaks support him openly, unashamed.

"It was an extraordinary revelation to me. Everyone was unusually careless and outspoken, and it was amazing how manifestly they echoed the feeling of this old Tory spokesman. . . . They were flushed and amused, but they left the impression on my mind of men irrevocably set upon narrow and cynical views of political life. For them the political struggle was a game, whose counters were human hate and human credulity; their real aim was just everyone's aim, the preservation of the class and way of living to which their lives were attuned."

So Remington, racked and self-conscious, but questioning to the end the justice of his rejection, passes from public life, conquered by lesser men and the unwritten laws of hypocrisy. It is right that the standard of public morality should be maintained; but there is no high value in a public profession which is regarded as merely formal, while private practice continues cynically lax. Yet there are few women who will not condone the "double standard," marrying men whom they know to have led unclean lives. Even Remington's wife accepts as normal the pre-marital experiences which he describes explicitly in the book. Such things are natural, for men. So long as they are not talked about, or publicly proclaimed, nothing really matters. The world will continue for a long time to believe that the best remedy for disease is ignorance, that silence in sufficient quantities will cure all evils.

THE NEW MACHIAVELLI

H. G. WELLS

CHAPTER THE THIRD

THE BREAKING POINT

II

I PARTED from Panmure at the corner of Aldington Street, and went my way alone.   But I did not go home, I turned westward and walked for a long way, and then struck northward aimlessly.   I was too miserable to go to my house.

I wandered about that night like a man who has discovered his Gods are dead.   I can look back now detached yet sympathetic upon that wild confusion of moods and impulses, and by it I think I can understand, oh! half the wrong-doing and blundering in the world.

I do not feel now the logical force of the process that must have convinced me then that I had made my sacrifice and spent my strength in vain.   At no time had I been under any illusion that the Tory party had higher ideals than any other party, yet it came to me like a thing newly discovered that the men I had to work with had for the most part no such dreams, no sense of any collective purpose, no atom of the faith I held.   They were just as immediately intent upon personal ends, just as limited by habits of thought, as the men in any other group or party.   Perhaps I had slipped unawares for a time into the delusions of a party man—but I do not think so.

No, it was the mood of profound despondency that had followed upon the abrupt cessation of my familiar intercourse with Isabel, that gave this fact that had always been present in my mind its quality of devastating revelation.   It seemed as though I had never seen before nor suspected the stupendous gap between the chaotic aims, the routine, the conventional acquiescences, the vulgarizations of the personal life, and that clearly conscious development and service of a collective thought and purpose at which my efforts aimed.   I had thought them but a little way apart, and now I saw they were separated by all the distance between earth and heaven.   I saw now in myself and every one around me, a concentration upon interests close at hand, an inability to detach oneself from the provocations, tendernesses, instinctive hates, dumb lusts and shy timidities that touched one at every point; and, save for rare exalted moments, a regardless-ness of broader aims and remoter possibilities that made the white passion of statecraft seem as unearthly and irrelevant to human life as the story an astronomer will tell, half proven but altogether incredible, of habitable planets and answering intelligences, suns' distances uncounted across the deep.   It seemed to me I had aspired too high and thought too far, had mocked my own littleness by presumption, had given the uttermost dear reality of life for a theorizer's dream.

All through that wandering agony of mine that night a dozen threads of thought interwove; now I was a soul speaking in protest to God against a task too cold and high for it, and now I was an angry man, scorned and pointed upon, who had let life cheat him of the ultimate pride of his soul.   Now I was the fool of ambition, who opened his box of gold to find blank emptiness, and now I was a spinner of flimsy thoughts, whose web tore to rags at a touch.   I realized for the first time how much I had come to depend upon the mind and faith of Isabel, how she had confirmed me and sustained me, how little strength I had to go on with our purposes now that she had vanished from my life.   She had been the incarnation of those great abstractions, the saving reality, the voice that answered back. There was no support that night in the things that had been.   We were alone together on the cliff for ever more!—that was very pretty in its way, but it had no truth whatever that could help me now, no ounce of sustaining value.   I wanted Isabel that night, no sentiment or memory of her, but Isabel alive,—to talk to me, to touch me, to hold me together.   I wanted unendurably the dusky gentleness of her presence, the consolation of her voice.

We were alone together on the cliff!   I startled a passing cabman into interest by laughing aloud at that magnificent and characteristic sentimentality.   What a lie it was, and how satisfying it had been.   That was just where we shouldn't remain.   We of all people had no distinction from that humanity whose lot is to forget.   We should go out to other interests, new experiences, new demands. That tall and intricate fabric of ambitious understandings we had built up together in our intimacy would be the first to go; and last perhaps to endure with us would be a few gross memories of sights and sounds, and trivial incidental excitements. . . .

I had a curious feeling that night that I had lost touch with life for a long time, and had now been reminded of its quality.   That infernal little don's parody of my ruling phrase, "Hate and coarse thinking," stuck in my thoughts like a poisoned dart, a centre of inflammation.   Just as a man who is debilitated has no longer the vitality to resist an infection, so my mind, slackened by the crisis of my separation from Isabel, could find no resistance to his emphatic

suggestion. It seemed to me that what he had said was overpower-
ingly true, not only of contemporary life, but of all possible human
life. Love is the rare thing, the treasured thing; you lock it away
jealously and watch, and well you may; hate and aggression and
force keep the streets and rule the world. And fine thinking is, in the
rough issues of life, weak thinking, is a balancing indecisive process,
discovers with disloyal impartiality a justice and a defect on each
disputing side. " Good honest men," as Dayton calls them, rule the
world, with a way of thinking out decisions like shooting cartloads
of bricks, and with a steadfast pleasure in hostility. Dayton liked
to call his antagonists " blackguards and scoundrels "—it justified
his opposition—the Lords were " scoundrels," all people richer than
he were " scoundrels," all Socialists, all troublesome poor people; he
liked to think of jails and justice being done. His public spirit was
saturated with the sombre joys of conflict and the pleasant thought
of condign punishment ·for all recalcitrant souls. That was the way
of it, I perceived. That had survival value, as the biologists say.
He was fool enough in politics to be a consistent and happy politician. . . .

Hate and coarse thinking; how the infernal truth of the phrase
beat me down that night! I couldn't remember that I had known
this all along, and that it did not really matter in the slightest degree. I had worked it all out long ago in other terms, when I had
seen how all parties stood for interests inevitably, and how the
purpose in life achieves itself, if it achieves itself at all, as a by
product of the war of individuals and classes. Hadn't I always
known that science and philosophy elaborate themselves in spite of
all the passion and narrowness of men, in spite of the vanities and
weakness of their servants, in spite of all the heated disorder of contemporary things? Wasn't it my own phrase to speak of " that
greater mind in men, in which we are but moments and transitorily
lit cells "? Hadn't I known that the spirit of man still speaks like a
thing that struggles out of mud and slime, and that the mere effort
to speak means choking and disaster? Hadn't I known that we who
think without fear and speak without discretion will not come to our
own for the next two thousand years?

It was the last was most forgotten of all that faith mislaid. Before mankind, in my vision that night, stretched new centuries of
confusion, vast stupid wars, hastily conceived laws, foolish temporary
triumphs of order, lapses, set-backs, despairs, catastrophes, new
beginnings, a multitudinous wilderness of time, a nigh plotless drama
of wrong-headed energies. In order to assuage my parting from
Isabel we had set ourselves to imagine great rewards for our separation, great personal rewards, we had promised ourselves success vis-

ible and shining in our lives. To console ourselves in our separation we had made out of the *Blue Weekly* and our young Tory movement preposterously enormous things—as though those poor fertilizing touches at the soil were indeed the germinating seeds of the millennium, as though a million lives such as ours had not to contribute before the beginning of the beginning. That poor pretence had failed. That magnificent proposition shriveled to nothing in the black loneliness of that night.

I saw that there were to be no such compensations. So far as my real services to mankind were concerned I had to live an unrecognized and unrewarded life. If I made successes it would be by the way. Our separation would alter nothing of that. My scandal would cling to me now for all my life, a thing affecting relationships, embarrassing and hampering my spirit. I should follow the common lot of those who live by the imagination, and follow it now in infinite loneliness of soul; the one good comforter, the one effectual familiar, was lost to me for ever; I should do good and evil together, no one caring to understand; I should produce much weary work, much bad-spirited work, much absolute evil; the good in me would be too often ill-expressed and missed or misinterpreted. In the end I might leave one gleaming flake or so amidst the slag heaps for a moment of postmortem sympathy. I was afraid beyond measure of my derelict self. Because I believed with all my soul in love and fine thinking, that did not mean that I should necessarily either love steadfastly or think finely. I remember how I fell talking to God —I think I talked out loud. "Why do I care for these things?" I cried, "when I can do so little! Why am I set apart from the jolly, thoughtless, fighting life of men? These dreams fade to nothingness, and leave me bare!"

Grotesque analogies arose in my mind. I discovered a strange parallelism between my now tattered phrase of "Love and fine thinking" and the "Love and the Word" of Christian thought. Was it possible the Christian propaganda had at the outset meant just that system of attitudes I had been feeling my way towards from the very beginning of my life? Had I spent a lifetime making my way back to Christ? It mocks humanity to think how Christ has been overlaid. I went along now, recalling long-neglected phrases and sentences; I had a new vision of that great central figure preaching love with hate and coarse thinking even in the disciples about Him, rising to a tidal wave at last in that clamor for Barabbas, and the public satisfaction in His fate. . . .

It's curious to think that hopeless love and a noisy disordered dinner should lead a man to these speculations, but they did. "He *did* mean that!" I said, and suddenly thought of what a bludgeon they'd made of His Christianity.   Athwart that perplexing, patient enigma sitting inaudibly among publicans and sinners, danced and gibbered a long procession of the champions of orthodoxy.   " He wasn't human," I said, and remembered that last despairing cry, " My God! My God! why hast Thou forsaken Me? "

" Oh, *He* forsakes every one," I said, flying out as a tired mind will, with an obvious repartee. . . .

I passed at a bound from such monstrous theology to a towering rage against the Baileys.   In an instant and with no sense of absurdity I wanted—in the intervals of love and fine thinking—to fling about that strenuously virtuous couple; I wanted to kick Keyhole of the *Peepshow* into the gutter and make a common massacre of all the prosperous rascaldom that makes a trade and rule of virtue.   I can still feel that transition.   In a moment I had reached that phase of weakly decisive anger which is for people of my temperament the concomitant of exhaustion.

" I will have her," I cried.   " By Heaven!   I *will* have her! Life mocks me and cheats me.   Nothing can be made good to me again. . . .   Why shouldn't I save what I can?   I can't save myself without her. . . ."

I remember myself—as a sort of anti-climax to that—rather tediously asking my way home.   I was somewhere in the neighborhood of Holland Park. . . .

It was then between one and two.   I felt that I could go home now without any risk of meeting Margaret.   It had been the thought of returning to Margaret that had sent me wandering that night. It is one of the ugliest facts I recall about that time of crisis, the intense aversion I felt for Margaret.   No sense of her goodness, her injury and nobility, and the enormous generosity of her forgiveness, sufficed to mitigate that.   I hope now that in this book I am able to give something of her silvery splendor, but all through this crisis I felt nothing of that.   There was a triumphant kindliness about her that I found intolerable.   She meant to be so kind to me, to offer unstinted consolation, to meet my needs, to supply just all she imagined Isabel had given me.

When I left Tarvrille's, I felt I could anticipate exactly how she would meet my homecoming.   She would be perplexed by my crumpled shirt front, on which I had spilt some drops of wine; she would overlook that by an effort, explain it sentimentally, resolve it should make no difference to her.   She would want to know who had been present, what we had talked about, show the alertest interest in whatever it was—it didn't matter what. . . .   No, I couldn't face her.

So I did not reach my study until two o'clock.

There, I remember, stood the new and very beautiful old silver candlesticks that she had set there two days since to please me—the foolish kindliness of it! But in her search for expression, Margaret heaped presents upon me. She had fitted these candlesticks with electric lights, and I must, I suppose, have lit them to write my note to Isabel. "Give me a word—the world aches without you," was all I scrawled, though I fully meant that she should come to me. I knew, though I ought not to have known, that now she had left her flat, she was with the Balfes—she was to have been married from the Balfes',—and I sent my letter there. And I went out into the silent square and posted the note forthwith, because I knew quite clearly that if I left it until morning I should never post it at all.

III

I had a curious revulsion of feeling that morning of our meeting. Overnight I had been full of self-pity, and eager for the comfort of Isabel's presence. But the ill-written scrawl in which she had replied had been full of the suggestion of her own weakness and misery. And when I saw her, my own selfish sorrows were altogether swept away by a wave of pitiful tenderness. Something had happened to her that I did not understand. She was manifestly ill. She came towards me wearily, she who had always borne herself so bravely; her shoulders seemed bent, and her eyes were tired, and her face white and drawn. All my life has been a narrow self-centred life; no brothers, no sisters or children or weak things had ever yet made any intimate appeal to me, and suddenly—I verily believe for the first time in my life!—I felt a great passion of protective ownership; I felt that here was something that I could die to shelter, something that meant more than joy or pride or splendid ambitions or splendid creation to me, a new kind of hold upon me, a new power in the world. Some sealed fountain was opened in my breast. I knew that I could love Isabel broken, Isabel beaten, Isabel ugly and in pain, more than I could love any sweet or delightful or glorious thing in life. I didn't care any more for anything in the world but Isabel, and that I should protect her. I trembled as I came near her, and could scarcely speak to her for the emotion that filled me. . . .

"I had your letter," I said.

"I had yours."

"Where can we talk?"

I remember my lame sentences. "We'll have a boat. That's best here."

I took her to the little boat-house, and there we hired a boat, and I rowed in silence under the bridge and into the shade of a tree.

The square gray stone masses of the Foreign Office loomed through the twigs, I remember, and a little space of grass separated us from the pathway and the scrutiny of passers-by. And there we talked.

"I had to write to you," I said.

"I had to come."

"When are you to be married?"

"Thursday week."

"Well?" I said. "But—can we?"

She leant forward and scrutinized my face with eyes wide open. "What do you mean?" she said at last in a whisper.

"Can we stand it? After all?"

I looked at her white face. "Can you?" I said.

She whispered. "Your career?"

Then suddenly her face was contorted,—she wept silently, exactly as a child tormented beyond endurance might suddenly weep. . . .

"Oh! I don't care," I cried, "now. I don't care. Damn the whole system of things! Damn all this patching of the irrevocable! I want to take care of you, Isabel! and have you with me."

"I can't stand it," she blubbered.

"You needn't stand it. I thought it was best for you. . . . I thought indeed it was best for you. I thought even you wanted it like that."

"Couldn't I live alone—as I meant to do?"

"No," I said, "you couldn't. You're not strong enough. I've thought of that. I've got to shelter you.

"And I want you," I went on. "I'm not strong enough—I can't stand life without you."

She stopped weeping, she made a great effort to control herself, and looked at me steadfastly for a moment. "I was going to kill myself," she whispered. "I was going to kill myself quietly—somehow. I meant to wait a bit and have an accident. I thought—you didn't understand. You were a man, and couldn't understand. . . ."

"People can't do as we thought we could do," I said. "We've gone too far together."

"Yes," she said, and I stared into her eyes.

"The horror of it," she whispered. "The horror of being handed over. It's only just begun to dawn upon me, seeing him now as I do. He tries to be kind to me. . . . I didn't know. I felt adventurous before. . . . It makes me feel like all the women in the world who have ever been owned and subdued. . . . It's not that he isn't the best of men, it's because I'm a part of you. . . . I can't go through with it. If I go through with it, I shall be left—robbed of pride—outraged—a woman beaten. . . ."

" I know," I said. " I know."

" I want to live alone. . . . I don't care for anything now but just escape. If you can help me. . . ."

" I must take you away. There's nothing for us but to go away together."

" But your work," she said, " your career! Margaret! Our promises! "

" We've made a mess of things, Isabel—or things have made a mess of us. I don't know which. Our flags are in the mud, anyhow. It's too late to save those other things! They have to go. You can't make terms with defeat. I thought it was Margaret needed me most. But it's you. And I need you. I didn't think of that either. I haven't a doubt left in the world now. We've got to leave everything rather than leave each other. I'm sure of it. Now we have gone so far. We've got to go right down to earth and begin again. . . . Dear, I *want* disgrace with you. . . ."

So I whispered to her as she sat crumpled together on the faded cushions of the boat, this white and weary young woman who had been so valiant and careless a girl. " I don't care," I said. " I don't care for anything, if I can save you out of the wreckage we have made together."

IV

The next day I went to the office of the *Blue Weekly* in order to get as much as possible of its affairs in working order before I left London with Isabel. I just missed Shoesmith in the lower office. Upstairs I found Britten amidst a pile of outside articles, methodically reading the title of each and sometimes the first half-dozen lines, and either dropping them in a growing heap on the floor for a clerk to return, or putting them aside for consideration. I interrupted him, squatted on the window-sill of the open window, and sketched out my ideas for the session.

" You're far-sighted," he remarked at something of mine which reached out ahead.

" I like to see things prepared," I answered.

" Yes," he said, and ripped open the envelope of a fresh aspirant. I was silent while he read.

" You're going away with Isabel Rivers," he said abruptly.

" Well! " I said, amazed.

" I know," he said, and lost his breath. " Not my business. Only——"

It was queer to find Britten afraid to say a thing.

" It's not playing the game," he said.

" What do you know? "

"Everything that matters."

"Some games," I said, "are too hard to play."

There came a pause between us.

"I didn't know you were watching all this," I said.

"Yes," he answered, after a pause, "I've watched."

"Sorry—sorry you don't approve."

"It means smashing such an infernal lot of things, Remington."

I did not answer.

"You're going away then?"

"Yes."

"Soon?"

"Right away."

"There's your wife."

"I know."

"Shoesmith—whom you're pledged to in a manner. You've just picked him out and made him conspicuous. Every one will know. Oh! of course—it's nothing to you. Honor——"

"I know."

"Common decency."

I nodded.

"All this movement of ours. That's what *I* care for most. . . . It's come to be a big thing, Remington."

"That will go on."

"We have a use for you—no one else quite fills it. No one. . . . I'm not sure it will go on."

"Do you think I haven't thought of all these things?"

He shrugged his shoulders, and rejected two papers unread.

"I knew," he remarked, "when you came back from America. You were alight with it." Then he let his bitterness gleam for a moment. "But I thought you would stick to your bargain."

"It's not so much choice as you think," I said.

"There's always a choice."

"No," I said.

He scrutinized my face.

"I can't live without her—I can't work. She's all mixed up with this—and everything. And besides, there's things you can't understand. There's feelings you've never felt. . . . You don't understand how much we've been to one another."

Britten frowned and thought.

"Some things one's *got* to do," he threw out.

"Some things one can't do."

"These infernal institutions——"

"Some one must begin," I said.

He shook his head. "Not *you*," he said. "No!"

He stretched out his hands on the desk before him, and spoke again.

"Remington," he said, "I've thought of this business day and night too. It matters to me. It matters immensely to me. In a way—it's a thing one doesn't often say to a man—I've loved you. I'm the sort of man who leads a narrow life. . . . But you've been something fine and good for me, since that time, do you remember? when we talked about Mecca together."

I nodded.

"Yes. And you'll always be something fine and good for me anyhow. I know things about you,—qualities—no mere act can destroy them. . . . Well, I can tell you, you're doing wrong. You're going on now like a man who is gripped and can't turn round. You're piling wrong on wrong. It was wrong for you two people ever to be lovers."

He paused.

"It gripped us hard," I said.

"Yes!—but in your position! And hers! It was vile!".

"You've not been tempted."

"How do you know? Anyhow—having done that, you ought to have stood the consequences and thought of other people. You could have ended it at the first pause for reflection. You didn't. You blundered again. You kept on. You owed a certain secrecy to all of us! You didn't keep it. You were careless. You made things worse. This engagement and this publicity——! Damn it, Remington!"

, "I know," I said, with smarting eyes. "Damn it!—with all my heart! It came of trying to patch. . . . You *can't* patch."

"And now, as I care for anything under heaven, Remington, you two ought to stand these last consequences—and part. You ought to part. Other people have to stand things! Other people have to part. You ought to. You say—what do you say? It's loss of so much life to lose each other. So is losing a hand or a leg. But it's what you've incurred. Amputate. Take your punishment—— After all, you chose it."

"Oh, damn!" I said, standing up and going to the window.

"Damn by all means. I never knew a topic so full of justifiable damns. But you two did choose it. You ought to stick to your undertaking."

I turned upon him with a snarl in my voice. "My dear Britten!" I cried. "Don't I *know* I'm doing wrong? Aren't I in a net? Suppose I don't go! Is there any right in that? Do you think we're going to be much to ourselves or any one after this parting? I've been thinking all last night of this business, trying it over and

over again from the beginning. How was it we went wrong? Since
I came back from America—I grant you *that*—but *since*, there's
never been a step that wasn't forced, that hadn't as much right in it
or more, as wrong. You talk as though I was a thing of steel that
could bend this way or that and never change. You talk as though
Isabel was a cat one could give to any kind owner. . . . We two are
things that change and grow and alter all the time. We're—so
interwoven that being parted now will leave us just misshapen crip-
ples. . . . You don't know the motives, you don't know the rush and
feel of things, you don't know how it was with us, and how it is with
us. You don't know the hunger for the mere sight of one another;
you don't know anything."

Britten looked at his finger-nails closely. His red face puckered
to a wry frown. " Haven't we all at times wanted the world put
back? " he grunted, and looked hard and close at one particular nail.

There was a long pause.

" I want her," I said, " and I'm going to have her. I'm too tired
for balancing the right or wrong of it any more. You can't separate
them. I saw her yesterday. . . . She's—ill. . . . I didn't think of
that. . . . I'd take her now, if death were just outside the door waiting for us."

" Torture? "

I thought " Yes."

" For her? "

" There isn't," I said.

" If there was? "

I made no answer.

" It's blind Want. And there's nothing ever been put into you
to stand against it. What are you going to do with the rest of your
lives? "

" No end of things."

" Nothing."

" I don't believe you are right," I said. " I believe we can save
something——"

Britten shook his head. " Some scraps of salvage won't excuse
you," he said.

His indignation rose. " In the middle of life! " he said. " No
man has a right to take his hand from the plough! "

He leant forward on his desk and opened an argumentative palm.
" You know, Remington," he said, " and I know, that if this could
be fended off for six months—if you could be clapped in prison, or
got out of the way somehow,—until this marriage was all over and
settled down for a year, say—you know then you two could meet,
curious, happy, as friends. Saved! You *know* it."

I turned and stared at him. "You're wrong, Britten," I said. "And does it matter if we could?"

I found that in talking to him I could frame the apologetics I had not been able to find for myself alone.

"I am certain of one thing, Britten. It is our duty not to hush up this scandal."

He raised his eyebrows. I perceive now the element of absurdity in me, but at the time I was as serious as a man who is burning.

"It's our duty," I went on, "to smash now openly in the sight of every one. I've got that as clean and plain—as prison whitewash. I am convinced that we have got to be public to the uttermost now —I mean it—until every corner of our world knows this story, knows it fully, adds it to the Parnell story and the Ashton Dean story and the Carmel story and the Witterslea story, and all the other stories that have picked man after man out of English public life, the men with active imaginations, the men of strong initiative. To think this tottering old-woman ridden Empire should dare to waste a man on such a score! You say I ought to be penitent——"

Britten shook his head and smiled very faintly.

"I'm boiling with indignation," I said. "I lay in bed last night and went through it all. What in God's name was to be expected of us but what has happened? I went through my life bit by bit last night, I recalled all I've had to do with virtue and women, and all I was told and how I was prepared. I was born into cowardice and debasement. We all are. Our generation's grimy with hypocrisy. I came to the most beautiful things in life—like peeping Tom of Coventry. I was never given a light, never given a touch of natural manhood by all this dingy, furtive, canting, humbugging English world. Thank God! I'll soon be out of it! The shame of it! The very savages in Australia initiate their children better than the English do to-day. Neither of us was ever given a view of what they call morality that didn't make it show as shabby subservience, as the meanest discretion, an abject submission to unreasonable prohibitions! meek surrender of mind and body to the dictation of pedants and old women and fools. We weren't taught—we were mumbled at! And when we found that the thing they called unclean, unclean, was Pagan beauty—God! it was a glory to sin, Britten, it was a pride and splendor like bathing in the sunlight after dust and grime!"

"Yes," said Britten. "That's all very well——"

I interrupted him. "I know there's a case—I'm beginning to think it a valid case against us; but we never met it! There's a steely pride in self-restraint, a nobility of chastity, but only for those who see and think and act—untrammeled and unafraid. The other thing; the current thing, why! it's worth as much as the chastity of a monkey kept in a cage by itself!" I put my foot in a chair, and urged my case upon him. "This is a dirty world, Britten, simply because it is a muddled world, and the thing you call morality is dirtier now than the thing you call immorality. Why don't the moralists pick their stuff out of the slime if they care for it, and wipe it?—damn them! I am burning now to say: ' Yes, we did this and this,' to all the world. All the world! . . . I will!'"

Britten rubbed the palm of his hand on the corner of his desk. "That's all very well, Remington," he said. "You mean to go."

He stopped and began again. "If you didn't know you were in the wrong you wouldn't be so damned rhetorical. You're in the wrong. It's as plain to you as it is to me. You're leaving a big work, you're leaving a wife who trusted you, to go and live with your jolly mistress . . . You won't see you're a statesman that matters, that no single man, maybe, might come to such influence as you in the next ten years. You're throwing yourself away and accusing your country of rejecting you."

He swung round upon his swivel at me. "Remington," he said, "have you forgotten the immense things our movement means?"

I thought. "Perhaps I *am* rhetorical," I said.

"But the things we might achieve! If you'd only stay now—even now! Oh! you'd suffer a little socially, but what of that? You'd be able to go on—perhaps all the better for hostility of the kind you'd get. You know, Remington—you *know*."

I thought and went back to his earlier point. "If I am rhetorical, at any rate it's a living feeling behind it. Yes, I remember all the implications of our aims—very splendid, very remote. But just now it's rather like offering to give a freezing man the sunlit Himalayas from end to end in return for his camp-fire. When you talk of me and my jolly mistress, it isn't fair. That misrepresents everything. I'm not going out of this—for delights. That's the sort of thing men like Snuffles and Keyhole imagine—that excites them! When I think of the things these creatures think! Ugh! But *you* know better? You know that physical passion that burns like a fire—ends clean. I'm going for love, Britten—if I sinned for passion. I'm going, Britten, because when I saw her the other day she *hurt* me. She hurt me damnably, Britten. . . . I've been a cold man—I've led a rhetorical life—you hit me with that word!—I put things in a windy way, I know, but what has got hold of me at last is her pain. She's ill. Don't you understand? She's a sick thing —a weak thing. She's no more a goddess than I'm a god. . . . I'm not in love with her now; I'm *raw* with love for her. I feel like a man that's been flayed. I have been flayed. . . . You don't begin to imagine the sort of helpless solicitude. . . . She's not going to do things easily; she's ill, and going to be very ill. Her courage fails. . . . It's hard to put things when one isn't rhetorical, but it's this, Britten—there are distresses that matter more than all the delights or achievements in the world. . . . For the most part, I expect to be Isabel's sick nurse. . . . I made her what she is—as I never made Margaret. I've made her—I've broken her. . . . I'm going with my own woman. The rest of my life and England, and so forth, must square itself to that. . . ."

V

I have a letter Margaret wrote me within a week of our flight. I cannot resist transcribing some of it here, because it lights things as no words of mine can do. It is a string of nearly inconsecutive thoughts written in pencil in a fine, tall, sprawling hand. Many words are underlined. It was in answer to one from me; but what I wrote has passed utterly from my mind. . . .

" Certainly," she says, " I want to hear from you, but I do not want to see you. There's a sort of abstract *you* that I want to go on with. Something I've made *out* of you. . . . I want to know things about you—but I don't want to see or feel or imagine. When some day I have got rid of my intolerable sense of proprietorship, it may be different. Then perhaps we may meet again. I think it is even more the loss of our political work and dreams that I am feeling than the loss of your presence. Aching loss. I thought so much of the things we were *doing* for the world—had given myself so unreservedly. You've left me with nothing to *do*. I am suddenly at loose ends. . . .

" We women are trained to be so dependent on a man. I've got no life of my own at all. It seems now to me that I wore my clothes even for you and your schemes. . . .

" After I have told myself a hundred times why this has happened, I ask again, ' Why did he give things up? Why did he give things up?' . . .

" It is just as though you were wilfully dead. . . .

" Then I ask again and again whether this thing need have happened at all, whether if I had had a warning, if I had understood better, I might not have adapted myself to your restless mind and made this catastrophe impossible. . . .

" Oh, my dear! why hadn't you the pluck to hurt me at the beginning, and tell me what you thought of me and life? You didn't give me a chance; not a chance. I suppose you couldn't. All these things you and I stood away from. You let my first repugnances repel you. . . ,

"It is strange to think after all these years that I should be asking myself, do I love you? have I loved you? In a sense I think I *hate* you. I feel you have taken my life, dragged it in your wake for a time, thrown it aside. I am resentful. Unfairly resentful, for why should I exact that you should watch and understand my life, when clearly I have understood so little of yours? But I am savage—savage at the wrecking of all you were to do.

"Oh, why—why did you give things up?

"No human being is his own to do what he likes with. You were not only pledged to my tiresome, ineffectual companionship, but to great purposes. They *are* great purposes. . . .

"If only I could take up your work as you leave it, with the strength you had—then indeed I feel I could let you go—you and your young mistress. . . . All that matters so little to me. . . .

"Yet I think I must indeed love you yourself in my slower way. At times I am mad with jealousy at the thought of all I hadn't the wit to give you. . . . I've always hidden my tears from you—and what was in my heart. It's my nature to hide—and you, you want things brought to you to see. You are so curious as to be almost cruel. You don't understand reserves. You have no mercy with restraints and reservations. You are not really a *civilized* man at all. You hate pretences—and not only pretences but decent coverings. . . .

"It's only after one has lost love and the chance of loving that slow people like myself find what they might have done. Why wasn't I bold and reckless and abandoned? It's as reasonable to ask that, I suppose, as to ask why my hair is fair. . . .

"I go on with these perhapses over and over again here when I find myself alone. . . .

"My dear, my dear, you can't think of the desolation of things —— I shall never go back to that house we furnished together, that was to have been a laboratory (do you remember calling it a laboratory?) in which you were to forge so much of the new order. . . .

"But, dear, if I can help you—even now—in any way—help both of you, I mean. . . . It tears me when I think of you poor and discredited. You will let me help you if I can—it will be the last wrong not to let me do that. . . .

"You had better not get ill. If you do, and I hear of it—I shall come after you with a troupe of doctors and nurses. If I am a failure as a wife, no one has ever said I was anything but a success as a district visitor. . . ."

There are other sheets, but I cannot tell whether they were written before or after the ones from which I have quoted. And most of them have little things too intimate to set down. But this oddly penetrating analysis of our differences must, I think, be given.

"There are all sorts of things I can't express about this and want to. There's this difference that has always been between us, that you like nakedness and wildness, and I, clothing and restraint. It goes through everything. You are always *talking* of order and system, and the splendid dream of the order that might replace the muddled system you hate, but by a sort of instinct you seem to want to break the law. I've watched you so closely. Now *I* want to obey laws, to make sacrifices, to follow rules. I don't want to make, but I do want to keep. You are at once makers and rebels, you and Isabel too. You're bad people—criminal people, I feel, and yet full of something the world must have. You're so much better than me, and so much viler. It may be there is no making without destruction, but it seems to me sometimes that it is nothing but an instinct for lawlessness that drives you. You remind me—do you remember?—of that time we went from Naples to Vesuvius, and walked over the hot new lava there. Do you remember how tired I was? I know it disappointed you that I was tired. One walked there in spite of the heat because there was a crust; like custom, like law. But directly a crust forms on things, you are restless to break down to the fire again. You talk of beauty, both of you, as something terrible, mysterious, imperative. *Your* beauty is something altogether different from anything I know or feel. It has pain in it. Yet you always speak as though it was something I ought to feel and am dishonest not to feel. *My* beauty is a quiet thing. You have always laughed at my feeling for old-fashioned chintz and blue china and Sheraton. But I like all these familiar *used* things. My beauty is *still* beauty, and yours is excitement. I know nothing of the fascination of the fire, or why one should go deliberately out of all the decent fine things of life to run dangers and be singed and tormented and destroyed. I don't understand. . . ."

VI

I remember very freshly the mood of our departure from London, the platform of Charing Cross with the big illuminated clock overhead, the bustle of porters and passengers with luggage, the shouting of newsboys and boys with flowers and sweets, and the groups of friends seeing travelers off by the boat train. Isabel sat very quiet and still in the compartment, and I stood upon the platform with the door open, with a curious reluctance to take the last step that should sever me from London's ground. I showed our tickets, and bought a handful of red roses for her. At last came the guards crying: "Take your seats," and I got in and closed the door on me. We had, thank Heaven! a compartment to ourselves. I let down the window and stared out.

There was a bustle of final adieux on the platform, a cry of "Stand away, please, stand away!" and the train was gliding slowly and smoothly out of the station.

I looked out upon the river as the train rumbled with slowly gathering pace across the bridge, and the bobbing black heads of the pedestrians in the footway, and the curve of the river and the glowing great hotels, and the lights and reflections and blacknesses of that old, familiar spectacle. Then with a common thought, we turned our eyes westward to where the pinnacles of Westminster and the shining clock tower rose hard and clear against the still, luminous sky.

"They'll be in Committee on the Reformatory Bill to-night," I said, a little stupidly.

"And so," I added, "good-bye to London!"

We said no more, but watched the south-side streets below— bright gleams of lights and movement, and the dark, dim, monstrous shapes of houses and factories. We ran through Waterloo Station, London Bridge, New Cross, St. John's. We said never a word. It seemed to me that for a time we had exhausted our emotions. We had escaped, we had cut our knot, we had accepted the last penalty of that headlong return of mine from Chicago a year and a half ago. That was all settled. That harvest of feelings we had reaped. I thought now only of London, of London as the symbol of all we were leaving and all we had lost in the world. I felt nothing now but an enormous and overwhelming regret. . . .

The train swayed and rattled on its way. We ran through old Bromstead, where once I had played with cities and armies on the nursery floor. The sprawling suburbs with their scattered lights gave way to dim tree-set country under a cloud-veiled, intermittently shining moon. We passed Cardcaster Place. Perhaps old Wardingham, that pillar of the old Conservatives, was there, fretting over his unsuccessful struggle with our young Toryism. Little he recked of this new turn of the wheel and how it would confirm his contempt of all our novelties. Perhaps some faint intimation drew him to the window to see, behind the stems of the young fir trees that bordered his domain, the little string of lighted carriage windows gliding southward. . . .

Suddenly I began to realize just what it was we were doing.

And now, indeed, I knew what London had been to me, London where I had been born and educated, the slovenly mother of my mind and all my ambitions. London and the empire! It seemed to me we

. must be going out to a world that was utterly empty. All our significance fell from us—and before us was no meaning any more. We
were leaving London; my hand, which had gripped so hungrily upon
its complex life, had been forced from it, my fingers left their hold.
That was over. I should never have a voice in public affairs again.
The inexorable unwritten law which forbids overt scandal sentenced
me. We were going out to a new life, a life that appeared in that
moment to be a mere shriveled remnant of life, a mere residuum of
sheltering and feeding and seeing amidst alien scenery and the sound
of unfamiliar tongues. We were going to live cheaply in a foreign
place, so cut off that I meet now the merest stray tourist, the commonest tweed-clad stranger with a mixture of shyness and hunger.
. . . And suddenly all the schemes I was leaving appeared fine and
adventurous and hopeful as they had never done before. How great
was this purpose I had relinquished, this bold and subtle remaking
of the English will! I had doubted so many things, and now suddenly I doubted my unimportance, doubted my right to this suicidal
abandonment. Was I not a trusted messenger, greatly trusted and
favored, who had turned aside by the way? Had I not, after all,
stood for far more than I had thought; was I not filching from that
dear great city of my birth and life, some vitally necessary· thing, a
key, a link, a reconciling clue in her political development that now
she might seek vaguely for in vain? What is one life against the
State? Ought I not to have sacrificed Isabel and all my passion and
sorrow for Isabel, and held to my thing—stuck to my thing?

I heard as though he had spoken it in the carriage Britten's " It
was a good game. No end of a game." And for the first time I
imagined the faces and voices of Crupp and Esmeer and Gane when
they learnt of this secret flight, this flight of which they were quite
unwarned. And Shoesmith might be there in the house—Shoesmith,
who was to have been married in four days—the thing might hit him
full in front of any kind of people. Cruel eyes might watch him.
Why the devil hadn't I written letters to warn them all? I could
have posted them five minutes before the train started. I had never
thought to that moment of the immense mess they would be in; how
the whole edifice would clatter about their ears. I had a sudden desire to stop the train and go back for a day, for two days, to set that
negligence right. My brain for a moment brightened, became animated and prolific of ideas. I thought of a brilliant line we might
have taken on that confounded Reformatory Bill. . . ..

That sort of thing was over. . . .

What indeed wasn't over? I passed to a vaguer, more multitudinous perception of disaster, the friends I had lost already since
Altiora began her campaign, the ampler remnant whom now I must

lose. I thought of people I had been merry with, people I had worked with and played with, the companions of talkative walks, the hostesses of houses that had once glowed with welcome for us both. I perceived we must lose them all. I saw life like a tree in late autumn that had once been rich and splendid with friends—and now the last brave dears would be hanging on doubtfully against the frosty chill of facts, twisting and tortured in the universal gale of indignation, trying to evade the cold blast of the truth. I had betrayed my party, my intimate friend, my wife, the wife whose devotion had made me what I was. For awhile the figure of Margaret, remote, wounded, shamed, dominated my mind, and the thought of my immense ingratitude. Damn them! they'd take it out of her too. I had a feeling that I wanted to go straight back and grip some one by the throat, some one talking ill of Margaret. They'd blame her for not keeping me, for letting things go so far. . . . I wanted the whole world to know how fine she was. I saw in imagination the busy, excited dinner tables at work upon us all, rather pleasantly excited, brightly indignant, merciless.

Well, it's the stuff we are! . . .

Then suddenly, stabbing me to the heart, came a vision of Margaret's tears and the sound of her voice saying, "Husband mine! Oh! husband mine! To see you cry! . . ."

I came out of a cloud of thoughts to discover the narrow compartment, with its feeble lamp overhead, and our rugs and handbaggage swaying on the rack, and Isabel, very still in front of me, gripping my wilting red roses tightly in her bare and ringless hand.

For a moment I could not understand her attitude, and then I perceived she was sitting bent together with her head averted from the light to hide the tears that were streaming down her face. She had not got her handkerchief out for fear that I should see this, but I saw her tears, dark drops of tears, upon her sleeve. . . .

I suppose she had been watching my expression, divining my thoughts.

For a time I stared at her and was motionless in a sort of still and weary amazement. Why had we done this injury to one another? *Why?* Then something stirred within me.

"*Isabel!*" I whispered.

She made no sign.

"Isabel!" I repeated, and then crossed over to her and crept closely to her, put my arm about her, and drew her wet cheek to mine.

She murmured, and put a hand upon my shoulder and clung to me.